CRITICAL AND EXEGETICAL

COMMENTARY

ON

THE NEW TESTAMENT.

BY

HEINRICH AUGUST WILHELM MEYER, Th.D.,

OBERCONSISTORIALRATH, HANNOVER.

From the German, with the Sanction of the Author.

13656

THE TRANSLATION REVISED AND EDITED BY

WILLIAM P. DICKSON, D.D.,

AND

WILLIAM STEWART, D.D.

PART I.—SECOND DIVISION.

THE GOSPELS OF MARK AND LUKE.

VOL. I.

EDINBURGH:

T. & T. CLARK, 38 GEORGE STREET.

MDCCCLXXXIII.

PRINTED BY MORRISON AND GIBB,

FOR

T. & T. CLARK, EDINBURGH.

LONDON, ...   HAMILTON, ADAMS, AND CO.

DUBLIN, ...   GEORGE HERBERT.

NEW YORK,   .   .   .   SCRIBNER AND WELFORD.

CRITICAL AND EXEGETICAL

HANDBOOK

TO THE

GOSPELS OF MARK AND LUKE.

BY

HEINRICH AUGUST WILHELM MEYER, Th.D.,

OBERCONSISTORIALRATH, HANNOVER.

TRANSLATED FROM THE FIFTH EDITION OF THE GERMAN BY

REV. ROBERT ERNEST WALLIS, Ph.D.

VOL. I.

THE TRANSLATION REVISED AND EDITED BY

WILLIAM P. DICKSON, D.D.,

PROFESSOR OF DIVINITY IN THE UNIVERSITY OF GLASGOW.

EDINBURGH:

T. & T. CLARK, 38 GEORGE STREET.

MDCCCLXXXIII.

PREFATORY NOTE BY THE EDITOR.

THE translation of the Commentary on the Gospels of Mark and Luke has been made from the fifth edition of the original—the last form in which the work had the advantage of Dr. Meyer's own corrections and additions. In the case of the Commentary on St. Matthew, the materials for a sixth edition had been carefully prepared by Dr. Meyer before his last illness; and the work was issued by its editor, Dr. Ritschl, substantially as the author had left it. The present portion has likewise been given forth since the author's death in what professes to be a "sixth edition worked up anew" by Dr. Bernhard Weiss; but it is so considerably changed in form and substance, that, whatever may be its value on its own account, it can no longer be regarded as the proper work of Meyer; and I have had no hesitation in deeming it my duty to present to the English reader the last form of the book as it came from the great master of exegesis, rather than to reproduce the manipulation which it has undergone at the hands of its new editor. A few sentences will suffice to explain the state of the case, and I should hope sufficiently to justify the course which I have taken.

In the preface to the first volume that was issued of this translation (Romans, vol. I.), when speaking of the marked advantage which Meyer's work possessed in having undergone successive revisions *at the hands of its author*, as compared with the rival work of de Wette, the revision of which passed early into other hands, I took occasion to remark on the strange and, as it appeared to me, unwarrantable procedure of Dr. Overbeck in overlaying de Wette's book on the Acts of the Apostles with a running commentary largely devoted to the combating of de Wette's views. Dr. Weiss can hardly

be charged with anything so unseemly as this; but he contrasts unfavourably with Dr. Overbeck in another respect.
The latter, even at the distance of twenty years after de Wette's
death, was careful to distinguish by brackets his own additions,
though forming two - thirds of the whole, from the original
author's text; but a strangely different course has been
adopted with the great work of Meyer. Within less than five
years after his death the Commentary on Mark and Luke has
been re-issued under his name; but he is spoken of throughout in the *third* person; his arrangement is discarded; his
critical verdicts are recast to a considerable extent on other
principles; his exegetical views are freely controverted; the
statements of the author are often superseded by those of
the editor; and, what is more, the character and complexion
of the Commentary are materially altered by the superinducing
on it of Dr. Weiss's special theories regarding the structure of
the Gospels and the relations of their parallel passages. In
other words, the work is no longer such as Meyer left it; it
is to a considerable extent a new book by another author,
and from a standpoint in various respects different.

Now, it may be at once granted that—if such a course were
allowable at all in the case of an author so recently removed
from us as Meyer, and of such a masterpiece of exegesis as
his Commentary—Dr. Weiss might well be chosen to carry
it out, for his investigations as to the relations of the Synoptic
Gospels, as well as his contributions to Biblical Theology, have
given him a foremost place among the critics and theologians
of the day. In his preface he suggests some more or less
plausible grounds for the course he has pursued, while indicating no small misgivings as to its legitimacy and its success.
The plan has met with partial approval in Germany; but
its propriety, as it seems to us, may well be questioned, on
account both of the respect due to so great a name, and
of the desirableness of permitting a reader, who buys a book
on the faith of the writer's reputation and of the title-page, to
have—with whatever else—at any rate the *entire* work of the
author in the form in which he left it. Weiss himself states
with regard to the work of Meyer, that "it contains such treasures

of erudite research, philological, archaeological, and biblico-theological; so laboriously collected and carefully grouped a summary of all different views on every passage of import-ance, drawn from the whole domain of the history of exegesis; and lastly, so exemplary a model of sober and strictly methodical exegesis, that generation after generation may learn from it." As the case stands with the re-issue of it, the reader has no security that he gets more of the views of Meyer, or their grounds, than the subjective judgment of Weiss may have deemed worthy of reproduction; while he does get a good deal for which, it is safe to say, Meyer would not have held himself responsible. I shall only add, that the plan of entrusting the revision of the several portions of the work to *different* editors, whose methods of procedure and standards of judgment are necessarily various, breaks up the unity and consistency of the Commentary as stamped through-out with the impress of its author; and introduces a confusion, which cannot but materially interfere with the pertinence of the numerous references from one portion of the Commen-tary to another (introduced by "see on," or "comp. on"), that form a main element of its value. I have therefore had little difficulty in coming to the conclusion that, having undertaken to issue the Commentary of Dr. Meyer in an English form, I ought to give it in its final shape as it came from himself, and not as it has been since transformed by another hand.

The translation, on which Dr. Wallis has expended a good deal of time and care, has been revised and carried through the press, in the case of the first volume, by myself, and, in that of the second, by my colleague and friend Dr. Stewart, who tells me that he has, as he went along, inserted [in square brackets] the readings of Tischendorf's *editio octava major*, which, as Dr. Meyer explains in his Preface (p. xi.), had not been carried beyond the earlier chapters of Mark's Gospel at the time of his sending to the press the fifth edition of the Handbook.

GLASGOW COLLEGE, *February* 1880.

THE AUTHOR'S PREFACE.

THE investigations as to the origin and mutual relations of the first three Gospels have again been pursued of late years with much vigour. A series of still unsettled questions has stimulated their prosecution; and the Christological discussions of the day, in which the authority of the evangelic records is of decisive importance, have imparted a peculiar and diversified interest of their own to the controversy, which has thus come to be of a more intensified and partisan character. That this critical ferment will last for some time longer, no one can doubt, who has given special attention to even the most prominent of the writings on the subject and compared their results with one another. And if, at the same time, we glance—as the two fields of inquiry, in fact, are not to be separated—from the Synoptic into the Johannine domain, in which very recently a valiant Swiss has raised the flaming sword, as if for a war of extermination, against the more popular [1] than strictly theological

---

[1] Of apologetic writings for cultivated non-theologians our day has produced many, and several that are excellent. Such writings—because their problems of themselves belong primarily and preponderantly to the province of professional theology—always occupy, in presence of the latter, a dubious position. For along with all the value of opportune and clever popularizing, there necessarily clings to them a certain incompleteness of proof and presentation, which may provoke the adversary at times to unfairness in his claims and in his criterion of judgment. It is indeed a material defect, when—as often—they deal with critical extravagances merely *in the way of repelling*, and leave untouched, or with a dubious mincing word evade, the necessary *concessions*, which in various important points are not to be refused to a sound, judicious, and thorough criticism. In this way there is no attempt to meet a justifiable requirement, and no clearness even as regards insight into the *status causae*.

work of a highly meritorious Saxon theologian whose laurels
belong to another field of criticism [Tischendorf], we cannot
but lament much impetuosity and even bitterness, which are
the more apt to come into play when the contest is a contest of principles.   Conflict in and by itself, indeed, over such
critical problems as belong to the exciting questions of the
present day in theology, is inevitable, and has its justification
in the end at which it aims,—the separating the dross of error
from the truth.   But the sharpness of passion should not
interpose to banish the charitable belief that an opponent,
even where he is chargeable with error, has been seeking the
truth and striving to serve it.   In so speaking we cannot
mean and desire that men should cry peace when there is
no peace.   But as we *cannot avail* aught against the truth,
so we ought never to *will* anything that is not pure—free
from selfish or even indecorous zeal—*for* the truth.[1]

Various as are the critical opinions of the present day on
the question of the Synoptic Gospels, *the* view seems ever
more evidently to be approaching final triumph, that among
the three Gospels (apart from the " Logia - collection " of
Matthew) Mark is the first.   The unfair judgments,[2] that may
still be heard about him, will gradually be put to silence; just
like Augustine's " pedissequus Matthaei," Griesbach's " copyist
of Matthew and Luke " will disappear from the arena of ancient
error.   This view derives special confirmation from the critical
contributions—some of them entering very thoroughly into the
subject—that have appeared since the publication of the fourth
edition of this Commentary, or, in other words, since 1860,
when we survey their aggregate results.   It will easily be

---

[1] The extravagance of criticism, which in various productions of the day far
transcends the boldness of Baur, does not advance the matter, bursts all the ties
even of historical possibility, turns things upside down, promotes the convenient
aversion—already, alas ! so widely diffused—to criticism generally, as if it were
an affair of unbelief, and works involuntarily into the hands of the *Jews,* who
gladly accept the alleged negative results as if they were settled matters, as may
be sufficiently seen from several writings of modern Jewish scholars.

[2] No one can pronounce a judgment of rejection over Mark more decidedly
than has been done, with *French* frivolity, by Eichthal (*les Évangiles,* 1863, I.
p. 51 ff.).

seen that I have sought [1] to give due heed to them, as well as generally to the latest literature relative to the subject, in their bearing on my purpose.

In reference to the critical remarks, I must call attention to the fact that only for the first four chapters of Mark could I take the readings of the text of Tischendorf from the new large edition (*editio octava*), which had only appeared up to that point; and for the sequel I had to quote them from the second edition of the *Synopsis Evangelica*. For I might not fall back on the *editio septima* (1859), because after issuing it Tischendorf modified essentially his critical procedure, and reverted to the principles of Lachmann, constituting in accordance with these the text of the second edition of the *Synopsis* (1864), and, of course, diverging much from that of the *editio septima*. I am

---

[1] Some minor works reached me too late for a consideration of their suggestions: *e.g.* Hilgenfeld, *Markus zwischen Matth. und Luk.*, in his *Zeitschr.* 1866, p. 82 ff.; Zahn, *Papias von Hierapolis*, in the *Stud. u. Krit.* 1866, p. 649 ff.; Stawars, *üb. d. Ordnung Abia*, in the *Theol. Quartalschr.* 1866, p. 201 ff.; also Volkmar, *Urspr. uns. Evangelien*, Zürich 1866, but chiefly in reference to John. The *Christologie des Neuen Testamentes* of Beyschlag, Berlin 1866, I have, to my regret, only been able to take into consideration here and there supplementarily, during the later progress of the printing. As I no longer had any fitting opportunity to express in the Commentary my view as to Beyschlag's development of the idea of the *Son of man*,—which he regards as the *Ideal* man, as the *ideal* of humanity,—I may here be allowed, on account of the Christological importance of the subject, frankly to state that the deductions of the author—however attractive they are, and however considerable the names of authority that may range themselves on the side of their result—have not been able to convince me. I cannot but think that the notion of the *Ideal* man, as well in Daniel as in the Gospels, is one brought to them and introduced, and not the one there given. I find that the only Synoptic passage which appears to favour this interpretation is Mark ii. 28. But even here it is, as I believe, only an appearance. For, firstly, the fundamental thought in this passage is not that of the *ideal*, but that of the *representative* of humanity, which is a different idea; secondly, even this conception does not attach to ὁ υἱὸς τοῦ ἀνθρώπου in itself, but to the whole conception of the *Messiah*, and would be the leading thought of the argument, even if quite *another* appellation of the Messiah were used. That Christ, although without prejudice to His personal pre-existence, was and is the Ideal of humanity, is accordant with Scripture; but it is not contained in ὁ υἱὸς τοῦ ἀνθρώπου, as, indeed, this expression in itself does not lexically contain the very slightest hint thereof.—We may add, that it is much to be wished that the antagonism, which the work of Beyschlag will still abundantly encounter and must needs encounter, may be kept clear of the passionate vehemence which it has already so largely experienced.

not quite free from hesitation as to this change of principles, whereby, instead of simply steering for the ideal goal as such, we are again directed, as in the case of Lachmann, only to an intermediate station, the actual reaching of which, especially if it is to be the text of the *second* century, must withal in numberless cases be uncertain.

In conclusion, may I be allowed, simply for those at a distance interested in my personal circumstances, to mention that since last autumn I have retired from my position as a member of the Royal Consistory here. "*Deus nobis haec otia fecit,*"—this I have (in another sense, indeed, than the Roman poet meant it) to acknowledge with humble thanks to the everlasting Love, which has in great long-suffering and grace upheld me during many most laborious and, in part, momentous years, and has at length helped me to get over the difficult step of retiring from the vocation bound up with my very inmost life. As nothing else than considerations of health, which I might not and could not withstand any longer, gave occasion to this change, and as for me especially it has been deeply painful to separate from the circle of the dear colleagues highly and gratefully esteemed by me,—with all of whom, amidst manifold diversity of our gifts and powers, I was bound in unity of spirit to the service of the one Lord, and, I venture to hope, may still continue bound,—it is a fervent joy to my heart, that in the partial co-operation which still remains assigned to me, especially by my continuing to take part in the theological examinations, there is not yet wholly dissolved the official bond of fellowship, which has always been to me so high a blessing in my position here.

Let the future, which is to be developed out of the blood-stained seed-sowing of the present not only for the fleeting existence of this world, but also for the eternal kingdom of the Lord, be committed to God, who turns the hearts of men as water-brooks, and will turn all things for the best to His people—the unknown and yet well known, the sorrowful and yet always rejoicing, the dying, and behold they live !

DR. MEYER.

HANNOVER, 10*th August* 1866.

EXEGETICAL LITERATURE.

————◆————

[For Commentaries embracing the whole New Testament, the Four Gospels as such, or the three Synoptic Gospels (including the chief Harmonies), see the list prefixed to the Commentary on the Gospel of St. Matthew. The following list contains Commentaries on the Gospel of St. Mark or on that of St. Luke, along with a few works of historical criticism relative to these Gospels. Works mainly of a popular or practical character have, with a few exceptions, been excluded, since, however valuable they may be on their own account, they have but little affinity with the strictly exegetical character of the present work. Monographs on chapters or sections are generally noticed by Meyer *in loc.* The editions quoted are usually the earliest; *al.* appended denotes that the book has been more or less frequently re-issued; † marks the date of the author's death; c. = *circa*, an approximation to it.]

ALEXANDER (Joseph Addison), D.D., † 1860, Prof. Bibl. and Eccl. Hist. at Princeton : The Gospel according to Mark explained.
8°, New York, 1858, al.

AMBROSIUS, † 397, Bishop of Milan : Expositio Evangelii secundum Lucam. [Opera.]

BAUR (Ferdinand Christian), † 1860, Prof. Theol. at Tübingen : Das Markusevangelium nach seinem Ursprung und Charakter.
8°, Tübing. 1851.

BORNEMANN (Friedrich August), † 1848, Pastor at Kirchberg : Scholia in Lucae Evangelium ad supplendos reliquorum interpretum commentarios. . . .
8°, Lips. 1830.

CATENAE. See CORDERIUS, NICETAS, and POSSINUS.

13

CORDERIUS [CORDIER] (Balthasar), † 1650, Jesuit: Catena sexaginta quinquePatrum Graecorum in S.Lucam. . . . Latinitate donata et annotationibus illustrata. . . .   2°, Antv. 1628.

COSTA (Isaac Da), Pastor at Amsterdam: Beschouwing van het Evangelie van Lucas.   8°, Amst. 1850–52.

ELSNER (Jakob), † 1750, Consistorialrath at Berlin: Commentarius critico - philologicus in Evangelium Marci . . . Edidit Ferd. Stosch.   4°, Traj. ad Rhen. 1773.

FORD (James), M.A., Prebendary of Exeter: The Gospel of St. Mark [and of St. Luke], illustrated from ancient and modern authors.   8°, Lond. 1849–51.

FRITZSCHE (Karl Friedrich August), † 1846, Prof. Theol. at Rostock: Evangelium Marci recensuit et cum commentariis perpetuis edidit D. Car. F. A. Fritzsche.   8°, Lips. 1830.

GODET (Frédéric), Prof. Theol. at Neuchâtel: Commentaire sur l'Evangile de saint Luc.   2 tomes.   8°, Neuchâtel, 1871. [Translated from the second French edition by E. W. Shalders and D. W. Cusin.   2 vols.   8°, Edin. 1875.]

HEUPEL (Georg Friedrich), Theological Tutor at Wittenberg: Marci Evangelium notis grammatico-historico-criticis illustratum.
            8°, Argent. 1716.

HILGENFELD (Adolf), Prof. Theol. at Jena: Das Markusevangelium nach seiner Composition, seiner Stellung in der Evangelien-Litteratur, seinem Ursprung und Charakter dargestellt.
            8°, Leip. 1850.

HOFMANN (Johann Christian Konrad von), † 1877, Prof. Theol. at Erlangen: Die Heilige Schrift Neuen Testamentes zusammenhängend untersucht.   Achter Theil.   Das Evangelium des Lukas.   Cap. i.–xxii. 66. . . .
            8°, Nördlingen, 1878.

JUNIUS (Franciscus) [FRANCOIS DU JON], † 1602, Prof. Theol. at Leyden: Analytica expositio Evangelii Marci.   [Opera.]

KLOSTERMANN (August), Prof. Theol. at Kiel: Das Markusevangelium nach seinem Quellenwerthe für die evangelische Geschichte.
            8°, Götting. 1867.

MICHELSEN (Jan Hendrik Adolf): Het Evangelie van Markus. 1 gedeelte.   8°, Amst 1867.

MORISON (James), D.D., Prof. Theol. to the Evangelical Union, Glasgow : A Commentary on the Gospel according to Mark.
8°, Lond. 1873.

MORUS (Samuel Friedrich Nathan), † 1792, Prof. Theol. at Leipzig : Praelectiones in Evangelium Lucae. Ed. K. A. Donat.
8°, Lip. 1795.

NICETAS Serrariensis, c. 1150, Bishop of Heraclea : Catena veterum Patrum in Lucae Evangelium, colligente Niceta. . . . [Mai, Scrip. Vet. Coll. ix.]

PAPE (Heinrich), † 1805 : Das Lucas-Evangelium umschrieben und erläutert. 2 Theile.   8°, Bremen, 1777-81.

PAREUS [WAENGLER] (David), † 1622, Prof. Theol. at Heidelberg : Adversaria in S. Marcum, S. Lucam . . . [Opera.]

PETTER (George), Min. at Bread, Sussex : A learned, pious, and practical commentary on the Gospel according to St. Mark. 2 vols.   2°, Lond. 1661.

PISCATOR [FISSCHER] (Johann), † 1626, Corrector at Herborn : Analysis logica Evangelii secundum Lucam.   8°, Sigenae, 1596, al.

POSSINUS (Peter), † c. 1650, Jesuit at Rome : Catena Graecorum Patrum in Marcum Graece et Latine. Interprete P. Possino.
2°, Romae, 1673.

REINHARD (Lorenz), † 1752, Superintendent at Büttstadt : Observationes philologicae et exegeticae in Evangelium Marci selectissimae.   4°, Lips. 1737.

SCHLEIERMACHER (Friedrich Daniel Ernst), † 1834, Prof. Theol. at Berlin : Ueber die Schriften des Lukas kritischer Versuch.
8°, Berl. 1817.
[Translated with an introduction by Connop Thirlwall, D.D.
8°, Lond. 1825.]

SCHOLTEN (Johan Hendrik), Prof. Theol. at Leyden : Het oudste Evangelie ; critisch onderzoek naar de samenstelling, de onderlinge verhouding, de historische waarde en den oorsprong der Evangelien naar Mattheus en Marcus.   8°, Leid. 1868.
Het Paulinisch Evangelie ; critisch onderzoek van het Evangelie naar Lucas, en seine verhouding tot Marcus, Mattheus, en die Handelingen.   8°, Leid. 1870.

SEGAAR (Carolus), † 1803, Prof. Theol. at Utrecht : Observationes philologicae et theologicae in Evangelii Lucae capita xi priora.
8°, Utrecht, 1766.

STEIN (Karl Wilhelm), Pastor at Niemegk : Commentar zu dem Evangelium des Lucas, nebst einem Anhange über den Brief au die
Laodicäer.   8°, Halle, 1830.
STELLA [ESTELLA] (Diego), † 1578, Spanish monk : In Evangelium
secundum Lucam enarrationes.   2 voll.
2°, Compluti, 1578, al.

TITUS Bostrensis? † c. 370 : Commentarius in Lucam.   [Bibl. Max.
Patrum. iv.]
TROLLOPE (William), M.A. : Commentary on St. Luke's Gospel.
12°, Lond. 1849.

VICTOR, Antiochenus, c. 400, Bishop of Antioch : Exegesis in Evangelium Marci.   Ex codd. Mosq. edidit Chr. F. Matthaei.
8°, Mosquae, 1775.
VINKE (Hendrik Egbert), † 1862, Prof. Theol. at Utrecht : Het
Nieuwe Testament met ophelderende en toepasslijke aanmer-
kingen.   8°, Utrecht, 1852–54.

WEISS (Bernhard), Prof. Theol. at Berlin : Das Markusevangelium
und seine synoptischen Parallelen erklärt.   8°, Berl. 1872.
Das Matthäusevangelium und seine Lucas-Parallelen erklärt.
8°, Halle, 1876.
WILLES (Bartus van), † 1844, Pastor at Niewland : Specimen herme-
neuticum de iis quae ab uno Marco sunt narrata aut
copiosius et explicatius ab eo exposita.
8°, Traj. ad Rhen. 1812.

THE GOSPEL OF MARK.

INTRODUCTION.

§ 1.—ON THE LIFE OF MARK.

THE evangelist Mark, a Jew by birth (Col. iv. 10 f.),
is the same[1] who, in the Acts of the Apostles, is
sometimes called *John Mark* (xii. 12, 25, xv. 37),
sometimes *John* only (xiii. 5, 13), sometimes only
Mark (xv. 39; comp. Col. iv. 10; 2 Tim. iv. 11; Philem. 24;
1 Pet. v. 13). His original name, therefore, was *John*;[2] and
the name *Mark, adopted* probably on his passing into the
service of the apostles, became the *prevailing* one in Christian
intercourse. *Mary* is named to us as his mother, who, at the
time of the execution of James the Elder, was an esteemed
Christian dwelling at Jerusalem, and in friendly relations
with Peter (Acts xii. 12). Jerusalem may therefore be regarded
as the birthplace of Mark. According to 1 Pet. v. 13, he was
converted by Peter (υἱός μου); he entered, however, into the
service of Barnabas and Paul, when they commenced their
missionary journeys (Acts xii. 25), but subsequently became
the occasion of a difference between them and of their separa-

---

[1] The supposition that there were *two different* Marks (Grotius, Calovius, and
several others, including Schleiermacher in the *Stud. u. Krit.* 1832, p. 760)
is absolutely without any sufficient foundation. It is nevertheless again taken
up by Kienlen in the *Stud. u. Krit.* 1843, p. 423 ff., and in opposition to the
tradition of the church further made use of for ascribing the Gospel not to the
Petrine, but to the Pauline Mark, whom Papias had already confounded with
the former.

[2] Thence Hitzig (*üb. Johannes Markus u. seine Schriften*, Zürich 1843) could
hold him to be the author of the Apocalypse, which, however, is decidedly
incorrect. See Lücke, *Einl. in d. Offenb.* p. 781.

tion from one another, when he accompanied Barnabas, whose
sister's son he was (see on Col. iv. 10), on his journey to
Cyprus (Acts xv. 36 ff.). It is probable that a want of
dauntless perseverance (Acts xiii. 13, xv. 38) had withdrawn
from him Paul's favour, without, however, hindering their
subsequent reunion. Of his further life and work nothing is
known to us in detail from the N. T. beyond the fact that
during Paul's imprisonment at Caesarea—according to the
usual view, at Rome (see on *Eph.*, Introd. § 2)—he was with
that apostle to his comfort (Col. iv. 10 f.; Philem. 24; comp.
2 Tim. iv. 11), and was at that time contemplating a journey
to Asia Minor (Col. iv. 10). At 1 Pet. v. 13 we find him
again with his spiritual father Peter in Babylon. His special
relation to Peter is specified by the unanimous testimony of
the ancient church as having been that of *interpreter* (ἑρμηνεύτης; Papias, in Eus. iii. 39; Iren. iii. 1, iii. 10, 6; Tertull.
contr. Marc. iv. 5; Eusebius, Jerome, *et al.*); and there exists absolutely no valid reason for *doubting* the statement, if only the
notion of ἑρμηνεύτης be taken not as meaning that Peter, being
himself insufficiently versed in Greek, caused what he delivered
in Aramaic to be reproduced in Greek by Mark (Kuinoel and
many others), or that Peter made use of him as *Latin* interpreter (Bleek), but rather as denoting the service of a *secretary*,
who had to write down the oral communications of his apostle,
whether from dictation or in a more free exercise of his own
activity, and thus became his interpreter *in writing* to others.
This view is plainly confirmed by Jerome, *ad Hedib.* 11:
" *Habebat ergo* (Paulus) *Titum interpretem* (in drawing up the
second Epistle to the Corinthians) *sicut et beatus Petrus Marcum,
cujus evangelium Petro narrante et illo scribente compositum est.
Denique et duae epistolae quae feruntur Petri, stilo inter se et
charactere discrepant structuraque verborum, ex quo intelligimus,
pro necessitate rerum diversis eum usum interpretibus.*"

The tradition, that Mark was with Peter in *Rome*, is not yet
attested, it is true, in the fragment of Papias, but is still very
ancient, as it is designated by Clem. Al. *Hypotyp.* 6, in Eus.
vi. 14, as παράδοσιν τῶν ἀνέκαθεν πρεσβυτέρων. It is not,
however, free from the suspicion of having arisen out of

1 Pet. v. 13, where Babylon was taken as a designation of Rome (Eus. ii. 15 ; Jerome, *Vir. ill.* 8). From Rome, after the death of that apostle (not so early as the eighth year of Nero, as Jerome states), he is said to have gone to *Alexandria,* and there—where, according to Eus. iii. 39, he is alleged to have founded the church[1]—to have died as bishop (Eus. ii. 16 ; Epiph. *Haer.* li. 6 ; Jerome, *Vir. ill.* 8), and, according to later tradition, in the character of a martyr (Niceph. ii. 43, *Martyrol. Rom.,* 25 Apr.).

§ 2.——ORIGIN OF THE GOSPEL.

It is related, first of all by *Papias* (in Eus. iii. 39), and then unanimously by the entire ancient church, that Mark wrote his Gospel under the special influence of Peter, whose ἑρμηνεύτης he was. This account is, according to Papias (see on Matt., Introd. p. 41 ff.), to be understood as amounting more precisely to this, that Mark made notes for himself after the discourses of Peter which he heard, and subsequently employed these in the composition of his Gospel. This original relation to the authority of Peter[2] could not but receive more precise delineation by tradition, as there grew up an increasing desire to see the non-apostolic writing invested with apostolic validity. Already, at a very early date, our Gospel was regarded directly as the Gospel of *Peter,* as even Justin, *c. Tryph.* 106, quotes it as τὰ ἀπομνημονεύματα Πέτρου (see on John, Introd. p. 9 f. ; Ritschl in the *theol. Jahrb.* 1851, p. 499 f. ; Köstlin, *Urspr. d. synopt. Evang.* p. 368 f. ; Weiss in

[1] That this occurred before the composition of the Epistle to the Romans, Thiersch concludes (*d. Kirche im apost. Zeitalt.* p. 104 f.) from Rom. xv. 19 ff. Certainly it is in itself probable that even at that early date Christianity existed, as in Rome, so also in Alexandria, where there was a very numerous body of Jews. Still the expression in Rom. *l.c.* is too indefinite as respects its geographical limits for any one to be able to maintain that Egypt belongs to the regions whereof Paul says that there is nothing more in them for him to do.

[2] Which, however, most of the later critics (comp. on Matt. p. 39), without sufficient warrant either from the testimony of Papias, or from other testimonies, or from internal grounds, refer back to a lost primitive Mark, from which our Mark first took its rise. So, too, Schenkel and Weizsäcker, *üb. d. Evang. Gesch.* 1864. Recently Weiss and Tischendorf have decidedly declared themselves against the hypothesis of a primitive Mark [*Urmarkus*].

the *Stud. u. Krit.* 1861, p. 677); and Tertull. *c. Macc.* iv. 5, says: "Marcus quod edidit evangelium, *Petri adfirmatur, cujus interpres Marcus*" (comp. Iren. iii. 1 : τὰ ὑπὸ Πέτρου κηρυσσόμενα ἐγγράφως ἡμῖν παραδέδωκε, similarly Origen in Eus. vi. 25). Still, however, there is no mention of any special *recognition* of the book on the part of Peter. Nothing can with any certainty be concluded from the fragmentary initial words of the Muratorian Canon (as has especially been attempted by Volkmar on Credner's *Gesch. d. Kanon*, p. 351 f.); and Clement, *Hypotyp.* 6, in Eus. vi. 14, expressly states that the publication of the Gospel, composed after the apostle's discourses, experienced at the hands of the latter neither a κωλύσαι nor a προτρέψασθαι. But in the course of tradition the apostolic confirmation also [1] does not fail to appear, and even Eusebius himself,[2] ii. 15, relates : γνόντα δὲ πραχθέν φασι τὸν ἀπόστολον . . . κυρῶσαί τε τὴν γραφὴν εἰς ἔντευξιν ταῖς ἐκκλησίαις. Comp. Epiph. *Haer.* li. 6 ; Jerome, *Vir. ill.* 8.

In the dependence—to which Papias testifies—of Mark on Petrine discourses and on notes made from them, there is not implied essentially and necessarily his independence of Matthew and Luke ; for if Mark, when he composed his Gospel, found already in existence the writings of Matthew and Luke, even although he rested on the testimony of Peter, the comparison of that testimony with those other two evangelists might still be of the highest importance to him, inasmuch as it might furnish to him partly confirmation, partly, in the event of want of accord between Matthew and Luke, decision, partly inducement for omissions, partly additions and modifications. And thus the matter would have to be conceived of, if the hypothesis of Griesbach (see Introd. to Matt. p. 35), which is still in substance upheld by many (including Saunier, Fritzsche, de Wette, Bleek, Baur, Delitzsch, Köstlin, Kahnis,

---

[1] The view which finds mention of the literary services of Mark even by Paul, namely at 2 Cor. viii. 18 (Storr, Hitzig), is a pure fancy.

[2] Eusebius does not here quote *Clement's* words, so that Clement would have here, compared with the previous passage, contradicted himself (Strauss, de Wette, and others), but he is narrating in his own person. See Credner, *Einl.* i. p. 113 ; Thiersch, *Hist. Standp.* p. 212 f.

and others), were the correct one.[1] But it is not the correct
one. For, apart from the fact that in any case Luke closes
the series of the Synoptics and is only to be placed after the
destruction of Jerusalem, our existing Gospel of Matthew
cannot have taken its present shape until *after* Mark (see
Introd. to Matt. p. 39 f.); and *prior to* Mark, as far as concerns
the relation of the latter to Matthew, there can only have
existed the *apostolic collection of Logia*, which became also the
first foundation of our Matthew. Mark must have made use
of *this*, although in general the presentation of the discourses
of Jesus has been with him so subordinate a feature, that we
may reasonably assume that he has taken for granted in his
readers an acquaintance with the teaching (comp. Holtzmann,
p. 385). But every kind of procedure in the way of epitome
and compilation (according to the hypothesis of Griesbach,
there would only be left to Mark as his own peculiar portions,
iv. 26–29, vii. 32–37, viii. 22–26, xi. 1–14, xiii. 33–37,
xvi. 6–11) is absolutely incompatible with the creative
life-like freshness and picturesqueness of detail, with the
accurate designation of the localities and situations in his
description,[2] with his taking no account of all the preliminary
history, with the clear objectivity and simple, firmly-knit
arrangement of his narratives, with the peculiar character of
that which he gives either in greater brevity or in greater detail
than the others. See especially, Ewald, *Jahrb.* II. p. 203 f.;

[1] The best conjoint view of all that can be said on behalf of this hypothesis is
given by Bleek in his *Beiträge*, p. 72 ff., and *Einl.* p. 243 ff. The most forcible
refutation is found in Holtzmann, *Synopt. Evang.* p. 113 ff., 344 ff. Comp.
Weiss in the *Stud. u. Krit.* 1861, p. 652 ff., 680 ff.

[2] Baur, *Markusevang.* p. 41, does Mark injustice, when he sees in his vividness of description merely the habit of seizing first of all on the most sensuously-
concrete conception. Köstlin and others speak of Mark's "mannerism." Weisse,
Evangelienfr. p. 73, rightly says : " in fact, nothing can be more dangerous to the
'*criticism of tendency*' than any kind of acknowledgment, be it ever so limited,
of the independence of Mark." Nevertheless, Eichthal (*les Evangiles*, Paris
1863) has found in the pictorial description of Mark a proof of subsequent
elaboration ; he is held to be the epitomizer of Matthew, whose Gospel nevertheless, as it now stands, is full of interpolations. And so Luke too is in many
ways interpolated. In this Eichthal goes to work with very uncritical licence,
and regards Mark as being much less interpolated, merely because he was from
the first looked on as of far less consequence (I. p. 267 ff.).

Weiss in the *Stud. u. Krit.* 1861, p. 67 ff., 646 ff.; Holtzmann, p. 284 f., 448 f. Besides, we do not find in Mark
the *peculiar* elements which Matthew and Luke (the latter
especially, ix. 51–xviii. 14) respectively have in matter and
manner; indeed, precisely in the passages where Mark does
not stand by their side (as in the preliminary history and in
discourses of Jesus), those two diverge even the furthest
from one another, while they in the main go together where
Mark presents himself as the intervening link. Such an intervening link between the two Mark could not be as a subsequent worker and compiler, but only as a previous worker
in the field, whose treatise—freshly moulded from the apostolic fountainhead in simplicity, objectivity, homogeneous-
ness, and historical continuity—furnished a chief basis, first, in
the gradual formation of our Matthew, and then also for Luke.
It is simply inconceivable that Mark could have passed over,
in particular, the rich materials which Luke has peculiar to
himself (as is still the opinion of Köstlin, p. 334), merely
from the endeavour after brevity and a laying aside of
everything anti-Jewish. As regards the origin of the Gospel
of Mark, we must accordingly abide simply by the testimony
of Papias: it is primarily to be traced back to the communications of Peter, and with this view admirably agrees
the characteristic discourse of the latter in Acts x. 36 ; in fact,
this discourse may be regarded as a *programme* of our Gospel.
Other special sources are not sufficiently recognisable,[1] apart
from the primitive evangelic tradition in general, under the
influence of which the companion of Paul, Barnabas, and Peter
of necessity came, and from the collection of *Logia* of Matthew,
which, as the most ancient (see on Matthew, Introd. p. 12 ff.)
document intended for the natives of Palestine, could not
have remained unknown to Mark, the inhabitant of Jerusalem.
Rightly have not only Weisse and Wilke, but also Lachmann,
Hitzig, Reuss, Ewald, Ritschl, Thiersch, Volkmar, Tobler,
Plitt, Holtzmann, Weiss, Schenkel, Weizsäcker, and others

---

[1] According to Fritzsche and Bleek, Mark is alleged to have used not merely
Matthew and Luke, but even the Gospel of John. The state of the case is
directly the reverse.

(see also Güder in Herzog's *Encykl.* IX. p. 47 f.), maintained the *primitive evangelic* character of Mark in relation to the rest of our Gospels, and thus there is taken " a great step towards finding our way in the labyrinth of Gospel-harmony" (Thiersch, *Kirche im Apost. Zeitalt.* p. 102), however strongly Baur and his school (Köstlin, in the most complex fashion) contend against it with their hypothesis of a special "tendency" (see § 3), and with the aid of a Papian primitive-Mark; while Hilgenfeld withal, following Augustine and Hug, insists upon the priority of Mark to Luke, and consequently on the intermediate position of Mark between Matthew and Luke.[1] According to the opinion of Delitzsch (*neue unters. üb. d. Entsteh. u. Anl. d. kanon. Evang.* I., 1853), in connection with his mistaken discovery (see on Matt. Introd. p. 36) that the writing of the evangelic history, proceeding in the footsteps of the Thora, was created by Matthew, the dependence of Mark on Matthew would appear as so great, that even the *possibility* of the converse relation vanishes before it,—a dependence which, we may add, Hilgenfeld thinks to explain by the dubious hypothesis, opening the door to much that is arbitrary, of a Gospel of Peter or of the Petrine-Roman tradition as an intermediate step (see on the other hand Baur, *Markusevang.* p. 119 ff.; Ritschl in the *theol. Jahrb.* 1851, p. 482 ff.; Weiss in the *Stud. u. Krit.* 1861, p. 691 ff.; Holtzmann in his *synopt. Evang.*).

The Gospel has *three main divisions,* of which the first goes as far as the choice of the Twelve (iii. 13), and the last begins from the setting out for Judaea (chap. x.).

REMARK 1.—Although Mark was chiefly dependent on the communications of Peter, still the Petrine *tendency* is not to be attributed to his Gospel (in opposition to Hilgenfeld), as appears by the very fact, that from his Gospel there is actually absent the saying of Jesus concerning the Rock of the church (Matt. xvi. 17). See generally, Baur in the *theol. Jahrb.* 1853, p. 56 ff., and *Markusevang.* p. 133 ff. Comp. on viii. 29; also Weiss in the *Stud. u. Krit.* 1861, p. 674 f.

[1] Especially since 1850, then in his long controversy with Baur, and once more in his *Kanon u. Kritik d. N. T.* 1863, and in his *Zeitschr.* 1864, p. 287 ff.

REMARK 2.—In making use of *particular passages* of Mark to prove his independence or dependence on the other Synoptics, the greatest caution is necessary, not to educe from our reading of them what is already in our own mind as the critical view of the relation. The experience of the most recent criticism is a warning against this, for in it very often what one takes to be *in his favour* is by another turned *against* him, according to the colouring imported by the subjectivity of each. Even from the O. T. citation in Mark i. 2, 3, compared with Matt. iii. 3, xi. 10, we cannot draw any inference either for (Ritschl) or against the dependence of Matthew on Mark; see Baur in the *theol. Jahrb.* 1853, p. 89 f. Comp. on i. 2 f.

§ 3.—PURPOSE, TIME, PLACE.

Like all the canonical Gospels, ours also has the *destined purpose* of historically proving the Messiahship of Jesus: it seeks to accomplish this especially by setting forth the *deeds* of Jesus, but in doing so does not bear any special dogmatic colour.[1] It leaves out of consideration the doctrinal differences that agitate the subsequent apostolic period, and goes to work quite objectively. We must not on this account, however, assume a *mediating* aim in the interest of the idea of catholicity, and consequently a neutral character accordant with that tendency [2] (Schwegler, Baur, Köstlin, and others, with more precise definitions various in kind), or a mediating between the Jewish-Christian Matthew and the Pauline Luke (Hilgenfeld), for assumptions of which sort it was thought that a welcome external support was to be found in the very fact, that Mark's place was from old assigned to him only after Matthew, and relatively (according to Clem. Al.) even only after Luke. The omission of a genealogy and preliminary history does not betray the design of a neutral attitude (Schwegler alleges even that a Docetic reference is implied), but simply points to a time for

[1] Not even the character of artistic construction, which (according to Hilgenfeld) is designed to turn on the contrast of light and shade. But the alternation of light and shade is involved in the course of the history, not in the artistic premeditation of a literary plan.

[2] According to Baur, even the name for this neutral and mediating Gospel is significantly chosen : "Mark," the interpreter of *Peter* and the companion of *Paul.*

its origin, in which, among Gentile Christians, such matters as these had not yet attained the importance of being regarded as elements of the Gospel.[1] And the work is composed for *Gentile Christians*, as is evident beyond any doubt from the total absence of proofs drawn from the O. T. (excepting only i. 2 f., see *in loc.*) and of Judaistic elements of doctrine (Köstlin, p. 314), as also from the comparison of many points of detail with the parallel passages in Matthew (see Holtzmann, p. 385 ff.). Comp. on x. 12, vii. 1 ff., xi. 17, and others.

With respect to the *time* of composition, the Gospel must, in accordance with the eschatological statements in chap. xiii. (see especially, vv. 13, 24, 30, 33), and because it preceded our Matthew, have been written at all events before the destruction of Jerusalem, although Weizsäcker concludes the contrary from the parable iv. 26—29 (see *in loc.*). This is more precisely defined by the statement of Irenaeus, iii. 1 (in Eus. v. 8), that Mark published the Gospel after the death (ἔξοδον, not: departure, as Mill, Grabe, Aberle, and others will have it[2]) of Peter and Paul. By this we must abide; and as there is not historical ground for going back to an earlier period (Hitzig: years 55–57; Schenkel, 45–58), the treating of that assertion of Irenaeus with suspicion, as if it might have flowed from 2 Pet. i. 15 (Eichhorn, Hug, Fritzsche), and were too much of a doctrinal nature (Weizsäcker), is unfounded. See Credner, I. p. 118. The account of Clement, *Hypotyp.* 6 (in Eus. *H. E.* vi. 14), that Mark published his Gospel while Peter was *still alive* in captivity at Rome, makes indeed but an inconsiderable difference in the definition of the time, yet was so welcome to the interest felt in its apostolic authority, that Eusebius not merely added the *confirmation* of the

---

[1] The opinion of Volkmar (*d. Relig. Jesu u. ihre erste Entwickelung*, 1857, and *geschichtstreue Theol.* 1858)—that the Gospel of Mark as an Epos is a *Pauline treatise with a set purpose* in opposition to the Judaistic reaction, and has as its presupposition the Judaistic *Apocalypse*, and that, having come into existence *under Titus*, it became the foundation for the rest of the Gospels—is a critical extravagance. See in opposition to it, Hilgenfeld in the *theol. Jahrb.* 1857, p. 387 ff., and in his *Zeitschr.* 1859, p. 252 ff., 1861, p. 190 ff., also in *Kanon u. Kritik*, p. 175 ff.

[2] See Hilgenfeld in his *Zeitschr.* 1864, p. 224.

treatise on the part of Peter (see § 2), but also transferred the
apostle's sojourn at Rome in question to the very earliest time
possible, namely, to the third year of Claudius (ten years after
the death of Christ), when Peter was said to have been there
together with Philo and Simon Magus (Eus. *H. E.* ii. 14, 15, 17),
which incorrect determination of the date of our Gospel was
in consequence adopted by Theophylact, Euthymius Zigabenus,
and others.   Later critics, who place Mark in point of time
after Matthew and Luke (Griesbach's hypothesis), or at least
after Matthew (Hilgenfeld), do not make it come into existence
till after the destruction of Jerusalem (de Wette, Bleek, and
others; Hilgenfeld: under Domitian), to which view Weisse
also ("under the influences of the lively impression of the
conquest") is inclined; Köstlin, assigning to the alleged older
Mark of Papias the date 65-70 A.D., makes the canonical
Gospel appear in the first decade of the second century.   Baur
puts it down still lower in the second century, as indeed he
assigns to the canonical Gospels in general no earlier date
than 130-170.

The *place* of composition is not known with certainty, but
the preponderant voice of ecclesiastical tradition (Clement,
Eusebius, Jerome, Epiphanius, and many others) names
Rome, which is not necessarily connected with the supposition that Mark wrote his Gospel while Peter was still alive,
and has no internal reasons against it, but still is not to
be made good by the Latin expressions which occur, as at
vi. 27, vii. 4, 8, xv. 39, 44, and explanations such as xv. 16,
xii. 42, or by x. 12, xv. 21.   Most of the later critics have
declared themselves in favour of the Roman origin (Gieseler,
Ewald, Hilgenfeld, Köstlin, Schwegler, Guerike, and several
others), and the evidence in its behalf can only gain in
weight from the fact that even at a very early period Alexandria was assigned to Mark as a sphere of labour.   It is
true that Chrysostom names *Alexandria* as the place of composition, but to this the less value is to be attached that
no Alexandrian confirms it.   Hence the *combination* of Rome
and Alexandria by the assumption of a *twofold* publication (Richard Simon, Lardner, Eichhorn) is unnecessary, and

cannot be made good, not even by the statement of Jerome: "Assumpto itaque Evangelio, quod ipse confecerat, perrexit Aegyptum."

§ 4.——PRIMARY LANGUAGE, ORIGINALITY, INTEGRITY.

Mark wrote *in Greek*, as the Fathers are unanimous either in presupposing or in expressly testifying. It is true that there occurs in the Peshito as a subscription, and in the Philoxenian on the margin (comp. also Ebedjesu, in Assem. *Bibl. Or.* III. 1, p. 9), the remark that at Rome he preached in the *Roman tongue;* and several manuscripts of the Greek text (see Scholz, p. xxx.; Tisch. p. 325) distinctly affirm that he *wrote* in Latin, but this entire statement is a hasty inference from the supposition that Mark wrote at *Rome* and for *Romans.* Nevertheless, to the Roman Catholics, in the interest of the Vulgate, it could not but be welcome, so that it was defended by Baronius (*ad ann.* 45, No. 39 ff.) and others. Since the days of Richard Simon, however, it has been again given up even among Catholic scholars. It was even given out that the Latin autograph was preserved in Venice, but that has long since been unmasked as a portion of the Vulgate (see Dobrowsky, *fragment. Pragense ev. St. Marci vulgo autographi,* Prag 1778; Michaelis, *orient. Bibl.* XIII. 108, *Einl.* II. p. 1073 ff.).

The *originality* of our Gospel has found *assailants* only in recent times, and that, indeed, on the ground of the account of Papias, on which its originality was formerly *based.* It was thought to be discovered that what Papias says of the Gospel of Mark does not suit our Gospel (see Schleiermacher in the *Stud. u. Krit.* 1832, p. 758 ff.; Credner, *Einl.* I, p. 123), and it was further inferred (see especially, Credner, *l.c.* and p. 205 [1]) that the Gospel in its present form could not be the

---

[1] Subsequently Credner (see his work, *das neue Test. nach Zweck, Ursprung, Inhalt,* 1843, II. p. 213 ff.) has declared *in favour of the genuineness* of our Gospel, and has looked upon the testimony of Papias as affirming that the order of events in the three Synoptics does not correspond to the reality. But even this does not follow from the words of Papias rightly apprehended.

work of Mark, but that another had worked up the notes
which Mark had made without regard to arrangement, and
thereby the εὐαγγέλιον κατὰ Μάρκον had come into existence.   In the further progress of criticism, the hypothesis was
developed of a *pre-canonical* or *primitive*-Mark [*Urmarkus*]
which had been an *Evangelium Petri*, a hypothesis variously
elaborated in particular by Baur, Köstlin, and others.
According to Köstlin, this primitive Gospel (which is held to
form the basis of Matthew also) was composed in Syria, and
formed, along with Matthew and Luke, a chief source for our
canonical Mark, which is alleged to be a later product of the
idea of catholicity.   But the assumption of an original
treatise that has been lost would only have a historical
point of support, in the event of the contents of the fragment
of Papias—so far as it speaks of the treatise of Mark—not
really suiting our canonical Mark.   But since, upon a correct
interpretation (see on Matt. Introd. p. 41 ff.), it contains
nothing with which our Mark is at variance, and therefore
affords no ground for the assertion that it is speaking of
another book ascribed to Mark, it remains the most ancient
and the most weighty historical testimony for the originality of our second Gospel, and at the same time for the high
historical value of its contents.   With this view, no doubt,
the much asserted dependence on Matthew—or on Matthew
and Luke—cannot subsist, because this runs directly counter
to the testimony of Papias; and to get rid of that testimony
is a proceeding which amounts to peremptory dogmatism
(de Wette), to arbitrary conjecture (Baur, *Markusevang.* p.
131 f., who alleges that Papias has combined things not
connected with each other, namely, the existence of the
Gospel of Mark, which, perhaps, had not been even known to
him, and the tradition of the discourses which Peter is alleged
to have delivered on his apostolic journeys), and to contradiction of history (as opposed to the testimonies of Irenaeus,
Clement, Eusebius), as if the Fathers, to whom at any rate
our Mark was very well known, would have only thus blindly
repeated the story of Papias.

On the supposition of the originality of our Mark, the comparison of Matthew and Luke, who made use of him, presents no constraining reason *for the view*, that the Gospel, in the form in which we possess it, has been preserved merely in a recension modified by various omissions, additions, and alterations (Ewald, comp. Hitzig, Weisse, Holtzmann, Schenkel, Weizsäcker, also Reuss, Köstlin, and others), or, indeed, that that form, in which his Gospel has been made use of in our Gospel of Matthew, as well as by Luke, was preceded by one still earlier (Ewald), especially as Mark has not always followed the most original tradition, and in accordance with the peculiar character of his book abstains from giving the longer discourses of Jesus, with the special exception of the eschatological in chap. xiii.; hence, also the Sermon on the Mount is not found in his Gospel,[1] and need not have stood between iii. 19 and iii. 20 (together with the narrative of the centurion at Capernaum). See on iii. 20, Remark.

As to the *integrity* of the Gospel, the only question to be considered is that of the genuineness of the concluding section, xvi. 6–20. See, regarding this, the critical remarks on chap. xvi.

[1] On the hypothesis of the Gospel being prepared with *a special purpose*, this discourse is regarded as having been omitted by Mark, because he did not wish to bring into remembrance the continuing obligation of the law, Matt. v. 17. See especially, Baur, *Evang.* p. 565. As if this would have been a sufficient reason for the exclusion of the entire discourse! Just as little as the alleged Ebionitic commencement of the discourse.

Εὐαγγέλιον κατὰ Μάρκον.

B F א have merely κατὰ Μάρκον. Others: τὸ κατὰ Μάρκον ἅγιον εὐαγγέλιον. Others: ἐκ τοῦ κ. Μ. ἁγίου εὐαγγελίου. Comp. on Matt. p. 45.

CHAPTER I.

Ver. 2. The *Recepta* has ἐν τοῖς προφήταις, following A E F G** H K M P S U V г, min. Iren. and other Fathers and vss. Defended by Rinck on account of Matt. iii. 3; placed by Lachm. in the margin. But Griesb. Scholz, Lachm. Tisch. have ἐν (ἐν τῷ, Lachm. Tisch.) Ἠσαΐᾳ (in Lachm. always with the spiritus lenis) τῷ προφήτῃ. So B D L Δ א, min. and many vss. and Fathers. Rightly; the *Recepta* was introduced because the quotation is from *two* prophets. — After ὁδόν σου Elz. has ἔμπροσθέν σου, from Matthew and Luke. — Ver. 5. πάντες] which in Elz. Scholz, and Fritzsche stands after ἐβαπτίζοντο, is rightly placed by Griesb. Lachm. and Tisch. after Ἱεροσολ. (B D L Δ א, min. vss. Or. Eus.). If καὶ ἐβαπτ. πάντες had been the original arrangement and πάντες had been put back, it would, conformably to usage (πᾶσα ἡ Ἰουδαία), have been placed before οἱ Ἱεροσολ. The *Recepta* is explained from the circumstance that πάντες was *omitted* (so still in min. and Brix.), and that it was then restored beside ἐβαπτίζοντο, because in Matt. iii. 5 also Ἱεροσόλυμα stands *alone*. — Ver. 10. ἀπό] So also Scholz. But Fritzsche, Lachm. Tisch. have ἐκ, which also Griesb. approved of, following B D L Δ א, min. Goth.; ἀπό is from Matt. iii. 16. — Ver. 11. ἐν ᾧ] Lachm. Tisch. have ἐν σοί, following B D L P א, min. vss. The latter is right; ἐν ᾧ is from Matt. iii. 17. — Ver. 13. Elz. Scholz, Fritzsche have ἐκεῖ after ἦν. It is wanting in A B D L א, min. vss. Or.; it was, however, very easily passed over as superfluous (K. min. omit ἐν τ. ἐρ.) between ἦν and ἐν. — Ver. 14. τῆς βασιλείας] is not found in B L א, min. vss. Or. It is regarded as suspicious by Griesb., deleted by Lachm. and Tisch. It is an addition in accordance with what follows. Comp. Matt. iv. 23. — Ver. 16. περιπατῶν δέ] Lachm. and Tisch.

read καὶ παράγων, which Griesb. also approved, following
B D L א, min. Vulg. It. *al.* The *Recepta* is from Matt. iv. 18,
from which place also came subsequently αὐτοῦ, instead of
which Σιμῶνος (Lachm.: τοῦ Σιμῶνος) is with Tisch. to be read,
according to B L M א. — ἀμφιβάλλ.] Elz. has βάλλοντας, contrary
to decisive evidence. From Matt. iv. 18. — Ver. 18. αὐτῶν] is,
with Lachm. and Tisch., following B C L א, min. vss., to be
deleted as a familiar addition, as also in ver. 31 αὐτῆς. — Ver. 19.
ἐκεῖθεν] is wanting in B D L, min. vss. Condemned by Griesb.,
deleted by Fritzsche and Tisch., bracketed by Lachm. From
Matt. iv. 21. — Ver. 21. The omission of εἰσελθών (Tisch.) is
attested indeed by C L Δ א, min. Syr. Copt. Colb. Or. (twice),
which assign various positions to ἐδιδ. (Tisch.: ἐδιδ. εἰς τ. συναγωγήν),
but might easily be produced by a clerical error on occasion of
the following εἰς, and it has the preponderance of the witnesses
against it. — Ver. 24. ἔα] is wanting in B D א*, min. Syr.
Perss. Arr. Aeth. Copt. Vulg. It. Aug. Deleted by Lachm. and
Tisch. The exclamation, which only occurs again in Luke
iv. 34, and is there more strongly attested, was the more easily
introduced here from that place. — Ver. 26. ἐξ αὐτοῦ] Lachm.:
ἀπ᾽ αὐτοῦ, without preponderating testimony. From Luke
iv. 35. — Ver. 27. Instead of πρὸς αὐτούς, read with Lachm., in
accordance with decisive evidence, πρὸς ἑαυτούς. Tisch., following only B א, has merely αὐτούς. — τί ἐστι τοῦτο; τίς ἡ διδαχὴ ἡ
καινὴ αὕτη; ὅτι κατ᾽ κ.τ.λ.] Lachm.: τί ἐστιν τοῦτο; διδαχὴ καινή· κατ᾽
κ.τ.λ. Just so Rinck and Tisch., who, however, connect διδ.
καινὴ κατ᾽ ἐξουσ. together. The authority of this reading depends
on B L Δ א, min.; it is to be preferred, since manifestly the
original διδαχὴ καινὴ κατ᾽ ἐξουσίαν was *conformed* to the question
in Luke, τίς ὁ λόγος αὕτος, ὅτι κ.τ.λ., and thus arose τίς ἡ διδαχὴ ἡ
καινὴ αὕτη, ὅτι. — Ver. 28. Instead of ἐξῆλθε δέ, preponderating
attestation favours καὶ ἐξῆλθεν (Lachm. Tisch.). — After εὐθύς
Tisch. has πανταχοῦ.[1] So B C L א** min. codd. It. Copt.
Rightly so; the superfluous word, which might easily be
regarded as inappropriate (א* min. omit εὐθύς also), dropped
away. — Ver. 31. εὐθέως] after πυρ. is wanting in B C L א, min.
Copt. Arm.; and D, Vulg. Cant. have it before ἀφῆκεν. Suspected by Griesb., deleted by Tisch. But it was easily omitted,
since Matt. viii. 15 and Luke iv. 39 have not this defining
word. — Ver. 38. After ἄγωμεν, B C L א, 33, Copt. Aeth. Arm.
Arr. Tisch. have ἀλλαχοῦ. To be adopted (comp. Bornem. in
the *Stud. u. Krit.* 1843, p. 127); being unnecessary and without corresponding element in Luke iv. 43, it was very easily

---

[1] In the text of the *Synops.* of Tisch. it is omitted by mistake.

passed over; comp. on πανταχοῦ, i. 28.—Instead of ἐξελήλυθα, B C L א, 33 have ἐξῆλθον, which Griesb. and Scholz have approved, and Tisch. has adopted. Rightly; the explanation of procession *from the Father* suggested the Johannine ἐλήλυθα, which, moreover, Δ and min. actually read.—Ver. 39. εἰς τὰς συναγωγάς] So also Griesb. Lachm. Tisch. on preponderant attestation. The *Recepta* ἐν ταῖς συναγωγαῖς is an emendation.—Ver. 40. καὶ γονυπετῶν αὐτόν] is wanting in B D G Γ, min. Cant. Ver. Verc. Colb. Germ. 1, Corb. 2. Deleted by Lachm.; omission through the homoeoteleuton. Had any addition been made from Matt. viii. 2, Luke v. 12, another expression would have been used. Tisch. has deleted αὐτόν, but following only L א, min. vss.—Ver. 41. ὁ δὲ Ἰησοῦς] B D א, 102, Cant. Verc. Corb. 2 have merely καί. So Lachm. and Tisch. But comp. Matt. viii. 3; Luke v. 13. From these passages comes also the omission of εἰπόντος αὐτοῦ, ver. 42, in B D L א, min. vss. Lachm. Tisch.—Ver. 44. μηδέν] deleted by Lachm., following A L L Δ א, min. vss. Vict. Theophyl. The omission occurred in conformity with Matt. viii. 4; Luke v. 14.— Ver. 45. Elz. reads πανταχόθεν. But πάντοθεν is decisively attested.

Vv. 1–4. As our canonical Matthew has a *superscription of his first section,* so also has Mark. This, however, does not embrace merely ver. 1, but ὡς γέγραπται . . . τὰς τρίβους αὐτοῦ *belongs also to the superscription,* so that with ver. 4 the section itself (which goes on to ver. 8, according to Ewald to ver. 15) begins. It is decisive in favour of this view, that with it there is nothing either to be supplied or to be put in parenthesis, and that it is in the highest degree appropriate not only to the simplicity of the style, but also to the peculiar historical standpoint of the author, seeing that he places the beginning of the Gospel, *i.e. the first announcement of the message of salvation as to the Messiah having appeared*— leaving out of view all the preliminary history in which this announcement was already included — in strictness only at the emergence of the Baptist; but *for this,* on account of the special importance of *this* initial point (and see also the remarks on vv. 21–28), he even, contrary to his custom, elsewhere appends a prophetic utterance, in conformity with which that ἀρχή took place in such a way and not otherwise than is related in ver. 4 ff. Moreover, in accordance with this, since the history of that ἀρχή itself does not begin till ver. 4, the want of a particle with ἐγένετο, ver. 4, is quite in order. Comp. Matt. i. 2. If, with Fritzsche, Lachmann,[1] Hitzig, Holtzmann, we construe : ἀρχὴ ... ἐγένετο Ἰωάννης βαπτίζων, then ὡς γέγραπται κ.τ.λ. becomes a parenthetical clause, in which case the *importance* of the Scripture proof has not due justice done to it, and the structure of the sentence becomes too complicated and clumsy for the simplicity of what follows. If we take merely ver. 1 as the superscription either of the first section only with Kuinoel and others, or of the entire Gospel with Erasmus, Bengel, Paulus, de Wette, and others, then ὡς γέγραπται becomes protasis of ἐγένετο κ.τ.λ., but thereby the citation, instead of being probative of the ἀρχή laid down by Mark, becomes a Scripture proof for the *emergence of John in itself,* and in that way loses its import- ant bearing, seeing that this emergence in itself did not need any scriptural voucher at all, and would not have received any, in accordance with Mark's abstinence from adducing Old Testament passages. Finally, if we supply after ver. 1 : *ἦν, the beginning . . . was, as it stands written* (Theophylact, Euthymius Zigabenus, Vatablus, Maldonatus, Jansen, Grotius, and others), doubtless the want of the article with ἀρχή is not against this course (see Winer, p. 113 [E. T. 154]), nor yet the want of a γάρ with ἐγένετο—an asyndeton which would rather conduce to the lively impressiveness of the representa- tion (comp. John i. 6); but it may well be urged that the supplying of ἦν is *unnecessary,* and even injurious to the vivid concrete representation. Moreover, in the very fact that

---

[1] The conjecture of Lachmann (*Stud. u. Krit.* 1830, p. 84, and *praefat.* II. p. vi.), that vv. 2, 3 are a later interpolation, is critically quite unwarranted. According to Ewald and Weizsäcker, p. 105, ver. 2 f. is not from the hand of the first author, but is inserted by the second editor ; in opposition to which, nevertheless, it is to be remarked that similar O. T. insertions, which might proceed from a second hand, are not found elsewhere in our Gospel. According to Holtzmann, p. 261, only the citation from Isaiah appeared in the primitive- Mark, and the evangelist further added the familiar passage of Malachi. In this way at all events,—as he allowed simply ἐν Ἡσαΐᾳ to stand,—he would have appropriated to Isaiah what belongs to Malachi ; and the difficulty would remain unsolved. There is therefore no call for the appeal to the primitive- Mark.

Mark just commences his book with the emergence of the
Baptist, there is ingenuously (without any purpose of contrast
to other Gospels, without neutral tendency, or the like) exhibited
the original type of the view which was taken of the Gospel
history,—a type which again, after the *terminus a quo* had been
extended in Matthew and Luke so as to embrace the preliminary
histories, presents itself in John, inasmuch as the latter, after
his general introduction and even in the course of it (ver. 6),
makes his historical commencement with the emergence of the
Baptist.   Undoubtedly, traditions of the preliminary history
were also known to Mark ; in leaving them unnoticed he does
not reject them, but still he does not find in them—lying as
they do back in the gloom prior to the great all-significant
epoch of the emergence of John—the ἀρχὴ τοῦ εὐαγγ.—Ἰησοῦ
Χριστοῦ] See on Matt. i. 1.   When the genitive with εὐαγγ. is
not a person, it is always genitive of the *object*, as εὐαγγ. τῆς
βασιλείας, τῆς σωτηρίας κ.τ.λ. (Matt. iv. 23 ; Eph. i. 13,
vi. 15, *al.*).   If Θεοῦ is associated therewith, it is the genitive
of the *subject* (i. 15 ; Rom. i. 1, xv. 16, *al.*), as is the case
also when μου stands with it (Rom. ii. 16, xvi. 25 ; 1 Thess.
i. 5, *al.*).   But if Χριστοῦ is associated therewith (Rom. i. 9,
xv. 19 ; 1 Cor. ix. 12, *al.*), it may be either the genitive
subjecti (*auctoris*) or the genitive *objecti*, a point which must
be determined entirely by the context.   In this case it decides
(see vv. 2–8) in favour of the latter.   Taken as genitive
subjecti (Ewald : " how Christ began to preach the gospel of
God "), τοῦ εὐαγγ. Ἰ. Χ. would have reference to ver. 14 f.;
but in that case the non-originality of vv. 2, 3 is presupposed.
— υἱοῦ τ. Θεοῦ] not as in Matt. i. 1, because Mark had
primarily in his view Gentile-Christian readers ;[1] see Introd.
§ 3.   This designation of the *Messiah* is used in the believing
consciousness of the *metaphysical* sonship of God (comp. on

---

[1] The absence of υἱοῦ τ. Θεοῦ in א, two min., and some Fathers (including Iren.
and Or.) has not so much critical importance as to warrant the deletion of these
words by Tischendorf (ed. maj. viii.).   In his *Synopsis*, Tischendorf had still
rightly preserved them.   The omission of them has just as little dogmatical
reason as the addition would have had.   But ἀρχὴ τοῦ εὐαγγ., as in itself a *complete* idea, was taken together with the following ὡς γίγρ. ; and thence all the
genitives, Ἰ. Χ. υ. τ. Θ., which could be dispensed with, were passed over the

Matt. iii. 17), and that in the Pauline and Petrine sense (see on Matt. p. 65 f.). The supernatural generation is by υἱοῦ τ. Θεοῦ neither assumed (Hilgenfeld) nor excluded (Köstlin); even vi. 3 proves nothing.— ἐν Ἡσαΐα] The following quotation combines Mal. iii. 1 and Isa. xl. 3. In this case, instead of all sorts of hypotheses (see them in Fritzsche), we must abide by the simple admission, that *by a mistake of memory* (of which, indeed, Porphyry made a bitter use, see Jerome, *ad Matt.* iii. 3) Mark thought of the whole of the words as to be found in Isaiah,—a mistake which, considering the affinity of the contents of the two sayings, and the pre-valence of their use and their interpretation, is all the more conceivable, as Isaiah was " copiosior et notior " (Bengel). A different judgment would have to be formed, if the passage of Isaiah *stood first* (see Surenhusius, καταλλ. p. 45). Matt. xxvii. 9 was a similar error of memory. According to Hengstenberg, *Christol.* III. p. 664, Mark has ascribed the entire passage to Isaiah, because Isaiah is the auctor *primarius*, to whom Malachi is related only as auctor *secundarius*, as expositor. A process of reflection is thus imputed to the evangelist, in which, moreover, it would be sufficiently strange that he should not *have placed first* the utterance of the auctor *primarius*, which is held to be *commented on* by that of the minor prophet.—As to the two passages themselves, see on Matt. iii. 3, xi. 10. The essential agreement in form of the first citation with Matt. xi. 10 cannot be used, in determining to which of the two evangelists the priority is due, as a means of proof (Anger and others, in favour of Matthew; Ritschl and others, in favour of Mark); it can only be used as a ground of confirmation, after a decision of this question has been other-wise arrived at. Just as little does the quotation form a proof for a *primitive-Mark*, in which, according to Holtzmann and

more readily by reason of the homoeoteleuta. So still in Ir. int. and Epiph. Others allowed at least Ἰησοῦ Χριστοῦ to remain, or restored these words Besides, υἱοῦ τ. Θεοῦ is precisely so characteristic of Mark's Gospel in contra-distinction to that of Matthew, that it could scarcely proceed from a transcriber, as, in fact, the very oldest vss. (and indeed *all* vss.) have read it; for which reason merely a sporadic diffusion is to be assigned to the reading without υἱοῦ τ. Θεοῦ.

others, it is alleged not to have held a place at all. — ἐγένετο] *might* be connected with βαπτίζων (Erasmus, Beza, Grotius, Kuinoel, and others), see Heindorf, *ad Plat. Soph.* p. 273 f.; Lobeck, *ad Aj.* 588; Kühner, II. p. 40. But the mention of the *emergence* of the Baptist is in keeping with the *beginning* of the history.[1] Hence : *there appeared John, baptizing in the desert.* Comp. John i. 6 ; 1 John ii. 18 ; 2 Pet. ii. 1 ; Xen. *Anab.* iii. 4. 49, iv. 3. 29, *al.* Comp. παραγίνεται, Matt. iii. 1, and on Phil. ii. 7. As to *the desert* (the *well-known* desert), see on Matt. iii. 1. — βάπτισμα μετανοίας] *a baptism involving an obligation to repentance* (see on Matt. iii. 2), genitive of the characteristic quality. — εἰς ἄφεσιν ἁμαρτ.] Comp. Luke iii. 3. The aim of this baptism, in order that men, prepared for the purpose by the μετάνοια, should receive forgiveness of sins from the Messiah. Comp. Euthymius Zigabenus. This is not an addition derived from a later Christian view (de Wette, comp. Weiss in the *Stud. u. Krit.* 1861, p. 61), but neither is it to be taken in such a sense as that John's baptism itself secured the forgiveness (Hofmann, *Schriftbew.* I. p. 606; Ewald). This baptism could, through its reference to the Mediator of the forgiveness who was approaching (John i. 29, 33, iii. 5 ; Acts ii. 38), give to those, who allowed themselves to be baptized and thereby undertook the obligation to repentance, the certain *prospect* of the ἄφεσις which was to be received only through Christ—promising, but not imparting it. Matthew has not the words, the passing over of which betrays an exercise of reflection upon the difference between John's and the Christian baptism.

Vv. 5–8. See on Matt. iii. 4, 5, 11; Luke iii. 7 ff. Matthew enters more into detail on John the Baptist; Mark has several particulars in a form more original. — πᾶσα ἡ Ἰουδ. κ.τ.λ.] Ἰουδ. is an adjective (see on John iii. 22), and χώρα is in contrast to the metropolis (see on John xi. 54 f.), the *whole Judaean region, and the people of Jerusalem collectively.*

[1] Ewald (comp. Hitzig) connects ἐγίνετο with κηρύσσων, reading ὁ βαπτίζων in accordance with B L Δ ℵ (comp. vi. 14), and omitting the subsequent καί with B, min. "John the Baptist was just preaching," etc. The critical witnesses for these readings are not the same, and not sufficiently strong; there has evidently been an alteration in accordance with Matt. iii. 1. Tischendorf has rightly reverted to the *Recepta.*

In πᾶσα and πάντες there is a popular *hyperbole.* — Ver. 6.
Instead of ἐσθίων, we must write, with Tischendorf, ἔσθων.[1]
— Ver. 7. ἔρχεται] *present :* "ut Christum intelligas jam
fuisse in via," Beza. — κύψας] belongs to the graphic character of Mark, whose delineation is here certainly more
original than that of Matthew. — ἐν πνεύμ. ἁγίῳ] The *fire*,
which Matthew (and Luke also) has in the connection of his
more comprehensive narrative, is not yet mentioned here, and
thus there is wanting a characteristic point, which, nevertheless,
appears not to be original. Comp. John i. 33 (in opposition to
Ewald, Köstlin, Holtzmann, and others). It would not have
been "abrupt" (Holtzmann) even in Mark.

Vv. 9-11. See on Matt. iii. 13-17 ; Luke iii. 21 f. — εἰς
τὸν Ἰορδάνην] Conception of *immersion.* Not so elsewhere
in the N. T.—εὐθύς] usual form in Mark ; we must, with
Tischendorf, read it here also. It belongs to ἀναβ. : *immediately* (after He was baptized) *coming up.* A hyperbaton
(Fritzsche refers εὐθ. to εἶδε) just as little occurs here as at
Matt. iii. 16. — εἶδε] Jesus, to whom also ἐπ' αὐτόν refers
(see on Matt. *l.c.*). Mark *harmonizes* with Matthew (in
opposition to Strauss, Weisse, de Wette), who gives a further
development of the history of the baptism, but whose ἀνεῴχ-
θησαν αὐτῷ οἱ οὐρ. presents itself in Mark under a more
directly definite form. In opposition to the context, Erasmus,
Beza, Heumann, Ebrard, and others hold that *John* is the subject.
— σχιζομένους, conveying a more vivid sensuous impression
than Matthew and Luke. — Lange's poetically naturalizing
process of explaining (*L. J.* II. 1, p. 182 ff.) the phenomena
at the baptism of Jesus is pure fancy when confronted with
the clearness and simplicity of the text. He transforms the
voice into the sense of God on Christ's part ; with which all
the chords of His life, even of His life of hearing, had
sounded in unison, and the voice had communicated itself
sympathetically to John also. The dove which John saw is

[1] See on this poetical form, which occurs also in the LXX. and Apocrypha,
Duncan, *Lex.*, ed. Rost, p. 457; Winer, p. 79 [E. T. 105]; Buttmann, *neut. Gr.*
p. 51 [E. T. 58]. Also at xii. 40, Luke vii. 33 f., **x. 7**, xxii. 30, this form
is to be read.

held to have been the hovering of a mysterious splendour, namely, a now manifested adjustment of the life of Christ with the higher world of light; the stars withal came forth in the dark blue sky, festally wreathing the earth (the opened heaven). All the more jejune is the naturalizing of Schenkel: that at the Jordan for the first time the divine destiny of Jesus dawned before His soul like a silver gleam from above, etc. See, moreover, the Remark subjoined to Matt. iii. 17.

Vv. 12, 13. See on Matt. iv. 1–11; Luke iv. 1 ff. — ἐκβάλλει] *He drives, urges Him forth;* more graphic than the ἀνήχθη of Matthew and the ἤγετο of Luke iv. 1. The sense of force and urgency is implied also in Matt. ix. 38. Observe the frequent use of the vividly realizing *praesens historicus.* — *And He was there* (ἐκεῖ, see the critical remarks) *in the desert* (whither the Spirit had driven Him), *i.e.* in *that region* of the desert, *during forty days, being tempted by Satan,* —a manifest *difference* of Mark (comp. also Luke) from Matthew, with whom it is not till *after* forty days that the temptations *begin.* Evasive interpretations are to be found in Krabbe, Ebrard, and others. — καὶ ἦν μετὰ τῶν θηρίων] *and He was with the wild beasts.* This is *usually*[1] taken as merely a graphic picture (according to de Wette: "a marvellous contrast" to the angels) of the awful solitude (Virg. *Aen.* iii. 646, and see Wetstein *in loc.*); but how remote would such a *poetic* representation be from the simple narrative! No, according to Mark, Jesus is to be conceived as *really surrounded by the wild beasts of the desert.* He is threatened in a twofold manner; Satan tempts Him, and the wild beasts encompass Him. The *typical* reference, according to which Christ is held to appear as the renewer of Paradise (Gen. i. 26 ; Usteri in the *Stud. u. Krit.* 1834, p. 789 ; Gfrörer, Olshausen, comp. Bengel, and also Baur, *Evang.* pp. 540, 564 ; Hilgenfeld, *Evang.* p. 126 ; Schenkel, Holtz-mann), is not indicated by anything in the text, and is foreign to it. The desert and the forty days remind us of *Moses* (Ex. xxiv. 48, xxxiv. 28; Deut. ix. 9, 18), not of *Adam.* — οἱ ἄγγελοι] The article denotes the category. — διηκόνουν αὐτῷ]

---

[1] So also von Engelhardt (*de Jesu Christi tentatione,* Dorp. 1858, p. 5).

There is no occasion at all, from the connection in Mark, to
understand this of the ministering *with food*, as in Matthew;
nor does the expression presuppose the representation of
Matthew (Weiss). On the contrary, we must simply abide
by the view that, according to Mark, is meant *the help which
gives protection against Satan and the wild beasts*. There is in
this respect also a difference from Matthew, that in the latter
Gospel the angels do not appear until after the termination
of the temptations. — The narrative of *Christ's temptation*
(regarding it, see on Matt. iv. 11, Remark) appears in Mark
in its oldest, almost still germinal, form. It is remarkable,
indeed, that in the further development of the evangelic
history (in Matthew and Luke) the wonderful element
ἦν μετὰ τῶν θηρίων (which, according to Hilgenfeld, merely
serves to colour and embellish the meagre extract), should have
remained unnoticed. But the entire interest attached itself
to Satan and to his anti-Messianic agency. The brevity[1]
with which Mark relates the temptation, and which quite
corresponds[2] to the still undeveloped *summary beginning of
the tradition*, is alleged by Baur to proceed from the circumstance that with Mark the matter still lay outside of the
historical sphere. Against this we may decisively urge the
very fact that he narrates it at all, and places the ἀρχὴ τοῦ
εὐαγγ. earlier. Comp. Köstlin, p. 322.

Ver. 14 f. See on Matt. iv. 12, 17; Luke iv. 14 f. — εἰς τ.
Γαλιλ.] in order to be more secure than in the place where
John had laboured; according to Ewald: "He might not
allow the work of the Baptist to fall to pieces." But this
would not furnish a motive for His appearing precisely *in
Galilee*. See Weizsäcker, p. 333. In Matthew also the
matter is conceived of as ἀναχώρησις. — κηρύσσων] *present*

[1] For the idea that κ. οἱ ἀγγ. διηκ. αὐτῷ is only the closing sentence of an
originally longer narration (Weisse, *Evangelienfr.* p. 163) is fanciful. Only the
short, compact account is in harmony with all that surrounds it. Weisse supposes that something has dropped out also after ver. 5 or 6, and after ver. 8.

[2] How awkwardly Mark would here have epitomized, if he had worked as an
epitomizer! How, in particular, would he have left unnoticed the rich moral
contents of the narrative in Matthew and Luke! Schleiermacher and de Wette
reproach him with doing so. Comp. also Bleek.

participle with ἦλθεν. See Dissen, *ad Pind. Ol.* vii. 14, p. 81; Bornemann, *ad Xen. Anab.* vii. 7. 17; Stallbaum, *ad Plat. Phaed.* p. 116 C. — τὸ εὐαγγ. τοῦ Θεοῦ] See on ver. 1. — ὅτι] recitative. — ὁ καιρός] *the period*, namely, which was to last until the setting up of the Messiah's kingdom, ὁ καιρὸς οὗτος, x. 30. It is conceived of as a *measure*. See on Gal. iv. 4. — πιστεύετε ἐν τῷ εὐαγγ.] *Believe on the gospel*. As to πιστ. with ἐν, see on Gal. iii. 26 ; Eph. i. 13 ; frequently in the LXX. The *object* of faith is conceived as that in which the faith is fixed and based. Fritzsche takes ἐν as *instrumental*: " per evangelium ad fidem adducimini." This is to be rejected, since the object of the faith would be *wanting*, and since τὸ εὐαγγ. is just the *news itself*, which Jesus gave in πεπλήρωται κ.τ.λ.

Vv. 16–20. See on Matt. iv. 18–22 (Luke v. 1 ff.). The narrative of Mark has the brevity and vividness of an original. Observe, however, how, according to all the evangelists, Jesus begins His work not with working miracles, but with teaching and collecting disciples.[1] This does not exclude the assumption that miracles essentially belonged to His daily work, and were even from the very beginning associated with His teaching, ver. 21 ff. — παράγων (see the critical remarks), *as He passed along by the sea*. This as well as ἀμφιβάλλ. ἐν τ. θαγ. (*casting around*) is part of the peculiar

---

[1] Comp. Weizsäcker, p. 364. But the teaching begins with the announcement of the kingdom, which has as its presupposition the Messianic self-consciousness (Weizsäcker, p. 425). Without reason Schenkel maintains, p. 370, that Jesus *could* not at all have regarded Himself at the beginning of His work as the Messiah. He might do so, *without* sharing the political Messianic hopes. See Schleiermacher, *L. J.* p. 250 f. ; Keim, *Geschichtl. Chr.* p. 44 f. But the view which makes the beginning of the teaching and miracle-working even precede the baptism (Schleiermacher) has absolutely no foundation in the N. T., not even in the history of the marriage feast at Cana. Nor yet can it be maintained, with Keim (p. 84), that the conviction of being the Messiah gained strength in Jesus gradually from His first emergence up to the decisiveness, which first makes itself manifest at Matt. xi., where He announces the *present* kingdom, no longer merely that which is *approaching*. For the *approaching* kingdom is throughout—only according to a relative conception of time—from the beginning onward to Luke xxi. 31 to be taken in an *eschatological* reference ; and it presupposes, therefore, a Messianic self-certainty in the Son of man, who with this announcement takes up the preaching of the Baptist.

vividness of representation that Mark loves. — Ver. 19. καὶ αὐτούς] et ipsos in nave, likewise in the ship. It does not belong to καταρτίζοντας (the *usual* view, in which there is assumed an imperfect comparison, which contemplates only the fishers' occupation generally, comp. on Matt. xv. 3), but merely to ἐν τῷ πλοίῳ, so that καταρτ. κ.τ.λ. then subjoins a further circumstance. The former explanation in the sense assigned to it would only be possible, if ἀμφιβάλλ., in ver. 16, and καταρτ. were included under *one* more general idea. — Ver. 20. μετὰ τ. μισθωτ.] peculiar to Mark. Any special purpose for this accuracy of detail is not apparent. It is an arbitrary supposition that it is intended to explain how the sons might leave their father without undutifulness (Paulus, Kuinoel, de Wette, Bleek, and others), in reference to which de Wette charges Mark with taking away from their resolution its nobleness.[1] It may, moreover, be *inferred*, that Zebedee carried on his business not altogether on a small scale, and perhaps was not without means. Comp. xvi. 1 ; Luke viii. 3 ; John xix. 27. Only no comparison with the " poverty of Peter " (Hilgenfeld) is to be imported.

Vv. 21–28. Comp. Luke iv. 31–37, who in substance follows Mark ; in opposition to the converse opinion of Baur, see especially Weiss, p. 653. Matthew, freely selecting, has not the history, but has, on the other hand, the more striking casting out of demons contained in Mark v. 1 ff. Mark lays special stress on these healings. — It is only with ver. 21 that Mark's peculiar mode of handling his materials begins,—the more detailed and graphic treatment, which presents a very marked contrast to the brevity of outline in the annalistic record of all that goes before. Perhaps up to this point he has followed an old documentary writing of this character ; and if this comprised also in its contents vv. 1–3, the introduction of the Bible quotation in vv. 2, 3, contrary to the usual custom

---

[1] With greater truth, because more naturally, it might be said that that trait places in so much stronger a light the *resignation* of those who were called, seeing that they forsook a business so successfully prosecuted. Comp. Ewald, p. 192. We may more surely affirm that it is just a mere feature of the detailed description peculiar to Mark. Comp. Weiss, *l.c.* p. 652.

of Mark elsewhere, is the more easily explained. And the fact that now for the first time an independent elaboration begins, is explained from the circumstance that precisely at this point Peter entered into the service of the Lord—from which point of time therefore begins what Peter in his doctrinal discourses had communicated of the doings and sayings of Christ, and Mark had heard and recorded (fragment of Papias).

Ver. 21. εἰσπορεύονται] Jesus and His four disciples. According to Mark, they go *away from the lake* to Capernaum, not from *Nazareth* (thus Victor Antiochenus, Theophylact, Euthymius Zigabenus, and others, following Luke), and not away *from the mount* (according to Matt. viii. 5). Matthew and Luke have differently restored the right historical sequence, the absence of which was felt in the abrupt report of Mark, ver. 21. They thus found here something of the ἔνια, which the fragment of Papias pronounced to be wanting in τάξις (see on Matt. Introd. p. 42 f.). — εὐθέως τοῖς σάββ.] *i.e. immediately on the next Sabbath,* not: on the several Sabbaths (Euthymius Zigabenus, Wolf, and many others), which is forbidden by εὐθέως. σάββατα, as in ii. 23; Matt. xii. 1; Luke iv. 6; Col. ii. 16. — ἐδίδασκε] *What,* Mark does not say, for he is more concerned with the powerful *impression,* with the marvellous *deed* of the teaching, the general tenor of which, we may add, ver. 14 f. does not leave in any doubt. This synagogue-discourse has nothing to do with the sermon on the Mount, as if it were intended to occupy the place of the latter (Hilgenfeld).

Ver. 22. Comp. Matt. vii. 28 f., where the notice of Mark is reproduced unaltered, but placed after the sermon on the Mount; and Luke iv. 32, where the second part of the observation is generalized and divested of the contrast. It is very far-fetched, however, in Hilgenfeld, who in ver. 22 sees a sure indication of dependence on Matthew, to find in the fact, that Mark already here makes *Capernaum* appear as the scene of the ministry of Jesus just as in ver. 29, the *Petrine* character of the Gospel. See, on the other hand, Baur in the *theol. Jahrb.* 1853, p. 56 ff. — As to ἦν διδάσκ. and ὡς ἐξουσ. ἔχων, see on Matt. vii. 28 f.

Ver. 23 f. Ἐν πνεύμ. ἀκαθάρτῳ] to be connected closely
with ἄνθρωπος : *a man in the power of an unclean spirit.* See
on ἐν Matthiae, p. 1141. Comp. v. 2 ; 2 Cor. xii. 2 ; Buttmann, *neut. Gr.* p. 84 [E. T. 96]. As to the *demoniacs,* see
on Matt. iv. 24 ; and as to the miracles of Jesus in general,
see on Matt. viii. 4. — ἀνέκραξε] *he cried aloud* (see Winer,
de verbor. cum praepos. compos. usu, III. p. 7), namely, the man,
who, however, speaks in the person of the demon. Comp.
Matt. viii. 29, where also, as here, the demon *immediately*
discerns the Messiah. — ἡμᾶς] me and those like to me.
" Communem inter se causam habent daemonia," Bengel. —
ἀπολέσαι] by relegation to Hades, like βασανίσαι in Matt. *l.c.*
— ὁ ἅγιος τοῦ θεοῦ] *the hallowed One of God* (John x. 36) κατ'
ἐξοχήν (see Origen and Victor Antiochenus in Possini *Catena*),
a characteristic designation of the *Messiah,* which here proceeds from the consciousness of the unholy demoniac nature
(Luke iv. 34; Acts iv. 27 ; Rev. iii. 7 ; John vi. 69). In a
lower sense priests and prophets were ἅγιοι τοῦ θεοῦ. See
Knapp, *Opusc.* I. p. 33 f. The demon does not name Him
thus as κολακεύων αὐτόν (Euthymius Zigabenus, and before
him Tertullian), but rather by way of giving to His ἦλθες
ἀπολέσαι ἡμᾶς the impress of hopeless certainty.

Ver. 25 f. Αὐτῷ] *to the demon,* who had spoken out of the
man.[1] — The demon, before he goes forth, once more gives
vent to his whole fury on the man by tearing (σπαράξαν) him.
Comp. ix. 26 ; Luke ix. 42.

Ver. 27. Πρὸς ἑαυτούς] is equivalent to πρὸς ἀλλήλους
(Luke iv. 36). The *reason* why the *reflexive* is used, is the
conception of the *contradistinction to others* (they discussed
among one another, not with Jesus and His disciples). See
Kühner, *ad Xen. Mem.* ii. 6. 20. Fritzsche explains : *apud
animum suum.* But συζητεῖν stands opposed to this, designating as it does action *in common,* ix. 10, xii. 28 ; Luke xx. 23,

[1] To refer φιμώθητι, with Strauss, II. p. 21, following older expositors, merely to
the demon's declaration of the Messiahship of Jesus, is, in view of the general
character of the word, arbitrary. It is the command of the victor in general:
Be silent and go out! Strauss appeals to i. 34, iii. 12. But these prohibitions
refer to the time *after* the going out.

xxiv. 15, *al.* ; so also in the classics. — τί ἐστι τοῦτο ;] a natural
demand in astonishment at what had happened *for more precise
information as to the circumstances of the case.*—In what follows
we must read : διδαχὴ καινὴ κατ' ἐξουσίαν· καὶ τοῖς πνεύμασι
τοῖς ἀκαθάρτοις . . . αὐτῷ ! See the critical remarks.   They
give vent by way of exclamation to what has thrown them
into such astonishment and is so incomprehensible to them,
and do so in the unperiodic mode of expression that is appropriate to excited feeling : *a doctrine new in power ! and He
commands the unclean spirits,* etc. ! They marvel at these
two marked points, as they have just perceived them in Jesus.
Lachmann attaches κατ' ἐξουσίαν to καὶ τοῖς πνεύμασι κ.τ.λ.
But this is manifestly opposed to the connection, according to
which κατ' ἐξουσίαν looks back to the foregoing ἦν γὰρ διδάσκων αὐτοὺς ὡς ἐξουσίαν ἔχων.   This applies also in opposition
to Ewald, who reads διδαχῇ καινῇ : " with new teaching He
powerfully commands even the devils."   A confused identifica-
tion of the teaching with the impression of the miraculous
action is here groundlessly discovered by Baur,[1] and used as
a proof of dependence on Luke iv. 36.   Even with the
Recepta ὅτι the two elements of the exclamation would be
very definitely correlative to the *two* elements of the ministry
of Jesus in the synagogue respectively.— κατ' ἐξουσίαν] defines
the reference of καινή : *new in respect to power,* which has never
yet occurred thus with the impress of higher authorization.

Ver. 28. Εἰς ὅλην τ. περίχ. τ. Γαλιλ.] not merely therefore
into Galilee itself, but also *into the whole region that surrounds
Galilee.*   Comp. Luke iii. 3, viii. 37.   This wide diffusion,
the expression of which is still further strengthened by πανταχοῦ (see the critical remarks), is not at variance with the
εὐθύς (Köstlin finds in the word " a mistaken fashion of
exaggeration "), which is to be estimated in accordance with
the lively popular mode of expression.   Criticism becomes

---

[1] Who holds that Mark has not been able to enter into Luke's mode of view,
but has kept to the διδαχή of Jesus in the sense of Matthew, without himself
rightly understanding in what relation the καινὴ διδαχή stood to the ἐπιτάσσειν
κ.τ.λ.   Baur, *Markusevang.* p. 11 ; comp. *theol. Jahrb.* 1853, p. 69 f.   See, on
the other hand, Hilgenfeld, *Evang.* p. 128.

confused by the stress laid on such points. — πανταχοῦ] with the verb of motion, as is often the case among the Greeks: *every-whither.* Comp. on ἀλλαχοῦ, ver. 38.—It is to be observed, we may add, that this first miracle, which Mark and Luke relate, is not *designated* by them *as the first.* Hence there is no inconsistency with John ii. 11 (in opposition to Strauss).

Vv. 29–39. In connection and narrative, Luke iv. 38–44 is parallel. But compare also Matt. viii. 14–17, which proceeds by way of abridgment.

Ver. 29 ff. See on Matt. viii. 14 f. — ἐξελθόντες] Jesus, Peter and Andrew. James and John are thereupon specially named as accompanying. — The short narrative is condensed, animated, graphic,[1] not subjected to elaboration, against which view the mention of *Andrew,* whom Matthew and Luke omit as a secondary person, cannot well be urged. Comp. Weiss, p. 654.

Ver. 32 f. ’Οψίας . . . ἥλιος] an exact specification of time (comp. Matthew *and* Luke) for the purpose of indicating that the close of the Sabbath had occurred. " Judaeos religio tenebat, quominus ante exitum sabbati aegrotos suos afferrent," Wetstein, and, earlier, Victor Antiochenus. — πρὸς αὐτόν] presupposes that before the evening He has returned again to His own dwelling (ii. 1, 15). It is not *Peter's* house that is meant. — πάντας τοὺς κ.τ.λ.] all whom they had.—Here and at ver. 34, as also at Matt. viii. 16, the naturally sick are *distinguished* from the demoniacs; comp. iii. 15. — ἡ πόλις ὅλη] comp. Matt. iii. 5. So also in the classical writers (Thuc. vii. 82. 1 ; Soph. *O. R.* 179) ; comp. Nägelsbach, *Anm. z. Ilias,* ed. 3, p. 103.

Ver. 34. πολλοὺς . . . πολλά] therefore not *all,* which, nevertheless, does not presuppose attempts that were without result. It was already *late,* and in various cases, moreover, the *conditions* of healing might be wanting. — ἤφιε] as in xi. 16.

---

[1] In this point of view the sickness is denoted by the words κατέκειτο πυρέσσ. as severe enough not to allow the event to be treated as a simple soothing of the over-excited nervous system (Schenkel). Mere psychological soothings of this kind would simply stand in utter disproportion to the sensation produced by Jesus as a worker of miracles.

Imperfect, from the form ἀφίω, with the augment on the preposition ; see Winer, p. 74 [E. T. 97]. — λαλεῖν . . . ὅτι] He allowed them not *to speak*, enjoined on them silence, *because* they knew Him. They would otherwise, had they been allowed to *speak*, have *said* that He was the Messiah. Kuinoel, Bleek, and others erroneously take it as if the expression was λέγειν . . . ὅτι. The two verbs (comp. on John viii. 43 ; Rom. iii. 19) are never interchanged in the N. T., not even in such passages as Rom. xv. 18 ; 2 Cor. xi. 17 ; 1 Thess. i. 8 ; hence "*to say that*" is never expressed by λαλεῖν, ὅτι. — As to the *reason* of the prohibition, see on v. 43 and Matt. viii. 4.

Vv. 35–39. Luke iv. 42–44 is less characteristic and more generalized. — ἔννυχον λίαν] *when it was still very dark.* ἔννυχον is the accusative neuter of the definition of time, as σήμερον, αὔριον, νέον, etc. The *word* itself is often found also in classical writers, but not this adverbial use of the accusative neuter (3 Macc. v. 5 ; see, however, Grimm *in loc.*). Comp. ἐννυχώτερον, Aesop, *Fab.* 79. The *plural* form ἔννυχα (in Lachmann and Tischendorf, following B C D L ℵ, min.) is, however, decisively attested, although likewise without sanction from Greek usage ;[1] in Soph. *Aj.* 930, πάννυχα is adjective. — ἐξῆλθε] out of his house, ver. 29. Comp. ii. 1. — κατεδίωξαν] only occurring here in the N. T., more significant than the simple form, expressive of the following *up till they reached* Him ; Thuc. ii. 84. 3 ; Polyb. vi. 42. 1 ; Ecclus. xxvii. 17 ; Ps. xxii. 18. — καὶ οἱ μετ' αὐτοῦ] Andrew, John, and James, ver. 29. Under this expression is already implied the conception of the historical prominent position of Peter. But such an expression does not betray any special *Petrine tendency* of the Gospel. — πάντες] puts Jesus in mind of the multitude of yesterday, vv. 32, 34. — ἀλλαχοῦ] with a verb of direction, comp. ver. 28 and on Matt. ii. 22. The following εἰς τὰς ἐχομ. κωμοπ., *into the nearest* (Herod. i. 134 ; Xen. *Anab.* i. 8, iv. 9 ; Joseph. *Antt.* xi. 8. 6, and frequently ; comp. Acts xiii. 44, xxi. 26) *villages*, is a more precise definition of ἀλλαχοῦ. See Bornemann, *Schol. in Luc.* iv. 23, v. 35, and

[1] Hesychius has the adverb νύχα, equivalent to νύκτωρ.

in the *Stud. u. Krit.* 1843, p. 127; Fritzsche, *ad Marc.* p. 22.
— κωμοπόλεις] *villages,* only used here in the N. T., but see
the passages in Wetstein. — εἰς τοῦτο γὰρ ἐξῆλθον] *for that*
(namely, to preach abroad also) *is the object for which I have
left the house,* ver. 35. Schenkel invents here quite a different
connection. In opposition to the context, others understand ἐξῆλθον of having come forth *from the Father.* So
Euthymius Zigabenus, Maldonatus, Grotius, Bengel, Lange,
and others; comp. Baumgarten-Crusius. A harmonizing with
Luke iv. 43.

Ver. 39. *Κηρύσσων εἰς τὰς συναγωγ. αὐτῶν κ.τ.λ.*] There
is the conception of *direction* in εἰς: announcing (the Gospel)
into their synagogues. He is conceived of as coming before
the assembly in the synagogue and speaking to them. Comp.
the well-known modes of expression: ἐς τὸν δῆμον εἰπεῖν, Thuc.
v. 45, εἰς τὴν στρατίαν εἰπεῖν, Xen. *Anab.* v. 6. 37; John
viii. 26, ταῦτα λέγω εἰς τὸν κόσμον. Comp. xiv. 10; Rom.
xvi. 26. The following εἰς ὅλην τὴν Γαλιλαίαν specifies the
geographical field, *into which* the κηρύσσειν εἰς τὰς συναγωγ.
αὐτ. *extended.* Comp. xiii. 10; Luke xxiv. 47. We may
add that this tour is not invented by Mark as a happier
substitute for the Gadarene journey of Matt. viii., as Hilgenfeld assumes it to be, which is a vagary in the interest
of antagonism to the independence of Mark. Holtzmann
appropriately observes that vv. 35-39 is one of the most
telling passages in favour of Mark's originality.

Vv. 40-45. Comp. on Matt. viii. 2-4, where this history
follows immediately after the sermon on the Mount, and that
in a shorter, more comprehensive form in accordance with
Mark. In Luke (v. 12 ff.) the narrative of the draught of
fishes is previously inserted. — γονυπετῶν αὐτόν] see on Matt.
xvii. 14. — Ver. 41.[1] σπλαγχνισθ.] subordinated to the
participle ἐκτείνας; see Winer, p. 308 [E. T. 433]; Dissen,
ad Dem. de Cor. p. 249. — Ver. 42. ἀπῆλθεν ἀπ' αὐτοῦ]

---

[1] If the leper had come to Jesus when he was already substantially healed, as
Schenkel in spite of ver. 45 thinks probable, what charlatanry would the Lord
have been practising at ver. 41 f.! And yet, even according to Schenkel (p. 373),
Mark is assumed to have had the narrative from the mouth of Peter.

so also Luke. But he has omitted the following κ. ἐκαθαρ., to which Matthew has adhered. — Ver. 43. ἐμβριμησάμ. αὐτῷ] *after He had been angry at him*, wrathfully addressed him (comp. xiv. 5, and on Matt. ix. 30). We are to conceive of a vehement *begone now! away hence!* With this is connected also the forcible ἐξέβαλεν. Observe the peculiar way in which Mark *depicts* how Jesus with very earnest zeal desired and urged the departure of the man that was healed. Moreover, the statement that the cure took place *in a house* (ἐξέβαλεν) is peculiar to Mark, who in the entire narrative is very original and cannot be following the colourless narrative of Luke (Bleek). It is true that, according to Lev. xiii. 46, comp. Num. v. 2, lepers were forbidden to enter into a house belonging to other people (see Ewald *in loc.*, and *Alterth.* p. 180); but the impulse towards Jesus and His aid caused the sick man to break through the barrier of the law, whence, moreover, may be explained the hurried and vehement deportment of Jesus. — Ver. 44. As to the prohibition, see on Matt. viii. 4, and on Mark v. 43. — The prefixing of σεαυτόν (*thyself*) is in keeping with the emotion, with which the withdrawal of the *person* is required. — περὶ τοῦ καθαρ. σου] *on account of thy cleansing, i.e.* in order to become Levitically clean. — Ver. 45. Comp. Luke v. 15 f. Mark has peculiar matter. — ἐξελθών] from the house. Comp. ver. 43. — ἤρξατο] εὐγνώμων ὢν ὁ λεπρὸς, οὐκ ἠνέσχετο σιγῇ καλύψαι τὴν εὐεργεσίαν, Euthymius Zigabenus. The *beginning* of this breach of the imposed silence is made prominent. — τὸν λόγον] Euthymius Zigabenus: ὃν εἴρηκεν αὐτῷ ὁ Χριστὸς, δηλαδὴ τὸ θέλω, καθαρίσθητι. So also Fritzsche. But Mark, in order to be intelligible, must have led men to this by a more precise designation pointing back to it. It is *the story,* i.e. *the narrative of the occurrence* (Luther appropriately has *the history*), not: *the matter* (so usually; even de Wette and Bleek), which λόγος in the N. T. never directly means (not even at ii. 2, viii. 32; Luke i. 4; Acts x. 36); as, indeed, also in classical writers (see Wolf, *ad Dem. Lept.* p. 277) it never absolutely means the matter in itself, but the point *spoken of,* the state of things that is *under discussion,* or the like.

As to the distinction between λόγος and φήμη, see Bremi, *ad
Isocr. Paneg.* p. 32. — μηκέτι] no longer, as He could hitherto.
— δύνασθαι] moral possibility, if, namely, He would not occasion any tumult. — καί] not: *and yet* (Kuinoel, de Wette,
Bleek, and others), but the simple *and*. Instead of going
publicly into the city, He was outside in solitary places, and
people came to Him from all quarters. A simple account of
what was connected with His sojourn in the solitude; He
did not withdraw from *this* concourse, but He would not
excite any sensation *in the city*.

CHAPTER II.

VER. 1. The *order* εἰσῆλθε πάλιν (Fritzsche, Lachm. Scholz) would need to be adopted on decisive evidence. But Tischendorf has εἰσελθὼν πάλιν without the subsequent καί, which Lachm. brackets. Rightly; the attestation by B D L ℵ, min. vss. is sufficient; the *Recepta* is an attempt to facilitate the construction by resolving it. — εἰς οἶκον] Lachm. Tisch. have ἐν οἴκῳ, following B D L ℵ, min. An interpretation. — Ver. 4. ἐφ᾽ ᾧ] Lachm.: ὅπου, according to B D L ℵ. So now also Tisch. Mechanical repetition from the foregoing. — Ver. 5. ἀφέωνται] B 28, 33 have ἀφίενται. So Lachm. and Tisch. here and at ver. 9 (where also ℵ has the same reading). But B has the same form at Matt. ix. 2. An emendation. — Elz. Scholz, Lachm. have σοί αἱ ἁμαρτίαι σου, the latter bracketing σου. But B D G L Δ ℵ, min. have σου αἱ ἁμαρτίαι (Griesb. Fritzsche, Tisch.). This reading is in Matt. ix. 2 exposed to the suspicion of having been taken up from ver. 5, where the *Recepta* has but very weak attestation, and from Matthew it passed easily over into our passage. There is the same diversity of reading also at ver. 9, but with the authorities so divided that in ver. 5 and ver. 9 only the *like* reading is warranted. — Ver. 7. λαλεῖ βλασφημίας] Lachm. Tisch. read λαλεῖ; βλασφημεῖ, following B D L ℵ, Vulg. It. Rightly; the *Recepta* has smoothed the expression in accordance with Luke. — Ver. 8. οὕτως] is deleted by Lachm. upon too weak evidence. — αὐτοί is adopted after οὕτως by Bengel, Matt. Griesb. Fritzsche, Scholz on very considerable evidence (A C Γ Δ, etc.). Being unnecessary and not understood, it was passed over. — Ver. 9. ἔγειρε] Elz. Rinck have ἔγειραι (1st aorist middle). The former is here quite decisively attested, and, indeed, in *all* places ἔγειρε is to be written, the active form of which the transcribers did not understand (see on Matt. ix. 5), and converted it into the middle forms ἔγειραι and ἐγείρου (B L 28 have here the latter form). The middle form ἐγείρεσθε is in stated use only in the *plural* (Matt. xxvi. 46; Mark xiv. 42; John xiv. 31), which affords no criterion for the singular. — After ἔγειρε Elz. Lachm.

Tisch. have καί, which C D L, min. vss. omit. An addition in accordance with Matt. ix. 5; Luke v. 23. — Instead of σου τὸν κραββ. we must read, with Lachm. Scholz, Tisch., in accordance with decisive testimony, τὸν κρ. σου. — παριπάτει] Tisch. ed. 8 : ὕπαγε, but against such decisive weight of evidence, that περιπάτει is not to be regarded as derived from the parallel passages, but ὕπαγε is to be referred to a gloss from ver. 11. — Ver. 10. Elz. has ἐπὶ τῆς γῆς after ἀφιέναι. So A E F G al. But B has ἀφ. ἁμ. ἐπὶ τ. γ.; C D L M Δ א, al. min. vss. have ἐπὶ τ. γ. ἀφ. ἁμ. So Griesb. Fritzsche, Lachm. Scholz, Tisch. ed. 8. The latter is a reading conformed to Matthew and Luke. The various readings have arisen through omission (Augustine) and diversity in the restoration of ἐπὶ τ. γ. The *Recepta* is to be restored, as there was no reason, either in the passage itself or from the parallel passages, for separating ἀφιέναι and ἁμαρτίας from one another by the insertion of ἐπὶ τ. γ. — Ver. 15. The reading κ. γίνεται κατακεῖσθαι (Tisch.) is based on B L א, and is to be preferred; ἐγένετο is from Matthew, and ἐν τῷ is explanatory. — Ver. 16. κ. οἱ γραμμ. κ. οἱ Φαρισ.] Tisch.: κ. γραμματεῖς τῶν Φαρισαίων, following B L Δ א, Lachm. in the margin. Rightly; the *Recepta* arose from the usual expression. But we are not, with Tisch. (following the same testimony), to insert καί before ἰδόντες, as this καί owes its origin to the erroneous connection of καὶ γραμμ. with ἠκολούθ. — The simple ὅτι (Tisch.), instead of τί ὅτι, is too feebly attested. — καὶ πίνει] is wanting, no doubt, in B D א, min. Cant. Verc. Ver. Corb. 2 (bracketed by Lachm.), but was omitted on account of Matt. ix. 11, from which place, moreover, C L D א, min. vss. Fathers have added ὁ διδάσκαλος ὑμῶν. — Ver. 17. After ἁμαρτ. Elz. has εἰς μετάνοιαν, which on decisive testimony is deleted as an addition from Luke v. 32 by Griesb. and the later editors. — Ver. 18. Griesb. Scholz, Lachm. Tisch. Fritzsche have rightly adopted οἱ Φαρισαῖοι instead of the *Recepta* οἱ τῶν Φαρισαίων. The former has decisive testimony in its favour, the latter is from Luke v. 33. — οἱ τῶν] Tisch.: οἱ μαθηταὶ τῶν, following B C* L א, 33. Rightly; the superfluous word was passed over. — Ver. 20. Instead of the *Recepta* ἐκείναις ταῖς ἡμέραις (which Fritzsche maintains), ἐκείνη τῇ ἡμέρᾳ is received by Griesb. Lachm. Scholz, Tisch. according to decisive evidence. The plural is from what precedes. — Ver. 21. The *Recepta* is καὶ οὐδείς, against decisive witnesses, which have not καί. — ἐπὶ ἱματίῳ παλαιῷ] Lachm. and Tisch.: ἐπὶ ἱμάτιον παλαιόν, according to B C D L א, 33. Rightly; it was altered in conformity with Matt. ix. 16. — αἴρει τὸ πλήρωμα αὐτοῦ τὸ καινὸν τοῦ παλαιοῦ] Many variations. A K Δ, min. Syr.

p.: αἴρει ἀπ᾽ αὐτοῦ τὸ πλ. τὸ καινὸν τοῦ παλ.; B L ℵ (yet without the first τό), min. Goth.: αἴρει τὸ πλ. ἀπ᾽ αὐτοῦ (B: ἀφ᾽ ἑαυτοῦ) τὸ καιν. τοῦ παλ. (so Lachm. and Tisch.); D, min. vss.: αἴρει τὸ πλ. τὸ καινὸν ἀπὸ τοῦ παλ. (so Rinck). The *Recepta* is to be rejected no less than the reading of D, etc. Both are from Matthew. Of the two readings that still remain, that of A, etc. is to be preferred, because in that of Lachm. and Tisch. the collocation of αἴρει τὸ πλ. likewise betrays its being shaped according to Matthew. Hence we read: αἴρει ἀπ᾽ αὐτοῦ τὸ πλήρωμα τὸ καινὸν τοῦ παλαιοῦ. — Ver. 22. ῥήσσει] Lachm. ῥήξει, following B C D L ℵ, 33, Vulg. codd. of It. So also Tisch. ed. 8. From Luke v. 37, whence also subsequently has come ὁ νέος, which Lachm. and Tisch. have deleted. — καὶ ὁ οἶνος . . . βλητέον] Instead of this there is simply to be read, with Tisch., following B L D, codd. of It.: καὶ ὁ οἶνος ἀπόλλυται καὶ οἱ ἀσκοί (B ℵ leave out of ἀλλὰ κ.τ.λ. only βλητέον). The *Recepta* is from the parallels. — Ver. 23. παραπορ.] Lachm.: διαπορ., following B C D. But comp. Luke vi. 1. — ὁδὸν ποιεῖν] Lachm.: ὁδοποιεῖν, only after B G H. — Ver. 24. ἐν] is on decisive evidence condemned by Griesb., deleted by Lachm. and Tisch. From ver. 23. — Ver. 25. αὐτός] after the first καί is suspected by Griesb., bracketed by Lachm., deleted by Fritzsche and Tisch. It is wanting indeed in B C D L ℵ, min. vss., but it was very easily mistaken in its reference, and passed over as cumbrous and superfluous, the more especially as it does not appear in the parallels. — Ver. 26. ἐπὶ Ἀβιάθαρ τοῦ ἀρχιερ.] is wanting in D, 271, Cant. Ver. Verc. Vind. Corb. 2. Condemned, after Beza, by Gratz (*neuer Versuch, d. Entst. d. drei erst. Ev. z. erkl.* p. 196), and Wassenbergh in Valckenaer, *Schol.* I. p. 23. An omission on account of the historical difficulty and the parallel passages. Only τοῦ before ἀρχ. has decisive evidence against it, and is rightly deleted by Lachm. and Tisch.

Vv. 1–12. Comp. on Matt. ix. 1–8; Luke v. 17–26. At the foundation of both lies the narrative of Mark, which they follow, however, with freedom (Matthew more by way of epitome), while not only Matthew but Luke also falls short of the vivid directness of Mark. — According to the reading εἰσελθών (see the critical remarks), this participle must be taken as anacoluthic in accordance with the conception of the logical subject of the following: *it was heard that He*, etc. See Buttmann, *neut. Gr.* p. 256 [E. T. 298].— δι᾽ ἡμερῶν] *interjectis diebus,* after the lapse of intervening days. See on Gal. ii. 1. — εἰς οἶκον ἔστι] just our: "He is into the house." The verb of rest assumes the previous motion; xiii. 16; John i. 18; Herod. i. 21, *al.* See Buttmann, p. 286 [E. T. 333]. Comp. even εἰς δόμους μένειν, Soph. *Aj.* 80, and Lobeck *in loc.;* Ellendt, *Lex. Soph.* I. 537. The house where Jesus dwelt is *meant* (but not expressly designated, which would have required the use of the article). — Ver. 2. μηκέτι] from the conception of the *increasing* crowd. — μηδέ] *not even* the space at the door, to say nothing of the house. Köstlin, p. 339, arbitrarily finds exaggeration here. — τὸν λόγον] κατ᾽ ἐξοχήν: the Gospel. Comp. viii. 32; Luke i. 2, *al.* — Vv. 3, 4. Here also Mark has the advantage of special vividness. Jesus is to be conceived of as in the *upper chamber,* ὑπερῷον (where the Rabbins also frequently taught, Lightfoot *in loc.;* Vitringa, *Synag.* p. 145 f.). Now, as the bearers could not bring the sick man near [1] to Him through the interior of the house by reason of the throng, they mounted by the stair, which led directly from the street to the roof, up to the latter, broke up—at the spot under which He was in the ὑπερῷον—the material of which the floor of the roof consisted, and let down the sick man through the opening thus made. The conception that Jesus was in the *vestibule,* and that the sick man was lowered down to Him after breaking off the parapet of the roof (Faber, Jahn, Köster, *Imman.* p. 166), is at variance with the words (ἀπεστέγασαν τὴν στέγην, comp. Luke v. 19), and is not required by ver. 2, where the crowd has filled the fore-court *because* the house itself, where Jesus is tarrying, is already occupied (see above on μηδέ, ver. 2); and a curious crowd is wont, if its closer approach is already precluded, to persevere stedfastly in its waiting, even at a distance, in the hope of some satisfaction. Moreover, the fact of the unroofing is a proof that in *that* house roof and upper chamber were either *not connected by a*

[1] Προσεγγίσαι, *active* (Aquila, 1 Sam. xxx. 7; Lucian, *Amor.* 53), hence the reading of Tischendorf, προσήνεγκαι, following B L ℵ, min. vss., is a correct interpretation of the word, which only occurs here in the N. T. This view is more in keeping with the vivid description than the usual intransitive *accedere.*

door (comp. Joseph. *Antt.* xiv. 15. 12), or that the door was
too narrow for the passage of the sick man upon his bed
(Hug, *Gutacht.* II. p. 23); and it is contrary to the simple
words to conceive, with Lightfoot and Olshausen, only of a
widening of an *already existing* doorway. Mark is not at
variance with Luke (Strauss), but both describe the same proceeding; and the transaction related by both bears in its very
peculiarity the stamp of truth, *in favour of* which in the case
of Mark the testimony of Peter is to be presumed, and *against*
which the assertion of the danger to those who were standing
below (Woolston, Strauss, Bruno Bauer) is of the less consequence, as the lifting up of the pieces of roofing is conceivable enough without the incurring of that risk, and the whole
proceeding, amidst the eager hurry of the people to render
possible that which otherwise was unattainable, in spite
of all its strangeness has no intrinsic improbability. — As
to κράββατος, or κράβατος, or κράβαττος (Lachmann and
Tischendorf), a *couch-bed,* a word rejected by the Atticists, see
Sturz, *Dial. Mac.* p. 175 f.; Lobeck, *ad Phryn.* p. 62 f. —
ἀφέωνται κ.τ.λ.] See on Matt. ix. 2. — Ver. 6. τῶν γραμματ.]
So correctly also Matthew. But Luke introduces already here
(too early, see in Mark ii. 16) the Pharisees as well. As to
διαλογιζ. comp. on Matt. xvi. 7. — Ver. 7. According to the
reading βλασφημεῖ (see the critical remarks), this word
answers to the question, *What speaketh this man thus?* by
saying *what* He speaks. — οὗτος οὕτω] *this* man in *this*
manner, an emphatic juxtaposition. The former is con-
temptuous (Matt. xiii. 54); the latter designates the special
and surprising manner, which is immediately pointed out in
what follows. — Ver. 8. Observe the intentional bringing into
prominence of the immediate knowledge of the thoughts. —
αὐτοί] is not the unaccented *they,* but designates with ἐν
ἑαυτοῖς, *ipsi in semet ipsis,* the element of *self-origination,* the
cogitationes sua sponte conceptas. — As to vv. 9–12,[1] see on

[1] Respecting the Messianic *designation*—which presupposes Messianic *consciousness*—coming from the mouth of Jesus: ὁ υἱὸς τοῦ ἀνθρώπου, see on Matt. viii. 20,
and the critical exposition of the different views by Holtzmann in Hilgenfeld's
Zeitschr. 1865, p. 212 ff., and Weizsäcker, p. 426 ff. Observe, however, that the

Matt. ix. 5–8, 33. — σοὶ λέγω] σοί prefixed with emphasis,
because the speaker now turns to the sick man. Comp. Luke
v. 24. According to Hilgenfeld, the "awkward structure of
the sentence," ver. 10 f., betrays the dependence on Matt. ix. 6.
Why, then, not the converse? — καὶ ἄρας κ.τ.λ.] Thus the
assurance of the remission of sins, according to Schenkel, must
have stimulated the paralyzed *elasticity of the nerves!* A
fancy substituted for the miracle. — οὕτως . . . εἴδομεν] not
equivalent to τοιοῦτο εἴδ. (see on Matt. ix. 33), but: *so we
have never seen,* i.e. *a sight* in such a fashion we have never
met with. Comp. the frequent ὡς ὁρᾶτε. It is not even
requisite to supply τί (Fritzsche), to say nothing of mentally
adding *the manifestation of the kingdom of God,* or the like.

Vv. 13–17. See on Matt. ix. 9–13; Luke v. 27–32.
Matthew deals with this in the way of abridgment, but he
has, nevertheless, retained at the end of the narrative the
highly appropriate quotation from Hos. vi. 6 (which Luke,
following Mark, has *not*), as an original element from the
collection of *Logia.* — ἐξῆλθε] out of Capernaum. Comp.
ver. 1. — πάλιν] looks back to i. 16. — Mark has peculiar to
himself the statements παρὰ τ. θάλασσαν as far as ἐδίδασκεν
αὐτούς, but it is arbitrary to refer them to his *subjective conception* (de Wette, comp. Köstlin, p. 335). — Ver. 14.
παράγων] *in passing along,* namely, by the sea, by the place
where Levi sat. Comp. ver. 16. — On *Levi* (*i.e.* Matthew)
and *Alphaeus,* who is not to be identified with the father
of James,[1] see Introd. to Matthew, § 1. Hilgenfeld, in his

passage before us, where Jesus thus early and in the face of His enemies, before
the people and before His disciples, and in the exercise of a divine plenary
power, characterizes Himself by this Danielic appellation, does not admit of the
set purpose of veiling that has been ascribed to His use of it (Ritschl, Weisse,
Colani, Holtzmann, and others). For the disciple especially the expression,
confirmed as it is, moreover, by John from his own lively recollection (see on
John i. 41), could not but be from the outset clear and unambiguous, and the
confession of Peter cannot be regarded as the gradually ripened fruit of the
insight now for the first time dawning. See on Matt. xvi. 13, 17. How correctly,
moreover, the people knew how to apprehend the Danielic designation of the
Messiah, is clearly apparent from John xii. 34.

[1] A confusion that actually arose in very early times, which had as its consequence the reading Ἰάκωβον (instead of Λευίν) in D, min., codd. in Or. and Vict.
and codd. of It.

Zeitschr. 1864, p. 301 f., tries by arbitrary expedients to make
out that Levi was not an apostle. — Ver. 15. ἐν τῇ οἰκίᾳ
αὐτοῦ] is understood by the expositors of the house *of Levi*.[1]
Comp. Vulg.: "in domo *illius.*" In itself this is possible,
but even in itself improbable, since by αὐτόν just before
Jesus was meant; and it is to be rejected, because subsequently it is said of those who sat at meat with Him, just as
it was previously of *Levi:* ἠκολούθησαν αὐτῷ. Moreover,
the absolute καλέσαι (*to invite*), ver. 17, which Matthew and
Mark have, while Luke adds εἰς μετάνοιαν, appears as a
thoughtful reference to the *host*, the καλεῖν on whose part
will transplant into the saving fellowship of His kingdom.
Accordingly, the account in Matthew (see on Matt. ix. 10)
has rightly taken up Mark's account which lies at its
foundation, but Luke has not (v. 29). It is not indeed
expressly said in our text that Jesus went again into the
city; this is nevertheless indirectly evident from the progress
of the narrative (παράγων . . . . ἠκολούθησαν αὐτῷ . . . .
κατακεῖσθαι κ.τ.λ.). — ἦσαν γὰρ πολλοὶ κ.τ.λ.] A statement
serving to elucidate the expression just used: πολλοὶ τελῶναι
κ.τ.λ., and in such a way that ἦσαν is prefixed with emphasis: *for there were many* (τελ. κ. ἁμαρτ.); there was no
lack of a multitude of such people, and they followed after
Jesus. Against the explanation of Kuinoel, Fritzsche, de
Wette, Bleek: *aderant,* it may be at once decisively urged that
such an illustrative statement would be unmeaning, and that
ἠκολούθησαν may not be turned into a pluperfect. And
mentally to supply with ἦσαν, as Bleek does: *at the calling of
Levi,* is erroneous, because the narrative lies quite beyond this
point of time. — Ver. 16. The corrected reading (see the
critical remarks) is to be explained: *and Pharisaic scribes
when they saw,* etc., *said to His disciples.* To attach this κ.
γραμμ. τ. Φαρισ. to the previous ἠκολούθ. (Tischendorf) is
unsuitable, because ἦσαν γὰρ πολλοί, taken by itself alone,
would be absolutely pleonastic, and because ἠκολούθ., in
accordance with the context, can only mean the following *of*

---

[1] Yet Bleek and Holtzmann have agreed with my view, and also Kahnis,
Dogm. I. p. 409 f.

adherents. — Respecting ἰδόντες κ.τ.λ., comp. on Matt. ix. 11.
Here the *direct* seeing (coming to Him) of the γραμματ. is
meant, not: *cum intelligerent* (Grotius and others, de Wette).
— τί ὅτι] *quid est, quod,* so that there needs to be supplied
after τί, not γέγονεν (Schaefer, *ad Bos. Ell.* p. 591), but
the simple ἐστί. Comp. Luke ii. 49; Acts v. 4, 9.

Vv. 18–22. See on Matt. ix. 14–17. Comp. Luke v.
33–38. — καὶ ἦσαν . . . νηστεύοντες] considered by Köstlin,
p. 339, as meaningless and beside the question, is taken by
the expositors as an " archaeological intimation" (de Wette,
comp. Fritzsche). There is nothing to indicate its being so
(how entirely different it is with vii. 3 f.!); we should at
least expect with νηστεύοντες some such general addition as
πολλά (Matt. ix. 14). It is to be explained: *And there were
the disciples of John,* etc., *engaged in fasting* (just at that time).
This *suggested* their question. This view is followed also by
Bleek and Holtzmann, the latter thinking, in the case of John's
disciples, of their fasting as mourners on account of the loss
of their master,—a view for which ver. 19 does not serve as
proof. — ἔρχονται κ.τ.λ.] *Both,* naturally by means of representatives from among them. The text does not yield anything else; so we are neither to understand the questioners
of ver. 16 (Ewald, Hilgenfeld), nor mentally to supply τινές
(Weisse, Wilke). In Matthew the *disciples of John* ask the
question, and this is to be regarded as historically the case (see
on Matt. ix. 17, Remark). — οἱ μαθηταὶ Ἰωάννου κ.τ.λ.] Not
inappropriate, but more definite and more suited to their party-
interest than ἡμεῖς (in opposition to de Wette). — σοί] *might*
be the dative (the disciples belonging to Thee), see Bernhardy,
p. 89; Kühner, II. p. 249. But in accordance with the use
—frequent also in the N. T.—of the emphatic σός, it is to be
taken as its plural. Comp. Luke v. 33. — Ver. 19. ὅσον
χρόνον κ.τ.λ.] superfluous in itself, but here suited to the solemn
answer. Comp. Bornemann, *Schol. in Luc.* p. xxxix. — μεθ᾽
ἑαυτῶν] *in the midst of themselves.* — Ver. 20. ἐν ἐκείνῃ τῇ
ἡμέρᾳ] Not a *negligence* (de Wette) or *impossibility* of expression
(Fritzsche), but: τότε is the *more general* statement of time:
then, when, namely, the case of the taking away shall have

occurred, and ἐν ἐκείνῃ τῇ ἡμέρᾳ is the *special* definition of
time subordinate to the τότε: *on that day,* ἐκεῖνος having
demonstrative force and consequently a *tragic* emphasis (on
that *atra dies !*). Comp. Bernhardy, p. 279. If the *plural*
were again used, the time previously designated by ἐλεύσ.
δὲ ἡμέραι would be once more expressed *on the whole and
in general,* and that likewise with solemnity, but not the
definite particular day. Aptly, moreover, Bengel remarks:
"Dies *unus* auferendi sponsi, dies *multi* ejusdem ablati et
absentis." The Lord from the beginning of His ministry had
made Himself familiar with the certainty of a violent death.
Comp. John ii. 19. — Ver. 21. εἰ δὲ μή] *In the contrary case,*
even after a negative clause, Buttmann, *neut. Gr.* p. 336 [E. T.
392], and see on 2 Cor. xi. 16.—The correct reading: αἴρει
ἀπ᾽ αὐτοῦ τὸ πλήρωμα τὸ καινὸν τοῦ παλαιοῦ (see the critical
remarks), is to be explained : *the new patch of the old* (garment)
breaks away from it. See on Matt. ix. 16 f. The *Recepta*
signifies: *his new patch* (that which is put on by him) *breaks
away from the old garment.* According to Ewald, αἴρει ἀφ᾽
ἑαυτοῦ ought to be read (following B, which, however, has the
ἀφ᾽ ἑαυτοῦ after τὸ πλήρωμα), and this is to be interpreted :
"thus the new filling up of the old becomes of itself
stronger." He compares the phrase ὁ λόγος αἴρει (*ratio
evincit,* Polyb. vi. 5. 5 ; comp. also Herod. ii. 33 ; Plat. *Crit.*
p. 48 C, *al.*), the meaning of which (reason *teaches it*) is,
however, here foreign to the subject. — Ver. 22. A combination from Matthew and Luke is here contained only in the
interpolated *Recepta.* See the critical remarks.—As to the form
ῥήσσω instead of ῥήγνυμι, see Ruhnken, *Ep. crit.* I. p. 26.

Vv. 23-28. See on Matt. xii. 1-8. Comp. Luke vi. 1-5,
who follows Mark in the order of events, which in Matthew is
different. — παραπορεύεσθαι] not: *to walk on, ambulare* (Vulgate, Luther, and many others, including de Wette), so that
παρά would refer indefinitely to *other* objects, but *to pass along
by.* Comp. Matt. xxvii. 39 ; Mark xi. 20, xv. 29. Jesus
passed *through* the corn-fields *alongside of these,* so that the
way that passed through the fields led Him on both sides
along by them. Just so ix. 30, and Deut. ii. 4. — ὁδὸν

ποιεῖν κ.τ.λ.] is *usually* explained as though it stood : ὁδὸν
ποιούμενοι τίλλειν τοὺς στάχυας, *to pluck the ears of corn as
they went.* Against the mode of expression, according to
which the main idea lies in the participial definition (see
Hermann, *ad Aj.* 1113 ; *Electr.* 1305 ; Stallbaum, *ad Plat.
Gorg.* p. 136 ; *Phil.* p. 58), there would be in itself nothing,
according to classical examples, to object ; but in the N. T.
this mode of expression does not occur (Winer, p. 316 [E. T.
443 f.]), and here in particular the active ποιεῖν is opposed
to it, since ὁδὸν ποιεῖν is always *viam sternere,* and ὁδὸν
ποιεῖσθαι (as also πορείαν ποιεῖσθαι) is *iter facere.* See Viger.
ed. Herm. p. 116 ; Kypke, I. p. 154 ; Krebs, p. 81 ; Winer,
p. 228 [E. T. 320]. Comp. also ὁδοποιεῖν (Xen. *Anab.* v.
1. 14 ; Dem. 1274, 26, frequently in the LXX.) and ὁδὸν
ὁδοποιεῖν ; Kühner, *ad Xen. Anab.* iv. 8. 8. The assumption
that Mark had missed this distinction is wholly without exegetical warrant, as is also the recourse to a Latinism (Krebs).
The only correct explanation is : *they began to make a way*
(to open a path) *by plucking the ears of corn;* not, as Bretschneider and Fritzsche alter the meaning of the words :
" evellisse spicas et factum esse, ut projectis, quum iis essent
demta grana, spicis *exprimeretur via.*" We must rather conceive of the field-path on which they are walking—perhaps at
a place where it leads through a field of corn which it inter-
sects—as overgrown with ears, so that they must of necessity,
in order to continue their journey, *make a path,* which they do
by *plucking the ears of corn* that stand in their way. According to Matthew and Luke, the chief point lies in the fact that
the disciples pluck the ears *and eat* them; and the Pharisees find
fault with their doing this—which *in itself is allowable*—on
the *Sabbath.* According to Mark, however, who has not a word[1]

---

[1] Mark has been blamed on this account. See Fritzsche, p. 69. But the very
evangelist, who knew how to narrate so vividly, should by no means have been
charged with such an awkwardness as the omission of the essential feature of the
connection—which is just what the latest harmonizing avers. It ought to have
been candidly noted that in Mark the object of the plucking of the ears is the ὁδὸν
ποιεῖν ; while in Matthew it is the *eating on account of hunger.* The occasions of
the necessity, in which the disciples were placed, are *different :* in the former
case, the ὁδοποιία ; in the latter, the hunger.

of the disciples eating, their act consists in this, that by the plucking of the ears of corn they *open a way through the field;* and the Pharisees, ver. 24, find fault that they do that, which *in itself is already unallowable,*[1] on the *Sabbath.* The justification of Jesus amounts then, ver. 25 ff., to the two points: (1) that according to David's precedent the proceeding of the disciples, as enjoined by *necessity,* is *by no means unallowable;* and (2) that the *Sabbath* makes no difference in the matter.—The origin of this difference itself is easily explained from the fact, that Jesus adduces the history of the *eating* of the shew-bread, by means of which also the *eating* of the ears of corn came into the tradition of this incident. Mark betrays by his ὁδὸν ποιεῖν abandoned by Matthew and Luke, and by the less obvious connection of it with the eating of the shew-bread, the original narrative, which perhaps proceeded from Peter himself. — τοὺς στάχυας] the article designates the ears of corn *that stood in the way.* — Ver. 24. They do not ask, as in Matthew and Luke, why the disciples do what is unallowable on the Sabbath, but *why they do on the Sabbath something* (already in itself) *unallowable.* — Ver. 25. αὐτός] and *He on His part,* replying to them. He put a *counter-question.* — ὅτε χρείαν ἔσχε] *In this* lies the analogy. The disciples also were by the circumstances compelled to the course which they took. The demonstrative force of this citation depends upon a conclusion *a majori ad minus.* David in a case of necessity dealt apparently unlawfully even with the shew-bread of the temple, which is yet far less lawful to be touched than the ears of grain in general. — Ver. 26. ἐπὶ Ἀβιάθαρ τοῦ ἀρχιερ.] *tempore Abiatharis pontificis maximi, i.e.* under the pontificate

---

[1] To this view Holtzmann and Hilgenfeld have acceded, as also Ritschl, *altkath. K.* p. 29 ; Schenkel, *Charakterbild,* p. 86 ; and as regards the ὁδὸν ποιεῖν in itself, also Lange. The defence of the usual explanation on the part of Krummel in the *allgem. K. Zeit.* 1864, No. 74, leaves the linguistic difficulty which stands in its way entirely unsolved. He should least of all have sought support from the reading of Lachmann (ὁδοποιεῖν) ; for this also never means anything else than *viam sternere,* and even in the middle voice only means *to make for oneself a path.* Weiss (*Jahrb. f. Deutsche Theol.* 1865, p. 363) calls my explanation "somewhat odd ;" this, however, can matter nothing, if only it is linguistically correct, and the usual one linguistically erroneous.

of Abiathar. Comp. Luke iii. 2 ; Matt. i. 11. According to
1 Sam. xxi. 1 ff., indeed, the high priest at that time was not
Abiathar, but his father (1 Sam. xxii. 20 ; Joseph. *Antt.* vi.
12. 6) *Ahimelech*. Mark has erroneously confounded these two,
which might the more easily occur from the remembrance of
David's friendship with Abiathar (1 Sam. xxii. 20 ff.). See
Korb in Winer's *krit. Journ.* IV. p. 295 ff. ; Paulus, Fritzsche,
de Wette, Bleek. The supposition that father and son both had
both names (Victor Antiochenus, Euthymius Zigabenus, Theophylact, Beza, Jansen, Heumann, Kuinoel, and many others),
is only apparently supported by 2 Sam. viii. 17, 1 Chron.
xviii. 16, comp. xxiv. 6, 31 ; as even apart from the fact
that these passages manifestly contain an erroneous statement
(comp. Thenius on 2 Sam. *l.c. ;* Bertheau judges otherwise,
d. Bücher der Chron. p. 181 f.), the reference of our quotation
applies to *no other* passage than to 1 Sam. xxi. Grotius
thought that the son had been the *substitute* of the father. Recourse has been had with equally ill success to a different interpretation of $\epsilon\pi\iota$; for, if it is assumed to be *coram* (Wetstein,
Scholz), 1 Sam. *l.c.* stands historically opposed to it ; but if
it is held to mean : *in the passage concerning Abiathar,* i.e.
there, where he is spoken of (xii. 26 ; Luke xx. 37), it is
opposed by the same historical authority, and by the consideration that the words do not stand immediately after
$\dot{a}\nu\dot{\epsilon}\gamma\nu\omega\tau\epsilon$ (in opposition to Michaelis and Saunier, *Quellen d.
Mark.* p. 58). — Ver. 27 f. $\kappa a\iota$ $\check{\epsilon}\lambda\epsilon\gamma$. $a\dot{v}\tau o\hat{\iota}\varsigma$] frequently used
for the introduction of a further important utterance of the
same subject who is speaking ; Bengel : " Sermonem iterum
exorsus." Comp. iv. 9. As Jesus has hitherto refuted the
reproach conveyed in $\dot{o}$ $o\dot{v}\kappa$ $\check{\epsilon}\xi\epsilon\sigma\tau\iota$, ver. 24, He now also refutes
the censure expressed by $\dot{\epsilon}\nu$ $\tau o\hat{\iota}\varsigma$ $\sigma\dot{a}\beta\beta a\sigma\iota\nu$, ver. 24. Namely :
as the Sabbath has been made (brought into existence, *i.e.*
ordained) *for the sake of man,* namely, as a means for his
highest moral ends (Gen. ii. 3 ; Ex. xx. 8 ff.), *not man for the
sake of the Sabbath,*[1] it follows thence : *the Messiah has to rule*

[1] Comp. *Mechilta* in Ex. xxxi. 13 : " Vobis sabbatum traditum est, et non vos
traditi estis sabbato." According to Baur, ver. 27 belongs to " the rational
explanations," which Mark is fond of prefixing by way of suggesting a motive

even over the Sabbath, so that thus the disciples, who *as my disciples* have acted under my permission, cannot be affected by any reproach in respect of the Sabbath. The inference ὥστε depends on the fact that the υἱὸς τοῦ ἀνθρώπου, *i.e.* the *Messiah* (not with Grotius and Fritzsche to be taken as *man* in general), is held *ex concesso* as the *representative head* of humanity.[1] On the mode of inference in general, comp. 1 Cor. xi. 9; 2 Macc. v. 19. — κύριος] emphatically at the beginning: is not dependent, but *Lord,*[2] etc.; whereby, however, is expressed not the prerogative of absolute *abolition* (see against this Matt. v. 17 ff., and the idea of the πλήρωσις of the law makes its appearance even in Mark vii. 15 ff., x. 5 ff., xii. 28 ff.), but the power of putting in the place of the external statutory Sabbath observance—while giving up the latter—something higher in keeping with the *idea* of the Sabbath, wherein lies the πλήρωσις of the Sabbath-law. Comp. Lechler in the *Stud. u. Krit.* 1854, p. 811; Weizsäcker, p. 391. — καί] *also,* along with other portions of His κυριότης.

for what is historically presented. To the same class he would assign ix. 39, vii. 15 ff. Weizsäcker finds in the passage before us a later reflection. This would only be admissible, if the idea *facilitated* the concluding inference, which is not the case, and if Mark were not in this narrative generally so *peculiar.* The connecting link of the argumentation preserved by him might more easily have been *omitted* as something foreign, than have been *added.*

[1] For Him, as such, in the judgment to be formed of the obligatory force of legal ordinances, the regulative standard is just the relation, in which man as a moral end to himself stands to the law. Comp. Ritschl, *altkathol. Kirche,* p. 29 ff.

[2] With this the *freedom of worship* is *given* as well as assigned to its necessary *limit,* but not generally *"proclaimed"* (Schenkel).

CHAPTER III.

VER. 2. Instead of παρετήρουν, read with Lachm. παρετηροῦντο, following A C* D Δ, min. The middle here and at Luke vi. 7 (comp. also Acts ix. 24) was not attended to. — κατηγορήσουσιν, instead of κατηγορήσωσιν, is not sufficiently attested by C D (Lachm.). — Ver. 3. Lachm. has τῷ τὴν χεῖρα ἔχοντι ξηράν, following B L 102, Verc. In favour of ξηράν C also tells, which has τῷ τ. ξηράν ἔχ. χ., and Δ א, which have τῷ τ. ξηρὰν χ. ἔχ. So Tisch. ed. 8. The *Recepta* τῷ ἐξηραμμένην ἔχοντι τὴν χεῖρα is from ver. 1. — Ver. 5. At the end Elz. has ὑγιὴς ὡς ἡ ἄλλη. This is indeed defended by Matthiae, but in opposition to decisive evidence. It is from Matt. xii. 13. — Ver. 7. The order of the words: μετὰ τῶν μαθητ. αὐτοῦ ἀνεχώρ. (Griesb. Lachm. Tisch.), instead of the *Recepta* ἀνεχώρ. μ. τ. μαθ. αὐτ., has in its favour B C D L Δ א, min. vss., and is on this evidence to be adopted, the more especially as the *Recepta* easily presented itself from the connection, according to which the important element for the progress of the narrative lies in ἀνεχώρ. — Instead of πρός (Elz. Scholz), Griesb. Fritzsche, Lachm. Tisch. have εἰς, which is attested, indeed, only by D H P, min. Theophyl., but was explained by πρός (in some min. by παρά) as a gloss. — ἠκολούθησαν] ἠκολούθησεν, in favour of which D, min. also concur by ἠκολούθει, is considerably attested, partly with, and partly without αὐτῷ (which Lachm. brackets). Approved by Griesb., adopted by Fritzsche and Lachm. The plural flowed mechanically from the conception of the multitude; αὐτῷ is supplied, and is with Tisch. to be deleted. — Ver. 8. ἀκούσαντες] Lachm. and Tisch. read ἀκούοντες, following only B Δ א, min. — Ver. 11. Instead of ἐθεώρει, προσέπιπτεν, and ἔκραζε, Fritzsche, Lachm. and Tisch. have the plurals, which also Griesb. approved. The evidence preponderates in favour of the latter, and the singulars are a grammatical but inappropriate correction. — Ver. 15. θεραπεύειν τὰς νόσους καί] is wanting in B C* L Δ א, 102, Copt. Deleted by Tisch. An addition, in recollection of Matt. x. 1. — Ver. 16. Fritzsche has πρῶτον Σιμῶνα before καὶ ἐπέθηκε, following only 13, 39, 124, 346. An addition from

Matt. x. 2, with a view to supply a construction.[1] — Ver. 18. Here,
too (comp. on Matt. x. 4), must be read in conformity to decisive
evidence, with Lachm. and Tisch., not Καναvίτην, but Καναναῖον.
— Ver. 20. μήτε] Read with Fritzsche and Lachm. μηδέ, which is
sufficiently attested and necessary as respects the sense. —
Ver. 27. The *Recepta* is : οὐ δύναται οὐδείς. So also Fritzsche and
Tisch., the latter having, in accordance with B C (?) L Δ ℵ, min.
vss., adopted ἀλλ᾽ previously (a connective addition). But οὐδείς
δύναται (Griesb. Matth. Scholz, Lachm.) is the more to be retained,
since the mechanical repetition of the οὐ δύναται was so readily
suggested from what precedes. — Ver. 28. The verbal order : τοῖς
υἱοῖς τῶν ἀνθρώπων τὰ ἁμαρτήματα (sanctioned by Griesb., adopted
by Lachm. and Tisch.), has, with A B C D L Δ ℵ, min. vss., the
balance of evidence in its favour, and is also to be accounted
genuine, as being the more unusual.—The *article* before βλασφ.
is adopted by Griesb. Fritzsche, Scholz, Lachm. Tisch. on decisive evidence ; it became absorbed through the preceding καί. —
ὅσας] Lachm. and Tisch. read ὅσα, following B D E* G H Δ Π*
ℵ, min. The *Recepta* is a correction. — Ver. 29. Elz. Fritzsche,
Scholz have κρίσεως (A C** E F G, etc. Syr.), instead of which
Griesb. approved ἁμαρτήματος (B L Δ ℵ ; D has ἁμαρτίας), and
this Lachm. and Tisch. have adopted. κρίσεως (al. κολάσεως) is a
gloss.—Ver. 31. The reading καὶ ἔρχονται (Lachm.) certainly has
preponderant evidence (D G ℵ, Tisch. ed. 8, have καὶ ἔρχεται),
but is a mechanical alteration, in which the retrospective reference of the οὖν was not attended to.—The *Recepta* is οἱ ἀδελφοὶ
καὶ ἡ μήτηρ αὐτοῦ. But B C D G L Δ ℵ, min. vss. have ἡ μήτηρ
αὐτοῦ κ. οἱ ἀδελφοὶ αὐτοῦ (Griesb. Scholz, Lachm. Tisch. ed. 8),
with which also the reading ἔρχεται is connected. Still the
Recepta (and that with αὐτοῦ repeated) is to be sustained, for
it became changed in consideration of the rank of the mother,
of ver. 32, and of the parallel passages. — φωνοῦντες] Lachm.
and Tisch. have καλοῦντες, following B C L ℵ, min. (A : ζητοῦντες).
Rightly ; the meaning of καλοῦντες was more precisely defined
by φωνοῦντες. — Ver. 32. The verbal order περὶ αὐτὸν ὄχλος (Lachm.
Tisch.) is preponderantly attested, as also is καὶ λέγουσιν (Lachm.
Tisch.) instead of εἶπον δέ. — The addition καὶ αἱ ἀδελφαί σου is
rightly adopted by Griesb. Matth. Scholz, Lachm. and Tisch.
It certainly has important evidence against it (B C G K L Δ Π ℵ,

[1] From the same design, moreover, we may explain the placing of καὶ ἐποίησιν
τοὺς δώδεκα at the beginning of the verse. So B C* Δ ℵ. Defended by Hitzig
and Ewald ; adopted by Tisch. In such awkwardly constructed passages
"correctio parit correctionem : alter enim alterum cupit antecellere ingenio"
(Matthiae, ed. min. *ad h. l.*).

Vulg. Copt. Arm. Aeth. Syr. utr.), and is rejected by Fritzsche ; but the words were omitted, because neither in ver. 31 nor in ver. 34 nor in the parallel passages are the sisters mentioned. Had it been interpolated, the addition would have been found already in ver. 31. — Ver. 33. Instead of ἤ, Lachm. and Tisch. ed. 8 have καί, following B C L V Δ ℵ, min. vss. A mechanical repetition from ver. 32 ; and comp. Matt. — Ver. 34. The verbal order : τοὺς περὶ αὐτ. κύκλῳ (Lachm. Tisch.), which is found in B C L Δ ℵ, min. Copt., arose from the fact, that the κύκλῳ, which with περιβλεψ. was superfluous, was omitted (so still in min. vss.), and then restored in the place that appeared fitting. — Ver. 35. The omission of γάρ (Lachm. Tisch.) is too weakly attested. On the other hand, μου after ἀδελφή is, with Lachm. and Tisch., following A B D L Δ ℵ, min. vss., to be deleted.

Vv. 1–6. See on Matt. xii. 9–14 ; comp. Luke vi. 6–11. The brief, vividly and sharply graphic account of Mark is in Matthew partly abridged, partly expanded. — πάλιν] see i. 21. — εἰς τ. συναγωγήν] at *Capernaum*. See ii. 15. — ἐξηραμμένην] "non ex utero, sed morbo aut vulnere ; haec vis participii," Bengel. More indefinitely Matthew (and Luke) : ξηράν. — παρετηροῦντο] of *hostile* observing, *spying* (comp. Luke vi. 7, *al.* ; Polyb. xvii. 3. 2 : ἐνεδρεύειν καὶ παρατηρεῖν), which, however, is implied, not in the middle, but in the context. — Ver. 3 ff. ἔγειρε εἰς τ. μέσον] *arise* (and step forth) *into the midst*. Comp. Luke vi. 8. — ἀγαθοποιῆσαι ἢ κακοποιῆσαι] *to act well* (Tob. xii. 13), *or to act ill* (Ecclus. xix. 25). Comp. καλῶς ποιεῖν, Matt. xii. 12 ; *Ep. ad Diogn.* 4 : God does not hinder καλόν τι ποιεῖν on the Sabbath day. The alternative must be such that the opponents cannot deny *the former* proposition, and therefore must be dumb. On this account it is not to be explained : *to render a benefit* (1 Macc. xi. 33), *or to inflict an injury* (Erasmus, Bengel, Beza, de Wette, Bleek, and others) ; for the former might be relatively negatived on account of the Sabbath-laws, the observance of which, however, could not be opposed to the idea of *acting well* (*i.e.* in conformity with the divine will). We can only decide the question on this ground, not from the *usus loquendi*, which in fact admits of either explanation. The reading in D : τι ἀγαθὸν ποιῆσαι,

MARK.   D

is a correct gloss of the late Greek word (Lobeck, *ad Phryn.*
p. 200), comp. 1 Pet. ii. 15, 20, iii. 6 ; 3 John 11. — ψυχὴν
σῶσαι] *to rescue a soul*, that it be not transferred to Hades,
but, on the contrary, the man may be preserved in life. Comp.
viii. 35, often also among Greek writers. This likewise could
not be denied, for " periculum vitae pellit sabbatum," *Joma*,
f. 84, 2. See the passages in Wetstein, *ad Matth.* xii. 10. —
ἀποκτεῖναι] to be taken by itself, not to be connected with
ψυχήν. At the foundation of the question of Jesus lies the conclusion from the general to the special; He carries the point
in question about the Sabbath healings back to the *moral
category*, in consequence of which a negative answer would be
absurd. The adversaries feel this; but instead of confessing
it they are *silent*, because they are *hardened*. — συλλυπού-
μενος] *feeling compassion over*, etc., Herod. ix. 94, vi. 39 ; Polyb.
vii. 3. 2 ; Aelian, *V. H.* vii. 3. Anger and compassion alter-
nated. The *preposition* denotes not the emotion of the heart
collectively, but the fellowship, into which the heart enters,
with the misfortune (in this case moral) of the persons concerned. Comp. Plato, *Pol.* v. p. 462 E. — ἀπεκατεστάθη] with
double augment (Winer, p. 67 [E. T. 84]) is, in accordance
with Lachmann, to be read. Comp. on Matt. xii. 13. — Ver. 6.
εὐθέως κ.τ.λ.] " crevit odium," Bengel. *They instituted a
consultation, in order that*, etc. Comp. on Matt. xxii. 5. That
the *Herodians* are introduced into this place erroneously
from Matt. xxii. 16 (see *in loc.*) is not to be maintained (de
Wette, Baur, Hilgenfeld). The sensation produced by the
working of Jesus (see vv. 7, 8) was sufficiently fitted to induce
their being now drawn by the Pharisees into the hostile effort.
Hence the mention of them here is no meaningless addition
(Köstlin).

Vv. 7–12. Comp. Matt. xii. 15 f., Luke vi. 17–19, who with
their difference of historical arrangement make but brief use
of the description in Mark, which is more accurate and more
fresh and does not blend heterogeneous elements (Hilgenfeld).
— εἰς] direction whither. — Ver. 8. Ἰδουμαία] on the south-
eastern border of Palestine.—A *point* is not to be placed, as
by Beza, Er. Schmid, and Fritzsche, after Ἰορδάνου, but—as

is required by the two distinct predicates based on the local
relations, ἠκολούθησεν and ἦλθον πρὸς αὐτόν—*before* καὶ ἀπὸ
τ. Ἰουδαίας. It is first of all stated, who *followed* Jesus from
Galilee, where He Himself was, to the sea, and then, from
καὶ ἀπὸ τ. Ἰουδ. onward, who *came to Him* from other regions.
Namely: *and from Judaea, and from Jerusalem, and from
Idumaea and Peraea* (καὶ πέραν τοῦ Ἰορδ. ; observe that here
ἀπό is not repeated), *and those* (the Jews) *about Tyre and
Sidon, in great multitudes* (πλῆθος πολύ belongs to the whole
as a more precise definition of the subject), *they came to Him.*
— Observe, moreover, the different position of πλῆθος in
vv. 7 and 8 ; in the one case the *greatness* of the mass of
people preponderates in the conception, in the other it is the
idea of the *mass of people itself.* — ἐποίει] *imperfect,* used of
the *continuous* doing. — Ver. 9. ἵνα] *What* He said to them is
conceived of as the design of the speaking (comp. on Matt.
iv. 3): *in order that a vessel should be continually at His service.*
— διὰ τὸν ὄχλον κ.τ.λ.] therefore not for the purpose of
crossing over ; ἔμελλε γὰρ ἐμβὰς εἰς αὐτὸ μὴ ἐνοχλεῖσθαι,
Euthymius Zigabenus. Comp. iv. 1 ; Matt. xiii. 2. It is not
said, however, that He wished to *teach* out of the vessel
(Kuinoel and others). — Ver. 10 f. Information regarding this
pressing towards Him. — ἐθεράπευσεν] not *sanaverat* (Castalio,
Kuinoel, Fritzsche), but *He healed* just at that time. The
ὥστε ἐπιπίπτειν αὐτῷ, *so that they fell upon Him,* depicts the
impetuous thronging unto Him of those seeking aid. " Ad-
mirabilis patientia et benignitas Domini," Bengel. προσέπιπτ.
αὐτῷ in ver. 11 is different: *they fell down before Him* (v. 33,
vii. 25). — μάστιγας] *plagues,* v. 29, 34 ; Luke vii. 21 ; Ps.
xxxv. 15 ; Ecclus. xl. 9 ; 2 Macc. vii. 37. In accordance
with the context: plagues *of sickness.* — τὰ πνεύματα κ.τ.λ.] a
statement in conformity with the appearance ; the sick people
identified themselves with the demons. — ὅταν] with the
praeterite indicative: whenever they saw Him, i.e. as soon as ever
they got sight of Him. See Winer, p. 276 [E. T. 388]. This
rare and late linguistic phenomenon is to be explained
to the effect, that the conception of the uncertain (ἄν) has
become completely blended with ὅτε, and the whole emphasis

rests upon this *whenever.* See Klotz, *ad Devar.* p. 690. It
does not mean: if they *ever saw* Him. — Ver. 12. ἵνα] design
of the πολλὰ ἐπετίμα αὐτοῖς (the demons). How colourless is
Matt. xii. 16! According to Hilgenfeld, Mark has *exaggerated.* As to the prohibition itself of their making Him
known as Messiah, comp. i. 43, and on Matt. viii. 4; Mark
v. 43.

Vv. 13–19. Comp. Matt. x. 2–4; Luke vi. 12–16. — τὸ
ὄρος] upon the mountain there. See on Matt. v. 1. — οὓς
ἤθελεν αὐτός] so that no one might come forward of his own
will. Jesus first of all made a wider selection, and then out
of this, ver. 14, the narrower one of the Twelve. To raise a
doubt of the actual selection of the latter (Schleiermacher, *L. J.*
p. 370), as if they to some extent had become apostles with
less of assent on Christ's part, is at variance also with John
vi. 70. — Ver. 14 f. ἐποίησε] *He made,* that is, *He ordained,
appointed.* Comp. Acts ii. 36; 1 Sam. xii. 6. On the clause
ἵνα ὦσι μετ᾽ αὐτοῦ, comp. Acts i. 21. — ἀποστέλλῃ αὐτούς]
namely, subsequently. See vi. 7. — καὶ ἔχειν] conjoined with
the κηρύσσειν as an aim of the sending forth, in which it
was contemplated that they were *to preach and to have power,*[1]
etc. Comp. vi. 7. The simple, naive detail of the appointment
and destination of the Twelve bears the stamp of originality,
not of elaboration after Matthew and Luke (Zeller in Hilgenfeld's *Zeitschrift,* 1865, p. 396 ff.). — Ver. 16 ff. Inexactly
enough Mark relates, instead of Simon's *appointment,* only his
being named; but he leaves his appointment to be thence understood of itself, and then, as if he had narrated it in connection with ἐποίησε, continues by καὶ Ἰάκωβον, which still
depends on ἐποίησε,—an awkwardness which is scarcely to be
attributed to a reflecting reviser.—As to the *arrangement—*
generally according to rank, but in Mark and Acts i. 13 giving
precedence to the three most intimate disciples—of the twelve

[1] Observe the *correctness* of the expression ἔχειν ἔξουσ. κ.τ.λ. (in opposition to
de Wette). For the destination of the apostles in fact was not: to teach *and
to drive out the demons,* but *to teach* and in so doing to possess the *power* of
driving out demons, in order that they might apply this power on appropriate occasion for the confirmation of their teaching. Comp. xvi. 20; 2 Cor.
xii. 12.

names in three quaternions, see on Matt. x. 2 ; Ewald, p. 205 f.
— Mark narrates the naming of Peter as having taken place *at
that time*, which is not incompatible with Matt. xvi. 18 (see
in loc.), although it is doubtless with John i. 43. — Ver. 17.
And He assigned to them names, (namely) *Boanerges.* The
plural ὀνόματα (for which D reads ὄνομα) depends on the
conception that the names bestowed on the *two* brothers are
included in Boanerges. *Boaνεργές*] حـنـدبـمـ, בְּנֵי רֶגֶשׁ. The
Sheva, according to Aramaic pronunciation (see Lightfoot) : *oa*.
רֶגֶשׁ, in the Hebrew, *a noisy crowd,* Ps. lv. 15 ; in the Syriac,
thunder ; comp. the Arabic رجس, *tonuit.*[1] The *historical
occasion* of this appellation is altogether unknown. It has
been sought in the *mighty eloquence* of the two (Victor Antiochenus, Theophylact, Euthymius Zigabenus, Calvin, Wetstein,
Michaelis, and others, comp. Luther's gloss) ; but it may be
objected to this view that such a quality could hardly have
appeared *at that time,* when the men had not yet taught ; and
also that in the case of John at least, a *thundering* eloquence
(as in Pericles ; Cic. *Orat.* 29) is not to be supposed.   Others
(Heumann, Kuinoel, comp. also Gurlitt in the *Stud. u. Krit.*
1829, p. 715 ff.) have understood it to be a name *of reproach,*
and referred it to Luke ix. 54, so that the meaningless, destructive power (Gurlitt) would be the point of comparison ; but the
time of the giving this name is not in accordance with this view,
as it is also in itself improbable, and at variance with the analogy of *Peter's* name, that Jesus should have converted a *reproach*
into a *name* and thereby have made it the signature of their
character ; to which we may add, that in Luke, *l.c.,* there is
nothing at all said about *thunder.*   Moreover, it is historically
demonstrable that the disciples were of *impetuous, ardent tem-
perament* (ix. 38 ; Luke ix. 54 ; comp. Matt. xx. 20 ff., and
Mark x. 35 ff.), and it is therefore not arbitrary to conjecture
that some special exhibition of this peculiarity at the time
suggested the name, of which, however, it is absolutely

---

[1] Jerome's reading (in Dan. i., Isa. lxii.) : *Benereem,* is an emendation (רעם,
thunder).

unknown for what reason it did not become *permanent*, like the name of Peter, and in fact is no further mentioned elsewhere, although it was given by *Jesus.* — Θαδδαῖον] see on Matt. x. 3. As to ὁ Καναναῖος, see on Matt. x. 4.

Vv. 20,[1] 21. Peculiar to Mark, but in unity of connection with ver. 22 f. — καὶ ἔρχ. εἰς οἶκον] The choice of the disciples, and what had to be said to them concerning it, was the important occasion for the preceding ascent of the mountain, ver. 13. Now they come back again to the house, namely, in *Capernaum*, as in ii. 2, to which also the subsequent πάλιν points back. De Wette is in error when he says that the following scene could by no means have taken place in the house. See, on the other hand, ver. 31 and Matt. xii. 46. Hilgenfeld finds in εἰς οἶκον even a misunderstanding of Matt. xiii. 1.—The accusation ὅτι ἐξέστη, ver. 21, and that expressed at ver. 22, ὅτι Βεελζεβοὺλ ἔχει, are analogous; and these accu-

---

[1] Before καὶ ἔρχονται εἰς οἶκον would be the place where Mark, if he had desired to take in the Sermon on the Mount, would have inserted it; and Ewald (as also Tobler, *die Evangelienfrage*, 1858, p. 14) assumes that the Gospel in its original form had actually contained that discourse, although abridged, in this place,—which Weiss (*Evangelienfrage*, p. 154 f.) concedes, laying decided stress on the abridgment on the ground of other abridged discourses in Mark. Nevertheless, the abrupt and unconnected mode of adding one account to another, as here by the καὶ ἔρχονται εἰς οἶκον, as well as the omission of longer discourses, are peculiar to Mark and in keeping with the originality of his work; further, it would be quite impossible to see why the discourse, if it had originally a place here, should have been entirely removed, whether we may conceive for ourselves its original contents and compass in the main according to Matthew or according to Luke. Ewald's view has, however, been followed by Holtzmann, whom Weiss, in the *Jahrb. f. Deutsche Theol.* 1864, p. 63 ff., and Weizsäcker, p. 46, with reason oppose, while Schenkel also regards the dropping out as probable, although as unintentional.—In respect of the absence from Mark of the history of the *centurion at Capernaum* (Matt. viii. 5 ff.; Luke vii. 1 ff.), the non-insertion of which Köstlin is only able to conceive of as arising from the neutral tendency of Mark, Ewald supposes that it originally stood in Mark likewise before καὶ ἔρχονται εἰς οἶκον, and that in Matthew and Luke it still has the tinge of Mark's language, in which respect ἱκανός and σκύλλειν are referred to (but comp. Matt. iii. 11, ix. 36; Luke iii. 16, viii. 49). Weiss, p. 161, finds the hypothesis of Ewald confirmed by the affinity of that history with the narrative of the Canaanitish woman, vii. 24 ff. Holtzmann appropriates the reasons of Ewald and Weiss; they are insufficient of themselves, and fall with the alleged disappearance of the Sermon on the Mount.

sations are the significant elements in Mark,[1] with whom ver. 22 still lacks the special historical information that is furnished by Matt. xii. 22 f. (comp. ix. 33 f.); Luke xi. 14. In the connection of Mark alone the retrospective reference to vv. 10–12 is sufficient; hence it is not to be supposed that in the primitive-Mark that cure of demoniacs given by Matthew and Luke must also have had a place (Holtzmann). See, moreover, Weiss, *l.c.* p. 80 ff. Mark, however, does not represent the mother and the brethren as "*confederates of the Pharisees*" (Baur, *Markusevang.* p. 23); their opinion ὅτι ἐξέστη is an error (not malicious), and their purpose is that of care for the security of Jesus. — αὐτούς] He and His disciples. — μηδέ] *not even*, to say nothing of being left otherwise undisturbed. Comp. ii. 2. According to Strauss, indeed, this is a "palpable exaggeration." — ἀκούσαντες] that He was again set upon by the multitude to such a degree, and was occupying Himself so excessively with them (with the healing of their demoniacs, ver. 22, and so on). — οἱ παρ' αὐτοῦ] *those on His side*, i.e. *His own* people. Comp. Xen. *Anab.* vi. 6. 24; *Cyrop.* vi. 2. 1; Polyb. xxiii. 1. 6; 1 Macc. ix. 44. See Bernhardy, p. 256. By this, however, the *disciples* cannot here be meant, as they are in the house with Jesus, ver. 20; but only, as is clearly proved by vv. 31, 32, *His mother, His brethren, His sisters.* — ἐξῆλθον] namely, not from a *place in Capernaum* (in opposition to ver. 20), but from the place where they were sojourning, from *Nazareth.* Comp. i. 9, vi. 3. It is not to be objected that the intelligence of the presence and action of Jesus in Capernaum could not have come to Nazareth so quickly, and that the family could not have come so quickly to Capernaum, as to admit of the latter being already there, after the reprimand of the scribes, vv. 23–30; for Mark does not say that that ἐξῆλθον, and the coming down of the scribes from Jerusalem, and the arrival of the mother, etc., happened *on the same day* whereon Jesus and the disciples had returned εἰς οἶκον. On the contrary, that intelligence arrived at Nazareth, where

---

[1] It is a hasty and unwarranted judgment that vv. 21, 22 appear in Mark as quite "misplaced," and find a much better place just before ver. 31 (so Weiss, *Evangelienfr.* p. 162).

His relatives were setting out, etc.; but from Jerusalem there
had already—when Jesus had returned to Capernaum and was
there so devoting Himself beyond measure to the people—come
down scribes, and these said, etc. This scene, therefore, with
the scribes who had come down was before the arrival of the
relatives of Jesus had taken place. — κρατῆσαι αὐτόν] *to lay
hold upon Him,*to possess themselves of Him. Comp. vi. 17, xii.
12, xiv. 1 ; Matt. xxvi. 4 ; Judg. xvi. 21 ; Tob. vi. 3 ; Polyb. viii.
20. 8, *al.* — ἔλεγον] namely, οἱ παρ᾽ αὐτοῦ. After ἐξῆλθον it is
arbitrary to supply, with others (including Ewald) : *people said,*
which Olshausen even refers to " the malicious Pharisees."
So also Paulus, while Bengel thinks of *messengers.* Let it be
observed that ἔλεγον, ver. 21, and ἔλεγον, ver. 22, correspond
to one another, and that therefore, as in ver. 22, so also in
ver. 21 there is the less reason to think of another subject
than that which *stands there.* — ἐξέστη] *He is out of his
mind,* has become frantic; 2 Cor. v. 13 ; Arist. *H. A.* vi. 22 :
ἐξίσταται καὶ μαίνεται, and see Wetstein. Comp. Xen. *Mem.*
i. 3. 12 : τοῦ φρονεῖν ἐξίστησιν. This strong meaning (erroneously rendered, however, by Luther : He *will* go out of his
mind) is contestably required by the forcible κρατῆσαι, as well
as by the subsequent still stronger analogous expression Βεελζεβοὺλ ἔχει. Hence it is not to be explained of a *swoon* or the
like, but is rightly rendered by the Vulgate : *in furorem versus
est.* To the relatives of Jesus, at that time still (John vii. 3)
unbelieving (according to Mark, even to *Mary,* which certainly does not agree with the preliminary history in Matthew
and Luke[1]), the extraordinary teaching and working of Jesus,
far transcending their sphere of vision, producing such a profound excitement among all the people, and which they knew
not how to reconcile with His domestic antecedents, were the

---

[1] It is entirely arbitrary for Theophylact, Beza, Maldonatus, Bisping, and
others to desire to exclude *Mary* from sharing in the judgment ὅτι ἐξέστη. No
better is the evasion in Olshausen, of a moment of weakness and of struggling
faith. Similarly Lange finds here a moment of eclipse in the life of Mary,
arising out of anxiety for her Son. If her Son had already been to her the
Messiah, how should she not have found in His marvellous working the very
confirmation of her faith in Him, and the begun fulfilment of the promises which
had once been so definitely made to her !

eccentric activity of the phrenzy which had taken possession
of Him.   Comp. Theophylact (who regards ἐξέστη as directly
equivalent to δαίμονα ἔχει), Erasmus, Beza, Calvin, Maldonatus,
Jansen, and others, including Fritzsche, de Wette, Bleek
(according to whom they considered Him as " at the least an
enthusiast "), Holtzmann, Weizsäcker, *et al.*   The omission of
the surprising historical trait in Matthew and Luke betrays
a later sifting process.

REMARKS.—To get rid of this simple meaning of ver. 21,
placed beyond doubt by the clear words, expositors have tried
very varied expedients.   Thus Euthymius Zigabenus, who in
other respects is right in his explanation, arbitrarily suggests for
the ἔλεγον the subject τινὲς φθονεροί, and adduces, even in his day,
two other but unsuitable explanations.[1]   According to Schoettgen and Wolf, the *disciples* (οἱ παρ᾽ αὐτοῦ) heard that so many
people were outside, and went forth *to restrain the multitude,*
and said: *the people* are frantic !   According to Griesbach and
Vater, the *disciples* likewise went forth after having heard *that
Jesus was teaching the people outside,* and wished *to bring* Jesus
in, for *people* were saying: " *nimia eum omnium virium conten-
tione debilitatum* velut insanire !"   According to Grotius, the
relatives of Jesus also dwelt at *Capernaum* (which, moreover,
Ewald, Lange, Bleek, and others suppose, although Mark has
not at all any notice like Matt. iv. 13); they come out of *their*
house, and wish to carry Jesus away from *the* house, where He
was so greatly thronged, for the *report*[2] had spread abroad (ἔλεγον
γάρ) that He had *fainted* (according to Ewald, *Gesch. Chr.* p. 334:
" had fallen into a phrenzy from exhaustion").   According to
Kuinoel, it is likewise obvious of itself *that Jesus has left
the house again and is teaching outside;* while the mother and
the brethren who are at home also go forth, in order to *bring
Jesus in* to eat, and they say, with the view of pressing back
the people: *maxime defatigatus est !*   Comp. Köster, *Imman.*
p. 185, according to whom they wish to *hold* Him on account
of *faintness.*   So again Linder in the *Stud. u. Krit.* 1862, p. 556.
According to Ebrard, § 70, notwithstanding the εἰς οἶκον and the

---

[1] 1. ἐξῆλθον οἱ οἰκεῖοι αὐτοῦ κρατῆσαι αὐτὸν, ἵνα μὴ ὑποχωρήσῃ, ἔλεγον γάρ τινες,
ὅτι ἐξέστη, ἤγουν ἀπέστη ἀπ᾽ αὐτῶν διὰ τὸν ὄχλον.   2. ἐξῆλθον . . . παραβοηθῆσαι,
ἔλεγον γάρ, ὅτι . . . παρελύθη τὸν τόνον τοῦ σώματος, ἄγαν κοπιάσας.

[2] Even Schleiermacher (*L. J.* p. 190 f.) presents the matter as if they had
learnt by *rumour* that He was in an *unsettled condition,* and that they thought
it better to *detain* Him (κρατεῖν) in domestic life.

πάλιν, Jesus is not in Capernaum, but *at the house of a host;* and
in spite of vv. 31, 32, οἱ παρ᾽ αὐτοῦ are *the people in this lodging,*[1]
who think, as they hear Him so zealously *teaching* (?), that He
is out of His mind, and go out to seize upon Him, but are at
once convinced of their error! According to Ammon, *L. J.* II.
p. 155, the people have gathered together round His dwelling,
while He is sitting at meat; He hastens into the midst of the
people, but is extricated by His friends out of the throng, because in their opinion He has fallen into a *faint.* Lange, *L. J.*
II. 2, p. 834, takes ἐξέστη rightly, but regards it as the presupposition of the *popular judgment,* into which the kinsfolk of Jesus had
with politic prudence entered, in order on this pretext to rescue
Him from the momentary danger, because they believed that
He did not sufficiently estimate this danger (namely, of having
broken with the hierarchical party). In this way we may read
everything, on which the matter is to depend, *between the lines.*
Schenkel also reads between the lines, that the relatives of Jesus
had been *persuaded* on the part of His enemies that He Himself
was a person possessed. It is aptly observed by Maldonatus:
" Hunc locum difficiliorem pietas facit . . . ; pio quodam
studio nonnulli rejecta verborum proprietate alias, quae minus
a pietate abhorrere viderentur, interpretationes quaesiverunt.
Nescio an, dum *pias* quaererent, *falsas* invenerint." According
to Köstlin, p. 342, Mark has, "after the manner of later prag-
matists," taken the ἔλεγον ὅτι ἐξέστη, which originally had the less
exceptionable sense of enthusiasm, as a malicious calumny.
Thus, indeed, what appears offensive is easily set aside and laid
upon the *compiler,* as is done, moreover, in another way by
Baur, *Evang.* p. 559.

Vv. 22–30. See on Matt. xii. 24–32, who narrates more
completely from the collection of Logia and historical tradition. Comp. Luke xi. 15–23, xii. 10. — And the scribes, etc.,
asserted a still worse charge. — Ver. 23. προσκαλεσάμ. αὐτούς]
De Wette is of opinion, without warrant, that this could only
have taken place in *the open air,* not in the house (ver. 20).
They were in the house along with, but further away from,
Jesus; He calls them to Him to speak with them. — σατανᾶς
σατανᾶν] not: one Satan . . . the other, but: Satan . . . himself; see on Matt. xii. 26. Comp. ὁ σατανᾶς . . . ἐφ᾽ ἑαυτόν,

[1] Kahnis (*Dogm.* I. p. 428 f.) also explains it of the *hosts* and *disciples* (not of
the mother and the brethren). He thinks that they wished to bring Him into
the house by saying that He was in the *ecstatic* state like *the prophets.*

ver. 26. The want of the article with the proper name is not opposed to this. — Ver. 24. Now, in order to make good this πῶς δύναται (*i.e.* οὐ δύναται κ.τ.λ.), there come, linked on by the simple *and* (not γάρ), two illustrative analogues (ἐν παραβολαῖς), after which at ver. 26, but likewise by the simple *and*, not by a particle of inference, is added the point, *quod erat demonstrandum.* This symmetrical progression by means of καί is *rhetorical;* it has something in it impressive, striking—a feature also presenting itself in the discourse as it proceeds *asyndetically* in vv. 27 and 28. — Ver. 28. The order of the words: πάντα ἀφεθ. τοῖς υἱοῖς τῶν ἀνθρώπων τὰ ἁμαρτήματα, places them so apart, as to lay a great emphasis on πάντα. See Bornemann and Herbst, *ad Xen. Mem.* ii. 10. 2. The expression τοῖς υἱοῖς τ. ἀνθρ., not a singular reminiscence from Matt. xii. 32 (Weiss), is rather a trait of Mark, depicting human weakness. — αἰωνίου ἁμαρτ.] namely, in respect of the *guilt,* "nunquam delendi," Beza. — Ver. 30. ὅτι ἔλεγον: (He spake thus) *because they said.* Comp. Luke xi. 18. — πνεῦμα ἀκάθαρτον] not again as at ver. 22 : Βεελζεβοὺλ ἔχει, because of the contrast with πνεῦμα τὸ ἅγιον. The less is it to be said that Mark places on a par the blasphemy against the *person* of Jesus (Matt. xii. 31 f.) and that against the Holy *Spirit* (Köstlin, p. 318), or that he has "already given up" the former blasphemy (Hilgenfeld). It is included, in fact, in ver. 28.

Vv. 31–35. See on Matt. xii. 46–50. Comp. Luke viii. 19–21. — ἔρχονται οὖν] οὖν points back, by way of resuming, to ver. 21. See Krüger, *Cyrop.* i. 5. 14; Klotz, *ad Devar.* p. 718. ἔρχονται corresponds with ἐξῆλθον, ver. 21, where Bengel pertinently observes: " Exitum sequetur τὸ *venire,* ver. 31." Ebrard resorts to harmonistic evasions. — οἱ ἀδελφοί] They are named at vi. 3. Of a "position *of guardianship* towards the Lord " (Lange), which they had wished to occupy, nothing is said either here or at John vii. 3, and here all the less that, in fact, the mother was present. — ἔξω] outside, *in front of the house,* ver. 20, Matt. xii. 47. — Ver. 32. The mention of the sisters *here for the first time* is an inaccuracy. — Ver. 34. περιβλεψ. κύκλῳ] Comp. vi. 6 ; Hom. *Od.* viii. 278 ;

Herod. iv. 182; Plat. *Phaed.* 72 B, and the passages in Sturz, *Lex. Xen.* II. p. 803 f.—The expressive looking round was here an entirely different thing from that of ver. 5. Bengel: "suavitate summa." How little did His actual mother and His reputed brothers and sisters as yet comprehend Him and His higher ministry :

CHAPTER IV.

Ver. 1. συνήχθη] Lachm. and Tisch. read συνάγεται, following B
C L Δ ℵ, min. Rightly; the alteration was made from Matt.
xiii. 2, partly to συνήχθησαν (so A, min.), partly to συνήχθη. —
Instead of πολύς, according to the same evidence, πλεῖστος is to
be adopted, with Tisch. — Ver. 3. τοῦ σπεῖραι] Lachm. and Tisch.
have merely σπεῖραι, following only B ℵ* 102. — Ver. 4. After
πετεινά Elz. has τοῦ οὐρανοῦ, in opposition to decisive evidence.
It is taken from Luke viii. 5. — Ver. 5. Instead of ἄλλο δέ read,
with Lachm. and Tisch., καὶ ἄλλο, according to B C L M** Δ ℵ,
min. vss. The *Recepta* is from Matt. xiii. 5. — Ver. 6. ἡλίου δὲ
ἀνατείλαντος] Lachm. and Tisch. read καὶ ὅτε ἀνέτειλεν ὁ ἥλιος,
following B C D L Δ ℵ, Copt. Vulg. Cant. Vind. Corb. 2, Rd.
The *Recepta* is from Matt. xiii. 6. — Ver. 8. ἄλλο] B C L ℵ, min.
have the reading ἀλλά (Fritzsche, Rinck, Tisch.). It is from
Matt., and was favoured by the tripartite division that follows.
— αὐξάνοντα] A B C D L Δ ℵ, 238 have αὐξανόμενον. Approved
by Griesb., adopted by Lachm. and Tisch. Rightly, because
the *intransitive* αὐξάνειν is the prevailing form in the N. T. —
Instead of the threefold repetition of ἐν, Tisch. has εἰς three
times, following B C* L Δ, min. Yet B L have ΕΙΣ once and
ΕΝ twice. The reading of Tisch. is to be regarded as original;
the ἐν, which is likewise strongly attested, was a gloss upon it, and
that reading then became easily taken and interpreted, in comparison with Matt. xiii. 8, as the numeral ἕν. In ver. 20 also
the ἕν is not to be written three times, but with all the uncials,
which have breathings and accents: ἐν, as also Tisch. has it. —
Ver. 9. ὁ ἔχων] Lachm. and Tisch. have ὃς ἔχει, following B C* D
Δ ℵ*. The *Recepta* is from Matt. xiii. 9; Luke viii. 8. — Ver. 10.
ἠρώτησαν] Fritzsche, Lachm. and Tisch. have ἠρώτων [1] on preponderant evidence (D has ἐπηρώτων). To be adopted. If the

---

[1] In ed. 8 Tisch., following C ℵ, has the form ἠρώτουν, which probably is only
a transcriber's error, as with still stronger evidence in its favour is the case
in Matt. xv. 23. The Ionic form of the verb in εω is entirely foreign to the
N. T.

imperfect had been introduced from Luke viii. 9, ἐπηρώτων would be more diffused. — τὴν ταραβολήν] Tisch. has τὰς παραβολάς, following B C L Δ ℵ, vss. The singular is a correction; comp. Luke. — Ver. 11. γνῶναι] is wanting in A B C* K L ℵ, min. Copt. Corb. 1. Suspected by Griesb., deleted by Lachm. and Tisch. An addition from Matt. xiii. 11; Luke viii. 10. With Tischendorf the words are to be arranged thus: ·. μυστ. δέδ. τ. βασ. — Ver. 12. τὰ ἀμαρτήματα] is wanting in B C L ℵ, min. Copt. Arm. Cr. (twice); condemned by Griesb., bracketed by Lachm., deleted by Fritzsche and Tisch. An addition, instead of which is found also τὰ παραπτώματα (min.). — Ver. 15. ἐν ταῖς καρδ. αὐτῶν] C L Δ ℵ, Copt. Syr. p. (in the margin) Colb.: ἐν αὐτοῖς (so Tisch.), and in favour of this B and min. testify by the reading εἰς αὐτούς. The *Recepta* is explanatory after Matt. xiii. 19, comp. Luke viii. 12, but at the same time its testimony is in favour of ἐν αὐτοῖς, not of εἰς αὐτούς. — Ver. 18. καὶ οὗτοι εἰσιν] Griesb. Lachm. Tisch. read καὶ ἄλλοί εἰσιν, following B C* D L Δ ℵ, Copt. Vulg. Cant. Ver. Colb. Vind. Germ. Corb. Rightly; the *Recepta* originated by mechanical process after vv. 15, 16, comp. ver. 20. When this οὗτοι came in, there emerged at once an incompatibility with the subsequent οὗτοί εἰσιν, therefore this *latter* was omitted (A C** E G H K M S U V π, min., Copt. Syr. p. Goth. Slav. Brix. Theophyl. Matth. and Fritzsche), while others removed the *first* οὗτοί εἰσιν (min. Arm.). — Ver. 19. τούτου after αἰῶνος is rightly deleted by Griesb., Fritzsche, Lach. and Tisch. in conformity with very considerable testimony. A current addition. — Ver. 20. οὗτοι] Tisch. has ἐκεῖνοι, following B C L Δ ℵ; οὗτοι is a mechanical repetition, and comp. Matt. and Luke. — Ver. 21. The order ἔρχεται ὁ λύχνος is to be adopted, with Lachm. and Tisch., according to B C D L Δ ℵ, min. vss. — ἐπιτεθῇ] τεθῇ is attested by B C L Δ ℵ, min. (so also Fritzsche, Lachm. and Tisch.; recommended, moreover, by Griesb.). The compound word is more precise in definition, and came in here and at Luke viii. 16. — Ver. 22. The τι (which Lachm. brackets) was easily omitted after ἐστι as being superfluous. — ὅ ἐὰν μή] many variations, among which ἐὰν μή has the strong attestation of A C K L, min. It is commended by Griesb., and is to be adopted. The apparent absurdity of the sense [1] suggested partly the addition of ὅ, partly, in conformity with what follows, readings with ἵνα, namely, ἀλλ' ἵνα (D, vss.) and ἐὰν μὴ ἵνα (so Lachm. Tisch., following B D ℵ), εἰ μὴ ἵνα (min.). — Ver. 24. After the second ὑμῖν, Elz. Fritzsche,

---

[1] The reading ἐὰν μή is in no wise absurd (Fritzsche, de Wette), but it gives the same logical analysis as x. 30. See *in loc.*

Scholz have τοῖς ἀκούουσιν, which also Lachm. and Tisch. on decisive evidence have deleted (it is a gloss), while Griesb. strikes out the whole καὶ προστεθ. ὑμῖν τοῖς ἀκ. (only in accordance with D G, Codd. It.), and Fritzsche places these words after ἀκούετε (according to Arm.). The course followed by Griesb. and Fritzsche must be rejected on account of the very weakness of the evidence; the reading of Griesb. arose from the fact that the eye of the transcriber passed from the first ὑμῖν directly to the second. — Ver. 25. ὃς γὰρ ἂν ἔχῃ] Lachm. and Tisch. have ὃς γὰρ ἔχει, following B C L Δ א, min., to which, moreover, D E* F, al. are added with the reading ὃς γὰρ ἂν ἔχει. According to this, ἔχει alone is to be read; ἂν was added probably in recollection of Luke viii. 18, and then ἔχει was transmuted into ἔχῃ. — Ver. 28. γάρ is to be deleted, with Lachm. and Tisch., following very important authorities. A connective addition, instead of which D has ὅτι αὐτ. — πλήρη σῖτον] Lachm. and Tisch. read πλήρης σῖτος, following B, to which D falls to be added with the reading πλήρης ὁ σῖτος. πλήρης σῖτος is the original, which it was thought necessary subsequently to help by a structural emendation. — Ver. 30. τίνι] B C L Δ א, min. Ver. have πῶς, which Griesb. has recommended, Fritzsche and Tisch. have adopted. τίνι is from Luke xiii. 18. — ἐν ποίᾳ παραβολῇ παραβάλωμεν αὐτήν] Fritzsche, Lachm. Tisch. have ἐν τίνι αὐτὴν παραβολῇ θῶμεν, following B C* L Δ א, min. Ver. Or. Rightly; ποίᾳ came in as a gloss upon τίνι, after the analogy of the preceding πῶς; and the more difficult θῶμεν was explained by παραβαλώμεν. — Ver. 31. κόκκον] Elz. Fritzsche, Tisch. read κόκκῳ, following B D Δ Π א. As after the second half of ver. 30 the accusative (Griesb. Scholz, Lachm.) more readily suggested itself (in connection with θῶμεν or παραβάλωμεν), the dative is to be preferred as the more difficult reading, which was the more easily supplanted by comparison of the different connections in Matt. xiii. 31; Luke xiii. 19. — μικρότερος] Lachm. reads μικρότερον, following B D L M Δ א, min. He adds, moreover, ὄν according to B L Δ א, omitting the subsequent ἐστί, and encloses τῶν ἐπὶ τῆς γῆς, which is wanting in C, Ver., in brackets. Tisch. also has μικρότερον ὄν, omitting ἐστί. The *Recepta* is to be retained; μικρότερον is a grammatical correction[1] that has originated from a comparison with Matt., and the added ὄν, having arisen from the writing twice over of the ON which had gone before, or from the marginal writing of ON over the final syllable of μικρότερΟΣ, dislodged the subsequent ἐστί, whereupon, doubtless,

---

[1] μείζων, too, ver. 32, became changed in codd. into μεῖζον. So A C E L V א, min. Tisch.

the connection was lost. — Ver. 34. *τ. μαθ. αὐτοῦ*] Tisch. reads
τ. ἰδίοις μαθ., following B C L Δ ℵ. Rightly ; the *Recepta* is the
usual expression. — Ver. 36. The reading *πλοῖα* instead of
πλοιάρια (as Elz. Fritzsche, Scholz have it) is so decisively
attested, that but for that circumstance the more rare *πλοιάρια*
would have to be defended. — Ver. 37. Instead of *αὐτὸ ἤδη
γεμίζεσθαι*, Griesb. approved, and Lachm. and Tisch. read, *ἤδη
γεμίζεσθαι τὸ πλοῖον*, following B C D L Δ ℵ** Copt. Syr. p. (in
the margin) Vulg. It. This latter is to be preferred ; the simple
mode of expression was smoothed. — Ver. 38. Instead of *ἐπι*
before *τ. πρ.*, Griesb. Fritzsche, Lachm. Tisch. read *ἐν* on decisive
evidence. — Ver. 40. *οὕτω*] is deleted by Lachm., following B D
L Δ ℵ, Copt. Aeth. Vulg. It., and subsequently, instead of *πῶς
οὐκ*, he has, with Griesb., *οὔπω* according to the same and other
authorities. But the *Recepta* is, with Tisch., to be maintained.
For in accordance with Matt. viii. 26 *οὕτω* was very easily
dropped, while *οὔπω* just as easily crept in as a modifying
expression, which at the same time dislodged the *πῶς*.

Vv. 1–9. See on Matt. xiii. 1–9. Comp. Luke viii. 4–8.
Matthew has here a group of parables from the collection of
Logia to the number of *seven*,—a later and richer selection
than Mark gives with his *three* similitudes, the second of
which, however (vv. 26–29), Matthew has not, because it
probably was not embraced in the collection of Logia. See
on ver. 26 ff. Matthew has worked by way of amplification,
and not Mark by way of reducing and weakening (Hilgenfeld).
— *πάλιν*, see iii. 7. — *ἤρξατο*] For from *καὶ συνάγεται* onward is related what happened *after the commencement* of His
teaching. — Ver. 2. *ἐν τῇ διδαχῇ αὐτοῦ*] *in His doctrinal discourse.* Of the many (*πολλά*) Mark adduces some. — Ver. 7.
συνέπνιξαν] *choked* the germinating seed, *com*pressing it. Comp.
Theophylact, *c. pl.* vi. 11. 6 : *δένδρα συμπνιγόμενα.* — Ver. 8.
ἀναβαίνοντα καὶ αὐξανόμενον (see the critical remarks) is
predicate of *καρπόν*, hence *ἐδίδου καρπόν* (and consequently
also *καρπὸν οὐκ ἔδωκε*, ver. 7) is to be understood not of the
grains of corn, but of the *corn-stalks* ascending and growing
(shooting upward and continuing to grow). The produce *of
the grains* is only mentioned in the sequel : *καὶ ἔφερεν
κ.τ.λ.* In the classics also *καρπός* means generally that which
grows in the field (Hom. *Il.* i. 156 ; Xen. *de venat.* v. 5; Plat.

Theaet. p. 149 E, *Crat.* p. 410 C), as in the German *Frucht,
Früchte.* Comp. καρποφορεῖ, ver. 28. — With the *Recepta* ἐν
τριάκοντα is to be taken as: *one bore thirty* (neuter: nothing
to be supplied), *i.e.* according to the connection: one grain,
which had been sown, bore thirty grains, another sixty, and
so on. On the *usus loquendi,* comp. Xen. *Hell.* vii. 4. 27: ἐν
μέρος ἔλαβον Ἀργεῖοι, ἐν δὲ Θηβαῖοι, ἐν δὲ Ἀρκάδες, ἐν δὲ
Μεσσήνιοι, Arist. *Eth. Nic.* vi. 1. 5 ; Ecclus. xxxi. 23 f.
With the reading εἰς τριάκοντα (see the critical remarks) we
must render: it bore *up to thirty,* and up to sixty, etc. If
ἐν τριάκοντα be read, the meaning is: it bore *in* (at the rate
of) thirty, etc., so that the fruit-bearing was consummated in
thirty, and so on. Observe, further, how ver. 8 has changed
the primitive form of the Logia-collection still preserved in
Matthew, especially as to the climax of the fruitfulness, which
in Matthew is descending, in Mark ascending. — Ver. 9. καὶ
ἔλεγεν] "pausa frequens, sermonibus gravissimis interposita,"
Bengel. Comp. ii. 27.

Vv. 10–20. See on Matt. xiii. 10–23. Comp. Luke viii.
9–15. — καταμόνας] therefore, according to Mark, no longer
in the ship, ver. 1. — οἱ περὶ αὐτόν] they who besides and next
after the Twelve were the more confidential disciples of Jesus.
A more precise definition than in Matthew and Luke. Of the
Seventy (Euthymius Zigabenus) Mark has no mention. We
may add that Matthew could not have *better* made use of the
expression οἱ περὶ αὐτὸν σὺν τοῖς δώδεκα (Holtzmann, who
therefore pronounces it not to belong to the primitive-Mark),
nor could he *not use it at all* (Weiss in the *Zeitschr. f. D. Theol.*
1864, p. 86 f.). He has only changed the detailed description of Mark into the usual expression, and he goes to work
in general less accurately in delineating the situation. — τὰς
παραβ.] see ver. 2. — Ver. 11. δέδοται] of the spiritual giving
brought about by making them capable of *knowing ;* hence
γνῶναι (which here is spurious) in Matthew and Luke. — τοῖς
ἔξω] that is, to those who are outside of our circle, *to the people.*
The sense of οἱ ἔξω is always determined by the contrast to
it. In the Epistles it is the *non-Christians* (1 Cor. v. 12 f. ;
Col. iv. 5 ; 1 Thess. iv. 12 ; 1 Tim. iii. 7). We are the less

entitled to discover here, with de Wette, an unsuitable ὕστερον
πρότερον of expression, seeing that the expression in itself so
relative does not even in the Talmud denote always the *non-
Jews* (Schoettgen, *ad* 1 Cor. v. 12 f.), but also those who do not
profess the doctrine of the הכמים—the היצונים ; see Lightfoot,
p. 609. — ἐν παραβ. τὰ πάντα γίνεται] ἐν παραβ. has the
emphasis : *in parables the whole is imparted to them,* so that
there is not communicated to them in addition the abstract
doctrine itself.   All that is delivered to them of the mystery
of the Messiah's kingdom—that is, of the divine counsel concerning it, which was first unveiled in the gospel—is conveyed
to them under a veil of parable, and not otherwise.   On γίνεται,
comp. Herod. ix. 46: ἡμῖν οἱ λόγοι γεγόνασι, Thucyd. v. 111, *al.*
— Ver. 12. ἵνα] not : *ita ut,* as Wolf, Bengel, Rosenmüller,
Kuinoel, and others would have it, but, as it *always* is (comp.
on Matt. i. 22), a pure *particle of design.*   The unbelieving
people are, by the very fact that the communications of the
mystery of the Messiah's kingdom are made to them in
parables and not otherwise, *intended* not to attain to insight
into this mystery, and thereby to conversion and forgiveness.   This idea of the *divine Nemesis* is expressed under a
remembrance of Isa. vi. 9, 10, which prophetic passage appears in Matthew (less originally) as a formal citation by
Jesus, and in an altered significance of bearing attended by a
weakening of its teleological point.   Baur, indeed, finds the
aim expressed in Mark (for it is in nowise to be explained
away) absolutely inconceivable ; but it is to be conceived of
as a mediate, not as a final, aim — a *"judicium divinum"*
(Bengel), which has a *paedagogic* purpose. — Ver. 13. After
Jesus, vv. 11, 12, has expressed the *right* of His disciples to
learn, not merely, like the unbelieving multitude, the parables
themselves, but also their meaning—the μυστήριον contained
in them — and has thus acknowledged their question in
ver. 10 as *justified,* He addresses Himself now, with a new
commencement of His discourse (καὶ λέγει αὐτοῖς, comp. vv. 21,
24, 26, 30, 35), to the purpose of *answering* that question, and
that with reference to the particular concrete parable, ver. 3 ff.
To *this* parable, which is conceived as having suggested the

general question of ver. 10 (hence τ. παραβολὴν ταύτην), He confines Himself, and introduces the exposition to be given with the words: *Know ye not this parable, and how shall ye* (in general) *understand all parables?* These words are merely intended to *lead back* in a lively manner, after the digression of vv. 11, 12, to the *point of the question* at ver. 10, the *reply* to which then begins at ver. 14 with respect to that special parable. A *reproach* is by some found in the words (*since unto you it is given,* etc., ver. 11, *it surprises me,* that ye know not, etc.). See Fritzsche and de Wette, the latter accusing Mark of placing quite inappropriately in the mouth of Jesus an *unseasonable* reproach. But Mark himself pronounces decisively against the entire supposition of this connection by his καὶ λέγει αὐτοῖς, whereby he *separates* the discourse of ver. 13 from what has gone before. If the assumed connection were correct, Mark must have omitted this introduction of a *new* portion of discourse, and instead of οὐκ οἴδατε must have used perhaps καὶ ὑμεῖς οὐκ οἴδατε, or some similar *link of connection* with what precedes. Moreover, ver. 13 is to be read *as one question* (comp. Lachmann and Tischendorf), and in such a way that καὶ πῶς κ.τ.λ. still depends on οὐκ οἴδατε (comp. Ewald); not, as Fritzsche would have it, in such a way that καί indicates the consequence, and there would result the meaning: "*Ye understand not this parable, and are ye to understand all parables?*" But this would rather result in the meaning: Ye understand not *this* parable; how is it, consequently, possible that ye shall understand *all* parables? And this would be a strange and unmeaning, because altogether self-evident consequence. Usually ver. 13 is divided into *two questions* (so, too, de Wette), and πάσας is taken as equivalent to: *all the rest;* but this is done quite without warrant, since the idea of λοιπάς would be precisely the *point* in virtue of the contrast which is assumed. — γνώσεσθε] *future,* because the disciples were not aware how they should attain to the understanding of the whole of the parables partly delivered already (ver. 2), partly still to be delivered in time to come. — The following interpretation of the parable, vv. 14–20, is "so vivid, rich, and peculiar, that there is good reason for finding in it words of Christ Himself,"

Ewald. — Ver. 15. Observe the difference between the local
ὅπου and the temporal ὅταν, in connection with which καί is
not adversative (Kuinoel, de Wette), but the simple conjunctive
and: The following are those (who are sown) *by the way-side:
then, when the teaching is sown and they shall have heard,
cometh straightway Satan*, etc. — Ver. 16. ὁμοίως] *in like
manner*, after an *analogous* figurative reference, in *symmetrical
further interpretation of the parable.*   Translate: *And the
following are in like manner those who are sown on the stony
ground:* (namely) *those who, when they shall have heard the
word, immediately receive it with joy; and they have not root
in themselves*, etc.   It is more in keeping with the simplicity
and vividness of the discourse not to take the καὶ οὐκ ἔχουσι
along with οἵ. — Ver. 18 f. *And there are others, who are sown
among the thorns; these are they who*, etc.   If ἀκούοντες be read,
—which, however, would arise more easily from the similar
parallel of Matthew than ἀκούσαντες (B C D L Δ ℵ, Tisch.)
from the dissimilar one of Luke,—the course of events is set
forth *from the outset*, whereas ἀκούσαντες sets it forth from
the standpoint of the result (*they have heard, and*, etc.). — τὰ
λοιπά] besides riches: sensual pleasure, honour, etc. — εἰσπορ.]
namely, into that place whither the word that is heard has
penetrated, into the heart.   The expression does not quite
fit into the parable itself; but this does not point to less
of originality (Weiss).   De Wette wrongly observes that
εἰσπορ. is probably an erroneous explanation of the πορευόμενοι in Luke. — Ver. 20. ἐν (not ἕν; see the critical remarks
on ver. 8) τριάκοντα κ.τ.λ. is, it is true, so far out of keeping,
that by retaining the numbers the discourse falls back from
the interpretation into the figure; but the very repetition of
the striking closing words of the parable, in which only the
preposition is here accidentally changed, betokens the set purpose of solemn emphasis.

Vv. 21–23.   Comp. Luke viii. 16 f.   *Meaning* (comp. Matt.
v. 15, x. 26): "the light, *i.e.* the knowledge of the μυστήριον
τῆς βασιλείας, which ye receive from me, ye are not to withhold from others, but to bring about its diffusion; for, as what
is concealed is not destined for concealment, but rather for

becoming manifest, so also is the mystery of the Messiah's kingdom."[1] These sayings, however, as far as ver. 25, have not their original place here, but belong to what (according to Papias) Mark wrote οὐ τάξει. Holtzmann judges otherwise, p. 81, in connection with his assumption of a primitive-Mark. The collection of Logia is sufficient as a source. Comp. Weiss in the *Jahrb. f. D. Theol.* 1864, p. 88. — ἔρχεται] *Doth the lamp then possibly come,* etc. ? ἔρχεσθαι is used of inanimate things which are *brought;* very frequently also in classical writers. — ὑπὸ τὸν μόδιον] See on Matt. v. 15. — κλίνην] a *table-couch.* Comp. vii. 4. After κλίνην there is only a comma to be placed: the question is *one* as far as τεθῇ. — According to the reading ἐὰν μὴ φανερ. (see the critical remarks), the rendering is: *nothing is hidden, if it shall not* (in future) *be made manifest.*[2] So surely and certainly does the φανέρωσις set in! — ἀλλ' ἵνα εἰς φαν. ἔλθῃ] The logical reference of ἀλλ' is found in a pregnant significance of ἀπόκρυφον: nor has there anything (after οὐδέ, τι is again to be mentally supplied) taken place as secret, *i.e. what is meant to be secret, but* what in such a case has come to pass, has the destination, etc.

Vv. 24, 25. Comp. Luke viii. 18. — βλέπετε] *Be heedful as to what ye hear;* how important it is rightly to understand what is delivered to you by me! — ἐν ᾧ μέτρῳ κ.τ.λ.] A ground of encouragement to heedfulness. It is otherwise in Matt. vii. 2. In our passage *the relation of heedfulness to*

---

[1] According to others, Jesus gives an allegorical exhortation to *virtue:* "ut lucerna candelabro imponenda est, sic vos oportet, discipuli, non quidem vitam umbratilem sine virtutis splendore agere; sed," etc., Fritzsche, comp. Theophylact, Grotius, and others. But the kindled light would, in fact, be already the symbol of virtue, and Jesus would forbid the exercise of it in secret! Moreover, this view is not required by ver. 20, since with ver. 21 a *new* portion of the discourse commences; and our view is not forbidden by ver. 11 (comp. ver. 34), since in ver. 11 Jesus is only speaking of the then unsusceptible multitude, and, if pushed to consistent *general* application, these words spoken at ver. 11 would quite annul the apostolic calling. *History* has refuted this general application. Erasmus, *Paraphr.,* aptly says : "Nolite putare me, quod nunc secreto vobis committo, perpetuo celatum esse velle ; . . . lux est per me in vobis accensa, ut vestro ministerio discutiat tenebras totius mundi."

[2] "Id fit successive in hoc saeculo, et fiet plene, quum lux omnia illustrabit, 1 Cor. iv. 5," Bengel.

the knowledge thereby to be attained is described. Euthymius Zigabenus well says: ἐν ᾧ μέτρῳ μετρεῖτε τὴν προσοχὴν, ἐν τῷ αὐτῷ μετρηθήσεται ὑμῖν ἡ γνῶσις, τουτέστιν
ὅσην εἰσφέρετε προσοχὴν, τοσαύτη παρασχεθήσεται ὑμῖν
γνῶσις, καὶ οὐ μόνον ἐν τῷ αὐτῷ μέτρῳ, ἀλλὰ καὶ πλέον. —
Ver. 25. Reason assigned for the foregoing καὶ προστε-
θήσεται. The application of the proverbial saying (comp.
Matt. xiii. 12, xxv. 29) is : For if ye (through heedfulness)
have become rich in knowledge, ye shall continually receive
still larger accession to this riches (that is just the προσ-
τεθήσεται); but if ye (through heedlessness) are poor in
knowledge, ye shall also lose even your little knowledge.
Euthymius Zigabenus erroneously refers δοθήσεται only to
the γνῶσις, and ἔχῃ to the προσοχήν. So also Theophylact.

Vv. 26–29. Jesus now continues, as is proved by ver. 33 f.
(in opposition to Baur, *Markusevang.* p. 28), His parabolic
discourses *to the people;* hence ἔλεγεν is here used without
αὐτοῖς (vv. 21, 24), and vv. 10–25 are to be regarded as an
inserted episode (in opposition to de Wette, *Einl.* § 94b, who
holds ὅτε δὲ ἐγένετο καταμόνας as absurd). — Mark alone has
the following parable, but in a form so thoughtful and so
characteristically different from Matt. xiii. 24 f., that it is without sufficient ground regarded (by Ewald, Hilgenfeld, Köstlin)
as founded on, or remodelled [1] from, Matt. *l.c.,* and therefore
as not originally belonging to this place,—a view with which
Weiss agrees, but traces the parable of Mark to the primitive
form in the collection of Logia, and holds the enemy that
sowed the tares, Matt. xiii., to have been brought into it by the
first evangelist; while Strauss (in Hilgenfeld's *Zeitschr.* 1863,
p. 209) has recourse to the *neutral* character of Mark, in
accordance with which he is held to have removed the ἐχθρὸς
ἄνθρωπος (by which *Paul* is meant!). See, on the other hand,
Klöpper in the *Jahrb. f. D. Theol.* 1864, p. 141 ff., who, with
Weizsäcker, discovers the point aimed at in the parable to
be that of antagonism to the vehement expectations of a
speedy commencement of the kingdom,—which, however,

---

[1] A "tame weakening," in the opinion of Hilgenfeld, comp. Strauss; "of a
secondary nature," in that of Weizsäcker.

must have been directly indicated, and is not even implied in Matt. xiii. (see ver. 37 ff.). Without foundation, Weizsäcker (p. 118) finds in the parable a proof that our Gospel of Mark was not written till after the destruction of Jerusalem, when the delaying of the Parousia had become evident. Here the establishment of the kingdom is not at all depicted under the specific form of the *Parousia*, and there is nothing said of a *delaying* of it. — ἡ βασιλεία τ. Θεοῦ] The *Messianic kingdom*, conceived of as *preparing* for its proximate appearance, and then (ver. 29) *appearing* at its time. — τὸν σπόρον] the seed concerned.—Observe the *aorist* βάλῃ, and then the *presents* which follow: *has* cast, and then *sleeps* and *arises*, etc. — νύκτα κ. ἡμέραν] With another form of conception the genitives might also be used here. See on the distinction, Kühner, II. p. 219. The prefixing of νύκτα is here occasioned by the order of καθεύδῃ καὶ ἐγείρ. See, further, on Luke ii. 37. Erasmus erroneously refers ἐγείρ. to the *seed*, which is only introduced as subject with βλαστ. — μηκύνηται] *is extended*, in so far, namely, as the *shoot* of the seed comes forth and mounts upwards (*increscat*, Vulgate). Comp. LXX. Isa. xliv. 14. In the shoot *the seed extends itself*. — ὡς οὐκ οἶδεν αὐτός] *in a way unknown to himself* (the sower); he himself knows not how it comes about. See the sequel. — αὐτομάτη] *of itself*, without man's assistance.[1] Comp. Hesiod, ἔργ. 118 ; Herod. ii. 94, viii. 138 ; and Wetstein *in loc.* — εἶτα πλήρης σῖτος ἐν τ. στ.] the *nominative* (see the critical remarks) with startling vividness brings before us the result as *standing by itself: then full* (developed to full size) *grain in the ear!* See on this nominative standing forth in rhetorical relief from the current construction, Bernhardy, p. 68 f. — Ver. 29. παραδῷ] is usually explained *intransitively*, in the sense : shall have delivered *itself* over, namely, by its ripeness to the harvesting. Many transitive verbs are confessedly thus used in an intransitive signification, in which case, however, it is inappropriate to supply ἑαυτόν (Kühner, II. p. 9 f.). So, in

[1] Hence there is no inconsistency with ver. 27 (Weiss). The germinative power of the seed is conditioned by the immanent power of the earth, which acts upon it.

particular, compounds of διδόναι (see Viger., ed. Herm. p. 132;
Valckenaer, *Diatr.* p. 233; Jacobs, *ad Philostr.* p. 363; Krüger,
§ 52. 2. 9); and see in general, Bernhardy, p. 339 f.; Winer,
p. 225 [E. T. 315]. But of this use of παραδιδόναι there
is found no quite certain instance [1] (not even in 1 Pet. ii. 23,
see Huther); moreover, the expression itself, "the fruit has
offered itself," would be foreign to the simplicity of the style,
and has a modern sound. Hence (comp. Kaeuffer, *de ζωῆς
αἰων. not.* p. 49) παραδιδ. is rather to be explained as *to allow*,
in accordance with well-known usage (Herod. v. 67, vii. 18;
Xen. *Anab.* vi. 6. 34; Polyb. iii. 12. 4): *but when the fruit
shall have allowed, i.e.* when it is sufficiently ripe. Quite
similar is the expression: τῆς ὥρας παραδιδούσης, Polyb.
xxii. 24. 9: *when the season permitted.* Bleek assents to this
view. — ἀποστέλλει τὸ δρέπανον] Comp. Joel iv. 13; Rev.
xiv. 15. — The *teaching* of the parable is: *Just as a man, after
performing the sowing, leaves the germination and growth, etc.,
without further intervention, to the earth's own power, but at
the time of ripening reaps the harvest, so the Messiah leaves the
ethical results and the new developments of life, which His word
is fitted to produce in the minds of men, to the moral self-activity
of the human heart, through which these results are worked
out in accordance with their destination* (to δικαιοσύνη —
this is the parabolic reference of the πλήρης σῖτος), *but will,
when the time for the establishment of His kingdom comes, cause
the δικαίους to be gathered into it* (by the angels, Matt. xxiv. 31;
these are the reapers, Matt. xiii. 39). The self-activity on
which stress is here laid does not exclude the operations of
divine grace, but the aim of the parable is just to render
prominent the former, not the latter. It is the one of the
two factors, and its separate treatment, keeping out of view
for the present the other, leaves the latter unaffected. Comp.
ver. 24. Bengel aptly observes on αὐτομάτη, ver. 28: "non
excluditur agricultura et coelestis pluvia solesque." Moreover,
Jesus must still for the present leave the mode of bringing
about the δικαιοσύνη (by means of His ἱλαστήριον and faith

[1] In Josh. xi. 19 the reading varies much and is doubtful; in Plat. *Phaedr.*
p. 250 E, παραδούς is not necessarily reflexive.

thereon) to the later development of His doctrine. But the
letting the matter take its course and folding the hands (Strauss)
are directly *excluded* by αὐτομάτη, although the parable is
opposed also to the conception of a so-called *plan* of Jesus.[1]

Vv. 30–32. See on Matt. xiii. 31 f. Comp. Luke xiii. 17 f.
— πῶς] *how* are we to bring the Messianic kingdom into
comparison ? — ἢ ἐν τίνι αὐτ. παραβολῇ θῶμεν (see the
critical remarks): *or in what parable are we to place it, set it
forth ?* The expression *inclusive of others* (*we*) is in keeping
with the *deliberative* form of discourse. The *hearers* are formally
taken into the consultation. The deviation from the normal
order of the words places the principal emphasis on τίνι. —
ὡς κόκκῳ σιν.] ὡς is correlative to the πῶς of ver. 30 : *so as
it is likened to a grain of mustard seed.* — The following [2] is
not a parable in the stricter sense (not a history), but a
comparison generally, the representation of the idea, borrowed
from the region of sense. Comp. iii. 23, vii. 17. See on
Matt. xiii. 3. — Observe the twofold ὅταν σπαρῇ, vv. 31, 32.
In the first the emphasis is on ὅταν, in the second on σπαρῇ.
" Exacte definit tempus illud, quum granum desinit esse
parvum et incipit fieri magnum," Bengel.

Ver. 33 f. Comp. Matt. xiii. 34. — From τοιαύταις it
follows that Mark knew yet more parables that were spoken
at that time. — καθὼς ἠδύναντο ἀκούειν] *As they were able*
(in virtue of their capacity) to *take in* the teaching. Not as
though they could have apprehended the inner *doctrinal
contents* of the parables (ver. 11), but they were capable of
apprehending the narrative *form*, the parabolic narrative *in
itself*, in which the teaching was veiled, so that they were thus
qualified only *in this form* (καθώς) to hear the doctrine.
Accordingly, ἀκούειν here is neither: *to understand*, nor
equivalent to βαστάζειν, John xvi. 12 (Bengel, Kuinoel, and
others), but the simple *to hear, to perceive.* — οὐκ ἐλάλει] *at*

---

[1] Comp. Schleiermacher, *L. J.* p. 348 ff.

[2] From the collection of Logia, and in a shape more original than Matthew
and Luke, who *add* the historical form. Mark would least of all have divested
it of this, if he had found it in existence. Comp. (in opposition to Holtzmann)
Weiss in the *Jahrb. f. D. Theol.* 1864, p. 93.

that time. See on Matt. xiii. 34. Baur indeed (see *Markus-evang.* p. 24 f.) will not allow a limitation to the teaching *at that time*, but would draw the conclusion that Mark has per-haps not even regarded the Sermon on the Mount, such as Matthew has it, as being historical, and has given the fore-going parables as a *substitute* for it. But Mark himself certainly has doctrinal utterances of Jesus enough, which are not parabolical.

Vv. 35–41. See on Matt. viii. 18, 23–27. Comp. Luke viii. 22–25. — ἐν ἐκείνῃ τῇ ἡμέρᾳ] ver. 1 f.; a difference in respect of time from Matt. viii. 18. Luke viii. 22 is alto-gether indefinite. — ὡς ἦν ἐν τῷ πλοίῳ] to be taken together ; *as He was in the ship* (comp. ver. 1) without delay for further preparation they take possession of Him.   For examples of this mode of expression, see Kypke and Fritzsche. — καὶ ἄλλα δέ] *but other ships also* (Hartung, *Partikell.* I. p. 182 ; Ellendt, *Lex. Soph.* I. p. 884) were in His train (μετ᾽ αὐτοῦ) during the voyage ; a characteristic descriptive trait in Mark. — Ver. 37. On λαῖλαψ ἀνέμου, comp. Hom. *Il.* xvii. 57 ; Anthol. Anacr. 82. On the accent of λαῖλαψ, see Lipsius, *gramm. Untersuch.* p. 36 f. — ἐπέβαλεν] *intransitive* (comp. on ver. 29, Plat. *Phaedr.* p. 248 A, and frequently) not *transitive*, so that the *storm* would be the subject (Vulgate, Luther, Zeger, Homberg, and several others). The τὰ δὲ κύματα, for this purpose prefixed, indicates itself as the subject. — Ver. 38. *And He Himself was at the stern*, laid down on the *pillow* that was there, *asleep.*   It was a part of the vessel intended for the sailors to sit or lie down, Poll. x. 40 ; more strictly, according to Smith (*Voyage and Shipwreck of St. Paul*, p. 296 ff.), the cushion of the rowers' bench. — Ver. 39. σιώπα, πεφίμωσο] *be silent ! be dumb !* asyndetic, and so much the more forcible (Nägelsbach, *Anm. z. Ilias*, ed. 3, p. 247, 359), Eur. *Hec.* 532. The sea is *personified ;* hence the less are we to con-jecture, with Schleiermacher, *L. J.* p. 230, that Jesus has addressed *the disciples* (ye shall see that it will immediately be still). — ἐκόπασεν ὁ ἄνεμος] Herod. vii. 191. Comp. Mark vi. 51 ; Matt. xiv. 32, from which passage de Wette arbitrarily derives the expression of Mark. — Ver. 40. πῶς]

how is it possible, etc. ? They had already so often been the
witnesses of His divine power,[1] under the protection of which
they needed not to tremble. — Ver. 41. ἐφοβήθησαν] not *the
people* (Grotius and others), which agrees with Matthew but not
with the context, but *the disciples,* who were thrown (psychologically) into *fear* at the quite extraordinary phenomenon,
and were not yet clear as to the divine *causa efficiens* in Jesus
(τίς ἄρα οὗτος, etc.). As to φοβεῖσθαι φόβον μέγαν, comp.
on Matt. ii. 10. On τίς ἄρα, in which the perplexity is not
expressed by the ἄρα, but is implied in the context (in
opposition to Hartung), and ἄρα means : *igitur, rebus ita
comparatis,* see Klotz, *ad Devar.* p. 176. Comp. Nägelsbach,
Anm. z. Ilias, ed. 3, p. 10 f.

REMARK.—The weakness of faith and of discernment on the
part of the disciples (ver. 40 f.) appears in Mark most strongly
of the Synoptics (comp. vi. 52, vii. 18, viii. 17, 18, 33, ix. 6, 19, 32,
34, x. 24, 32, 35, xiv. 40). Ritschl in the *theol. Jahrb.* 1851,
p. 517 ff., has rightly availed himself of this point on behalf of
Mark's originality ; since a later softening—yet without set purpose and naturally unbiassed, and hence not even consistent—
is at any rate more probable than a subsequent aggravation of
this censure. The remarks of Baur in opposition (*theol. Jahrb.*
1853, p. 88 f.) are unimportant, and would amount to this, that
Mark, who is assumed withal to be neutral, would in this point
have even outstripped Luke. Comp. Holtzmann, p. 435 f.

[1] With this agrees neither the half-naturalizing view of Lange, *L. J.* II.
p. 314, that the *immediate* causes of the calm setting in lay in the atmosphere,
and that so far the threatening word of Jesus was *prophetical* (comp.
Schleiermacher) ; nor the complete breaking up of the miracle by Schenkel, who
makes the matter amount simply to this, that Jesus by virtue of His confidence in
God and foresight of His destination exercised a peaceful and soothing sway
among the disciples, although these were possessed of nautical knowledge and He
was not. Keim, p. 123, adds, moreover, a prayer previous to the command of
Jesus, assuming that then *God* acted, and Jesus was only His interpreter. Of all
this, however, there is nothing in the text. See rather ver. 41, which also
testifies against the resolution of the natural miracle suggested by Weizsäcker.

CHAPTER V.

VER. 1. Γαδαρηνῶν] Here also, as in Matt. viii. 28, occur the various readings Γερασηνῶν (B D א* Vulg. Sax. Nyss., so Lachm. and Tisch.) and Γεργεσηνῶν (L Δ א** min. Arr. Copt. Aeth. Arm. Or.). The *Recepta* is to be retained, according to A C E, etc., with Fritzsche and Scholz. See on Matt. — Ver. 2. ἐξελθόντος αὐτοῦ] is here more strongly attested (B C L Δ א, min. Ver. Brix., to which D also with ἐξελθόντων αὐτῶν falls to be added) than in Matt. viii. 28. To be adopted, with Lachm. and Tisch.; ἐξελθόντι αὐτῷ (Elz.) is from the parallel passages. — εὐθέως] which Lachm. has deleted, is only wanting in B, Syr. Arm. Ver. Brix. Vind. Colb. Corb. 2. The omission is explained from the parallels, from which also has arisen the reading ὑπήντησεν (B C D L Δ א, min. Lachm.). — Ver. 3. οὔτε] B C D L Δ א 33 have οὐδέ. So Fritzsche, Lachm. Tisch.; and of necessity rightly. — ἁλύσεσιν] Lachm. and Tisch. have ἁλύσει, following B C L 33, Colb.; the *Recepta* is from what follows. — οὐδείς] Lachm. and Tisch. have οὐκέτι οὐδείς, following B C* D L Δ א, min. Vulg. It. Arm. Looking to the peculiarity of this notice and the accumulation of the negatives, we must recognise this as correct. — Ver. 7. εἶπε] λέγει has preponderating evidence; approved by Griesb., adopted by Fritzsche, Lachm. and Tisch.; εἶπε is from Luke viii. 28. But Mark is fond of the historical present. In ver. 9 also the simple λέγει αὐτῷ (instead of ἀπεκρίθη λέγων in Elz.) is rightly adopted by Griesb. on preponderant evidence. — Ver. 9. Λεγεών] B* C D L Δ א* 69, Syr. Copt. It. Vulg. have Λεγιών, and this Lachm. and Tisch. have adopted. The *Recepta* is from Luke. — Ver. 11. Instead of πρὸς τῷ ὄρει, Elz. has πρὸς τὰ ὄρη, in opposition to decisive evidence. — Ver. 12. After αὐτόν Elz. Matt. have πάντες, which Lachm. brackets and Tisch. deletes. It is wanting in B C D K L M Δ א, min. vss. Afterwards Elz. Matth. Scholz, Lachm. have οἱ δαίμονες, which Griesb. rejected, and Fritzsche and Tisch. have deleted, following B C L Δ א, min. Copt. Aeth. The *Recepta* πάντες οἱ δαίμονες is to be maintained; these words were omitted in accordance with the parallels; but they are quite in keeping with Mark's

graphic manner. — Ver. 13. ἦσαν δέ] is on considerable evidence
to be deleted as supplied (Tisch.). — Ver. 14. Instead of ἀπήγγ.
Elz. has ἀνήγγ. But the former is decisively attested. —
ἐξῆλθον] has come in from Matt. and Luke instead of the genuine
ἦλθον (A B K L M U ℵ** min. vss.), which Griesb. approved,
Lachm. and Tisch. have adopted. — Ver. 15. The omission of
the καί before ἱματ. (Tisch.) proceeded from Luke. — Ver. 18.
ἐμβάντος] A B C D K L M Δ ℵ, min. Vulg. It. have ἐμβαίνοντος.
Approved by Griesb., adopted by Fritzsche, Lachm. and
Tisch. The *Recepta* is from Luke viii. 37. — Ver. 19. Instead
of καί οὐκ, Elz. has ὁ δὲ 'Ιησοῦς οὐκ, against decisive evidence. —
ἀνάγγειλον] Lachm. Tisch. have ἀπάγγειλον, following B C Δ ℵ
50, 258. A mechanical change in conformity to ver. 14.
— Instead of πεποίηκε, Elz. has ἐποίησε, contrary to decisive
evidence. — Ver. 22. ἰδού] before ἔρχ. is wanting in B D L Δ ℵ
102, vss. (also Vulg. It.). Suspected by Griesb., bracketed
by Lachm., deleted by Fritzsche and Tisch. From Luke
viii. 41, contrary to the usage of Mark. — Ver. 23. παρεκάλει]
A C L ℵ, min. have παρακαλεῖ. Recommended by Griesb. and
Scholz, adopted by Fritzsche and Tisch. The imperfect is
from Luke viii. 41; the present is in keeping with Mark's
manner. — The reading ἵνα σωθῇ καὶ ζήσῃ has preponderant
attestation by B C D L Δ ℵ, min. (adopted by Lachm. and Tisch.);
ὅπως (Elz. Fritzsche, Scholz) instead of ἵνα may be suspected of
being an amendment of style, and the more current ζήσεται
flowed easily from Matt. ix. 18. — Ver. 25. τις] is wanting in
A B C L Δ ℵ, min. Vulg. Ver. Vind. Colb. Corb. Condemned
by Griesb., deleted by Fritzsche and Lachm., and justly so;
the weight of evidence is too strong against it, to admit of the
omission of a word so indifferent for the sense being explained
from the parallels. — Ver. 26. Instead of αὐτῆς, Elz. Tisch. have
ἑαυτῆς, against so preponderant evidence that it is manifestly
the result of a gloss, as also is the omission of παρ' (D, min. Syr.
utr. Vulg. It.). — Instead of περί, Tisch. has τὰ περί. So B C*
Δ ℵ. τά, being superfluous, dropped out after the preceding
syllables. — Ver. 33. ἐπ' αὐτῇ] ἐπ' is wanting in B C D L ℵ, min.
Syr. Copt. Verc. Bracketed by Lachm., deleted by Tisch.
That ΑΥΤΗ is not the *nominative* belonging to the following
verb (as it is understood in Cant. Corb. Vind.) was noted in the
form of gloss, sometimes by ἐπ', sometimes by ἐν (F Δ). —
Ver. 36. εὐθέως] deleted by Tisch. following B D L Δ ℵ, min. Syr.
Arr. Perss. Copt. Aeth. Arm. Vulg. It. But regarded as superfluous, nay, as disturbing and incompatible with the following
reading παρακούσας, it became omitted the more easily in accord-

ance with Luke viii. 50. — ἀκούσας] B L Δ ℵ have παρακούσας.
So Tisch. and Ewald also. Rightly; although the attestation of
the vss. is wanting (only one Cod. of the It. has *neglexit*). The
difficulty of the not understood compound occasioned the sub-
stitution for it of the current simple form. — Ver. 38. ἔρχεται]
A B C D F Δ ℵ, min. vss. have ἔρχονται. So Lachm. and Tisch.
The plural might just as well have been introduced from what
precedes, as the singular from what follows and Matt. ix. 23.
But the preponderance of the witnesses is decisive in favour of
the plural. — After θόρυβον Griesb. Scholz, Lachm. Tisch. have,
on preponderant evidence, added καί. Being superfluous, it was
the more easily absorbed by the first syllable of κλαίοντας. —
Ver. 40. ὁ δέ] Lachm. has αὐτὸς δέ, on evidence considerable doubtless, but not decisive. From Luke viii. 54. — After παιδίον Elz.
and Scholz have ἀνακείμενον, which Lachm. has bracketed, Tisch.
has deleted. It is wanting in B D L Δ ℵ, min. vss. An addition by way of gloss, instead of which are also found κείμενον,
κατακείμενον, and other readings.

Vv. 1–20. See on Matt. viii. 28–34. Comp. Luke viii.
26–39. The narrative of the former follows a briefer and
more general tradition; that of the latter attaches itself to
Mark, yet with distinctive traits and not without obliteration of
the original. — Ver. 2. ἐξελθόντος αὐτοῦ . . . ἀπήντησεν αὐτῷ]
The *genitive absolute* brings the point of time more strongly
into prominence than would be done by the dative under the
normal construction. See Dissen, *ad Dem. de Cor.* p. 307,
135 ; Pflugk, *ad Eur. Med.* 910 ; Winer, p. 186 [E. T. 259].
— ἄνθρωπος ἐν πνεύματι ἀκ. See on i. 23. — Ver. 3. οὐδὲ
ἀλύσει οὐκέτι οὐδεὶς κ.τ.λ. (see the critical remarks): *not even
with a chain could thenceforth any one*, etc. So fierce and
strong was he now, that all attempts of that kind, which had
previously been made with success, no longer availed with
him (οὐκέτι). On the accumulation of negatives, see Lobeck,
Paralip. p. 57 f. — Ver. 4. διὰ τὸ αὐτὸν κ.τ.λ.] *because* he often
. . . was chained. See Matthaei, p. 1259. — πέδαι are *fetters*,
but ἀλύσεις need not therefore be exactly *manacles*, as the expositors wish to take it,—a sense at variance with the general
signification of the word in itself, as well as with ver. 3. It
means here also nothing else than *chains; let them be put
upon any part of the body whatever*, he rent them asunder ;

but the *fetters* in particular (which might consist of cords) he *rubbed to pieces* (συντετρῖφθαι, to be accented with a circumflex). — Ver. 5. *He was continually in the tombs and in the mountains, screaming and cutting himself with stones.* — Ver. 6. ἀπὸ μακρόθεν] as in Matt. xxv. 58. — Ver. 7. ὁρκίζω σε τὸν Θεόν] not *inappropriate* in the mouth of the demoniac (de Wette, Strauss), but in keeping with the address υἱὲ τ. Θεοῦ τ. ὑψ., and with the *desperate* condition, in which the πνεῦμα ἀκάθαρτον sees himself to be. On ὁρκίζω as a Greek word (Acts xix. 13; 1 Thess. v. 27), see Lobeck, *ad Phryn.* p. 361. — μή με βασανίσ.] is not—as in Matthew, where πρὸ καιροῦ is associated with it—to be understood of the torment of *Hades,* but of *tormenting generally,* and that by the execution of the ἔξελθε, ver. 8. The possessed man, identifying himself with his demon, dreads the pains, convulsions, etc. of the going forth. Subsequently, at ver. 10, where he has surrendered himself to the inevitable going forth, his prayer is different. Observe, moreover, how here the command of Jesus (ver. 8) has as its result in the sick man an immediate consciousness of the necessity of the going forth, but not the immediate going forth itself. — Ver. 8. ἔλεγε γάρ] *for he said,* of course *before* the suppliant address of the demoniac. A subjoined statement of the reason, without any need for conceiving the imperfect in a pluperfect sense. — Ver. 9. The demoniac power in this sufferer is conceived and represented as an aggregate—combined into unity—of numerous demoniacal individualities, which only separate in the going forth and distribute themselves into the bodies of the swine. The fixed idea of the man concerning this manifold-unity of the demoniac nature that possessed him had also suggested to him the name : *Legion* (the word is also used in Rabbinic Hebrew ליגיון, see Buxtorf, *Lex. Talm.* p. 1123 ; Lightfoot, p. 612),—a name which, known to him from the Roman soldiery, corresponds to the paradoxical state of his disordered imagination, and its explanation added by the sick man himself (ὅτι πολλοί ἐσμεν ; otherwise in Luke), is intended to move Jesus the more to compassion. — Ver. 10. ἔξω τῆς χώρας] According to Mark, the demons desire not to be sent *out of the Gadarene region,* in which hitherto they had pleasure; according to Luke (comp. Matt.: πρὸ καιροῦ), they wish not to be sent *into the nether world*. A difference of tradition; but the one that Luke followed is a remodelling in accordance with the result (in opposition to Baur), and was not included originally also in the account of Mark (in opposition to Ewald, *Jahrb*. VII. p. 65). — Ver. 13. ὡς δισχίλιοι] without ἦσαν δέ (see the critical remarks) is in apposition to ἡ ἀγέλη. Only Mark gives this *number*, and that quite in his way of mentioning particulars. According to Baur, *Markusevang*. p. 43, it is a trait of his " affectation of knowing details;" according to Wilke, an interpolation; according to Bleek, an exaggerating later tradition. — Ver. 15. ἦλθον] the townsmen and the possessors of the farms. Here is meant generally the coming of the people to the place of the occurrence; subsequently, by κ. ἔρχονται πρὸς τ. Ἰησοῦν, is meant the special act of the coming *to Jesus*. — καθήμ.] He who was before so fierce and intractable was sitting peacefully. So transformed was his condition. — ἱματισμένον] which in his unhealed state would not have been the case. This Mark leaves to be *presupposed* (comp. Hilgenfeld, *Markusevang*. p. 41); Luke has expressly *narrated* it, viii. 27. It might be told in either way, without the latter of necessity betraying *subsequent elaboration* on the narrator's part (Wilke), or the former betraying an (*inexact*) *use* of a precursor's work (Fritzsche, de Wette, and others, including Baur), as indeed the assumption that *originally* there stood in Mark, ver. 3, an addition as in Luke viii. 27 (Ewald), is unnecessary. — The verb ἱματίζω is not preserved except in this place and at Luke viii. 35. — τὸν ἐσχηκ. τ. Δεγ.] contrast, " ad emphasin miraculi," Erasmus. — Ver. 16. καὶ περὶ τ. χοίρ.] still belongs to διηγήσ. — Ver. 17. ἤρξαντο] The first impression, ver. 15, had been: καὶ ἐφοβήθησαν, under which they do not as yet interfere with Jesus. But now, after hearing the particulars of the case, ver. 16, *they begin*, etc. According to Fritzsche, it is indicated: " Jesum *statim* se sivisse permoveri." In this the correlation of καὶ ἐφοβήθησαν and καὶ ἤρξαντο is overlooked. — Ver. 18. ἐμβαίνοντος αὐτοῦ] *at the* embarkation. — παρεκάλει κ.τ.λ.] entreaty of grateful love, to remain with his benefactor. Fear of the demons was hardly included as a motive (μὴ χωρὶς αὐτοῦ τοῦτον εὑρόντες πάλιν ἐπιπηδήσωσιν αὐτῷ, Euthymius Zigabenus ; comp. Victor Antiochenus, Theophylact, Grotius), since after the destruction of the swine the man is cured of his fixed idea and is σωφρονῶν. — Ver. 19. οὐκ ἀφῆκεν αὐτόν] *He permitted him not. Wherefore?* appears from what follows. He was to abide in his native place as a witness and proclaimer of the marvellous deliverance, that he had experienced from God through Jesus, and *in this way* to serve the work of Christ. According to Hilgenfeld, Mark by this trait betrays his Jewish-Christianity, which is a sheer figment. — ὁ κύριος] God. — καὶ ἠλέησέ σε] *and how much He had compassion on thee* (when He caused thee to be set free from the demons, aorist). It is still to be construed with ὅσα, but zeugmatically, so that now ὅσα is to be taken *adverbially* (Kühner, II. p. 220). On ὅσος, *quam insignis,* comp. Ellendt, *Lex. Soph.* II. p. 377. — Ver. 20. ἤρξατο] a graphic delineation from the starting-point. — Δεκαπόλει] See on Matt. iv. 25. — ἐποίησεν] aorist, like ἠλέησε. On the other hand, in ver. 19, πεποίηκε, which is conceived of from the point of time of the speaker, at which the fact subsists completed and continuing in its effects. — ὁ Ἰησοῦς] ὁ μὲν Χριστὸς μετριοφρονῶν τῷ πατρὶ τὸ ἔργον ἀνέθηκεν· ὁ δὲ θεραπευθεὶς εὐγνωμονῶν τῷ Χριστῷ τοῦτο ἀνετίθει, Euthymius Zigabenus. — The circumstance, moreover, that Jesus did not here forbid the diffusion of the matter (see on v. 43 ; Matt. viii. 4), but *enjoined* it, may be explained from the locality (Peraea), where He was less known, and where concourse around His person was not to be apprehended as in Galilee.

Vv. 21–24. See on Matt. ix. 1, 18. Comp. Luke viii. 40–42, who also keeps to the order of events. — παρὰ τὴν θάλ.] a point of difference from Matthew, according to whom Jairus makes his appearance at Capernaum at the lodging of Jesus. See on Matt. ix. 18. — Ver. 23. ὅτι] recitative. — τὸ θυγάτριόν μου] Comp. Athen. xiii. p. 581 C; Long. i. 6 ; Plut. *Mor.* p. 179 E; Lucian, *Tox.* 22. This diminutive expression of paternal tenderness is peculiar to Mark. Comp. vii. 25. It does not occur elsewhere in the N. T. — ἐσχάτως ἔχει] a late

MARK. F

Greek phrase. See Wetstein and Kypke, also Lobeck, *ad Phryn.* p. 389. — ἵνα ἐλθὼν κ.τ.λ.] His excitement amidst grief and hope speaks incoherently. We may understand before ἵνα : *this I say*, in order that, etc. This is still simpler and more natural than the taking it *imperatively*, by supplying *volo* or the like (see on xii. 19).

Vv. 25–34. See on Matt. ix. 20–22 ; Luke viii. 43–48. — Ver. 26. Mark depicts with stronger lines than Luke, and far more strongly than Matthew. — τὰ παρ' αὐτοῦ] *what was of her means.* How manifold were the prescriptions of the Jewish *physicians* for women suffering from haemorrhage, and what experiments they were wont to try upon them, may be seen in Lightfoot, p. 614 f. — Ver. 27. ἀκούσασα] subordinated as a prior point to the following ἐλθοῦσα. Comp. on i. 41. — The characteristic addition τοῦ κρασπέδου in Matt. ix. 20, Luke viii. 44, would be well suited to the graphic representation of Mark (according to Ewald, it has only come to be omitted in the existing form of Mark), but may proceed from a later shape of the tradition. — Ver. 28. ἔλεγε γάρ] without ἐν ἑαυτῇ (see the critical remarks) does not mean : *for she thought* (Kuinoel, and many others), which, moreover, אמר used absolutely never does mean, not even in Gen. xxvi. 9, but : *for she said.* She *actually* said it, to others, or for and to herself ; a vivid representation. — Ver. 29. ἡ πηγὴ τ. αἵμ. αὐτ.] like מְקוֹר דָּמִים (Lev. xii. 7, xx. 18), not a euphemistic designation of the *parts themselves* affected by the haemorrhage, but designation of the seat of the issue of blood in them. — τῷ σώματι] διὰ τοῦ σώματος μηκέτι ῥαινομένου τοῖς σταλαγμοῖς, Euthymius Zigabenus. Still this by itself could not as yet give the certainty of the *recovery.* Hence rather : through the feeling of the being strong and well, which suddenly passed through her body. — μάστιγος] as at iii. 10. — Ver. 30. ἐπιγνούς] stronger than the previous ἔγνω. — ἐν ἑαυτῷ] in His own consciousness, therefore immediately, not in virtue of an externally perceptible effect. — τὴν ἐξ αὐτοῦ δύν. ἐξελθ.] *the power gone forth from Him. What* feeling in Jesus was, according to Mark's representation, the medium of His discerning this efflux of power that had occurred, we are not informed. The tradi-

tion, as it has expressed itself in this trait in Mark and Luke
(comp. on Matt. ix. 22), has disturbed this part of the narrative
by the view of an efflux of power independent of the will of
Jesus, but brought about on the part of the woman by her faith
(comp. Strauss, II. p. 89), the recognition of which on the part of
Jesus occurred *at once*, but yet not until *after it had taken
place.* This is, with Weiss and others (in opposition to Holtzmann and Weizsäcker), to be conceded as a trait of *later* origin,
and not to be dealt with by artificial explanations at variance
with the words of the passage (in opposition to Ebrard and
Lange), or to be concealed by evasive expedients (Olshausen,
Krabbe, and many others). It does not, however, affect the
simpler *tenor* of the history, *which we read in Matthew.* Calovius
made use of the passage against the Calvinists, "*vim divinam
carni Christi derogantes.*" — τίς μου ἥψατο τῶν ἱμ.] *who has
touched me on the clothes?* Jesus knew that by means of the
clothes-touching power had gone out of Him, but not, *to whom.*
The disciples, unacquainted with the reason of this question,
are astonished at it, seeing that Jesus is in the midst of
the crowd, ver. 31. In Olshausen, Ebrard, Lange,[1] and older
commentators, there are arbitrary attempts to explain away
that ignorance. — Ver. 32. περιεβλέπετο ἰδεῖν] namely, by any
resulting effect that might make manifest the reception of the
power. The *feminine* τὴν τ. ποιήσασαν is said from the
standpoint of the already known fact. — Ver. 33. πᾶσαν τὴν
ἀλήθειαν] *the whole truth,* so that she kept back nothing and
altered nothing. Comp. Plat. *Apol.* p. 17 B, 20 D ; Soph.
Trach. 91; and see Krüger on *Thuc.* vi. 87. 1. — εἰς εἰρήνην]
לְשָׁלוֹם, 1 Sam. i. 17; 2 Sam. xv. 9; Luke vii. 50, *al.: unto
bliss,* unto future happiness. In ἐν εἰρήνῃ (Judg. xviii. 6 ;
Luke ii. 29 ; Acts xvi. 36 ; Jas. ii. 16) the happy state is conceived of as combined with the ὕπαγε, as simultaneous. — ἴσθι
ὑγιὴς κ.τ.λ.] definitive *confirmation* of the recovery, which
Schenkel indeed refers merely to the woman's "religious excitement of mind" as its cause.

---

[1] According to Lange, for example, the conduct of Jesus only amounts to an
appearance; "He let His eyes move *as if* (?) inquiringly over the crowd"
(περιεβλέπ. ἰδεῖν κ.τ.λ.).

Vv. 35–43. See on Matt. ix. 23–25. Comp. Luke viii. 49–56. The former greatly abridges and compresses more than Luke, who, however, does not come up to the vivid originality of the representation of Mark. — ἀπὸ τοῦ ἀρχισυν.] τουτέστιν ἀπὸ τῆς οἰκείας τοῦ ἀρχισυν., Euthymius Zigabenus. — ἔτι] since now there is no longer room for help. — Ver. 36. According to the reading παρακούσας, this (comp. Matt. xviii. 17) is to be taken as the opposite of ὑπακούειν, namely: *immediately He left this speech unnoticed;* He did not heed it for one moment, but let it remain as it was, and said, etc. In this way is set forth the *decided certainty.*[1] He has heard the announcement (ver. 35), but at once let it pass unattended to. Ewald is incorrect in saying that He *acted* as if he *had failed to hear* it. That He did *not* fail to hear it, and, moreover, did not *act* as if He had, is in fact shown just by the μὴ φοβοῦ κ.τ.λ. which he addresses to Jairus. The Itala in the Cod. Pal. (e. in Tisch.) correctly has *neglexit.* — μὴ φοβοῦ κ.τ.λ.] as though now all were lost, all deliverance cut off. — Ver. 37. According to Mark, Jesus sends back the rest (disciples and others who were following Him) *before* the house; according to Luke viii. 51, in the house. — Ver. 38. θόρυβον καὶ κλαίοντας κ. ἀλαλ.] *an uproar and* (especially) *people weeping and wailing.* The first καί attaches to the general term θόρυβον the special elements that belong to it, as in i. 5, and frequently. ἀλαλάζω not merely used of the cry of conflict and rejoicing, but also, although rarely, of the *cry of anguish and lamentation.* See Plutarch, *Luc.* 28; Eur. *El.* 843. — Ver. 39. εἰσελθών] into the house. A later point of time than at ver. 38. — Ver. 40. ἐκβαλών] irritated, commanding; He *ejected* them. Among the πάντας, those who are named immediately afterwards (παραλαμβ. κ.τ.λ.) are *not* included, and so not the three disciples (in opposition to Baur). — Ver. 41. ταλιθά, κούμι] טְלִיתָא קוּמִי, *puella, surge.* It is a feature of Mark's vivid concrete way of description to give significant words *in Hebrew,* with their interpretation, iii. 18, vii. 12, 34, xiv. 36. On the Aramaean טליתא, see Buxtorf, *Lex. Talm.* p.

---

[1] Which, however, all the more precludes the thought of a mere *apparent* death of the maiden (such as Schleiermacher and Schenkel assume).

875. — τὸ κοράσιον] nominative with the article in the imperative address, Bernhardy, p. 67 ; Kühner, II. 155. — σοὶ λέγω]
a free addition of Mark, " ut sensum vocantis atque imperantis
exprimeret" (Jerome). — ἔγειρε] out of the sleep, ver. 39. —
Ver. 42. ἦν γὰρ ἐτῶν δώδεκα] not as giving a reason for the
word κοράσιον (Euthymius Zigabenus, Fritzsche), but in explanation of the previous remark, that the maiden arose and
walked about ; she was no longer a *little* child.   Bengel
appropriately observes : " rediit ad statum aetati congruentem."
The circumstance that she was just in the *period of development*
(Paulus) is certainly in keeping with the thought of an apparent
death, but is alien to the connection. — Ver. 43. διεστείλατο]
He gave them urgently (πολλά) injunction, command.   See
on Matt. xvi. 20. — αὐτοῖς] those brought in at ver. 40. — ἵνα]
the purpose of the διεστείλ. πολλά.   Comp. Matt. xvi. 20 ;
Mark vii. 36, ix. 9. — γνῷ [1]] τοῦτο : namely, this course of the
matter.   The *prohibition itself*, as only the three disciples and
the child's parents were present (ver. 40), has in it nothing
unsuitable, any more than at i. 44, vii. 36, viii. 26.   When
Jesus heals publicly in presence of the multitude there is not
found even in Mark, except in the cases of the expulsion of
demons, i. 34, iii. 12, any prohibition of the kind (ii. 11 f.,
iii. 5, v. 34, ix. 27, x. 52).   Mark therefore ought not to have
been subjected to the imputation of a tendency to make the
sensation produced by the healings of Jesus " appear altogether
great and important" (Köstlin, p. 317 ; comp. Baur, *Markusevang.* p. 54) by His design of wishing to hinder it ; or of the
endeavour to leave out of view the unsusceptible mass of the
people, and to bestow His attention solely on the susceptible
circle of the disciples (Hilgenfeld, *Evang.* p. 135).   In our
history the quickening to life again in itself could not, of
course, be kept secret (see, on the contrary, Matt. ix. 26), but
probably the more detailed circumstances of the way of its

[1] The subjunctive form γνοῖ (like δοῖ, etc.), which Lachmann and Tischendorf
have (comp. ix. 30 ; Luke xix. 15), has important codices in its favour (A B D L)
and against it (including ℵ), but it is unknown to the N. T. elsewhere, and has
perhaps only crept in by error of the transcribers from the language of common
life.

accomplishment might. Jesus, although He was from the outset certain of being the promised Messiah (in opposition to Schenkel), by such prohibitions did *as much as on His part He could* to oppose the kindling of precipitate Messianic fanaticism and popular commotion. He could not prevent their want of success in individual cases (i. 45, vii. 36); but it is just the frequent occurrence of those prohibitions that gives so sure attestation of their historical character in general. Comp. Ewald, *Jahrb.* I. p. 117 f. It is quite as historical and characteristic, that Jesus never forbade the propagation of His *teachings.* With His *Messiahship* He was afraid of arousing a premature sensation (viii. 30, ix. 9; Matt. xvi. 20, xvii. 9), such as His miraculous healings were calculated in the most direct and hazardous way to excite among the people. — καὶ εἶπε δοθῆναι κ.τ.λ.] not for dietetic reasons, nor yet in order that the revival should not be regarded as only apparent (Theophylact, Euthymius Zigabenus), but in order to prove that the child was delivered, not only from death, but also *from her sickness.*

CHAPTER VI.

VER. 1. Instead of ἦλθεν, we must read with Tisch., following B C L Δ ℵ, ἔρχεται. ἦλἱεν was introduced in accordance with the preceding ἐξῆλθεν. — Ver. 2. After αὐτῷ (instead of which B C L Δ ℵ, as before, read τούτῳ; so Tisch.) Elz. has ὅτι, which Fritzsche defends. But the evidence on the other side so preponderates, that ὅτι must be regarded as an inserted connective addition, instead of which C* D K, min. give ἵνα (and then γίνωνται), while B L Δ ℵ have changed γίνονται into γινόμεναι, which is only another attempt to help the construction, although it is adopted (with αἱ before διά upon too weak evidence) by Tisch. — Ver. 3. ὁ τέκτων] The reading ὁ τοῦ τέκτονος υἱός (and then merely καὶ Μαρίας), although adopted by Fritzsche, is much too weakly attested, and is from Matt. xiii. 35. — Ἰωσῆ] The form Ἰωσῆτος (Lachm. Tisch.) has in its favour B D L Δ, min. vss. Ἰωσήφ (ℵ, 121, Aeth. Vulg. codd. of the It.) is here too weakly attested, and is from Matt. xiii. 55. — Ver. 9. The Recepta, defended by Rinck, Fritzsche, is ἐνδύσασθαι. But ἐνδύσησθε (so Griesb. Scholz, Lachm. Tisch.) has decisive attestation; it was altered on account of the construction. — Ver. 11. ὅσοι ἂν] Tisch. has ὃς ἂν τόπος (and afterwards δέξηται), following B L Δ ℵ, min. Copt. Syr. p. (in the margin). A peculiar and original reading, which became altered partly by the omission of τόπος (C* ? min.), partly by ὅσοι, in accordance with the parallels. — After αὐτοῖς Elz. Matth. Fritzsche, Scholz, have: ἀμὴν λέγω ὑμῖν, ἀνεκτότερον ἔσται Σοδόμοις ἢ Γομόῤῥοις ἐν ἡμέρᾳ κρίσεως, ἢ τῇ πόλει ἐκείνῃ, which is not found in B C D L Δ ℵ, min. vss. An addition in accordance with Matt. x. 15. — Ver. 12. ἐκήρυξαν (Tisch.), instead of the Recepta ἐκήρυσσον, is still more strongly attested than μετανοῶσιν (Lachm. Tisch.). The former is to be adopted from B C D L Δ ℵ; the latter has in its favour B D L, but easily originated as the shorter form from the Recepta μετανοήσωσι. — Ver. 14. ἔλεγεν] Fritzsche, Lachm. have ἔλεγον only, following B D, 6, 271, Cant. Ver. Verc. Mart. Corb. Aug. Beda (D has ἐλέγοσαν). An alteration in accordance with ver. 15; comp. ver. 16. — ἐκ νεκρ. ἠγέρθη]

Lachm. Tisch. have ἐγήγερται ἐκ νεκρ., following B D L Δ ℵ, min.; but A K, min. Theophyl. have ἐκ νεκρ. ἀνέστη. The latter is right; ἀνέστη became supplanted by means of the parallel passages and ver. 16. — Ver. 15. δέ after the first ἄλλοι is wanting in Elz. Fritzsche, but is guaranteed by decisive evidence. Decisive evidence condemns the ἤ read before ὡς in Elz. and Fritzsche. — Ver. 16. οὗτός ἐστιν, αὐτὸς ἠγ.] B D L Δ, min. Vulg. Cant. Colb. Corb. Germ. 1, 2, Mm. Or. have merely οὗτος ἠγ. So Griesb. Fritzsche, Scholz, Tisch. (Lachm. has bracketed ἐστ. αὐτ.). Certainly the *Recepta* might have arisen out of Matt. xiv. 2. But, if merely οὗτος ἠγ. were original, it would not be at all easy to see why it should have been altered and added to. On the other hand, the transcribers might easily pass over from ουΤΟΣ at once to αυΤΟΣ. Therefore the *Recepta* is to be maintained, and to be regarded as made use of by Matthew. — ἐκ νεκρῶν] is, in accordance with Tisch., to be deleted as an addition, since in B L Δ ℵ, vss. it is altogether wanting; in D it stands before ἠγ.; and in C, Or. it is exchanged for ἀπὸ τ. νεκρ. — Ver. 17. The article before φυλακῇ is deleted, in accordance with decisive evidence. — Ver. 19. ἤθελεν] Lachm. has ἐζήτει, although only following C* Cant. Ver. Verc. Vind. Colb. An interpretation. — Ver. 21. ἐποίει] B C D L Δ ℵ, min. have ἐποίησεν. So Lachm. But the reading of Tisch. is to be preferred: ἠπόρει; see the exegetical remarks. — Ver. 22. αὐτῆς] B D L Δ ℵ, min. have αὐτοῦ. A wrong emendation. — καὶ ἀρεσάσ.] B C* L Δ ℵ have ἤρεσεν. So Lachm. and Tisch., the latter then, upon like attestation, having ὁ δὲ βασ. εἶπεν (Lachm., following A, has εἶπε δὲ ὁ βασ.). Rightly; the *Recepta* is a mechanical continuation of the participles, which was then followed by the omission of δέ (Elz. has: εἶπεν ὁ βασ.). — Ver. 24. αἰτήσομαι] αἰτήσωμαι is decisively attested; commended by Griesb., and adopted by Fritzsche, Lachm. and Tisch. — Ver. 30. πάντα καί] This καί has evidence so considerable against it that it is condemned by Griesb. and deleted by Fritzsche, Lachm. and Tisch. But how easily might the quite superfluous and even disturbing word come to be passed over! — Ver. 33. After ὑπάγοντας Elz. has οἱ ὄχλοι, in opposition to decisive evidence; taken from Matt. and Luke. — After ἐπέγνωσαν (for which Lachm., following B* D, reads ἔγνωσαν) Elz. Scholz have αὐτόν, which is not found in B D, min. Arm. Perss. Vulg. It., while A K L M U Δ ℵ, min., vss. have αὐτούς. So Tisch. But αὐτόν and αὐτούς are additions by way of gloss. — ἐκεῖ] Elz. Scholz have: ἐκεῖ, καὶ προῆλθον αὐτοὺς καὶ συνῆλθον πρὸς αὐτόν. Griesb.: καὶ ἦλθον ἐκεῖ. Fritzsche: ἐκεῖ καὶ ἦλθον πρὸς αὐτόν. Lachm. Tisch.: ἐκεῖ καὶ προῆλθον αὐτούς. So, too, Rinck, *Lucubr.*

crit. p. 298. The latter reading (B L א) is to be regarded as the original one, and the variations are to be derived from the fact that προσῆλθον was written instead of προῆλθον. Thus arose the corruption καὶ προσῆλθον αὐτούς (so still L, min.). This corruption was then subjected to very various glosses, namely, καὶ προσῆλθον πρὸς αὐτούς (220, 225, Arr.), καὶ προσῆλθον αὐτοῖς (Δ), καὶ συνῆλθον αὐτοῦ (D, Ver.), καὶ συνέδραμον πρὸς αὐτόν (A), καὶ συνῆλθον πρὸς αὐτόν (Elz.), *al.;* which glosses partly supplanted the original καὶ προῆλθον αὐτούς (D, min. vss.), partly appeared by its side with or without restoration of the genuine προῆλθον. The reading of Griesb. has far too little attestation, and leaves the origin of the variations inexplicable. For the reading of Fritzsche there is no attestation; it is to be put on the footing of a conjecture. — Ver. 34. After εἶδεν Elz. and Scholz have ὁ Ἰησοῦς, which in witnesses deserving of consideration is either wanting or differently placed. An addition. — ἐπ᾽ αὐτοῖς] Lachm. and Tisch. have ἐπ᾽ αὐτούς, following important witnesses; the *Recepta* is from Matt. xiv. 14 (where it is the original reading). — Ver. 36. ἄρτους· τί γὰρ φάγωσιν οὐκ ἔχουσιν] B L Δ, min. Copt. Cant. Verc. Corb. Vind. have merely τί φάγωσιν, which Griesb. approves and Tisch. reads. D has merely τι φαγεῖν, which Fritzsche reads, adding, however, without any evidence: οὐ γὰρ ἔχουσιν. Lachm. has [ἄρτους·] τί [γὰρ] φάγωσιν [οὐκ ἔχουσιν]. The reading of Griesb. is to be preferred; ἄρτους was written in the margin as a gloss, and adopted into the text. Thus arose ἄρτους, τι φάγωσιν (comp. א: βρώματα τι φάγωσιν, Vulg.: "cibos, quos manducent"). This was then filled up from viii. 2, Matt. xv. 32, in the way in which the *Recepta* has it. The reading of D (merely τι φαγεῖν) would be preferable, if it were better attested. — Ver. 37. δῶμεν] Lachm. has δώσομεν, following A B (?) L Δ 65, It. Vulg. Comp. D א, min., which have δώσωμεν. The future is original; not being understood, it was changed into δῶμεν, and mechanically into δώσωμεν (Tisch.). — Ver. 38. καί before ἴδετε is wanting in B D L א, min. vss., and is an addition which Griesb. has condemned, Lachm. has bracketed, and Tisch. has deleted. — Ver. 39. ἀνακλῖναι] Lachm. has ἀνακλιθῆναι, not sufficiently attested from Matt. xiv. 19. — Ver. 40. Instead of ἀνά, Lachm. and Tisch. have κατά both times, in accordance with B D א, Copt. Rightly; ἀνά is from Luke ix. 14. — Ver. 44. Elz. has after ἄρτους: ὡσεί, in opposition to decisive evidence. — Ver. 45. ἀπολύσῃ] Lachm. and Tisch. have ἀπολύει, following B D L Δ א 1. The *Recepta* is from Matt. xiv. 22. — Ver. 48. εἶδεν] B D L Δ א, min. Vulg. It. Copt. have ἰδών. So Lachm. and Tisch., omitting the subsequent καί before περί. Rightly; the

participle was changed into εἶδεν, because the parenthetic nature
of the following ἦν γὰρ . . . αὐτοῖς was not observed. — Ver.
51. καὶ ἐθαύμαζον] is wanting, it is true, in B L Δ א, min. Copt.
Vulg. Vind. Colb. Rd., and is condemned by Griesb., bracketed
by Lachm., cancelled by Tisch.; but after ἐξίσταντο it was, as
the weaker expression, more easily passed over than added. —
Ver. 52. The order αὐτῶν ἡ καρδ. is, with Scholz, Lachm. Tisch.,
to be preferred on far preponderating evidence. — Ver. 54.
After αὐτόν Lachm. has bracketed οἱ ἄνδρες τοῦ τόπου ἐκείνου, which
A G Δ, min. vss. read; from Matt. xiv. 35. — Ver. 55. ἐκεῖ] is
not found in B L Δ א, 102, Copt. Vulg. Vind. Brix. Colb.
Deleted by Lachm. and Tisch. Passed over as superfluous. —
Ver. 56. ἥπτοντο] Lachm. reads ἥψαντο, following B D L Δ א,
min. Matt. xiv. 36.

Vv. 1–6. See on Matt. xiii. 54–58, who follows Mark with
slight abbreviations and unessential changes. As respects the
question of *position*, some advocates of the priority of Matthew
have attributed to Mark an unthinking mechanism (Saunier),
others a very artistic grouping (Hilgenfeld, who holds that
the insusceptibility of the people was here to be represented
as attaining its climax). — The narrative itself is not to be
identified with that of Luke iv. 16 ff. See on Matt. — ἐξῆλθεν
ἐκεῖθεν] from the house of Jairus. Matthew has an entirely
different historical connection, based on a distinct tradition,
in which he may have furnished the more correct τάξις. —
ἤρξατο] for the *first emergence* and its result are meant to be
narrated. — After elimination of ὅτι, the words from πόθεν
to αὐτῷ are to be taken together as an interrogative sentence,
and καὶ δυνάμεις on to γίνονται forms again a separate
question of astonishment. — δυνάμεις τοιαῦται] presupposes
that they have *heard* of the miracles that Jesus had done
(in Capernaum and elsewhere); these they now bring into
association with His teaching. — διὰ τῶν χειρ. αὐτοῦ] that is,
by *laying on of His hands*, by *taking hold of*, touching, and the
like; ver. 5. Comp. Acts v. 12, xix. 11. — Ver. 3. ὁ τέκτων]
According to the custom of the nation and of the Rabbins
(Lightfoot, p. 616; Schoettgen, II. p. 898; Gfrörer in the
Tub. Zeitschr. 1838, p. 166 ff.), Jesus Himself had learned
a handicraft. Comp. Justin. *c. Tryph.* 88, p. 316, where

it is related that He made¹ ploughs and yokes; Origen,
c. *Celsum,* vi. 4. 3, where Celsus ridicules the custom;
Theodoret, *H. E.* iii. 23 ; *Evang. infant.* 38 ; and see generally,
Thilo, *ad Cod. Apocr.* I. p. 368 f. The circumstance that Mark
has not written ὁ τοῦ τέκτονος υἱός, as in Matt. xiii. 55, is
alleged by Hilgenfeld, *Evang.* p. 135 (" Mark tolerates not
the paternity of Joseph even in the mouth of the Naza-
renes "), Baur, *Markusevangel.* p. 138, and Bleek, to point
to the view of the divine procreation of Jesus. As though
Mark would not have had opportunity and skill enough to
bring forward this view otherwise with clearness and definitely !
The expression of Matthew is not even to be explained from
an offence taken at τέκτων (Holtzmann, Weizsäcker), but simply
bears the character of *the* reflection, that along with the
mother the *father* also would have been mentioned. And
certainly it is singular, considering the completeness of the
specification of the members of the families, that Joseph is
not also designated. That he was already dead, is the usual
but not certain assumption (see on John vi. 42). In any
case, however, he has at an early date fallen into the back-
ground in the evangelical tradition, and in fact disappeared :
and the narrative of Mark, in so far as he names only the
mother, is a reflection of this state of things according
to the customary appellation among the people, without any
special design. Hence there is no sufficient reason for sup-
posing that in the primitive-Mark the words ran: ὁ τέκτων,
ὁ υἱὸς Ἰωσήφ (Holtzmann). — Ἰωσῆ] Matthew, by way of
correction, has Ἰωσήφ. See on Matt. xiii. 55. The brother
of James *of Alphaeus* was called *Joses.* See on Matt. xxvii. 56 ;
Mark xv. 40. — Ver. 4. The generic προφήτης is not to be

---

¹ Whether exactly "with an *ideal* meaning," so that they became *symbols*
under His hand, as Lange, *L. J.* II. p. 154, thinks, may be fitly left to the
fancy which is fond of inventing such things. No less fanciful is Lange's
strange idea that the brothers of Jesus (in whom, however, he sees sons of his
brother Alphaeus adopted by Joseph) would hardly have allowed Him to work
much, because they saw in Him the glory of Israel! Comp., on the other hand,
iii. 21; John vii. 5.—We may add that, according to the opinion of Baur,
Mark here, with his ὁ τέκτων, "stands quite on the boundary line between the
canonical and the apocryphal" (*Markusevang.* p. 47).

misapplied (so Schenkel) to make good the opinion that Jesus
had not yet regarded Himself as the *Messiah*. — καὶ ἐν τοῖς
συγγ. κ.τ.λ.[1]] graphic fulness of detail; native town, kinsfolk,
house, proceeding from the wider to the narrower circle; not
a glance back at iii. 20 (Baur, p. 23). — Ver. 5. οὐκ ἠδύνατο]
neither means *noluit* (Verc. Vind. Brix. Germ. 2), nor is ἠδύν.
superfluous; but see on Matt. xiii. 58. Theophylact says
well: οὐχ ὅτι αὐτὸς ἀσθενὴς ἦν, ἀλλ᾽ ὅτι ἐκεῖνοι ἄπιστοι ἦσαν.
— Ver. 6. διὰ τὴν ἀπιστ. αὐτῶν] *on account of* their unbelief.
Διά is never thus used with θαυμάζειν in the N. T. (not
even in John vii. 21) and in the LXX. But the unbelief is
conceived not as the *object*, but as the *cause* of the wondering.
Comp. Ael. *V. H.* xii. 6, xiv. 36: αὐτὸν θαυμάζομεν διὰ τὰ
ἔργα. Jesus Himself had not expected such a degree of
insusceptibility in His native town. Only a few among the
sick themselves (ver. 5) met Him with the necessary condition
of faith. — καὶ περιῆγε κ.τ.λ.] seeking in the country a better
field for His ministry. — κύκλῳ] as iii. 34, belonging to περιῆγε.

Vv. 7–13. Comp. Matt. x. 1–14; Luke ix. 1–6. Mark
here adopts, with abridgment and sifting, from the collection
of Logia what was essentially relevant to his purpose; Luke
follows him, not without obliteration and generalizing of individual traits. — ἤρξατο] He now began that sending forth, to
which they were destined in virtue of their calling; its continuance was their whole future calling, from the standpoint
of which Mark wrote his ἤρξατο. — δύο δύο] *binos, in pairs.*
Ecclus. xxxvi. 25. A Hebraism; Winer, p. 223 [E. T.
312]. The Greek says κατά, ἀνά, εἰς δύο, or even συνδύο
(see Valckenaer, *ad Herod.* p. 311; Heindorf, *ad Plat. Parm.*
p. 239). *Wherefore* in pairs? "Ad plenam testimonii fidem,"
Grotius. Comp. Luke vii. 19, ix. 1. — Ver. 8. αἴρωσιν]
should take up, in order to carry it with them, 1 Macc. iv. 30.
— εἰ μὴ ῥάβδον μόνον] The variation in Matthew and Luke

---

[1] The form συγγινεῦσι, which, though erroneous, had been in use, is here
recommended by Buttmann, *neut. Gr.* p. 22 [E. T. 25]; and it is so adequately
attested by B D** E F G, *al.* (in ℵ* the words κ. ἐ. τ. συγγ. are wanting) that
it is, with Tischendorf, to be adopted. In Luke ii. 44 the attestation is much
weaker. Mark has not further used the word.

betokens the introduction of exaggeration,[1] but not a misunderstanding of the clear words (Weiss). There is an
attempt at a mingling of interpretations at variance with the
words in Ebrard, p. 382 ; Lange, *L. J.* II. 2, p. 712. It
ultimately comes to this, that εἰ μὴ ῥ. μ. is intended to mean :
at most a staff. Even Bleek has recourse to the unfounded
refinement, that the staff in Mark is meant only for *support*,
not as a *weapon of defence.* — Ver. 9. ἀλλ᾽ ὑποδεδεμ. σανδάλ.]
There is no difference from μηδὲ ὑποδήματα, Matt. x. 10, not
even a correction of this expression (Bleek, comp. Holtzmann).
See on Matt. *l.c.* The meaning is, that they should be
satisfied with the simple light foot-covering of *sandals,* in
contrast with the proper *calceus* (ὑπόδημα κοῖλον), which had
upper leather, and the use of which was derived from the
Phoenicians and Babylonians (Leyrer in Herzog's *Encykl.* VII.
p. 729). Comp. Acts xii. 8. The construction is *anacoluthic,*
as though παρήγγειλεν αὐτοῖς πορεύεσθαι had been previously
said. Then the discourse changes again, going over from the
obliqua into the *directa* (ἐνδύσησθε). See Kühner, II. p. 598 f.,
and *ad Xen. Mem.* i. 4. 15, iii. 5. 14, iv. 4. 5. A lively non-
periodic mode of representing the matter ; comp. Buttmann,
neut. Gr. p. 330 [E. T. 384 f.]. — Ver. 10. καὶ ἔλεγ. αὐτ.] a new
portion of the directions given on that occasion. Comp. on
iv. 13. — ἐκεῖ] in this house: but ἐκεῖθεν : from this τόπος (see
the critical remarks). — Ver. 11. εἰς μαρτύριον αὐτοῖς] *which
is to serve them for a testimony,* namely, of that which the
shaking off of the dust expresses, *that they are placed on a
footing of equality with heathens.* Comp. on Matt. x. 14. —
Ver. 12 f. ἵνα] the aim of the ἐκήρυξαν. — ἤλειφον ἐλαίῳ] The
anointing with oil (the mention of which in this place is held
by Baur, on account of Jas. v. 14, to betray a later date) was
very frequently applied medically in the case of external and
internal ailments. See Lightfoot, p. 304, 617 ; Schoettgen,
I. p. 1033 ; Wetstein *in loc.* But the assumption that the
apostles had healed *by the natural virtue of the oil* (Paulus,
Weisse), is at variance with the context, which narrates their

---

[1] Inverting the matter, Baur holds that the "*reasoning*" Mark had *modified*
the expression. Comp. Holtzmann and Hilgenfeld.

miraculous action. Nevertheless it is also wholly unwarranted to regard the application of the oil in this case
merely as a *symbol;* either of the working of miracles for
the purpose of awakening faith (Beza, Fritzsche, comp. Weizsäcker), or of the bodily and spiritual refreshment (Euthymius
Zigabenus), or of the divine compassion (Theophylact, Calvin),
or to find in it merely an *arousing of the attention* (Russwurm
in the *Stud. u. Krit.* 1830, p. 866), or, yet again, a later magi-
cal mingling of the supernatural and the natural (de Wette).
In opposition to the latter view the pertinent remark of
Euthymius Zigabenus holds good : εἰκὸς δὲ, καὶ τοῦτο παρὰ
τοῦ κυρίου διδαχθῆναι τοὺς ἀποστόλους. Comp. Jas. v. 14.
The anointing is rather, as is also the application of spittle
on the part of Jesus Himself (vii. 33, viii. 23 ; John ix. 6),
to be looked upon as a *conductor of the supernatural healing
power,* analogous to the laying on of hands in ver. 5, so that
the faith was the *causa apprehendens,* the miraculous power
the *causa efficiens,* and the oil was the *medians,* therefore
without independent power of healing, and not even necessary,
where the way of *immediate* operation was, probably in accordance with the susceptibility of the persons concerned, adopted
by the Healer, as Jesus also heals the blind man of Jericho
without any application of spittle, x. 46 f. The passage
before us has nothing to do with the *unctio extrema* (in opposition to Maldonatus and many others), although Bisping still
thinks that he discovers here at least a *type* thereof.

Vv. 14–16. See on Matt. xiv. 1, 2. Comp. Luke ix. 7–9.
Mark bears the impress of the original in his circumstantiality and want of polish in form. — ὁ βασιλεύς] in the
wider sense ἀδιαφόρως χρώμενος τῷ ὀνόματι (Theophylact) :
the prince (comp. the ἄρχων βασιλεύς of the Athenians, and
the like), a more popular but less accurate term than in
Matthew and Luke : ὁ τετράρχης. Comp. Matt. ii. 22. —
φανερὸν γὰρ ἐγέν. τ. ὄν. αὐτοῦ] is not to be put in a parenthesis, since it does not interrupt the construction, but assigns
the reason for the ἤκουσεν, after which the narrative proceeds
with καὶ ἔλεγεν.—As *object* to ἤκουσεν (generalized in Matthew
and Luke) we cannot, without arbitrariness, think of aught

but the contents of vv. 12, 13. Comp. ἀκούσας, ver. 16.
Antipas heard that the disciples of Jesus preached and did
such miracles. Then comes the explanation assigning the
reason for this : *for His name became known, i.e.* for it did not
remain a secret, that these itinerant teachers and miracle-
workers were working as empowered *by Jesus.* Comp. also
Holtzmann, p. 83. According to Grotius, Griesbach, and
Paulus (also Rettig in the *Stud. u. Krit.* 1838, p. 797), the
object of ἤκουσεν is : τὸ ὄνομα αὐτοῦ, so that φαν. γ. ἐγέν.
would be parenthetic. This is at variance with the simple
style of the evangelist. According to de Wette, Mark has
been led by the alleged parenthesis φανερὸν ... αὐτοῦ to forget
the object, so that merely something indefinite, perhaps ταῦτα,
would have to be supplied. But what carelessness ! and still
the question remains, to what the ταῦτα applies. Ewald
(comp. Bengel) takes φανερὸν ... προφητῶν as a parenthesis,
which was intended to explain *what* Herod heard, and holds
that in ver. 16 the ἤκουσεν of ver. 14 is again taken up (that
instead of ἔλεγεν in ver. 14 ἔλεγον is to be read, which
Hilgenfeld also prefers ; see the critical remarks). But the
explanation thus resorted to is not in keeping with the simple
style of the evangelist elsewhere (in the case of Paul it would
create no difficulty). — ὁ βαπτίζων] substantival (see on
Matt. ii. 20). Observe with what delicacy the set evangelic expression ὁ βαπτιστής is not put into the mouth of
Antipas ; he speaks from a more extraneous standpoint.
Moreover, it is clear from our passage that *before* the death
of John he can have had no knowledge of Jesus and His
working. — διὰ τοῦτο] πρότερον γὰρ ὁ Ἰωάννης οὐδὲν σημεῖον
ἐποίησεν· ἀπὸ δὲ τῆς ἀναστάσεως ἐνόμισεν ὁ Ἡρώδης προσ-
λαβεῖν αὐτὸν τῶν σημείων τὴν ἐργασίαν, Theophylact. — αἱ
δυνάμεις] *the powers* κατ᾽ ἐξοχήν, *i.e.* the *miraculous* powers,
the effluence *of which* he saw now also in the working of the
disciples. — Ver. 15. The difference between these assertions
is that *some* gave Him out to be *the Elias,* and so to be *the*
prophet who was of an altogether special and distinguished
character and destination ; but others said : *He is a prophet
like one of the prophets, i.e.* (comp. Judg. xvi. 7, 11), a *usual,*

ordinary prophet, one out of the category of prophets in general, not quite the exceptional and exalted prophet Elias. Comp. Ewald, p. 258 f. The interpolation of ἤ before ὡς could only be occasioned by the expression not being understood.[1] — Ver. 16. ἀκούσας] namely, these different judgments. Mark now relates the *more special* occasion of the utterance of Herod. — ὃν . . . Ἰωάννην] a familiar form of attraction. See Winer, p. 148 [E. T. 205]. — ἐγώ] has the stress of an evil conscience. *Mockery* (Weizsäcker) is, in accordance with ver. 14 f., not to be thought of. — οὗτος] anaphorically with emphasis (Kühner, *ad Xen. Mem.* ii. 1. 19): *this* is he. — αὐτός] the emphatic *He, precisely he,* for designation of the identity. Observe the urgent expression of certainty, which the terror-stricken man gives to his conception : *This one* it is: *He* is risen !

Vv. 17–29. See on Matt. xiv. 3–12. Mark narrates more circumstantially[2] and with more peculiar originality; see especially ver. 20, the contents of which, indeed, are held by Baur to rest on a deduction from Matt. xiv. 9. — αὐτός] is a commentary upon the ἐγώ of ver. 16. Herod *himself,* namely, etc. — ἐν φυλακῇ] *in a prison,* without the article. At ver. 28, on the other hand, *with* the article. Comp. 1 Macc. ix. 53; Thuc. iii. 34; Plut. *Mor.* p. 162 B; Plat. *Leg.* ix. 864 E: ἐν δημοσίῳ δεσμῷ δεθείς. — Vv. 19, 20. The θέλειν αὐτὸν ἀποκτεῖναι is here, in variation from Matthew, denied in the case of Herod. It is not merely an *apparent* variation (Ebrard, p. 384; Lange), but a real one, wherein Mark's narrative betrays a later shape of the tradition (in opposition to Schneckenburger, *erst. kan. Ev.* p. 86 f.); while with Matthew Josephus also, *Antt.* xviii. 5. 2, attributes to Herod the intention of putting to death. Comp. Strauss, I. p. 396 f. As to ἐνεῖχεν (*she gave close heed to him*), see on Luke xi. 53. —

[1] The *Recepta* ὅτι προφ. ἐστίν, ἢ ὡς εἷς τῶν προφ. would have to be explained : *he is a prophet, or* (at least) *like to one of the prophets.*

[2] Mentioning even the name of *Philip.* Josephus, *Antt.* xviii. 5. 4, names him by the *family* name *Herodes,* which does not necessitate the supposition of a confusion as to the name on the part of Mark (Ewald, *Gesch. Chr.* p. 51). Only we may not understand Philip the *tetrarch,* but a half-brother of his, bearing a similar name. See on Matt. xiv. 3.

ἐφοβεῖτο] *he feared* him; he was afraid that this holy man, if
he suffered him to be put to death, would bring misfortune
upon him.   From this fear arose also the utterance contained
in vv. 14, 16 : " Herodem non timuit Johannes," Bengel. —
συνετήρει] not: *magni eum faciebat* (Erasmus, Grotius, Fritzsche,
de Wette), which the word does not mean, but *he guarded him*
(Matt. ix. 17 ; Luke v. 38 ; Tob. iii. 15 ; 2 Macc. xii. 42 ;
Polyb. iv. 60. 10 ; Herodian, ii. 1. 11), *i.e.* he did not abandon
him, but took care that no harm happened to him : "*custodiebat
eum*," Vulg. Comp. Jansen, Hammond, Bengel, who pertinently
adds by way of explanation : " contra Herodiadem ; " and also
Bleek. According to Ewald, it is: "*he gave heed to him*." Comp.
Ecclus. iv. 20, xxvii. 12. But this thought is contained already in
what precedes and in what follows. The compound strengthens
the idea of the simple verb, designating its action as entire
and undivided.—ἀκούσας] when he had heard him. Observe
afterwards the emphasis of ἡδέως (and *gladly* he heard him). —
πολλὰ ἐποίει] namely, which he had heard from John. Very
characteristic is the reading : π. ἠπόρει, which has the strongest
internal probability of being genuine, although only attested
by B L א, Copt.[1]—We may add that all the imperfects apply
to the *time of the imprisonment*, and are not to be taken as
pluperfects (Grotius, Bolten). The ἤκουε took place when
Herod was actually present (as was now the case ; see on
Matt. xiv. 10 f.) in Machaerus ; it is possible also that he had
him sent for now and then to his seat at Tiberias. But in
any case the expressions of Mark point to a longer period of
imprisonment than Wieseler, p. 297, assumes. — Ver. 21. ἡμέρας
εὐκαίρου] εὔκαιρος, in reference to time, means nothing else
than *at the right time*, hence : *a rightly-timed, fitting, appropriate day* (Beza, Grotius, Jansen, Fritzsche, de Wette, Ewald,
Bleek, and many others). Comp. Heb. iv. 16 ; Ps. civ. 27 ;
2 Macc. xiv. 29 ; Soph. *O. C.* 32 ; Herodian, i. 4. 7, i. 9. 15,
v. 8. 16 ; and see Plat. *Def.* p. 413 C. Mark makes use of

---

[1] Comp. Buttmann in the *Stud. u. Krit.* 1860, p. 349. It is to be explained:
he was perplexed about many things ; what he heard from John was so heart-
searching and so closely touched him. On ἀπορεῖν τι as equivalent to περί τινος,
see Krüger on *Thuc.* v. 40. 3 ; Heindorf, *ad Plat. Crat.* p. 409 D.

this predicate, having before his mind *the purpose of Herodias,*
ver. 19, which hitherto had not been able to find any
fitting point of time for its execution on account of the
tetrarch's relation to John.[1] Grotius well says : " opportuna
insidiatrici, quae vino, amore et adulatorum conspiratione
facile sperabat impelli posse nutantem mariti animum." Others
(Hammond, Wolf, Paulus, Kuinoel) have explained it contrary
to linguistic usage as : *dies festivus* (יום טוב). At the most,
according to a later use of εὐκαιρεῖν (Phrynich. p. 125; comp.
below, ver. 31), ἡμέρα εὔκαιρος might mean : *a day, on which one
has convenient time, i.e.* a *leisure* day (comp. εὐκαίρως ἔχειν,
to be at leisure, Polyb. v. 26. 10, *al.,* εὐκαιρία, leisure), which,
however, in the connection would be inappropriate, and very
different from the idea of a *dies festivus.* — On μεγιστᾶνες,
magnates, a word in current use from the Macedonian period,
see Kypke, I. p. 167; Sturz, *Dial. Mac.* p. 182; Lobeck, *ad
Phryn.* p. 197. — καὶ τοῖς πρώτοις τῆς Γαλ.] The first two
were the chief men of the civil and military service *of the
tetrarch.* Moreover, the principal men *of Galilee,* people who
were not in his service ("status provinciales," Bengel), were
called in. — Ver. 22. αὐτῆς τῆς Ἡρωδ.] *of Herodias herself.*
The king was to be captivated with all the greater certainty
by Herodias' *own daughter;* another dancer would not have
made the same impression upon him. — Ver. 23. ἕως ἡμίσους
κ.τ.λ.] in accordance with Esth. v. 3. See in general, Köster,
Erläut. p. 194. It is thus that the unprincipled man, carried
away by feeling, promises. The *contracted* form of the genitive belongs to the later manner of writing. Lobeck, *ad Phryn.*
p. 347. The article was not requisite. Heindorf, *ad Phaed.*
p. 176. — Ver. 25. Observe the *pertness* of the wanton damsel.
As to θέλω ἵνα (x. 35 : *I will that thou shouldst,* etc.), see on
Luke vi. 31. — Ver. 26. περίλυπος] on account of what was
observed at ver. 20. — διὰ τοὺς ὅρκους κ. τ. συνανακ.] emphatically put first, as the determining motive. — αὐτὴν ἀθετῆσαι]
eam repudiare. Examples of ἀθετεῖν, referred to persons (comp.

---

[1] The *appropriateness* of the day is then stated in detail by ὅτε Ἡρώδης κ.τ.λ.
Hence I do not deem it fitting to write, with Lachmann (comp. his *Prolegom.*
p. xliii.), ὅ, τι.

Heliod. vii. 26 : εἰς ὅρκους ἀθετοῦμαι), may be seen in Kypke,
I. p. 167 f. The use of the word in general belongs to the
later Greek. Frequent in Polybius. — Ver. 27. σπεκουλάτωρα]
a *watcher*, *i.e.* one of his *body-guard*. On them also devolved
the execution of capital punishment (Seneca, *de ira*, i. 16,
benef. iii. 25, *al.* ; Wetstein *in loc.*). The Latin word (not
spiculator, from their being armed with the *spiculum*, as Beza
and many others hold) is also adopted into the Hebrew ספקלטור.
See Lightfoot and Schoettgen, also Buxtorf, *Lex. Talm.* p.
1533. The spelling σπεκουλάτορα (Lachm. Tisch.) has decisive
attestation.

Vv. 30-44. See on Matt. xiv. 13–21. Comp. Luke ix.
10–17. The latter, but not Matthew, follows Mark also in
connecting it with what goes before; Matthew in dealing
with it abridges very much, still more than Luke. On the
connection of the narrative in Matthew, which altogether
deviates from Mark, see on Matt. xiv. 13. Mark has filled
up the gap, which presented itself in the continuity of the
history by the absence of the disciples who were sent forth,
with the episode of the death of John, and now makes the
disciples return, for whom, after the performance and report
of their work, Jesus has contemplated some rest in privacy,
but is hampered as to this by the thronging crowd. — ἀπόσ-
τολοι] only used here in Mark, but "apta huic loco appellatio," Bengel. — συνάγονται] returning from their mission,
ver. 7. — πάντα] *What?* is told by the following καί . . .
καί : as well . . . as also. — Ver. 31. ὑμεῖς αὐτοί] *vos ipsi*
(Stallb. *ad Plat. Phaed.* p. 63 C ; Kühner, § 630, A 3), *ye*
for yourselves, ye for your own persons, without the attendance
of the people. Comp. on Rom. vii. 25. See the following
ἦσαν γὰρ κ.τ.λ. — καὶ οὐδὲ φαγεῖν] Comp. ii. 2, iii. 20. — Ver.
33. *And many saw them depart and perceived it*, namely, what
was the object in this ὑπάγειν, whither the ὑπάγοντες wished
to go (vv. 31, 32), so that thereby the intention of remaining
alone was thwarted. πολλοί is the subject of both verbs. —
πεζῇ] emphatically *prefixed*. They came partly round the
lake, partly from its sides, *by land*. — ἐκεῖ] namely, to the
ἔρημος τόπος, whither Jesus with the disciples directed His

course. — προῆλθον αὐτούς] *they anticipated them.* Comp.
Luke xxii. 47. Not so used among the Greeks, with whom,
nevertheless, φθάνειν τινά (Valck. *ad Eur. Phoen.* 982), and
even προθεῖν τινά (Ael. *N. A.* vii. 26; Oppian. *Hal.* iv. 431)
is analogously used. — Ver. 34. ἐξελθών] not as in Matt.
xiv. 14, but *from the ship,* as is required by the previous
προῆλθον αὐτούς. In ver. 32 there was not as yet reported
the *arrival* at the retired place, but the *direction of the course*
thither. — ἤρξατο] His sympathy outweighed the intention,
under which He had repaired with the disciples to this place,
and He *began* to teach. — Ver. 35 ff. καὶ ἤδη ὥρας πολλ. γενομ.]
and when much of the day-time had already passed (comp. subsequently: καὶ ἤδη ὥρα πολλή), that is, when the day-time
was already far advanced, τῆς ὥρας ἐγένετο ὀψέ, Dem. 541
pen. Πολύς, according to very frequent usage, applied to *time.*
Comp. Dion. Hal. ii. 54: ἐμάχοντο . . . ἄχρι πολλῆς ὥρας;
Polyb. v. 8. 3; Joseph. *Antt.* viii. 4. 3. — λέγουσιν] more
exactly in John vi. 7. — δηναρ. διακοσ.] Comp. John vi. 7,
by whom this trait of the history, passed over by Matthew and
Luke, not a mere addition of Mark (Bleek, Hilgenfeld), is confirmed. That the *contents of the treasure-chest* consisted exactly
of two hundred denarii (Grotius and others) is not clear from
the text. The disciples, on an approximate hasty estimate,
certainly much too small (amounting to about £7, 13s., and
consequently not quite one-third of a penny per man), specify
a sum *as that which would be required.* It is otherwise at
John vi. 7. Moreover, the answer of the disciples bears the
stamp of a certain irritated *surprise* at the suggestion δότε
αὐτοῖς κ.τ.λ.,—a giving, however, which was afterwards to be
realized, ver. 41.—With the reading δώσομεν, ver. 37 (see
the critical remarks), the note of interrogation is to be placed,
with Lachmann, after ἄρτους, so that καί is then the *con-
secutive; and so shall we,* etc. The reading ἀπελθόντες on to
φαγεῖν together *without interrogation* (Ewald, Tischendorf),
is less in keeping with the whole very vivid colouring, which
in vv. 37–40 exhibits a very circumstantial graphic representation, but not a paraphrase (Weiss). — Ver. 39 f. συμπόσια
συμπόσια] *Accusatives: after the fashion of a meal,* so that the

whole were distributed into companies for the meal. The *distri-butive* designation, as also πρασιαὶ πρασιαί (*areolatim*, so that they were arranged like beds in the garden), is a Hebraism, as at ver. 7. The individual divisions consisted *partly of a hundred, partly of fifty* (not 150, Heupel, Wetstein). — χλωρῷ] Mark depicts; it was *spring* (John vi. 4). — εὐλό-γησε] refers to the prayer at a meal. It is otherwise in Luke. See on Matt. xiv. 19. — Ver. 41. καὶ τ. δύο ἰχθ.] *also the two fishes.* — ἐμέρισε πᾶσι] namely, *by means of the apostles,* as with the loaves. — Ver. 43. *And they took up of fragments twelve full baskets,* in which, however, κλασμάτων is emphati-cally *prefixed.* Yet probably Mark wrote κλάσματα δώδεκα κοφίνων πληρώματα (so Tischendorf), which, indeed, is only attested fully by B, and incompletely by L, Δ, min. (which read κοφίνους), as well as by ﬡ, which has κλασμάτων δώδ. κοφίνων πληρώματα, but was very easily subjected to gloss and alteration from the five parallel passages. This reading is to be explained: *and they took up as fragments fillings of twelve baskets, i.e.* they took up in fragments twelve baskets full. — καὶ ἀπὸ τ. ἰχθ.] *also of the fishes,* that it might not be thought that the κλάσματα had been merely fragments *of bread.* Fritzsche without probability goes beyond the twelve baskets, and imports the idea : " and further in addition some remnants of the fishes," so that τί is supplied (so also Grotius and Bleek). — Why ver. 44 should have been copied, not from Mark, but from Matt. xiv. 21 (Holtzmann), it is not easy to see. — τοὺς ἄρτους] These had been the principal food (comp. ver. 52) ; to their number corresponded also that of those who were satisfied.

Vv. 45–56. Comp. on Matt. xiv. 22–36. The latter abridges indeed, but adds, probably from a tradition [1] not known to Mark, the intervening scene xiv. 28–31. The con-clusion has remained peculiar to Mark. — ἠνάγκασε κ.τ.λ.]

---

[1] According to Hilgenfeld, Mark purposely suppressed the incident under the influence of a Petrine tendency, because Peter had shown weakness of faith. In this case he would have been inconsistent enough in narratives such as at viii. 33. Weizsäcker rightly recognises in Matt. *l.c.* the later representation, which, however, is merely a further embellishment not belonging to history.

remaining behind *alone,* He could the more easily withdraw
Himself unobserved from the people. — τὸ πλοῖον] *the ship,*
in which they had come. — Βηθσαϊδάν] The place on the
western coast of the lake, in *Galilee,* is meant, Matt. xi. 21. See
ver. 53, viii. 22 ; John vi. 17. In opposition to Wieseler and
Lange, who understand the *eastern* Bethsaida, see on Matt.
xiv. 22, Remark. As to the relation of this statement to Luke
ix. 10, see *in loc.* — ἀπολύει (see the critical remarks) is to be
explained from the peculiarity of the Greek in introducing in
the direct mode of expression in oblique discourse, by which
means the representation gains in liveliness. See Kühner, II.
p. 594 f., and *ad Xen. Anab.* i. 3. 14 ; Bernhardy, p. 389. —
ἀποταξάμ. αὐτοῖς] *after He had taken leave of them* (of the
people), an expression of later Greek. See Lobeck, *ad Phryn.*
p. 24 ; Wetstein *in loc.* — Ver. 48. A point is to be placed,
with Lachmann and Tischendorf, after θαλάσσης, and then a
colon after αὐτούς ; but ἦν γὰρ ὁ ἄνεμ. ἐναντ. αὐτ. is a parenthesis. *When He had seen them in distress* (ἰδών, see the
critical remarks), this induced Him about the fourth watch of
the night to come to them walking on the sea (not upon its
shore). His purpose therein was to help them (ver. 51) ; but
the initiative in this matter was to come from the side of the
disciples ; therefore He wished to pass by before the ship, in
order to be observed by them (ver. 49). — περὶ τετάρτ. φυλακ.]
The difficulties suggested by the lateness of the time at which
they were still sailing, after having already ὀψίας γενομένης
reached the middle of the lake (Strauss, B. Bauer), are quite
explained by the violence of the contrary wind. Comp.
Ebrard, p. 392 ; Robinson, *Pal.* III. p. 527, 572. — παρελ-
θεῖν αὐτούς] The Vulgate rightly has : *praeterire eos* (Hom. *Il.*
viii. 239 ; Plat. *Alc.* i. 123 B), not : " to come over (the lake)
to them," Ewald (yet comp. his *Gesch. Chr.* p. 365). This is
at variance with the New Testament usage, although poets (as
Eur. *Med.* 1137, 1275) join παρέρχεσθαι, to come to any one,
with the accusative ; moreover, after ἔρχεται πρὸς αὐτούς the
remark would be superfluous. It might mean : He wished
to *overtake* them (*antevertere,* see Hom. *Od.* viii. 230 ; Sturz,
Lex. Xen. III. p. 453 ; Ameis and Nägelsbach on Hom. *Il.* i.

132), but the primary and most usual meaning is quite appropriate. — Ver. 51. ἐκ περισσοῦ] is further strengthened by λίαν: *very much above all measure.* Comp. λίαν ἄγαν (Meineke, *Menand.* p. 152), and similar expressions (Lobeck, *Paralip.* p. 62), also λίαν βέλτιστα, Plat. *Eryx.* p. 393 E. — ἐν ἑαυτοῖς] *in their own hearts,* without giving vent to their feelings in utterances, as at iv. 14. — ἐθαύμαζον] The imperfect denotes (comp. Acts ii. 7) the continuance of the feeling after the first amazement. — Ver. 52. γάρ] *for they attained not to understanding in the matter of the loaves* (on occasion of that marvellous feeding with bread, ver. 41 ff.); otherwise they would, by virtue of the insight acquired on occasion of that work of Christ, have known how to judge correctly of the present new miracle, in which the same divine power had operated through Him,[1] and they would not have fallen into such boundless surprise and astonishment. Bengel says correctly: "Debuerant a pane ad mare concludere." De Wette unjustly describes it as "an observation belonging to the craving for miracles;" and Hilgenfeld arbitrarily, as "a foil" to glorify the confession of Peter. — ἦν γὰρ κ.τ.λ.] informs us of the internal *reason* of their not attaining insight in the matter of the loaves; their heart, *i.e.* the seat of their internal vital activity (Beck, *Seelenlehre,* p. 67; Delitzsch, *Psych.* p. 248 ff.), was withal in a state of hardening, wherein they were as to mind and disposition obtuse and inaccessible to the higher knowledge and its practically determining influence. Comp. viii. 7. — Ver. 53. διαπεράσ.] points back to ver. 45. — ἐπὶ τ. γῆν Γεννησ.] not: *into* the country, but *unto* the country of Gennesareth; for the landing (προσωρμίσθ.) and disembarking *does not follow till afterwards.* — Ver. 55. περιδραμόντες] in order to fetch the sick. — ἤρξατο] belongs to the description of the quick result. *Immediately* they knew Him, they ran round about and began, etc. — περιφέρειν] is not inappro-

---

[1] Mark therefore regarded the walking on the sea quite differently from Lange, *L. J.* II. p. 287 f., for this latter finds the pith of the miracle in the complete divine *equanimity* of the mind of Jesus, and in respect of that even says: "the dog falls into the water and swims, but the man falls into it and is drowned," namely, by his alarm, instead of poising himself amidst the waves in the triumphant equanimity of his mind. This is an extravagance of naturalizing.

priate (Fritzsche), which would only be the case, if it were
necessary to suppose that the *individual* sick man had been
carried *about*. But it is to be understood *summarily* of the
sick; these were *carried about*—one hither, another thither,
wherever Jesus was at the time (comp. ver. 56).— Hence
ὅπου ἤκουον, ὅτι ἐκεῖ ἐστι cannot mean: *from all the places,
at which* (ὅπου) *they heard that He was there* (in the region
of Gennesareth), but *both* ὅπου and ἐκεῖ, although we may not
blend them after the analogy of the Hebrew אֲשֶׁר־שָׁם into the
simple *ubi* (Beza, Grotius, Wetstein, and many others), must
denote the (changing, see ver. 56) abode of Jesus. They
brought the sick round about *to the places, at which they were
told that He was to be found there*. We may conceive that
the people before going forth with their sick first make inquiry
in the surrounding places, whether Jesus is there. Wherever
on this inquiry they hear that He is present, thither they bring
the sick. — Ver. 56. εἰς κώμ. ἢ πόλεις] therefore not merely
limiting Himself to the small district of Gennesareth, where
He had landed. The following ἐν ταῖς ἀγοραῖς, however, is not
in keeping with ἀγρός (country-places). A want of precision,
which has suggested the reading ἐν ταῖς πλατείαις in D, Vulg.
It. The expression is zeugmatic. — κἂν τοῦ κρασπ. κ.τ.λ.]
comp. v. 28. As to the mode of expression, see Acts v. 15;
2 Cor. xi. 16. — ὅσοι ἂν ἥπτοντο] *all whosoever*, in the several
cases. Comp. above: ὅπου ἂν εἰσεπορεύετο. See Hermann, *de
part. ἄν*, p. 26 ff.; Klotz, *ad Devar*. p. 145; Buttmann, *neut.
Gr*. p. 186 f. [E. T. 216]. — ἐσώζοντο] analogously to the case
of the woman with an issue of blood, v. 29, 30, yet not independent of the knowledge and will of Jesus. And αὐτοῦ
refers to *Jesus*, no matter *where* they touched Him.

CHAPTER VII.

VER. 2. ἄρτους] Lachm. and Tisch. read τοὺς ἄρτους, following
B D L Δ, min. Rightly; the article was passed over, because
it was regarded as superfluous. The reading ἄρτον (Fritzsche)
has in its favour only ℵ, min. and vss., and is from Matt. xv. 2. —
After ἄρτους Elz. and Fritzsche have ἐμέμψαντο, which, however,
is absent from witnesses so important, that it must be regarded
as an addition; instead of it D has κατέγνωσαν. — Ver. 5. ἔπειτα]
B D L ℵ, min. Syr. Copt. Vulg. It. have καί (Δ has ἔπειτα καί).
Recommended by Griesb., and adopted by Fritzsche, Lachm.
and Tisch. Rightly; ἔπειτα was written on the margin on
account of the construction, and then displaced the καί. —
κοιναῖς] Elz. Scholz have ἀνίπτοις, in opposition to B D ℵ, min.
vss. An interpretation. — Ver. 8. γάρ] is wanting in B D L Δ ℵ,
min. Copt. Arm. It. Goth. Lachm. Tisch. A connecting addition. — βαπτισμοὺς . . . ποιεῖτε is wanting in B L Δ ℵ, min. Copt.
Arm. There are many variations in detail. Bracketed by
Lachm. ed. min., deleted by Fritzsche, and now also by Tisch.
Rightly restored again by Lachm. ed. maj. For, if it were an
interpolation from vv. 4 and 13, there would be inserted, as at
ver. 4, ποτηρίων καὶ ξεστῶν, and, as in ver. 13, not ἄλλα; moreover,
an interpolator would certainly not have forgotten the washing
of hands. The explanatory comment of Mark, vv. 3, 4, tells
precisely in favour of the genuineness, for the joint-mention of
the ποτηρίων κ. ξεστῶν in that place has its reason in these words
of Jesus, ver. 8. And why should there have been an interpolation, since the reproach of the Pharisees did not at all con-
cern the pitchers and cups? This apparent inappropriateness
of the words, however, as well as in general their descriptive
character, strikingly contrasting with the conciseness of the
context, might have occasioned their omission, which was
furthered and rendered more widespread by the circumstance
that a church-lesson concluded with ἀνθρώπων. — Ver. 12. καί]
deleted by Lachm. and Tisch., following B D ℵ, min. Copt. Cant.
Ver. Verc. Corb. Vind. Colb. Omitted as confusing, because the
apodosis was found here. — Ver. 14. πάντα] B D L Δ ℵ, Syr.

p. (in the margin) Copt. Aeth. Sax. Vulg. It. have πάλιν. Recommended by Griesb., adopted by Fritzsche, Lachm. Tisch.
Rightly; πάντα was written in the margin on account of the following πάντες, and the more easily supplanted the πάλιν, because
the latter finds no definite reference in what has preceded. —
Instead of ἀκούετε and συνίετε, Lachm. and Tisch. have ἀκούσατε
and σύνετε, following B D H L Δ. The *Recepta* is from Matt.
xv. 10. — Ver. 15. The reading τὰ ἐκ τοῦ ἀνθρώπου ἐκπορευόμενα
(Lachm. Tisch.) has in its favour B D L Δ ℵ, 33, Copt. Goth.
Aeth. Pers. p. Vulg. It. The *Recepta* τὰ ἐκπορ. ἀπ’ αὐτοῦ appears
to have originated from the copyist, in the case of the above
reading, passing over from the first ἐκ to the second (ἐκπορ.).
Thus came the reading τὰ ἐκπορευόμενα, which is still found in
min. Then, after the analogy of the preceding εἰς αὐτόν, in some
cases ἀπ’ αὐτοῦ, in others ἐξ αὐτοῦ (min. Fritzsche) was supplied.
— Ver. 16 is wanting in B L ℵ, min. Copt. Suspected by Mill
and Fritzsche as an interpolation at the conclusion of the church-
lesson; deleted by Tisch. But the witnesses on behalf of the
omission, in the absence of internal reasons which might occasion an interpolation (in accordance with iv. 23; comp., on the
other hand, Matt. xv. 11), are too weak. — Ver. 17. περὶ τῆς
παραβ.] B D L Δ ℵ, min. It. Vulg. have τὴν παραβολήν. Approved
by Griesb., adopted by Fritzsche, Lachm. Tisch. The *Recepta*
is a gloss. — Ver. 19. καθαρίζον] A B E F G H L S X Δ ℵ, min.
Or. Chrys. have καθαρίζων (D : καταρίζει). So Lachm. and Tisch.
Not a transcriber's error, but correct (see the exegetical remarks),
and needlessly emended by the neuter. — Ver. 24. μεθόρια]
Lachm. and Tisch. have ὅρια, following B D L Δ ℵ, min. Or.
But μεθόρια does not occur elsewhere in the N. T., and was supplanted by the current ὅρια (comp. Matt. xv. 22). — καὶ Σιδῶνος]
is wanting in D L Δ 28, Cant. Ver. Verc. Corb. Vind. Or. Suspected by Griesb., deleted by Fritzsche and Tisch., comp. Ewald.
Rightly; the familiarity of the collocation "Tyre and Sidon"
and Matt. xv. 21 have introduced the καὶ Σιδῶνος, which also
came in at ver. 31, and there supplanted the original reading
ἦλθε διὰ Σιδῶνος (approved by Griesb., adopted by Fritzsche,
Lachm. Tisch., in conformity with B D L Δ ℵ, 33, Arr. Copt.
Aeth. Syr. hier. Vulg. Sax. It.), and changed it into the *Recepta*
καὶ Σιδῶνος ἦλθεν. — Ver. 25. ἀκούσασα γὰρ γυνή] Tisch. has ἀλλ’
εὐθὺς ἀκούσασα γυνή, following B L Δ ℵ, 33, vss. The witnesses
are very much divided (D : γυνὴ δὲ εὐθέως ὡς ἀκούσασα); but the
reading of Tisch. is, considering this division, sufficiently attested,
and in keeping with the character of Mark; it is therefore to
be preferred. — Ver. 26. Instead of ἐκβάλῃ (Griesb. Scholz, Lachm.

Tisch.) Elz. has *ἐκβάλλῃ*. The evidence for the aorist is not decisive, and the present is in keeping with Mark's manner. — Ver. 27. Instead of *ὁ δὲ Ἰησοῦς εἶπεν* Lachm. and Tisch. have *καὶ ἔλεγεν*, following B L Δ ℵ, 33, Copt. Cant. (D has *καὶ λέγει*; Vulg.: *qui dixit*). The *Recepta* is an alteration arising from comparison of Matt. xv. 26. — Ver. 28. *ἐσθίει*] Lachm. and Tisch. have *ἐσθίουσιν*, following B D L Δ ℵ, min. The *Recepta* is from Matthew. — Ver. 30. Lachm. and Tisch. have adopted the transposition: *τὸ παιδίον βεβλημένον* (instead of *τὴν θυγατ. βεβλημένην*) *ἐπὶ τὴν κλίνην κ. τὸ δαιμόν. ἐξεληλυθός*, following B D L Δ ℵ, min. vss. (yet with variations in detail). The *Recepta* is to be retained; the above transposition is to be explained by the fact that the transcriber passed over from the *καί* after *ἐξεληλυθός* immediately to the *καί* in ver. 31. Thus *καὶ τὴν θυγατ.* down to *κλίνης* was omitted, and afterwards restored at the wrong, but apparently more suitable place. From the circumstance that *θυγ. . . . κλίνης*, and not *τὸ δαιμόν. ἐξεληλ.*, is the clause omitted and restored, may be explained the fact that all the variations in detail are found not in the latter, but in the former words. — Ver. 31. See on ver. 24. — As in iii. 7, so also here, instead of *πρός* we must read, with Griesb. Fritzsche, Lachm., following evidence of considerable weight, *εἰς*. — Ver. 32. After *κωφόν* Lachm. and Tisch. have *καί*, following B D Δ ℵ, vss. A connecting addition. — Ver. 35. *εὐθέως*] is wanting in B D ℵ, min. vss. Deleted by Lachm. and Tisch. Rightly; the more frequent in Mark, and the more appropriate it is in this place, the more difficult it was of omission, and the easier of addition; here also in a different order. — Instead of *διηνοίχθησαν* Lachm. and Tisch. have *ἠνοίγησαν*, following B D Δ ℵ, 1 (L has *ἠνοίχθησαν*). The *Recepta* arose from the previous *διανοίχθητι*. — Ver. 36. *αὐτός*] is wanting in A B L X Δ ℵ, min. Vulg. Lachm. Tisch.; but superfluous as it is in itself, how easily it was absorbed by the following *αὐτοῖς*! — Before *μᾶλλον* Lachm. and Tisch. have *αὐτοί*, following B D L Δ ℵ, min. Copt. Goth. Syr. Arm. To be adopted; correlative to the *αὐτός*, but passed over, as not being recognised in this reference and so regarded as superfluous.

Vv. 1-16. See on Matt. xv. 1-11. The occasion of the discussion, only hinted at in Matt. ver. 2, is expressly narrated by Mark in vv. 1, 2, and with a detailed explanation of the matter, vv. 3, 4. Throughout the section Matthew has abridgments, transpositions, and alterations (in opposition to Hilgenfeld and Weiss). — *συνάγονται*] is simply: *there come together*, there

assemble themselves (ii. 2, iv. 1, v. 21, vi. 30). The suggestion of a *procedure of the synagogue* (Lange), or of a formal
deputation (Weizsäcker), is purely gratuitous. — ἐλθόντες]
applies to both; on the notice itself, comp. iii. 22. — With
the reading καὶ ἐπερωτῶσιν, ver. 5 (see the critical remarks),
a full stop is not to be placed after ver. 1, as by Lachmann
and Tischendorf, but the participial construction, begun with
ἐλθόντες, runs on easily and simply as far as ἄρτους, where a
period is to be inserted. Then follows the explanatory remark,
vv. 3, 4, which does not interrupt the construction, and therefore is not, as usually, to be placed in a parenthesis. But
with καὶ ἐπερωτῶσιν in ver. 5 a new sentence begins, which
continues the narrative. — ἰδόντες] not in Jerusalem (Lange),
but on their present arrival, when this gave them a welcome
pretext for calling Jesus to account. — τοῦτ᾽ ἔστιν ἀνίπτοις]
Mark explains for his Gentile readers (for whom also the
explanation that follows was regarded by him as necessary)
in *what sense* the κοιναῖς is meant. Valckenaer, Wassenbergh,
and Fritzsche without ground, and against all the evidence,
have declared the words a gloss.[1] See, on the other hand,
Bornemann, *Schol. in Luc.* p. xl. The ἀνίπτοις (Hom. *Il.* vii.
266; Hesiod, *Op.* 725; Lucian. *Rhet. praec.* 14) stands in
contrast with the *prescribed* washing. Theophylact well says:
ἀνίπτοις χερσὶν ἤσθιον ἀπεριέργως καὶ ἀπλῶς. — Ver. 3.
πάντες οἱ ᾿Ιουδ.] A more popular expression — not to be
strained — indicating the general diffusion of the Pharisaic
maxims among the people. — πυγμῇ] Vulg.: *crebro* (after which
Luther: *manchmal*); Gothic: *ufta* (often); Syr.: *diligenter*[2]—
translations of an ancient reading πυκνά (as in א) or πυκνῶς
(*heartily*), which is not, with Schulz and Tischendorf (comp.
Ewald), to be regarded as original, but as an emendation
(comp. Luke v. 33), as indeed πυγμῇ itself cannot be made to
bear the meaning of πυκνά (in opposition to Casaubon). The
only true explanation is the instrumental one; so that they

---

[1] Wilke holds the entire passage, vv. 2–4, as well as καὶ ... ποιεῖτε, ver. 13,
to be a later interpolation.
[2] Some Codd. of the It. have *pugillo*, some *primo*, some *momento*, some *crebro*,
some *subinde*. Aeth. agrees with Syr.; and Copt. Syr. p. with Vulgate.

place the closed fist in the hollow of the hand, rub and roll the former in the latter, and in this manner wash their hands (νίψωνται) *with the fist.* Comp. Beza, Fritzsche. Similarly Scaliger, Grotius, Calovius, and others, except that they represent the matter as if the text were πυγμὴν ... ταῖς χερσί. The explanations : μέχρι τοῦ ἀγκῶνος (Theophylact, Euthymius Zigabenus), and : *"up to the wrist"* (Lightfoot, Bengel), correspond neither with the case nor with the signification of the word. Finally, had some peculiar *ritual form* of washing been meant (" in which they take the one fist full of water, and so pour it over the other hand *held up, that it runs off towards the arm"* (Paulus); comp. Drusius, Cameron, Schoettgen, Wetstein, Rosenmüller), Mark would with the mere πυγμῇ have expressed himself as unintelligibly as possible, and a ritual reference so precise would certainly have needed an explanatory remark for his Gentile readers. — Ver. 4. καὶ ἀπὸ ἀγορᾶς] The addition in D, ἐὰν ἔλθωσι, is a correct interpretation : *from market* (when they come from the market) *they eat not.* A pregnant form of expression, which is frequent also in classical writers. See Kypke and Loesner ; Winer, *Gr.* p. 547 [E. T. 776] ; Fritzsche *in loc.* In this case ἐὰν μὴ βαπτισ. is not to be understood of *washing the hands* (Lightfoot, Wetstein), but of *immersion,* which the word in classic Greek and in the N. T. everywhere denotes, *i.e.* in this case, according to the context : *to take a bath.* So also Luke xi. 38. Comp. Ecclus. xxxi. 25 ; Judith xii. 7. Having come from market, where they may have contracted pollution through contact with the crowd, they eat not, without having first *bathed.* The statement proceeds *by way of climax ;* before eating they observe the washing of hands *always,* but the *bathing, when they come from market* and wish to eat. Accordingly it is obvious that the interpretation of Paulus, Kuinoel, Olshausen, Lange, Bleek : " they eat not *what has been bought* from the market, *without having washed it,"* is erroneous both in linguistic usage (active immersion is always βαπτίζειν, not βαπτίζεσθαι) and in respect of the sense, to which the notion of special strictness would have required to be *mentally supplied.* — βαπτισμούς] is likewise to be understood of the

cleansing of things ceremonially impure, which might be
effected partly by *immersion,* partly (κλινῶν) by mere *sprink-
ling;* so that βαπτισμ. applies *by way of zeugma* to all the
four cases. — By the *cups* and *jugs* are meant vessels *of wood,*
for mention of the *copper vessels* (χαλκίων) follows, and *earthen*
vessels, when they were ceremonially defiled, were *broken into
pieces* (Lev. xv. 12). See Keil, *Archäol.* I. § 56 ; Saalschütz,
Mos. Recht, I. p. 269. — κλινῶν] not *couches in general* (de Wette),
for the whole context refers to *eating;* but *couches for meals,
triclinia* (iv. 21 ; Luke viii. 16 ; Xen. *Cyr.* viii. 2. 6 ; Herod.
ix. 16), which were rendered unclean by persons affected with
haemorrhage, leprosy, and the like (Lightfoot, p. 620 f.). —
Ver. 5. With καὶ ἐπερωτ. a new sentence begins. See above
on vv. 1, 2. — Ver. 6. Mark has not the counter-question
recorded in Matt. xv. 3, and he gives the two portions of
Christ's answer in inverted order, so that with him the leading
thought precedes, while with Matthew it follows. This order
of itself, as well as the ironical καλῶς prefixed to both portions, indicates the form in Mark as the more original. Comp.
Weizsäcker, p. 76. The order in Matthew betrays the set
purpose of placing the law before the prophets. The agreement of the quotation from Isa. xxix. 13 with Matt. xv. 8 f.
is wrongly adduced in opposition to this view (Hilgenfeld);
it is to be traced back to the collection of Logia, since it
belongs to the speech of *Christ.* — Ver. 8. ἀφέντες and κρα-
τεῖτε (2 Thess. ii. 15) are intentionally chosen as correlative.
— ἀλλὰ παρόμοια τοιαῦτα πολλά] Such accumulations of
homoeoteleuta were not avoided even by classical writers. See
Lobeck, *Paralip.* p. 53 f. τοιαῦτα defines παρόμοια as respects
the category of quality. — Ver. 9. καλῶς] *Excellently, nobly,*—
ironical. 2 Cor. xi. 4; Soph. *Ant.* 735 ; Arist. *Av.* 139 ;
Ael. *V. H.* i. 16. Not so in ver. 6. — ἵνα] " vere accusantur,
etsi hypocritae non putarent, hanc suam esse intentionem"
(Bengel). — Ver. 11. κορβᾶν] קָרְבָּן = δῶρον, namely, to the
temple.[1] See on Matt. xv. 5. — The construction is altogether

---

[1] The following is Luther's gloss: "is, in brief, as much as to say : Dear
father, I would gladly give it to thee. But it is Korban ; I employ it better
by giving it to God than to thee, and it is of more service to thee also."

the same as that in Matt. *l.c.*, so that after ὠφελ. there is an
aposiopesis (*he is thus bound to this vow*), and ver. 12 continues the reproving discourse of Jesus, setting forth what the
Pharisees do in pursuance of that maxim. — Ver. 12. οὐκέτι]
no more, after the point of the occurrence of the κορβᾶν;
previously they had nothing to oppose to it. — Ver. 13. ἦ
παρεδώκ.] *quam tradidistis.* The tradition, which they receive
from their predecessors, they have again transmitted to their
disciples. — καὶ παρόμοια κ.τ.λ.] a repetition of solemn
rebuke (comp. ver. 8). — Ver. 14. πάλιν (see the critical
remarks) has no *express* reference in the connection. But it
is to be conceived that after the emergence of the Pharisees,
ver. 1, Jesus sent away for a time the people that surrounded
Him (vi. 56); now *He calls them back to Him again.* Comp.
xv. 13. — Ver. 15. There is no comma to be placed after
ἀνθρώπου. — ἐκεῖνα] emphasizing the contrast to that which is
εἰσπορευόμενον. Observe, further, the *circumstantiality* of the
entire mode of expression in ver. 15, exhibiting the *importance* of the teaching given.

Vv. 17–23. See on Matt. xv. 12–20; the conversation,
which is recorded in this latter vv. 12–14, is by him inserted
from the Logia here as in an appropriate place. — εἰς οἶκον]
peculiar to Mark in this place : *into a house.* Jesus is still
in the land of Gennesareth (vi. 53), where He is wandering
about. — ἐπηρώτων κ.τ.λ.] According to Matt. xv. 15, Peter
was the spokesman, the non-mention of whose name in the
passage before us is alleged by Hilgenfeld to betoken the
Petrinism of Mark, who prefers to divert the reproach upon
all the disciples in general; but it in truth betokens the *older*
representation of the scene. — Ver. 18. οὕτω] *siccine, accordingly,* since you must ask this question. Comp. on 1 Cor. vi. 5.
— καὶ ὑμεῖς] like persons, who have not the benefit of my
guidance (οἱ ἔξω, iv. 11). — Ver. 19.[1] οὐκ εἰσπορ. αὐτοῦ εἰς τ.
καρδ.] *it enters not into his heart.* — The word ἀφεδρών does not

---

[1] The contents of ver. 19, very appropriate as they are for popular argument
in the way of naive sensuous representation, are unfairly criticised by Baur, *krit.
Unters.* p. 554, and *Markusev.* p. 55, as awkward and unsuitable ; and in this
view Köstlin, p. 326, agrees with him.

occur among the Greeks, but ἄφοδος. — The reading καθαρίζον
(see the critical remarks) would have to be explained : *which*
(*i.e.* which ἐκπορεύεσθαι εἰς τὸν ἀφεδρῶνα) *makes pure the*
whole of the food (that is eaten), inasmuch, namely, as thereby
every impurity passes away from it (by means of the excre-
ments). Thus καθαρίζον would be an appositional addition,
which contains the judgment upon the εἰς τὸν ἀφεδρῶνα
ἐκπορεύεται. See Kühner, II. p. 146 ; Winer, p. 549 [E. T.
778]; Fritzsche *in loc.* But the latter arbitrarily changes
καθαρίζον into the meaning : " puros esse *declarat,*" in so far,
namely, as all food, clean and unclean, would come digested
into the ἀφεδρών. With the reading καθαρίζων we must
explain : *which* (the draught) *makes pure the whole of the food,*
inasmuch as it is the place destined for the purpose of receiving the impurities therefrom (the excretions). Thus καθαρίζων
refers to τὸν ἀφεδρῶνα, and is put not in the accusative, but in
the nominative, as though καὶ ὁ ἀφεδρὼν δέχεται or something
similar had been said previously, so that the ἀφεδρών appears
as the *logical subject.* Comp. the similar application of the
anacoluthic nominative participle among the Greeks (Richter,
de anacol. I. p. 7 ; Bernhardy, p. 53 ; Krüger, § 56. 9. 4),
according to which it is not necessary, as with Buttmann, *neut.*
Gr. p. 68 [E. T. 78], to assume the abbreviation of a relative
clause. Comp. also Stallb. *ad Plat. Phaed.* p. 81 A. Moreover, the connection of the course of the matter presented from
ὅτι onward requires that καὶ εἰς τ. ἀφεδρῶνα ἐκπορ. should still
be dependent on ὅτι (in opposition to Fritzsche). — Ver. 21 f.
διαλογισμοὶ οἱ κακοί] is specialized by all that follows, which
therefore is to be taken as the *thoughts* actually presenting
themselves, as the *prava consilia* realized. — The following
catalogue betrays later enrichment when compared with that
of Matthew, and there is not manifest any *principium dividendi*
beyond the fact that (with the exception of ἀσέλγεια, *excess,*
especially unchaste excess; see on Rom. xiii. 13 ; Gal. v. 19)
matters approximately homogeneous are placed together. —
πονηρίαι] *malignities, ill-wills,* Rom. i. 29 ; Eph. iv. 31 ;
Col. iii. 8. — ὀφθαλμὸς πονηρ.] an envious eye, as at Matt.
xx. 15. — ἀφροσύνη] *unreason,* morally irrational conduct,

Wisd. xii. 23. Foolishness of moral practice. Comp. on Eph.
v. 17; Beck, *Seelenl.* p. 63 (its opposite is σωφροσύνη), not
merely *in loquendo,* to which, moreover, ὑπερηφανία (*arro-
gance*) is arbitrarily limited (in opposition to Luther's gloss;
Fritzsche also, and de Wette, and many others). — Ver. 23.
As of all good, so also of all evil, *the heart* is the inmost life-
seat. See Delitzsch, *Psych.* p. 250.

Vv. 24–30. See on Matt. xv. 21–29, who in vv. 23–25 has
added what is certainly original. — ἐκεῖθεν] out of the land of
Gennesareth, vi. 53. — εἰς τὰ μεθόρια Τύρου] *into the regions
bordering on Tyre* (Xen. *Cyr.* i. 4. 16; Thuc. ii. 27. 2, iv. 56.
2, iv. 99; Herodian, v. 4. 11; Lucian, *V. H.* i. 20). It is not,
withal, said even here (comp. Matt. xv. 21) that Jesus had now
left Galilee and betaken Himself into Gentile territory. He went
into the Galilean regions bordering on Tyre (the tribe of Asher).
According to Mark, it was only in further prosecution of His
journey (ver. 31) that He went through Phoenicia, and even
through Sidon, merely, however, as a traveller, and without
any sojourn. The explanation of Erasmus and Kypke: into the
region *between* Tyre and Sidon, is set aside by the spuriousness
of καὶ Σιδῶνος. — εἰς οἰκίαν] *into a house.* Comp. ver. 17. It
was doubtless the house of one who honoured Him. — οὐδένα
ἤθελε γνῶναι] not: *He wished to know no one* (Fritzsche, Ewald),
but: *He wished that no one should know it.* See the sequel.
Matthew does not relate this wish to remain concealed; the
remark is one of those peculiar traits in which Mark is so
rich. But he has no purpose of thereby explaining the subsequent refusal of aid on the part of Jesus from another
ground than that mentioned by Matt. xv. 24 (de Wette, Hilgenfeld), since Mark also at ver. 27 narrates in substance the
same ground of refusal. — ἠδυνήθη] corresponds to the ἤθελε:
He *wished* . . . and *could* not. — ἧς αὐτῆς] See Winer, p. 134
[E. T. 184]. On θυγάτρ., comp. v. 23. — Ver. 26. Ἑλληνίς]
a Gentile woman, not a Jewess, Acts xvii. 12. — *Syrophoenice*
means *Phoenicia* (belonging to the province of Syria), as distinguished from the Λιβοφοίνικες (Strabo, xvii. 3, p. 835) in
Libya. The (unusual) form Συροφοινίκισσα is, with Wetstein,
Griesbach, Scholz, and Lachmann, to be received on account

MARK. H

of the preponderance of the witnesses in its favour, with which
are to be classed those which read Συραφοινίκισσα or Σύρα
Φοινίκισσα (so Tischendorf), which is explanatory (a Phoenician Syrian). The Recepta Συροφοίνισσα (so also Fritzsche) is
an emendation, since Φοίνισσα was the familiar name for a
Phoenician woman (Xen. Hell. iii. 4. 1, iv. 3. 6; Herodian, v. 3. 2).
But the form Συροφοινίκισσα is not formed from Συροφοίνιξ
(Luc. D. Concil. 4), but from Φοινίκη. The Χαναναία of Matthew
is substantially the same. See on Matt. xv. 22. — ἐκβάλλῃ] (see
the critical remarks) present subjunctive, makes the thought of
the woman present, and belongs to the vividness of the graphic
delineation; Klotz, ad Devar. p. 618. — Ver. 27. πρῶτον]
certainly a modification in accordance with later tradition,
intended to convey the meaning: it is not yet competent for
Gentiles also to lay claim to my saving ministry; the primary
claim, which must be satisfied before it comes to you, is that of
the Jews.[1] It is the idea of the Ἰουδαίῳ τε πρῶτον καὶ Ἕλληνι,
Rom. i. 16, which has already come in here, added not exactly
in a doctrinal sense (Keim), but out of the consciousness of the
subsequent course of things and without set purpose—to say
nothing of an anti-Judaistic purpose in opposition to Matthew
(Hilgenfeld), which would rather have led to the omission of
the entire narrative. But in general the presentation of this
history in Matthew bears, especially as regards the episode
with the disciples, the stamp of greater originality, which is to
be explained from a more exact use of the collection of Logia
through simple reproduction of their words. Ewald finds in
that episode another genuine remnant from the primitive document of Mark. Comp. also Holtzmann, p. 192. — Ver. 29.
διὰ τοῦτον τὸν λόγον ὕπαγε] on account of this saying (which
gives evidence of so strong a confidence in me), go thy way.
In ὕπαγε is implied the promise of compliance, hence it is
fittingly associated with διὰ τοῦτον τ. λ. Comp. Matt.
viii. 13; Mark v. 34. — Ver. 30. εὗρε κ.τ.λ.] "Vis verbi in-
venit cadit potius super participium quam super nomen"

[1] According to Schenkel, indeed, Jesus was not at all in earnest with this
answer of harsh declinature, and this the woman perceived. But see on Matt.,
and comp. Keim, geschichtl. Chr. p. 61 f.

(Bengel). — βεβλημ. ἐπὶ τ. κλίνην] weary and exhausted, but
κειμένην ἐν εἰρήνῃ, Euthymius Zigabenus, which the demon
did not previously permit.

Vv. 31–37. A narrative peculiar to Mark. Matthew, at xv.
30, 31—here foregoing details, of which he has already related
many — only states in general that Jesus, having after the
occurrence with the Canaanitish woman returned to the lake,
healed many sick, among whom there were also *deaf* persons.
Mark has preserved a special incident from the evangelic
tradition, and did not coin it himself (Hilgenfeld). — πάλιν
ἐξελθών] his reference to ἀπῆλθεν εἰς, ver. 24. — διὰ Σιδῶνος]
(see the critical remarks) : He turned Himself therefore from
the region of Tyre first in a northern direction, and went
through Sidon (we cannot tell what may have been the more
immediate inducement to take this route) in order to return
thence to the lake. If we should take Σιδῶνος not of the
city, but of the *region* of Sidon (Σιδονία, Hom. *Od.* xiii. 285 ;
Ewald, Lange also and Lichtenstein), the analogy of Τύρου
would be opposed to us, as indeed both names always
designate *the cities themselves.* — ἀνὰ μέσον τῶν ὁρίων τ.
Δεκαπόλεως] He came (as he journeyed) *through the midst*
(Matt. xiii. 25 ; 1 Cor. vi. 5 ; Rev. vii. 17) *of the regions
belonging to Decapolis,* so that He thus from Sidon arrived at
the Sea of Galilee, not on this side, but on the farther side of
Jordan (comp. on Matt. iv. 25), and there the subsequent cure,
and then the feeding the multitude, viii. 1, occurred, viii. 10.
— Ver. 32. κωφὸν μογιλάλον] is erroneously interpreted :
a deaf man with a difficulty of utterance (see Beza, Grotius,
Maldonatus, de Wette, Bleek, and many others). Although,
according to its composition and according to Aëtius in Beck.
Anecd. p. 100, 22, μογιλάλος means *speaking with difficulty,*
it corresponds in the LXX. to the אִלֵּם, *dumb.* See Isaiah
xxxv. 6. Comp. Aquila, Symmachus, and Theodotion, Ex.
iv. 11. Hence it is to be understood as : a *deaf-mute* (Vulgate,
Luther, Calovius, and many others, including Ewald), which is
also confirmed by ἀλάλους, ver. 37, and is not refuted by ἐλάλει
ὀρθῶς, ver. 35. The reading μογγιλάλον, *speaking hollowly*
(B** E F H L X Γ Δ, Matthaei), is accordingly excluded of

itself as inappropriate (comp. also ver. 35). — Ver. 33. The question *why Jesus took aside the sick man apart from the people*, cannot without arbitrariness be otherwise answered than to the effect that He adopted this measure for the sake of an entirely undisturbed *rapport* between Himself and the sick man, such as must have appeared to Him requisite, *in the very case of this sick man*, to the efficacy of the spittle and of the touch.   Other explanations resorted to are purely fanciful, such as : that Jesus wished to make no parade (Victor Antiochenus, Theophylact, Euthymius Zigabenus, and many others); that in this region, which was not purely Jewish, He wished to avoid attracting dangerous attention (Lange); that He did not wish to foster the superstition of the spectators (Reinhard, *Opusc.* II. p. 140).   De Wette conjectures that the circumstance belongs to the *element of mystery*, with which Mark invests the healings.   But it is just in respect of the two cases of the application *of spittle* (here and at viii. 23) that he relates the withdrawing from the crowd ; an inclination to the mysterious would have betrayed itself also in the presenting of the many other miracles.   According to Baur, Mark wished to direct the attention of his readers to this precise kind of miraculous cure.   This would amount to a fiction in a physiological interest.   The *spittle* [1] (like the oil in vi. 13) is to be regarded as the *vehicle* of the miraculous power.   Comp. on John ix. 6.   It is not, however, to be supposed that Jesus wished in any wise to *veil* the marvellous element of the cures (Lange, *L. J.* II. 1, p. 282), which would amount to untruthfulness, and would widely differ from the enveloping of the truth in parable. — πτύσας] namely, on the tongue of the patient ; [2] this was *previous to* the touching of the tongue (comp. i. 41, viii. 22, x. 13), which was done with the

---

[1] According to Baur, there is betrayed in the narrative of the πτύειν, as also at vi. 13, "the more material notion of miracle in a later age."   But it cannot at all be shown that the later age had a more material conception of the miracles of Jesus.

[2] As in viii. 23 He spits into the eyes of the blind man.   It is not therefore to be conceived that Jesus spat on His own fingers and so applied His spittle to the tongue of the sick man (Lange, Bleek, and older commentators), for this Mark would certainly in his graphic manner have *said*.

fingers, and not the mode of the touching itself. — Ver. 34 f. ἐστέναξε] Euthymius Zigabenus well says : ἐπικαμπτόμενος τοῖς πάθεσι τοῦ ἀνθρώπου (comp. Grotius and Fritzsche). Certainly (see ἀναβλ. εἰς τ. οὐρανόν) it was a sigh of *prayer* (de Wette and many others), and yet a *sigh :* on account of painful sympathy. Comp. viii. 12, also iii. 5. It is reading between the lines to say, with Lange, that in this half-heathen region duller forms of faith rendered His work difficult for Him; or with Hofmann (*Schriftbew.* II. 2, p. 352), that He saw in the deaf-mute an image of His people incapable of the hearing of faith and of the utterance of confession (comp. Erasmus, *Paraphr.*). — ἐφφαθά] ܐܬܦܬܚ, imperative Ethpael. — διανοίχθητι] *be opened,* namely, in respect of the closed ears and the bound tongue. See what follows. — αἱ ἀκοαί] *the ears,* as often in classic use (Eur. *Phoen.* 1494; Luc. *Philop.* 1; Herodian, iv. 5. 3 ; comp. 2 Macc. xv. 39). — ἐλύθη κ.τ.λ.] The tongue, with which one cannot speak, is conceived as *bound* (comp. the classical στόμα λύειν, γλώσσας λύειν, and see Wetstein), therefore the expression does not justify the supposition of any other cause of the dumbness beside the deafness. — ὀρθῶς] consequently, no longer venting itself in inarticulate, irregular, stuttering sounds, as deaf-mutes attempt to do, but *rightly,* quite regularly and normally. — Ver. 36. αὐτοῖς] *to those present,* to whom He now returned with the man that was cured. — αὐτός] and the subsequent αὐτοί (see the critical remarks) correspond to one another : *He on His part* . . . *they on their part.* — ὅσον . . . μᾶλλον περισσότερον] *however much He enjoined* (forbade) *them, still far more they published it.* They exceeded the degree of the prohibition by the *yet* far greater degree in which they made it known. So transported were they by the miracle, that the prohibition only heightened their zeal, and they prosecuted the κηρύσσειν with still greater energy than if He had not interdicted it to them. As to this prohibition without result generally, comp. on v. 43. — μᾶλλον[1]] along

---

[1] Here in the sense of "*only all the more.*" See Stallb. *ad Plat. Rep.* iii. p. 397 A; Nägelsbach's note on the *Iliad,* ed. 3, p. 227.

with another comparative, strengthens the latter.   See on
Phil. i. 23; Hermann, *ad Viger.* p. 719 f.; Stallbaum, *ad
Phaed.* p. 79 E; Pflugk, *ad Hecub.* 377. — Ver. 37. καλῶς
πάντα πεποίηκε] Let πεποίηκε be distinguished from the
subsequent ποιεῖ.   The former relates to the miraculous cure
at that time, which has taken place and is now accomplished
(*perfect*); and καὶ (*even*) τοὺς κωφοὺς ποιεῖ κ.τ.λ. is the
general judgment deduced from this concrete case.   In this
judgment, however, the *generic* plurals κωφούς, ἀλάλους are
quite in their place, and do not prove (in opposition to
Köstlin, p. 347) that a source of which Mark here availed
himself contained *several* cures of deaf and dumb people. —
τ. ἀλάλ. λαλ.] *the speechless to speak.*   On ἄλαλος, comp.
Plut. *Mor.* p. 438 B; Ps. xxxvii. 14, xxx. 22.

CHAPTER VIII.

VER. 1. παμπόλλου] B D G L M N Δ א, min. Arr. Copt. Aeth.
Arm. Goth. Vulg. It. have πάλιν πολλοῦ. Recommended by
Griesb., adopted by Lachm. Tisch. But the former being an
ἅπαξ λεγόμ. in the N. T., might very easily have been changed
into πάλιν πολλοῦ, as πάλιν was used in Mark so frequently, and
in this place (it is otherwise at vii. 14) was so appropriate. —
Ver. 2. Instead of ἡμέραι, Elz. has ἡμέρας. A correction, in
opposition to decisive evidence, as is Matt. xv. 32. — μοί] is,
according to B D, with Lachm., to be deleted as a supplementary
addition. It is from Matt. xv. 32. — Ver. 3. ἤκουσιν] As A D א,
min. have ἥκασιν (so Lachm.), and B L Δ Copt. have εἰσίν (so
Tisch.), ἤκουσιν is condemned by preponderant counter-evidence.
But as, moreover, almost all the versions deviate from the simple
εἰσίν, we must abide by the reading of Lachm. If εἰσίν had been
glossed by a verb of *coming*, the praeterite ἧκα, not elsewhere
found in the N. T., would hardly have been the word chosen for
that purpose. Mark has the verb ἥκειν only in this place. —
Ver. 6. παρήγγειλε] B D L Δ א have παραγγέλλει. So Lachm.
and Tisch. Rightly; the historical present was lost in the
connection with the praeterite. — Ver. 7. εὐλογήσας εἶπε παραθεῖναι καὶ αὐτά] Many variations. Griesb. regards merely εὐλογ.
εἶπε παραθεῖναι as genuine. Lachm. has ταῦτα εὐλογ. εἶπεν παρατε-
θῆναι καὶ αὐτά. Fritzsche: εὐλογ. εἶπε παραθ. αὐτά. Tisch.: εὐλογ.
αὐτὰ παρέθηκεν. It may be urged against Griesbach, that a
reading without any pronoun has not been preserved at all in
the Codd. In the midst of the confusion of readings that has
arisen from the double pronoun, that one is to be retained
which has in its favour the relatively greatest agreement of the
most important uncials. And this is: εὐλογήσας αὐτὰ (B C L
Δ א, min. Copt.) εἶπεν καὶ ταῦτα παρατιθέναι (B L Δ א**, to which,
on account of the pronoun and its position, C also falls to be
added with: εἶπεν καὶ ταῦτα παράθετε). This consensus is more
important than that which Lachm. has followed (principally
relying upon A). The reading of Tisch., simple as it is, and not
giving occasion to variation, is too weakly attested by א*. —

Ver. 9. οἱ φαγόντες] is wanting in B L Δ ℵ, min. Copt. Condemned by Griesb., deleted by Tisch. It is from vi. 44. —
Ver. 12. σημ. ἐπιζητεῖ] Schulz, Lachm. Tisch. read ζητεῖ σημ., in
accordance with B C D L Δ ℵ, min. vss. The *Recepta* is from
Matt. xvi. 4. — Ver. 13. ἐμβὰς πάλιν] B C D L Δ ℵ, min. Copt.
Arm. have πάλιν ἐμβάς. This is to be adopted, with Fritzsche,
Lachm. Tisch., as the better attested order. — εἰς τὸ πλοῖον] Lachm.
reads εἰς πλοῖον, following A E F G M S V X, min. Fritzsche
and Tisch. have entirely deleted it, following B C L Δ ℵ, Corb.,
Germ. 1, Tol. The latter is right; ἐμβάς had its notion completed. — Ver. 16. λέγοντες] is wanting in B D ℵ, min. It.
Deleted by Lachm. and Tisch.; the former has subsequently,
with B, min. It., ἔχουσιν (comp. D: εἶχον). As well λέγοντες as
the first person of the verb was introduced in accordance with
Matt. xvi. 7. — Ver. 17. ἔτι] is wanting in B C D L Δ ℵ, min.
Copt. Verc. Lachm. and Tisch. As well the omission as the
addition might have been occasioned by the last syllables of
συνίετε; but more easily the addition, as the connection (οὔπω)
so readily suggested an ἔτι. — Ver. 21. πῶς οὐ] Lachm. has πῶς
οὔπω, following A D M U X, min. Syr. utr. Perss. Goth. Vulg. It.
Theophyl. Tisch. has merely οὔπω, following C K L Δ ℵ, min.
The latter is to be regarded as the original. To this οὔπω, πῶς
was added (Lachm.) from Matt. xvi. 11; and in accordance
with the same parallel, πῶς οὔπω passed into πῶς οὐ (B, Elz.). —
Ver. 22. ἔρχεται] ἔρχονται is rightly approved by Griesb., and
adopted by Lachm. and Tisch. See on v. 38. — Ver. 24. ὡς
δένδρα] Lachm. and Tisch. read ὅτι ὡς δένδρα ὁρῶ, following
decisive evidence. The *Recepta* is an abbreviation to help
the construction. — Ver. 25. καὶ ἐποίησεν αὐτὸν ἀναβλέψαι] Many
various readings; but not such as to warrant the total condemnation of the words (Griesb.), since they are only wanting
in a few vss. The most fully attested is καὶ διέβλεψεν, and this
is adopted by Tisch., following B C* L Δ ℵ, min. Copt. Aeth.
Καὶ διέβλεψεν, not being understood, was variously glossed. —
ἐνέβλεψε] Lachm. Tisch., following B L ℵ** min. (Δ, min. have
ἀνέβλεπεν), read ἐνέβλεπεν, which is to be adopted, as the aorist
was easily introduced mechanically from what preceded.—
Instead of ἅπαντα (approved by Griesb., adopted by Fritzsche,
Scholz, Lachm. Tisch.), Elz. has ἅπαντας. But the former is
attested by B C D L M Δ ℵ, min. vss., also Vulg. It. (D has
πάντα). ἅπαντας is to be regarded as an emendation, on account
of τοὺς ἀνθρώπους, ver. 24. — Ver. 26. μηδὲ εἰς . . . κώμῃ] very
many variations, arising out of the apparent inappropriateness
of the meaning; but not such as to justify the striking out of

the second half of the sentence (μηδὲ εἴπῃς τινὶ ἐν τ. κώμῃ), with Tisch. (B L ℵ, min. Copt.). In this way it was sought to help the matter by abbreviation. Others amplified (Vulg. It.) and altered (D). — Ver. 28. ἕνα] Lachm. Tisch. have ὅτι εἷς, following B C* L ℵ, Copt. The *Recepta* is an alteration on account of the construction. If ὅτι εἷς had come in in accordance with Luke ix. 19, ἀνέστη would also be found in Codd. — Ver. 29. λέγει αὐτοῖς] B C D* L Δ ℵ, 53, Copt. Cant. Verc. Corb. Colb. have ἐπηρώτα αὐτούς. Recommended by Griesb., approved by Schulz, adopted by Lachm. and Tisch.; the *Recepta* is from Matt. xvi. 15. — Ver. 31. ἀπό] B C D G K L ℵ, min. have ὑπό. Recommended by Griesb., adopted by Fritzsche, Lachm. Tisch.; ἀπό is from the parallel passages. — Ver. 34. Instead of ἀκολουθεῖν (which Griesb. Scholz, and Tisch. have adopted), Elz. Fritzsche, Lachm. read ἐλθεῖν. Both readings have weighty attestation; but ἐλθεῖν is from Matt. xvi. 24. — Ver. 35. Instead of τ. ἑαυτοῦ ψυχήν in the second half of the verse (Griesb. Scholz), Elz. Fritzsche, Lachm. Tisch. have τ. αὐτοῦ ψ., again following A B C* L Δ ℵ. From the preceding clause, and in keeping with the parallel passages. — Ver. 36. ἄνθρωπον] read, with Lachm. and Tisch., following A C* D, min. Or.: τὸν ἄνθρωπον. As well the omission of the article as the reading ἄνθρωπος (E F G H L M X Γ Δ ℵ* min.) is from the parallels. — Ver. 37. ἢ τί] Tisch. reads τί γάρ, following B L Δ ℵ, 28, Copt. Or.; ἢ τί is from Matt. xvi. 26.

Vv. 1–10. See on Matt. xv. 32–39. — ἐν ἐκ. τ. ἡμέρ.] An unessential difference from Matthew, but still a difference. — παμπ. ὄχλου ὄντος] *when very many people were there.* The presence of such a crowd is intelligible enough after the miraculous cure that has just been related (in opposition to Holtzmann, p. 85). On εἶναι, equivalent to παρεῖναι, comp. xv. 40; John vii. 39; Dorvill. *Charit.* p. 600. On πάμπολυς, only found in this place in the N. T., see Wetstein. Comp. Plato, *Legg.* vii. p. 819 A (πάμπολυς ... ὄχλος), *Polit.* p. 291 A; Lucian, *Herm.* 61. — Ver. 2. In the nominative ἡμέραι τρεῖς, Hilgenfeld finds an indication of dependence on Matt. xv. 32. Why not the converse? — Ver. 3. τινὲς γὰρ κ.τ.λ.] information peculiar to Mark concerning the previous ἐκλυθ. ἐν τῇ ὁδῷ, but still belonging to the words *of Jesus:* hence ἥκασιν (Lobeck, ad *Phryn.* p. 744), *have come;* not: *had come* (Luther). — Ver. 4. πόθεν] *With surprise* the disciples thus ask, as on the

desert surface (ἐπ᾽ ἐρημίας) there is no place *whence* loaves
for their satisfaction were to be obtained. — Ver. 7. Mark
(it is otherwise in Matthew) narrates in this place (otherwise
at vi. 41) two separate actions in respect of the loaves and the
fishes.—According to the reading : καὶ εὐλογήσας αὐτὰ εἶπεν
καὶ ταῦτα παρατιθέναι (see the critical remarks), we must
translate : *and after He had blessed them, He bade set these also
before them.*—With the small fishes thus, according to Mark,
Jesus performs a special *consecration* (comp. on Matt. xiv. 19),
as to which, however, in εὐλογ. there is nothing to be found of
itself higher than in εὐχαρ. (Lange : " the pre-celebration of
the glorious success "). The thanksgiving of Jesus *was* a
prayer of praise (comp. 1 Cor. xiv. 16). On εὐλογεῖν, with
accusative of the object, comp. Luke ix. 16, 1 Cor. x. 16,—
in the sense, namely, of uttering over the object a prayer of
praise (ברכה), blessing it. — Ver. 8. περισσ. κλασμ. ἑπτὰ σπυρ.,
remains left over in pieces seven baskets. The *definition of
measure* is added, according to the Greek usage, in the form
of an *apposition ;* Kühner, II. p. 117. — Ver. 10. Δαλμανουθά,
named nowhere else, was doubtless (comp. Matt. xv. 39) a
village or hamlet on the *western side* of the lake, in the neighbourhood of Magdala (or else Magada ; see on Matt. xv. 39).
See Robinson, III. p. 530 f. Ewald, indeed, *Gesch. Chr.* p. 376
(comp. Lightfoot), conjectures that in *Dalmanutha* we have the
Galilean pronunciation of the name of the town צלמון, where,
according to the Mishna, many Jews dwelt. But comp. on
Matt. xv. 39. The present village *Delhemija* (Robinson, III.
p. 514, 530) lies too far to the south, immediately above the
influx of the Hieromax, *eastward* from the Jordan. — The
specification of *a better-known* place in Matthew betrays itself
as *later;* although Baur thinks, that by such variations Mark
probably only wished to give himself a semblance of being
independent.

Vv. 11–13. See on Matt. xvi. 1–4, who narrates more
fully out of the collection of Logia, and from the tradition adds
the Sadducees. — ἐξῆλθον] namely, from their dwellings in the
district there. A trait of graphic circumstantiality. Lange
imports the idea : as spies out of an ambush. But it is not

easy to see why ver. 11 should fitly attach itself, not to the history of the miraculous feeding (which could not but serve to enhance the sensation produced by Jesus), but to vii. 37 (Holtzmann). Between Dalmanutha and the place of the feeding there lay in fact only the lake. — ἤρξαντο συζ. αὐτῷ] *How* they made the beginning of disputing with Him, is told by ζητοῦντες κ.τ.λ.: *so that they asked,* etc. — Ver. 12. ἀναστενάξας] *after that He had heaved a sigh* (comp. vii. 34), namely, at the hardened unbelief of those men.[1] A picturesque feature here peculiar to Mark. Comp. vii. 34. — τί] *why*—in painful certainty of the *want of result,* which would be associated with the granting of their request. " Tota hujus orationis indoles intelligitur ex *pronuntiatione,*" Beza. — εἰ δοθήσεται] a thoroughly Hebraistic expression of asseveration (*never* shall, etc.), by the well-known suppression of the apodosis. See Köster, *Erläut.* p. 104 ff.; Winer, p. 444 [E. T. 627]. According to Mark, therefore (who has not the significant saying as to the sign of Jonas adopted by Matthew from the collection of Logia already at x. 39 ff., and in this case at xvi. 4), a σημεῖον is altogether refused to this generation of Pharisees.[2] *For them*—these hardened ones, for whom the signs already given *did not suffice*—*none* should be given; the σημεῖα, which Jesus gave everywhere, were in fact sufficient even for their conversion, if they had only been willing to attend to and profit by them. — πάλιν ἐμβάς] without εἰς τὸ πλοῖον (see the critical remarks), which is, however, by means of πάλιν obvious from ver. 10. Comp. Xen. *Cyrop.* v. 7. 7: ὥστε ἐμβαίνειν, ὁπόταν Νότος πνέῃ, Dem. 29. 26, and many other places in the classical writers. — εἰς τὸ πέραν] to the *eastern* side of the lake (comp. ver. 10). Holtzmann is wrong in saying that Jesus here passes over for the *second* time to the *western* side; see on ver. 22.

Vv. 14–21. See on Matt. xvi. 5–11, whose narrative is

---

[1] This is all that is shown by the following painful question. Lange arbitrarily holds that Jesus sighed on account of the commencement of His separation from the dominant popular party; that there was, at the same time, a forbearing reservation of His judicial power, and so forth.

[2] By passing over the sign of Jonas, Mark has effaced the *point* of the answer, which Matthew and Luke have furnished.

less concise and more explanatory. — ἐπελάθοντο] quite as
in Matt. xvi. 6, and therefore not: *viderunt se oblitos esse*
(Fritzsche, Kuinoel). *The disciples* (ver. 15) form the subject,
as is evident of itself; for they ought to have taken care as to
the provision of bread, but *forgot* it. — εἰ μὴ ἕνα κ.τ.λ.] a
statement, which is quite in keeping with the peculiarity of
Mark, and perhaps proceeds from Peter (in opposition to
Hilgenfeld). — Ver. 15. ὁρᾶτε is *absolute;* and ἀπὸ τῆς ζ. κ.τ.λ.
belongs only to βλέπετε, the construction of which with ἀπό
(comp. xii. 33) is not, with Tittmann, *Synon.* p. 114, and
Kuinoel, to be analysed: *avertere oculos,* but: take heed *on
account of,* etc. Comp. προσέχειν ἀπό (Matt. xvi. 6); φόβος
ἀπὸ τῶν πολεμίων (Xen. *Cyr.* iii. 3. 53), *al.* — τῆς ζύμης τῶν
Φαρισαίων] According to Matthew (see on xvi. 6), ζύμη is
a figure for pernicious *doctrine,* and there appears no reason for
assuming any other reference here, such as to the *mali mores,*
the character (Bleek, Holtzmann), the *mental tendency* (Schenkel),
and the like. See on Matt. xvi. 6. Jesus warns against the
soul-perilling *doctrines,* which at that time proceeded as well
from the leaders of the *hierarchy* (the Pharisees) as from
the *political* head (Herod Antipas). Herod was a frivolous,
voluptuous, unprincipled man (see Ewald, *Gesch. Chr.* p.
47 f.); and the *morally vile principles and maxims,* given
forth by him, and propagated by the Jews who adhered to
him (the Herodians, iii. 6; see on Matt. xxii. 16), are the
ζύμη Ἡρώδου. A wrong attempt at harmonizing will have it
that Herod is mentioned (Heupel) as a *Sadducee* (which, however,
he never was; see on Matt. xiv. 2), because Matt. xvi. 6 has
καὶ Σαδδουκαίων. — Ver. 16. According to the correct reading
(see the critical remarks): *and they considered with one another,*
that they would have no bread. With respect to the indicative
present ἔχουσι, comp. on vi. 45, and Dissen, *ad Dem. de Cor.*
p. 203. — Vv. 19, 20. This *dialogue* form is characteristic of
Mark's *vivid mode of representation.* — πόσων σπυρίδ. πληρώματα κλασμάτων] See on vi. 43. Observe here, also, as
well as in Matthew, the alternation of κοφίνους and σπυρίδων,
in accordance with vi. 43 and viii. 8. — By the fact that, after
those two miraculous feedings, they still could take thought

one with another about *want of bread*, they show how much
they still lack discernment. The reproach of vv. 17, 18 [1]
refers to this. But in οὔπω συνίετε, ver. 21 (see the critical
remarks), the οὔπω applies to the instruction that has just
been catechetically conveyed vv. 19, 20, and is therefore a
later οὔπω than that in ver. 17, standing related thereto *by way
of climax.* Schenkel regards as incorrect all that is said of this
reference to the miraculous feedings, in consistency with his
view that these did not happen at all in the manner narrated.

Vv. 22—26 are found in Mark only. — It is not the Bethsaida situated on the *western* shore of the lake (vi. 45) that is
here meant (Theophylact, Euthymius Zigabenus, Heumann,
Heupel, Köstlin, Holtzmann; comp. Bleek and several others),
but the north-*eastern* Bethsaida, completed by the tetrarch
Philip (called also *Julias,* in honour of the daughter of Augustus;
see Josephus, *Bell.* ii. 9. 1, iii. 3. 5 ; *Antt.* xviii. 2. 1, xviii.
4. 6 ; Plin. *N. H.* v. 15 ; Wieseler, *chronol. Synopse*, p. 273 f. ;
Robinson, *Pal.* III. p. 566 f.; Ritter, *Erdk.* XV. p. 280 ; Ewald,
Gesch. Chr. p. 46), from which Jesus goes forth and comes
northwards into the region of Caesarea-Philippi (ver. 27) ; see
ver. 13. The weakly-attested reading Βηθανίαν (D, Cod. It.)
is an ancient alteration, from geographical ignorance of any
other Bethsaida than the western one. Ewald, indeed, following Paulus, has again (*Gesch. Chr.* p. 378) preferred this
reading, because Bethsaida Julias was not a κώμη, ver. 26 ;
but it was Philip who first *raised* it to the rank of a city, and
hence its designation as a village may still have been retained,
or may have been used inaccurately by Mark.— The blind
man was not *born* blind. See ver. 24. — Ver. 23. ἐξήγαγεν]
see on vii. 33. — The *spitting* is to be apprehended as at
vii. 33. As in that place, so here also, Jesus held it as
necessary to do more than had been prayed for. — Ver. 24.
ἀναβλέψας] *after he had looked up* (vi. 41, vii. 34). Erasmus
erroneously interprets it : *to become seeing again* (x. 51), which

---

[1] On the thought of ver. 18, comp., besides Isa. vi. 9 f., Xen. *Cyr.* iii. 1.
27 : ὦ θαυμασιώτατε ἄνθρωπε, σὺ δέ γε οὐδὲ ὁρῶν γινώσκεις, οὐδὲ ἀκούων μέμνησαι,
Dem. 797. 3 : οὕτως ὁρῶντες . . . ὥστε τὸ τῆς παροιμίας ὁρῶντας μὴ ὁρᾶν καὶ ἀκούοντας
μὴ ἀκούειν.

is only conveyed in καὶ ἀποκατεστ. κ.τ.λ. — According to the
reading ὅτι ὡς δένδρα ὁρῶ περιπατοῦντας (see the critical
remarks) : I see the men, *for like trees I perceive persons walking
about*, I observe people walking who look like trees (so un-
shapely and large). This was the first stage of seeing, when
the objects appeared in vague outline and enlarged. More
harsh is Ewald's construction, which takes ὅτι as the *recitative*, that indicates a new commencement of the discourse.—
We cannot decide *why* Jesus did not heal the blind man per-
fectly at once, but gradually. But it is certain that the agency
does not lose, by reason of its being gradual, the character
of an instantaneous operation. Comp. Holtzmann, p. 507 ;
Euthymius Zigabenus : ἀτελῶς δὲ τὸν τυφλὸν τοῦτον ἐθερά-
πευσεν ὡς ἀτελῶς πιστεύοντα· διὸ καὶ ἐπηρώτησεν αὐτὸν, εἴ τι
βλέπει, ἵνα μικρὸν ἀναβλέψας ἀπὸ τῆς μικρᾶς ὄψεως πιστεύσῃ
τελεώτερον, καὶ ἰαθῇ τελεώτερον· σοφὸς γάρ ἐστιν ἰατρός.
Comp. Victor Antiochenus and Theophylact. So usually.
According to Olshausen, a process too much accelerated would
have been *hurtful* to the blind man. This is an arbitrary
limitation of the miraculous power of Jesus (see, on the other
hand, Strauss, II. p. 66). According to Lange, Jesus desired
in this quiet district, and at this momentous time, " to *subdue*
the powerful effect of His miracles." As though the miracle
would not even as it occurred have been powerful enough.
According to Strauss, the gradual character is merely part of
Mark's effort after *vividness* of representation.[1] A notion unwarranted in itself, and contrary to the analogy of Mark's other
narratives of miracles. — Ver. 25. καὶ διέβλεψεν (see the critical
remarks) : *and he looked stedfastly* (Plato, *Phaed.* p. 86 D ; comp.
on Matt. vii. 5), and was restored. This stedfast look, which
he now gave, so that people saw that he fixed his eyes
on definite objects, was the result of the healing influence
upon his eyes, which he experienced by means of this second

---

[1] In fact, Baur, *Markusev.* p. 58, thinks that thereby the writer was only
making a display of his physiological knowledge on the theory of vision. And
Hilgenfeld says, that Mark desired to set forth the gradual transition of the
disciples from spiritual not-seeing to seeing primarily in the case of one
corporeally blind. Thus the procedure *related* by Mark would be *invented* by
Mark !

laying on of hands, and which the restoration immediately
followed. — καὶ ἐνέβλεπεν (see the critical remarks) τηλαυγῶς
ἅπαντα] Notice the *imperfect*, which defines the visual activity
from this time *continuing;* and how keen this was! *He saw
everything from afar,* so that he needed not to come *close* in
order to behold it clearly. ἐμβλέπειν, *intueri,* see Xen. *Mem.*
iii. 11. 10, *al.* In the classical writers used with τινί (*Cyrop.*
i. 3. 2; Plat. *Pol.* x. p. 609 D), but also with τινά (Anthol.
xi. 3). τηλαυγῶς (*far-shining*) with ἐμβλέπειν denotes that
the objects at a distance shone clearly into his eyes. Comp.
Diod. Sic. i. 50: τηλαυγέστερον ὁρᾶν, Suidas: τηλαυγές,
πόῤῥωθεν φαῖνον. — Ver. 26. εἰς οἶκον αὐτοῦ] He did not
dwell in Bethsaida, but was from elsewhere, and was brought
to Jesus at Bethsaida. See the sequel. — μηδὲ εἰς τ. κώμην
κ.τ.λ.] This μηδέ is not wrong, as de Wette and Fritzsche
judge, under the impression that it ought to be μή only; but
it means: *not even:* so now Winer also, p. 434 [E. T. 614].
The blind man had come with Jesus *from the village;* the
healing had taken place outside *in front of the village;* now
He sends him away to his house; He desires that he shall
not remain in this region, and says: *not even into the village*
(although it is so near, and thou hast just been in it) *enter
thou.* The second μηδέ is: *nor yet.*—The second clause, μηδὲ
εἴπῃς κ.τ.λ., is no doubt rendered quite superfluous by the
first; but Fritzsche pertinently remarks: "Jesu graviter inter-
dicentis cupiditatem et ardorem adumbrari . . . Non enim, qui
commoto animo loquuntur, verba appendere solent." Grotius,
Calovius, Bengel, Lange, and various others take τινὶ ἐν τ. κώμῃ
to mean: *to one of the inhabitants of the village* (who may meet
thee outside). A makeshift occasioned by their own addition.
And why should not Mark have simply written τινι ἐκ τῆς
κώμης? As to the prohibition in general, comp. on v. 43.

Vv. 27–38. See on Matt. xvi. 13–27. Comp. Luke ix.
18–26. — ἐξῆλθεν] from Bethsaida (Julias), ver. 22. — εἰς
τ. κώμας Καισαρ.] into the villages belonging to the region of
Caesarea. — Ver. 28. With the reading ὅτι εἰς τῶν προφητῶν
(see the critical remarks), εἶ is to be supplied. Matthew was the
more careful to insert the name of *Jeremiah* from the collection

of Logia, because he wrote for Jews.—Ver. 29. Mark and Luke omit what Matthew relates in vv. 17-19. Generally, Matthew is here fuller and more original in drawing from the collection of Logia. According to Victor Antiochenus and Theophylact (comp. Wetstein, Michaelis, and others), Mark has omitted it on purpose : ἵνα μὴ δόξῃ χαριζόμενος τῷ Πέτρῳ κ.τ.λ. According to B. Bauer, the narrative of Matthew has only originated from the consciousness of the hierarchy. Both these views are arbitrary, and the latter rests on quite a groundless presupposition. As the remarkable saying of Jesus to Peter, even if it had been omitted in the collection of Logia (Holtzmann), cannot have been unknown to Mark and cannot have its place supplied by iii. 16, it must be assumed that he purposely abstained from including it in this narrative, and that probably from some sort of consideration, which appeared to him necessary, for Gentile-Christian readers.[1] Thus he appears to have foregone its insertion from higher motives. To Luke, with his Paulinism, this passing over of the matter was welcome. The omission furnishes no argument against the Petrine *derivation* of our Gospel (in opposition to Baur, *Markusevang.* p. 133 f.), but it is doubtless irreconcilable with its subserving a *special* Petrine *interest*, such as is strongly urged by Hilgenfeld and Köstlin. Comp. Baur in the *theol. Jahrb.* 1853, p. 58 f. And to invoke the conception of a *mediating* Petrinism (see especially, Köstlin, p. 366 f.), is to enter on a field too vague and belonging to later times. Observe, moreover, that we have here as yet the *simplest* form of Peter's confession. The confession itself has not now for the first time come to maturity, but it is a confirmation of the faith that has remained unchangeable from the beginning. Comp. on Matt. xv. 17. — Ver. 31.[2] τῶν πρεσβ. κ. τῶν ἀρχ. κ. τῶν

---

[1] Beza, however, justly asks : " Quis crediderit, vel ipsum Petrum vel Marcum praeteriturum fuisse illud *Tu es Petrus*, si ecclesiae Christianae fundamentum in his verbis situm esse existimassent ? "

[2] The view that Jesus Himself now for the first time clearly foresaw His death (Weizsäcker, p. 475 ; Keim, *geschichtl. Chr.* p. 45), conflicts, even apart from the narrative of John, with ii. 20. Comp. on Matt. xvi. 21. Moreover, we cannot get rid of the mention of the Parousia, Matt. x. 23, and the interpretation of the sign of Jonah, Matt. xii. 39 f. (comp. on Luke xi. 30).

γραμμ.] Although these three form one corporation (the Sanhedrim), still each class is *specially* brought before us by repetition of the article, which is done *with rhetorical solemnity.* — μετὰ τρεῖς ἡμέρ.] *after the lapse of three days.* Comp. Matt. xxvii. 63. More definitely, but *ex eventu*, Matt. and Luke have : τῇ τρίτῃ ἡμέρᾳ, with which μετὰ τρ. ἡμ., according to the popular way of expression, is not at variance. See Krebs, *Obs.* p. 97 f. — Ver. 32. καὶ παρρησίᾳ κ.τ.λ.] a significant feature introduced by Mark, with the view of suggesting a still more definite motive for Peter's subsequent conduct : *and openly* (without reserve, frankly and freely) *He spoke the word* (ver. 31). παρρησίᾳ stands opposed to speaking in mere hints, obscurely, figuratively (John xi. 14, xvi. 25, 29). — ἐπιτιμ.] *to make reproaches,* namely, ὡς εἰς θάνατον ῥίπτοντ ἑαυτὸν ἐξὸν μηδὲν παθεῖν, Theophylact. But "Petrus dum *increpat, increpationem* meretur," Bengel. Comp. ἐπετίμησε, ver. 33. — Ver. 33. καὶ ἰδὼν τοὺς μαθητὰς αὐτοῦ] when He had turned Himself towards him *and beheld His disciples.* The latter clause gives more definitely the reason for the stern outburst of the censure of Jesus ; He could not *but set an example* to the disciples, whom He beheld as witnesses of the scene. Moreover, in ἐπιστραφείς there is a different conception from that of στραφείς, Matt. xvi. 23. — Ver. 34. Jesus now makes a pause ; for what He has to say now is to be said *to all* who follow Him. Hence He calls to Him the multitude that accompanies Him, etc. Mark alone has clearly this trait, by which the ὄχλος is expressly brought upon the scene also (Luke at ix. 23 relates after him, but with less clearness). Comp. vii. 14. This is to be explained by the originality of the Gospel, not by the πρὸς πάντας of Luke ix. 23 (which de Wette thinks Mark misunderstood). Comp. Hilgenfeld, *Markusevang.* p. 61. — ὅστις] *quicunque,* not at variance with the sense (Fritzsche), but as appropriate as εἴ τις. — ἀκολουθ.] both times in the *same* sense of discipleship. See, moreover, on Matt. x. 38. — Ver. 35. See on Matt. x. 39. τ. ἑαυτοῦ ψ.] expression of *self-sacrifice ;* His *own soul* He spares not. — Ver. 37. τί γάρ (see the critical remarks) gives the reason for the negative sense of the previous question. —

MARK. I

Ver. 38. γάρ] proves from the law of the retribution, which
Jesus will fully carry out, that no ransom can be given,
etc.   *Whosoever shall have been ashamed to receive me and my
doctrines—of Him the Messiah shall also be ashamed* (shall not
receive him for His kingdom, as being unworthy) *at the
Parousia!*   As to ἐπαισχυνθ., comp. on Rom. i. 16. — τῇ
μοιχαλίδι] see on Matt. xii. 39.   This bringing into prominence of the contrast with the Lord and His words, by
means of ἐν τῇ γενεᾷ . . . ἁμαρτωλῷ, is only given here in
the vivid delineation of Mark; and there is conveyed in it a
deterrent power, namely, from making common cause with this
γενεά by the denial of Christ.   The comparison of Matt. xii.
39, xvi. 4, is not, on account of the very dissimilarity of the
expressions, to be used either for or against the originality of
Mark, against which, according to Weiss, also σώσει, ver. 35
(Matt.: εὑρήσει, which Luke also has), is supposed to tell.
Nevertheless, κ. τοῦ εὐαγγελίου, ver. 35, is an addition of
later tradition. — ὁ υἱὸς τ. ἀνθρώπ.] Bengel aptly says : "Nunc
non *ego*, sed *filius hominis*, quae appellatio singularem cum
adventu glorioso visibili nexum habet."   Comp. xiv. 62. — And
as to this mighty decision, how *soon* shall it emerge! ix. 1.
What warning and encouragement in this promise!

CHAPTER IX.

VER. 1. The arrangement: ὧδε τῶν ἑστηκ., in Tisch., following B D* and one codex of the It., is correct; τῶν ὧδε ἑστηκ. is from the parallels. — Ver. 3. ἐγένετο] Lachm. and Tisch. have ἐγένοντο, following a considerable amount of evidence. The singular is a correction in recollection of Matt. xvii. 2. — ὡς χιών] is wanting in B C L Δ 1, Sahid. Arm. Aeth. Cant. Condemned by Griesb., deleted by Tisch. But had it been interpolated, it would not have been ὡς χιών (comp. Matt. xxviii. 3), but ὡς τὸ φῶς, that would have been supplied from Matt. xvii. 2, as Or. min. actually have. — Before λευκᾶναι, B C L Δ ℵ, min. vss. Or. have οὕτως, which Tisch. has adopted. Rightly; as it was found to be superfluous and cumbrous, it was omitted. — Ver. 6. Elz. Fritzsche, Scholz, Lachm. have λαλήσῃ. But a preponderance of evidence favours λαλήσει, which, with Matth., is the more to be preferred, as the future seemed objectionable to copyists lacking nice discernment; hence also in ℵ, Or. the reading ἀπεκρίθη (according to ver. 5), whence again proceeded, as an emendation, ἀποκριθῇ (Tisch., following B C* L Δ, min. Copt.). — ἦσαν γὰρ ἔκφοβοι] is, with Lachm. and Tisch., following B C D L Δ ℵ 33, Copt. Sahid. It. Chrys., to be changed into ἔκφ. γ. ἐγένοντο. — Ver. 7. ἦλθε] B C L Δ ℵ, Syr. in the margin, Copt. Arm. have ἐγένετο. Recommended by Griesb. It is from Luke ix. 35. — After νεφέλης Elz. Lachm. have λέγουσα, in opposition to very considerable witnesses (yet not to A D L Δ; the latter has λέγων). From Matt. xvii. 5. — αὐτοῦ ἀκούετε] Lachm. Tisch. have ἀκ. αὐτ. The *Recepta* is from the parallels. — Ver. 8. ἀλλά] B D ℵ, min. vss. have εἰ μή, which Lachm. has adopted. From Matt. xvii. 8. — Ver. 10. τὸ ἐκ νεκρῶν ἀναστῆναι] D, min. Syr. Perss. Vulg. Jer. have ὅταν ἐκ ν. ἀναστῇ. So Fritzsche (retaining τό); already recommended by Griesb., following Mill and Bengel. A gloss, for the sake of more accurate definition. — Ver. 11. Before οἱ γραμμ. Tisch. has οἱ Φαρισ. καί, only following L ℵ, Vulg. codd. It. It would, with stronger attestation, require to be adopted on account of Matt. xvii. 10. — Ver. 12. ἀποκρ. εἶπεν] B C L Δ ℵ, Syr. Perss. p. Copt. have ἔφη. Commended by Griesb.,

adopted by Tisch.   Rightly; the more prevalent expression
crept in from Matth.; ἔφη is only further found in the *Text. rec.*
of Mark at xiv. 29. — ἀποκαθιστᾷ] on decisive evidence read, with
Lachm. Tisch., ἀποκαθιστάνει. — Ver. 15. ἰδὼν αὐτ. ἐξεθαμβήθη] B C
D I L Δ ℵ, min. vss. have ἰδόντες αὐτ. ἐξεθαμβήθησαν.   Rightly
approved by Griesb., adopted by Fritzsche, Lachm. Tisch.   Not
the plural, but the singular had its origin in correction. —
Ver. 16. Instead of ἐπηρ. αὐτούς Elz. Scholz have ἐπηρ. τοὺς γραμματεῖς, which Lachm. has in the margin.   But B D L Δ ℵ, min.
Copt. Arm. Aeth. Vulg. It. have αὐτούς; τοὺς γραμματεῖς is plainly
an interpretation in accordance with ver. 14. — Ver. 17. Following B C D L Δ ℵ, 33, Copt. Cant. Ver. Verc. read, with Lachm.
and Tisch., καὶ ἀπεκρίθη αὐτῷ εἷς ἐκ. τ. ὄχλ. — Ver. 18. After ὀδόντας
Elz. Scholz have αὐτοῦ; it is wanting in B C* D L Δ ℵ, min.
Vulg. It.   By Lachm. it is only bracketed, by Tisch. deleted.
A familiar addition. — Ver. 19. Instead of αὐτοῖς Elz. has αὐτῷ,
which Rinck, *Lucubr. crit.* p. 300, defends.   But αὐτοῖς has preponderant attestation, and was changed, as the Father has just
spoken, into the singular. — Ver. 20. ἐσπάραξεν] B C L Δ ℵ, 33
have συνεσπάραξεν.   So Lachm. Tisch.   It is from Luke ix. 42.
The reading ἐτάραξεν in D also tells in favour of the *Recepta.* —
Ver. 21. ἐκ παιδιόθεν (Lachm. Tisch.) is found in B C G I L Δ ℵ,
min., and is, moreover, supported by D, Chrys., which have ἐκ
παιδός.   The pleonastic ἐκ was passed over. — Ver. 22. πῦρ]
Griesb. Fritzsche, Scholz have τὸ πῦρ, following A E F G K M
V Γ, min.   From Matth. — δύνασαι] Lachm. and Tisch. have
δύνῃ here and at ver. 23, following B D I L Δ ℵ, min.   To be
adopted; the usual form was substituted. — Ver. 23. πιστεῦσαι]
is, with Tisch. (comp. Ewald), following B C* L Δ ℵ, min. Copt.
Arm. Aeth. Arr., to be deleted.   An addition to the simple εἰ
δύνῃ, which was not understood. — Ver. 24. μετὰ δακρ.] is wanting in A* B C* L Δ ℵ, 28, Copt. Aeth. Arm.   Rightly deleted
by Lachm. and Tisch.   It is a gloss on κράξας. — After πιστεύω
Elz. Fritzsche have κύριε, in opposition to preponderant evidence.
— Ver. 26. κράξαν . . . σπαράξαν] Griesb. Lachm. Tisch. have
κράξας . . . σπαράξας, following B C* D L ℵ, min. (Δ has κράξας
. . . σπαράξαν); the neuter is a correction. — αὐτόν] is, in accordance with nearly the same witnesses and vss., to be deleted,
with Griesb. and Tisch. (Lachm. has bracketed it). — πολλούς]
Lachm. and Tisch. have τοὺς πολλούς, following A B L Δ ℵ, 33.
The article, in itself superfluous, was more easily omitted than
added. — Ver. 27. αὐτὸν τῆς χειρός] Lachm. Tisch. have τῆς χειρ.
αὐτοῦ, following B D L Δ ℵ, min. Copt. Arm. Vulg. It. Vict.   A
gloss (comp. i. 31, v. 41, viii. 23; Matt. ix. 25; Luke viii. 54).

— Ver. 28. The genitives εἰσελθόντος αὐτοῦ (Lachm. Tisch.) are found in B C D L Δ ℵ, min.; they are, however, to be regarded as an emendation (it is otherwise at ver. 2) on account of the double αὐτόν. — Ver. 29. The omission of κ. νηστείᾳ (Tisch.) is sufficiently attested by B ℵ* and one codex of the It., since the addition from Matthew so very easily suggested itself. — Ver. 30. παρεπορεύοντο] Lachm. has ἐπορεύοντο, following only B* D, Verc. Brix. Colb. The compound, not being understood, was set aside. — Ver. 31. τῇ τρίτῃ ἡμέρᾳ] B C* D L Δ ℵ, vss. have μετὰ τρεῖς ἡμέρας; approved by Griesb., adopted by Lachm. and Tisch. From viii. 31. If τ. τρίτῃ ἡμ. had been introduced from the parallel (in this case, Luke), this would rather have been done at viii. 31 (from Matt. and Luke), where it has but very weak attestation. — Ver. 33. ἦλθεν] Lachm. and Tisch. have ἦλθον, following B D ℵ, min. Syr. Pers. W, Vulg. It. (exc. Brix.). Not sufficiently attested for adoption, since at any rate the plural, after ver. 30, occurred more readily to the transcribers. — Before διελογ. Elz. Fritzsche, Scholz have πρὸς ἑαυτούς, which Griesb. condemned, Lachm. and Tisch. have deleted. It is wanting in B C D L Δ ℵ, vss., also in Vulg. It. (exc. Brix.), while several cursives place it *after* διελογ., and it is to be regarded as added for more precise definition. — Ver. 34. ἐν τῇ ὁδῷ] is wanting in A D Δ, Goth. Cant. Ver. Verc. Brix. Vind. Bracketed by Lachm., deleted by Fritzsche. But, if it had been added from ver. 33, it would appear *before* διελέχθ. Understood of itself, it was easily overlooked. — Ver. 38. ἀπεκρίθη δέ] B L Δ ℵ, Syr. Copt. Tisch. have merely ἔφη. Rightly; comp. on ver. 12. — The *Recepta,* Lachm. Tisch. read: ἐν τῷ ὀνόμ. σου. Griesb. Scholz have deleted ἐν. The witnesses on both sides are strong. The simple dative was more precisely defined partly, in accordance with the usual conception "in the name," by ἐν, partly, in accordance with vv. 37, 39, by ἐπί (so Fritzsche, although following only U, min.). — After δαιμόνια Elz. Scholz, Fritzsche, Lachm. Tisch. have: ὃς οὐκ ἀκολουθεῖ ἡμῖν. But this is wanting in B C L Δ ℵ, min. Syr. Arr. Perss. Aeth. Copt. Brix., while D X, min. vss., including Vulg. It. (exc. Brix.), omit the following ὅτι οὐκ ἀκολ. ἡμῖν (so Schulz, Fritzsche, Rinck). Accordingly Griesb. regards both as an addition from Luke. But both are to be retained. The former dropped out, because Luke has it not; witnesses, which had the former reading, left out the latter as superfluous and cumbrous. If it had been a gloss from Luke, μεθ' ἡμῶν would have been written instead of ἡμῖν; but this only occurs in L. — ἐκωλύσαμεν] B D L Δ ℵ, min. have ἐκωλύομεν. So Rinck and Tisch. The aorist is from Luke. —

Ver. 40. Elz. Fritzsche, Tisch. have both times ἡμῶν. But A D E
F G H K M S V Γ, min. and most of the vss., including Vulg. and
It., read ὑμῶν; ἡμῶν is an emendation, as it is also in Luke ix. 50.
— Ver. 41. Elz. has : ἐν τῷ ὀνόμ. μου. But τῷ and μου are wanting
in very considerable witnesses, which condemn, although not
unanimously, both readings as additions. — Before οὐ μή, ὅτι is
to be adopted, following B C* D L Δ ℵ, min., with Fritzsche,
Lachm. and Tisch. — Lachm. and Tisch. read ἀπολέσει, following
only B D E, min. — Ver. 42. After μικρῶν Fritzsche, Lachm.
have τούτων, in accordance, doubtless, with A B C** D L N Δ ℵ,
min. vss., including Vulg. It.; but from Matt. xviii. 6, whence also
has come the reading μύλος ὀνικός (Lachm. Tisch., following B C D
L Δ ℵ, min. vss., including Vulg. and It.). — Ver. 43. καλόν σοί ἐστι]
Lachm. and Tisch. rightly read : καλόν ἐστίν σε, following B C L
Δ ℵ, min. Verc. The *Recepta* is from Matt. xviii. 8 ; but to
derive thence the order εἰσελθεῖν εἰς τ. ζ. (Fritzsche, Lachm.
Tisch.) is forbidden by its decisive attestation. — Ver. 45. σοί] σε
is still more strongly attested here than at ver. 43, and is likewise
to be adopted (with Scholz, Lachm. and Tisch.). — εἰς τὸ πῦρ τὸ
ἄσβεστον] is wanting in B C L Δ ℵ, min. vss. Condemned by
Griesb., bracketed by Lachm., deleted by Tisch. Even in ver. 43
the words are wanting in some, although far weaker witnesses.
They are to be retained in ver. 43 (had there been an interpolation, we should have expected εἰς τὸ πῦρ τὸ αἰώνιον, in accordance with Matt. xviii. 8), but in ver. 45 they are to be struck
out as a mechanical repetition from ver. 43. — The words ὅπου
ὁ σκώληξ αὐτῶν οὐ τελευτᾷ καὶ τὸ πῦρ οὐ σβέννυται are only found in
all witnesses at ver. 48, whereas in vv. 44 and 46 they are
wanting in B C Δ ℵ, min. Copt. Arm. They are, with Tisch.,
to be deleted in vv. 44 and 46. They were written on the
margin from ver. 48. — Ver. 47. τοῦ πυρός] falls, according to
B D L Δ ℵ, min. Arr. Copt. Arm. Slav. Cant. Verc. Colb. Corb.,
with Lachm. and Tisch., to be struck out. From Matt.
xviii. 9. — Ver. 50. Instead of the third ἅλας there is to be
adopted ἅλα, with Lachm. and Tisch., following A* B D L Δ ℵ,
1, 28, 209. ἅλας is a mechanical repetition.

Ver. 1. See on Matt. xvi. 28. Comp. Luke ix. 27. — εἰσὶ
τινὲς ὧδε κ.τ.λ.] see the critical remarks : *there are some here
among the bystanders.* — ἐληλυθ.] *having come ;* otherwise conceived of in Matthew : ἐρχόμενον. — ἐν δυνάμει] *in power ;*
comp. Rom. i. 3. When, moreover, in this place the coming
of the *kingdom* is spoken of, it is the same nearness of the

Parousia that is meant (comp. on Matt. vi. 10), as at Matt. xvi. 28 (in opposition to Schwegler, I. p. 467 ; Baur, *Evang.* p. 561 ; Köstlin, p. 383) ; not the constituting of the church (Bleek), nor the emergence of the *idea* of the kingdom of God into historical realization (Weisse, *Evangelienfr.* p. 232), the triumph of the gospel (Schenkel), and the like. See viii. 38. With interpretations of this nature the specification of time εἰσὶ τινὲς κ.τ.λ.—pointing as it does to the term of the existing generation—is not at all in keeping.

Vv. 2[1]-13. See on Matt. xvii. 1-12, where on the whole the narrative is presented in its most original form ; Matthew has followed a tradition mostly more accurate (in opposition to Schenkel and Weizsäcker) than Mark, and altogether more so than Luke ix. 28-36 f. — τὸν Ἰάκ. κ. Ἰωάνν.] The one article embraces the *pair of brothers.* — Ver. 3. ἐγένοντο] *plural* (see the critical remarks), indicates the *different* articles of clothing, which became white (a vivid delineation), see Kühner, *ad Xen. Anab.* I. 2. 33. — οἷα γναφεὺς κ.τ.λ.] *i.e.* of such nature (they became) as that a fuller on earth is not able to furnish such a whiteness (οὕτως λευκᾶναι, see the critical remarks). ἐπὶ τῆς γῆς is added with reference to the *heavenly* nature of that lustre. Bengel well says, moreover : " χιών natura, λευκᾶναι arte." — Ver. 6.[2] τί λαλήσει] *what he shall say* (*future,* see the critical remarks), not inappropriate (Fritzsche) ; but ᾔδει has reference to the point of time, when Peter was just desiring to begin the utterance of what is said at ver. 5 ; and τί λαλήσει expresses the unknown more strongly and more vividly than the deliberative τί λαλήσῃ

---

[1] A definite specification of time, similar to μεθ᾽ ἡμέρας ἓξ in this case, is only found again in Mark at xiv. 1, and there, too, of a very important turning-point of the history.

[2] In this remark (by way of excuse) about Peter Hilgenfeld finds Petrinism ; and Baur, a dependence of the writer on Luke ix. 33. As to the latter, the converse is the case. The former springs from the endeavour to discover *tendency* everywhere, even when, as here, it is the most innocent explanatory remark, in which indeed Baur only sees (*Markusev.* p. 68) the character of incompleteness in the writer's combination of the other two Gospels. In opposition to such unfairness, however, Holtzmann, p. 88 f. 194, goes too far in his defence of Mark, inasmuch as he does not even acknowledge the excusing character of the οὐ γὰρ ᾔδει κ.τ.λ., which even Bleek, Weiss, and Hilgenfeld have recognised.

(what he *should* say). — ἔκφοβοι γὰρ ἐγένοντο (see the critical remarks): *for they became full of terror* (Heb. xii. 21 ; Deut. ix. 19 ; Plut. *Fab.* 6 ; Arist. *Physiogn.* 6), namely, by reason of the *appearances*, vv. 3, 4. — Ver. 7. καὶ ἐγένετο] *and there became* (there arose, came into manifestation) a cloud. Comp. Luke ix. 34. — Ver. 8. *And of a sudden,* having looked around, *they saw,* etc. ἐξάπινα occurs only here in the N. T., frequently in the LXX., but elsewhere is rare and late. — οὐδένα] applies to the *persons who had appeared* ; hence ἀλλά is : *but, on the contrary,* not equivalent to εἰ μή (Beza, and many others), which Matthew has. — The *fear* of the disciples is presented by Matt. xvii. 6 with more of psychological accuracy as only *subsequent to* the voice (this is the climax of the event), but in such a manner that they fall down, and Jesus Himself delivers them from it. The saying about building tabernacles does not bear the impress of confusion, as Mark presents it, but that of a still fresh ingenuous joy at the ravishing spectacle ; nor yet does it bear the impress of drowsiness, as Luke designates it, whose expression, according to Baur's opinion (see *Markusevang.* p. 69), Mark has only wished to modify ; comp. Baur's very unfavourable judgment on the narrative of Mark in general in the *theol. Jahrb.* 1853, p. 82 f. In Luke the later tradition betrays itself ; see on Luke ix. 28 ff., and Holtzmann, p. 224 f. But all three narratives in this particular, as also in their other features, stand opposed to the boldness of Schenkel, who (following Weisse) reduces the whole matter to this, that Jesus had by His *instructive teaching* made the two representatives of the old covenant *appear* to the three confidential disciples on the mountain *in a right light,* in the light of His *own Messianic destination;* while, on the other hand, Weizsäcker abides by a vision as the culmination of a deeper process of faith. And assuredly a visionary element was combined with the marvellous event. See on Matt. xvii. 12, Remark. — Ver. 10. τὸν λόγον] what Jesus had just said to them, ver. 9, not the occurrence of the glorification (Beza) ; see the following question. — ἐκράτησαν] *kept the saying fast ;* did not let it go out of their consideration, "*non neglectim habuerunt* " (Bengel). Comp. Test. XII. patr. p. 683 : ἐν ψυχῇ σου μὴ κρατήσῃς δόλον, Ecclus. xxi. 14 : πᾶσαν γνῶσιν οὐ κρατήσει. Comp. Bar. iv. 1 ; Cant. iii. 4 : ἐκράτησα αὐτὸν καὶ οὐκ ἀφῆκα αὐτόν. To explain it in harmony with the ἐσίγησαν in Luke ix. 36, we must neither attach to the κρατεῖν *in itself* the meaning : *to keep concealed* (on behalf of which Theodotion, Dan. v. 12, and the Scholiast *Aesch. Choëph.* 78, have wrongly been appealed to), nor bring out that meaning by the addition to it of πρὸς ἑαυτούς (Vulg. : *continuerunt apud se ;* comp. Erasmus, Luther, Beza, Lachmann, Ewald, and many others, including even Euthymius Zigabenus ; see, on the other hand, ver. 16, i. 27 ; Luke xxii. 23 ; Acts ix. 29 ; comp. Schulz) ; but simply explain it with Fritzsche, comp. Bretschneider : *they held fast to the prohibition of Jesus,* that is, they were silent on the matter. But this entire explanation does not agree with πρὸς ἑαυτοὺς συζητοῦντες κ.τ.λ., wherein is contained the accompanying *more precise definition* of the κρατεῖν τὸν λόγον. — πρὸς ἑαυτούς prefixed with emphasis : *among themselves discussing,* not questioning Jesus thereupon. To *Him* they have *another* question, ver. 11. Comp. on i. 27. — τί ἐστι τὸ ἐκ νεκρ. ἀναστ.] relates not to the resurrection of the dead in general (which was familiar as a conception, and expected in fact as a *Messianic* work), but to the rising *just mentioned by Jesus,* namely, that the *Messiah* would rise from the dead, which, in fact, presupposed His *dying,* and on that account was so startling and enigmatical to the disciples. Comp. ver. 32 ; John xii. 34. And in reference to the historical character of the prediction of the resurrection, see on Matt. xvi. 21. — Ver. 11. ὅτι λέγουσιν κ.τ.λ.] *wherefore say,* etc. ; that, indeed, is not in keeping with thy prohibition ! It is, with Lachmann, to be written : ὅ, τι (" *quod est* διὰ τί, *simillimum illi notissimo* εἰ *interrogativo,*" Praefat. p. xliii.) ; and the *indirect* character of the question (Thucyd. i. 90. 4) lies in the thought that governs it : *I would fain know,* or the like. See Stallbaum, *ad Plat. Euth.* p. 271 A ; Lücke on John viii. 25, p. 311 f. ; Buttmann, *neut. Gr.* p. 218 [E. T. 253]. Comp. ver. 28, and Homer, *Il.* x. 142 : ὅ, τι δὴ χρειὼ τόσον ἵκει,

Barnab. 7, and Dressel *in loc.* Ewald likewise appropriately takes ὅτι as the *recitativum,* so that the question would be veiled in an affirmative clause (but at ver. 28 : *wherefore*). Comp. Bleek. Still the *bashful* expression, which according to our view the *question* has, appears more in keeping with the circumstances. — Ver. 12. Ἠλίας . . . πάντα] a concession of the correctness of the doctrinal proposition (comp. on Matt. xvii. 11), the theoretical form of which (hence the *present*) is retained.[1] Bengel appropriately says : " Praesens indefinitum uti Matt. ii. 4." — What follows is, with Heinsius and Lachmann, to be punctuated thus : καὶ πῶς γέγραπται ἐπὶ τὸν υἱὸν τοῦ ἀνθρώπου ; ἵνα πολλὰ πάθῃ κ. ἐξουδ. : *and how stands it written as to the Son of man? He is to suffer many things, and be set at nought.* The truth of that proposition of *Elias* as the theocratic restorer, who is destined to precede the Messiah, has side by side with it the Scriptural testimony of the *suffering of the Messiah.* καί is the simple *and,* linking what stands written of the *Messiah* to what was said of *Elias.* Mark ought, after beginning the construction of the discourse with μέν, to have followed it up by δέ ; but he passes over in an ana-coluthic fashion from the form of *contrast* with which he began into the *subjunctive.* See Nägelsbach on the *Iliad,* Exc. i. p. 173 ; Maetzner, *ad Antiph.* p. 257 ; Klotz, *ad Devar.* p. 659. The *answer* follows in ἵνα κ.τ.λ., and that conceived under *the form of the design* of the γέγραπται ἐπὶ τ. υἱὸν κ.τ.λ. The *entire* καὶ πῶς . . . ἐξουδ. is *usually* regarded as a question, containing an *objection* against the prevailing way in which that doctrine regarding Elias was understood : *But how does it agree with this, that it is written of the Messiah that He is to suffer many things?* The *solution* would then be given in ver. 13 : " Verum enim vero mihi credite, Elias *venit,* non est talis apparitio expectanda, qualem expectant Judaei, *jam venit Elias,* Johannes baptista . . . et eum tractarunt, etc., neque ergo mihi meliora sunt speranda," Kuinoel. Comp. Euthy-mius Zigabenus, Theophylact, Grotius, Bengel, and many others,

---

[1] The conjecture of Hitzig in the *Züricher Monatsschr.* 1856, p. 64 : ἀποκαθισ-ταναι, is quite as unnecessary as it is grammatically clumsy.

including de Wette. In substance so also Hofmann, *Weissag. und Erfüll.* II. p. 80 f. In opposition to this entire view, it may be decisively urged that it would need an *adversative* particle instead of καί, and that, in ver. 13, instead of ὅτι καὶ Ἠλίας ἐλήλυθε, the expression would have run: ὅτι καὶ ἐλήλυθεν Ἠλίας. Fritzsche, following the reading[1] καθώς too weakly attested (instead of καὶ πῶς), says : " Quod Judaici doctores perhibent, venturum esse Eliam, non minus certum est, quam e V. T. oraculis illud, fore ut ego Messias multa exantlem." But Fritzsche himself does not fail to see the want of internal connection herein, and hence he *conjectures* as to vv. 12, 13 : Ἠλίας μὲν ἐλθὼν πρῶτον, ἀποκαθιστᾷ πάντα· ἀλλὰ λέγω ὑμῖν, ὅτι καὶ ἐποίησαν αὐτῷ ὅσα ἠθέλησαν, καθὼς γέγραπται ἐπὶ τὸν υἱὸν τοῦ ἀνθρώπου, ἵνα πολλὰ κ.τ.λ. Ewald also, with whom Holtzmann agrees, comes ultimately to a conjecture that in Mark, ver. 13, there is wanting before καθὼς γέγραπται the clause of Matt. xvii. 12 : οὕτως καὶ ὁ υἱὸς τοῦ ἀνθρώπου μέλλει πάσχειν ὑπ᾽ αὐτῶν. He supposes the discourse to have proceeded thus : "*What is said in Malachi iii. of Elias—that, coming before the Messiah, he shall restore all things—retains, doubtless, its truth; but also what the Holy Scripture says about a suffering of the Messiah (as in Isa. liii. 7 f.) must be fulfilled; if, thus, both are to be true, the Elias who is to precede the historical Messiah must in fact have come already, and have been mistaken and set at nought by men, just in the same way as, according to the Holy Scripture, this destiny awaits the Messiah Himself.*" [In this view it is at the same time assumed that the clause, ver. 12, καὶ πῶς γέγραπται κ.τ.λ. is omitted in Matthew.] According to Mark, however, as his narrative lies before us,[2] the discourse of Jesus rather contains a *syllogism with a suppressed conclusion,*—in such a way, namely, that the *major proposition* is conveyed in ver. 12, and the *minor*

---

[1] Which Linder also follows in the *Stud. u. Krit.* 1862, p. 558, arbitrarily enough supplying a *fiet*.

[2] Which does not exhibit a *distinction* between Scripture and fulfilment, as Weizsäcker judges, but *the harmony* of the two. Weizsäcker is also mistaken in his extending the question from πῶς to ἐξουδ. Accordingly it is assumed to have the meaning, that the Messiah's suffering, according to the prevailing view, is *not* treated of.

in ver. 13 : "the doctrine of the prior advent and the prior work of *Elias* is correct, and *of the Messiah* it is written that He has to endure much suffering and setting at nought (ver. 12). But I say unto you, that *Elias* also (before the Messiah) has come, and they have done to him everything that they have pleased, according to the Scripture (ver. 13)." The suppressed *conclusion* is: "consequently there is now impending *over the Messiah* the Scriptural destiny of suffering, since the fate of the Elias is already fulfilled." The suppression of this sad closing inference, to which Matthew, ver. 12, gives *expression*, is dictated by tender forbearance towards the disciples, whom, after so transporting a vision, the Lord will not now introduce any further into the gloomy future. This is assuredly an original feature, in which Mark has the advantage over the narrative of Matthew, who in this history has, on the whole, the more original account.[1] — $\dot{\epsilon}\xi o\upsilon\delta\epsilon\nu\omega\theta\hat{\eta}$] The form $\dot{\epsilon}\xi o\upsilon\delta\epsilon\nu\eta\theta\hat{\eta}$ (Lachmann), as being that which is less prevalent in the LXX., is to be preferred. On the later Greek character of the word in general (only used here in the N. T. —not in 2 Cor. x. 10), see Lobeck, *ad Phryn.* p. 182. The *signification* may be either: *to be esteemed as nothing* (*contemnatur*, Vulgate, and most expositors), as Ps. xv. 4, liii. 6; 1 Macc. iii. 14; Ecclus. xxxiv. 22; or: *to be annihilated*, as Ps. xliv. 6 (5), lx. 14, cxix. 117; Judith xiii. 17; Ecclus. xlvii. 7. The latter is here most in harmony with the context after $\pi o\lambda\lambda\grave{\alpha}$ $\pi\alpha\theta\hat{\eta}$. — Ver. 13. $\dot{\alpha}\lambda\lambda\acute{\alpha}$] is the continuative *jam vero, atqui*, which introduces a new thought in contrast with the previous one. If the continuation of the discourse were formed purely syllogistically (consequently without $\lambda\acute{\epsilon}\gamma\omega$ $\dot{\upsilon}\mu\hat{\iota}\nu$, $\ddot{o}\tau\iota$), the classical language would have chosen $\dot{\alpha}\lambda\lambda\grave{\alpha}$ $\mu\acute{\eta}\nu$ (Becker, *Anecd.* II. p. 839). — $\kappa\alpha\grave{\iota}$ $\dot{\textrm{H}}\lambda\acute{\iota}\alpha\varsigma$] *Elias also*, not merely the Messiah. That the latter had come, was to the disciples undoubted; but as to the advent of the Elias they had scruples. The *second* $\kappa\alpha\acute{\iota}$ therefore is *and*. De Wette

---

[1] Holtzmann thinks that in the question and answer *Mark* lays the stress upon the *resurrection of the dead*, while *Matthew* emphasizes the *appearance of Elias*. But in Mark too the disciples *ask no question whatever* about the rising from the dead, but only have their difficulties about it *among themselves*.

wrongly considers the two uses of καί as corresponding, *et . . . et;* in that case καὶ ἐλήλ. Ἠλίας must have been read. — καθὼς γέγραπται ἐπ' αὐτόν] has reference to the immediately preceding καὶ ἐποίησαν κ.τ.λ., not to Ἠλίας ἐλήλ., as Euthymius Zigabenus, Robert Stephens, Heinsius, Clericus, Homberg, Wolf, Bengel, and many others ambiguously connect it. But in these words Jesus does not *mean* what is written of the unworthy treatment *of the prophets in general* (Kuinoel), against which may be urged the definite ἐπ' αὐτόν, but what the Scripture relates of the *fate of Elias* (1 Kings xix.) as type of the fate *of John.* Comp. Grotius, Wetstein, Fritzsche. See also Hengstenberg, *Christol.* III. 2, p. 89. The reference to a *lost* writing (a conjecture of Bleek) is very unnecessary.

Vv. 14–29. See on Matt. xvii. 14–21. Comp. Luke ix. 37–43. The narrative of Mark is more original, characteristic, fresher, and, for the most part, more detailed than the other two. — συζητ.] according to vv. 16–18, on occasion of the circumstance that the disciples had not been able to perform the cure, and so concerning their power of miracles which was now so doubtful. — ἐξεθαμβ.] *they were very much amazed* (Orph. *Arg.* 1217 ; Ecclus. xxx. 9 ; Polyb. xx. 10. 9 : ἔκθαμβοι γεγονότες; in the N. T., used by Mark only). But *at what?* Euthymius Zigabenus leaves the open choice between two explanations : *either* at the approach of Jesus so exactly opportune, *or* at the brightness of His countenance (καὶ γὰρ εἰκὸς ἐφέλκεσθαί τινα χάριν ἐκ τῆς μεταμορφώσεως, comp. Bengel, de Wette, Bisping). But the *latter* must have been *expressed;* moreover, this cause of astonishment would rather have been followed by a remaining at a distance than a προστρέχειν and ἀσπάζειν. Hence (comp. also Bleek) the *first* explanation of Euthymius Zigabenus (comp. Theophylact and Victor Antiochenus) is, in accordance with the connection, to be preferred. It was *the amazement of joyously startled surprise,* that, whilst the disciples, who had not been able to help, were in so critical a situation, as was also the father with his unfortunate son, just at that moment the mighty miracle-worker Himself came to their aid. According to Fritzsche, there is denoted generally : " *quanta fuerit Jesu . . . et admiratio in plebe et*

veneratio." Much too general and aloof from the context.
According to Lange, what is meant is, " the *starting back* of a
multitude, that had become somewhat *profanely* disposed, at
the sudden emergence of a manifestation *of punishment.*" But
Mark has nothing of these psychological presuppositions, and
προστρέχοντες κ.τ.λ. is not in keeping therewith. According
to Baur, *Markusev.* p. 70, Mark has only attributed to the
people the impression, "with which *he himself* accompanied
the Lord, as He descended from the mount of transfiguration."
With such modes of dealing all exegesis is at an end. —
Ver. 16. ἐπηρώτ. αὐτούς] This αὐτούς cannot without arbitrariness be referred to any but those mentioned immediately
before—therefore to the *people*,[1] who are accordingly to be
conceived, ver. 14, as likewise taking part in the συζητεῖν, so
that there συζητοῦντας also applies jointly to the ὄχλον πολύν.
So also Bleek; comp. Ewald.   The usual reference to the
γραμματεῖς is consequently to be rejected (although Fritzsche
adopts this, and Lange, who, however, assumes a *sympathetic*
participation of the people); and so, too, is the reference to the
disciples and scribes (Griesbach, Paulus, Kuinoel), or merely to
the disciples (Mill, Bengel).   From the above reference it is
plain at the same time that in what follows there must be
written, not πρὸς αὐτούς (so *usually ;* hence also the readings
πρὸς ἑαυτούς, A ℵ*, and ἐν ὑμῖν, D, Vulg.), but πρὸς αὐτούς
(with Bengel, Fritzsche, Lachmann, Tischendorf), since αὐτούς,
like αὐτοῖς in ver. 14, applies to the *disciples.* — Ver. 17. The
father, included among this ὄχλος, begins to speak *in the
natural impulse of the paternal heart,* not as if no other would
have *ventured* to do so (Euthymius Zigabenus, Bengel,
de Wette).   He is designated, in apt delineation of what
occurred, as εἷς ἐκ τ. ὄχλου, since it is by his utterance that
he first shows himself as father. — πρός σε] that is, thither,
where I might presume Thy presence, because Thy disciples
were there. — ἄλαλον] according to the point of view, that the
condition of the sick man is the effect of the same condition
in the demon.   Comp. Luke xi. 14; Wetstein *in loc.* —
Ver. 18. καὶ ὅπου ἂν κ.τ.λ.] *and wherever he has taken hold*

---

[1] To whose ἠσπάζοντο αὐτόν Jesus replies with His question.

of him. The possession (ver. 17) is *not* conceived *as constant*, but as such that the demon leaves the sick man (epileptic) at times, and then again returns into him (Matt. xii. 44), and lays hold of him, etc. Hence ver. 35 : μηκέτι εἰσέλθῃς εἰς αὐτόν. The ἔχοντα of ver. 17 is not opposed to this (de Wette), for the son *had* the demon—even although at intervals the latter left him—so long as the μηκέτι εἰσέλθῃς was not yet realized. — ῥήσσει] *he tears him,* which convulsive effect is not more precisely to be defined (Euthymius Zigabenus and many others : καταβάλλει εἰς γῆν). See on the word, Ruhnken, *ep. crit.* I. p. 26 ; Duncan, *Lex.,* ed. Rost, p. 1016. Comp. ῥάσσειν (of the gladiators); Salmasius, *ad Ach. Tat.* p. 657 ; and Jacobs, p. 821. — ἀφρίζει] change of the subject; Winer, p. 556 [E. T. 787]. The permanent effect of these paroxysms is : ξηραίνεται, *becomes withered,* wasted away. Comp. iii. 1. See generally the description of the *morbus comitialis* in Celsus, III. 23. — εἶπον . . . ἵνα] *I told it . . . that they.* — Ver. 19. αὐτοῖς] the disciples, ver. 18. See, moreover, on Matt. xvii. 17. — Ver. 20. ἰδὼν αὐτὸν κ.τ.λ.] when the demoniac (not : the demon, Bleek) had looked upon Jesus, the demon tore him (the patient). On the anacoluthic use of the *nominative participle,* see Matthiae, *ad Eurip. Phoen.* 283 ; Bernhardy, p. 479 ; Winer, p. 501 [E. T. 711]. Comp. also Nägelsbach, *Anm. z. Ilias,* ed. 3, p. 385 f. — ἐπὶ τ. γῆς] belongs to πεσών (comp. xiv. 35 ; Xen. *Cyr.* iv. 5. 54). — Vv. 21-24. It is only the specially graphic Mark that has this dialogue. — Ver. 21. ὡς] Particle of time : how long ago is it, *when this fell upon him ?* — Ver. 22. καὶ εἰς πῦρ] *even into fire.* In John xv. 6 also the article is not necessary (in opposition to Fritzsche), although critically attested. — εἴ τι δύνῃ] Euthymius Zigabenus rightly says : ὁρᾶς, πῶς οὐκ εἶχε πίστιν ἀδίστακτον. Hence the answer of Jesus at ver. 23 ; hence also the utterance of the father at ver. 24, who felt his faith not to be sufficiently strong. On the form δύνῃ instead of δύνασαι, see Lobeck, *ad Phryn.* p. 359. — ἡμῖν] the father *of the family* speaks. — Ver. 23. After deletion of πιστεῦσαι (see the critical remarks), τὸ εἰ δύνῃ is to be regarded (Winer, p. 163, 506 [E. T. 225, 718]) as *nominative absolute: The " if thou canst"*

. . . "*Everything is possible to him that believeth,*" *i.e.* as far as concerns thy just expressed "*if thou canst,*" the matter depends on the *faith;* the *believer* is able to attain *everything.* The article embracing the εἰ δύνῃ substantivally (Kühner, § 492) takes up the word just spoken by the father, and puts it with lively emphasis without connecting it with the further construction, in order to link its fulfilment to the petitioner's own faith. Griesbach, Tischendorf, Ewald take τὸ εἰ δύνῃ *interrogatively,* and πάντα δύν. τ. πιστ. as answering it: "Tune dubitans *si potes* aiebas? Nihil non in ejus, qui confidat, gratiam fieri potest," Griesbach. Comp. Ewald: *Askest thou that: if thou canst?* etc. But the assumption of *a question* is not indicated by the non-interrogative address of the father (whence we should have expected τί τὸ εἰ δύνῃ, or the like), and so we are not warranted in mentally supplying an *aiebas* or *askest thou?* Comp. Bornemann in the *Stud. u. Krit.* 1843, p. 122. With the *Recepta* πιστεῦσαι or δύνῃ the explanation is: *if thou canst believe* (I will help thee); *everything is possible,* etc., in which interpretation, however, the τό is without warrant disregarded, as if it were of no significance (but comp. Matt. xix. 18; Luke xxii. 37), and taken only "as a sign of quotation of the direct discourse" (de Wette). So also Linder in the *Stud. u. Krit.* 1862, p. 559. Lachmann[1] places no point at all after πιστεῦσαι, and we might accordingly explain it thus: *if thou art in a position to believe that everything is possible to him that believeth* (so in my second edition). But even thus the τό causes difficulty, and the thought and the expression would be too diffuse, not in keeping with the concise representation of Mark, especially in so impassioned a connection. Lange takes it thus: "the *if thou canst* means: canst *believe.*" How enigmatically would Jesus have so spoken! Bleek takes εἰ *interrogatively.* But neither the deliberative character of this question (see on Matt. xii. 10) nor the τό would be appropriate. Bengel's interpretation also

---

[1] Who nevertheless, *Praef.* II. p. vii., conjectures ΠΙΣΤΩΣΑΙ: "Istud si potes," in quo dubitatio est, facito ut certum et confirmatum des, ut fiat "potes." Ingenious, but very artificial; and πιστοῦν only occurs in the N. T. at 2 Tim. iii. 14.

is impossible : '· Hoc, *si potes credere*, res est ; hoc· agitur."
But he well observes on the state of the case : " Omnipotentiae
divinae se fides hominis quasi organon accommodat ad recipien-
dum, vel etiam ad agendum." Fritzsche has *conjectured* either :
εἶπεν αὐτῷ· εἰ δύνασαι ; πίστευε· πάντα δυνατὰ κ.τ.λ., or : εἶπεν
αὐτῷ· τί ἐστι τὸ εἰ δύνασαι ; πίστευε· πάντα κ.τ.λ., and Bornemann, *l.c.* p. 123 : εἶπεν αὐτῷ τὸ πάντα δυνατὰ τῷ πιστ. —
Ver. 24. βοήθει μου τῇ ἀπιστίᾳ] *help me unbelieving ;* refuse
me not Thy help, notwithstanding my unbelief. Calovius,
Bengel,[1] and many others render : *assist my unbelief*, strengthen
my weak faith, which, however, is at variance with the contextual meaning of βοήθει (ver. 22). Moreover, the answer
of the father, who has just said πιστεύω, but immediately
afterwards, in consideration of the greatness of the issue made
to depend on his faith, designates this faith in respect of its
degree as ἀπιστία, is quite in keeping with the alternation of
vehemently excited feeling. Victor Antiochenus rightly says :
διάφορός ἐστιν ἡ πίστις· ἡ μὲν εἰσαγωγικὴ, ἡ δὲ τελεία.— The
substantive τῇ ἀπιστίᾳ brings more strongly into prominence
the condition than would have been done by an adjective. See
Winer, p. 211 [E. T. 296]. And the prefixed μου represents
at the same time the *mihi* of interest (v. 30 ; Rom. xi. 14,
and frequently Stallbaum, *ad Plat. Phaed.* p. 117 A) : *render
for me to my unbelief Thy help.* — Ver. 25. ὅτι ἐπισυντρέχει
ὄχλος] *that people were thereupon running together.* He wished
to avoid still greater publicity. — ἐγώ] emphatically, in contrast
to the disciples. — μηκέτι] *no more,* as hitherto. See on ver. 18.
— Ver. 26. κράξας . . . σπαράξας] κράξας : *crying out,* not
speaking. The *masculines* belong to the *constructio κατὰ
σύνεσιν* ; Mark has conceived to himself the πνεῦμα as a
person (as δαίμων), and has used the attributive participles
accordingly, not therefore by mistake (Fritzsche, de Wette).
Comp. Xen. *Cyr.* vii. 3. 8 : φεῦ, ὦ ἀγαθὴ καὶ πιστὴ ψυχὴ, οἴχῃ
δὴ ἀπολιπὼν ἡμᾶς ; see in general, Matthiae, p. 975 ; Bornemann in the *Sächs. Stud.* 1846, p. 40. — τοὺς πολλούς] the
multitude. The entire description is true and lifelike, and
does not aim, as Hilgenfeld thinks, at attaining a very great

[1] Who, however, also admits our view.

miracle.— Ver. 28 f. εἰς οἶκον] as vii. 17.— ὅτι] is to be
written ὅ,τι, and, as at ver. 11, to be explained as *wherefore*.
— τοῦτο τ. γένος] *this kind of demons* — a view of the
words which Ewald also, in his *Gesch. Chr.* p. 385 (not in
his *Evang.* p. 78, 277), recognises " in the present Mark," but
not in Matthew. — ἐν οὐδενί] *by nothing*, by no means.   That
prayer (κ. νηστ. is not genuine) is meant as a *means of increasing faith* (Matt. xvii. 20), Mark does not *say* indeed, but it
follows from ver. 19 ; hence it is not to be concluded that the
utterance contains in his case the sense of *a reproach* that the
disciples had not prayed (and fasted) enough (de Wette).

   Vv. 30–32. Comp. Matt. xvii. 22 f., who abridges, and
Luke ix. 43–45. — ἐκεῖθεν] out of the region of Caesarea
Philippi, viii. 27. — παρεπορεύοντο] *they journeyed along
through Galilee, i.e.* they passed through in such a way, that
(until Capernaum, ver. 33) they never tarried anywhere.
Comp. Deut. ii. 4, 14 ; Bar. iv. 43 ; also Mark ii. 23.
The travelling *along by-ways* (Lange) is not implied in the
verb. — καὶ οὐκ ἤθελεν, ἵνα τὶς γνῷ (Lachmann, Tischendorf
read γνοῖ; see on v. 43): similar to vii. 24.   But here
(ἵνα) the contents of the wish is conceived as its *design*.
The *reason* why Jesus wished to journey unknown is given by
ἐδίδασκε γὰρ κ.τ.λ., ver. 31, for which deeply grave instruction
He desired to be entirely undisturbed with His disciples.
This ἐδίδασκε was the continuance of the ἤρξατο διδάσκειν
of viii. 31 ; hence there is no reason for understanding in the
passage before us not the Twelve, but the scattered adherents
in Galilee (Lange). Moreover, αὐτούς in ver. 33 is decisive
against this. Comp. ver. 35. — παραδίδοται] the near and
certain future realized as present. — καὶ ἀποκτανθείς] has in
it something solemn. Comp. Pflugk, *ad Eur. Hec.* 25. —
Ver. 32. The instructions of Jesus were so opposed to their
Messianic expectations, that they not only did not comprehend
them, but they, moreover, shrank from any more precise disclosure concerning the inconceivable gloomy fate before them.

   Vv. 33–37. See on Matt. xviii. 1–5. Comp. Luke ix.
46–48.   Only Matt. xvii. 24 ff. has the history of the
stater. Of subordinate importance, perhaps also belonging to

a more local tradition, it seems to have remained unknown to
Mark, with which view κ. ἦλθ. εἰς Καπ. in ver. 33 is not
at variance (in opposition to de Wette). — Mark is more
original in the historical introduction of the point in question,
ver. 33 f., whereas Matt. xviii. 3, 4 has rightly completed the
narrative from the collection of Logia, but has, on the other
hand, withdrawn from the conclusion in ver. 5 its completeness, as it appears in Mark ver. 37 (Matthew has the thought
already at x. 40). — ἐν τῇ ὁδῷ] See ver. 30. — ἐσιώπων]
from being conscience - struck. — πρὸς ἀλλήλ.] emphatically
prefixed : *with one another*, so that they *one against the other*
claimed the higher place. It was not the *general* question
τίς μείζων *in abstracto*, but the *concrete* question of *personal* jealousy in their own *circle of disciples.* — τίς μείζων]
This brief, certainly primitive, interrogation is in Matthew
more precisely defined by ἐν τῇ βασιλ. τ. οὐρ. from the
answer (ver. 3). This more precise definition, however, is
not, with Beza, Heupel, and many others, to be imported also
here, but it stands simply : *who is of higher rank*, although it
is self-evident that they had *also* included in their view their
position in the kingdom of heaven. — καθίσας ἐφών. τοὺς
δώδεκα] by way of solemn preparation. — *If a man desires to
be of the first rank, he must*, etc. This ἔσται expresses the
result (comp. on Matt. xx. 26 f.),—the state of things that will
arise in consequence of that wish,—and thereby defines the
right θέλειν πρῶτ. εἶναι. — Ver. 36 does not come in un-
connectedly (Weisse, Holtzmann), but the progression is :
" Of *all* servants, even of the *least*, the affectionate reception of
whom is a service shown to myself," etc. — ἐναγκαλισ.] *after
he had embraced it.* Comp. x. 16. An original trait, which is
only found in Mark. The verb occurs only in Mark, but is
frequent in the classical writers.—Ver. 37. οὐκ . . . ἀλλά] not
non tam . . . quam, but with conscious rhetorical emphasis
the ἐμὲ δέχεται is *absolutely* negatived (comp. Matt. x. 20),
which is intended to denote in the strongest degree the *importance* of the reception of such a child (a child-like unassuming
believer, see on Matt. xviii. 5) to fraternal loving fellowship.
See Winer, p. 439 ff. [E. T. 623 ff.]; Klotz, *ad Devar.* p. 9 f.

Vv. 38–40. Comp. Luke ix. 49, 50 (not in Matthew). The *connection of thought* lies in ἐπὶ τῷ ὀνόμ. μου . . . τῷ ὀνόμ. σου; the disciples had done the opposite of the δέχεσθαι in the case of one, *who had uttered the name of Jesus.* Comp. Schleiermacher, *Luk.* p. 153 f.; Fritzsche, Olshausen, Ebrard, p. 447 f. So *John* came to his question. Bengel well says: " dubitationem hanc videtur in pectore aliquamdiu gessisse, dum opportune eam promeret." But Strauss, I. p. 642, and de Wette (comp. also Bleek), attribute this connection of thought merely to the *reporter* (*Luke*, whom Mark follows), who, on the ground of the ἐπὶ τῷ ὀνόμ. μου, has inserted just *here* the traditional fragment. This is improbable; such casual annexations are more natural in real living dialogue, and the reflection of the reporter would have found more appropriate places for their insertion, such as after vi. 30. — τῷ ὀνόμ. σου.] *by means of Thy name,* by the utterance of it. Comp. Matt. vii. 22; Acts iii. 6, xix. 13. The exorcist in our passage was not an impostor, but a believer; yet not one belonging to the constant followers of Jesus, although his faith was not perhaps merely elementary, but, on the contrary, even capable of miracles. What he had done appeared to the disciples as a privilege still reserved for the narrower circle, and as an usurpation outside of it. — ὃς οὐκ ἀκολ. ἡμῖν, and then again ὅτι οὐκ ἀκολ. ἡμῖν] John brings this point *very urgently* forward as the motive of the disciples' procedure (it is no "intolerabilis loquacitas," of which Fritzsche accuses the *textus receptus*). — ἐκωλύομεν (see the critical remarks): the *imperfect,* following the aorist, makes us *dwell on* the *main point* of the narrative. See Kühner, II. p. 74. — Ver. 39 f. *Application:* Of such a man, who, even without belonging to our circle, has nevertheless attained to such an energetic faith in me as to do a miracle on the basis of my name, there is no reason to apprehend any speedy change into reviling enmity against me. His *experience* will retain him for us, even although he has not come to his authorization, as ye have, in the way of immediate fellowship with me. It is obvious, moreover, from this passage how powerfully the word and work of Jesus had awakened in individuals even beyond the circle of His constant followers a higher power, which even performed miracles; thus sparks, from which flamed forth the power of a higher life, had fallen and kindled beyond the circle of disciples, and Jesus desires to see the results unchecked. Some have found in this man who followed not with the company of the Twelve the *Pauline Christians,* whom Mark makes to be judged of by Jesus only with more tenderness and tolerance than at Matt. vii. 21 f. (Hilgenfeld, *Evang.* p. 140 [1]) ; this is more than exaggerated ingenuity; it is the invention of a criticism, the results of which are its own presuppositions. — The construction is regular, and δυνήσεται designates the *ethical* possibility. — ταχύ] soon (Matt. v. 25, *al.*; Ecclus. vi. 18, xlviii. 20 ; Plato, *Conv.* p. 184 A; *Tim.* p. 73 A; Xen. *Cyr.* i. 1. 1), not: *lightly,* which might be signified by τάχα, Rom. v. 7; Philem. 15.

Ver. 41. See on Matt. x. 42. There is nothing opposed to the assumption that Jesus uttered such a saying *here also,* and generally on several occasions. — γάρ refers, by way of assigning a reason, to what immediately precedes, in so far, namely, as the *high significance of their position in the world* is contained in ὃς οὐκ ἔστι καθ᾽ ὑμῶν, ὑπὲρ ὑμῶν ἔστιν. " For ye are such important persons as the Messiah's disciples in the world, that he who shows to you the smallest service of love," etc. — ἐν ὀνόματι ὅτι κ.τ.λ.] so that this rendering of service *has its impelling reason* in the name, in the characteristic designation, that ye are Messiah's disciples, *i.e. for the sake of the name.* Comp. Winer, p. 346 f. [E. T. 484]. On εἶναί τινος, *addictum esse alicui,* see Bremi, *ad Dem. Phil.* III. p. 125, 56 ; Seidler, *ad Eur. El.* 1098; Ast, *Lex. Plat.* I. p. 621.

Vv. 42–48. See on Matt. xviii. 6–9. Comp. Luke xvii. 1–4. Jesus now reverts to the demeanour towards the lowly modest believers, as whose lively type the little child was still standing before Him (ver. 36), and administers the

[1] See also his *Zeitschr.* 1864, p. 317 f., where likewise quite untenable grounds are adduced for the above opinion. In the answer of Jesus, Eichthal sees even a specimen of good but *not moral tactics,* and holds that the narrative is an interpolation.

warning that none should give offence to such child-like ones
(ver. 42).   To comply with this, we need the most decided
sternness towards ourselves and self-denial, so as not to be
seduced by ourselves to evil and thereby to incur everlasting
torment (vv. 43–48).   This simple course of the address is
often mistaken, and even de Wette (comp. Saunier, p. 111,
Köstlin, Baur) thought that Mark had allowed himself to be
drawn out of the connection by Luke.   The source from
which Mark draws is the collection of Logia. — καλόν . . .
μᾶλλον] namely, than that he should have accomplished such
a seduction. — περίκειται and βέβληται bring vividly before
us the state of the case, in which he *is* sunk with the
millstone round his neck. — Ver. 43 ff.   Observe, according to
the corrected text (see the critical remarks), how in the three
references to the everlasting torment (which, indeed, according
to Köstlin, p. 349, are alleged to be in the taste of a later
time) it is only at the end, in the case of the third, ver. 47,
that the awful ὅπου ὁ σκώληξ κ.τ.λ., ver. 48, comes in
and affectingly winds up the representation. — Ver. 48.   A
figurative designation of the extremely painful and endless
punishments of hell (not merely the terrors of conscience), in
accordance with Isa. lxvi. 24 (comp. Ecclus. vii. 17 ; Judith
xvi. 17).   Against the *literal* understanding of the worm and
the fire it may be urged that in reality (in opposition to
Augustine, *de civit.* xxi. 9) the two together are incompatible,
and, moreover, that ἁλί, ver. 49, the counterpart of πυρί, is to
be understood *figuratively*.

Ver. 49.   Without any parallel; but the very fact of its
enigmatical peculiarity [1] tells in favour of its originality (in
opposition to de Wette, Weiss, and many others).   See on the
passage, Schott, *Opusc.* II. p. 5 ff., and *Dissert.* 1819 ; Grohmann in the *bibl. Stud. Sächs. Geistl.* 1844, p. 91 ff. ; Bähr in

---

[1] Baur judges very harshly on the subject (*Markusev.* p. 79), holding that
Mark in this independent conclusion, ver. 49 f., gives only a new proof how
little he could accomplish from his own resources, inasmuch as the thought only
externally annexed is obscure, awkward, and without unity of conception.   By
Hilgenfeld the discourse is alleged to be a mitigation of the harsh saying as to
cutting off the hand and the foot, and so to confirm the later position of Mark
after Matthew.   According to Weiss, vv. 49, 50 are " an artificial elaboration "

the *Stud. u. Krit.* 1849, p. 673; Lindemann in the *Mecklenb. Zeitschr.* 1864, p. 299 ff. In order to its correct interpretation the following points must be kept closely in view: (1) The logical connection (γάρ) is argumentative, and that in such a way that γάρ is related to the πῦρ in ver. 48 (because to this the πυρί must correspond), not to the entire thought, ver. 43 ff. (2) Πᾶς cannot be *every disciple* (Lindemann), nor yet can it be *every one* in general, but it must, in accordance with the context, be limited to those who are designated in the 48th verse by αὐτῶν (comp. Luke vi. 40), because afterwards with πᾶσα θυσία *another* class is distinguished from that meant by πᾶς, and something opposed to what is predicated of the latter is affirmed of it. (3) Πυρί and ἁλί are contrasts; like the latter, so also the former can only be explained *instrumentally* (not therefore: *for* the fire, as Baumgarten-Crusius and Linder in the *Stud. u. Krit.* 1854, p. 515, will have it), and the former can, according to the context, apply to nothing else than to the fire *of hell*, not to the fire of trial (1 Cor. iii. 13), as Theophylact and others (including Köstlin, p. 326 f.) would take it, nor yet to the sanctifying fire of the *divine word* (Lindemann). (4) Καί may not be taken as: *just as* (ὡς, καθώς), to which, following the majority, Lindemann also ultimately comes, but which καί never expresses; but rather: *and*, joining on to those who are meant by πᾶς and its predicate *others* with another predicate. (5) *The two futures* must be taken in a purely temporal sense; and in accordance with the context (vv. 43–48) can only be referred to the time of the Messianic decision at the establishment of the kingdom. Hence, also, (6) it is beyond doubt that πᾶσα θυσία cannot apply to *actual* sacrifices, but must denote *men,* who in an *allegorical* sense may be called sacrifices. (7) The meaning of ἁλισθήσεται may not be apprehended as deviating from the meaning (presupposed by Jesus as well

of Matt. v. 13. But how specifically different are the two utterances! And what would there have been to *elaborate* in the plain saying of Matt. v. 13 ? and to elaborate *in such a way ?* According to Weizsäcker, ver. 49 f. is only added here "on account of the assonance as respects the figure." This would amount to mere mechanical work. Holtzmann, however, justly maintains the independent conception of the (primitive-) Mark.

known) which the application of salt in sacrifices had (see
Lev. ii. 13, where meat-offerings are spoken of; comp. in
respect of the animal offerings, Ezek. xliii. 24; Joseph. *Antt.*
iii. 9. 1; and see in general, Lund. *Jüd. Heiligth.*, ed. Wolf,
p. 648; Ewald, *Alterth.* p. 37; Bähr, *Symbol. d. Mos. Cult.*
II. p. 324; and *Stud. u. Krit. l.c.* p. 675 ff.; Knobel on Lev.
p. 369 f.). It was, namely, *salt of the covenant* (מלח ברית) *of
God* (comp. also Num. xviii. 19; 2 Chron. xiii. 5), *i.e.* it
represented symbolically the covenant with Jehovah as
regarded its imperishableness,—represented that the sacrifice
was offered in accordance therewith, and for the renewing
thereof. Comp. Pressel in Herzog's *Encykl.* XIII. p. 343 f. —
Consequently we must translate and explain : " With warrant
I speak of their *fire* (ver. 48); for *every one* of those who come
into Gehenna *will be salted* therein *with fire, i.e.* none of them
will escape the doom of having represented in him by means
of fire that which is done in sacrifices by means of salt,
namely, the imperishable validity of the divine covenant, *and*
(to add now the *argumentum e contrario* for my assertion
concerning the fire, ver. 48) *every sacrifice, i.e.* every pious
man unseduced, who, as such, resembles a (pure) sacrifice
(comp. Rom. xii. 1), *shall be salted with salt, i.e.* he shall at his
entrance into the Messianic kingdom (comp. εἰσελθεῖν εἰς τ.
ζωήν, vv. 43–47), by reception of higher wisdom (comp.
ver. 50; Col. iv. 6; and as to the subject-matter, 1 Cor. xiii.
9–12), represent in himself that validity of the divine covenant,
as in the case of an actual sacrifice this is effected by its
becoming salted." Accordingly, it is in brief : *for in every one
of them the ever-during validity of the divine covenant shall be
represented by means of fire, and in every pious person resembling
a sacrifice this shall be accomplished by the communication of
higher wisdom.* It is to be observed, further : (1) that the
figure of the salt of the covenant refers, in the case of those
condemned to Gehenna, to the *threatening* aspect of the
divine covenant, in the case of the pious, to its aspect
of promise; (2) that Jesus does not accidentally set forth
the pious as a sacrifice, but is induced to do so by the
fact He has just been speaking of ethical self-sacrifice by

cutting off the hand, the foot, etc. And the conception of
sacrifice, under which He regards the pious, suggests to Him
as a designation of its destined counterpart the sacrificial
expression ἁλίζεσθαι. (3) Analogous to the twofold distinction
of ἁλίζεσθαι in the passage before us, although different in
the figurative conception, is the βαπτίζειν πυρί and πνεύματι
ἁγίῳ, Matt. iii. 11. — Of the many *diverging* explanations,
which in the light of what has just been stated are opposed
to the context, or to the language of the passage, or to both,
we may note historically the following :—(1) Euthymius Zigabenus : πᾶς πιστὸς πυρὶ τῆς πρὸς θεὸν πίστεως, ἢ τῆς πρὸς
τὸν πλησίον ἀγάπης ἁλισθήσεται, ἤγουν τὴν σηπεδόνα (corruption) τῆς κακίας ἀποβαλεῖ . . . πᾶσα θυσία πνευματικὴ,
εἴτε δι᾽ εὐχῆς, εἴτε δι᾽ ἐλεημοσύνης, εἴτε τρόπον ἕτερον γινομένη,
τῷ ἅλατι τῆς πίστεως ἢ τῆς ἀγάπης ἁλισθήσεται, εἴτουν
ἁλισθῆναι ὀφείλει. (2) Luther : " In the O. T. every sacrifice
was salted, and of every sacrifice something was burnt up with
fire. This Christ here indicates and explains it spiritually,
*namely, that through the gospel, as through a fire and salt, the
old man becomes crucified, seared, and well salted ; for our body
is the true sacrifice,* Rom. xii." He is followed by Spanheim,
Calovius, L. Cappel, and others: a similar view is given by
Beza, and in substance again by Lindemann.[1] (3) Grotius :
" Omnino aliqua desumtio homini debetur, aut per modum
saliturae (extirpation of the desires), aut per modum incendii
(in hell) ; haec impiorum est, illa piorum ; " the godless are
likened to the whole burnt-offerings, the pious to the *mincha.*
He is followed by Hammond, comp. Clericus and Schleusner.
(4) Lightfoot : " Nam unusquisque eorum ipso igne salietur,
ita ut inconsumtibilis fiat et in aeternum duret torquendus,
prout sal tuetur a corruptione : . . . at is, qui vero Deo victima, condietur sale gratiae ad incorruptionem gloriae." Wolf
and Michaelis follow this view ; comp. also Jablonsky, *Opusc.*
II. p. 458 ff. (5) Rosenmüller (comp. Storr, *Opusc.* II.
p. 210 ff.): " Quivis enim horum hominum perpetuo igni
cruciabitur ; . . . sed quivis homo Deo consecratus sale

[1] "As every sacrifice is salted by salt, *i.e.* by the word of God is made a holy
offering, so also every disciple is to be salted by fire [of the divine word]."

verae sapientiae praeparari debet ad aeternam felicitatem."
(6) Kuinoel (taking πῦρ, with Flacius and others, as a figurative designation of *sufferings*) : " Quilibet sectatorum meorum
calamitatibus (these are held to be the pains that arise by
suppression of the desires) veluti saliri, praeparari debet, quo
consequatur salutem, sicuti omnes oblationes sale condiri, praeparari debent, quo sint oblationes Deo acceptae." (7) Schott :
" *Quivis illorum hominum (qui supplicio Geennae sunt obnoxii)
nunc demum hoc igne sale (quod ipsis in vita terrestri
versantibus defuit) imbuetur, i.e.* nunc demum poenis vitae
futurae discet resipiscere. *Alio sensu illi salientur, quam
victimae Deo sacrae, de quibus loco illo scriptum legitur: victima
quaevis sale est conspergenda.* His enim similes sunt homines
in hac vita terrestri animis suis sapientiae divinae sale imbu-
endis prospicientes." (8) According to Fritzsche, γάρ assigns
the reason of the exhortation to suffer rather the loss of
members of their body than to let themselves be seduced, and
the meaning is (in the main as according to Kuinoel, comp.
Vatablus) : " Quippe omnes (in general) aerumnis ad vitae
aeternae felicitatem praeparabuntur, sicut omnes victimae e
Mosis decreto sale sunt ad immolationem praeparandae." So
in substance also Bleek. (9) Olshausen : " On account of the
general sinfulness of the race every one must be salted with
fire, whether by entering voluntarily upon self-denial and
earnest cleansing from sins, or by being carried involuntarily
to the place of punishment ; and therefore [in order to be the
symbolical type of this spiritual transaction] every sacrifice
is (as is written) to be salted with salt." [1] Similarly Lange.
(10) According to de Wette, πυρὶ ἁλίζεσθαι is nearly (?) tantamount to " the receiving by purification the holy seasoning and
consecration (of purity and wisdom)," and καί is comparative.
(11) Grohmann takes the first clause in substance as does
Olshausen, and the second thus : " as every sacrifice shall be
made savoury with salt, so also shall every one, who desires to
offer himself as a sacrifice to God, be salted,—that is, shall from
without, by sufferings, privations, and the like, be stirred up,

---

[1] According to Olshausen, we are to find here an authentic explanation as to
the significance of the sacrifices, and of the ritual of their salting.

quickened, and pervaded by a higher, fresh spiritual power."
(12) Bähr : " As according to the law there must in no sacrifice be wanting the symbol of the covenant of sanctification
that consecrates it the salt ; so also must every one be purified
and refined in and with the sacrifice of self-surrender ; . . .
this refining process, far from being of a destructive nature, is
rather the very thing which preserves and maintains unto
true and eternal life." (13) According to Ewald, the meaning
is that every one who yields to seductive impulses, because
he allows the salt—wherewith from the beginning God has
seasoned man's spirit—to become insipid, must first be salted
again by the fire of hell, in order that this sacrifice may not
remain without the salt which, according to Lev. ii. 13,
belongs to every sacrifice ; no other salt (no other purification)
is left save the fire of hell itself, when the salt in man has
become savourless. (14) By Hilgenfeld the *fire* is alleged to
be even that of internal desire, through which (this is held to
mean : by *overcoming* the desire !) one is said to be salted, *i.e.*
led to Christian wisdom ; thereby one is to offer a sacrifice
of which the salt is Christian discernment. — This great
diversity of interpretation is a proof of the obscurity of the
utterance, which probably was spoken by Jesus in an explanatory connection which has not been preserved.—The second
clause of the verse has been held by Gersdorf, p. 376 f., on
linguistic grounds that are wholly untenable, to be spurious ;
and, as it is wanting also in B L Δ ℵ, min. and some vss. (on
account of the twice occurring ἀλισθήσ. by transcriber's error),
it is declared also by Schulz to be a gloss.

Ver. 50. Καλὸν . . . ἀρτύσετε] a maxim of experience
drawn from common life, in which . τὸ ἅλας is to be taken
literally. Then follows with ἔχετε κ.τ.λ. the *application,* in
which the *spiritual* meaning of the salt (*wisdom,* see on
ver. 49, and Buxtorf, *Lex. Talm.* p. 1208) emerges. The
connection with what precedes is : In order to experience in
yourselves on the establishment of the kingdom the truth :
πᾶσα θυσία ἀλὶ ἀλισθήσεται, ye must—seeing that salt, which
in itself is so excellent a thing, when it has become insipid,
can in no wise be restored—*preserve* in your hearts the salt of

true wisdom [1] and withal be *peaceful* one with another.
Against both the disciples had sinned by their dispute about
precedence (ver. 34), from which the entire discourse of
Jesus, ver. 35 ff., had started, and to which He now again at
the close points back.   This contest about precedence had
been *foolish* (opposed to the ἅλας) and *unpeaceful.* — ἐὰν δὲ τὸ
ἅλας ἄναλον κ.τ.λ.] Comp. on Matt. v. 13. — αὐτὸ ἀρτύσετε]
wherewith shall ye restore it? so that it shall again be provided with saline efficacy (comp. on Col. iv. 6). — ἔχετε]
emphatically placed first : *keep, preserve,* which is not done, if
the analogue of the ἄναλον γίνεσθαι sets in with you. — ἐν
ἑαυτοῖς] *in yourselves,* correlative to the subsequent ἐν ἀλλή-
λοις (*reciprocally*).   Comp. Bengel : " prius officium respectu
nostri, alterum erga alios." — ἅλα (see the critical remarks)
from ὁ ἅλς.   See Lobeck, *Paralip.* p. 93. — καὶ εἰρην. ἐν ἀλλ.]
The annexing of this exhortation was also suggested by the
conception of the salt, since the salt was *symbol of a covenant.*
Hence the course of thought : *And*—whereof ye are likewise
reminded by the symbolic significance of salt—*live in peace
one with another.*

[1] Comp. Ignat. *ad Magnes.* 10 : ἀλίσθητε ἐν αὐτῷ (Χριστῷ), ἵνα μὴ διαφθαρῇ τις ἐν ὑμῖν.

CHAPTER X.

VER. 1. διὰ τοῦ] is wanting in C** D G Δ, min. Syr. Pers. Aeth. Goth. Vulg. It. On the other hand, B C* L ℵ, Copt. have καί. So rightly Lachm. and Tisch. This καί was, in some cases, deleted in accordance with Matt. xix. 1; in others, more precisely defined by the description contained in διὰ τοῦ. — Ver. 4. With Lachm. and Tisch. the order ἐπέτρεψεν Μωϋσῆς, following B C D L Δ, min., is to be preferred. — Ver. 6. ὁ Θεός is wanting in B C L Δ ℵ, Copt. Colb. Corb. Bracketed by Lachm., deleted by Tisch. An addition by way of gloss, which appeared necessary here, although not at Matt. xix. 4. — Ver. 7. πρὸς τ. γυν.] Lachm. has τῇ γυναικί, following A C L N Δ, min. codd. It. Jer. From Matthew. Tisch. has now again deleted κ. προσκολλ. πρὸς τ. γυν. αὐτοῦ, nevertheless only following B ℵ, Goth. It lies under a strong suspicion of being an addition from Matthew. — Ver. 10. εἰς τὴν οἰκίαν] So also Lachm. and Tisch., following B D L Δ ℵ, min. Cant. Ver. The Recepta ἐν τῇ οἰκίᾳ (Fritzsche, Scholz) is an emendation. — αὐτοῦ περὶ τοῦ αὐτοῦ] On decisive evidence we must read, with Fritzsche, Lachm., and Tisch., merely περὶ τούτου. The first αὐτοῦ is a current addition to οἱ μαθηταί; by τοῦ αὐτοῦ (D : τοῦ αὐτοῦ λόγου) τούτου was glossed for the purpose of more precise definition. — Ver. 12. Tischendorf's reading: καὶ ἐὰν αὐτὴ ἀπολύσασα τὸν ἄνδρα αὐτῆς γαμήσῃ (B C L ℵ and Δ, which, however, has καί before γαμ.), is a stylistic emendation. — γαμηθῇ ἄλλῳ] Lachm. Tisch. have γαμήσῃ ἄλλον, following B C* D L Δ ℵ, min. A mechanical repetition from ver. 11 (whence Δ has even ἄλλην instead of ἄλλον !). — Ver. 14. Before μή Elz. Fritzsche, Lachm. have καί, which is wanting in witnesses deserving consideration, and is added from the parallels. — Ver. 16. Instead of ηὐλόγει Lachm. (as also Scholz) has εὐλόγει. But B C Δ ℵ, min. Vict. have κατευλόγει (L N : κατηυλ.). It is to be adopted, with Tisch.; this compound, which does not elsewhere occur in the N. T., was unfamiliar to the transcribers. Its position before τιθείς (omitting the last αὐτά) is attested by B C L Δ ℵ, min. Copt. Syr. p. ms. Vict. (Fritzsche, Tisch.). But it was precisely the threefold αὐτά that gave occasion to error and correction. — Ver. 19. The

arrangement μὴ φον., μὴ μοιχ. (Lachm. Tisch.), is found in B C Δ
ℵ** min. Copt. Ar. Colb.; but it is from Matt. xix. 18. — Ver.
21. The article before πτωχοῖς is wanting in witnesses of such
preponderating character (condemned by Griesb., deleted by
Fritzsche, Lachm.) that it appears (as also in Matt. xix. 21) as
an addition. — ἄρας τὸν σταυρόν] is wanting in B C D Δ ℵ, 406,
Copt. Vulg. It. Clem. Hilar. Aug. Ambr. Other witnesses have
it before δεῦρο. Bracketed by Lachm. But how easily the
words were passed over, as the parallels have nothing of the
kind! — Ver. 24. τοὺς πεποιθότας ἐπὶ τοῖς χρήμ.] is not found in
B Δ ℵ, Copt. ms. Deleted by Tisch. But if it had been added,
the addition would have been made in accordance with the text
of Matt. or Luke, or according to ver. 23. The omission was
meant in the interest of stricter morality, which regarded
the πεποιθότας, etc., as quite excluded. — Ver. 25. διελθεῖν]
The εἰσελθεῖν, commended by Griesb., adopted by Tisch., has
indeed considerable attestation, but it is from Matt. ix. 24,
and in this case the significant change of the verbs in Mark was
not observed. — Ver. 28. ἠκολουθήσαμεν] Lachm. and Tisch. have
ἠκολουθήκαμεν, following B C D. A mechanical similarity of formation with ἀφήκαμεν, occurring also in some witnesses in
Matthew and Luke. — Ver. 29. Only B Δ ℵ (ἐ. αὐτῷ ὁ Ἰ.), Copt.
have the simple ἔφη ὁ Ἰησ. (Tisch.) instead of ἀποκρ. ὁ Ἰ. εἶπεν,
but they are correct. Comp. on ix. 12, 38. — ἢ πατέρα ἢ μητέρα]
The reverse order is found in B C Δ 106, Copt. Goth. Colb. Brix.
Lachm. and Tisch. It is to be preferred. ἢ πατέρα was in some
cases placed first, in accordance with the natural relation; in
some cases also, in consideration of ver. 30, it was altogether
omitted (D, Cant. Verc. Corb. Harl.). On account of ver. 30
ἢ γυναῖκα has also been omitted (B D Δ ℵ, min. Copt. Arm.
Vulg. It. Or. Lachm. Tisch.). — After καί the second ἕνεκεν is
added by Griesb. and Tisch., following preponderating evidence.
The omission is explained from viii. 35. — Ver. 30. μητέρας]
Lachm. has μητέρα, following A C D, Verss.; the plural was
objectionable. — Ver. 31. The article before the second ἔσχατοι
is indeed deleted by Griesb. Lachm. Tisch.; but following
Matt. xix. 30 it dropped out so easily, and, moreover, it is
found still in such important testimonies, that it must be
restored. — Ver. 32. καὶ ἀκολουθ.] B C* L Δ ℵ, 1, Copt. have οἱ
δὲ ἀκολουθ. This is rightly followed by Ewald, and is now
adopted by Tisch. The οἱ δέ not being understood was set
aside by καί. But the attestation is to be the more regarded
as sufficient, that D K, min. Verc. Ver. Chrys. are not to be
reckoned in favour of the *Recepta*, because they altogether

omit κ. ἀκολ. ἐφοβ., of which omission the homoioteleuton was manifestly the cause. — Ver. 33. The article before γραμμ. (Elz.) is, with Scholz and Tisch. (in opposition to Griesb. Matth. Fritzsche, and Lachm.), to be maintained. The testimony in favour of its omission is not preponderating, and comp. Matt. xx. 18. — Ver. 34. The order ἐμπτύσουσιν αὐτ. κ. μαστιγ. αὐτ. (Lachm. Tisch. Rinck) is found in B C L Δ ℵ, min. vss., including Vulg. and codd. It. But the ἐμπαίξ. and ἐμπτύσ. were considered as *belonging together.* Comp. Luke xviii. 33. — Elz. has τῇ τρίτῃ ἡμέρᾳ; so also Fritzsche, Scholz. But B C D L Δ ℵ, vss. have μετὰ τρεῖς ἡμέρας. Approved by Griesb. Schulz, adopted by Lachm. Tisch. The *Recepta* is to be maintained. See on ix. 31. — Ver. 35. After αἰτήσ. Fritzsche, Lachm. Tisch. have σε, following A B C L Δ ℵ** min. vss. To be adopted. It was easily passed over as being superfluous. D K have it *before* the verb. An incorrect restoration. ℵ* has entirely omitted ὅ ἐάν down to δὸς ἡμῖν. — Ver. 36. ποιῆσαί με ὑμῖν] Lachm. Tisch. have ποιήσω ὑμῖν, which was also approved by Griesb. An alteration in remembrance of passages such as x. 51, xiv. 12, Matt. xx. 32, in which also the bare subjunctive was sometimes completed by ἵνα ποιήσω. — Ver. 38. Instead of καί (in Elz. Scholz, Fritzsche) read, with Rinck, Lachm. and Tisch., ἤ, which Griesb. also approved, following B C* D L Δ ℵ, min. Copt. Arm. Ar. Vulg. It. Or.; καί came from ver. 39. — In ver. 40 also ἤ is to be adopted on almost the same evidence (with Rinck, Lachm., and Tisch.); καί is from Matt. xx. 23. — After εὐων. Elz. has μου, which is deleted on decisive evidence. — Ver. 42. Read καὶ προσκαλ. αὐτοὺς ὁ Ἰησοῦς, with Lachm. and Tisch., following B C D L Δ ℵ, 406, Syr. Copt. codd. It. The *Recepta* is from Matt. xx. 25. — Ver. 43. Instead of the first ἔσται, Lachm. and Tisch. have ἐστίν, which Schulz also approved, in accordance with B C* D L Δ ℵ, Vulg. It. The future came in from Matt., and on account of what follows. — Ver. 44. ὑμῶν γενέσθαι] Lachm. has ἐν ὑμῖν εἶναι, following important evidence, but it is from Matt. xx. 27. — Ver. 46. After τυφλός read with Tisch. προσαίτης, omitting the subsequent προσαιτῶν. So B L Δ Copt. Comp. ℵ, τυφλὸς καὶ προσαίτης. The *Recepta* is from Luke xviii. 35. — Ver. 47. ὁ υἱός] Lachm. has υἱέ, following B C L Δ ℵ, min. From Luke. Comp. ver. 48. — Ver. 49. αὐτὸν φωνηθῆναι] B C L Δ ℵ, min. Copt. have φωνήσατε αὐτόν. So Fritzsche and Tisch. And rightly; the accusative with the infinitive was introduced through the fact of ἐκέλευσεν being written instead of εἶπεν, after Luke xviii. 40 (so still Ev. 48, It. Vulg.), and remained, after εἶπεν was restored, the more easily because Luke has it also.

— ἔγειρε] See on ii. 9. — Ver. 50. ἀναστάς] Lachm. and Tisch.
have ἀναπηδήσας, according to B D L Δ ℵ, min. vss. (including
Vulg. It.) Or. The *Recepta* is a "scriptorum jejunitas" that
mistakes the peculiarity of Mark (Tisch.). — Ver. 51. The form
ῥαββουνί (Elz. ῥαββονί) has decisive evidence. — Ver. 52. Instead
of τῷ Ἰησοῦ (Elz., Scholz, Rinck), A B C D L Δ ℵ have αὐτῷ
(Tisch.), which attestation is decisive.

Vv. 1–9. See on Matt. xix. 1–8. — κἀκεῖθεν] points back
to ix. 33. — καὶ πέραν τοῦ Ἰορδάνου] see the critical remarks.
He came to the borders of Judaea, *and that* (see Fritzsche,
Quaest. Luc. p. 9 ff.; Hartung, *Partikell.* I. p. 145) *on the
further side of Jordan*, "ipsa Samaria ad dextram relicta"
(Beza). At Jericho He came again to this side, ver. 46.
See, moreover, on Matt. xix. 1. — καὶ συμπορ. κ.τ.λ.] *And
there gather together to Him again crowds of people.* πάλιν,
for previously, at ix. 30 ff., He had withdrawn Himself from
the people. — Ver. 2. Mark has not the properly *tempting
element* in the question, but it is found in Matt.: κατὰ
πᾶσαν αἰτίαν (see on Matt. xix. 3). That this element was
not also preserved in *the* tradition which Mark here follows,
may very naturally be explained from the *reply* of Jesus,
which ran *unconditionally* (even according to Matt. vv. 4–6).
Mark therefore has not the *original* form of the question
(Bleek, Weiss, Holtzmann, Schenkel, Harless, *Ehescheid.* p.
30), nor does he make the question be put more *captiously*
(Fritzsche), nor has he made use of Matthew incorrectly, or
with alterations consonant to his own reflection (Saunier,
Baur), because the Jewish points of dispute as to divorce were
to him indifferent (Köstlin); but he follows a defective tradition, which in this particular is completed and corrected in
Matthew. De Wette's conjecture is arbitrary, that Mark
presupposes that the Pharisees had already heard of the view
of Jesus on divorce, and wished to induce Him to a *renewed*
declaration on the subject. The perilous element of the
question does not turn on the divorce of *Herod* (Ewald, Lange).
See on Matthew. — Ver. 3. Here also the tradition, which
Mark follows, deviates from Matthew, who represents that
the commandment of Moses is brought into question not by

Jesus, but by the Pharisees, and that as an objection against the answer of Jesus. But it is more natural and more forcible that the reply of Jesus should start immediately from Deut. xxiv. 1, and should first elicit this Mosaic ἐντολή—on the right estimation of which depended the point at issue—from the mouth of the questioners themselves, in order thereupon to attach to it what follows. — Ver. 4. ἐπέτρεψε] emphatically prefixed (see the critical remarks): Moses *permitted*, in saying which their ἔξεστιν, ver. 2, is present to their minds. See, moreover, on Matt. v. 31. They prudently refrain from saying ἐνετείλατο. — Ver. 5. τ. ἐντολὴν ταύτ.] the commandment of the putting forth a writing of divorcement. — Ver. 6. The *subject* (as ὁ Θεός is not genuine) is to be taken out of κτίσεως (ὁ κτιστής). See Kühner, II. p. 36, 4. — Ver. 7. Christ makes Adam's words at Gen. ii. 44 *His own*. It is otherwise, but less directly and concisely, given in Matthew. — ἔνεκεν τούτου] because God created men as male and female—in order to correspond with this arrangement of the Creator. — The *futures* indicate what *will happen* in cases of marrying according to God's ordinance.

Vv. 10–12. See on Matt. xix. 9. The two evangelists differ from one another here in respect of the place, of the persons to whom Jesus is speaking, and partially of the contents of what He says. Certainly Matthew has furnished the original shape of the matter, since what Mark makes Jesus say only in the house and merely to His disciples (ver. 11 with the not original amplification of ver. 12) is withal an essential element of the reply to the Pharisees, and does not bear the character of a special private instruction, whereas the private communication to the disciples, Matt. xix. 10–12, which as such is just as appropriate as it is original, is indeed "the crown of the whole" (Ewald). — εἰς τὴν οἰκίαν] *having come into the house* (in which at that time they were lodging). The same brevity of expression occurs at xiii. 9. — πάλιν οἱ μαθηταί] *again the disciples*, as previously the Pharisees. — περὶ τούτου] (see the critical remarks): *upon this subject.* — Ver. 11. ἐπ᾽ αὐτήν] *in reference to her*, the woman that is put away.[1] — Mark has not the μὴ ἐπὶ πορνείᾳ (Matt.), which makes no essential difference, as this ground of divorce is obvious of itself as such. See on Matt. v. 32. Comp. also Hofmann, *Schriftbew.* II. 2, p. 410. — Ver. 12. καὶ ἐὰν γυνὴ ἀπολύσῃ κ.τ.λ.] Matthew has quite a different saying. The narrative of Mark is certainly not original (in opposition to Schenkel), but puts into the mouth of Jesus what was the custom among the *Greeks* and *Romans*, namely, that the wife also might be the divorcing party, and very often actually was so (see on 1 Cor. vii. 13, and Wetstein *in loc.*; also Danz in Meuschen, *N. T. ex Talm. ill.* p. 680 ff.), which was not competent to the *Jewish* wife (Deut. xxiv. 1; Josephus, *Antt.* xv. 7. 10), for the instances of *Michal* (1 Sam. xxv. 41), of *Herodias* (Matt. xiv. 4 f.), and of *Salome* (Josephus, *Antt.* xv. 7. 10) are abnormal in respect of their rank; and the cases in which, according to the Rabbins, the wife might require that the husband should give her a writing of divorcement (see Saalschütz, *Mos. R.* p. 806 f.) do not belong to the question here, where the wife herself is the party who puts away. The proposition in the passage before us is derived from an *Hellenic* amplification of the tradition,[2] which, however, in Matthew is again excluded. Comp. Harless, p. 25 f. According to Kuinoel (comp. Lange), Jesus purposed to give to the apostles, as future teachers of the *Gentiles*, the instruction requisite for judging in such a case. But He must have *said* as much, as the *question* had reference to the *Jewish* relation of divorce. — μοιχᾶται] the subject is the *woman* (comp. v. 11), not the ἄλλος. Moreover, Grotius appropriately says: "Mulier ergo, cum domina sui non sit . . . omnino adulterium committit, non interpretatione aliqua aut per consequentiam, sed directe. Ideo non debuit hic addi ἐπ᾽ αὐτόν."

[1] Observe that Jesus here of necessity presupposes the acknowledgment of the principle of *monogamy*. Theophylact and many others, including Lange, Ewald, and Bleek, have erroneously referred αὐτήν to the *second* wife. Erasmus appropriately says: "in injuriam illius." Comp. Calvin and Bengel: "in illam." It is only thus that its emphatic bearing is brought out; the marrying of the *second* wife makes him an adulterer towards the *first*.

[2] According to Baur, from a *reflection* of Mark on the equal rights of the two sexes.

Vv. 13–16. See on Matt. xix. 13–15, who gives the narrative only by way of extract. Comp. Luke xviii. 15–17. — ἅψεται] From the mere *touch* on the part of the holy man, who assuredly was also known as a friend of children, they hoped to derive blessing for their children. So too Luke. It is otherwise in Matthew, in whose account, instead of the *touch*, there is already introduced here the more definite *laying on of hands*, which was performed by Jesus at ver. 16. — Ver. 14. ἠγανάκτησε] " propter impedimentum amori suo a discipulis oblatum " (Bengel). — Ver. 15 is also adopted by Luke xviii. 17, but not by the abbreviating Matthew. *Whosoever shall not have received the kingdom of the Messiah as a child, i.e.* in the moral condition, which resembles the innocence of childhood (comp. Matt. xviii. 3); Theophylact appropriately says: τῶν ἐχόντων ἐξ ἀσκήσεως τὴν ἀκακίαν, ἣν τὰ παιδία ἔχουσιν ἀπὸ φύσεως. — In δέξηται the kingdom (which the coming Messiah establishes) is conceived as *coming* (ix. 1 ; Matt. vi. 10 ; Luke xvii. 20, *al.*). It is erroneous to explain the βασιλ. τ. Θεοῦ as *the preaching* of the kingdom (Theophylact, Euthymius Zigabenus, Kuinoel, and many others). — Ver. 16. ἐναγκαλ.] as at ix. 36. — κατηυλόγ.] only occurs in this place in the New Testament; it is stronger than the simple form, Plut. *Amator.* 4 ; Tob. xi. 1, 17. It expresses here the *earnestness* of His interest. How *much more* did Christ do than was asked of Him !

Vv. 17–27. See on Matt. xix. 16–26. Comp. Luke xviii. 18–27. As well in the question at ver. 17, and in the answer of Jesus vv. 18, 19, as also in the account of the address to the disciples ver. 23 f., and in several little peculiar traits, the narrative of Mark is more concrete and more direct. — εἰς ὁδόν] out of the house, ver. 10, in order to prosecute His journey, ver. 32. — γονυπετ.] not inappropriate (de Wette), but, in connection with προσδραμών, representing the earnestness of the inquiry ; both words are peculiar to the graphic Mark. With an accusative, as at i. 40. See on Matt. xvii. 14. — Ver. 18. The variation from Matthew is so far unessential, as in the latter also the predicate ἀγαθός is attributed to God only. But in Matthew it has become necessary to give to it, in the relation to the question, a turn which betrays more a later moulding under reflection[1] than the simple and direct primitive form, which we still find in Mark and Luke. — τί με λέγεις ἀγαθόν; οὐδεὶς κ.τ.λ.] Ingeniously and clearly Jesus makes use of the address διδάσκαλε ἀγαθέ, in order to direct the questioner to the highest moral Ideal, in whose commands is given the solution of the question (ver. 19). He did this in such a manner as *to turn aside from Himself and to ascribe to God only* the predicate ἀγαθός, which had been used by the young man in the customary meaning of holding one in esteem (*excellent teacher*, Plat. *Men.* p. 93 C; comp. the familiar Attic ὦ ἀγαθέ or ὦ 'γαθέ; and see Dorvill. *ad Charit.* p. 642), but is taken up by Jesus in the eminent and absolute sense. "Thou art wrong in calling me good; this predicate, in its complete conception, belongs to none save One,—that is, God." Comp. Ch. F. Fritzsche in Fritzschior. *Opusc.* p. 78 ff. This declaration, however, is no evidence against the *sinlessness* of Jesus; rather it is the true expression of the necessary moral distance, which the human consciousness— even the sinless consciousness, as being human—recognises between itself and the absolute perfection of God.[2] For the human sinlessness is of necessity relative, and even in the case of Jesus was conditioned by the divine-human development that was subject to growth (Luke ii. 52; Heb. v. 8; Luke iv. 13, xxii. 28; comp. Ullmann in the *Stud. u. Krit.* 1842, p. 700); the absolute being-good, that excludes all having become and becoming so, pertains only to God, who is "verae bonitatis canon et archetypus" (Beza). Even the man Jesus had to wrestle until He attained the victory and peace

---

[1] This primitive form is alleged, indeed, by Hilgenfeld (in the *theol. Jahrb.* 1857, p. 414 ff. ; comp. in his *Zeitschr.* 1863, p. 364 f.) to have been no longer preserved even in Mark and Luke. He finds it rather in the form of the words which has been preserved in Justin, *c. Tryph.* 101, and among the Marcosians (similarly in Marcion): τί με λέγ. ἀγαθόν; εἷς ἐστὶν ἀγαθὸς, ὁ πατήρ μου, ὁ ἐν τοῖς οὐρανοῖς ; and holds these words to have been altered, in order to deprive them of their probative force in favour of the Gnostic distinction between the perfect God and the imperfect Creator of the world. But the Gnostic exegesis might find this probative force just as suitably in our form of the text (in behalf of which Justin, *Apolog.* i. 16, testifies), if it laid stress, in the εἷς ὁ Θεός, on the reference to the supreme God, the Father of Christ. See also on Luke xviii. 19.

[2] Comp. Dorner, *Jesu sündlose Vollkommenh.* p. 14.

of the cross.[1] This is overlooked from dogmatic misunderstanding in the often attempted (see as early as Augustine,
c. Maxim. iii. 23 ; Ambros. de fide, ii. 1) and variously-turned
makeshift (see Theophylact, Erasmus, Bengel, Olshausen,
Ebrard ; comp. also Lange, II. 2, p. 1106 f.), that Jesus rejected
that predicate only from the standpoint of the questioner (if
thou regardest me as only a human teacher, then thou art
wrong in calling me good, etc.). Wimmer (in the Stud. u.
Krit. 1845, p. 115 ff.) thinks that the young man had been
ambitious, had said διδάσκαλε ἀγαθέ as captatio benevolentiae,
and presupposed the existence of ambition also in Jesus ; that,
therefore, Jesus wished to point his attention by the τί με
λέγεις ἀγαθόν to his fault, and by the οὐδεὶς ἀγαθὸς κ.τ.λ. to
bring to his knowledge the unique condition of all being-good,
in the sense : "Nobody is to be called good, if the only God
be not called good, i.e. if He be not assumed and posited as
the only condition of all goodness." In this explanation the
premisses are imported, and the interpretation itself is incorrect;
since with οὐδεὶς κ.τ.λ., λέγεται cannot be supplied, but only
ἐστί, as it so frequently is in general propositions (Kühner, II.
p. 40), and since οὐδεὶς εἰ μή means nothing else than nemo
nisi, i.e. according to the sense, no one except (Klotz, ad Devar.
p. 524). — Ver. 19. The certainly original position of the
μὴ φονεύσ. is to be regarded as having at that time become
traditional. Comp. Weizsäcker, p. 356. — μὴ ἀποστερ.] is not
a renewed expression of the seventh commandment (Heupel,
Fritzsche), against which may be urged its position, as well as
the unsuitableness of adducing it twice ; neither is it an expression of the tenth commandment, as far as the coveting
applies to the plundering another of his property (Bengel,
Wetstein, Olshausen, de Wette), against which may be urged
the meaning of the word, which, moreover, does not permit us
to think of a comprehension of all the previous commands (Beza,
Lange) ; but it applies to Deut. xxiv. 14 (οὐκ ἀποστερήσεις
μισθὸν πένητος, where the Roman edition has οὐκ ἀπαδικήσεις
μ. π.), to which also Mal. iii. 3, Ecclus. iv. 1, refer. Comp.
also LXX. Ex. xxi. 10. Jesus, however, quotes the originally

[1] Comp. Keim, geschichil. Chr. p. 39 ff., and, moreover, at p. 108 ff.

special command according to its *moral universality: thou shalt
not withhold.* According to Kuinoel, He is thinking of Lev.
xix. 13 (οὐκ ἀδικήσεις κ.τ.λ.), with which, however, the characteristic ἀποστερήσῃς is not in accordance. Least of all can it
be taken together with τίμα κ.τ.λ., so that it would be the pro·
hibitory aspect of the commanding τίμα κ.τ.λ. (so Hofmann,
Schriftbew. II. 2, p. 391), against which may be decisively urged
the similarity of form to the preceding *independent* commands,
as well as the hallowed and just as *independent* τίμα κ.τ.λ.; moreover, Mark must have written μὴ ἀποστερ. τιμὴν τὸν πατέρα
κ.τ.λ., in order to be understood. In Matthew this command
does not appear; while, on the other hand, he has the ἀγαπήσεις τὸν πλησίον κ.τ.λ., which is wanting in Mark and Luke.
These are various forms of the tradition. But since ἀγαπήσεις
κ.τ.λ. (which also occurred in the Gospel of the Hebrews) is
most appropriate and characteristic, and the μὴ ἀποστερήσῃς is so peculiar that it could hardly have been added as
an appendix to the tradition, Ewald's conjecture (*Jahrb.* I.
p. 132) that the original *number* of these commandments was
seven is not improbable. That which did not occur in the
Decalogue was more easily omitted than (in opposition to
Weizsäcker) added. — Ver. 20. διδάσκαλε] not ἀγαθέ again.
— Ver. 21. ἠγάπησεν αὐτόν] means nothing else than: He
loved him, felt a love of esteem (*dilectio*) for him, *conceived an
affection for him,* which impression He derived from the
ἐμβλέπειν αὐτῷ. He read at once in his countenance genuine
anxiety and effort for everlasting salvation, and at the same
time fervid confidence in Himself. The conception of *meritum
de congruo* is altogether foreign to the passage. Grotius appropriately remarks: "amat Christus non virtutes tantum, sed et
semina virtutum, suo tamen gradu." The explanation: *blandis
eum compellavit verbis* (Casaubon, Wolf, Grotius, Wetstein, Kuinoel, Vater, Fritzsche, and others), is founded merely on the
passage in Homer, *Od.* xxiii. 214, where, nevertheless, it is to
be explained likewise as *to love.*[1] — ἕν σοι ὑστερεῖ] see on John

---

[1] Penelope in this passage says to her husband: be not angry that *I loved thee
not thus* (ὧδ᾽ ἀγάπησα) as soon as I saw thee,—namely, thus as *I do now,* when
I have embraced thee, etc., v. 207 f.

ii. 2. Yet, instead of σοι, according to B C M D ℵ, min., σε
is, with Tischendorf, to be read. Comp. Ps. xxiii. 1. The σοι
occurred more readily (comp. Luke) to the transcribers. — ἄρας
τ. σταυρ.] Matt. xvi. 24; Mark viii. 34. It *completes* the
weighty demand of that which he still lacks for the attainment
of salvation; which demand, however, instead of bringing
salutarily to his knowledge the relation of his own inward life
to the divine law, was the rock on which he made shipwreck.
— Ver. 22. στυγνάσας] *having become sullen, out of humour.*
Except in the Schol. *Aesch. Pers.* 470, and Matt. xvi. 3, the verb
only occurs again in the LXX. at Ezek. xxvii. 35, xxviii. 19,
xxxii. 10. — ἦν γὰρ ἔχων] *for he was in possession* of much
wealth. — Ver. 23. On the significant and solemn περιβλέπειν,
comp. iii. 5, 34; Luke vi. 10. Comp. also ἐμβλέψας, vv. 21,
27. — οἱ τὰ χρήματα ἔχοντες] The article τά is to be explained
summarily. The possessions are regarded as an existing whole,
which is possessed by the class of the wealthy. — Ver. 24. The
repetition of the utterance of Jesus is touched with emotion
(τέκνα) and milder (τοὺς πεποιθότας κ.τ.λ.), but then, at ver. 25,
again declaring the state of the case with decision and with
enhanced energy,—an alternation of feeling, which is to be
acknowledged (in opposition to Fritzsche), and which involves
so much of what is peculiar and psychologically true, that even
in τοὺς πεποιθότας κ.τ.λ. there is not to be found a *modification* by tradition interpreting the matter in an *anti-Ebionitic*
sense, or a *mitigation* found to be necessary in a *subsequent*
age (Baur, Köstlin, p. 329, Hilgenfeld, Holtzmann). These
words, which are intended to disclose the moral ground of the
case as it stands, belong, in fact, essentially to the scene preserved by Mark in its original form. — Ver. 25. διὰ τῆς τρυμαλ.
κ.τ.λ.] *through the eye of the needle.* The two articles are *generic;*
see Bernhardy, p. 315. Observe also the vivid change : *to go
through . . . to enter into.* — Ver. 26. καί] at the beginning of
the question : " cum vi auctiva ita ponitur, ut is, qui interrogat,
cum admiratione quadam alterius orationem excipere ex eaque
conclusionem ducere significetur, qua alterius sententia con-
futetur." Kühner, *ad Xen. Mem.* i. 3. 10 ; Hartung, *Partikell.*
I. p. 146 f. Comp. John ix. 36, xiv. 22.

Vv. 28–31. See on Matt. xix. 27–30 ; Luke xviii. 28–30.
Matthew is in part more complete (ver. 28 coming certainly
under this description), in part abridging (ver. 29), but, even
with this abridgment, more original. See on Matt. xix. 29.
— ἤρξατο] "spe ex verbis salvatoris concepta," Bengel. —
The question in Matthew, τί ἄρα ἔσται ἡμ., is obvious of
itself, even although unexpressed (not omitted by Mark in the
Petrine interest, as Hilgenfeld thinks), and Jesus understood
it. — Ver. 29 f. The logical link of the two clauses is : *No
one has forsaken*, etc., *if he shall not have* (at some time)
received, i.e. if the latter event does not occur, the former has
not taken place ; the hundredfold compensation is so certain,
that its non - occurrence would presuppose the not having
forsaken. The association of thought in iv. 22 (not in Matt.
xxvi. 42) is altogether similar. Instead of the ἤ, there is introduced in the second half of the clause καί ; which is : *and
respectively*. The *principle of division* of ver. 30 is : He is
(1) to receive a hundredfold now, in the period prior to the
manifestation of the Messiah, namely, a hundred times as
many houses, brothers, etc. ; and (2) to receive in the
coming period (" jam in adventu est," Bengel), after the
Parousia, the everlasting life of the Messiah's kingdom. — The
plurals, which express the number a hundred, plainly show
that the promised compensation in the καιρὸς οὗτος is not to
be understood literally, but generally, of *very abundant compensation*. Nevertheless, the delicate feeling of Jesus has not
said γυναῖκας also. So much the more clumsy was Julian's
scoff (see Theophylact) that the Christians were, moreover,
to receive a hundred wives ! The promise was *realized*, in
respect of the καιρὸς οὗτος, by the reciprocal *manifestations
of love*,[1] and by the wealth in *spiritual* possessions, 2 Cor.
vi. 8–10 ; by which passage is illustrated, at the same time,
in a noble example, the μετὰ διωγμῶν (comp. Matt. v. 10 ff.,

---

[1] Comp. Luther's gloss: "He who believeth must suffer persecution, and
stake everything upon his faith. Nevertheless he has enough ; whithersoever
he comes, he finds father, mother, brethren, possessions more than ever he
could forsake." See, *e.g.*, on μητέρας, Rom. xvi. 13 ; on τέκνα, 1 Cor. iv. 14 ff. ;
on ἀδελφούς, all the Epistles of the New Testament and the Acts of the Apostles
(also ii. 44).

x. 23, xiii. 21, xxiii. 34). The latter does not mean: *after persecutions* (Heinsius conjectured μετὰ διωγμόν, as also a few min. read), but: *inter persecutiones* (in the midst of persecutions, where one "omnium auxilio destitui videtur," Jansen), designating the *accompanying* circumstances (Bernhardy, p. 255), the shadow of which *makes prominent* the light of the promise. — Ver. 31. *But many*—so independent is the greater or lower reception of reward in the life eternal of the earlier or later coming to me—*many that are first shall be last, and they that are last* shall in many cases *be first* (see on Matt. xix. 30, xx. 16); so that the one shall be equalized with the other in respect of the measuring out of the degree of reward. A doctrine assuredly, which, after the general promise of the great recompense in ver. 29 f., was quite in its place to furnish a wholesome check to the ebullition of greediness for reward in the question of the disciples, ver. 28 (for the *disciples*, doubtless, belonged to the πρῶτοι). There is therefore the less reason to attribute, with Weiss, a different meaning to the utterance in Mark from that which it has in Matthew.

Vv. 32–34. See on Matt. xx. 17–19. Comp. Luke xviii. 31–33. Mark is more detailed and more characteristic than Matthew. — ἦσαν δὲ ἐν τῇ ὁδῷ] The occurrence with the rich young man had happened, *while they went out* εἰς ὁδόν, ver. 17 ; now they were *on the way* (ἀναβαίνοντες is not to be taken with ἦσαν). Jesus moves on before " more intrepidi ducis" (Grotius), and the disciples *were amazed ; but they who followed were afraid*,[1] for the foreboding of a serious and grave future had taken hold of them, and they beheld Him thus incessantly *going*, and themselves *being led*, to meet it ! See vv. 24–26, the μετὰ διωγμ., ver. 30, and the declaration, ver. 31. Comp. John xi. 7–16. — πάλιν] refers neither to xi. 31 (de Wette), where there is nothing said of any παραλαμβάνειν, nor to ix. 35 (Fritzsche), where the ἐφώνησε

---

[1] According to the reading οἱ δὲ ἀκολ. ἐφοβοῦντο ; see the critical remarks. The matter, namely, is to be conceived in this way, that the majority of the disciples *stayed behind* on the way in perplexity, but those among them who *followed* Jesus as He went forward did so only *fearfully*. As to this use of οἱ δέ, see on Matt. xxviii. 17.

τοὺς δώδεκα, which happened *in the house*, is withal something entirely different; but to—what is just related—the
partial separation of Jesus from His disciples on the way,
after they had previously gone *together*. Only in part had
they followed Him fearfully; most of them had remained
behind on the way amazed; He now made a pause, and
took again to Himself all the Twelve (hence in this place
there is put not merely αὐτούς, but τοὺς δώδεκα). — ἤρξατο]
so that He broke the previous silence. — Ver. 34. The *Gentiles*
are the subject of ἐμπαίξ. as far as ἀποκτ. (comp. Matthew).
Instead of ἀποκτενοῦσιν Matthew has the definite, but certainly later, *crucifying*.

Vv. 35-45. See on Matt. xx. 20-28. Luke has not this
scene. — As to the variation from Matt. xx. 20 f., where the
peculiar putting forward of the mother is (in opposition to
Holtzmann, Weizsäcker, and others) to be regarded as the
historically correct form, see on Matthew. — θέλομεν, ἵνα] as
at vi. 25 ; John xvii. 24 ; and comp. on Luke vi. 35. — Ver. 37.
ἐν τῇ δόξῃ σου] not : *when thou hast attained to Thy glory* (de
Wette), but : *in Thy glory*, which will surround us then, when
we sit so near to Thee. — Ver. 38. ἤ] *or*, in other words. —
The *presents* πίνω and βαπτίζομαι *picture the matter as being
realized*. The *cup* and *baptism* of Jesus represent *martyrdom*.
In the case of the figure of *baptism*, however (which latter
Matthew by way of abridgment omits ; it is alleged by Baur
that Mark has taken it from Luke xii. 50), the point of the
similitude lies in the being *submerged*, not in the *purification*
(forgiveness of sins), as the Fathers have apprehended the
baptism of blood (see Suicer, I. p. 627), which is not appropriate
to *Jesus*. Comp. the classical use of καταδύειν and βαπτίζειν,
to plunge (*immergere*) into sufferings, sorrows, and the like
(Xen. *Cyrop.* vi. 1. 37 ; Wesseling, *ad Diod.* I. p. 433). On
the construction, comp. Ael. *H. A.* iii. 42 : ὁ πορφυρίων
λούεται τὸ τῶν περιστερῶν λουτρόν, *al.* See in general,
Lobeck, *Paralip.* p. 520. — Ver. 40. ἤ] *or else* on the left,
not put inappropriately (Fritzsche) ; the disciples had desired
both places of honour, and therefore Jesus now says that *none*
depends on Him, whether the sitting be on the right hand *or*

else on the left. — ἀλλ᾽ οἷς ἡτοίμασται] Matthew has added the correctly explanatory amplification: ὑπὸ τοῦ πατρός μου. — Ver. 41. ἤρξαντο] Jesus, namely, at once appeased their indignation. — Ver. 42. οἱ δοκοῦντες ἄρχειν] peculiar to Mark and original, denoting the *essential* basis of the Gentile rule, — the *having the repute of* rulers, — not equivalent to οἱ ἄρχοντες (Gataker, Raphel, Homberg, Kypke, Rosenmüller, and many more), but: "qui censentur imperare, *i.e.* quos gentes habent et agnoscunt, quorum imperio pareant" (Beza, comp. Casaubon and Grotius). Comp. Gal. ii. 9; Winer, p. 540 [E. T. 766]; Möller, *neue Ansichten*, p. 158 ff., who, however, as Fritzsche also, explains: *who imagine themselves to rule*, which in itself (as τῶν ἐθνῶν refers to the *Gentiles*, whose rulers were no shadow-kings) and in respect of the context (which requires the general idea of *rulers*) is unsuitable. Compare, moreover, the close echo of the passage before us in Luke xxii. 25 from tradition. — Ver. 43. The reading ἐστίν is as little inappropriate (in opposition to Fritzsche) as Matt. xx. 26. — Ver. 45. καὶ γάρ] *for even.* As the master, so the disciples, Rom. xv. 3.

Vv. 46–52. See on Matt. xx. 29–34. Comp. Luke xviii. 35–43. Matthew has abridged the narrative, and, following a later tradition (comp. on Matt. viii. 28), doubled the persons. Only Mark has the *name* of the blind man, which is not interpolated (Wilke), and certainly is from trustworthy tradition. — Βαρτίμαιος] The patronymic בַּר טִמְאַי, as was often the case (comp. Βαρθολομαῖος, Βαριησοῦς, Βαρσαββᾶς), had become altogether a proper name, so that Mark even expressly prefixes to it ὁ υἱὸς Τιμαίου, which, however, may be accounted for by the fact of Timaeus being *well known*, possibly as having become a *Christian* of note. — τυφλὸς προσαίτης] (see the critical remarks): *a blind beggar.* — Ver. 47. "Magna fides, quod caecus filium Davidis appellat, quem ei Nazaraeum praedicabat populus," Bengel. — Ver. 49. θάρσει, ἔγειρε, φωνεῖ σε] a hasty *asyndeton.* Comp. Nägelsbach, *Anm. z. Ilias*, ed. 3, p. 80. — Ver. 50. ἀποβαλ. τὸ ἱμάτ.] depicts the joyous eagerness, with which also the ἀναπηδήσας is in keeping (see the critical remarks). Comp.

Hom. *Il.* ii. 183 : βῆ δὲ θέειν, ἀπὸ δὲ χλαῖναν βάλε, Acts
iii. 8 ; Dem. 403, 5. — Ver. 51. ῥαββουνί] רַבּוֹנִי, usually :
domine mi. See Buxtorf, *Lex. Talm.* p. 2179. Yet the
yod, as in רבי, may also be only *paragogic* (Drusius, Michaelis,
Fritzsche) ; and this latter view is precisely on account of
the analogy of רבי more probable, and is confirmed by the
interpretation διδάσκαλε in John xx. 16. The form רבוני is,
we may add, more respectful than רבי. Comp. Drusius.

CHAPTER XI.

VER. 1. Lachm. and Tisch. read (instead of ε.ς Βηθφ. κ. Βηθ.) merely καὶ εἰς Βηθανίαν; but the evidence is not sufficient (D, Vulg. codd. It. Or. (twice) Jer.) to entitle us to derive the *Recepta* from Luke xix. 29. An old clerical error, occasioned by the similar beginnings of the two local names; and καί was inserted to connect them. C ℵ have εἰς Βηθφ. κ. εἰς Βηθ. If this were the original form, the omission would occur still more easily. — The form 'Ιεροσόλυμα is to be adopted, with Fritzsche, Lachm. and Tisch., following B C D L Δ ℵ, min. Sahid. Or. 'Ιερουσαλήμ does not occur elsewhere in Mark, and only in Matthew at xxiii. 37 (see *in loc.*); in Luke it is the usual form. — ἀποστέλλει] Lachm. reads ἀπέστειλεν, in opposition to decisive evidence. It is from the parallels. — Ver. 2. οὐδείς] Lachm. has οὐδεὶς οὔπω; Fritzsche: οὐδέπω οὐδείς. The latter is much too weakly attested. The former has considerable attestation, but with a different position of the οὔπω (Tisch. οὐδ. ἀνθρ. οὔπω), instead of which A has πώποτε (from Luke). The *Recepta* is to be defended; the idea expressed in *adhuc* was very variously brought in. — λύσαντες αὐτὸν ἀγάγετε] B C L Δ ℵ, Copt. Sahid. Vulg. It. Or. have λύσατε αὐτὸν καὶ φέρετε. Approved by Griesb., adopted by Tisch. (Lachm. has λύσατε αὐτ. κ. ἀγάγετε). Rightly; the *Recepta* is from Luke xix. 30; comp. Matt. xxi. 2, whence also originated the reading of Lachm. — Ver. 3. ἀποστέλλει] Elz. Fritzsche have ἀποστελεῖ, in opposition to decisive evidence. Comp. on Matt. xxi. 3. — πάλιν, which B C* D L Δ ℵ, min. Verc. Colb. Or. (twice) read, although it is adopted by Tisch., is an addition from misunderstanding; the reader probably being misled by ὧδε, and taking the words as being still a portion of what was to be said by the disciples. — Ver. 4. The article before πῶλον (Elz.) is, in accordance with decisive evidence, deleted. — Ver. 6. Instead of εἶπεν (so also Lachm. and Tisch.) Elz. Scholz have ἐνετείλατο. But εἶπεν is so weightily attested by B C L Δ ℵ, min. Or. Copt. Aeth. Sahid. Arm. Or. that ἐνετείλατο appears a gloss. D has εἰρήκει, which likewise tells in favour of εἶπεν, and is only a change into the pluperfect. — Ver. 7.

ἤγαγον] B L Δ ℵ** Or. have φέρουσιν; approved by Griesb.,
adopted by Tisch. The *Recepta* is from the parallel passages. —
ἐπέβαλον] B C D L Δ ℵ, min. Vulg. Cant. Ver. Corb. Vind. Or.
have ἐπιβάλλουσιν. Adopted by Griesb. Fritzsche, Lachm. Tisch.
The *Recepta* was derived from the reading ἤγαγον. — ἐπ᾽ αὐτῷ]
B C D L Δ ℵ, min. have ἐπ᾽ αὐτόν, which Griesb. approved,
Fritzsche, Lachm. Tisch. adopted. The *Recepta* is a mechanical
repetition of the previous αὐτῷ. — Ver. 8. δένδρων] B C L Δ ℵ,
Syr. p. (in the margin) Or. Sahid. have ἀγρῶν, which Fritzsche
and Tisch. have rightly adopted. With Tisch., however,
instead of the whole passage ἔκοπτον . . . ὁδόν we must read briefly
and simply: κόψαντες ἐκ τῶν ἀγρῶν. The *Recepta* is an expansion
from Matthew, whence also came λέγοντες in ver. 9. This is wanting in B C L Δ ℵ, min. Copt. Sahid. Colb. Corb. Or., is regarded
as suspicious by Griesb. and Lachm., and is deleted by Tisch. —
Ver. 10. After βασιλεία Elz. has ἐν ὀνόματι κυρίου, against preponderating evidence. An awkward repetition from ver. 9. —
Ver. 11. καὶ εἰς τ. ἱερόν] καί is wanting in B C L M Δ ℵ, min.
Syr. Arr. Copt. Perss. Arm. Vulg. It. Or. Lachm. Tisch.; inserted by way of connection. — Ver. 13. Τὸ μακρόθεν, with Griesb.,
Fritzsche, Lachm. Scholz, Tisch., there is to be added ἀπό, upon
preponderating evidence. Comp. v. 6. — Ver. 14. The arrange-
ment εἰς τ. αἱ. ἐκ. σ., as well as μηδείς (instead of οὐδείς in Elz.), is
decisively attested. — Ver. 17. λέγων αὐτοῖς] B C L Δ ℵ, min.
Copt. have καὶ ἔλεγεν αὐτοῖς. So Tisch. The *Recepta* is from
Luke. — ἐποιήσατε] B L Δ, Or. have πεποιήκατε. Adopted by
Tisch. The aorist, in itself more familiar, came from Luke.
Comp. on Matt. xxi. 13. — Ver. 18. The arrangement οἱ
ἀρχιερεῖς κ. οἱ γραμμ. is decisively attested (Fritzsche, Lachm.
Tisch.), as is also the subjunctive ἀπολέσωσιν (Fritzsche, Lachm.
Tisch.) instead of ἀπολέσουσιν. — Ver. 19. ὅτε] B C K L Δ ℵ, min.
have ὅταν. Wrongly adopted by Tisch. Comp. his *Proleg.*
p. lvii. Unsuitable (otherwise at iii. 11), and to be regarded
as an ancient clerical error. — ἐξεπορεύετο] A B K M Δ, min.
vss. have ἐξεπορεύοντο. So Fritzsche, Lachm. But how natural
it was here to bring in the same number, as in the case of
παραπορ., ver. 20! — Ver. 20. The order πρωΐ παραπορ. is not
necessary (in opposition to Fritzsche), but suggested itself most
naturally after ver. 19, on which account, however, παραπορ.
πρωΐ (B C D L Δ ℵ, min. Ver. Cant.) is precisely to be preferred, with Lachm. and Tisch. — Ver. 23. γάρ] is wanting in
B D U ℵ, min. vss. Deleted by Lachm. and Tisch. A connective addition. — λέγει] Lachm. and Tisch. have λαλεῖ, following B L N Δ ℵ, min.; the more familiar λέγ. slipped in

involuntarily. — ὃ ἐὰν εἴπῃ] is wanting in B C D L Δ ℵ, min. Copt. Vulg. It. Deleted by Fritzsche and Tisch., condemned also by Griesb. A confusing gloss, following the foregoing ὃς ἂν εἴπῃ. — Ver. 24. ἄν] is wanting in B C D L Δ ℵ, min. An addition from Matt. xxi. 22. — προσευχόμενοι] B C D L Δ ℵ, Cant. Verc. Colb. Corb. Cypr. have προσεύχεσθε καί. So Lachm. and Tisch. The participle is an emendation, because it was thought necessary (comp. Matt. xxi. 22) to make ὅσα dependent on αἰτεῖσθε. — λαμβάνετε] B C L Δ ℵ, Copt. have ἐλάβετε. Commended by Griesb., adopted by Lachm. and Tisch. Rightly ; the aorist was not understood, and was changed partly into the present, partly into the future (D). — Ver. 25. στήκητε] A C D H L M, min. have στήκετε. So Lachm. and Tisch. The *Recepta* is an emendation introduced from ignorance. — Ver. 26.[1]] is wanting in B L S Δ ℵ, min. Copt. Arm. codd. It. Suspected by Fritzsche, deleted by Tisch. But the evidence in favour of omission is the less sufficient for its condemnation, that the words do not closely agree with Matt. vi. 15, from which place they are said to have come in, but present deviations which are in no wise to be attributed to the mechanical transcribers. The omission is explained from the homoeoteleuton of vv. 25 and 26. But what M., min. further add after ver. 26 is an interpolation from Matt. vii. 7, 8. — Ver. 28. Instead of καὶ τίς read, with Tisch., ἢ τίς, which is considerably attested and is supplanted by καὶ τίς in Matthew. — Ver. 29. κἀγώ] Tisch. has deleted this, in accordance with B C ? L Δ ; and Lachm., following A K, min. Arm. Germ. 2, Goth., has placed it *before* ὑμᾶς. It has come in from the parallels. — Ver. 30. Before Ἰωάνν. here, as in Matt. xxi. 25, τό is to be adopted, with Fritzsche, Lachm. Tisch., in accordance with important testimony. It was passed over as superfluous ; in Luke it is too weakly attested. — Ver. 31. ἐλογίζοντο] B C D G K L M Δ ℵ** min. read : διελογίζοντο, which Griesb. has commended, Schulz has approved, Fritzsche, Lachm. have adopted. With this preponderance of evidence it is the less to be derived from Matt. xxi. 25, in proportion to the facility with which the syllable ΔΙ might be lost in the two last letters of the preceding ΚΑΙ. ℵ* has the manifest clerical error προσελογίζοντο, which, however, does not presuppose the simple form. — οὖν] is wanting in A C* L M X Δ, min. vss. Deleted by Fritzsche, Lachm. It is from the parallels. — Elz. and Fritzsche have afterwards at ver. 32: ἀλλ' ἐὰν εἴπωμεν. But ἐάν has against it decisive evidence, and is an addition easily misunderstood.

---

[1] Ver. 26 is wanting in all the original editions of Luther's translation.

— ὅτι ὄντως] Tisch. has ὄντως ὅτι, following B C L א** min.   The *Recepta* is a transposition for the sake of facility.

Vv. 1–11. See on Matt. xxi. 1–11.   Comp. Luke xix. 29–44.   Mark narrates with greater freshness and particularity than Matthew, who partly abridges, but partly also already comments (vv. 4, 5) and completes (ver. 10 f.). — εἰς Βηθφ. κ. Βηθ.] a more precise local definition to εἰς Ἱεροσ.: *when they come into the neighbourhood of Jerusalem*, (namely) *into the neighbourhood of Bethphage and Bethany*, which places are situated *on the Mount of Olives*.   Comp. the double εἰς, ver. 11. — Ver. 2. εἰς τὴν κώμην κ.τ.λ.] Bethphage, which was first named as the nearest to them.   See also Matt. xxi. 1 f., where Bethany as explanatory is omitted. — πῶλον] without more precise definition, but, as is obvious of itself, the foal of an *ass*.   Judg. x. 4, xii. 14; Zech. ix. 9; Gen. xlix. 11. — ἐφ' ὃν οὐδεὶς κ.τ.λ.] This notice, which in Matthew is not adopted[1] into the narrative, is an addition supplied by reflective tradition, arising out of the sacred destination of the animal (for to a sacred purpose creatures as yet unused were applied, Num. xix. 2; Deut. xxi. 3; 1 Sam. vi. 7; Wetstein *in loc.*).   Comp. Strauss, II. p. 276 f. — On φέρετε (see the critical remarks), comp. Gen. xlvii. 16: φέρετε τὰ κτήνη ὑμῶν, Hom. *Od.* iii. 117.   Therefore it is not unsuitable (Fritzsche); even the *change of the tenses* (λύσατε . . . φέρετε) has nothing objectionable in it.   See Kühner, II. p. 80. — Ver. 3. τί] *wherefore;* to this corresponds the subsequent ὅτι, *because*. — καὶ εὐθέως κ.τ.λ.] this *Jesus* says; it is not the *disciples* who are to say it (Origen; comp. the critical remarks), whereby a paltry trait would be introduced into the commission. — ὧδε, *hither*, Plato, *Prot.* p. 328 D; Soph. *Trach.* 496; *O. T.* 7; *El.* 1149.   Not yet so used in Homer. — Ver. 4. εὗρον . . . ἀμφόδου] a description characteristic of Mark; τὸ ἄμφοδον and ἡ ἄμφοδος (comp. ἀμφόδιον in Lucian, *Rhet. praec.* 24, 25) is not simply *the way*, but the *way that leads round (winding way)*.   Jer. xvii. 27, xlvii.

---

[1] By no means obvious of itself, moreover, in the case of the ass's *colt* in the narrative of Matthew, since it was already large enough for riding,—in opposition to Lange and others.

27; Aristot. *de part. ani.* III. 2, p. 663, 36 (codd., see Lobeck, *Paralip.* p. 248), and the examples in Wetstein, also Koenig and Schaefer, *ad Gregor. Cor.* p. 505. — Ver. 5. τί ποιεῖτε κ.τ.λ.] Comp. Acts xxi. 13. — Ver. 8. On the only correct form στιβάς, not στοιβάς, see Fritzsche. The *meaning* is: *litter*, ἀπὸ ῥάβδων καὶ χλωρῶν χόρτων στρῶσις καὶ φύλ-λων, Hesychius. Very frequent in the classical writers. Litter (branches and leaves) was cut from the fields that were near (ἀγρῶν, see the critical remarks). — Ver. 10. ἡ ἐρχομένη βασιλεία τοῦ πατρ. ἡμ. Δ.] *i.e. the coming kingdom of the Messiah.* Its approaching manifestation, on the eve of occurring with the entry of the Messiah, was seen in the riding of Jesus into Jerusalem. And it is called *the kingdom of David,* so far as it is the fulfilment of the type given in the kingdom of David, as David himself is a type of the Messiah, who is even *called* David among the Rabbins (Schoettgen, *Hor.* II. p. 10 f.). Mark did not *avoid* mention of the "*Son* of David" (in opposition to Hilgenfeld; comp. x. 47, xii. 35), but Matthew added it; in both cases without special aim. The personal expression, however (comp. Luke: βασιλεύς, which Weizsäcker regards as the most original), easily came into the tradition. — Ver. 11. εἰς Ἱεροσ. εἰς τὸ ἱερόν] After the rejection of καί (see the critical remarks) the second εἰς is to be understood as *a more precise specification,* similar to that in ver. 1. — ὀψίας ἤδη οὔσης τῆς ὥρας] *as the hour was already late.* ὀψίας is here an adjective. Taken as a substantive, τῆς ὥρας (evening of the day-time) would not be applicable to it; expressions with ὀψέ (as Dem. 541, ult. ὀψὲ τῆς ὥρας ἐγίγνετο, Xen. *Hell.* ii. 1. 14, *al.*) are different. On the adjective ὄψιος, see Lobeck, *ad Phryn.* p. 51. It was already the time of day, which in the classical writers is called ὀψία δείλη (Herod. viii. 6; Thuc. viii. 26; Polyb. vii. 16. 4; Ruhnken, *Tim.* p. 75). According to Matthew and Luke, it was immediately after His entry, and not on the next day (Mark, vv. 12, 15 ff.) that Jesus purified the temple. A real difference; Matthew has not only *narrated* the cleansing of the temple as occurring at once along with the entry, but *assumed* it so (in opposition to Ebrard, Lange, and many others); Mark, however, is original; the day's work is completed with the Messianic entry itself, and only a visit to the temple and the significant look round about it forms the close. What the Messiah has still further to do, follows on the morrow. This at the same time in opposition to Baur (*Markusevang.* p. 89), who sees in the narrative of Mark only the later work of sober reflection adjusting the course of events; and in opposition to Hilgenfeld, who accuses Mark of an essential impropriety. — περιβλεψάμ. πάντα is a preparatory significant statement in view of the measure of cleansing purposed on the morrow. The look around was itself deeply serious, sorrowful, judicial (comp. iii. 5, 34), not as though He Himself had now for the first time beheld the temple and thus had never previously come to the feast (Schenkel).

Vv. 12–14. Comp. on Matt. xxi. 18–20, whose more compressed narrative represents a later form taken by the tradition. — εἰ ἄρα] *whether under these circumstances* (see Klotz, *ad Devar.* p. 178 f.)—namely, since the tree had leaves, which in fact in the case of fig-trees come *after* the fruits. Comp. on Matt. xxi. 19. — οὐ γὰρ ἦν καιρὸς σύκων] not inappropriate (Köstlin), but rightly giving information whence it happened that Jesus found nothing but leaves only.[1] If it had been the time for figs (*June*, when the *Boccôre* ripens, comp. Matt. xxiv. 32) He would have found fruits also as well as the leaves, and would not have been deceived by the abnormal foliage of the tree. The objections against this logical connection—on the one hand, that figs of the previous year that had hung through the winter might still have been on the tree; on the other, that from οὐ γὰρ ἦν καιρ. σύκ. the fruitlessness of the tree would appear quite natural, and therefore not be justified as an occasion for cursing it (comp. de Wette, Strauss, Schenkel; according to Bruno Bauer, Mark made the remark on account of Hos. ix. 10)—are quite irrelevant; for (1) Figs *that have hung through the winter* were

[1] Not as to the point, that only a symbolical demonstration was here in question (Weizsäcker, p. 92). Nobody could have gathered this from these words without some more precise indication, since the symbolical nature of the event is wholly independent of them.

not at all associated with a tree's *being in leaf*, but might also be found on trees without leaves; the *leafy* tree promised *summer figs*, but had none,[1] because in the month Nisan it was not the time for figs, so that thus the presence of foliage which, in spite of the earliness of the time of year, justified the conclusion from the nature of the fig-tree that there would be fruit upon it, was only a deceptive anomaly. (2) The tree presents itself as deserving a curse, because, having *leaves* it ought also to have had *fruit;* the οὐ γὰρ ἦν κ. σ. would only make it appear as blameless if it had had no *leaves ;* hence even with our simply literal apprehension of the words there in no wise results an over-hasty judicial sentence.   It is almost incredible how the simple and logically appropriate meaning of the words has been distorted, in order to avoid representing Jesus as seeking figs out of the fig-season.   Such explanations, however, deserve no refutation ; *e.g.* that of Hammond, Clericus, Homberg, Paulus, Olshausen, Lange, *L. J.* II. 1, p. 321 : for it was *not a good fig-year* (see, on the other hand, Strauss, II. p. 220 f.); that of Abresch, *Lect. Arist.* p. 16, and Triller, *ad Thom. M.* p. 490 : for it was not a *place suitable for figs ;* the *interrogative* view of Majus, *Obss.* I. p. 7 : "*nonne* enim tempus erat ficuum ? ;" that of Heinsius and Knatchbull : "*ubi enim fuit, tempus erat ficuum*" (so that οὖ would have to be read) ; the notion of Mill, that Jesus only *feigned* as if He were seeking figs, in order merely to do a miracle (Victor Antiochenus and Euthymius Zigabenus had already taken even His hunger as simulated ; compare recently again Hofmann, p. 374) ; the view of Kuinoel (comp. Dahme in Henke's *Magaz.* I. 2, p. 252) : for it was *not yet* (οὐ = οὔπω) *fig-harvest ;* compare also Baumgarten-Crusius.   Fritzsche has the correct view, although he reproaches Mark with having subjoined the notice " *non elegantissime*," whereas it very correctly states why Jesus, *notwithstanding the leaves of* the tree, found no *fruits.*   Toup (*Emendatt. in Suid.* II. p. 218 f.), Tittmann (*Opusc.* p. 509), and Wassenbergh (in Valckenaer, *Schol.* I.

---

[1] No fruit indeed, even *that had hung through the winter ;* but this Jesus had not *sought,* since the *presence of leaves* had induced Him to expect fruit—namely, fruit *before the time* (comp. Tobler, *Denkbl. aus Jerus.* p. 101 ff.).

p. 18) have even declared themselves against the genuineness of the words in spite of all the critical evidence ! Bornemann (in opposition to Wassenbergh) in the *Schol. in Luc.* p. xlix. f., and in the *Stud. u. Krit.* 1843, p. 131 ff., comes back again essentially to the interpretation of Hammond, and explains : " for it was *not favourable weather* for figs." But καιρός could only acquire the meaning of "favourable weather" by more precise definition *in the context*, as in the passage quoted by Bornemann, Eur. *Hec.* 587, by θεόθεν, and hence this interpretation is not even favoured by the reading ὁ γὰρ καιρὸς οὐκ ἦν σύκων (B C* L Δ ℵ, Copt. Syr. ; so Tischendorf), *for the time was not fig-time*, which reading easily originated from an ὁ καιρός written on the margin by way of supplement, whence also is to be derived the reading of Lachmann (following D, Or.) : οὐ γ. ἦν ὁ καιρὸς σ. De Wette finds the words " *absolutely incomprehensible.*"[1] Comp. also Baur, *Markusev.* p. 90, according to whom, however, Mark here only betrays his poverty in any resources of his own, as he is alleged by Hilgenfeld only to make the case worse involuntarily. — Ver. 14. ἀποκριθείς] Appropriately Bengel adds : " arbori fructum neganti." — φάγοι] According to Mark (it is otherwise in Matt. xxi. 19) the cursing is expressed in the form of *a wish*, as *imprecation*, Acts viii. 20. — καὶ ἤκουον οἱ μαθ. αὐτοῦ] a preparation for ver. 20.

Vv. 15–19. See on Matt. xxi. 12–17. Comp. Luke xix. 45–48. Matthew deals with this partly by abbreviating, partly also by adding what is peculiar and certainly original (vv. 14–16). — ἤρξατο ἐκβάλλειν] but afterwards : κατέστρεψε, so that thus the latter occurred after the beginning and before the ending of the expulsion. — Ver. 16. ἵνα] The object of the permission is conceived as its *purpose*. The form ἤφιε, as i. 34. — διενέγκῃ σκεῦος διὰ τοῦ ἱεροῦ] In the estimation also of the Rabbins it was accounted a desecration of the temple, if anybody carried the implements of common life (σκεῦος, household furniture, pots, and the like) through

---

[1] Nay, they even compelled Bleek to the conjecture that the event had occurred *at another time of year*, possibly in the previous year at the Feast of Tabernacles (John vii.).

the temple-enclosure, διὰ τοῦ ἱεροῦ (not ναοῦ), in order to save himself a circuit; they extended this even to the synagogues. See Lightfoot, p. 632 f.; Wetstein *in loc.* Olshausen is mistaken in explaining διαφέρειν as *to carry to and fro;* and Kuinoel and Olshausen, following Beza and Grotius, arbitrarily limit σκεῦος to implements used *for the purpose of gain.* — Ver. 17. ἐδίδασκε] on what subject? What follows leaves no doubt as to the principal theme of this teaching. — πᾶσι τοῖς ἔθνεσιν] *Dativus commodi:* (destined) *for all nations,—* which has reference in Isa. lvi. 7 to the fact that even the strangers dwelling among the Israelites were to return with them to the Holy Land (Ezra ii. 43 ff., vii. 7; Neh. iii. 26, xi. 21), where they were to present their offerings in the temple (according to the Israelitish command, Lev. xvii. 8 ff., xxii. 19 ff.; Num. xv. 14 ff.). Only Mark (not Matthew and Luke) has taken up the πᾶσι τοῖς ἔθνεσιν from Isaiah, which probably has its reason not only in more careful quotation (Fritzsche, de Wette, Holtzmann, Bleek), but, inasmuch as it is an *honourable* mention of the Gentiles, in the *Gentile-Christian* interest, without, however, thereby indicating that Jesus had desired to announce the *new spiritual temple* of His church (Schenkel), which *point* of the action does not emerge in any of the evangelists, since they had failed to perceive it, or had suppressed it. — Ver. 18. ἀπολέσωσιν] (see the critical remarks): how they *were to destroy* Him, deliberative. The *future* of the *Recepta* (how they *should destroy* Him) would designate the realization as indubitable (the question only still remaining as to the kind and manner of the destruction). See Kühner, II. p. 489 f.; Stallbaum, *ad Plat. Symp.* p. 225 C. — ἐφοβοῦντο γὰρ αὐτόν] The reason why they sought to destroy Him. — ἐπὶ τῇ διδαχῇ, αὐτοῦ] which He, namely, had just set forth, ver. 17, after the cleansing of the temple. Baur arbitrarily suggests that Mark has dexterously inwoven the διδάσκειν from Luke. — ὅτε ὀψὲ ἐγένετο] on that day, ver. 12; hence not ὅταν (see the critical remarks).

Vv. 20—24. Comp. on Matt. xxi. 20—22. But according to Matthew the tree withered away *forthwith after the cursing,* so that the following conversation *immediately* attached itself

thereto. A later form moulded in accordance with the immediate result in other miracles. If Mark had separated the
miracle into two acts in order to give to it the more importance (see Köstlin, p. 335) he would have reckoned erroneously,
as the immediate result is the greater and therefore the more
in keeping with a " later reflection " (Hilgenfeld). But this
variation of the tradition has nothing to do with the view that
the entire history is only a legendary formation from Luke
xiii. (in opposition to Schenkel). — παραπορευόμενοι πρωΐ]
Fritzsche is wrong in rejecting this order, because " πρωΐ is
opposed to the preceding ὀψέ." In fact παραπορ. is the
leading idea (and *passing by* in the morning), pointing out the
modal definition to the following εἶδον κ.τ.λ. — Ver. 22.
πίστιν Θεοῦ] *confidence in God ;* genitive of the object. Comp.
Acts iii. 16 ; Rom. iii. 22 ; Gal. ii. 20, iii. 22 ; Eph. iii. 8 ;
Dem. 300, 10 ; Eur. *Med.* 414. — Ver. 24. διὰ τοῦτο] because
the confidence has so great effect. — ὅτι ἐλάβετε] (see the
critical remarks) : The *praeterite* is not " *ineptum* " (Fritzsche),
but the *having received,* which one believes has its ground *in
the counsel of God.* Comp. xiii. 20. The real *de facto* bestowal
is future (ἔσται ὑμῖν).

Vv. 25, 26. Comp. Matt. vi. 14 f. To the exhortation to
confidence in prayer, according to Mark, Jesus links on another
principal requisite of being heard—namely, the necessity of
forgiving in order to obtain forgiveness. And how appropriate is this to guard against a false conclusion from the
occurrence with the fig-tree ! Nevertheless (in opposition to
Holtzmann) it is hardly here original, but introduced [1] into
this connection by Mark from the collection of Logia in the
way of thoughtful redaction, not of unadjusted insertion (Hilgenfeld). — στήκετε] Comp. on ἑστῶτες, Matt. vi. 5. The
indication is not incorrect, but ἄν has its relation merely to
the particle ὅτε, and does not affect the verb ; see on iii. 11.
— Ver. 26. Observe the *antithesis,* in which οὐκ (not μή, as

---

[1] Which, however, is not, with Weiss in the *Jahrb. f. D. Theol.* 1864, p. 63,
to be supported by the argument that Mark has nowhere else the expression : ὁ
πατὴρ ὁ ἐν τοῖς οὐρ. For Mark has no place at all, in which this designation would
have been applicable instead of another that he has used.

in Matthew) is closely associated with ἀφίετε and constitutes
with it *one* idea (Hermann, *ad Vig.* p. 831 ; Winer, p. 423 f.
[E. T. 597 f.] ; Buttmann, *neut. Gr.* p. 297 [E. T. 346]).

Vv. 27-33. See on Matt. xxi. 23-27.   Comp. Luke
xx. 1-8.   Matthew abridges little, but yet remains not so
directly vivid. — περιπατοῦντος] According to Matthew and
Luke Jesus *taught*, which, however, is not excluded by Mark's
statement. — Ver. 28. ταῦτα] the *cleansing of the temple*,
comp. on Matt. xxi. 23. — ἵνα ταῦτα ποιῇς] not a paraphrase
of the infinitive, but: *in order that thou mayest do these things*,
purpose of τὴν ἐξουσίαν τ. ἔδωκεν. — Ver. 29. ἐπερωτήσω]
not : *post interrogabo* (Fritzsche), but, as always in the N. T. :
to inquire of, so that ἐπί expresses the direction.   Comp.
Plat. *Soph.* p. 249 E : δικαίως ἂν ἐπερωτηθεῖμεν ἅπερ αὐτοὶ
τότε ἠρωτῶμεν (be *inquired of*, as we ourselves *asked questions*). — Ver. 31. οὖν] *therefore*, since it comes from heaven. —
Ver. 32. ἀλλ᾽ εἴπωμεν· ἐξ ἀνθρώπων] Here is to be placed a
note of interrogation (Complutensian, Lachmann, Tischendorf) ;
but are we to say : of men ? a question of doubtful reflection !
Rinck, *Lucubr. crit.* p. 306, aptly remarks on what follows :
"Respondet Marcus suo nomine, idque elegantissime fecisse
videtur, quoniam haud facile quisquam sibi ipse aperte
timorem adscribere consuevit."   Comp. Buttmann, *neut. Gr.*
p. 330 [E. T. 385]. — εἶχον τὸν Ἰωάννην ὄντως, ὅτι προφ.
ἦν] (see the critical remarks): *they really perceived* (per-
spectum habebant, see Ast, *Lex. Plat.* I. p. 873) *that John* (in
his lifetime) *was a prophet.*   Ἰωάννην . . . ὅτι is to be taken
according to the well-known attraction ; see Winer, p. 551
[E. T. 781] ; Buttmann, p. 322 [E. T. 376].

CHAPTER XII.

VER. 1. λέγειν] B G L Δ ℵ, min. Syr. Vulg. It. have λαλεῖν. So Lachm. and Tisch. The testimony of the codd. in favour of λέγειν remains doubtless strong enough, nevertheless λαλεῖν is to be preferred, because there immediately follows *what* Jesus said, and therefore the change into λέγειν was readily suggested. Comp. iii. 23. — Ver. 3. οἱ δέ] Lachm. Tisch. have καί, following B D L Δ ℵ, min. Copt. Cant. Ver. Verc. Vind. It is from Matt. xxi. 25. — Ver. 4. λιθοβολήσ.] is wanting in B D L Δ ℵ, min. Copt. Arm. Vulg. It. Almost all the above witnesses have afterwards instead of ἀπέστ. ἠτιμωμ.: ἠτίμησαν. Fritzsche, Lachm. Tisch. have followed the former omission and this reading, and rightly; λιθοβολ. is a gloss on ἐκεφαλ. from Matt. xxi. 35, and ἀπέστ. ἠτιμωμένον is a reading conformed to the conclusion of ver. 3. — Ver. 5. καὶ ἄλλον] Elz. Scholz have καὶ πάλιν ἄλλ., in opposition to preponderating evidence; πάλιν is a mechanical repetition from ver. 4. — Instead of τούς is to be written οὕς both times, following B L Δ ℵ, min. with Fritzsche, Lachm. Tisch. — The Aeolic form ἀποκτέννοντες is on decisive evidence to be adopted, with Fritzsche, Lachm. Tisch. Comp. the critical remarks on Matt. x. 28. — Ver. 6. The arrangement ἕνα ἔχων υἱόν is required by decisive evidence (Fritzsche, Lachm., comp. Tisch.), of which, however, B C** L Δ ℵ, 33 have εἶχεν instead of ἔχων (so Tisch. rightly, as ἔχων is an emendation of the construction). Almost the same witnesses omit the οὖν after ἔτι; it is, with Tisch., to be deleted as a connective addition, as, moreover, αὐτοῦ after ἀγαπ. is a decidedly condemned mechanical addition. — Ver. 8. Such preponderating evidence is in favour of the superfluous αὐτόν after ἐξέβαλ., that it is to be adopted with Lachm. and Tisch. — Ver. 14. οἱ δέ] B C D L Δ ℵ, 33, Copt. codd. of the It. have καί. So Fritzsche, Lachm. From Luke xx. 21, whence also many variations with ἐπηρώτων have come into our passage. — Ver. 17. The arrangement τὰ Καίσαρος ἀπόδ. Καίσαρι (Tisch.) is to be preferred, in accordance with B C L Δ ℵ, 28, Syr. Copt. The placing of ἀπόδοτε first (Elz. Lachm.) is from the parallels. — ἐθαύμασαν] Lachm. has ἐθαύμαζον.

But among the codd. which read the imperfect (B D L Δ א), B א have ἐξεθαύμαζον (D* has ἐξεθαυμάζοντο). This ἐξεθαύμαζον (Tisch.) is to be preferred. The simple form and the aorist are from the parallels. — Ver. 18. ἐπηρώτησαν] Lachm. Tisch. have ἐπηρώτων, following B C D L Δ א, 33 ; the aorist is from the parallels. — Ver. 19. τὴν γυναῖκα αὐτοῦ] αὐτοῦ is wanting in B C L Δ א, min. Copt., and is from Matthew. — Ver. 20. After ἑπτά Elz. Fritzsche have οὖν, against decisive evidence; it is from Luke xx. 29 ; instead of which some other witnesses have δέ (from Matthew). — Ver. 21. καὶ οὐδὲ αὐτὸς ἀφῆκε] B C L Δ א, 33, Copt. have μὴ καταλιπών. Approved by Bornemann in the *Stud. u. Krit.* 1843, p. 133, adopted by Tisch. But if the *Recepta* had originated from what precedes and follows, it would have run simply καὶ οὐκ ἀφῆκε; the καὶ οὐδὲ αὐτός does not look like the result of a gloss, and might even become offensive on account of its emphasis. — Ver. 22. ἔλαβον αὐτήν] is wanting in B M, min. Colb., also C L Δ א, min. Copt., which, moreover, omit καί before οὐκ. Fritzsche has deleted ἔλαβον αὐτ., Lachm. has merely bracketed it; Tisch. has struck out, besides ἔλαβ. αὐτ., the καί also before οὐκ. Rightly; the short reading: καὶ οἱ ἑπτὰ οὐκ ἀφῆκαν σπέρμα, was completed in conformity with ver. 21. — ἐσχάτη] Fritzsche, Lachm. Tisch. have ἔσχατον, certainly on considerable attestation; but it is an emendation (comp. Matthew and Luke : ὕστερον), on account of the difference of the genders (ἐσχ. feminine, πάντ. masculine). — The order καὶ ἡ γυνὴ ἀπέθ. is, with Fritzsche, Lachm., Tisch., to be adopted. The *Recepta* is from the parallels. — Ver. 23. After ἐν τῇ Elz. Lachm. Scholz have οὖν, which important witnesses omit, others place after ἀναστ. From the parallels. — ὅταν ἀναστῶσι] is wanting in B C D L Δ א, min. vss. Condemned by Griesb., bracketed by Lachm. It is to be maintained, for there was no occasion for any gloss ; its absolute superfluousness, however, the absence of any such addition in the parallels, and the similarity of ἀναστάσει and ἀναστῶσι, occasioned the omission. — Ver. 25. γαμίσκονται] A F H, min. have ἐκγαμίσκονται. B C G L U Δ א, min. have γαμίζονται. Consequently the testimonies in favour of the *Recepta* are left so weak (even D falls away, having γαμίζουσιν), and γαμίζονται has so much the preponderance, that it is, with Fritzsche, Lachm. Tisch., to be adopted. Comp. on Matt. xxii. 30. — Before ἐν Elz. has οἱ. The weight of the evidence is divided. But since this οἱ after ἄγγελΟΙ was more easily dropped out than brought in (by being written twice over), and is wanting also in Matthew, it is to be maintained. — Ver. 26. Instead of τοῦ βάτου Elz. has τῆς βάτου, in opposition to decisive evidence. —

Decisive evidence condemns in ver. 27 the article before Θεός,
and then Θεός before ζώντων; just as also ὑμεῖς οὖν before πολὺ
πλανᾶσθε is, following B C L Δ ℵ, Copt., to be struck out, with
Tisch., as being an addition to these short pithy words.—Ver. 28.
εἰδώς] Fritzsche, Lachm. Tisch. have ἰδών (Fritzsche: καὶ ἰδών).
So, with or without καί (which is a connective interpolation), in
C D L ℵ* min. vss., including Syr. Arm. Vulg. It. Aug. But
these witnesses are not preponderating, and εἰδώς might easily
seem unsuitable and give way to the more usual ἰδών; comp.
ver. 34.—The order ἀπεκρίθη αὐτοῖς has been preferred by Schulz,
Fritzsche, and Tisch. (following Gersd. p. 526), in accordance
with B C L Δ ℵ, min. Copt. Theophylact. But it was just the
customary placing of the pronoun after the verb that occasioned
the inversion of the words, in which the *intention* with which
αὐτοῖς was prefixed was not observed. It is otherwise at xiv. 40.
— Instead of πάντων Elz. has πασῶν, contrary to decisive evidence.
—Ver. 29. The *Recepta* is ὅτι πρώτη πασῶν τῶν ἐντολῶν. Very many
variations. Griesb. and Fritzsche have ὅτι πρώτη πάντων ἐντολή,
following A, min. Scholz reads ὅτι πρ. πάντων τῶν ἐντολῶν, following E F G H S, min. Lachm. has ὅτι πρ. πάντων [ἐντολή ἐστιν].
Tisch. has ὅτι πρώτη ἐστιν, following B L Δ ℵ, Copt. The latter is
the original form, which, according to the question of ver. 28 and
its various readings, was variously amplified, and in the process
ἐστίν was partly dropped.—Ver. 30. αὕτη πρώτη ἐντολή] is wanting in B E L Δ ℵ, Copt. Deleted by Tisch. An addition in
accordance with Matthew, with variations in details, following
vv. 28, 29.—Ver. 31. Instead of καὶ δευτ. read, with Tisch.,
merely δευτ.—Elz. Griesb. Scholz have ὁμοία αὕτη; Fritzsche,
Lachm. have ὁμ. αὐτῇ; Tisch. merely αὕτη. The last is attested
by B L Δ ℵ, Copt., and is to be preferred, since ὁμοία very
readily suggested itself to be written on the margin from
Matthew.—Ver. 32. After εἷς ἔστι Elz. has Θεός; a supplement in
opposition to preponderant evidence.—Ver. 33. καὶ ἐξ ὅλης τῆς
ψυχ.] is wanting in B L Δ ℵ, min. Copt. Verc. Marcell. in Eus.
Condemned by Rinck, bracketed by Lachm., deleted by Tisch.
But if it were an addition, it would have been inserted after
καρδίας (comp. ver. 30). On the other hand, the arrangement
different from ver. 30 might easily draw after it the omission.
—The article before θυσιῶν (in Elz.) is decisively condemned.—
Ver. 36. γάρ] is wanting in B L Δ ℵ, min. Copt. Verc., while D,
Arm. read καὶ αὐτός, and Colb. Corb. have *autem*. Lachm. has
bracketed γάρ, and Tisch. has deleted it. The latter is right.
The connection was variously supplied.—Ver. 37. οὖν] is wanting in B D L Δ ℵ, min. copt. Syr. p. codd. It. Hil. Bracketed

by Lachm., deleted by Tisch. An addition from the parallels. — Ver. 43. εἶπεν] instead of the *Recepta* λέγει (which Scholz, Rinck, Tisch. defend), is decisively attested, as also is ἔβαλε (Lachm.) instead of the *Recepta* βέβληκε. In place of βαλόντ. (Elz.), βαλλόντ. must be written on decisive attestation.

Vv. 1–12. See on Matt. xxi. 33–46. Comp. Luke xx. 9–19. Matthew makes another kindred parable precede, which was undoubtedly likewise original, and to be found in the collection of Logia (vv. 28–32), and he enriches the application of the parable before us in an equally original manner; while, we may add, the presentation in Mark is simpler and more fresh, not related to that of Matthew in the way of heightened and artificial effect (Weiss). — ἤρξατο] after that dismissal of the chief priests, etc. — αὐτοῖς] therefore not as Luke has it : πρὸς τὸν λαόν, to which also Matthew is opposed. — ἐν παρα-βολαῖς] *parabolically*. The plural expression is *generic ;* comp. iii. 22, iv. 2. Hence it is not surprising (Hilgenfeld). Comp. also John xvi. 24. — Ver. 2. According to Mark and Luke, the lord receives *a part* of the fruits; the rest is the reward of the vine-dressers. It is otherwise in Matthew. — Ver. 4. Observe how compendiously Matthew sums up the contents of vv. 4, 5.[1] — κἀκεῖνον] The conception of *maltreatment* lies at the foundation of the comparative *also,* just as at ver. 5. Comp. on Matt. xv. 3. — ἐκεφαλαίωσαν] *they beat him on the head.* The word is not further preserved in this signification (Vulg.: *in capite vulnerarunt*), but only in the meaning: *to gather up as regards the main substance, to set forth summarily* (Thuc. iii. 67. 5, viii. 53. 1 ; Herod. iii. 159 ; Ecclus. xxxv. 8) ; but this is wholly inappropriate in this place, since it is not, with Wakefield, *Silv. crit.* II. p. 76 f., to be changed into the meaning : " *they made short work with him.*"[2] We have here a

---

[1] All the less ought the several δοῦλοι to be *specifically* defined ; as, for instance, according to Victor Antiochenus, by the first servant is held to be meant *Elias* and the contemporary prophets ; by the second, *Isaiah, Hosea,* and *Amos ;* by the third, *Ezekiel* and *Daniel.* That the expression in vv. 2–4 is in the *singular,* notwithstanding the *plurality* of prophets, cannot in a *figurative* discourse be surprising, and cannot justify the conjecture that here *another* parable—of the three *years of Christ's ministry*—has been interwoven (Weizsäcker).

[2] This explanation is set aside by αὐτόν, which, moreover, is opposed to the

veritable *solecism;* Mark confounded κεφαλαιόω with κεφαλίζω, perhaps after the analogy of γναθόω and γυιόω (Lobeck, *ad Phryn.* p. 95). — ἠτίμησαν (see the critical remarks): *they dishonoured him, treated him disgracefully,* the general statement after the special ἐκεφαλ. The word is poetical, especially epic (Hom. *Il.* i. 11, ix. 111; *Od.* xvi. 274, *al.;* Pind. *Pyth.* ix. 138; Soph. *Aj.* 1108; Ellendt, *Lex. Soph.* I. p. 251), as also in *this* sense the later form ἀτιμόω, of frequent use in the LXX. (Eur. *Hel.* 462, *al.*), which in the prose writers is used in the sense of inflicting dishonour by depriving of the rights of citizenship (also in Xen. *Ath.* i. 14, where ἀτιμοῦσι is to be read). — Ver. 5. κ. πολλοὺς ἄλλους] Here we have to supply: *they maltreated*—the *dominant* idea in what is previously narrated (comp. κἀκεῖνον, vv. 4, 5, where this conception lay at the root of the καί), and to which the subsequent elements δέροντες and ἀποκτεννόντες are subordinated. Comp. Buttmann, *neut. Gr.* p. 252 [E. T. 293]. But Mark does not write " in a disorderly and slipshod manner," as de Wette supposes, but just like the best classical writers, who leave the finite verb to be supplied from the context in the case of participles and other instances. See Bornemann, *ad Xen. Sympos.* iv. 53; Hermann, *ad Viger.* p. 770; Nägelsbach, *Anm. z. Ilias,* ed. 3, p. 179. — Ver. 6. The ἔτι ἕνα εἶχεν υἱὸν ἀγ. (see the critical remarks), which is peculiar to the graphic Mark, has in it something touching, to which the bringing of ἕνα into prominence by the unusual position assigned to it contributes. Then, in vivid connection therewith stands the contrast of vv. 7, 8; and the trait of the parable contained in ver. 7 f. certainly does not owe its introduction to Mark (Weiss). — Ver. 8. Not a *hysteron proteron* (Grotius, Heumann, de Wette), a mistake, which is with the greatest injustice imputed to the vividly graphic *Mark;* but a different representation from that of Matthew and Luke: *they killed him, and threw him* (the slain) *out of the vineyard.* In the latter there is the tragic element of outrage even against the

view of Theophylact: συνετέλεσαν καὶ ἐκορύφωσαν τὴν ὑβριν. The *middle* is used in Greek with an accusative of the person (τινά), but in the sense: *briefly to describe any one.* See Plat. *Pol.* ix. p. 576 B.

corpse, which is not, however, intended to be applied by way
of special interpretation to Jesus. — Ver. 9. ἐλεύσεται κ.τ.λ.]
not an answer of the *Pharisees* (Vatablus, Kuinoel, following
Matt. xxi. 41); but *Jesus Himself* is represented by Mark as
replying to His own question.[1] — Ver. 10. οὐδέ] What Jesus
has set before them in the way of parable concerning the
rejection of the Messiah and His divine justification, *is also
prophesied in the Scripture*, Ps. cxviii. 22 ; hence He continues :
have ye not also read this Scripture, etc.? On γραφή, that
which is drawn up in writing, used of *individual passages of
Scripture*, comp. Luke iv. 21; John xix. 37; Acts i. 16,
viii. 35. — Ver. 12. καὶ ἐφοβ. τ. ὄχλ.] καί connects adversative clauses without changing its signification, Hartung,
Partikell. I. p. 147 f.; Winer, p. 388 [E. T. 545]. It is an
emphatic *and* in the sense of: *and yet*. Especially frequent
in John. — The words ἔγνωσαν γὰρ . . . εἶπε, which are not
to be put in a parenthesis, are regarded as illogically placed
(see Beza, Heupel, Fritzsche, Baur, Hilgenfeld, and others),
and are held to have their proper place after κρατῆσαι. But
wrongly.   Only let ἔγνωσαν be referred not, with these interpreters, to the chief priests, scribes, and elders, but to the
ὄχλος, which was witness of the transaction in the temple-
court. If the people had not observed that Jesus was speaking the parable in reference to (πρός) them (the chief priests,
etc., as the γεωργούς), these might have ventured to lay hold
on Him; but, as it was, they might not venture on this, but
had to stand in awe of the people, who would have seen at
once in the arrest of Jesus the *fulfilment* of the parable, and
would have interested themselves on His behalf. The chief
priests, etc., were cunning enough to avoid this association,
and left Him and went their way. In this manner also Luke
xx. 19 is to be understood ; he follows Mark.

Vv. 13–17. See on Matt. xxii. 15–22. Comp. Luke
xx. 20–26. Mark is more concise and vivid than Matthew.
— ἀποστέλλουσι] the chief priests, scribes, and elders (xi. 27),

---

[1] That the opponents themselves are compelled to pronounce judgment (Matthew),
appears an original trait. But the *form* of their answer in Matthew (κακοὺς
κακῶς κ.τ.λ.) betrays, as compared with Mark, a later artificial manipulation.

whereas Matthew inaccurately refers this new and grave temptation to the Pharisees as its authors. — *ἵνα αὐτ. ἀγρεύσ. λόγῳ*] *in order that they* (these messengers) *might ensnare Him by means of an utterance, i.e.* by means of a question, which they were to address to Him. See ver. 14. Comp. xi. 29. The *hunting* term ἀγρεύω is frequently even in the classical writers transferred to *men*, who are got into the hunter's power as a prey. See Valckenaer, *ad Herod.* vii. 162; Jacobs, *ad· Anthol.* VII. p. 193. In a good sense also, as in Xen. *Mem.* iii. 11. 7 : τὸ πλεῖστον ἄξιον ἄγρευμα φίλους θηράσειν. — Ver. 14. ἐπ' ἀληθείας] equivalent to ἀληθῶς, Luke iv. 25, xx. 21, xxii. 59, iv. 27, x. 34. See Wetstein *in loc.;* Schaefer, *Melet.* p. 83; Fritzsche, *Quaest. Luc.* p. 137 f. — δῶμεν, ἢ μὴ δ.] The previous question was theoretical and general, this is practical and definite. — Ver. 15. εἰδώς] as knowing hearts (John ii. 25). Comp. Matt. xii. 25; Luke vi. 8, xi. 17. — τ. ὑπόκρισιν] "Discere cupientium praeferebant speciem, cum animus calumniam strueret," Grotius. — Ver. 17. Observe the more striking order of the words in Mark : *what is Caesar's, pay to Caesar,* etc. — ἐξεθαύμαζον] see the critical remarks. The *aorist* would merely narrate historically ; the *imperfect depicts,* and is therefore not inappropriate (in opposition to Fritzsche) ; see Kühner, II. p. 73, and *ad Xen. Anab.* vii. 1. 13. Comp. v. 20, vi. 6. The *compound* ἐκθαυμ. strengthens the notion ; Ecclus. xxvii. 23, xliii. 18 ; 4 Macc. xvii. 17, also in the later Greek writers, but not further used in the N. T.

Vv. 18–27.[1] See on Matt. xxii. 23–33, who narrates more briefly and smoothly. Comp. Luke xx. 27–40. — ἐπηρώτων] Imperfect, as at ver. 17. — Ver. 19. ὅτι is recitative, and ἵνα is the *imperative* to be explained by the *volo* that lies at the root of the expression (see on 2 Cor. viii. 7 ; Eph. v. 33). Comp. on ὅτι before the imperative, Plat. *Crit.* p. 50 C : ἴσως ἂν εἴποιεν (the laws), ὅτι . . . μὴ θαύμαζε τὰ λεγόμενα. — The

---

[1] Hitzig, *Joh. Mark.* p. 219 ff., places the *Pericope of the adulteress,* John vii. 53 ff., after ver. 17, wherein Holtzmann, p. 92 ff., comparing it with Luke xxi. 37 f., so far follows him as to assume that it had stood in the *primitive-Mark,* and had been omitted by all the three Synoptists. Hilgenfeld (in his *Zeitschr.* 1863, p. 317) continues to attribute it to John. It probably belonged originally to one of the sources of Luke that are unknown to us.

ἐπιγαμβρεύσει, which Matthew has here, is a later annexation to the original text of the law. Anger, *Diss.* II. p. 32, takes another view (in favour of Matthew). — Ver. 20. ἑπτά] emphatically prefixed, and introduced in a vivid way without οὖν. — Ver. 21. καὶ οὐδὲ αὐτός] *and also not he.* — καὶ ὁ τρίτος ὡσαύτ.] namely, he took her and died without children ; comp. what has gone before. — Ver. 23. ὅταν ἀναστῶσι] *when they shall have risen,* not an epexegesis of ἐν τῇ ἀναστάσει : but the discourse goes from the general to the particular, so that *the seven brothers and the woman* is the subject of ἀναστῶσι. — Ver. 24. διὰ τοῦτο] does not point back to what has gone before ("ipse sermo vester prodit errorem vestrum," Bengel), which must have been *expressed,* but *forward* to the participle which follows : do ye not err *on this account, because* ye do not understand ? See Maetzner, *ad Antiph.* p. 219 ; Bornemann in the *Stud. u. Krit.* 1843, p. 137 f. ; Winer, p. 146 f. [E. T. 201 f.]. — Ver. 25. ὅταν . . . ἀναστῶσιν] generally, not as at ver. 23. — γαμίζονται] The form γαμίσκω (Arist. *Pol.* vii. 14. 4) is not indeed to be read here (see the critical remarks), but neither is it, with Fritzsche, altogether to be banished out of the N. T. It is beyond doubt genuine in Luke xx. 34 f. — Ver. 26. ὅτι ἐγείρονται] *that* they, namely, etc. ; this is the conclusion to be proved—the *doctrinal position* denied by the interrogators. — ἐπὶ τοῦ βάτου] belongs to what has preceded (in opposition to Beza) as a more precise specification of ἐν τῷ βιβλ. M. : *at the* (well-known) *thorn-bush, i.e.* there, where it is spoken of, Ex. iii. 6. See on quotations of a similar kind, Jablonsky, *Bibl. Hebr.* praef. § 37 ; Fritzsche, ad Rom. xi. 2. Polybius, Theophrastus, and others have βάτος as *masculine.* It usually occurs as *feminine* (Luke xx. 37 ; Deut. xxxiii. 16), but at Ex. iii. 2-4, likewise as masculine. — Ver. 27. According to the amended text (see the critical remarks) : *He is not God of dead men, but of living ! Much ye err !*

Vv. 28-34. See on Matt. xxii. 34-40. — Mark, however, has much that is peculiar, especially through the characteristic and certainly original amplification in vv. 32-34. — The *participles* are to be so apportioned, that ἀκούσας is subordinated

to the προσελθών, and εἰδώς belongs to ἐπηρώτηρεν as its
determining motive. — εἰδώς] not inappropriate (Fritzsche, de
Wette); but the scribe *knew* from his listening how aptly Jesus
had answered *them* (αὐτοῖς, emphatically placed *before* ἀπεκρ.);
and therefore he hoped that He would also give to him an
apt reply. — πάντων] *neuter.* Compare Xen. *Mem.* iv. 7. 70:
ὁ δὲ ἥλιος . . . πάντων λαμπρότατος ὤν, Thucyd. vii. 52. 2.
See Winer, p. 160 [E. T. 222]; Dorvill. *ad Charit.* p. 549.
— Vv. 29, 30. Deut. vi. 4, 5. This principle of morality,
which binds all duties into unity (see J. Müller, *v. d. Sünde,*
I. p. 140 f.), was named pre-eminently קריאה, or also from the
initial word שׁמע, and it was the custom to utter the words
daily, morning and evening. See Vitringa, *Synag.* ii. 3. 15;
Buxtorf, *Synag.* 9. — ἰσχύος] LXX. δυνάμεως. It is the
moral strength, which makes itself known in the overcoming
of hindrances and in energetic activity. Comp. Beck, *bibl.
Seelenl.* p. 112 f., and on Eph. i. 19. Matthew has not this
point, but Luke has at x. 27.[1] — Ver. 32. After διδάσκαλε
there is only to be placed a comma, so that ἐπ' ἀληθείας
(comp. on ver. 14) is a more precise definition of καλῶς. —
ὅτι εἷς ἐστι] *that He is one.* The subject is obvious of itself
from what precedes. As in the former passage of Scripture,
ver. 29, so also here the mention of the unity of God is the
premiss for the duty that follows; hence it is not an improbable trait (Köstlin, p. 351), which Mark has introduced here
in the striving after completeness and with reference to the
Gentile world. — Ver. 33. συνέσεως] a similar notion instead
of a repetition of διανοίας, ver. 30. It is the moral intelligence which comprehends and understands the relation in
question. Its opposite is ἀσύνετος (Rom. i. 21, 31), Dem.
1394, 4: ἀρετῆς ἁπάσης ἀρχὴ ἡ σύνεσις. Comp. on Col.
i. 9. — ὁλοκαυτ.] "Nobilissima species sacrificiorum," Bengel.
πάντων τῶν applies inclusively to θυσιῶν. Krüger, § 58.
3. 2. — Ver. 34. ἰδὼν αὐτὸν, ὅτι] Attraction, as at xi. 32 and
frequently. — νουνεχῶς] *intelligently,* only here in the N. T.

---

[1] The variations of the words in Matthew, Mark, and Luke represent different
forms of the Greek tradition as remembered, which arose independently of the
LXX. (for no evangelist has δύναμις, which is in the LXX.).

Polybius associates it with φρονίμως (i. 83. 3) and πραγ-
ματικῶς (ii. 13. 1, v. 88. 2).　On the character of the word
as Greek, instead of which the Attics say νουνεχόντως (its
opposite : ἀφρόνως, Isocr. v. 7), see Lobeck, *ad Phryn.* p. 599.
— οὐ μακρὰν κ.τ.λ.] The (future) kingdom of the Messiah is
conceived as the common *goal.*　Those who are fitted for the
membership of this kingdom are *near* to this goal ; those who
are unfitted are *remote* from it.　Hence the meaning : There
is not much lacking to thee, that thou mightest be received
into the kingdom at its establishment.　Rightly does Jesus
give him this testimony, because in the frankly and eagerly
avowed agreement of his religious-moral judgment with the
answer of Jesus there was already implied a germ of faith
promising much. — καὶ οὐδεὶς οὐκέτι κ.τ.λ.] not inappropriate
(de Wette, Baur, Hilgenfeld, Bleek) ; but it was just this
peculiar victory of Jesus—that now the result of the questioning was even agreement with Him—which took from all
the further courage, etc.

REMARK.—The difference, arising from Matthew's bringing
forward the scribe as πειράζων (and how naturally in the bearing of the matter this point of view suggested itself !), is not to
be set aside, as, for instance, by Ebrard, p. 493,[1] who by virtue
of harmonizing combination alters ver. 34 thus : "When Jesus
saw how the man of sincere mind quite forgot over the truth
of the case the matter of his pride," etc.　The variation is to be
explained by the fact, that the design of the questioner was
from the very first differently conceived of and passed over in
different forms into the tradition ; not by the supposition, that
Mark did not understand and hence omitted the trait of special
temptation (Weiss), or had been induced by Luke xx. 39 to adopt
a milder view (Baur).　Nor has Matthew remodelled the narrative
(Weiss) ; but he has followed *that* tradition which best fitted into
his context.　The wholly peculiar position of the matter in Mark
tells in favour of the correctness and originality of his narrative.

---

[1] He follows the method of reconciliation proposed by Theophylact : πρῶτον
μὲν αὐτὸν ὡς πειράζοντα ἐρωτῆσαι· εἶτα ὠφιληθέντα ἀπὸ τῆς ἀποκρίσεως τοῦ Χριστοῦ καὶ
νουνεχῶς ἀποκριθέντα ἐπαινεθῆναι.　Comp. Grotius and others, including already
Victor Antiochenus and the anonymous writer in Possini *Cat.* ; Lange, again,
in substance takes the same view, while Bleek simply acknowledges the variation, and Hilgenfeld represents Mark as importing his own theology into the
conversation.

MARK.　　　　　　　　　　　　　　　　N

Vv. 35–37. See on Matt. xxii. 41–46. Comp. Luke xx. 41–44.—Mark is distinguished from Matthew in this respect, that the latter represents Jesus as laying the theological problem before *the assembled Pharisees*, and then relates that they were *thereby* brought to silence, so that they put no further questions to Him ; whereas Mark relates that *the conversation as to the most important commandment* had had this result, and thereafter Jesus had thrown out *before the people*, while He was teaching (vv. 37, 35), the question respecting the Son of David. — ἀποκριθείς] The following question to the people is a reply—publicly exposing the theological helplessness of the scribes—to the silence, to which they had just seen themselves reduced by the very fact that one of their number had even given his entire approval to Jesus. The scribes are still present. But it is not to *themselves* that Jesus puts His question ; He utters it before the *people*, but in express *reference* to the γραμματεῖς. They may therefore give information also before the people, if they can. If they cannot, they stand there the more completely vanquished and put to shame. And they cannot, because to them the divine lineage of the Messiah, in virtue of which as David's descendant He is yet David's Lord, remained veiled and unperceived ;—we may conceive after πόθεν υἱὸς αὐτοῦ ἐστιν the *pause* of this silence and this confusion. So peculiar is this whole position of the matter in Mark, that it appears to be (in opposition to Hilgenfeld and Baur) original. — πῶς] *how then ?* "Quomodo consistere potest, quod dicunt," Grotius.—The twofold emphatic αὐτὸς Δαν. places the declaration of *David himself* in contrast to the point held by *the scribes*. — καὶ πόθεν] breaking in with surprise. Comp. Luke i. 43. πόθεν is the *causal* unde : *whence comes it that.*[1] Comp. Plat. *Phaedr.* p. 269 D.; Dem. 241, 17 ; Wolf, *ad Lept.* p. 238. — ὁ πολὺς ὄχλ.] *the multitude*

[1] In opposition to the whole N. T., the question is, according to Schenkel (comp. Strauss), intended to exhibit the Davidic descent of the Messiah as a *phantom*. This descent in fact forms of necessity *the presupposition* of the words καὶ πόθεν κ.τ.λ., the *concessum* on the part of Jesus Himself. And it is the postulate of the whole of the N. T. Christology, from Matt. i. 1 to Rev. xxii. 16. Comp., moreover, the appropriate remarks of Beyschlag, *Christol. d. N. T.* p. 61 f. But the *pre-existence* of Jesus, which certainly must have

of people, which was present. — ἤκουεν αὐτοῦ ἡδέως] a triumph
over those put to silence.

Vv. 38-40. Comp. on Matt. xxiii. 1, 6, 7 (14). Mark
gives only a short fragment (and Luke xx. 45-47 follows
him) of the great and vehement original speech of severe
rebuke, which Matthew has adopted in full from the collection of Logia. — βλέπετε ἀπό] as viii. 15. — τῶν θελόντων]
quippe qui volunt, desire, *i.e. lay claim to* as a privilege.
" *Velle* saepe rem per se indifferentem malam facit," Bengel.
— ἐν στολαῖς] *i.e.* in long stately *robes,* as στολή, even without
more precise definition, is frequently used (1 Macc. vi. 16 ;
Luke xv. 22 ; Marc. Anton. i. 7). Grotius well remarks that
the στολή is "gravitatis index." — καὶ ἀσπασμούς] governed
by θελόντων. See Winer, p. 509 [E. T. 722]. — Ver. 40.
οἱ κατεσθίοντες κ.τ.λ.] is usually not separated from what
precedes, so that the nominative would come in instead of the
genitive, bringing into more independent and emphatic prominence the description of their character. See Bernhardy,
p. 68 f. ; Buttmann, *neut. Gram.* p. 69 [E. T. 79]. But it is
more suited to the vehement emotion of the discourse (with
which also the asyndetic form of ver. 40 is in keeping), along
with Grotius, Bengel, Lachmann, Tischendorf, Ewald (doubt-
fully also Winer, p. 165 [E. T. 228]), to begin with οἱ
κατεσθίοντες a new sentence, which runs on to κρίμα : *the
devourers of widows' houses . . . these shall* (in the Messianic
judgment) *receive a greater condemnation !* — καί] is the simple
copula : *those devouring widows' houses and* (and withal) *by
way of pretence uttering long prayers* (in order to conceal under
them their pitiless greed). — τῶν χηρῶν] ὑπεισήρχοντο γὰρ
τὰς ἀπροστατεύτους γυναῖκας ὡς δῆθεν προστάται αὐτῶν
ἐσόμενοι, Theophylact. — καὶ προφάσει μακρὰ προσευχ.]
προσχήματι εὐλαβείας καὶ ὑποκρίσει ἀπατῶντες τοὺς ἀφελεσ-
τέρους, Theophylact. — περισσότερον κρίμα] ὅσῳ δὲ μᾶλλον
τετίμηνται παρὰ τῷ λαῷ καὶ τὴν τιμὴν εἰς βλάβην ἕλκουσι,

been in His *consciousness* when He asked the question, is not *expressed* (in
some such way as in John viii. 58), nor is the recognition of it claimed *for
the Psalmist* by ἐν πνεύματι. The latter merely asserts that David, *as a prophet,*
designated his Son as his Lord.

τοσούτῳ μᾶλλον καταδικασθήσονται· δυνατοὶ γὰρ δυνατῶς ἐτασθήσονται, Victor Antiochenus.

Vv. 41–44. Comp. Luke xxi. 1–4. It is surprising that this highly characteristic and original episode, which according to Eichthal, indeed, is an interpolation and repeated by Luke, has not been adopted in Matthew. But after the great rebuking discourse and its solemn close, the little isolated picture seems not to have found a place. — τοῦ γαζοφυλακίου] comp. Josephus, *Antt.* xix. 6. 1, where Agrippa hangs a golden chain ὑπὲρ τὸ γαζοφυλάκιον. According to the Rabbins it consisted of thirteen trumpet-shaped brazen chests (שׁוֹפָרוֹת), and was in the fore-court of the women. It was destined for the reception of pious contributions for the temple, as well as of the temple-tribute. See, generally, Lightfoot, *Hor.* p. 539 f.; Reland, *Antt.* i. 8. 14. The treasure-chambers (γαζοφυλάκια) in Josephus, *Bell.* v. 5. 2 and vi. 5. 2, have no bearing here. Comp. Ebrard, p. 495. The word itself (comp. John viii. 20) is found also in the Greek writers (Strabo, ii. p. 319), and frequently in the LXX. and the Apocrypha. — χαλκόν] not *money in general* (Grotius, Fritzsche, and others), but *copper money*, which *most of the people* gave. See Beza. — ἔβαλλον] *imperfect*, as at vv. 17, 18. The reading ἔβαλον (Fritzsche) is too weakly attested, and is not necessary. — Ver. 42 f. μία] in contrast with the πολλοί πλούσιοι: *one single poor widow.* A λεπτόν, so called from its smallness (Xen. *Cyr.* i. 4. 11 : τὸ λεπτότατον τοῦ χαλκοῦ νομίσματος), was ⅛th of an as in copper. See on Matt. v. 26. It is the same definition in the Talmud, that two פרוטות make a קדריונטס; see Lightfoot, p. 638 f.—On the fact that it is not "a *quadrans*" but λεπτὰ δύο, that is mentioned, Bengel has aptly remarked: "quorum unum vidua retinere potuerat." The Rabbinical ordinance: "Non ponat homo λεπτόν in cistam eleemosynarum" (*Bava bathra* f. 10. 2), has no bearing here (in opposition to Schoettgen), for here we have not to do with *alms.* — προσκαλεσάμ.] "de re magna," Bengel. — πλεῖον πάντων] is said *according to the scale of means;* all the rest still kept back much for themselves, the widow nothing (see what follows),—a sacrifice which Jesus estimates in its *moral* greatness; τὴν ἑαυτῆς προαίρεσιν ἐπεδείξατο εὐπορωτέραν τῆς δυνάμεως, Theophylact. — The *present* participle βαλλόντων (see the critical remarks) is not inappropriate (Fritzsche), but designates *those who were throwing*, whose βάλλειν was *present*, when the widow ἔβαλε. — Ver. 44. ἐκ τῆς ὑστερήσ. αὐτῆς] (not αὑτῆς) is the antithesis of ἐκ τοῦ περισσ. αὐτ. in ver. 43. Comp. 2 Cor. viii. 14; Phil. iv. 12. Out of her want, out of her destitution, she has cast in all that (in cash) she possessed, her whole (present) means of subsistence. Observe the earnest twofold designation. On βίος, *victus, that whereby one lives*, comp. Luke viii. 43, xv. 12, 30; Hesiod, *Op.* 230; Xen. *Mem.* iii. 11. 6; Soph. *Phil.* 919, 1266; Dem. 869, 25; Plat. *Gorg.* p. 486 D; and Stallbaum *in loc.*

CHAPTER XIII.

VER. 2. ἀποκριθείς] is, with Tisch., to be deleted, as at xi. 33, following B L ℵ, min. vss. — Ver. 2. ὧδε is adopted before λίθος by Griesb. Fritzsche, Scholz, Lachm., in accordance doubtless with B D G L U Δ ℵ, min. vss., but it is an addition from Matt. xxiv. 2. It is genuine in Matthew alone, where, moreover, it is not wanting in any of the codices. — Ver. 4. εἰπέ] B D L ℵ, min. have εἰπόν. So Fritzsche, Lachm. Tisch. This rarer form is to be adopted in accordance with so considerable testimony ; εἰπέ is from Matthew. — With Tisch., following B L ℵ, we must write ταῦτα συντελ. πάντα; different attempts to rectify the order produced the variations. — Ver. 8. Before the second ἔσονται we must, with Tisch., delete καί, in accordance with B L ℵ**. — καὶ ταραχαί] Suspected by Griesb., struck out by Lachm. and Tisch., in accordance with B D L ℵ, Copt. Aeth. Erp. Vulg. It. Vict. But wherefore and whence was it to have been introduced ? On the other hand, it was very easily lost in the following ἀρχαί. — Ver. 9. ἀρχαί] B D K L U Δ ℵ, min. vss. Vulg. It. also have ἀρχή, which is commended by Griesb., adopted by Fritzsche, Scholz, Lachm. Tisch.; from Matt. xxiv. 8. — Ver. 11. Instead of ἄγωσιν Elz. has ἀγάγωσιν, in opposition to decisive evidence. — μηδὲ μελετᾶτε] is wanting in B D L ℵ, min. Copt. Aeth. Ar. p. Erp. Vulg. It. Vigil. Condemned by Griesb., bracketed by Lachm., deleted by Tisch. But the Homoioteleuton the more easily occasioned the omission of the words, since they *follow immediately after* τί λαλήσητε. Luke xxi. 14, moreover, testifies in favour of their genuineness. — Ver. 14. After ἐρημώσεως Elz. Scholz, Fritzsche (Lachm. in brackets) have: τὸ ῥηθὲν ὑπὸ Δανιὴλ τοῦ προφήτου, which words are not found in B D L ℵ, Copt. Arm. It. Vulg. Sax. Aug. They are from Matthew. — ἑστώς] Lachm. has ἑστηκός, following D 28 ; Tisch. has ἑστηκότα, following B L ℵ. Fritzsche : ἑστός, according to A E F G H V Δ, min. Under these circumstances the *Recepta* has preponderant evidence against it ; it is from Matt. xxiv. 15. Of the other readings ἑστηκός is to

be adopted, because B L ℵ also testify in its favour by ἐστηκότα; [1]
while ἑστός likewise betrays its origin from Matthew (var.; see the
critical remarks on Matt. xxiv. 15). — Ver. 16. ὤν] is wanting in
B D L Δ ℵ, min. Lachm. Tisch. But how easily it dropt out
after ἀγρΟΝ! the more easily, because ὤν stood also in ver. 15.
— Ver. 18. ἡ φυγὴ ὑμῶν] is wanting in B D L Δ ℵ* min. Arm.
Vulg. It., and in other witnesses is represented by ταῦτα. Condemned by Griesb. and Rinck, deleted by Fritzsche, Lachm.
Tisch. Rightly so; it is from Matt. xxiv. 20, from which place
also codd. and vss. have after χειμῶνος added: μηδὲ σαββάτῳ, or
μηδὲ σαββάτου, or ἢ σαββάτου, and the like. — Ver. 19. ἧς] Lachm.
Tisch. have ἤν, following B C* L ℵ, 28. A correction. The
omission of ἧς ἔκτ. ὁ Θεός in D 27, Arm. codd. It. is explained
by the superfluousness of the words. — Ver. 21. The omission
of ἤ, which Griesb., following Mill, commended, and Fritzsche
and Tisch. have carried out, is too weakly attested. In itself it
might as well have been added from Matthew as omitted in
accordance with Luke. — Instead of πιστεύετε Elz. has πιστεύσητε,
in opposition to preponderant evidence; it is from Matt. xxiv.
23. — Ver. 22. Although only on the evidence of D, min.
codd. It., ψευδόχριστοι καί is to be deleted, and ποιήσουσιν is to be
written instead of δώσουσι. Moreover (with Tisch.), καί is to be
omitted before τοὺς ἐκλ. (B D ℵ). The *Recepta* is a filling up
from Matthew. — Ver. 23. ἰδοῦ] is wanting in B L 28, Copt
Aeth. Verc. Bracketed by Lachm., deleted by Tisch. An
addition from Matthew. — Ver. 25. τοῦ οὐρανοῦ ἔσονται] A B C ℵ,
min. vss. have ἔσονται ἐκ τοῦ οὐρανοῦ. So Fritzsche, Lachm. Tisch.
Instead of ἐκπίπτ. B C D L ℵ, min. codd. It. have πίπτοντες (so
Fritzsche, Lachm. Tisch.). Thus the most important codices
are *against* the *Recepta* (D has οἱ ἐκ τοῦ οὐρανοῦ ἔσονται πίπτοντες),
in place of which the best attested of these readings are to be
adopted. Internal grounds are wanting; but if it had been
altered from Matthew, ἀπό would have been found instead of ἐκ.
— Ver. 27. αὐτοῦ] after ἀγγέλ. is wanting in B D L, Copt. Cant.
Verc. Vind. Corb. Bracketed by Lachm., deleted by Tisch.; it
is from Matthew. — Ver. 28. The verbal order ἤδη ὁ κλάδος
αὐτῆς (Fritzsche, Lachm.) has preponderating evidence, but it
is from Matthew. The manifold transpositions in the codices
would have no motive, if the reading of Lachm. had been
the original, as in the case of Matthew no variation is
found. — γινώσκετε] A B** D L Δ, min. have γινώσκεται, which is
approved by Schulz and adopted by Fritzsche and Tisch. The

---

[1] The masculine was introduced by the reference, frequent in the Fathers, to
the statue (τὸν ἀνδριάντα) of the conqueror.

Recepta is from the parallels. — Ver. 31. Instead of παρελεύσεταί, Elz. Lachm. Tisch. have παρελεύσονται. The plural (B D K U Γ ℵ) is to be maintained here and at Luke xxi. 33; the remembrance of the well-known saying from Matth. suggested παρελεύσεται in the *singular*. Moreover, it tells in favour of the *plural*, that B L ℵ, min. (Tisch.) have παρελεύσονται again afterwards instead of παρέλθωσι, although this is a mechanical repetition. — Ver. 32. Instead of ἤ Elz. has καί, in opposition to decisive evidence. — Ver. 33. καὶ προσεύχεσθε] is wanting in B D 122, Cant. Verc. Colb. Tolet. Deleted by Lachm. Rightly; an addition that easily occurred (comp. Matt. xxvi. 41 and the parallels). — Ver. 34. καί is to be deleted before ἑκάστῳ (with Lachm. and Tisch.), in conformity with B C* D L ℵ, min. codd. It. — Ver. 37. Between ἅ in Elz. Scholz, and ὅ which Griesb. has approved, and Fritzsche, Lachm. have adopted, the evidence is very much divided. But ὅ is an unnecessary emendation, although it is now preferred by Tisch. (B C ℵ, etc.). D, codd. It. have ἐγὼ δὲ λ. ὑμ. γρηγ.

Vv. 1–8. See on Matt. xxiv. 1–8. Comp. Luke xxi. 5–11. Mark has preserved the *introduction* in its original historical form. But Matthew *has the discourse itself*, although more artistically elaborated, in its greatest completeness from the collection of Logia and with some use of Mark; and that down to the consummation of the last judgment.[1] — ποταποὶ λίθοι] *quales lapides!* ᾠκοδομήθη ὁ ναὸς ἐκ λίθων μὲν λευκῶν τε καὶ καρτερῶν, τὸ μέγεθος ἑκάστων περὶ πέντε καὶ εἴκοσι πηχῶν ἐπὶ μῆκος, ὀκτὼ δὲ ὕψος, εὖρος δὲ περὶ δώδεκα, Joseph. *Antt.* xv. 11. 3. See Ottii *Spicileg.* p. 175. *Who* uttered the exclamation? (Was it Peter? or Andrew?) Probably Mark himself did not know. — On the ποταπός belonging to later usage, see Lobeck, *ad Phryn.* p. 56 f.; Fritzsche, p. 554 f. — Ver. 2. ὃς οὐ μὴ καταλ.] for οὐ μή in the relative clause, see Winer, p. 450 [E. T. 635 f.] The conception here is: there shall certainly be no stone left upon the other, which

---

[1] Weizsäcker, p. 125, conjectures from Barnabas 4 (ℵ), where a saying of Enoch is quoted about the shortening (συντέτμηκεν) of the days of the final offence (comp. ver. 20; Matt. xxiv. 22), that the properly apocalyptic elements of the discourse as to the future are of Jewish origin, from an Apocalypse of Enoch; but the conjecture rests on much too bold and hasty an inference, hazarded as it is on a single thought, which Jesus Himself might very fairly share with the Jewish consciousness in general.

(in the further course of the destruction) would be secure from being thrown down. Comp. Luke xviii. 30. — Ver. 3. As previously, Mark here also relates more vividly (κατέναντι τοῦ ἱεροῦ) and more accurately (Πέτρος κ.τ.λ.) than Matthew. According to de Wette (comp. Saunier, p. 132; Strauss, Baur), Mark is induced to the latter statement by the κατ' ἰδίαν of Matthew—a specimen of the great injustice which is done to Mark as an alleged compiler. — εἰπόν] Thus, and not εἶπον, is this imperative (which is also current among the Attic writers; see Lobeck, *ad Phryn.* p. 348) to be accented in the N. T. See Winer, p. 49 [E. T. 58]. — τὸ σημεῖον] *scil.* ἔσται: *what will be the fore-token* (which appears), *when* all this destruction is to enter on its fulfilment? — ταῦτα συντελ. πάντα] (see the critical remarks) applies not to the *buildings* of the temple (Fritzsche, who takes συντελεῖσθαι as *simul exscindi*, comp. Beza), but, just like ταῦτα, to the *destruction* announced at ver. 2. To explain it of "*the whole world*" (as ταῦτα is well known to be so used by the philosophers, Bernhardy, p. 280) or of "*all things of the Parousia*" (Lange), is a forced course at variance with the context, occasioned by Matt. xxiv. 3 [1] (in opposition to Grotius, Bengel). Moreover, the state of the case is here *climactic;* hence, while previously there stood merely ταῦτα, now πάντα is added; previously: ἔσται, now συντελεῖσθαι (*be consummated*). — Ver. 5. Jesus now begins His detailed explanation as to the matter (ἤρξατο). — Ver. 7. τὸ τέλος] the end of the tribulation (see ver. 9), not the end of *the world* (so even Dorner, Lange, Bleek), which only sets in *after* the end of the tribulation. See on Matt. xxiv. 6. — Ver. 8. καὶ ἔσονται ... καὶ ἔσονται] solemnly. — καὶ ταραχαί] Famines *and* (therewith connected) *disturbances*, not exactly *revolts* (Griesbach), which the context does not suggest, but more general. Plat. *Legg.* ix. p. 861 A: ταραχή τε καὶ ἀξυμφωνία. *Theaet.* p. 168 A: ταρ. καὶ ἀπορία, *Alc.* ii. p. 146, 15: ταρ,

---

[1] Nevertheless, between the passage before us and Matt. *l.c.* there is no essential diversity, since the disciples conceived of the destruction of Jerusalem as immediately preceding the Parousia. See on Matt. xxiv. 3. Comp. also Dorner, *de orat. Chr. eschatologica*, p. 45.

τε καὶ ἀνομία, 2 Macc. xiii. 16. Comp. τάραχος, Acts xii. 18, xix. 23.

Vv. 9–13. See on Matt. xxiv. 9, xiv. 10–13 ; Luke xxi. 12–18. Mark has here interwoven some things from the discourse which is found at Matt. x. 17–22. — ἀρχαί] pre-fixed with emphasis : *beginnings* of sorrows (comp. τὸ τέλος, ver. 7) are these. — βλέπετε δὲ κ.τ.λ.] *but look ye* (ye on your part, in the midst of these sorrows that surround you) *to your-selves,* how *your own conduct* must be. Comp. on βλέπ. ἑαυτ., 2 John 8 ; Gal. vi. 1. — συνέδρια] *judicial assemblies,* as Matt. x. 17. — καὶ εἰς συναγωγ.] attaches itself, as εἰς συνέδρια precedes, most naturally *to this* (Luther, Castalio, Erasmus, Beza, Calovius, Elz., Lachmann), so that with δαρήσεσθε begins a further step of the description. The more usual connection with δαρήσεσθε, preferred also by Buttmann, *neut. Gr.* p. 287 [E. T. 333] and Bleek, is inadmissible, because εἰς cannot be taken in the pregnant meaning (instead of ἐν ; for the element of " motion towards " is not implied in δαρήσ.), and because the explanation (see my first edition): *ye shall be brought under blows of scourges into synagogues* (comp. Bengel, Lange), is not accordant with fact, since the scourging took place *in* the syna-gogues ; see on Matt. x. 17 ; Acts xxii. 19. That δαρήσ. comes in asyndetically, is in keeping with the emotional character of the discourse. — εἰς μαρτύρ. αὐτοῖς] *i.e.* in order that a testi-mony may be given to them, the rulers and kings, namely, regarding me (comp. previously ἕνεκεν ἐμοῦ), regarding my person and my work (not : " intrepidi, quo causam meam defendatis, animi," Fritzsche)—which, no doubt, involves their inexcusableness in the event of their unbelief ; but it is arbitrary to explain the dative here just as if it were εἰς κατηγορίαν κ. ἔλεγχον αὐτῶν (Euthymius Zigabenus, Theophy-lact, and many others). Comp. on Matt. x. 18. — Ver. 10. And this your vocation fraught with suffering will not soon pass away ; *among all nations* (πάντα has the emphasis) *must first* (before the end of the sorrows appears, comp. ἀρχαὶ ὠδίνων, ver. 9), etc. These words are neither disturbing nor inappropriate (as Köstlin judges, p. 352, comp. Schenkel and Weiss) ; they substantially agree with Matt. xxiv. 14, and do

not betray a "more advanced position in point of time" on
Mark's part (Hilgenfeld), nor are they concocted by the latter
out of κ. τοῖς ἔθνεσιν, Matt. x. 18 (Weiss). — Ver. 11.
μελετᾶτε the proper word *for the studying of discourses.* See
Wetstein. The opposite of extemporizing. Comp. Dem. 1129,
9 : μελετᾶν τὴν ἀπολογίαν ὑπὲρ ἑαυτῶν. — δοθῇ] has the
emphasis. — οὐ γάρ ἐστε ὑμεῖς] of *them* it is *absolutely* denied
that they are the speakers. Comp. on Matt. x. 20. — Ver. 12.
See on Matt. x. 21. From that hostile delivering up, however (comp. παραδιδόντες, ver. 11), neither the relationship of
brother nor of child, etc., will protect my confessors. — Ver. 13.
ὑπομείνας] according to the context here : *in the confession
of my name.* See above, διὰ τὸ ὄνομά μου. See, moreover,
on Matt. xxiv. 13. The τέλος is that of the ὠδίνων, ver. 9,
not that "of the theocratic period of the world's history"
(Schenkel).

Vv. 14-23. See on Matt. xxiv. 15–26. Comp. Luke xxi.
20–24, who, however, has freely elements that are peculiar.
— ὅπου οὐ δεῖ] thoughtful, but more indefinite designation of
the sacred *temple - area* than in Matthew, where the more
definite expression, as well as the reference by name (not
merely suggested by the use of the set expression τὸ βδέλ. τ.
ἐρημ.) to Dan. ix. 27, betrays a later manipulation. — Ver. 16.
ὁ εἰς τὸν ἀγρὸν ὤν] *he who is* (has gone) *into the field.* See on
ii. 1. — Ver. 18. Mark has, with a view to his Gentile-Christian readers, passed over the μηδὲ σαββάτῳ, which was in the
collection of Logia, in Matt. xxiv. 20. — Ver. 19. ἔσονται
. . . θλίψις] "Tempori adscribitur res, quae in tempore fit ;
una et continua erit calamitas," Wetstein. — οἵα οὐ γέγονε
κ.τ.λ.] Comp. Plato, *Rep.* vi. p. 492 E : οὔτε γὰρ γίγνεται, οὔτε
γέγονεν, οὔτ' οὖν μὴ γένηται. — τοιαύτη] after οἵα. See
Fritzsche, *ad Marc.* p. 14 ; Kühner, II. p. 527. — κτίσεως ἧς
ἔκτισ. ὁ Θεός] Comp. ver. 20 : διὰ τοὺς ἐκλεκτοὺς οὓς ἐξελέξατο,
Herod. iii. 147 : ἐντολάς τε, τὰς . . . ἐνετέλλετο, Philostr.
V. Ap. iv. 13. 150 : τῆς μήνιδος ἣν ἐμήνισας. The mode of
expression has for its object "gravius eandem notionem bis
iterari," Lobeck, *Paralip.* p. 522. A contrast with the Jewish
state as a human κτίσις (Lange) is fanciful. κτίσις, *that*

which is created, see on Rom. viii. 19. — ἀποπλαν.] 1 Tim.
vi. 10. — Ver. 23. In Matthew at this point the saying about
the lightning and the carcase, which certainly belongs originally to this place, is added (vv. 27, 28).

Vv. 24–27. See on Matt. xxiv. 29–31. Comp. Luke
xxi. 25–28. — ἀλλ'] breaking off and leading over to a new
subject. Hartung, *Partikell.* II. p. 34 f. — ἐν ἐκείναις τ. ἡμέρ.
μετὰ τ. θλίψ. ἐκ.] Thus in Mark also the Parousia is predicted
as setting in *immediately* after the destruction of Jerusalem,
since it is still to follow *in those days*[1] (comp. vv. 19, 20).
The εὐθέως of Matthew is not thereby *avoided* (de Wette,
Bleek, and others), but this εὐθέως is only a still more express
and more direct definition, which tradition has given to the
saying. To refer ἐν ἐκ. τ. ἡμ. to the times of the church
that are still continuing, is an exegetical impossibility. Even
Baur and Hilgenfeld are in error in holding that Mark has
conceived of the Parousia as *at least not following so immediately close* upon the destruction. — Ver. 25. οἱ ἀστέρες
τοῦ οὐρανοῦ κ.τ.λ.] *the stars of heaven* shall be, etc., which is
more simple (comp. Rev. vi. 13) than that which is likewise linguistically correct : *the stars* shall *from heaven*, etc.
(Hom. *Od.* xiv. 31, *Il.* xi. 179 ; Soph. *Aj.* 1156 ; Aesch.
ii. 34 ; Gal. v. 4 ; 2 Pet. iii. 17). — ἔσονται ἐκπίπτ.] more
graphic and vividly realizing than the simple πεσοῦνται
(Matt.). — Ver. 26. Mark has not *the order of sequence* of the
event, as Matthew depicts it ; he relates *summarily*. —
Ver. 27. ἀπ' ἄκρου γῆς ἕως ἄκρου οὐρανοῦ] *From the outmost border of the earth* (conceived as a flat surface) shall
the ἐπισυνάγειν begin, and be carried through even to the
opposite end, *where the outmost border of the heaven* (κατὰ
τὸ φαινόμενον of the horizon) sets limit to the earth. The
expression is *more poetical* than in Matthew ; it is the

---

[1] It is, in fact, to impute great thoughtlessness and stupidity to Mark, if
people can believe, with Baur, *Markusev.* p. 101, that Mark did not write till
after Matthew and Luke, and yet did not allow himself to be deterred by all
that had intervened between the composition of Matthew's Gospel and his
own, from speaking of the nearness of the Parousia in the same expressions
as Matthew used. This course must certainly be followed, if the composition of
Mark (comp. also Köstlin, p. 383) is brought down to so late a date.

more arbitrary to think (with Bleek) in the case of γῆς of those still living, and in that of οὐρ. of those who sleep in bliss.

Vv. 28–32. See on Matt. xxiv. 32–36. Comp. Luke xxi. 29–33. — αὐτῆς] prefixed with emphasis (see the critical remarks) as the subject that serves for the comparison : When *of it the branch* shall have already become tender, so that thus *its* development has already *so far* advanced. The *singular* ὁ κλάδος, *the shoot*, belongs to the *concrete* representation. — τὸ θέρος] is an image of the Messianic period also in the *Test. XII. Patr.* p. 725. — Ver. 30. ἡ γενεὰ αὕτη] i.e. the *present generation*, which γενεά with αὕτη means throughout in the N. T., Matt. xi. 16, xii. 41, 42, 45, xxiii. 36 ; Mark viii. 12, 13 ; Luke vii. 31, xi. 29, 30, 31, 32, 50, 51. Comp. Heb. iii. 10 (Lachmann). Nevertheless, and although Jesus has just (ver. 29) presupposed of the disciples in general, that they would *live to see* the Parousia—an assumption which, moreover, underlies the exhortations of ver. 33 ff.—although, too, the context does not present the slightest trace of a reference to *the Jewish people*, there has been an endeavour very recently to uphold this reference ; see especially Dorner, p. 75 ff. The word never means *people*,[1] but may in the signification *race, progenies*, receive possibly by virtue of the *connection* the approximate *sense* of *people*, which, however, is not the case here. See, moreover, on Matt. xxiv. 34. — οὐδὲ ὁ υἱός] Observe the *climax*: the *angels*, the *Son*, the *Father*. Jesus thus confesses in the most unequivocal words that the day and hour of His Parousia *are unknown*[2] to Himself, to Him the Son of God (see subsequently ὁ πατήρ),—

[1] The signification "people" is rightly not given either by Spitzner on Homer, *Il.* Exc. ix. 2, or in Stephani *Thes.*, ed. Hase, II. p. 559 f.; in the latter there are specified—(1) *genus*, progenies ; (2) *generatio*, genitura ; (3) *aetas*, seculum. Comp. Becker, *Anecd.* p. 231, 11; also Ellendt, *Lex. Soph.* I. p. 353.

[2] Matthew has not οὐδὲ ὁ υἱός ; according to Köstlin, Holtzmann, and others, he is held to have omitted it on account of its dogmatic difficulty. But this is to carry back the scruples of later prepossession into the apostolic age. Zeller (in Hilgenfeld's *Zeitschr.* 1865, p. 308 ff.) finds in the words, because they attribute to Christ a nature exalted above the angels, an indication that our Mark was not written until the first half of the second century ; but his view is founded on erroneous assumptions with respect to the origin of the Epistles to the Colossians,

a confession of non-omniscience, which cannot surprise us (comp. Acts i. 7) when we consider the human limitation (comp. Luke ii. 52) into which the Son of God had entered (comp. on x. 18), — a confession, nevertheless, which has elicited from the antipathy to Arianism some strange devices to evade it, as when Athanasius and other Fathers (in Suicer, *Thes.* II. p. 163 f.) gave it as their judgment that Jesus meant the not-knowing of His *human nature* only (Gregor. *Epist.* viii. 42: " *in* natura quidem humanitatis novit diem et horam, non *ex* natura humanitatis novit "); while Augustine, *de Genesi c. Manich.* 22, *de Trinit.* i. 12, and others were of opinion that He did not know it *for His disciples*, in so far as He had not been commissioned by God to reveal it unto them. See in later times, especially Wetstein. Similarly Victor Antiochenus also and Theophylact suggest that He desired, as a wise Teacher, to keep it concealed from the disciples, although He was aware of it. Lange, *L. J.* II. 3, p. 1280, invents the view that He *willed* not to know it (in contrast with the sinful wish to know on the part of the disciples), for there was no call in the horizon of His life for His *reflecting* on that day. So, in his view, it was likewise with the angels in heaven. The Lutheran orthodoxy asserts that κατὰ κτῆσιν He was omniscient, but that κατὰ χρῆσιν He had not everything *in promptu*.[1] See Calovius. Ambrosius, *de fide,* v. 8, cut the knot, and declared that οὐδὲ ὁ υἱός was an interpolation of the Arians. Nevertheless it is contained *implicite* also in the εἰ μὴ ὁ πατὴρ μόνος of Matthew, even although it may not have stood originally in the collection of Logia, but rather is to be attributed to the love of details in Mark, whose dependence not on our Matthew (Baur, *Markusev.* p. 102, comp. his *neut. Theol.* p. 102), but on the

---

Ephesians, and Philippians, and of the fourth Gospel. Moreover, Paul places Christ above the angels in other passages (Rom. viii. 38 ; 2 Thess. i. 7), and even as early as in the history of the temptation they *minister* to Him. Zeller believes that he gathers the like conclusion in respect of the date of the composition of our Gospel (and of that of Luke also), but under analogous incorrect combinations, *from the fact* that Mark (and Luke) attaches so studious importance to the narratives of the expulsion of demons.

[1] See, on the other hand, Thomasius, *Chr. Pers. u. Werk.* II. p. 156 f.

apostle's collection of Logia, may be recognised in this more precise explanation.

Vv. 33–37. Comp. Matt. xxiv. 42, 44 ff., xxv. 14. By way of an energetic conclusion Mark has here a passage, which has been formed by the aggregation of several different portions—belonging to this connection, and most completely preserved in Matthew from the collection of Logia—on the part of tradition or of the evangelist himself into a well-adjusted, compact, and imposing unity. — Ver. 34. ὡς] an *anantapodoton*, as at Matt. xxv. 14. See *in loc.* With ὡς the plan of the discourse was, after ver. 34, to subjoin : *so do I also bid you : watch !* Instead of this, after ἵνα γρηγορῇ, with an abandonment of the plan of sentence introduced by ὡς, there follows at once, with striking and vivid effect, the exhortation itself : γρηγορεῖτε, which now, just because the ὡς is forgotten, is linked on by οὖν. — ἀπόδημος] is not equivalent to ἀποδημῶν (Matt. xxv. 14), but : *who has taken a journey.* Pind. *Pyth.* iv. 8 ; Plut. *Mor.* p. 299 E. At the same time ἐνετεί-λατο is not to be taken as a *pluperfect*, but : " *as a traveller, when he had left his house, after having given to his slaves the authority and to each one his work, gave to the doorkeeper also command, in order that he should watch.*" In this we have to observe : (1) the ἐνετείλατο took place after the ἀπόδημος had gone out of his house ; (2) καὶ δοὺς κ.τ.λ., in which καί is *also*, is subordinate to the ἀφεὶς κ.τ.λ., because *prior to* the leaving of the house ; (3) ἄνθρωπος ἀπόδημ.] forms *one* notion : *a man finding himself on a journey, a traveller ;* comp. ἄνθρω-πος ὁδίτης, Hom. *Il.* xvi. 263 ; *Od.* xiii. 123 ; ἄνθρ. ἔμπορος, Matt. xiii. 45, *al. ;* (4) the ἐξουσία, the authority *concerned* in the case, is according to the context the control over the household. This He gave *to all in common ;* and, moreover, to *every one in particular* the special business which he had to execute. Fritzsche is wrong in making the participles ἀφείς . . . καὶ δούς dependent on ἀπόδημος : " homo, qui relicta domo sua et commissa servis procuratione assignatoque suo cuique penso peregre abfuit." Against this may be urged, partly that ἀφεὶς τ. οἰκ. αὐτοῦ would be a quite superfluous definition to ἀπόδημος, partly that δοὺς κ.τ.λ. would need to stand

before ἀφεὶς κ.τ.λ., because the man *first* made the arrangement and *then* left the house. — Ver. 35. γρηγορεῖτε οὖν] the
apostles thus are here compared with the *doorkeeper.* — As
to the *four watches of the night*, see on Matt. xiv. 24.   They
belong to the *pictorial effect* of the parable; the *night*-season
is in keeping with the figurative γρηγορεῖτε, without exactly
expressing " a dark and sad time " (Lange).   Singularly at
variance with the text as it stands, Theophylact and many
others interpret it of the four ages of human life. — Ver. 37.
The reference to *one* thought is not at variance with the use
of the plural ἄ (see the critical remarks).   See Kühner, *ad
Xen. Anab.* iii. 5. 5. — πᾶσι] to all who confess me.

CHAPTER XIV.

VER. 2. δέ] B C* D L ℵ, vss. have γάρ. So Lachm. and Tisch.
The *Recepta* is from Matt. xxvi. 5. — Ver. 3. καί before συντρ. is,
with Tisch., following B L ℵ, Copt., to be deleted. A connective addition. — τὸ ἀλάβ.] Fritzsche, Lachm. read τὸν ἀλάβ., which
is attested by A D E F H K S U V X Γ, min. Tisch., following
B C L Δ ℵ**, has τὴν ἀλάβ., and this is to be preferred. The
ignorance of the transcribers brought in τό and τόν. — κατά] is
wanting in B C L Δ ℵ, min. Deleted by Lachm. and Tisch.
A supplement, instead of which D has ἐπί. — Ver. 4. καὶ λέγοντες]
is with Tisch., in accordance with B C* L ℵ, Copt., to be deleted.
It is a gloss after Matthew, instead of which D reads καὶ ἔλεγον.
— Ver. 5. τὸ μύρον] is wanting in Elz., but is decisively attested.
The omission is explained from Matt. xxvi. 9 (where τοῦτο alone
is genuine). The preponderance of evidence forbids the supposition that it is an interpolation from John xii. 5. D, min.
have it *before* τοῦτο, and in ℵ τοῦτο is wanting. — Ver. 6. Instead
of ἐν ἐμοί Elz. has εἰς ἐμέ, in opposition to decisive evidence. It
is from Matthew. — Ver. 8. αὕτη] is only wanting, indeed, in
B L ℵ, min. Copt. Syr. utr. (bracketed by Lachm.), but is rightly
deleted by Tisch. It is an addition, which is not found till after
ἐποίησεν in Δ. Comp. Matt. xxvi. 12. — Ver. 9. After ἀμήν very
considerable evidence supports δέ, which Lachm. has bracketed,
Tisch. has adopted. It is to be adopted; the omission occurred
conformably to the usual expression of Mark, in accordance
with Matt. xxvi. 13. — τοῦτο] is wanting in B D L ℵ, min. Cant.
Verc. Vind. Corb. Bracketed by Lachm., deleted by Tisch. It
is from Matt. xxvi. 13. — Ver. 14. After κατάλυμα Griesb.
Fritzsche, Lachm. (in brackets) Tisch. read μου, following B C
D L Δ ℵ, min. Sax. Vulg. It. (not all the codices). As μου has
this strong attestation and yet is superfluous, and as it does
not occur at Luke xxii. 11, it is to be held as genuine. — Ver. 15.
The form ἀνάγαιον (Elz.: ἀνώγεον) is decisively attested. — Before
ἐκεῖ is to be read with Tisch. καί, in accordance with B C D L
ℵ, 346, vss. It dropped out in accordance with Luke xxii. 12.
— Ver. 19. καὶ ἄλλως· μήτι ἐγώ] is wanting in B C L P Δ ℵ,
min. vss., including Syr., utr. Vulg. After the example of earlier

MARK.   O

editors, suspected by Griesb., rejected by Schulz, struck out by
Fritzsche and Tisch. But the omission might just as easily
have been brought about by means of the preceding μήτι ἐγώ as
by reason of the startling and even offensive superfluousness of
the words, which, moreover, are not found in Matthew, whereas
no reason for their being added can at all be conceived of
without arbitrary hypotheses. — After λάβετε, ver. 22, Elz. has
φάγετε, in opposition to decisive evidence. From Matthew.
— Ver. 23. The article before ποτήριον (deleted by Lachm.
and Tisch.) has in this place even stronger evidence against
it than in Matt. xxvi. 27, and is, as there, to be struck out. —
Ver. 24. τὸ τῆς] This τό is, as in Matt. xxvi. 28, to be deleted
on considerable evidence with Tisch. (Lachm. has bracketed
it). — καινῆς] is wanting in B C D L ℵ, Copt. Cant. Deleted
by Tisch., and rightly, as also at Matt. xxvi. 28. — περί] B C D
L Δ ℵ, min.: ὑπέρ. So Lachm. and Tisch. Περί is from Matthew,
from whom also codd. and vss. have added εἰς ἄφεσιν ἀμαρτ. —
Ver. 27. ἐν ἐμοὶ ἐν τῇ νυκτὶ ταύτῃ] So Elz. and the editors,
except Fritzsche and Tisch., read after σκάνδαλ. Yet Mill and
Griesb. condemned the words. They are decisively to be rejected
as an addition from Matt. xxvi. 31, as they are wholly wanting
in preponderant witnesses, while others merely omit ἐν ἐμοί, and
others still ἐν τῇ νυκτὶ ταύτῃ. Lachm. has the latter in brackets.
— διασκορπισθήσεται is an emendation (comp. on Matt. xxvi. 31),
instead of which, with Lachm. and Tisch., διασκορπισθήσονται is to
be read, and that with Tisch., after πρόβατα (B C D L ℵ, min.). —
Ver. 29. καὶ εἰ] Fritzsche, Tisch. read εἰ καί. Either is appropriate, and with the evidence divided no decision can be arrived
at, even if εἰ καί was introduced in Matthew. — Ver. 30. σύ after
ὅτι is wanting in Elz., in opposition to decisive evidence. — ἐν
τῇ νυκτὶ ταύτῃ] B C D L ℵ, min. Lachm. Tisch. have ταύτῃ
τῇ νυκτί. Rightly; if this order of words were from Matt.
xxvi. 34, the ἐν also would not be left out in it. — In what
follows τρίς με ἀπ. is, with Lachm. and Tisch., to be written.
The received order is from Matthew. — Ver. 31. ἐκ περισσοῦ]
B C D ℵ, min. have ἐκπερισσῶς. So Lachm. and Tisch. Rightly;
the unusual word was partly exchanged for the simple περισσῶς
(L, min.), partly glossed by ἐκ περισσοῦ. — ἔλεγε] Lachm. and
Tisch. have ἐλάλει, following B D L ℵ. The Recepta is a correction. Comp. on xi. 23. — μᾶλλον] is wanting in B C D L ℵ, vss.,
including Vulg., It. Deleted by Lachm. and Tisch. A gloss on ἐκ
περισσοῦ; hence min. have it also before these words (comp. vii. 36),
and this course Fritzsche has followed. — Ver. 35. As at Matt.
xxvi. 39, so here also προσελθών is strongly attested, but it is to be

rejected. — Ver. 36. τὸ ποτήρ. ἀπ' ἐμοῦ τοῦτο] D, Hil. : τοῦτο τ. π. ἀπ' ἐμοῦ; K M : ἀπ' ἐμοῦ τ. π. τ.; A B C G L U X Δ א, min. Or. vss., including Vulg.: τ. π. τοῦτο ἀπ' ἐμοῦ. In this variety of readings the last is so preponderantly attested that it is, with Fritzsche, Lachm. Tisch., to be adopted. — Ver. 40. ὑποστρέψας] Lachm. has πάλιν ἐλθών, following B L א, Copt. Pers. w. Ar. p. (D and cod. It. have merely ἐλθών). πάλιν ἐλθών is the more to be preferred, seeing that Mark is fond of the word πάλιν, and that he nowhere has the word ὑποστρέφω. But transcribers referred and joined the πάλιν to εὗρ. αὐτοὺς καθεύδ., in accordance with which ἐλθών then became glossed and supplanted by ὑποστρέψ. Accordingly the subsequent πάλιν, which by Elz. Scholz, Tisch. is read after αὐτούς, and is not found in B D L א, min. vss., is, with Lachm., to be deleted. — Instead of καταβαρυνόμενοι, Elz. Scholz have βεβαρημένοι, in opposition to preponderant evidence. It is from Matthew. — Ver. 41. Elz. Scholz, Tisch. have τὸ λοιπόν. But the article has come in from Matthew, in opposition to considerable evidence. — Ver. 43. After Ἰούδας Fritzsche has Ἰσκαριώτης, Lachm. and Tisch. ὁ Ἰσκαρ.; and this addition, some-times with, sometimes without the article, is found in witnesses of weight (but not in B א). Rightly; the omission is explained from the parallels. — ὤν] after εἷς has against it such decisive evidence that it cannot be maintained by means of the parallels, nor even by ver. 10. It is to be deleted, with Fritzsche, Lachm. Tisch. — πολύς] is wanting in B L א, min. vss. Condemned by Rinck, bracketed by Lachm., deleted by Tisch. From Matthew. — Ver. 45. Lachm. only reads ῥαββί once, following B C* D L M Δ א, min. vss., including Vulg., codd. It. But this reading is from Matt. xxvi. 49, whence also χαῖρε has intruded into codd. and vss. — Ver. 46. ἐπ' αὐτὸν τ. χεῖρας αὐτῶν] Many various readings, of which Lachm. has τ. χεῖρας ἐπ' αὐτ.; Tisch. : τ. χεῖρας αὐτῷ. The latter is attested by B D L א** min. vss., and is to be pre-ferred as the less usual (see on Acts xii. 1, the exegetical remarks), which was altered in accordance with Matt. xxvi. 50. — Ver. 47. τις] has, it is true, important evidence against it; but, as being superfluous, and, moreover, as not occurring in Matt. xxvi. 51, it might have been so easily passed over, that it may not be deleted, with Lachm. and Tisch. — Instead of ὠτίον read, with Lachm. and Tisch., following B D א, 1, ὠτάριον. The former is from Matthew. — Ver. 48. The form ἐξήλθατε (Fritzsche, Lachm. Tisch.) is decisively attested. — Ver. 51. εἷς τις νεανίσκ.] Lachm. Tisch. read νεανίσκ. τις, following B C L א, Copt. Syr. It. Vulg. (D : νεανίσκ. δέ τις, without καί). The *Recepta* is to be maintained; νεανίσκος τις is the most prevalent mode of

expression. — Instead of ἠκολούθει, read, in accordance with B C
L א, συνηκολούθει (so Lachm. and Tisch.). The current simple
form has crept in also at v. 37. — οἱ νεανίσκοι] is wanting in
B C* D L Δ א, Syr. Arr. Pers. Copt. It. Vulg. Theophylact.
Rightly condemned by Griesb. (but see his *Comm. crit.* p. 179)
and Rinck, deleted by Fritzsche, Lachm. Tisch. It came in by
means of the gloss τὸν νεανίσκον, which was written in the margin
beside αὐτόν, as Slav. still renders τὸν νεανίσκον instead of αὐτὸν οἱ
νεανίσκοι. The τὸν νεανίσκον written in the margin was easily
changed into οἱ νεανίσκοι, since the absence of a fitting subject
for κρατοῦσιν might be felt. — Ver. 52. ἀπ᾿ αὐτῶν] bracketed by
Lachm., deleted by Tisch., has considerable testimony against
it; yet, as being quite superfluous, it was more easily passed
over than added. — Ver. 53. αὐτῷ after συνέρχ. is wanting in
D L Δ א, Vulg. It. Or. Deleted by Tisch. An omission from
misunderstanding. — Ver. 65. ἔβαλλον] Lachm. and Tisch. have
ἔλαβον on decisive evidence. ἔλαβον not being understood, was
variously altered. — Ver. 67. Ἰησοῦ ἦσθα] B C L א have ἦσθε τοῦ
Ἰησοῦ. So Lachm. and Tisch. D Δ, min. vss., including Vulg. and
codd. It., have τοῦ Ἰησ. *before* τοῦ Ναζ. The latter is in accordance with the usual mode of expression, and with Matt. xxvi. 69.
ἦσθα τοῦ Ἰησοῦ is to be adopted; this τοῦ Ἰησοῦ following was
omitted (so still in min., Fritzsche), and was then variously
restored. — Ver. 68. οὐκ . . . οὐδέ] Lachm. has οὔτε . . . οὔτε, following B D L א, Eus. So now Tisch. also; and rightly. See
Matthew. — τί σὺ λέγεις] Lachm. and Tisch. have σὺ τί λέγεις,
following B C L Δ א, min. Rightly; σύ was omitted (so still
in D, Vulg. It.), and then was restored at the place that first presented itself after τί. — καὶ ἀλέκτωρ ἐφώνησε] is wanting, indeed,
in B L א, Copt. Colb. (bracketed by Lachm.); but the omission is
manifestly caused by comparison with Matthew. — Ver. 70. καὶ
ἡ λαλία σου ὁμοιάζει] So Elz. Scholz, Fritzsche, after Γαλιλ. εἶ. But
the words are wanting in B C D L א, min. Copt. Sahid. Vulg.
codd. It. Eus. Aug. Condemned by Griesb., deleted by Lachm.
and Tisch. An interpolation from Matt. xxvi. 73, in accordance
with the very old reading in that place (D, codd. It.), ὁμοιάζει.
If the words were genuine, they would hardly have been passed
over, containing, as they do, so familiar and noteworthy a particular of the history; the appeal to the homoeoteleuton is not
sufficient. — Ver. 71. Instead of ὀμνύειν (comp. Matthew), ὀμνύναι
is sufficiently vouched for by B E H L S U V X Γ, min. —
Ver. 72. εὐθέως after καί is wanting in Elz., but it is attested by
B D G L א (which, with L, has not ἐκ δευτ.), min. Syr. Arr. Aeth.
Arm. Vulg. codd. It. Eus., and adopted by Griesb. Fritzsche,

Scholz, Lachm. Nevertheless it was far easier for it to be
introduced from Matt. xxvi. 74 than for it, with its prevalent
use and appropriateness, to be omitted. Hence, on the important evidence for its omission (including A C), it is, with
Tisch., to be struck out. — Instead of τὸ ῥῆμα ὅ, the *Recepta* has
τοῦ ῥήματος οὗ, in opposition to decisive witnesses, among which,
however, A B C L Δ ℵ, min. Copt. Sahid. read τὸ ῥῆμα ὡς. Lachm.
and Tisch. have the latter; and with this preponderant attestation, it is to be regarded as original (followed also by Luke
xxii. 61).

Vv. 1, 2. See on Matt. xxvi. 2–5. Comp. Luke xxii. 1, 2.
Including this short introduction of simple historical tenor
(in which Luke follows him), Mark is, in the entire narrative
of the passion, *generally* more original, fresh, and free from
later additions and amplifications of tradition than Matthew
(comp. Weiss, 1861, p. 52 ff.), although the latter again is
the more original in various details. — τὸ πάσχα κ. τὰ ἄζυμα]
the Passover and the unleavened (חמצות), *i.e.* the *feast* of the
Passover and (which it likewise is) of the unleavened. Comp.
3 Esdr. i. 19 : ἠγάγοσαν ... τὸ πάσχα καὶ τὴν ἑορτὴν τῶν
ἀζύμων. On τὰ ἄζυμα as a designation of the *feast*, comp.
3 Esdr. i. 10 : ἔχοντες τὰ ἄζυμα κατὰ τὰς φυλάς. — ἔλεγον
γάρ] This γάρ (see the critical remarks) informs us of the
reason of the ἐζήτουν πῶς previously said; for the feast
was in their way, so that they could not at once proceed,
but believed that they must let it first go quietly by, so
that no tumult might occur. Victor Antiochenus remarks :
τὴν μὲν ἑορτὴν ὑπερθέσθαι βούλονται· οὐ συγχωροῦντο δὲ,
ἐπειδὴ τὴν προφητείαν ἔδει πληροῦσθαι τὴν ἐν τῇ νομικῇ
διατυπώσει, ἐν ᾗ τὸ πάσχα ἐδύετο, μηνὶ πρώτῳ τεσσαρεσκαιδε-
κάτῃ ἡμέρᾳ· ἐν τούτῳ γὰρ τῷ μηνὶ καὶ ἐν ταύτῃ τῇ ἡμέρᾳ τὸ
ἀληθινὸν πάσχα ἔδει θυτῆναι. A view right in itself; not,
however, according to the Synoptic, but according to the Johannine account of the day of the death of Jesus. — ἔσται] *shall
be*, certainty of what was otherwise to be expected. Hartung,
Partikell. II. p. 140.

Vv. 3–9.[1] See on Matt. xxvi. 6–13. Comp. John xii. 1–8,

[1] Holtzmann, p. 95, attributes to this episode the significant purpose of introducing the attitude of the betrayer, whose psychological crisis had now set in,

who also has the peculiar expression πιστικῆς, either directly
from Mark, or from the form of tradition from which Mark
also adopted it.   Luke has at vii. 36 ff. a history of an
anointing, but a different one. — μύρου νάρδου] On the costli-
ness of this, see Pliny, *H. N.* xiii. 2. — πιστικῆς] See on
this word, Fritzsche *in loc.*, and in the *Hall. Lit. Z.* 1840,
p. 179 ff.; Lücke on John xii. 3 ; Winer, p. 89 [E. T. 121];
Wichelhaus, *Leidensgesch.* p. 74 f.; Stephani *Thes.*, ed. Hase, VI.
p. 1117.   πιστικός, in demonstrable usage, means nothing else
than (1) *convincing, persuading* (Xen. *Cyrop.* i. 6. 10 : πιστικω-
τέρους . . . λόγους, Plato, *Gorg.* p. 455 A: ὁ ῥήτωρ ἐστι . . .
πιστικὸς μόνον), thus being equivalent to πειστικός ; (2) *faith-
ful, trustworthy* (Artemidorus, *Oneir.* ii. 32, p. 121: γυνὴ
πιστικὴ καὶ οἰκουρός, comp. πιστικῶς, Plut. *Pel.* 8; Scymn. *orb.
descr.* 42), thus equivalent to πιστός.   The latter signification
is here to be maintained: nard, *on which* one can rely, i.e.
unadulterated *genuine* nard, as Eusebius, *Demonstr. ev.* 9, calls
the gospel the εὐφροσύνη τοῦ πιστικοῦ τῆς καινῆς διαθήκης
κράματος (where the contextual reference to the drinking lies
not in πιστικοῦ, but in κράματος).   The opposite is "*pseudo-
nardus*" (Plin. *H. N.* xii. 12. 26), with which the genuine
nard was often adulterated (comp. also Dioscor. *mat. med.*
i. 6 f.).   This is the explanation already given by Theophylact,
Euthymius Zigabenus (both of whom, however, add that a
special *kind* of nard may also be intended), and most of the
older and more recent commentators (Lücke is not decided).
But Fritzsche (following Casaubon, Beza, Erasmus Schmid,
Maldonatus, and others of the older expositors quoted by Wolf,
who deduce it from πίνω) derives it from πιπίσκω, and
explains it as *nardus potabilis.*   Certainly anointing oils, and
especially oil of spikenard, were *drunk* mingled with wine
(Athen. xv. p. 689 ; Lucian, *Nigrin.* 31 ; Juvenal, *Sat.* vi. 303 ;
Hirtius, *de bell. Hisp.* 33. 5 ; Plin. *H. N.* xiv. 19. 5 ; and see
in general, Hermann, *Privatalterth.* § 26. 8, 9); but the actual

in making advances to meet the Sanhedrim.   But this could only be the case,
if Mark and Matthew had *named* Judas as the murmurer.   Now Mark has
τινές in general, and Matthew designates οἱ μαθηταί as the murmurers.   John is
the first to name Judas.

usus loquendi stands decidedly opposed to this view, for according to it πιστός doubtless (Aesch. *Prom.* 478 ; Lobeck, *Technol.* p. 131) has the signification of *drinkable*, but not πιστικός, even apart from the facts that the *context* does not point to *this* quality, and that it is asserted not of the *ointment*, but of the *nard* (the plant). The *usus loquendi*, moreover, is decisive against all other explanations, such as that of the Vulgate (comp. Castalio, Hammond, Grotius, Wetstein, Rosenmüller) : *spicati ;* [1] and that of Scaliger : *pounded nard* (equivalent to πιστικῆς), from πτίσσω, although this etymology *in itself* would be possible (Lobeck, *Paralip.* p. 31). Others have derived πιστικῆς from the proper name of some unknown place (*Pistic nard*), as did Augustine ; but this was a *cutting of the knot.*[2] — πολυτελοῦς] belongs to μύρου, not to νάρδου, which has its epithet already, and see ver. 5. Comp. Matt. xxvi. 7. — συντρίψασα] neither : *she rubbed it and poured,* etc. (Kypke), nor : *she shook* the vessel (Knatchbull, Hammond, Wakefield, *Silv. crit.* V. p. 57), but : *she broke it* (Ecclus. xxi. 14 ; Bar. vi. 17 ; Dem. 845, 18 ; Xen., *et al.*), namely, the narrow (Plin. *H. N.* ix. 35) neck of the vessel, for she had destined the *entire* contents for Jesus, nothing to be reserved. — τὴν ἀλάβ.] ἀλάβαστρος occurs in all the three genders, and the codices vary accordingly. See the critical remarks. — αὐτοῦ τῆς κεφαλῆς] (see the critical remarks) *on him upon the head,* without the preposition usual in other cases (Plato, *Rep.* iii. p. 397 E), κατά before τῆς κεφαλῆς (Plato, *Leg.* vii. p. 814 D ; Herod. iv. 62). — Ver. 4. *But there were some, who grumbled to one another* (uttered grumblings to one another). πρὸς ἑαυτ., as at xi. 31, x. 26, *al. What* they

[1] Mark having retained the Latin word, but having given to it another form. See also Estius, *Annot.* p. 892.—Several codd. of the It., too, have the translation *spicati ;* others : *pistici,* Verc. : *optimi.*

[2] Still the *possibility* of its being the adjective of a local name may not be called in question. In fact, the Scholiast, Aesch. *Pers.* 1, expressly says : τάδε μὲν Περσῶν πιστὰ καλεῖται . . . πόλις ἐστι Περσῶν Πίστειρα καλουμένη, ἣν συγκόψας ὁ ποιητὴς Πίστα ἔφη. Lobeck, *Pathol.* p. 282, remarks on this : "Somnium hoc est, sed nititur observatione licentiae popularis, qua nomina peregrina varie et multipliciter interpolantur." On the taking of it as a local designation depends the translation *pistici,* which the Vulgate also, along with codd. of It., has in John xii. 3, although in the present passage it gives *spicati.*

murmured, is contained in what follows, without καὶ λέγοντες.
Comp. the use of θαυμάζειν, *mirabundum quaerere*, in Sturz,
Lex. Xen. II. p. 511 f. — Ver. 5. ἐνεβρίμ. αὐτῇ] *they were
angry at her.* Comp. i. 43. — Ver. 7. καὶ ὅταν θέλητε κ.τ.λ.]
certainly an amplifying addition of tradition, found neither in
Matthew nor in John. — Ver. 8. *What she was able* (to do)
*she has done ; the greatest work of love which was possible to her,
she has done.* Comp. Xen. *Mem.* ii. 1. 30 : διὰ τὸ μηδὲν
ἔχειν, ὅ τι ποιῇς. — προέλαβε κ.τ.λ.] *Beforehand she hath
anointed my body on behalf of embalming* (in order thereby to
embalm it). A classical writer would have said προλαβοῦσα
ἐμύρισε (Xen. *Cyr.* i. 2. 3 ; Thuc. iii. 3 ; Dem. 44, 3, *al.*).
Passages with the *infinitive* from Josephus may be seen in
Kypke, I. 192. We may add that the expression in Mark
already betrays the *explanatory* tradition. — Ver. 9. εἰς ὅλον
τ. κόσμον] as in i. 39. The relation to ὅπου is as at Matt.
xxvi. 13.

Vv. 10, 11. See on Matt. xxvi. 14–16. Comp. Luke
xxii. 3–6. — εἷς τῶν δώδεκα] has a tragic stress.

Vv. 12–16. See on Matt. xxvi. 17–19. Comp. Luke
xxii. 7–13. The *marvellous* character of the ordering of the
repast, which is not as yet found in Matthew with his simple
πρὸς τὸν δεῖνα, points in Mark and Luke to a later form of
the tradition (in opposition to Ewald, Weiss, Holtzmann, and
others), as Bleek also assumes. Comp. Matt. xxvi. 18. This
form may easily, under the influence of the conception of our
Lord's prophetic character (comp. xi. 2 f.), have originated
through the circumstance, that the two disciples met the
servant of the δεῖνα, to whom Jesus sent them, in the street
with a pitcher of water. Assuredly *original*, however, is the
sending of only *two* disciples in Mark, whom thereupon Luke
xxii. 8 *names.* — ὅτε τ. πάσχα ἔθυον] *on which day they
killed the paschal lamb* (Ex. xii. 21 ; Deut. xvi. 2 ; 3 Esdr.
i. 1, vii. 12), which occurred on the 14th Nisan in the after-
noon.[1] See on Matt. xxvi. 17. — Ver. 13. ἄνθρωπος] The

----

[1] Neither here nor elsewhere have the Synoptics expressed themselves
ambiguously as to the day of the Last Supper. See Hilgenfeld in his *Zeitschr.*
1865, p. 96 ff. (in opposition to Aberle in the *theol. Quartalschr.* IV. p. 548 ff.).

connection (see ver. 14) shows that the man in question was a *slave;* his occupation was the carrying of water, Deut. xxix. 10 ; Josh. ix. 21 ; Wetstein *in loc.* — κεράμιον ὕδατος] *an earthen vessel with water.* Comp. ἀλάβαστρον μύρου, ver. 3. " The *water pitcher* reminds one of the beginning of a meal, for which the hands are washed," Ewald. — Ver. 14. τὸ κατάλυμά μου] *the lodging destined for me,* in which (ὅπου) I, etc. The word κατάλ., *lodging, quarters,* is bad Greek, Thom. M. p. 501. But see Pollux, i. 73, and Eustathius, *ad Od.* iv. 146, 33, Rom. — Ver. 15. αὐτός] *He himself,* the master of the house. On the form ἀνάγαιον instead of ἀνώγαιον (Xen. *Anab.* v. 4. 29), which is preserved in the old lexicographers, see Fritzsche *in loc. ;* Buttmann, *neut. Gr.* p. 12 [E. T. 13]. In signification it is equivalent to ὑπερῷον, עֲלִיָּה, *upper chamber,* used as a place of prayer and of assembling together. Comp. on ii. 3, and see on Acts i. 13. — The attributes which follow are thus to be distributed : *he will show you a large upper chamber spread,* i.e. laid with carpets, *in readiness.* — ἑτοιμάσ. ἡμῖν] *arrange for us,* make preparation for us. Comp. Luke ix. 52.

Vv. 17–25. See on Matt. xxvi. 20–29. Comp. Luke xxii. 14–23. — μετὰ τῶν δώδεκα] Those two are to be conceived as having returned after the preparation. — Ver. 18 f. ὁ ἐσθίων μετ᾽ ἐμοῦ] not said for the purpose of making known the fact, but the expression of deeply painful emotion. — εἷς καθεῖς] *man by man.* See on this expression of late Greek, wherein the preposition is adverbial, Wetstein *in loc. ;* Winer, p. 223 [E. T. 312] ; Buttmann, *neut. Gr.* p. 27 [E. T. 30]. — καὶ ἄλλος] an inaccuracy of expression, as though there had been previously said not εἷς καθεῖς, but merely εἷς. *Mark* in particular might be led into this inaccuracy by his *graphic* manner. — Ver. 20. ὁ ἐμβαπτ.] not *at this moment,* and so not a definite designation of the traitor (as Bleek will have it), for after ver. 19 it is certain that the eating was not immediately proceeded with (comp. on Matt. xxvi. 23) ; but neither is it generally : " qui mecum *vesci consuevit,*" Beza ; but, like ὁ ἐσθίων μετ᾽ ἐμοῦ, ver. 18, *referring generally to this meal,* and withal more precisely indicating the traitor to this extent, that he was one of those who reclined nearest to Jesus, and who ate with Him *out of the same dish.* According to Lange, indeed, the hand of Judas made a "movement playing the hypocrite," and met the hand of the Lord, while the latter was still in the dish, in order with apparent ingenuousness to receive the morsel. A harmonistic play of fancy, whereof nothing appears in the text. — Ver. 24. εἶπεν] namely, *while they drank,* not *before* the drinking. A deviation from Matthew and Luke, but not inappropriate, as Jesus gives the explanation not *afterwards* (in opposition to de Wette), but *at the time of* the drinking[1] (ἐστί). A very immaterial difference, to be explained not from Mark's mere love for alteration (de Wette), but from a diversity of the tradition, in respect to which, however, the greater simplicity and independence on the form of the ecclesiastical observance, which mark the narrative in Mark, tell in favour of its originality (in opposition to Baur). — τὸ αἷμά μου τῆς διαθήκης] *my covenant-blood,* as Matt. xxvi. 28. The definition, "the *new* covenant," came in later; as also "*for the forgiveness of sins*" is a more precise specification from a further stage of development.[2] Comp. on Matt. xxvi. 28. And the direction, "*Do this in remembrance of me,*" is first added in Paul (twice over) and in Luke. See on 1 Cor. xi. 24.

Vv. 26–31. See on Matt. xxvi. 30–35. — Ver. 29. καὶ εἰ] *even if.* On the difference between this and εἰ καί (which here occurs as a various reading), see Klotz, *ad Devar.* p. 519 f. — ἀλλ'] in the apodosis of a connecting sentence, *at certe ;* see Heindorf, *ad Plat. Soph.* p. 341 f.; Klotz, p. 93. — Ver. 30. σύ] has the emphasis of the contrast with ἀλλ' οὐκ ἐγώ. — σήμερον ταύτῃ τῇ νυκτί] (see the critical remarks) impassioned climax: *to-day, in this* night. As to πρὶν ἤ, see on Matt. i. 18. — δίς] a later form assumed by the utterance than in Matthew. Comp. vv. 68, 72. Even John xiii. 38 has it not. There was no occasion for a later simplification (Weiss), if the

---

[1] Comp. also Rückert, *Abendm.* p. 72.

[2] But observe how *the idea of reconciliation* is already in the case of Mark implied in the simple ὑπὲρ πολλῶν. Even Baur (*neut. Theol.* p. 102) acknowledges this, but thinks that these very words contain a later modification of the narrative.

characteristic δίς was there from the first. — Ver. 31. ἐκπερισσῶς ἐλάλει] (see the critical remarks): but *he was speaking
exceedingly much.* Observe the difference between this ἐλάλει
and the subsequent ἔλεγον (comp. on i. 34); the latter is the
simple, definite *saying;* the former, with ἐκπερισσῶς, is in
keeping with the passionate nature of Peter not even yet
silenced by ver. 30. The word ἐκπερισσ. is not preserved
elsewhere. — ἀπαρνήσομαι] οὐ μή, with the future (see Ellendt,
Lex. Soph. II. p. 410 ff.), denotes the right sure expectation.
Comp. on Matt. xxvi. 35.

Vv. 32–42. Comp. on Matt. xxvi. 36–46. Comp. Luke
xxii. 40–46. — Ver. 33. ἐκθαμβεῖσθαι] used in this place of
the *anguish* (otherwise at ix. 15). The word occurs in the N. T.
only in Mark, who uses strongly graphic language. Comp.
xvi. 5, 6. Matthew, with more psychological suitableness, has
λυπεῖσθαι. — ἕως θανάτου] See on Matt. xxvi. 38, and comp.
Ecclus. xxxvii. 2; Clem. 1 Cor. 4: ζῆλος ἐποίησεν Ἰωσὴφ
μέχρι θανάτου διωχθῆναι, *Test. XII. Patr.* p. 520. — παρέλθῃ
ἀπ᾽ αὐτοῦ] Comp. *Test. XII. Patr.* p. 527: ηὔξατο ... ἵνα
παρέλθῃ ἀπ᾽ ἐμοῦ ἡ ὀργὴ κυρίου. — ἡ ὥρα] the hour κατ᾽
ἐξοχήν, *hora fatalis.* It passes over from the man, when the
latter is spared from undergoing its destiny. — Ver. 36.
Ἀββᾶ] אַבָּא; *so* spoke Jesus in prayer to His Father. This
mode of address assumed among the Greek-speaking Christians
the nature of a *proper name,* and the fervour of the feeling of
childship added, moreover, the *appellative* address ὁ πατήρ,—a
juxtaposition, which gradually became so *hallowed by usage*
that here Mark even places it in the very mouth of Jesus,
which is an involuntary *Hysteron proteron.* The *usual* view,
that ὁ πατήρ is an addition by way of interpreting, is quite
out of place in the fervent address of prayer. See on Rom.
viii. 15. Against the objections of Fritzsche, see on Gal.
iv. 6. — παρένεγκε] *carry away past.* Hahn was wrong,
Theol. d. N. T. I. p. 209 f., in deducing from the passage (and
from Luke xxii. 24) that Jesus had been tempted by His
σάρξ. Every temptation came to Him from without. But
in this place He gives utterance only to His purely human
feeling, and that with unconditional subordination to God,

whereby there is exhibited even in that very feeling His μὴ γνῶναι ἁμαρτίαν, which is incompatible with incitements to sin from His own σάρξ. — ἀλλ᾽ οὐ] The following interrogative τί shows how the utterance emotionally broken off is here to be completed. Hence somewhat in this way: *but there comes not into question,* not : ἀλλ᾽ οὐ γενέσθω. — Ver. 41. καθεύδετε λοιπὸν κ.τ.λ.] as at Matt. xxvi. 45, painful irony: *sleep on now, and take your rest!* Hardly has Jesus thus spoken when He sees Judas approach with his band (vv. 42, 43). Then His mood of painful irony breaks off, and with urgent *earnestness* He now goes on in hasty, unconnected exclamations : *there is enough* (of sleep) ! *the hour is come! see, the Son of man is delivered into the hands of sinners !* arise, let us go (to meet this decisive crisis) ! *see, my betrayer is at hand !* It is only this view of ἀπέχει, according to which it refers to the *sleep* of the disciples, that corresponds to the immediate connection with what goes before (καθεύδετε κ.τ.λ.) and follows ; and how natural is the change of mood, occasioned by the approaching betrayers ! All the more original is the representation. Comp. Erasmus, Bengel (" suas jam peractas habet sopor vices ; nunc alia res est "), Kuinoel, Ewald, Bleek. Hence it is not: there is enough *of watching* (Hammond, Fritzsche). The *usus loquendi* of ἀπέχει, *sufficit* (Vulgate), depends on the passages, which certainly are only few and late, but certain, (pseudo-) Anacreon, xxviii. 33 ; Cyrill. *in Hagg.* ii. 9, even although the gloss of Hesychius : ἀπέχει, ἀπόχρη, ἐξαρκεῖ, is critically very uncertain.[1] Others interpret at variance with linguistic usage : *abest,* sc. *anxietas mea* (see Heumann, Thiess), or *the betrayer* (Bornemann in the *Stud. u. Krit.* 1843, p. 103 f.) ; ἀπέχειν, in fact, does not mean

---

[1] See Buttmann in the *Stud. u. Krit.* 1858, p. 506. He would leave ἀπέχει without any idea to complete it, and that in the sense : *it is accomplished, it is the time of fulfilment, the end is come,* just as Grotius, *ad Matt.* xxvi. 45 (*peractum est*), and as the codex Brixiensis has, *adest finis,* while D and min. add to ἀπέχει : τὸ τέλος. The view deserves consideration. Still the usual *it is enough* is more in keeping with the empirical use, as it is preserved in the two passages of Anacreon and Cyril ; moreover, it gives rise to a doubt in the matter, that Jesus should have spoken a word equivalent to the τετέλεσται of John xix. 30 even *now,* when the consummation was only just beginning.

the being removed *in itself,* but denotes the *distance* (Xen. *Anab.* iv. 3. 5 ; Polyb. i. 19. 5 ; 2 Macc. xi. 5, xii. 29). Lange also is linguistically wrong in rendering : " *it is all over with it,*" *it will do no longer.* The comparison of οὐδὲν ἀπέχει, *nothing stands in the way,*—in which, in fact, ἀπέχει is not intransitive, but active,—is altogether irrelevant.

Vv. 43–52. See on Matt. xxvi. 47–56. Comp. Luke xxii. 47–53. The brief, vivid, terse narrative, especially as regards the blow of the sword and the young man that fled (which are alleged by Wilke to be interpolated), testifies to its originality. — δεδώκει] without augment. See Winer, p. 67 f. [E. T. 84 f.]. — σύσσημον] *a concerted signal,* belongs to the later Greek. See Wetstein and Kypke, Sturz, *Dial. Al.* p. 196. — ἀσφαλῶς] *securely,* so that He cannot escape. Comp. Acts xvi. 23. — Ver. 45. ῥαββί, ῥαββί] The betrayer himself is under excitement. — Ver. 49. ἀλλ᾽ ἵνα κ.τ.λ.] *sc. :* ὡς ἐπὶ λῃστὴν ἐξήλθατε κ.τ.λ., ver. 48. Comp. John ix. 3, i. 8, xiii. 18. — Ver. 50. It would have been more exact to name the subject (the disciples). — Ver. 51 f. συνηκολούθει αὐτῷ] (see the critical remarks) : *he followed Him along with,* was included among those who accompanied Jesus in the garden. — σινδόνα] a *garment* like a shirt, made of cotton cloth or of linen (see Bast, *ep. crit.* p. 180), in which people slept. " Atque ita hic juvenis lecto exsilierat," Grotius. — ἐπὶ γυμνοῦ] not to be supplemented by σώματος, but a neuter substantive. Comp. τὰ γυμνά, the *nakedness,* and see in general Kühner, II. p. 118. — If οἱ νεανίσκοι were genuine, it would not have to be explained as *the soldiers* (Casaubon, Grotius, de Wette), since the context makes no mention of such, but generally : *the young people,* who were to be found in the ὄχλος, ver. 43. — *Who the young man was,* is not to be defined more precisely than as : *an adherent of Jesus,*[1] *but not one of the Twelve.* The latter point follows not from ver. 50 (for this young man also, in fact, had fled), but from the designation εἶς τις νεανίσκ. in itself, as well as from the fact that he already had on the night-dress, and therefore had not been in the company at the

[1] Not possibly *Saul* (the subsequent Apostle Paul), who had run after Him from curiosity, as Ewald, *Gesch. der apost. Zeit.* p. 339, conjectures.

table.   There was no justification, therefore, for guessing at
John (Ambrose, Chrysostom, Gregory, *Moral.* xiv. 23), while
others have even concluded from the one garment that it was
James the Just, the brother of the Lord (Epiphanius, *Haer.*
lxxxvii. 13, as also in Theophylact).   There are other precarious
hypotheses, such as: a youth from the house where Jesus had
eaten the Passover (Victor Antiochenus and Theophylact), or
from a neighbouring farm (Grotius), or *Mark himself* (Olshausen,
Bisping).   The latter is assumed also by Lange, who calls
him a "premature Joseph of Arimathea;" and likewise by
Lichtenstein, who, by a series of combinations, identifies the
evangelist with a son of the master of the house where the
Passover took place.   Casaubon aptly remarks: "quis fuerit
hic juvenis quaerere curiosum est et vanum, quando inveniri
τὸ ζητούμενον non potest."   Probably Mark himself did not
know his name. — It must be left undetermined, too, whence
(possibly from Peter?) he learned this little episode,[1] which
was probably passed over by Matthew and Luke only on
account of its unimportance. — γυμνός] " pudorem vicit timor
in magno periculo," Bengel.

Vv. 53, 54. See on Matt. xxvi. 57 f.   Comp. Luke xxii.
54 f. — πρὸς τ. ἀρχιερ.] *i.e. Caiaphas*, not *Annas*, as appears
from Matthew. — συνέρχονται αὐτῷ] is usually explained:
they come together to Him (the high priest), in which case the
dative is either taken as that of the direction (Fritzsche), or
is made to depend upon συν: *with him*, i.e. *at his house*, they
assemble.   But always in the N. T. (Luke xxiii. 55; Acts
i. 21, ix. 39, *al.*), even in John xi. 33, συνέρχεσθαί τινι means:
to come with any one, una cum aliquo venire (comp. Winer, p.
193 [E. T. 269]); and αὐτῷ, in accordance with the following
ἠκολούθησεν αὐτῷ, is most naturally to be referred to *Jesus*.
Hence: *and there came with Him* all the chief priests,[2] *i.e.* at
the same time, as Jesus is led in, there come also all the

---

[1] According to Baur, only a piquant addition of Mark; according to Hilgenfeld, it is connected with Mark's conception of a more extended circle of
disciples (ii. 14?).

[2] *Whither?* is clearly shown from the context, namely, to the ἀρχιερεύς.   This
in opposition to Wieseler, *Synops.* p. 406.

chief priests, etc., who, namely, had been bespoken for this time of the arranged arrest of the delinquent. This view of the meaning, far from being out of place, is quite in keeping with the *vivid* representation of Mark. — πρὸς τὸ φῶς] *at the fire-light*, Luke xxii. 56. See Raphel, *Polyb.* p. 151 ; Sturz, *Lex. Xen.* IV. p. 519 f. According to Baur, indeed, this is an expression unsuitably borrowed from Luke.

Vv. 55–65. See on Matt. xxvi. 59–68. — Ver. 56. καὶ ἴσαι κ.τ.λ.] *and the testimonies were not alike*[1] (consonant, agreeing). At least *two* witnesses had to agree together ; Deut. xvii. 6, xix. 15 ; Lightfoot, p. 658 ; Michaelis, *Mos. R.* § 299 ; Saalschütz, p. 604. The καί is the simple : *and.* Many testified falsely and dissimilarly. — Ver. 58. ἡμεῖς] *we*, on our part : the ἐγώ also which follows has corresponding emphasis. — χειροποίητον ... ἄλλον ἀχειροποίητον] peculiar to Mark, but certainly (comp. on xv. 29) a later form of the tradition resulting from reflection (at variance with John's own interpretation) as to the meaning of the utterance in John ii. 19, according to which there was found in that saying a reference to the new spiritual worship of God, which in a short time Christ should put in the place of the old temple-service. Comp. Acts vi. 14. Matthew is here more simple and more original. — ἀχειροπ.] is an appositional more precise definition to ἄλλον. See van Hengel, *Annotat.* p. 55 ff. Comp. on Luke xxiii. 32. — Ver. 59. οὐδὲ οὕτως] and *not even thus* (when they gave *this* statement) was their testimony consonant. The different witnesses must therefore have given utterance to not unimportant variations in details (not merely in their mode of apprehending the saying, as Schenkel would have it). It is plain from this that one witness was not heard in the presence of the other. Comp. Michaelis, *Mos. R.* § 299, p. 97. Others, like Erasmus, Grotius, Calovius, in opposition to linguistic usage and to the context (see ver. 56), hold that ἴσος is here and at ver. 56 : *sufficiens.* — Ver. 60. *Two* questions, as at Matt. xxvi. 62. If we assume only one,

---

[1] It is not to be accented ἴσος, as in Homer, but ἴσος, as with the Attic and later writers. See Fritzsche *in loc.;* Bentley, *ad Menandr. fragm.*, p. 533, ed. Meinek.; Brunck, *ad Arist. Plut.* 1113 ; Lipsius, *grammat. Unters.* p. 24.

like the Vulgate, and take τί for ὅ,τι : *answerest thou nothing
to that, which*, etc. (Bornemann in the *Stud. u. Krit.* 1843, p.
120 f. ; Lachmann, Tischendorf, Ewald, Bleek, and various
others), it is true that the construction ἀποκρίνεσθαί τι is not
opposed to it (see on Matthew), but the address is less expressive of the anxiety and urgency that are here natural to the
questioner. Buttmann, *neut. Gr.* p. 217 [E. T. 251], harshly
suggests that "hearing" should be supplied before ὅ,τι. —
Ver. 61. Well known *parallelismus antitheticus*, with emphasis.
Inversely at Acts xviii. 9. — ὁ εὐλογητός] κατ᾿ ἐξοχήν, הַבָּרוּךְ,
God. Used absolutely thus only here in the N. T. The *Sanctus
benedictus* of the Rabbins is well known (Schoettgen, *ad Rom.*
ix. 5). The expression makes us feel the *blasphemy*, which would
be involved in the affirmation. But it is this affirmation which
the high priest *wishes* (hence the form of his question : *Thou
art* the Messiah ?), and Jesus *gives* it, but with what a majestic
addition in this deep humiliation ! — Ver. 62. The ἀπ᾿ ἄρτι in
Matt. xxvi. 64, which is wanting in Mark, and which requires
for what follows the *figurative* meaning, is characteristic and
certainly original. On μετὰ τ. νεφελ., comp. Dan. vii. 13 (עַם) ;
Rev. i. 7. That *figurative* meaning is, moreover, required in
Mark by ἐκ δεξιῶν καθήμ. τ. δυν., although Keim finds in this
interpretation "arbitrariness without measure." Luke only,
xxii. 69, while abbreviating and altering the saying, presents
the *literal* meaning. — Ver. 63. τοὺς χιτῶνας] a more accurate
statement, in accordance with the custom of rending the gar-
ments, than the general τὰ ἱμάτια in Matt. xxvi. 65 ; see *in
loc.* People of rank wore *two* under-garments (Winer, *Realw.*) ;
hence τοὺς χιτ. — Ver. 64. κατέκριναν κ.τ.λ.] *they condemned
Him, to be guilty of death*.[1] On κατακρ. with an infinitive,

---

[1] This was the result, which was already from the outset a settled point with
the court, and to the bringing about of which the judicial procedure had merely
to lend the form of legality. The defence of the procedure in Saalschütz, *Mos. R.*
p. 623 ff., only amounts to a pitiful *semblance* of right. Against the fact as it
stood, that Jesus claimed to be the Messiah, they had no law ; this claim, therefore, was brought into the sphere of the *spiritual* tribunal under the title of
blasphemy, and before the *Roman* tribunal under that of high treason. And
into the question as to the ground and truth of the claim—although in the
confession of Jesus there was implied the *exceptio veritatis*—they prudently did
not enter at all.

comp. Herod. vi. 85, ix. 93; Xen. *Hier.* vii. 10. — Ver. 65.
ἤρξαντο] when the "guilty!" had been uttered. A vivid
representation of the sequel. — τινές] comp. previously οἱ δὲ
πάντες, hence: some of the *Sanhedrists.* *The servants,* i.e.
the servants of the court, follow afterwards. — προφήτευσον]
usually: who struck thee, according to the amplifying narratives of Matthew and Luke; Mark, however, does not say this,
but generally: *prophesy!* which as Messiah thou must be able
to do! They wish to bring Him to *prophesy* by the κολαφίζειν!
The narrative of Mark, regarded as an *abbreviation* (Holtzmann),
would be a singularity without motive. Matthew and Luke
followed another tradition. The veiling of the face must,
according to Mark, be considered merely as *mocking mummery.*
— And after some of the Sanhedrists had thus mocked and
maltreated Him, *the servants received Him with strokes of the*
rod. To them He was delivered for custody until further
orders. This is the meaning according to the reading ἔλαβον
(see the critical remarks). On the explanation of the reading
ἔβαλλον, *they struck Him,* see Bornemann in the *Stud. u. Krit.*
1843, p. 138. As to ῥαπίσμασιν, see on Matt. xxvi. 67
The *dative* denotes the form, the accompanying circumstances,
with which on the part of the servants the ἔλαβον took place.
Bernhardy, p. 100 f. Comp. the Latin *accipere aliquem ver-*
beribus (Cic. *Tusc.* ii. 14. 34).

Vv. 66–72. See Matt. xxvi. 69–75. Comp. Luke xxii.
56–62. — κάτω] *below,* in contrast to the buildings that were
situated higher, which surrounded the court-yard (see on Matt.
xxvi. 3). — Ver. 68. οὔτε οἶδα, οὔτε ἐπίσταμαι] (see the
critical remarks) *I neither know nor do I understand.* Thus
the two verbs that are negatived are far more closely connected
(conceived under *one* common leading idea) than by οὐκ . . .
οὐδέ. See Klotz, *ad Devar.* p. 706 f. On the manner of the
denial in the passage before us, comp. *Test. XII. patr.* p. 715:
οὐκ οἶδα ὃ λέγεις. The *doubling* of the expression denotes
earnestness; Bornemann, *Schol. in Luk.* p. xxxi. f. — προ-
αύλιον] Somewhat otherwise in Matt. xxvi. 71. See *in loc.*
— καὶ ἀλ. ἐφ.] *and a cock crew;* peculiar to Mark in accordance with xiv. 30. — Ver. 69. ἡ παιδίσκη] consequently the

MARK. P

same; a difference from Matt. xxvi. 71.　It is still otherwise
in Luke xxii. 58. — πάλιν] would, if it belonged to ἰδοῦσα
αὐτόν (as taken usually), stand before these words, since it
would have logical emphasis in reference to ἰδοῦσα, ver. 67.
Comp. subsequently πάλιν ἠρνεῖτο.　Hence it is, with Erasmus,
Luther, Grotius, and Fritzsche, to be attached to ἤρξατο, on
which account, moreover, C L Δ ℵ have placed it only after
ἤρξ.　So Tischendorf.　Still the word on the whole is critically
suspicious, although it is quite wanting only in B M, vss.: the
addition of it was natural enough, even although the λέγειν
here is not addressed again to Peter. — ἤρξατο] graphic. —
Ver. 70. ἠρνεῖτο] Tempus *adumbrativum* (as so often in
Mark).　The second πάλιν introduces a *renewed* address, and
this, indeed, ensued *on the part of those who were standing
by.*　Hence it is not: πάλιν ἔλεγον οἱ παρ., but: πάλιν οἱ
παρ. ἔλεγον. — καὶ γὰρ Γαλιλ. εἶ] *for thou art also a Galilean ;*
i.e. for, besides whatever else betrays thee, thou art, moreover, a
Galilean.　They observed this from his dialect, as Matthew,
following a later shape of the tradition, specifies. — ἐπιβαλών]
not: *coepit* flere (Vulg. It. Goth. Copt. Syr. Euthymius Zigabenus, Luther, Castalio, Calvin, Heinsius, Loesner, Michaelis,
Kuinoel, and others), as D actually has ἤρξατο κλαίειν,
which certainly also those versions have read; expressed with
ἐπιβάλλειν, it must have run ἐπέβαλε κλαίειν, and this would
only mean: he threw himself on, set himself to, the weeping (comp. Erasmus and Vatablus: "prorupit in fletum ;" see
also Bengel) ; nor yet: *cum se foras projecisset* (Beza, Raphel,
Vater, and various others), since ἐπιβαλών might doubtless
mean: when he had rushed away, but not: when he had
rushed out,—an alteration of the meaning which Matt. xxvi. 75,
Luke xxii. 62, by no means warrant;[1] nor yet: *veste capiti
injecta* flevit (Theophylact, Salmasius, *de foen. Trap.* p. 272 ;
Calovius, L. Bos, Wolf, Elsner, Krebs, Fischer, Rosenmüller,

---

[1] Lange : "*he rushed out thereupon,*" namely, *on the cock crowing* as the
awakening cry of Christ.　"First a rushing out as if he had an external
purpose, then a painful absorption into himself and weeping. . . . Outside he
found that the cry went inward and upward, and now he paused, and wept."
A characteristic piece of fancy.

Paulus, Fritzsche, and others [1]), which presupposes a supplement not warranted in the context and without precedent in
connection with ἐπιβάλλειν, and would, moreover, require the
middle voice; neither, and that for the same reason, is it:
after he had cast his eyes upon Jesus (Hammond, Palairet);
nor: *addens*, i.e. *praeterea* (Grotius), which is at variance with
linguistic usage, or *repetitis vicibus* flevit (Clericus, Heupel,
Münthe, Bleek), which would presuppose a weeping as having
already previously occurred (Theophrastus, *Char.* 8; Diodorus
Siculus, p. 345 B).   Ewald is linguistically correct in rendering: Breaking in with the tears of deep repentance upon the
sound of the cock arousing him.   See Polyb. i. 80. 1, xxiii.
1. 8; Stephani *Thes.*, ed. Hase, III. p. 1526; Schweighäuser,
Lex. Polyb. p. 244 f.   Thus we should have to conceive of a
loud weeping, answering, as it were, to the cock-crowing.
From a linguistic point of view Casaubon is already correct
(κατανοήσας); then Wetstein, Kypke, Glöckler, de Wette, Bornemann (in the *Stud. u. Krit.* 1843, p. 139), Buttmann, *neut. Gr.*
p. 127 [E. T. 145]: *when he had attended thereto*, namely, to
this ῥῆμα of Jesus, when he had directed his reflection to it.
See the examples for this undoubted use of ἐπιβάλλειν with
and without τὸν νοῦν or τὴν διάνοιαν, in Wetstein, p. 632 f.;
Kypke, I. p. 196 f.   The latter mode of taking it (allowed
also by Beza) appears more in accordance with the context,
because ἀνεμνήσθη κ.τ.λ. precedes, so that ἐπιβαλών corresponds to the ἀνεμνήσθη as the further mental action that
linked itself thereto, and now had as its result the weeping.
Peter *remembers* the word, *reflects* thereupon, *weeps!*

[1] So also Linder in the *Stud. u. Krit.* 1862, p. 562 f., inappropriately comparing περιβάλλειν, and appealing to 2 Kings viii. 15 (where the word, however,
does not at all stand absolutely) and to Lev. xiii. 45 (where the middle voice
is used).

CHAPTER XV.

VER. 1. ἐπὶ τὸ πρωΐ] B C D L ℵ 46, Or. Lachm. Tisch. have merely πρωΐ. But why should ἐπὶ τό have been added? The omission is easily explained from the fact that the transcribers had the simple conception *mane* (Vulg.; comp. Matt. xxvii. 1). — Instead of ποιήσ. Tisch. has ἑτοιμάσ., following only C L ℵ, without min. vss. and Fathers. But it is worthy of consideration, as ποιήσ. might easily come from iii. 6. — Ver. 4. καταμαρτ.] B C D ℵ, Copt. Aeth. It. Vulg. have κατηγοροῦσιν. So Lachm. and Tisch.; the *Recepta* is from Matt. xxvii. 13. — Ver. 7. συστασιαστῶν] Fritzsche, Lachm. Tisch. have στασιαστῶν, following B C D K ℵ, min. Sahid. But how easily the syllable ΣΥ dropped away before ΣΤ, even although no scruple might be felt at the unusual συστασ.! ΣΥ has scarcely been added to make it undoubted that Barabbas was himself an insurgent with the others (Fritzsche), which assuredly apart from this every transcriber found in the words. — Ver. 8. ἀναβοήσας] Lachm. Tisch. have ἀναβάς, following B D ℵ* Copt. Sahid. Goth. Vulg. It. Approved also by Schulz and Rinck. The ἀναβάς was not understood, and, in accordance with what follows (vv. 13, 14), it was awkwardly changed into the ἀναβοήσας, which was as yet in this place premature. — Ver. 12. ὃν λέγετε] Lachm. has deleted this, on too slight evidence. If it had been added, it would have taken the form τὸν λεγόμενον from Matt. xxvii. 22. But τόν is to be adopted before βασιλ. (with Fritzsche, Lachm. Tisch.), according to A B C Δ ℵ, min., to which also D may be added as reading τῷ βασιλ. Out of the swerving from ὃν to τόν is explained the omission of ὃν λέγετε, which happened the more easily after ver. 9. — Ver. 14. The reading περισσῶς (Lachm.), instead of the *Recepta* περισσοτέρως, is so decisively attested that it may not be derived from Matt. xxvii. 23. Somewhat more weakly, but still so considerably, is ἔκρεζον (Lachm.) in the sequel attested (A D G K M, min.; Δ: ἔκραζαν), that this also is to be adopted, and ἔκραζαν is to be regarded as a repetition from ver. 13. — Ver. 17. ἐνδύουσιν] Fritzsche, Lachm. Tisch. have ἐνδιδύσκουσιν, which Griesb. also recommended, and Schulz

approved, following B C D F Δ א, min. Rightly; the familiar
verb supplanted the unusual one. — Ver. 18. The *Recepta*
βασιλεῦ is to be maintained; ὁ βασιλεύς (Griesb. Scholz) is
from Matthew and John. The evidence is divided. — Ver. 20.
σταυρώσωσιν] Lachm. and Tisch. have σταυρώσουσιν, following A C
D L P Δ, min. (B has not got ἵνα σταυρ. αὐτ. at all). With this
preponderant attestation, and as the subjunctive so easily
intruded itself, the future is to be adopted. — Ver. 22. Before
Γολγ. Fritzsche and Tisch. have τόν, following B C** F L Δ א,
min. Rightly; the article, superfluous in itself, was left out
in accordance with Matthew. — Ver. 23. πιεῖν] is with Tisch.,
following B C* L Δ א, Copt. Arm., to be struck out as being an
addition from Matt. xxvii. 34. — Ver. 24. Instead of διαμερίζονται
Elz. has διεμέριζον, in opposition to all the uncials. — Ver. 28. The
whole of this verse is wanting in A B C D X א, min. Cant. Sahid.
Condemned by Griesb., Schulz, and Fritzsche, deleted by Tisch.
It is an ancient, but in the case of Mark a foreign, interpolation from a recollection of Luke xxii. 37 (comp. John xix. 24).
— Ver. 29. ἐν τρισὶν ἡμ. οἰκοδ.] Lachm. and Tisch. have οἰκ. τρ. ἡμ.
As well the omission of ἐν as the putting of οἰκ. first, is sufficiently well attested to make the *Recepta* appear as an alteration
in accordance with Matt. xxvii. 40. — Ver. 30. καὶ κατάβα]
Lachm. Tisch. have καταβάς, following B D L Δ א, Copt. Vulg.
codd. It. The *Recepta* is a resolution of the participle;
comp. P, min.: καὶ κατάβηθι (in accordance with Matthew). —
Ver. 33. καὶ γενομ. (Lachm. and Tisch.) is to be adopted instead
of γενομ. δέ on preponderating evidence; but in ver. 34 the *Recepta*
τῇ ὥρᾳ τῇ ἐνάτῃ is, following A C E G, etc., to be maintained. —
Lachm. Tisch. read τῇ ἐνάτῃ ὥρᾳ, which suggested itself in accordance with Matt. xxvii. 46. — Ver. 34. The words ἐλωΐ κ.τ.λ. are
very variously written in codd. and vss. The *Recepta* λαμμᾶ
is in any case rejected by the evidence; between the forms
λιμά (Lachm.), λαμά (Tisch.), and λεμᾶ (Fritzsche), in the equal
division of the evidence, there is no coming to a decision. —
Ver. 36. τε] has important but not preponderating evidence
against it; it is deleted by Lachm. and Tisch. But if it had
been added, καὶ περιθ. would have been written (Matt. xxvii. 48),
which, however, is only found in a few cursives. On the other
hand, previously instead of εἷς, τις is to be read with Tisch., and
the following καί to be deleted with Lachm. The *Recepta* is
moulded after Matthew. — Ver. 39. κράξας] is wanting only in
B L א Copt. Ar. (deleted by Tisch.), and easily became objectionable. — The arrangement οὗτος ὁ ἄνθρωπ. in Lachm. and Tisch.
is attested by B D L Δ א, min. The *Recepta* is from Luke

xxiii. 47. — Ver. 41. αἲ καί] Lachm. and Tisch. have merely αἲ.
So also Rinck. But the collocation of the two almost similar
syllables was the occasion of the dropping away partly of αἲ
(A C L Δ, min. vss.), partly of καί (B ℵ, min. vss.). — Ver. 42.
The reading πρὸς σάββατον in Lachm. (instead of προσάββατον) is
nothing but a clerical error. — Ver. 43. ἦλθεν] Decisive evidence
gives ἐλθών. So Matthaei, Fritzsche, Lachm. Tisch., approved
also by Griesb. ἐλθὼν . . . τολμ. εἰσῆλθε was resolved into ἦλθεν
. . . καὶ τ. ἐ. This καί before τολμ. occurs still in min. Syr. utr.
Vulg. Euthym. — Ver. 44. πάλαι] Lachm. has ἤδη, in accordance
with B D, Syr. hier. Arm. Copt. Goth. Vulg. It. Theophyl. A
repetition of the previous ἤδη. — Ver. 45. σῶμα] B D L ℵ: πτῶμα.
So Lachm. and Tisch. Rightly; σῶμα appeared more worthy.
— Ver. 46. καί before καθελ. is wanting in B D L ℵ, Copt.
Lachm. Tisch. A connective addition. — κατέθηκεν] B C** D
L ℵ, min. have ἔθηκεν. So Fritzsche, Lachm. But how easily
the syllable κατ dropped out after καί, especially since Matthew
and Luke also only have the simple form! — Ver. 47. τίθεται]
In accordance with decisive evidence read, with Lachm. and
Tisch., τέθειται.

Ver. 1. See on Matt. xxvii. 1, 2. Comp. Luke xxiii. 1. —
ἐπὶ τὸ πρωΐ] *on the morning* (xiii. 35), *i.e. during the early
morning*, so that ἐπί expresses the duration stretching itself
out. Bernhardy, p. 252. Comp. Acts iii. 1, iv. 5. As to συμβ.
ποι., comp. on iii. 6. They made a consultation. According
to the more significant reading ἑτοιμάσ. (see the critical
remarks), they *arranged* such an one, *they set it on foot.*
On what subject? the sequel informs us, namely, on the
delivering over to the Procurator. — καὶ ὅλον τὸ συνέδρ.] *and
indeed the whole Sanhedrim.* Mark has already observed, xiv. 53
(πάντες), that the assembly was a *full* one, and with manifest
design brings it into prominence once more. " Synedrium
septuaginta unius seniorum non necesse est, ut sedeant omnes
. . . cum vero necesse est, ut congregentur omnes, *congregentur
omnes,*" Maimonides, *Sanhedr.* 3 in Lightfoot, p. 639.

Vv. 2–5. See on Matt. xxvii. 11–14. Comp. Luke xxiii.
2 f. Matthew has here inserted from the evangelic tradition
elsewhere the tragical end of Judas, just as Luke has the discussion with Herod; Mark abides simply and plainly by the
main matter in hand; nor has he in the sequel the dream of

Pilate's wife, or the latter's washing of his hands.   Doubts, however, as to the historical character of these facts are not to be deduced from this silence; only the tradition had narrower and wider spheres of its historical material. — Ver. 4. πάλιν] See ver. 2. — Ver. 5. οὐκέτι] At ver. 2 he had still answered.

Vv. 6–14. See on Matt. xxvii. 15–23.   Comp. Luke xxiii. 13–23. — Ver. 6. ἀπέλυεν] " Imperfectum ubi *solere* notat, non nisi de re ad certum tempus restricta dicitur," Hermann, *ad Viger.* p. 746. — ὅνπερ] *quem quidem* (Klotz, *ad Devar.* p. 724), *the very one whom they,* etc. — Ver. 7. μετὰ τῶν συστασιαστ.] *with his fellow-insurgents.* συστασι-αστής occurs again only in Josephus, *Antt.* xiv. 2. 1.   In the classical writers it is συστασιώτης (Herod. v. 70. 124; Strabo, xiv. p. 708). — ἐν τῇ στάσει] *in the insurrection in question,* just indicated by συστασιαστ.   It is hardly assumed by Mark as *well known;* to us it is entirely unknown.[1]   But Bengel well remarks : " crimen Pilato suspectissimum." — Ver. 8. What Matthew represents as brought about by Pilate, Mark makes to appear as if it were suggested by the people themselves.   An unessential variation. — ἀναβάς] *having gone up* before the palace of Pilate (see the critical remarks). — αἰτεῖσθαι, καθώς] *so to demand, as,* to institute a demand *accordingly, as; i.e.* according to the real meaning : *to demand that, which.*   See Lobeck, *ad Phryn.* p. 427 ; Schaef. *O. C.* 1124. — Ver. 9. τὸν βασιλέα τ. Ἰουδ.] not inappropriate (Köstlin), but said in bitterness against the chief priests, etc., as John xviii. 39. — Ver. 10. ἐγίνωσκε] *he perceived;* Matthew has ᾔδει, but Mark represents the matter *as it originated.* — Ver. 11. ἵνα μᾶλλον] aim of the ἀνέσεισαν (comp. Buttmann, *neut. Gr.* p. 204 [E. T. 236]), *in order that he* (Pilate) *rather,* etc., in order that this result might be brought about. — Ver. 13. πάλιν] supposes a responsive cry already given after ver. 11 on the instigation of the chief priests.   An inexact simplicity of narration.

Vv. 15–20. See on Matt. xxvii. 26–31.   Comp. Luke

[1] If it was not the rising on account of the aqueduct (comp. on Luke xiii. 1), as Ewald supposes.

xxiii. 24, 25. — τὸ ἱκανὸν ποιῆσαι] *satisfacere*, to do what
was enough, to content them. See examples from Diog.
Laert., Appian, and so forth, in Wetstein and Kypke. Comp.
λαμβάνειν τὸ ἱκανόν, Acts xvii. 9. — Ver. 16. Matthew has :
εἰς τὸ πραιτώριον ; the vividly descriptive Mark has : ἔσω
τῆς αὐλῆς, ὅ ἐστι πραιτώριον, *into the interior of the court, which
is the praetorium,* for they did not bring Him into the *house*
and call the cohorts together thither, but into the inner *court*
surrounded by the buildings (*the court-yard*) which formed
the area of the praetorium, so that, when people went from
without into this court through the portal (πυλών, comp. on
Matt. xxvi. 71) they found themselves *in the praetorium*.
Accordingly αὐλή is not in this place to be translated *palace*
(see on Matt. xxvi. 3), but *court*, as always in the N. T.
Comp. xiv. 66, 54. — On the ὅ attracted by the predicative
substantive, comp. Winer, p. 150 [E. T. 206]. — πορφύραν]
a purple robe. Matthew specifies the robe *more definitely*
(χλαμύδα), and the colour *differently* (κοκκίνην), following
another tradition. — Ver. 18. ἤρξαντο] after that investiture ;
a new act.

Ver. 21. See on Matt. xxvii. 32. Comp. Luke xxiii. 26.
— ἵνα σταυρώσουσιν] See the critical remarks. On the
future after ἵνα, see Winer, p. 257 f. [E. T. 360 f.]. — Only
Mark designates Simon by his *sons.* Whether *Alexander* be
identical with the person named at Acts xix. 33, or with the
one at 1 Tim. i. 20, 2 Tim. ii. 17, or with neither of these
two, is just as much a matter of uncertainty, as is the
possible identity of *Rufus* with the person mentioned at
Rom. xvi. 13. Mark takes for granted that both of them were
known, hence they doubtless were *Christians* of mark ; comp.
x. 46. But how frequent were these names, and how many
of the Christians that were *at that time* well known we know
nothing of ! As to ἀγγαρ., see on Matt. v. 41. The notice
ἐρχόμενον ἀπ᾽ ἀγροῦ, which Luke also, following Mark, gives
(but not Matthew), is one of the traces which are left in
the Synoptical narratives that the day of the crucifixion was
not the first day of the feast (see on John xviii. 28). Comp.
Bleek, *Beitr.* p. 137 ; Ebrard, p. 513. It is not, indeed,

specified *how far* Simon had come from the country (comp.
xvi. 12) to the city, but there is no *limitation* added having
reference to the circumstances of the festal Sabbath, so that
the quite open and general nature of the remark, in connection
with the other tokens of a work-day (vv. 42, 46 ; Luke xxiii.
56 ; Matt. xxvii. 59 f.), certainly suggests to us such a work-day.
The ἀγγαρεύοντες being the Roman soldiers, there is the less
room on the basis of the text for thinking, with Lange, of a
popular jest, which had just laid hold of a *Sabbath-breaker* who
happened to come up.

Vv. 22–27. See on Matt. xxvii. 33–38. Comp. Luke
xxiii. 33 f., who here narrates summarily, but yet not without
bringing in a deeply vivid and original trait (ver. 34), and
has previously the episode of the daughters of Jerusalem. —
τὸν Γολγοθᾶ τόπον] Γολγ. corresponds to the subsequent
κρανίου, and is therefore to be regarded as a *genitive.* According to Mark, the place was called the *"place of Golgotha,"*
which name (ὅ) interpreted is equivalent to *"place of a skull."*
— Ver. 23. ἐδίδουν] *they offered.* This is implied in the
imperfect. See Bernhardy, p. 373. — ἐσμυρνισμ.] See, on
this custom of giving to criminals wine mingled with *myrrh*
or similar bitter and strong ingredients for the purpose of
blunting their sense of feeling, Wetstein *in loc.* ; Dougtaeus,
Anal. II. p. 42. — Ver. 24. ἐπ' αὐτά] according to Ps.
xxii. 19 : *upon them* (the clothes were lying there), as Acts
i. 26. Whether the *casting of the lot* was done by dice, or
by the shaking of the lot-tokens in a vessel (helmet), so that
the first that fell out decided for the person indicated by it
(see Duncan, *Lex.,* ed. Rost, p. 635), is a question that must
be left open. — τίς τί ἄρῃ] *i.e. who should receive anything,
and what he was to receive.* See, on this blending of two
interrogative clauses, Bernhardy, p. 444 ; Ellendt, *Lex. Soph.*
II. p. 824 ; Winer, p. 553 [E. T. 783]. — Ver. 25. This
specification of time (comp. ver. 33), which is not, with Baur
and Hilgenfeld, to be derived from the mere consideration of
symmetry (of the third hour to that of ver. 33), is in keeping
with Matt. xxvii. 45 ; Luke xxiii. 44. As to the difference,
however, from John xix. 14, according to which, at about the

sixth hour, Jesus still stood before Pilate, and as to the attempts at reconciliation made in respect thereof, see on John. — καὶ ἐστ. αὐτ.] ἐστ. is not to be translated as a pluperfect (Fritzsche), but : and it was the third hour, *and they crucified Him*, i.e. *when they crucified Him ;*[1] as also in classical writers after the specification of the time the fact is often linked on by the simple καί. See Thuc. i. 50, iii. 108 ; Xen. *Anab.* ii. 1. 7, vii. 4. 12. Comp. on Luke xix. 43. Stallbaum, *ad Plat. Symp.* p. 220 C.

Vv. 29–41. See on Matt. xxvii. 39–56. Comp. Luke xxiii. 35–49. — οὐά] the Latin *vah !* an exclamation of (here ironical) *amazement.* Dio Cass. lxiii. 20 ; Arrian, *Epict.* iii. 23. 24 ; Wetstein *in loc.* — ὁ καταλύων κ.τ.λ.] gives us a glimpse of the *original* affirmation of the witnesses, as it is preserved in Matt. xxvi. 61 (not in Mark xiv. 58). — Ver. 31. πρὸς ἀλλήλ., *inter se invicem,* belongs to ἐμπαίζ. — Ver. 32. *Let the Messiah the King of Israel* come down now, etc.,—a bitter mockery ! The ὁ Χριστός applies to the confession before the supreme council, xiv. 61 f., and ὁ βασιλ. τ. Ἰσρ. to that before Pilate, ver. 2. Moreover, we may attach either the two forms of address (Lachmann, Tischendorf), or the first of them (Ewald), to what precedes. But the customary mode of apprehending it as a *double* address at the head of what follows is more in keeping with the malicious triumph. — πιστεύσ.] namely, that He is the Messiah, the King of Israel. καὶ οἱ συνεσταυρ.] agrees with Matthew, but not with Luke. See on Matt. xxvii. 44. It is to be assumed that Mark had no knowledge of the narrative of Luke xxiii. 39 ff., and that the scene related by Luke belongs to a later tradition, in which had been preserved more special traits of the great

---

[1] Euthymius Zigabenus here gives a warning illustration of forced harmonizing : ἦν δέ, φησιν, ὥρα τρίτη, ὅτε δηλονότι ἤρξατο πάσχειν ὑπὸ τῶν στρατιωτῶν τοῦ Πιλάτου. Εἶτα τὸ ἑξῆς ἀναγνωστέον καθ᾽ ἑαυτό· καὶ ἐσταύρωσαν αὐτὸν, ἐν ἕκτῃ δηλαδὴ ὥρᾳ. So also Luther in his gloss, and Fr. Schmid ; comp. Calovius : "hora tertia *inde a traditione Pilato facta.*" With more shrewdness Grotius suggests : "jam audita erat tuba horae ter'iae, *quod dici solebat donec caneret tuba horae sextae.*" In the main even at this day Roman Catholics (see Friedlieb and Bisping) similarly still make out of the third hour the second quarter of the day (9 to 12 o'clock).

event of the crucifixion, but with which the historical character of the exceedingly characteristic scene is not lost. See on Luke, *l.c.* — Ver. 34.[1] ἐλωΐ] the Syriac form for אֵלִי (Matthew), which latter appears to have been what Jesus uttered, as is to be inferred from the scoff: Ἠλίαν φωνεῖ. — Ver. 36. λέγων] a difference from Matt. xxvii. 49, whose account is more original (in opposition to Holtzmann), because to *remove* the aspect of *friendliness* must appear more in keeping with the *later* development. In consequence of this difference, moreover, ἄφετε is to be understood quite otherwise than ἄφες in Matthew, namely, *allow it,* what I am doing, *let me have my way,*—which has reference to the scoffing conception, as though the proffered draught would preserve the life till Elias should come. The view that in ver. 35 f. *friends* of Jesus are meant who misunderstood His cry of ἐλωΐ, and one of whom had wished still to cheer Him as regards the possible coming of Elias (Ewald, *Gesch. Chr.* p. 490), is in itself improbable even on account of the well-known cry of the Psalm, as indeed the ἄφετε, ἴδωμεν κ.τ.λ., comp. ver. 30, sounds only like malicious mockery. — Ver. 37. ἐξέπνευσε] *He breathed out, i.e.* He *died.* It is often used in this meaning absolutely in the Greek writers (Soph. *Aj.* 1025; Plut. *Arist.* 20). — Ver. 39. According to Mark, the centurion concluded from the fact of Jesus dying *after having cried out in such a manner,* i.e. *with so loud a voice* (ver. 37), that He was a hero. The extraordinary power (οὕτω δεσποτικῶς ἐξέπνευσε, Theophylact, comp. Victor Antiochenus: μετ᾽ ἐξουσίας ἀπέθανε) which the Crucified One manifested in His very departing, made on the Gentile this impression—in which his judgment was naturally guided by the circumstance that he had heard (Matt. xxvii. 40) of the charge brought against Jesus, that He claimed to be Son of God. According to others (as Michaelis, Kuinoel, de Wette), the *unexpectedly*

[1] Mark has only this one of the sayings of Jesus on the cross, and Schenkel regards only this one as absolutely undoubted,—in which opinion he does great injustice specially to John. Schleiermacher, *L. J.* p. 451, takes offence at this very saying, and only finds it conceivable as a *reference to the whole twenty-second Psalm.*

speedy dying of Jesus, who had just before emitted a vigorous cry, made that impression upon the Gentile, who saw in it *a favour of the gods.* But in order to express this, there would have been necessary under the circumstances before ἐξέπν. an accompanying definition, such as ἤδη or εὐθέως. Baur, *Markusev.* p. 108 f., illustrates the remark even from the crying out of the *demons* as they went forth (i. 26, v. 7, ix. 26); holding that Mark correspondingly conceived of the forcible separation of the higher spirit, through which Jesus had been the Son of God,—therefore after a Gnostic manner. Comp. also Hilgenfeld and Köstlin. Wrongly; because opposed to the doctrine of the entire N. T. regarding Christ the *born* Son of God, as indeed the heathen centurion, according to the measure of his conception of sons of God, could not conceive of Him otherwise. We may add that the circumstantial and plain statement of motive, as given by Matthew and Luke for the centurion's judgment, betrays the later manipulators (Zeller in Hilgenfeld's *Zeitschr.* 1865, p. 385 ff., gives a contrary opinion), to whom Mark in this place seemed obscure or unsatisfactory. — ἦν] in His life. — Ver. 40. ἦσαν] *aderant;* comp. viii. 1. — — καὶ Μαρ.] among others *also* Mary. — τοῦ μικροῦ] cannot according to the meaning of the word be without arbitrariness explained as: *the younger,* although the James designated *is* the so-called Younger, but as: *the little* (of *stature,* comp. Luke xix. 3). Hom. *Il.* v. 801: Τυδεύς τοι μικρὸς μὲν ἔην δέμας, Xen. *Cyr.* viii. 4. 20. An appeal is wrongly made to Judg. vi. 15, where in fact μικρός is not the youngest, but the least, that is, the weakest in warlike aptitude. — Mark does not name *Salome,* but he *indicates* her. According to John xix. 25, she was the sister of the mother of Jesus. Comp. also Ewald, *Gesch. Chr.* p. 171. Thus there are *three* women here recorded by Mark. So also Matt. xxvii. 56. To *distinguish* the Mary of James from the mother of Joses, so that *four* should be adduced (Ewald, *l.c.* p. 324), there appears to be no sufficient ground (comp. the Remark after ver. 47); on the contrary, Mark and Matthew would have here expressed themselves in a way very liable to be misunderstood; comp. on Matthew. — Ver. 41. αἲ καὶ κ.τ.λ.] as they were *now* in the company around Jesus, so *also* they were, while He was in Galilee, in His train. αἵ applies, we may add, to the three who were *named*. Beside these there were among the women present yet many *others*, who had gone up with Him to Jerusalem.

Vv. 42–47. See on Matt. xxvii. 57–61. Comp. Luke xxiii. 50–56. — ἐπεί as far as προσάββ. gives the reason why Joseph, when the even had come, etc. With the commencement of the Sabbath (on Friday after sunset) the business of the taking away, etc., would not have been allowable.[1] Hence the words are *not* to be put in parenthesis. Mark has not ἐπεί elsewhere, and it is noteworthy that John also, xix. 31, has it here precisely at the mention of the παρασκευή, and in his Gospel the word only occurs elsewhere in xiii. 29. Certainly this is no accidental agreement; perhaps it arose through a common primitive evangelic document, which John, however, worked up differently. — ὅ ἐστι προσάββ.] *which*—namely, the expression παρασκευή—*is as much as Sabbath-eve*, the day before the Sabbath. On προσάββ., comp. Judith viii. 6. — Ver. 43. The breaking of the legs, John xix. 31 ff., preceded this request for the dead body, and it is to be supposed that Joseph at the same time communicated to Pilate how in the case of Jesus, because He was already dead, the breaking of the legs was not applied. — ὁ ἀπὸ Ἀριμαθ.] The article designates the *well-known* man. See Kühner, *ad Xen. Anab.* iii. 1. 5, iv. 6. 20. — εὐσχήμων βουλευτ.] is usually explained: *a counsellor of rank*. See on the later use of εὐσχήμ., in contrast with the *plebeians*, Wetstein *in loc.*; Phryn. p. 333 and Lobeck thereupon; Acts xiii. 50, xvii. 12. But, as the characteristic of *rank* is already involved in βουλευτής, there is the less reason to depart from the old classical meaning of the word. Hence: a *seemly*, *stately* counsellor, so that the nobleness (the σεμνότης) of his external appearance and deportment is brought into prominence. — That by βουλευτής is

---

[1] Here, therefore, is no trace that that *Friday itself* was already a festal day, although it was really so according to the narrative otherwise of the Synoptics— also a remnant of the original (Johannine) conception of the day of the death of Jesus. Comp. on ver. 21. Bleek, *Beitr.* p. 115 ff.

meant a *member of the Sanhedrim*,[1] may be rightly concluded
from Luke xxiii. 51. This is in opposition to Erasmus,
Casaubon, Hammond, Michaelis, and many others, who conceive of him as a *member of a council at Arimathea*. — καὶ
αὐτός] *on his part also*, like other adherents of Jesus. Comp.
John xix. 38. — προσδεχόμ.] comp. Luke ii. 25, 38; Acts
xxiii. 21, xxiv. 15. — τὴν βασιλ. τοῦ Θεοῦ] *the kingdom of
the Messiah*, whose near manifestation—that subject-matter of
fervent expectation for the devout ones of Israel—Jesus had
announced. The idea of the kingdom is not *Petrine* (Lange),
but one belonging to primitive Christianity generally. — τολ-
μήσας] *having emboldened himself*, absolutely; see Maetzner,
ad Antiph. p. 173. Comp. Rom. x. 20. — Ver. 44. εἰ ἤδη
τέθνηκε] he wondered *if He were already dead* (*perfect*; on the
other hand, afterwards the historic *aorist: had died*). It is
plain that Pilate had had *experience*, how slowly those who
were crucified were accustomed to die. εἰ after θαυμάζω
denotes that the matter is not as yet assumed to be beyond a
doubt. See Boissonade, *ad Philostr. Her.* p. 424; Kühner, II.
p. 480 f.; Frotscher, *Hier.* i. 6; Dissen, *ad Dem. de cor.* p. 195.
— πάλαι] the opposite of ἄρτι. *Whether He had died* (not
just only now, but) *already earlier*. He wished, namely, to
be sure that he was giving away the body as actually dead.
See on πάλαι, *dudum*, as a relative antithesis to the present
time, Wolf, *ad Plat. Symp.* p. 20; Stallbaum, *ad Apol. Socr.*
p. 18 B. — Ver. 45. ἐδωρήσατο] *he bestowed as a gift*, without
therefore requiring money for it. Instances of the opposite
(as Cic. *Verr.* v. 46; Justin, ix. 4. 6) may be seen in Wetstein.
— Ver. 46. καθαιρεῖν] the proper word for the taking away
from the cross, Latin: *detrahere, refigere*. Comp. ver. 36.
See Raphel, *Polyb.* p. 157; Kypke and Loesner *in loc.* — λελατ.
ἐκ πέτρας] *hewn out of a rock*. Comp. Matt. xxvii. 60. The
same fact is expressed in Mark according to the conception

---

[1] The participation of Nicodemus in the action (John xix. 39) forms one of the
special facts which John alone offers us from his recollection. But the attempt
to identify Joseph with Nicodemus (Krenkel in Hilgenfeld's *Zeitschr.* 1865, p.
438 ff.) can only be made, if the fourth Gospel be regarded as non-apostolic, and
even then not without great arbitrariness.

from whence; and in Matthew, according to the conception *wherein.* Of the fact that the grave *belonged* to Joseph, Mark gives no hint, neither do Luke and John ; see on Matt. xxvii. 60. — ποῦ τέθειται] The *perfect* (see the critical remarks) indicates that the women, after the burial had taken place, went thither and beheld *where He has been laid,* where He lies. The *present* would indicate that they looked on *at the burial.*

REMARK.—In ver. 47, instead of 'Ιωσῆ Lachmann and Tischendorf have adopted ἡ 'Ιωσῆτος, following B Δ (L has merely 'Ιωσῆτος) ℵ**, as they also at ver. 40 have 'Ιωσῆτος, following B D L Δ ℵ** (in which case, however, B prefixes ἡ). This is simply a Greek form of the Hebrew name (comp. the critical remarks on vi. 3), and probably, on the strength of this considerable attestation, original, as also is the article ἡ, which is found in A B C G Δ ℵ**. Another reading is ἡ 'Ιωσήφ, which occurs in A, 258, Vulg. Gat. Prag. Rd., and is preferred by Wieseler, *chronol. Synopse,* p. 427 f., who here understands the daughter or wife of the *counsellor Joseph of Arimathea,* and so quite a different Mary from the Mary of James. But (1) this reading has the very great preponderance of evidence opposed to it; (2) it is easily explained whence it originated, namely, out of the correct reading of Matt. xiii. 55 ('Ιωσήφ, see *in loc.*), from which place the name of *Joseph* found its way into many of the witnesses (including Vulg. and codd. It.), not only at Mark vi. 3, but also at xv. 40 (Aeth. Vulg. It. Aug.) and xv. 47; while the underlying motive for conforming the name of *Joses* to that of *Joseph* the brother of Jesus, Matt. xiii. 55, might be found as well in the assumption of the identity of the brethren of Jesus with the sons of Alphaeus, as in the error, which likewise was already ancient (see Theophylact), that *the mother of Jesus* is meant and is designated as the *stepmother* of James and Joses. (3) A Mary *of Joseph* is never named among the women of the Gospel history. But (4) if *Joseph* had been the *counsellor* just previously mentioned, Mark would have written not merely M. ἡ 'Ιωσήφ, but M. ἡ τοῦ 'Ιωσήφ., and would, moreover, assuming only some accuracy on his part, have *indicated* the relation of kinship, which he has not omitted even at ver. 40, where, withal, the relation of Mary to James and Joses was well enough known. Finally, (5) the association of Mary *of Magdala* in the passage before us of itself entitles us to suppose that Mary would also have been one of the women who followed Jesus *from Galilee* (ver. 41), as indeed at xvi. 1 *these* two friends are again named. On the whole we must abide by the *Maria Josis* at the passage before us. Mark, in the passage where he mentions her for the first time, ver. 40, names her *completely* according to her *two* sons (comp. Matt. xxvii. 56), and then—because she was wont to be designated both as *Maria Jacobi* (comp. Luke xxiv. 10) and as *Maria Josis*—at ver. 47 in the latter, and at xvi. 1 in the former manner, both of which differing modes of designation (ver. 47, xvi. 1) either occurred so accidentally and involuntarily, or perhaps were occasioned by different sources of which Mark made use.

CHAPTER XVI.

Ver. 2. τῆς μιᾶς] Lachm. has μιᾷ τῶν, following B 1. From John xx. 1, as is also τῇ μιᾷ τῶν in L Δ ℵ, Eus. Tisch. — Ver. 8. After ἐξελθ. Elz. has ταχύ, in opposition to decisive evidence, from Matt. xxviii. 8. — Ver. 9. ἀφ᾽ ἧς] Lachm. has παρ᾽ ἧς, following C D L 33. Rightly; ἀφ᾽ is from Luke viii. 2. — Ver. 14. After ἐγηγερμ. A C* X Δ, min. Syr. p. Ar. p. Erp. Arm. have ἐκ νεκρῶν, which Lachm. has adopted. A mechanical addition. — Vv. 17, 18. The omission of καιναῖς, as well as the addition of καὶ ἐν ταῖς χερσίν before ὄφεις, is too feebly attested. The latter is an exegetical addition, which, when adopted, absorbed the preceding καιναῖς. — Instead of βλάψη Elz. has βλάψει, in opposition to decisive evidence. — Ver. 19. After κύριος read, with Lachm. and Tisch., Ἰησοῦς, which is found in C* K L Δ, min. most of the vss. and Ir. As an addition in the way of gloss, there would be absolutely no motive for it. On the other hand, possibly on occasion of the abbreviation ΚΣ., ΙΣ., it dropped out the more easily, as the expression ὁ κύριος Ἰησοῦς is infrequent in the Gospels.

The entire section from vv. 9–20 is a non-genuine conclusion of the Gospel, not composed by Mark. The *external* grounds for this view are: (1) The section is wanting in B ℵ, Arm. mss. Ar. vat. and in cod. K of the It. (in Tisch.), which has another short apocryphal conclusion (comp. subsequently the passage in L), and is designated in 137, 138 with an asterisk. (2) Euseb. *ad Marin.* qu. 1 (in Mai, *Script. vet. nov. coll.* I. p. 61 f.), declares that σχεδὸν ἐν ἅπασι τοῖς ἀντιγράφοις the Gospel closes with ἐφοβοῦντο γάρ. Comp. qu. 3, p. 72, where he names the manuscripts which contain the section only τινα τῶν ἀντιγράφων. The same authority in Victor Ant. ed. Matth. II. p. 208, states that Mark has not related any appearance of the risen Lord that occurred to the disciples. (3) Jerome, *ad Hedib.* qu. 3; Gregor. Nyss. *orat. 2 de resurr. Chr.;* Vict. Ant. ed. Matth. II. p. 120; Sever. Ant. in Montfauc. *Bibl. Coisl.* p. 74, and the Scholia in several codd. in Scholz and Tisch., attest that the passage was wanting in very many manuscripts

MARK. Q

(Jerome: "omnibus Graeciae libris paene"). (4) According to Syr. Philox. in the margin, and according to L, several codd. had an entirely different ending[1] of the Gospel. (5) Justin Martyr and Clem. Al. do not indicate any use made by them of the section (how precarious is the resemblance of Justin, *Apol.* I. 45 with ver. 20!); and Eusebius has his Canons only as far as ver. 8, as, indeed, also in codd. A U and many min. the numbers really reach only thus far,[2] while certainly in C E H K M V they are carried on to the very end. These external reasons are the less to be rejected, seeing that it is not a question of a single word or of a single passage of the context, but of an entire section so essential and important, the omission of which, moreover, deprives the whole Gospel of completeness; and seeing that the way in which the passage gradually passed over into the greater part of the codd. is sufficiently explained from Euseb. *ad Marin.* qu. 1, p. 62 (ἄλλος δέ τις οὐδ᾽ ὁτιοῦν τολμῶν ἀθετεῖν τῶν ὁπωσοῦν ἐν τῇ τῶν εὐαγγελίων γραφῇ φερομένων, διπλῆν εἶναί φησι τὴν ἀνάγνωσιν, ὡς καὶ ἐν ἑτέροις πολλοῖς, ἑκατέραν τε παραδεκτέαν ὑπάρχειν, τῷ μὴ μᾶλλον ταύτην ἐκείνης, ἢ ἐκείνην ταύτης, παρὰ τοῖς πιστοῖς καὶ εὐλαβέσιν ἐγκρίνεσθαι). See Credner, *Einl.* I. p. 107. And when Euthymius Zigabenus, II. p. 183, designates those who condemn the section as τινὲς τῶν ἐξηγητῶν, not, however, himself contradicting them, the less importance is to be attached to this after the far older testimonies of Eusebius, and others, from which is apparent not the exegetical, but the *critical* point of view of the condemnation. Moreover, this external evidence against the genuineness finds in the section itself an *internal confirmation*, since with ver. 9 there suddenly sets in a process of excerpt-making in contrast with the previous character of the narration, while the entire section in general contains none of Mark's peculiarities (no εὐθέως, no πάλιν, etc.,—and what a brevity, devoid of

---

[1] Namely: πάντα δὲ τὰ παρηγγελμένα τοῖς περὶ τὸν Πέτρον συντόμως ἐξήγγειλαν· μετὰ δὲ ταῦτα καὶ αὐτὸς ὁ Ἰησοῦς ἀπὸ ἀνατολῆς καὶ ἄχρι δύσεως ἐξαπέστειλε δι᾽ αὐτῶν τὸ ἱερὸν καὶ ἄφθαρτον κήρυγμα τῆς αἰωνίου σωτηρίας. After that L goes on: ἔστην δὲ καὶ ταῦτα φερόμενα μετὰ τὸ ἐφοβοῦντο γάρ· ἀναστὰς δὲ κ.τ.λ.

[2] Vv. 15–18 occur in the Evang. Nicod. 14, in Thilo, p. 618; Tischendorf, p. 242 f. They *might* therefore have already appeared in the Acts of Pilate, which composition, as is well known, is worked up in the *Gospel of Nicodemus.* Ritschl, in the *theol. Jahrb.* 1851, p. 527, would infer this from Tertullian, *Apol.* 21. But scarcely with warrant, for Tertullian, *l.c.*, where there is contained an excerpt from the Acts of Pilate, is founded upon the tradition in *the Acts of the Apostles,* foreign to the Synoptics, regarding *the forty days.*

vividness and clearness on the part of the compiler!); in individual expressions it is quite at variance with the sharply defined manner throughout of Mark (see the notes on the passages in detail, and Zeller in the *theol. Jahrb.* 1843, p. 450); it does not, moreover, presuppose what has been previously related (see especially ver. 9 : ἀφ᾽ ἧς ἐκβεβλ. ἑπτὰ δαιμ., and the want of any account of the meeting in *Galilee* that was promised at ver. 7), and has even apocryphal disfigurements (ver. 18 : ὄφεις ... βλάψῃ). — If, in accordance with all this, the section before us is decidedly to be declared spurious, it is at the same time evident that the Gospel is *without any conclusion:* for the announcement of ver. 7, and the last words ἐφοβοῦντο γάρ themselves, decisively show that Mark did not intend to conclude his treatise with these words. But whether *Mark himself* left the Gospel unfinished, or whether the conclusion has been *lost,* cannot be ascertained, and all conjectures on this subject are arbitrary. In the latter case the lost concluding section may have been similar to the concluding section of Matthew (namely, xxviii. 9, 10, and 16–20), but must, nevertheless, after ver. 8 have contained some incident, by means of which the angelic announcement of ver. 6 f. was still, even in spite of the women's silence in ver. 8, conveyed to the disciples. Just as little with reference to the apocryphal fragment[1] itself, vv. 9–20,—which already in very early times (although not by Mark himself, in opposition to Michaelis, Hug, Guericke, Ebrard, and others) was incorporated with the Gospel as a conclusion (even Syr. has it; and Iren. *Haer.* iii. 10. 6 quotes ver. 19, and Hippol. vv. 17, 18),—is there anything more definite to be established than that it was composed independently of our Gospel, in which case the point remains withal undecided whether the author was a Jewish or a Gentile Christian (Credner), as indeed at least πρώτη σαββάτων, ver. 9 (in opposition to Credner), might be used by one who had been a Jew and had become conversant with Hellenic life. — *Against* the genuineness the following have declared themselves: Michaelis (*Auferstehungsgesch.* p. 179 ff. ; *Einl.* p. 1059 f.), Thies, Bolten, Griesbach, Gratz, Bertholdt, Rosenmüller, Schulthess in Tzschirner's *Anal.* III. 3; Schulz, Fritzsche, Schott (*Isag.* p. 94 ff., contrary to his *Opusc.* II. p. 129 ff.), Paulus (*exeget. Handb.*), Credner, Wieseler (*Commentat. num. loci Marc.* xvi. 9–20 *et Joh.* xxi. *genuini sint,* etc., Gott. 1839), Neudecker,

---

[1] That it is a *fragment,* which originally stood in connection with matter preceding, is plain from the fact that in ver. 9 the subject, ὁ Ἰησοῦς, is not named.

Tischendorf, Ritschl, Ewald, Reuss, Anger, Zeller, Hitzig (who, however, regards Luke as the author), Schenkel, Weiss, Holtzmann, Keim, and various others, including Hofmann (*Schriftbew.* II. 2, p. 4). *In favour of* the genuineness : Richard Simon (*hist. crit.* p. 114 f.), Mill, Wolf, Bengel, Matthaei, Eichhorn, Storr, Kuinoel, Hug, Feilmoser, Vater, Saunier, Scholz, Rinck (*Lucubr. crit.* p. 311 ff.), de Wette, Schwarz, Guericke, Olshausen, Ebrard, Lange, Bleek, Bisping, Schleiermacher also, and various others.[1]   Lachmann, too, has adopted the section, as according to his critical principles it was necessary to do, since it is found in most of the uncials (only B ℵ have it not), Vulg. It. Syr., etc. We may add that he did not regard it as genuine (see *Stud. u. Krit.* 1830, p. 843).

Vv. 1–8. See on Matt. xxviii. 1–8. Comp. Luke xxiv. 1–11. — διαγενομ. τοῦ σαββ.] *i.e.* on *Saturday after sunset.* See ver. 2. A difference from Luke xxiii. 56, which is neither to be got rid of, with Ebrard and Lange, by a distortion of the clear narrative of Luke ; nor, with Beza, Er. Schmid, Grotius, Wolf, Rosenmüller, and others, by taking ἠγόρασαν as a *pluperfect.* For examples of διαγίνεσθαι used *of the lapse of an intervening time* (Dem. 541. 10, 833. 14 ; Acts xxv. 13, xxvii. 9), see Raphel, *Polyb.* p. 157 ; Wetstein *in loc.* — They bought *aromatic herbs* (ἀρώματα, Xen. *Anab.* i. 5. 1 ; *Polyb.* xiii. 9. 5) to mingle them with ointment, and so to anoint the dead body therewith (ἀλείψ.). This is no contradiction of John xix. 40. See on Matt. xxvii. 59. — Ver. 2 f. πρωΐ] with the *genitive.* Comp. Herod. ix. 101, and see generally, Krüger, § 47. 10. 4. — τῆς μιᾶς σαββ.] *on the Sunday.* See on Matt. xxviii. 1. — ἀνατειλαντ. τοῦ ἡλίου] *after sunrise ;* not : when the sun *rose* (Ebrard, Hug, following Grotius, Heupel, Wolf, Heumann, Paulus, and others), or : *was about to rise* (so Krebs, Hitzig), or : *had begun to rise* (Lange), which would be ἀνατέλλοντος, as is actually the

---

[1] Köstlin, p. 378 ff., ascribes the section to the alleged second manipulator of the Gospel. Lange conjectures (see his *L. J.* I. p. 166) that an incomplete work of Mark reached the Christian public earlier than that which was subsequently completed. According to Hilgenfeld, the section is not without a genuine groundwork, but the primitive form can no longer be ascertained ; the evangelist appears " to have become unfaithful to his chief guide Matthew, in order to finish well by means of an older representation."

reading of D. A difference from John xx. 1, and also from
Luke xxiv. 1; nor will it suit well even with the πρωΐ
strengthened by λίαν; we must conceive it so, that the
sun had *only just* appeared above the horizon. — πρὸς
ἑαυτούς] in communication with each other. But of a Roman
watch they know nothing. — ἐκ τῆς θύρας] The stone
was rolled *into* the entrance of the tomb, and so closed
the tomb, John xx. 1. — Ver. 4. ἦν γὰρ μέγας σφόδρα]
Wassenbergh in Valckenaer, *Schol.* II. p. 35, would transpose
this back to ver. 3 after μνημείου, as has actually been
done in D. Most expositors (including Fritzsche, de Wette,
Bleek) proceed thus *as respects the meaning;* holding that γάρ
brings in the reason for ver. 3. An arbitrary view; it refers
to what immediately precedes. *After they had looked up*
(their look was previously cast down) *they beheld* ("contempla-
bantur cum animi intentione," see Tittmann, *Synon.* p. 120 f.)
that the stone was rolled away; for (specification of the reason
how it happened that this perception could not escape them
after their looking up, but the fact of its having been rolled
away must of necessity meet their eyes) *it was very great.*
Let us conceive to ourselves the very large stone *lying
close by the door of the tomb.* Its rolling away, however,
had not occurred while they were beside it, as in Matthew,
but previously; so also Luke xxiv. 2, 23; John xx. 1.
As to σφόδρα at *the end*, comp. on Matt. ii. 10. — Ver. 5.
νεανίσκον] Mark and Luke (who, however, differ in the
number: ἄνδρες δύο) relate the angelic appearance as it
presented itself (κατὰ τὸ φαινόμενον); Matthew (who, however, places it not in the tomb, but upon the stone), as that
which it actually *was* (ἄγγελος κυρίου). On the form of *a
young man* assumed by the angel, comp. 2 Macc. iii. 26;
Joseph. *Antt.* v. 8. 2 f., and Gen. xix. 5 f. — ἐν τ. δεξ.] on
the right hand in the tomb from the entrance, therefore to
the left hand of the place where the body would lie. —
Ver. 6. Simple *asyndeta* in the lively eagerness of the discourse. — Ver. 7. ἀλλ'] *breaking off*, before the summons
which suddenly intervened, Kühner, II. p. 439; Ellendt,
Lex. Soph. I. p. 78 f. — καὶ τῷ Πέτρῳ] to His disciples *and*

(among these especially) *to Peter.* Comp. i. 5; Acts i. 14;
and see Grotius. The special prominence of Peter is explained
by the ascendancy and precedence, which by means of Jesus
Himself (Matt. xvi. 18) he possessed as *primus inter pares*
(" dux apostolici coetus," Grotius; comp. also Mark ix. 2,
xiv. 33), not by the *denial* of Peter, to whom the announcement is held to have given the assurance of forgiveness
(Theophylact, Euthymius Zigabenus, Victor Antiochenus,
Calovius, Heumann, Kuinoel, Lange, and others), which is
assumed with all the greater arbitrariness without any indication in the text, seeing that possibly Peter might have concluded just the contrary. — ὅτι] recitative, so that ὑμᾶς and
ὑμῖν apply to the *disciples* as in Matthew. — καθὼς εἶπεν
ὑμῖν] xiv. 28. It relates to the *whole* of what precedes:
προάγει ὑμᾶς κ.τ.λ. *and* ἐκεῖ αὐτ. ὄψ. The latter was *indirectly*
contained in xiv. 28.—The circumstance that here *preparation
is made for* a narrative of a meeting together in Galilee, but
no such account subsequently *follows*, is an argument justly
brought to bear against the genuineness of ver. 9 ff. That
the women did not execute the angel's charge (ver. 8), does
not alter the course of the matter as it had been indicated by
the angel; and to explain that inconsistency by the fact that
the ascension does not well agree with the Galilean meeting,
is inadmissible, because Mark, according to our passage and
xiv. 28, must of necessity have assumed such a meeting,[1]
consequently there was nothing to hinder him from representing Jesus as journeying to Galilee, and then again returning
to Judaea for the ascension (in opposition to de Wette). —
Ver. 8. δέ] explicative, hence also γάρ has found its way
into codd. and vss. (Lachmann, Tischendorf). — οὐδενὶ οὐδὲν

---

[1] It is characteristic of Schenkel that he assumes the Gospel to have *really*
closed with ver. 8, and that it is "mere unproved conjecture" (p. 319) that
the conclusion is lost. Such a supposition doubtless lay in his interest as
opposed to the bodily resurrection; but even ver. 7 and xiv. 28 ought to have
made him too prudent not to see (p. 333) in the absence of any appearances of the
risen Lord in Mark the weightiest evidence in favour of the early composition
of his Gospel, whereas he comes ·to the unhistorical conclusion that Peter did
not touch on these appearances in his discourses. See Acts x. 40 f., and previously ii. 32, iii. 15.

εἶπον] The suggestion that we should, with Grotius, Heupel, Kuinoel, and many more, mentally supply: *on the way*, is devised for the sake of Luke xxiv. 9 ; rather is it implied, that from fear and amazement they left the bidding of the angel at ver. 7 unfulfilled. It is otherwise in Matt. xxviii. 8. That subsequently they *told* the commission given to them by the angel, is self-evident ; but they did not *execute* it. — εἶχε δὲ αὐτὰς κ.τ.λ.] Hom. *Il.* vi. 137 ; Herod. iv. 15 ; Soph. *Phil.* 681 ; also in the LXX.

Vv. 9, 10. Now begins the apocryphal fragment of some other evangelical treatise (doubtless written very much in the way of epitome), which has been added as a conclusion of our Gospel. In it, first of all, the appearance related at John xx. 14–18 is given in a meagre abstract, in which the remark, which in Mark's connection was here wholly inappropriate (at the most its place would have been xv. 40), πὰρ ἧς ἐκβεβλ. ἑπτὰ δαιμ., is to be explained *by the fact*, that this casting out of demons was related in the writing to which the portion had originally belonged (comp. Luke viii. 2). — πρωΐ πρώτῃ σαββ.] is joined by Beza, Castalio, Heupel, Wolf, Rosenmüller, Paulus, Fritzsche, de Wette, Ewald, and others with ἀναστὰς δέ, but by Severus of Antioch, Gregory of Nyssa, Theophylact, Euthymius Zigabenus, Victor, Grotius, Mill, Bengel, Kuinoel, Schulthess, and others, with ἐφάνη. We cannot decide the point, since we do not know the connection with what went before, in which the fragment originally occurred. If it were an integral part of our Gospel, it would have to be connected with ἐφάνη, since ver. 2 already presupposes the time of the resurrection having taken place, and now in the progress of the narrative the question was not about *this* specification of time, but about the fact that Jesus on the very same morning made His first appearance. — As well πρώτῃ as the singular σαββάτου (comp. Luke xviii. 12) is surprising after ver. 2. Yet it is to be conceded that even Mark himself *might* so vary the expressions. — παρ᾽ ἧς] (see the critical remarks): *away from whom* (French: *de chez*). See Matthiae, p. 1378. The expression with ἐκβάλλειν is not elsewhere found in the N. T. — Ver. 10. Foreign to Mark is here—(1) ἐκείνη, which never occurs (comp. iv. 11, vii. 15, xii. 4 f., xiv. 21) in his Gospel so devoid of emphasis as in this case. As unemphatic stands κἀκεῖνοι in ver. 11, but not at ver 13, as also ἐκείνοις in ver. 13 and ἐκεῖνοι at ver. 20 are emphatic. (2) πορευθεῖσα, which word Mark, often as he had occasion for it, never uses, while in this short section it occurs *three* times (vv. 12, 15). Moreover, (3) the circumlocution τοῖς μετ᾽ αὐτοῦ γενομένοις, instead of τοῖς μαθηταῖς αὐτοῦ (the latter does not occur at all in the section), is foreign to the Gospels. The μαθηταί in the *more extended* sense are *meant*, the apostles and the rest of the companions of Jesus; the apostles *alone* are designated at ver. 14 by οἱ ἔνδεκα, as at Luke xxiv. 9, 33; Acts ii. 14. — πενθοῦσι κ. κλαίουσι] who *were mourning and weeping*. Comp. Luke vi. 25, although to *derive* the words from this passage (Schulthess) is arbitrary.

Ver. 11. Comp. Luke xxiv. 10, 11; John xx. 18. — The fact that θεᾶσθαι apart from this section does not occur in Mark, forms, considering the frequency of the use of the word elsewhere, one of the signs of a strange hand. By ἐθεάθη is not merely *indicated* that He had been *seen*, but that He had been *gazed upon*. Comp. ver. 14, and see Tittmann, *Synon.* p. 120 f. — ἀπιστεῖν does not occur in Mark except here and at ver. 16, but is altogether of rare occurrence in the N. T. (even in Luke only in chap. xxiv.)

Vv. 12, 13. A meagre statement of the contents of Luke xxiv. 13–35, yet provided with a traditional explanation (ἐν ἑτέρᾳ μορφῇ), and presenting a variation (οὐδὲ ἐκείνοις ἐπίστευσαν) which betrays as its source [1] not Luke himself, but a divergent tradition. — μετὰ ταῦτα] (*after what was narrated* in vv. 9–11) does not occur at all in Mark, often as he *might* have written it: it is an expression *foreign* to him. *How long* after, does not appear. According to Luke, it was still on the same day. — ἐξ αὐτῶν] τῶν μετ᾽ αὐτοῦ γενομένων, ver. 10.

---

[1] De Wette wrongly thinks (following Storr, Kuinoel, and others) here and repeatedly, that an interpolator would not have allowed himself to extract so *freely*. Our author, in fact, wrote not *as an interpolator of Mark* (how unskilfully otherwise must he have gone to work !), but *independently of Mark*, for the purpose of completing whose Gospel, however, this fragment was subsequently used.

— περιπατοῦσιν] *euntibus*, not while they stood or sat or lay, but *as they walked*. More precise information is then given in πορευομένοις εἰς ἀγρόν : *while they went into the country*. — ἐφανερώθη] ver. 14; John xxi. 1, *He became visible to them*, was brought to view. The expression does not directly point to a "ghostlike" appearance (in opposition to de Wette), since it does not of itself, although it does by ἐν ἑτέρᾳ μορφῇ, point to a supernatural element in the bodily mode of appearance of the risen Lord. This ἐν ἑτέρᾳ μορφῇ is not to be referred to other clothing and to an alleged disfigurement of the face by the sufferings borne on the cross (comp. Grotius, Heumann, Bolten, Paulus, Kuinoel, and others), but to the *bodily form*, that was *different* from what His previous form had been,—which the tradition here followed assumed in order to explain the circumstance that the disciples, Luke xxiv. 16, did not recognise Jesus who walked and spoke with them. — Ver. 13. κἀκεῖνοι] *these also*, as Mary had done, ver. 10. — τοῖς λοιποῖς] to the others γενομένοις μετ᾽ αὐτοῦ, vv. 10, 12. — οὐδὲ ἐκείνοις ἐπίστ.] *not even them* did they believe. A difference of the tradition from that of Luke xxiv. 34, not a confusion with Luke xxiv. 41, which belongs to the *following* appearance (in opposition to Schulthess, Fritzsche, de Wette). It is boundless arbitrariness of harmonizing to assume, as do Augustine, *de consens. evang.* iii. 25, Theophylact, and others, including Kuinoel, that under λέγοντας in Luke xxiv. 34, and also under the unbelievers in the passage before us, we are to think only of *some,* and those *different* at the two places ; while Calvin makes the distribution in such a manner, that they had doubted *at first,* but had *afterwards* believed ! Bengel gives it conversely. According to Lange, too, they had been believing, but by the message of the disciples of Emmaus they were led into new doubt. Where does this appear ? According to the text, they believed neither the Magdalene nor even the disciples of Emmaus.

Ver. 14. Ὕστερον] not found elsewhere in Mark, *does not* mean : *at last* (Vulgate, Luther, Beza, Schulthess, and many others), although, according to our text, this appearance was the last (comp. Matt. xxi. 37), but : *afterwards, subsequently* (Matt.

iv. 2, xxi. 29; John xiii. 36), which certainly is a very indefinite specification. — The narrative of this appearance confuses very different elements with one another. It is manifestly (see ver. 15) the appearance which according to Matt. xxviii. 16 took place on the mountain in Galilee; but ἀνακειμένοις (*as they reclined at table*) introduces an altogether different scenery and locality, and perhaps arose from a confusion with the incident contained [1] in Luke xxiv. 42 f., or Acts i. 4 (according to the view of συναλιζόμενος as *convescens*); while also the reproaching of the unbelief is here out of place, and appears to have been introduced from some confusion with the history of Thomas, John xx., and with the notice contained in Luke xxiv. 25; for which the circumstance mentioned at the appearance on the mountain, Matt. xxviii. 17 (οἱ δὲ ἐδίστασαν), furnished a certain basis. — αὐτοῖς τοῖς ἔνδεκα] *ipsis undecim*. Observe the ascending gradation in the three appearances— (1) to Mary; (2) to two of His earlier companions; (3) *to the eleven themselves*. Of other appearances *in the circle of the eleven* our author knows nothing; to him *this* was the *only one*. See ver. 19. — ὅτι] equivalent to εἰς ἐκεῖνο ὅτι, Luke xvi. 3; John ii. 18, ix. 17, xi. 51, xvi. 9; 2 Cor. i. 18, xi. 10.

Ver. 15. Continuation of *the same* act of speaking. — πάσῃ τῇ κτίσει] *to the whole creation*, i.e. *to all creatures*, by which expression, however, in this place, as in Col. i. 23, all *men* are designated, as those who are created κατ' ἐξοχήν, as the Rabbinic הבריות is also used (see Lightfoot, p. 673, and Wetstein *in loc.*). Not merely the *Gentiles* (who are called by the Rabbins contemptuously הבריות, see Lightfoot, *l.c.*) are meant, as Lightfoot, Hammond, Knatchbull, and others would have it. This would be in accordance neither with ver. 16 f., where the discourse is of *all* believers without distinction, nor with ἐκήρυξαν πανταχοῦ, ver. 20, wherein is included the *entire* missionary activity, not merely the preaching to the *Gentiles*. Comp. on πάντα τὰ ἔθνη, Matt. xxviii. 19. Nor yet is there a pointing in τῇ κτίσει at the *glorification of the whole of nature* (Lange, comp. Bengel) by means of the gospel (comp.

---

[1] Beza, Calovius, and others wrongly explain ἀνακειμ. as: *una sedentibus*. Comp. xiv. 18.

Rom. viii.), which is wholly foreign to the conception, as plainly appears from what follows (ὁ . . . ὁ δέ). As in Col. *l.c.*, so here also the designation of the universal scope of the apostolic destination by πάσῃ τῇ κτίσει has in it something of *solemnity*.

Ver. 16. *He who shall have become believing* (see on Rom. xiii. 11), *and have been baptized, shall attain the Messianic salvation* (on the establishment of the kingdom). The *necessity* of baptism—of baptism, namely, regarded as a necessary *divinely ordained consequent* of the having become believing, without, however (as Calvin has observed), being regarded as *dimidia salutis causa*—is here (comp. John iii. 5) expressed for all *new converts*, but not for the *children of Christians* (see on 1 Cor. vii. 14). — ὁ δὲ ἀπιστήσας] That in the case of such *baptism* had not occurred, is obvious of itself; refusal of faith necessarily excluded baptism, since such persons despised the salvation offered in the preaching of faith. In the case of a baptism *without* faith, therefore, the necessary subjective *causa salutis* would be wanting.

Ver. 17. Σημεῖα] marvellous significant appearances for the divine confirmation of their faith. Comp. 1 Cor. xiv. 22. — τοῖς πιστεύσουσι] *those who have become believing*, generically. The limitation to *the teachers*, especially the apostles and seventy disciples (Kuinoel), is erroneous. See ver. 16. The σημεῖα adduced indeed actually occurred with the *believers* as such, not merely with the teachers. See 1 Cor. xii. Yet in reference to the serpents and deadly drinks, see on ver. 18. Moreover, Jesus does not mean that *every one* of these signs shall come to pass in the case of *every one*, but in one case this, in another that one. Comp. 1 Cor. xii. 4. — παρακολ.] *shall follow* them that believe, shall *accompany* them, after they have become believers. The word, except in Luke i. 3, is foreign to all the four evangelists, but comp. 1 Tim. iv. 6; 2 Tim. iii. 10. — ταῦτα] *which follow.* See Krüger, *Xen. Anab.* ii. 2. 2; Kühner, *ad Anab.* ii. 5. 10. — ἐν τῷ ὀνόματί μου] *in my name*, which they confess, shall *the ground* be, that they, etc. It refers to *all* the particulars which follow. — δαιμ. ἐκβαλ.] Comp. ix. 38. — γλώσσ. λαλ. καιναῖς] *to speak with new languages.* The ecstatic *glossolalia*

(see on 1 Cor. xii. 10), which first appeared at the event of
Pentecost, and then, moreover, in Acts x. 46 and xix. 6,
and is especially known from the Corinthian church, had been
converted by the tradition with reference to the Pentecostal
occurrence into a speaking in *languages* different from the
mother-tongue (see on Acts ii. 4). And such is the speaking
in *new* languages mentioned in the passage before us, in
such languages, that is, as they could not previously speak,
which were new and strange *to the speakers*. Hereby the
writer betrays that he is writing in the *sub-apostolic* period,
since he, like Luke in reference to the Pentecostal miracle,
imports into the first age of the church a conception of the
glossolalia intensified by legend ; nay, he makes the phenomenon
thereby conceived as a speaking in strange languages to be
even a common possession of believers, while Luke limits it
solely to the unique event of Pentecost. We must accordingly
understand the γλώσσ. λαλεῖν καιναῖς of our text, not in the
sense of the speaking *with tongues*, 1 Cor. xii.–xiv., but in the
sense of the much more wonderful speaking *of languages*, Acts
ii., as it certainly is in keeping with the two strange particulars that immediately follow. Hence every rationalizing
attempt to explain away the concrete designation derived,
without any doubt as to the meaning of the author, from the
Acts of the Apostles, is here as erroneous as it is in the case
of Acts ii., whether recourse be had to generalities, such as
the newness of the utterance of the Christian spirit (Hilgenfeld), or the new formation of the spirit-world by the new
word of the Spirit (Lange), the ecstatic speaking on religious
subjects (Bleek), or others. Against such expedients, comp.
Keim in Herzog, *Encykl.* XVIII. p. 687 ff. The ecstatic
phenomena of Montanism and of the Irvingites present no
analogy *with the passage before us*, because our passage has to
do with *languages*, not with tongues. Euthymius Zigabenus :
γλώσσαις ξέναις, διαλέκτοις ἀλλοεθνέσιν.

Ver. 18. Ὄφεις ἀροῦσι] *They shall lift up serpents* (take
them into the hand and lift them up). Such a thing is not
known from the history of the apostolic times (what took
place with the adder on the hand of Paul in Acts xxviii. 2 ff.

is different) ; it would, moreover, be too much like juggling
for a σημεῖον of believers, and betrays quite the character
of apocryphal legend, for which, perhaps, a traditional distortion of the fact recorded in Acts xxviii. 2 f. furnished a
basis, whilst the serpent-charming so widely diffused in the
East (Elsner, *Obss.* p. 168 ; Wetstein *in loc.;* Winer, *Realw.*)
by analogy supplied material enough.   The promise in Luke
x. 19 is specifically distinct.   Others have adopted for αἴρειν
the meaning of *taking out of the way* (John xvii. 5 ; Matt.
xxiv. 39; Acts xxi. 36), and have understood it either of the
driving away, banishing (Luther, Heumann, Paulus), or of the
destroying of the serpents (Euthymius Zigabenus, Theophylact,
both of whom, however, give also the option of the correct
explanation) ; but the expression would be inappropriate and
singular, and the thing itself in the connection would not be
sufficiently marvellous.   The meaning : " *to plant* serpents *as
signs of victory with healing effect*," in which actual serpents
would have to be thought of, but according to their symbolical
significance, has a place only in the fancy of Lange excited
by John iii. 14, not in the text.   The singular thought must
at least have been indicated by the addition of the essentially
necessary word σημεῖα (Isa. v. 26, xi. 12), as the classical
writers express *raising a signal* by αἴρειν σημεῖον (comp.
Thuc. i. 49. 1, and Krüger thereon). — κἂν θανάσ. τι πίωσιν
κ.τ.λ.] Likewise an apocryphal appendage, not from the direct
contemplation of the life of believers in the apostolic age.
The practice of condemning to the cup of poison gave material
for it.   But it is not to be supposed that the legend of the
harmless poison-draught of *John* (comp. also the story of *Justus
Barsabas* related by Papias in Euseb. *H. E.* iii. 39) suggested
our passage (in opposition to de Wette and older expositors),
because the legend in question does not occur till so late
(except in Abdias, *hist. apost.* v. 20, and the *Acta Joh.* in
Tischendorf, p. 266 ff., not mentioned till Augustine) ; it rather
appears to have formed itself on occasion of Matt. xx. 23
from our passage, or to have developed itself [1] out of the same

[1] Lange knows how to rationalize this σημεῖον also. In his view, there is
symbolically expressed "the subjective restoration of life to invulnerability."

conception whence our expression arose, as did other similar traditions (see Fabricius *in Abd.* p. 576). On θανάσιμον, which only occurs here in the N. T., equivalent to θανατηφόρον (Jas. iii. 8), see Wetstein, and Stallbaum, *ad Plat. Rep.* p. 610 C. — καλῶς ἕξουσιν] the sick.[1] Comp. Acts xxviii. 8 f.

Vv. 19, 20. *The Lord Jesus therefore* (see the critical remarks). οὖν annexes what now emerged as the final result of that last meeting of Jesus with the eleven, and that as well in reference to the Lord (ver. 19) as in reference also to the disciples (ver. 20); hence μὲν . . . δέ. Accordingly, the transition by means of μὲν οὖν is not incongruous (Fritzsche), but logically correct. But the *expression* μὲν οὖν, as well as ὁ κύριος Ἰησοῦς, is entirely foreign to Mark, frequently as he had occasion to use both, and therefore is one of the marks of another author. — μετὰ τὸ λαλῆσαι αὐτοῖς] cannot be referred without harmonistic violence to anything else than the discourses *just uttered*, vv. 14–18 (Theophylact well says: ταῦτα δὲ λαλήσας), not to the *collective discourses of the forty days* (Augustine, Euthymius Zigabenus, Maldonatus, Bengel, Kuinoel, Lange, and others); and with this in substance agrees Ebrard, p. 597, who, like Grotius and others, finds in vv. 15-18 the account of all that Jesus had said in His several appearances after His resurrection. The forty days are quite irreconcilable with the narrative before us generally, as well as with Luke xxiv. 44. But if Jesus, *after having discoursed to the disciples*, vv. 14-18, was taken up into heaven (ἀνελήφθη, see Acts x. 16, i. 2, xi. 22 ; 1 Tim. iii. 16 ; Luke ix. 51), it is not withal to be gathered from this *very compendious* account, that the

---

Christ is held to declare that the poison-cup would not harm His people, primarily in the symbolical sense, just as it did not harm Socrates in his soul; but also in the typical sense: that the life of believers would be ever more and more strengthened to the overcoming of all hurtful influences, and would in many cases, even in the literal sense, miraculously overcome them. This is to put into, and take out of the passage, exactly what pleases subjectivity.

[1] Not the believers who heal (Lange: "they on their part shall enjoy perfect health"). This perverted meaning would need at least to have been suggested by the use of καὶ αὐτοί (and they on their part).

writer makes Jesus pass *from the room where they were at meat* to heaven (Strauss, B. Bauer), any more than from ἐκεῖνοι δὲ ἐξελθόντες it is to be held that the apostles immediately after the ascension departed into all the world. The representation of vv. 19, 20 is so evidently limited only to the *outlines* of the subsequent history, that between the μετὰ τὸ λαλῆσαι αὐτοῖς and the ἀνελήφθη there is at least, as may be understood of itself, sufficient space for a *going forth of Jesus with the disciples* (comp. Luke xxiv. 50), even although the forty days do not belong to the evangelical tradition, but first appear in the Acts of the Apostles. *How* the writer conceived of the ascension, whether as visible or invisible, his words do not show, and it must remain quite a question undetermined. — καὶ ἐκάθισεν ἐκ δεξιῶν τ. Θεοῦ] reported, it is true, not as an object of sense-perception (in opposition to Schulthess), but as a *consequence, that had set in,* of the ἀνελήφθη; not, however, to be explained away as a merely *symbolical* expression (so, for example, Euthymius Zigabenus: τὸ μὲν καθίσαι δηλοῖ ἀνάπαυσιν καὶ ἀπόλαυσιν τῆς θείας βασιλείας· τὸ δὲ ἐκ δεξιῶν τοῦ Θεοῦ οἰκείωσιν καὶ ὁμοτιμίαν πρὸς τὸν πατέρα, Kuinoel : " cum Deo regnat et summa felicitate perfruitur "), but to be left as a *local fact,* as actual occupation of a seat on the divine throne (comp. on Matt. vi. 9 ; see on Eph. i. 20), from which hereafter He will descend to judgment. Comp. Ch. F. Fritzsche, *nova opusc.* p. 209 ff. — As to the ascension generally, see on Luke xxiv. 51.

Ver. 20. With the ascension the evangelic history was at its end. The writer was only now concerned to add a *conclusion* in keeping with the commission given by Jesus in ver. 15. He does this by means of a *brief summary of the apostolic ministry,* by which the injunction of Jesus, ver. 15, had been fulfilled, whereas all unfolding of its special details lay beyond the limits of the *evangelic,* and belonged to the region of the *apostolic,* history ; hence even the effusion of the Spirit is not narrated here. — ἐκεῖνοι] the ἔνδεκα, ver. 14. — δέ] prepared for by μέν, ver. 19. — ἐξελθόντες] namely, forth from the place, in which at the time of the ascension they sojourned. Comp. πορευθέντες, ver. 15 ; *Jerusalem* is meant. — πανταχοῦ]

By way of popular hyperbole; hence not to be used as a proof in favour of the composition not having taken place till after the death of the apostles (in opposition to Fritzsche), comp. Rom. x. 18; Col. i. 6. — τοῦ κυρίου] nor *God* (Grotius, and also Fritzsche, comparing 1 Cor. iii. 9; Heb. ii. 4), but *Christ*, as in ver. 19. The σημεῖα are wrought by the exalted One. Comp. Matt. xxviii. 20. That the writer has made use of Heb. ii. 3, 4 (Schulthess, Fritzsche), is, considering the prevalence of the thought and the dissimilarity of the words, arbitrarily assumed. — διὰ τῶν ἐπακολουθ. σημείων] *by the signs that followed* (the λόγος). The *article* denotes the signs *spoken of,* which are promised at vv. 17, 18, and indeed promised as accompanying those *who had become believers;* hence it is erroneous to think, as the expositors do, of the miracles *performed by the apostles.* The confirmation of the apostolic preaching was found in the fact that *in the case of those who had become believers by means of that preaching* the σημεῖα promised at vv. 17, 18 occurred. — ἐπακολουθ. is foreign to all the Gospels; it occurs elsewhere in the N. T. in 1 Tim. v. 10, 24; 1 Pet. ii. 21; in classical Greek it is very frequently used.

REMARK.—The fragment before us, vv. 9–18, compared with the parallel passages of the other Gospels and with Acts i. 3, presents a remarkable proof how uncertain and varied was the tradition on the subject of the appearances of the Risen Lord (see on Matt. xxviii. 10). Similarly ver. 19, comp. with Luke xxiv. 50 f., Acts i. 9 ff., shows us in what an uncertain and varied manner tradition had possessed itself of the fact of the ascension, indubitable as in itself it is, and based on the unanimous teaching of the apostles.

THE GOSPEL OF LUKE.

B

THE GOSPEL OF LUKE.

INTRODUCTION.

§ 1.—ON THE LIFE OF LUKE.

EXCEPTING what the Acts of the Apostles and the Pauline Epistles contain as to the circumstances of Luke's life, — and to this Irenaeus also, with whom begins the testimony of the church concerning Luke as the author of the Gospel, still confines himself, *Haer.* iii. 14. 1,—nothing is historically certain concerning him. According to Eusebius, *H. E.* iii. 4, Jerome, Theophylact, Euthymius Zigabenus, and others, he was a native of Antioch,—a statement, which has not failed down to the most recent times to find acceptance (Hug, Guericke, Thiersch), but is destitute of all proof, and probably originated from a confusion of the name with *Lucius*, Acts xiii. 1. Luke is not to be identified either with this latter or with the Lucius that occurs in Rom. xvi. 21 (in opposition to Origen, Tiele, and others); for the name *Lukas* may be abbreviated from *Lucanus* (some codd. of the Itala have " secundum *Lucanum* " in the superscription and in subscriptions), or from *Lucilius* (see Grotius, and Sturz, *Dial. Mac.* p. 135), but not from *Lucius*.[1] Comp. Lekebusch, *Composit. d. Apostelgesch.* p. 390. Moreover, in the *Constitt. ap.* vi. 18. 5, Luke is expressly distinguished from Lucius.

---

[1] How freely the Greeks dealt in different forms of the same name, may be seen generally in Lobeck, *Patholog.* p. 504 ff.—The notion of Lange (*L. J.* p. 153, 168), that Luke is the person named *Aristion* in the fragment of Papias, quoted by Eusebius, iii. 39 (ἀριστεύειν = *lucere!*), is a preposterous fancy.

Whether he was a Jew by birth or a Gentile, is decided by
Col. iv. 11, 14, where Luke is distinguished from those
whom Paul calls οἱ ὄντες ἐκ περιτομῆς.[1] But it must be
left an open question whether he was before his conversion a
Jewish proselyte (Isidorus Hispalensis); the probability of
which it is at least very unsafe to deduce from his accurate
acquaintance with Jewish relations (in opposition to Kuinoel,
Riehm, *de fontibus Act. Ap.* p. 17 f., Guericke, Bleek). As to
his civil calling he was *a physician* (Col. iv. 14); and the very
late account (Nicephorus, *H. E.* ii. 43) that he had been at
the same time *a painter*, is an unhistorical legend. When and
how he became a Christian is unknown. Tradition, although
only from the time of Epiphanius (*Haer.* li. 12; also the pseudo-
Origenes, *de recta in Deum fide*, in Orig. *Opp.*, ed. de la Rue,
I. p. 806; Hippolytus, Theophylact, Euthymius Zigabenus,
Nicephorus Callistus, and others), places him among the
Seventy disciples,[2] whereas Luke i. 1 f. furnishes his own
testimony that he was *not* an eye-witness. Comp. Estius,
Annot. p. 902 f. The origin of this legend is explained from
the fact that only Luke has the account about the Seventy (in
opposition to Hug, who finds in this circumstance a confirmation of that statement). He was a highly esteemed assistant
of Paul and companion to him, from the time when he joined
the apostle on his second missionary journey at Troas, where
he, perhaps, had dwelt till then (Acts xvi. 10). We find
him thereafter with the apostle in Macedonia (Acts xvi. 11 ff.),
as well as on the third missionary journey at Troas, Miletus,

[1] This passage tells against everything with which Tiele in the *Stud. u. Krit.*
1858, p. 753 ff. has attempted to make good that Luke was a Jew by birth. His
reasons are based especially on the Hebraisms occurring in Luke, but lose their
importance partly in view of the like character which, it is to be assumed,
marked the writings made use of as sources, partly in view of the Jewish-Greek
nature of the evangelic language current in the church, to which Luke had
become habituated. The passage in the Colossians, moreover, has its meaning
wrongly turned by Tiele, as is also done by Hofmann, *Schriftbew.* II. 2, p. 99,
who starts from the postulate, which is utterly incapable of proof, that *all* the
N. T. writings are of Israelitish origin. See on Col. iv. 11, 14.

[2] According to some mentioned by Theophylact, he is alleged to have been
one of the two disciples going to Emmaus, which Lange, *L. J.* I. p. 252, considers probable. See on xxiv. 13.

etc. (Acts xx. 5–xxi. 18). In the imprisonment at Caesarea he was also with him (Acts xxiv. 23 ; Col. iv. 14 ; Philem. 24), and then accompanied him to Rome, Acts xxvii. 1–xxviii. 16 (comp. also 2 Tim. iv. 11). At this point the historical information concerning him ceases ; beyond, there is only uncertain and diversified tradition (see Credner, I. p. 126 f.), which, since the time of Gregory of Nazianzus, makes him even a martyr (*Martyrol. Rom.:* 18 Oct.), yet not unanimously, since accounts of a natural death also slip in. *Where* he died, remains a question ; certainly not in Rome with Paul, as Holtzmann conjectures, for his writings are far later. His bones are said by Jerome to have been brought from Achaia to Constantinople in the reign of Constantius.

§ 2.——ORIGIN OF THE GOSPEL.

On the origin of his Gospel—which falls to be divided into three principal portions, of which the middle one begins with the departure for Jerusalem, ix. 51, and extends to xviii. 30— Luke himself, i. 1–4, gives authentic information. According to his own statement, he composed his historical work (the continuation of which is the Acts of the Apostles) on the basis of the *tradition of eye-witnesses,* and having regard to the *written* evangelic compositions which already existed in great numbers, with critical investigation on his own part, aiming at completeness and correct arrangement. Those earlier compositions, too, had been drawn from apostolic tradition, but did not suffice for his special object; for which reason, however, to think merely of Jewish-Christian writings and their relation to Paulinism is unwarranted. One of his principal documentary sources was— although this has been called in question for very insufficient reasons (Weizsäcker, p. 17 ; see on vi. 14 f.)—the Gospel of Mark. Assuming this, as in view of the priority of Mark among the three Synoptics it must of necessity be assumed, it may be matter of doubt whether Matthew also in his present form was made use of by him (according to Baur and others, even as principal source) or not (Ewald, Reuss, Weiss, Holtzmann, Plitt, Schenkel, Weizsäcker, and others). At any rate he has worked up the apostle's collection of Logia in part, not seldom, in fact, more completely and with more critical sifting withal than our Matthew in his treatise. As, however, this collection of Logia was already worked up into the Gospel of Matthew; and as the Gospel invested with this authority, it is *a priori* to be presumed, could hardly remain unknown and unheeded by Luke in his researches, but, on the contrary, his having regard to it in those passages, where Luke agrees with Matthew in opposition to Mark, presents itself without arbitrariness as the simplest hypothesis;[1] our first Gospel also is doubtless to be reckoned among the sources of Luke, but yet with the limitation, that for him Mark, who represented more the primitive Gospel and was less Judaizing, was of far greater importance, and that generally in his relation to Matthew he went to work with a critical independence,[2] which presupposes that he did not measure the share of the apostle in the first Gospel according to the later view (comp. Kahnis, *Dogm.* I. p. 411), but on the contrary

---

[1] If a use of *our* Matthew by Luke is quite rejected, recourse must be had to the hypothesis (see especially, Weiss in the *Jahrb. f. Deutsch. Theol.* 1865, p. 319 ff.) that the apostolic *collection of Logia* already contained very much *historical matter*, and thereby already presented the type of the later Gospels. But in this way we again encounter the unknown quantity of a written primitive Gospel, while we come into collision with the testimony of Papias. And yet this primitive collection of historical matter in connection with the λογία is held to have excluded not only the history of the birth and childhood, but also the history of the Passion from Matt. xxvi. 6–12 onward; which latter exclusion, if once we impute to the λογία an historical framework and woof in the measure thought of, is hardly conceivable in view of the importance of the history of the Passion and Resurrection. I am afraid that by following Weiss, instead of the συγγραφὴ τῶν λογίων, which Papias claims for Matthew, we get already an historical ἐξήγησις—even if only dealing aggregately—oddly breaking off, moreover, with the history of the Passion; instead of the unknown primitive-Mark, an unknown primitive-Matthew.

[2] As decisive against the supposition that Luke knew our Matthew, ii. 39 is cited (see especially, Weiss and Holtzmann), and the genealogy of Jesus, so far as it goes by way of Nathan,—ii. 39 being held to show that the preliminary history of Matthew did not lie within the horizon of Luke. Certainly it did not lie within it; for he has *critically eliminated* it, and given *another*, which lay in *his* horizon. And the fact that he gave a genealogical table not according to the royal line of descent, in which, nevertheless, Christ remained just as well the Son of David, is likewise entirely accordant with the *critical* task of the *later* work; for genealogies according to the royal line were certainly the *most*

had no hesitation[1] in preferring other sources (as in the preliminary history). And other sources were available for him, partly oral in the apostolic tradition which he sought completely to investigate, partly written in the Gospel literature which had already become copious. Such written sources may in general be sufficiently recognised; they are most readily discernible in the preliminary history and in the account of the journeying (see on ix. 51), but not always certainly definable as respects their compass and in their original form, least of all in so far as to assume them to be only Jewish-Christian, especially from the south of Palestine (Köstlin, comp. Holtzmann, p. 166). The arrangement which places Mark only after Luke involves us, when we inquire after the sources of the latter, in the greatest difficulty and arbitrariness, since Luke cannot possibly be merely a free elaboration of Matthew (Baur), and even the taking in of tradition and of written sources *without* Mark (de Wette, Kahnis, Bleek, and others) is in no wise sufficient. The placing of Mark as intermediate between Matthew and Luke, stedfastly contended for by Hilgenfeld in particular, would, if it were in other respects allowable, not raise up such invincible difficulties for our question, and at least would not require the hypothesis of Hilgenfeld, that our Matthew is a freer *revision* of the strictly Jewish-Christian writing which formed its basis, or even (see the *Zeitschr. f. wiss. Theol.* 1864, p. 333) a *tertiary* formation, any more than it would need the insertion of a Petrine gospel between Matthew and Mark (Hilgenfeld, Köstlin).

To carry back our Gospel in respect of its origin to *apostolic authority* was a matter of importance to the ancient church in the interest of the canon; and the connection of Luke with *Paul* very naturally offered itself. Hence even Irenaeus, *Haer.*

---

ancient. Only people should be in earnest in attributing to him the *critical* procedure, which he himself, i. 3, affirms of his work, also in relation to the Gospel of Matthew. Schenkel in particular (p. 345) lightly pronounces judgment over the criticism of the third Gospel.

[1] We may dispense with the hypothesis, improbable even in itself, that Luke made use of Matthew according to an older and shorter redaction (de Wette and others), which is alleged to derive support especially from the gap between ix. 17 and 18 compared with Matt. xiv. 22–xvi. 12.

iii. 1, quoted by Eusebius, v. 8, states: Λουκᾶς δὲ ὁ ἀκόλουθος Παύλου τὸ ὑπ᾽ ἐκείνου κηρυσσόμενον εὐαγγέλιον ἐν βιβλίῳ κατέθετο (comp. iii. 14. 1 f.); and already Origen, Eusebius, and Jerome find our Gospel of Luke designated in the expression of Paul τὸ εὐαγγέλιόν μου. See the further testimonies in Credner, I. p. 146 ff. As regards this ecclesiastical tradition, there is to be conceded a general and indirect influence of the apostle, not merely in reference to doctrine, inasmuch as in Luke the stamp of Pauline Christianity is unmistakeably apparent, but also in part as respects the historical matter,[1] since certainly Paul must, in accordance with his interest, his calling, and his associations, be supposed to have had, at least in the leading points, a more precise knowledge of the circumstances of the life of Jesus, His doctrine, and deeds. Comp. 1 Cor. xi. 23 ff., xv. 1 ff. But the generality and indirectness of such an influence explain the fact, that in his preface Luke himself does not include any appeal to this relation; the proper sources from which he drew (and he wrote, in fact, long after the apostle's death) were different. As a *Pauline* Gospel, ours was the one of which *Marcion* laid hold. How he mutilated and altered it, is evident from the numerous fragments in Tertullian, Epiphanius, Jerome, the pseudo-Origen, and others.

REMARK 1.—The view, acutely elaborated by Schleiermacher, that the whole Gospel is a stringing together of written documents (*krit. Versuch über d. Schriften d. Luk.* I. Berl. 1837), is refuted at once by i. 3, and by the peculiar literary character of Luke, which is observable throughout. See H. Planck, *Obss. de Lucae evang. analysi critica a Schleierm. propos.*, Gött. 1819; Roediger, *Symbolae ad N. T. evangelia potiss. pertin.*, Hal. 1827. And this literary peculiarity is the same which is also prominent throughout the Acts of the Apostles. See, besides the proofs advanced by Credner and others, especially Lekebusch, *Composit. d. Apostelgesch.* p. 37 ff.; Zeller, *Apostelgesch.* p. 414 ff.

REMARK 2.—The investigation recently pursued, after the earlier precedents of Semler, Löffler, and others, especially by

---

[1] In reference to this, Thiersch, *K. im apost. Zeitalt.* p. 158, 177, is bold enough arbitrarily to assume that Paul had procured for Luke written records in accordance with 2 Tim. iv. 13.

Ritschl (formerly), Baur, and Schwegler,[1] in opposition to Hahn (*d. Evang. Marcions in s. urspr. Gestalt.*, Königsb. 1823), to prove that the Gospel of Marcion was the *primitive-Luke*, has reverted —and that indeed partially by means of these critics themselves, following the example of Hilgenfeld, *krit. Unters.* 1850, p. 389 ff.—more and more to the view that has commonly prevailed since Tertullian's time, that Marcion abbreviated and altered Luke. Most thoroughly has this been the case with Volkmar (*theol. Jahrb.* 1850, p. 110 ff., and in his treatise, *das Evangel. Marcions, u. Revis. d. neueren Unters.*, Leip. 1852), with whom Köstlin, *Urspr. u. Composit. d. synopt. Ev.* 1853, p. 302 ff., essentially agrees. Comp. Hilgenfeld in the *theol. Jahrb.* 1853, p. 192 ff.; Zeller, *Apostelgesch.* p. 11 ff. The opinion that the Gospel of Marcion was the pre-canonical form of the present Luke, may be looked upon as set aside; and the attacks and wheelings about of the Tübingen criticism have rendered in that respect an essential service. See Franck in the *Stud. u. Krit.* 1855, p. 296 ff.; and on the history of the whole discussion, Bleek, *Einl.* p. 126 ff. For the Gospel of Marcion itself,— which has been *ex auctoritate veter. monum. descr.* by Hahn,— see Thilo, *Cod. Apocr.* I. p. 401 ff.

§ 3.—OCCASION AND OBJECT, TIME AND PLACE OF COMPOSITION.

The historical work consisting of two divisions (Gospel and Acts of the Apostles), which Luke himself characterizes as a critico-systematic (ver. 3) presentation of the facts of Christianity (ver. 1), was *occasioned* by the relation, not more pre-

---

[1] Ritschl, *d. Evang. Marcions u. d. kanon. Ev. d. Luk., e. krit. Unters.*, Tüb. 1846 ; Baur, *krit. Unters. üb. d. kanon. Evangelien*, Tüb. 1847, p. 393 ff. ; Schwegler, *nachapost. Zeitalt.* I. p. 261 ff. See, on the other hand, Harting: *quaestionem de Marcione Lucani evang. adulteratore*, etc., *novo examini submisit*, Utrecht 1849.—Ritschl has subsequently, in the *theol. Jahrb.* 1851, p. 528 f., confessed : "The hypothesis propounded by me, that Marcion did not alter the Gospel of Luke, but that his Gospel is a step towards the canonical Luke, I regard as refuted by Volkmar and Hilgenfeld. Any one who considers the onesided exaggeration with which Hahn has defended the customary view, will know how to excuse my being led by him to an opposite onesidedness." According to Baur, *Markusevangel.* 1851, p. 191 ff., Marcion had before him at least an older text of Luke, in many respects different from the canonical one. Certainly the text of Luke which was before Marcion may have had individual readings more original than our witnesses exhibit ; and it is in general, so far as we can distinguish it, to be regarded as tantamount to a very ancient manuscript. But still Volkmar and Hilgenfeld often overestimate its readings.

cisely known to us, in which the author stood to a certain *Theophilus*, for whom he *made it his aim* to bring about by this presentation of the history a knowledge of the trust-worthiness of the Christian instruction that he had received. See vv. 1–4.   Unhappily, as to this Theophilus, who, how-ever, assuredly is no merely fictitious personage (Epiphanius, Heumann, and the Saxon Anonymus), nothing is known to us with certainty ; for all the various statements as to his rank, native country, etc. (see Credner, *Einl.* I. p. 144 f.), are destitute of proof, not excepting even the supposition which is found as early as Eutychius (*Annal. Alex.*, ed. Selden et Pocock, I. p. 334), that he was an *Italian*, or, more precisely, a *Roman* [1] (Hug, Eichhorn, and many others, including Ewald and Holtzmann).   It is, although likewise not certain, accord-ing to Acts xxiii. 26, xxiv. 3, xxvi. 25, probable, that the address κράτιστε points to a man *of rank* (comp. Otto in *Ep. ad Diogn.*, ed. 2, p. 53 f.) ; and from the Pauline doctrinal character of the historical work, considering that it was to serve as a confirmation of the instruction enjoyed by Theophilus, it is to be concluded that he was a *follower of Paul ;* in saying which, however, *the very* point whether he was a Jewish or a Gentile Christian cannot be determined, although, looking to the Pauline author and character of the book, the latter is probable.   The Clementine *Recognitiones*, x. 71, make him to be a man of high rank in *Antioch ;* and against this very ancient testimony [2] there is nothing substantial to object, if it

---

[1] Whether this follows from the passage of the Muratorian Canon as to the Acts of the Apostles (Ewald, *Jahrb.* VIII. p. 126 ; *Gesch. d. apost. Zeitalt.* p. 40) is, considering the great corruption of the text, very doubtful.   At least the very indication, according to which Theophilus would appear as living in Rome, would be introduced into the fragment only by conjecture, and that, indeed, as daring a conjecture as Ewald gives.   The text, namely, is, in his view, to be thus restored : "*Acta omnium apostolorum sub uno libro scripta Lucas optimo Theophilo comprehendit, omittens quae sub praesentia ejus singula gerebantur, sicut et non modo passionem Petri evidenter decerpit* (or *decollat*), *sed et profectionem*," etc.

[2] With which the circumstance is easily reconcilable that in the *Constitut. Ap.* vii. 46. 1 he is adduced as the third bishop of *Caesarea.*   And that in that place *our* Theophilus is meant, is more than probable from the context, where almost none but New Testament names are mentioned.

be conceded that, even without being an Italian, he might be acquainted with the localities named in Acts xxviii. 12, 13, 15, without more precise specification. The idea that Luke, in composing the work, has had in view other readers also besides Theophilus, not *merely* Gentile Christians (Tiele), is not excluded by i. 3 f., although the treatise was *primarily* destined for Theophilus and only by his means reached a wider circle of readers, and then gradually, after the analogy of the N. T. Epistles, became the common property of Christendom. The *Pauline* standpoint of the author generally, and especially his *universalistic* standpoint, have been of essential influence on the selection and presentation of the matter in his Gospel, yet by no means to such an extent that we should have to substitute for the objectively historical character of the work,—according to which it had to pay due respect to the Judaistic elements actually given in the history itself,—a character of *subjective set purpose shaping* the book, as if its aim were to accommodate the Judaizing picture of the Messiah to the views of Paulinism and to convert the Judaistic conceptions into the Pauline form (Zeller, *Apostel-gesch.* p. 439), or to exalt Paulinism at the expense of Jewish Christianity and to place the twelve apostles in a position of inferiority to Paul (Baur, Hilgenfeld). See especially, Weiss in the *Stud. u. Krit.* 1861, p. 708 ff.; Holtzmann, p. 389 ff. If the author had such a set purpose, even if taken only in Zeller's sense, he would have gone to work with an inconsistency that is incomprehensible (not in keeping with that purpose, as Zeller thinks); and we should, in fact, be compelled to support the hypothesis by the further assumption that the original work had contained neither the preliminary history nor a number of other portions (according to Baur, iv. 16–30, v. 39, x. 22, xii. 6 f., xiii. 1–5, xvi. 17, xix. 18–46, xxi. 18, also probably xi. 30–32, 49–51, xiii. 28–35, and perhaps xxii. 30), and had only been brought into its present form by the agency of a later *rédacteur* taking a middle course (Baur, *Markusevang.* p. 223 ff.). Baur regards this latter as the author of the Acts of the Apostles. See, on the other hand, Zeller, *Apostelgesch.* p. 446 ff.

The composition of the Gospel, placed by the Fathers as early as fifteen years after the ascension, by Thiersch, *K. im apost. Zeitalt.* p. 158, and by various others as early as the time of Paul's imprisonment in Caesarea, is usually (and still by Ebrard and Guericke) referred to the time soon after the apostle's two years' sojourn in Rome, which is narrated at the conclusion of the Acts of the Apostles. But as this conclusion is not available for any such definition of time (see Introd. to the Acts of the Apostles, § 3), and as, in fact, Luke xxi. 24 f. (compared with Matt. xxiv. 29) already presupposes the destruction of Jerusalem, and places between this catastrophe and the Parousia a period of indefinite duration (ἄχρις πληρωθῶσι καιροὶ ἐθνῶν), Luke must have written within these καιροὶ ἐθνῶν, and so not till *after the destruction of Jerusalem,* as is rightly assumed by Credner, de Wette, Bleek, Zeller, Reuss, Lekebusch (*Composit. d. Apostelgesch.* p. 413 ff.); Köstlin, p. 286 ff.; Güder in Herzog's *Encykl.;* Tobler, *Evangelienfr.,* Zürich 1858, p. 29. See especially, Ewald, *Jahrb.* III. p. 142 f.; Holtzmann, p. 404 ff. With this also agrees the reflection, which so often presents itself in the Gospel, of the oppressed and sorrowful condition of the Christians, as it must have been at the time of the composition. Comp. on vi. 20 ff. Still xxi. 32 forbids us to assign too late a date,—as Baur, Zeller (110–130 after Christ), Hilgenfeld (100–110) do, extending the duration of the γενεά to a Roman *seculum* (in spite of ix. 27),—even although no criterion is to be derived from Acts viii. 26 for a more precise definition of the date of the Book of Acts, and so far also of the Gospel (Hug : during the Jewish war ; Lekebusch : soon after it). John wrote still later than Luke, and thus there remains for the latter as the time of composition the decade 70–80, beyond which there is no going either forward or backward. The testimony of Irenaeus, iii. 1, that Luke wrote after the death of Peter and Paul, may be reconciled approximately with this, but resists every later date,—and the more, the later it is. The *Protevangelium Jacobi,* which contains historical references to Matthew and Luke (Tischendorf : " *Wann wurden unsere Evangelien verfasst ?* " 1865,

p. 30 ff.), fails to give any more exact limitation of time, as the date of its own composition cannot be fixed with certainty. Whether in its present form it was used by Justin in particular, is very questionable. Still more doubtful is the position of the *Acta Pilati.* In the *Epistle* of Barnabas 19, the parallel with Luke vi. 30 is not genuine (according to the Sinaitic).

Where the Gospel was written is utterly unknown ; the statements of tradition vary (Jerome, *præf. in Matth.* : " in *Achaiae Boeotiaeque* partibus ; " the Syriac : in *Alexandria magna,* comp. Grabe, *Spicileg. patr.* I. p. 32 f.) ; and conjectures pointing to *Caesarea* (Michaelis, Kuinoel, Schott, Thiersch, and others), *Rome* (Hug, Ewald, Zeller, Lekebusch, Holtzmann, and others), *Achaia and Macedonia* (Hilgenfeld in his *Zeitschr.* 1858, p. 594 ; 1851, p. 179), and *Asia Minor* (Köstlin), are not capable of proof.

§ 4.—GENUINENESS AND INTEGRITY.

The author does not name himself ; but the unanimous tradition of the ancient church, which in this express statement reaches as far back as Irenaeus (*Haer.* iii. 1, i. 27. 2, iii. 14. 3 f., iii. 10. 1), designates *Luke* as the author (see also the Syriac and the Canon of Muratori) ; in opposition to which there does not arise from the book itself any difficulty making it necessary to abide merely by the general view of a Pauline Gentile-Christian (but not Luke) as the author, as Hilgenfeld does on account of its alleged late composition. Papias, in Eusebius, iii. 39, does not mention Luke, which, however, cannot matter much, since it is after all only a *fragment* which has been preserved to us from the book of Papias. Moreover, the circumstance that Marcion appropriated to himself this very Gospel, presupposes that he regarded it as the work of a disciple of the Apostle Paul ; indeed, the disciples of Marcion, according to Tertullian, *c. Marc.* iv. 5, attributed it directly to Paul himself, as also the Saxon Anonymus preposterously enough has again done. The unanimous tradition of the church is treated with contempt by the precarious assertion, that the authorship of Luke was only

inferred from the narrative of travel in the Book of Acts at a
time when there was a desire to possess among the Gospels
of the church also a Pauline one (Köstlin, p. 291).   That our
Gospel—which, we may add, was made use of by Justin (see
Semisch, *Denkw. Justins*, p. 142 ff.; Zeller, *Apostelgesch.* p.
26 ff.[1]), and in the Clementine Homilies (see Uhlhorn,
Homil. u. Recognit. des Clemens, p. 120 ff.; Zeller, p. 53 ff.)—
is not as yet quoted in the Apostolic Fathers (not even in the
Epistle of Barnabas), is sufficiently to be explained on the
general ground of their preference for oral tradition,[2] and
by the further circumstance, that this Gospel in the first instance was only a private document.

REMARK.—That the person who, in the narrative of travel
in the Book of Acts, speaks in the first person (*we*) is neither
Timothy nor Silas, see Introd. to Acts, § 1.

The *integrity* of the work has, no doubt, been impugned, as
far as the genuineness of i. 5 ff. and ch. ii. has been called in
question; but see the critical remarks on ch. ii.

---

[1] Comp. also Credner, *Gesch. d. Kanon*, p. 45.   He, nevertheless, in this, his
last work, calls in question Justin's direct *use* of our Gospels, and only concedes
that he *knew* them, and in particular that of Luke.

[2] See Gieseler, *Entsteh. d. schriftl. Evangelien*, p. 149 ff.

Εὐαγγέλιον κατὰ Λουκᾶν.

B F ℵ have only *κατὰ Λουκᾶν.* Others: *τὸ κατὰ Λουκᾶν ἅγιον*
εὐαγγ. Others: *ἐκ τοῦ κατὰ Λ.* Others: *ἐκ τοῦ κ. Λ. (ἁγίου)*
εὐαγγελίου. See on Matthew.

CHAPTER I.

Ver. 5. *ἡ γυνὴ αὐτοῦ*] B C* D L X ℵ, min. codd. It. Jer. Aug.
Beda have *γυνὴ αὐτῷ.* Approved by Griesb., adopted by Lachm.
and Tisch. The *Recepta* is an exegetical alteration—which also
holds true of the order of the words at ver. 10 in Elz. *τοῦ λαοῦ*
ἦν, instead of which *ἦν τοῦ λαοῦ* is preponderatingly attested.
— Ver. 14. Instead of *γενέσει,* Elz. has *γεννήσει,* in opposition to
decisive evidence. From *γεννήσει,* ver. 13. Comp. on Matt.
i. 18. — Ver. 20: *πληρωθήσονται*] D, Or. have *πλησθήσονται.* If
it were more strongly attested, it would have to be adopted
(comp. on xxi. 22). — Ver. 27. The form *ἐμνηστευμ.* (Lachm.
Tisch.), instead of the reduplicated *μεμνηστευμ.,* has in this place,
and still more at ii. 5, such important codd. in its favour, that
it is to be preferred, and *μεμνηστευμ.* must be attributed to the
transcribers (Deut. xxii. 23, xx. 7). — Ver. 28. *ὁ ἄγγελος*] is
wanting in B L, min. Copt. Suspected by Griesb., deleted by
Tisch. ; the more rightly, that in F Δ ℵ, 69, Syr. Arm. Brix. Rd.
Corb. it is placed after *αὐτήν,* and was more easily supplied than
omitted. — *εὐλογημένη σὺ ἐν γυν.*] is wanting in B L ℵ, min. Copt.
Sahid. Arm. Syr. hier. Damasc. Suspected by Griesb., deleted
by Tisch. An addition from ver. 42, whence, also, in some
witnesses there has been added, *καὶ εὐλογημένος ὁ καρπὸς τῆς κοιλίας*
σου. — Ver. 29. Elz. Scholz, Lachm. have *ἡ δὲ ἰδοῦσα διεταράχθη*
ἐπὶ τῷ λόγῳ αὐτοῦ. Griesb. and Tisch. have *ἡ δὲ ἐπὶ τῷ λόγῳ*
διεταράχθη. So B D L X ℵ, min. Arm. Cant. Damasc. (D:
ἐταράχθη). This reading is to be preferred. From ΔE the
transcriber passed immediately to ΔΙΕ*ταράχθη* (hence, also,
in D, the mere simple form), by which means *ἐπὶ τῷ λόγῳ*
dropped out, and this is still wanting in C* min. The bare *ἡ*
δὲ διεταράχθη was then glossed by *ἰδοῦσα* (comp. ver. 12)

(*another* gloss was: *cum audisset*, Vulg. *al.*), which, being
adopted *before* διεταρ., was the cause of ἐπὶ τῷ λόγῳ being placed
after διεταρ. when it was restored (in which case, for the most
part, αὐτοῦ was inserted also). — Ver. 35. After γεννώμ. C, min.
and many vss. and Fathers (see especially, Athanasius), as also
Valentinus in the *Philos.*, have ἐκ σοῦ (yet with the variations
de te and *in te*), and this Lachmann has adopted in brackets.
A more precisely defining, and withal doctrinally suggested
addition (comp. Matt. i. 16; Gal. iv. 4). — Ver. 36. The form
συγγενίς is to be adopted, with Lachm. and Tisch., following
A C*** D E G H L Δ ℵ, min.　συγγενής is a correction. — Instead
of γήρει, Elz. has γήρᾳ, in opposition to decisive evidence.
— Ver. 37. παρὰ τῷ Θεῷ] Tisch. has παρὰ τοῦ Θεοῦ, following B D
L ℵ; the dative suggested itself as being closer to the prevailing conception (Gen. xviii. 14). — Ver. 41. The verbal order:
τὸν ἀσπασμὸν τῆς Μαρ. ἡ ᾿Ελισ. (Lachm. Tisch.), is attested with
sufficient weight to induce us to recognise ἡ ᾿Ελισ. τ. ἀσπ. τ.
Μαρ. (Elz.) as a transposition. — Ver. 44. Following B C D* F
L ℵ, Vulg. It. Or., the verbal order of the *Recepta* ἐν ἀγαλλ.
τὸ βρέφος is to be maintained (Griesb. Scholz have τὸ βρεφ.
ἐν ἀγαλλ.). — Ver. 49. μεγαλεῖα] Lachm. Tisch. read μεγάλα,
in accordance with B D* L ℵ 130. So also probably Vulg.
It., *magna* (not *magnalia*, as at Acts ii. 11). To be preferred,
since μεγαλεῖα might easily have been introduced as a more
exact definition by a recollection of Ps. lxxi. 19. — Ver. 50. εἰς
γενεὰς γενεῶν] Very many variations, among which εἰς γενεὰς καὶ
γενεάς (Tisch.) is the best attested, by B C* L Syr. Copt. codd.
It. Vulg. ms. Aug.; next to this, but far more feebly, εἰς γενεὰν
καὶ γενεάν (commended by Griesb.). The former is to be preferred; the *Recepta*, although strongly attested, arose out of
the current expression *in saecula saeculorum.* — Ver. 55. The
Codd. are divided between εἰς τὸν αἰῶνα (Elz. Lachm. Tisch.) and
ἕως αἰῶνος (Griesb. Scholz). The former has the stronger attestation, but is the expression so current in the N. T. that ἕως,
etc., which does not occur elsewhere in the N. T., but is in keeping with the usage of the LXX. after τ. σπέρμ. αὐτοῦ (Gen. xiii.
15, etc.), here deserves the preference. — Ver. 59. ὀγδόῃ ἡμέρᾳ]
B C D L ℵ, min. have ἡμέρᾳ τῇ ὀγδόῃ. Approved by Griesb.,
adopted by Lachm. and Tisch. Preponderantly attested, and
therefore to be preferred. — Ver. 61. ἐν τῇ συγγενείᾳ σου] Lachm.
and Tisch. read ἐκ τῆς συγγενείας σου, following A B C* L Δ Λ ℵ,
min. Copt. Chron. Pasch. The latter is to be preferred, in place
of which the former more readily occurred to the pen of the
copyists. — Ver. 62. αὐτόν] B D F G ℵ, min. have αὐτό. So

Lachm. and Tisch. Rightly; the reference to τὸ παιδίον, ver. 59, was left unnoticed, and the masculine was mechanically put in κατὰ σύνεσιν. — Ver. 66. καὶ χείρ] Lachm. Tisch. have καὶ γὰρ χείρ, following B C* D L ℵ, Copt. Aeth. Vulg. It. Goth. Approved by Rinck also, who, however, rejects ἦν on too slight evidence. γάρ is the rather to be adopted, because of the facility with which it may have dropt out on occasion of the similarly sounding χείρ which follows, and of the difficulty with which another connective particle was inserted after the already connecting καί. — Ver. 70. τῶν ἀγ. τῶν] the second τῶν, deleted by Tisch., is wanting in B L Δ ℵ, min. Or. Eus. An omission by a clerical error. — Ver. 75. After ἡμέρας Elz. has τῆς ζωῆς, in opposition to decisive evidence. — Ver. 76. καὶ σύ] Tisch. has καὶ σὺ δέ (so also Scholz, following Bornem. in Rosenm. *Repert.* II. p. 259), on very considerable evidence; καὶ . . . δέ was often mutilated by copyists lacking discernment.

Ver. 1.[1] Ἐπειδήπερ] *Quoniam quidem, since indeed,* not found elsewhere in the N. T., nor in the LXX., or the Apocrypha; frequent in classical writers, see Hartung, *Partikell.* I. p. 342 f. Observe that ἐπειδή denotes the fact, assumed as known, in such a way "ut quae inde evenerint et secuta sint, nunc adhuc durent," Ellendt, *Lex. Soph.* I. p. 640. — πολλοί] Christian writers, whose works for the most part are not preserved.[2] The apocryphal Gospels still extant are of a later date; *Mark,* however, is in any case meant to be included. The Gospel of *Matthew* too, in its present form which was then already in existence, cannot have remained unknown to Luke; and in using the word πολλοί he must have thought

---

[1] According to Baur and others, this preface, vv. 1–4, was only added by the last hand that manipulated our Gospel, after the middle of the second century. Thus, the Gospel would bear on the face of it untruth *in concreto.* Ewald aptly observes, *Jahrb.* II. p. 182 f., of this preamble, that in its homely simplicity, modesty, and brevity, it may be called the model of a preface to an historical work. See on the prologue, Holtzmann, p. 243 ff. Aberle in the *Tüb. Quartalschr.* 1863, 1, p. 84 ff., in a peculiar but untenable way makes use of this prologue as proof for the allegation that our Gospel was occasioned by the accusation of Paul (and of the whole Christian body) in Rome; holding that the prologue must therefore have been composed with the intention of its being interpreted in more senses than one. See, on the other hand, Hilgenfeld in his *Zeitschr.* 1864, p. 443 ff. The whole hypothesis falls to the ground at once before the fact that Luke did not write till after the destruction of Jerusalem.

[2] There is not the remotest ground for thinking of non-Christian books written in hostility to Christianity (Aberle in the *theol. Quart.* 1855, p. 173 ff.).

of it with others (see Introd. § 2), although not as an *apostolic* writing, because the πολλοί are *distinct* from the eye-witnesses, ver. 2. The *apostolic collection of Logia* was no διήγησις περὶ τῶν κ.τ.λ., and its author, as an apostle, belonged not to the πολλοί, but to the ἀπ᾽ ἀρχῆς αὐτόπται. But the *Gospel to the Hebrews*, if and so far as it had then already assumed shape, belonged to the attempts of the πολλοί. — ἐπεχείρησαν] *have undertaken*, said under a sense of the *loftiness and difficulty* of the task, Acts xix. 13. In the N. T. only used in Luke ; frequently in the classical writers. Comp. also Ulpian, p. 159 (in Valckenaer): ἐπειδήπερ περὶ τούτου πολλοὶ ἐπεχείρησαν ἀπολογήσασθαι. Neither in the word in itself, nor by comparing it with what Luke, ver. 3, says of his own work, is there to be found, with Köstlin, Ebrard, Lekebusch, and older writers, any indication of *insufficiency* in those endeavours *in general*, which Origen,[1] Ambrosius, Theophylact, Calovius, and various others even referred to their *contrast* with the *inspired* Gospels. But for *his special purpose* he judged none of those preliminary works as sufficient. — διήγησιν] *a narrative;* see especially, Plato, *Rep.* iii. p. 392 D ; Arist. *Rhet.* iii. 16 ; 2 Macc. ii. 32. Observe the *singular*. Of the πολλοί each one attempted a narrative περὶ τῶν κ.τ.λ., thus comprising the evangelic whole. Loose leaves or detached essays (Ebrard) Luke does not mention. — ἀνατάξασθαι] *to set up according to order*, Plut. *Moral.* p. 968 C, εὐτρεπίσασθαι, Hesychius. Neither διήγησ. nor ἀνατάσσ. occurs elsewhere in the N. T. — περὶ τῶν πεπληροφορ. ἐν ἡμῖν πραγμ.] *of the facts that have attained to full conviction among us* (Christians). πληροφορεῖν, to bring to full conviction, may be associated also with an accusative *of the thing*, which is brought to full acknowledgment (2 Tim. iv. 5); hence in a passive sense : πληροφορεῖταί τι, something attains to full belief (2 Tim. iv. 17), it is brought to full conviction (πληροφορία πίστεως, Heb. x. 22) among others. So here (it is otherwise where πληροφορεῖσθαι is said of a *person*, as Rom. iv. 21, xiv. 5 ; Col. iv. 12 ; Ignat. *ad Magnes.* viii. 10 ; Eccles.

---

[1] In Jerome : "Matthaeus quippe et Marcus et Johannes et Lucas non sunt conati scribere, sed *scripserunt*." Comp. Euthymius Zigabenus.

viii. 11 ; Phot. *Bibl.* p. 41, 29). Rightly so taken by the
Fathers (Theophylact : οὐ γὰρ ἁπλῶς κατὰ ψιλὴν παράδοσιν
εἰσὶ τὰ τοῦ Χριστοῦ, ἀλλ᾽ ἐν ἀληθείᾳ καὶ πίστει βεβαίᾳ καὶ
μετὰ πάσης πληροφορίας), Erasmus, Beza, Calvin, Grotius,
Valckenaer, and many others, including Olshausen and Ewald.
The explanation : "quae in nobis completae sunt" (Vulgate),
which have fully *happened, run their course* among us (Luther,
Hammond, Paulus, de Wette, Ebrard, Köstlin, Bleek, and
others), is opposed to usage, as πληροφορεῖν is never, even in
2 Tim. iv. 5, equivalent to πληροῦν, and therefore it cannot
be conceived as applying, either, with Schneckenburger (comp.
Lekebusch, p. 30), to the *fulfilment of God's counsel and promise* through the life of the Messiah, which besides would be
entirely imported; or, with Baur, *to the idea of Christianity
realized* as regards its full contents, under which the Pauline
Christianity was essentially included.

Ver. 2. Καθώς] neither *quatenus,* nor belonging to πεπληροφ.
(in opposition, as respects both, to Kuinoel, as respects the
latter also to Olshausen), but introducing the *How,* the *modal
definition* of ἀνατάξ. διήγησιν. — παρέδοσαν] *have delivered.* It
is equally erroneous to refer this merely to *written* (Königsm.
de fontibus, etc., in Pott's *Sylloge,* III. p. 231 ; Hug), or merely
to *oral* communication, although in the historical circumstances the latter was by far the preponderating.[1] Holtzmann
appropriately remarks : "The subjects of παρέδοσαν and the
πολλοί are not distinguished from one another as respects
the categories of the oral and written, but as respects those
of primary and secondary authority." For the πολλοί, as
for Luke himself, who associates himself with them by κἀμοί,
the παράδοσις of the αὐτόπται was the proper source, in accordance with which therefore he must have critically sifted the
attempts of those πολλοί, so far as he knew them (ver. 3). —
ἀπ᾽ ἀρχῆς] namely, of those πραγμάτων. But it is not the
time of *the birth of Jesus* that is meant (so most commentators,
including Kuinoel and Olshausen), but that of the *entrance of
Jesus on His ministry* (Euthymius Zigabenus, de Wette) ; comp.

[1] Of the *written* materials of this παράδοσις of the αὐτόπται we know with certainty only the λόγια of Matthew according to Papias.

John xv. 27; Acts i. 21 f., which explanation is not "auda-
cious" (Olshausen), but necessary, because the αὐτόπται καὶ
ὑπηρέται τοῦ λόγου are the *same* persons, and therefore under
the αὐτόπται there are not to be understood, in addition to
the first disciples, Mary also and other members of the family.
ἀπ᾽ ἀρχῆς therefore is not to be taken absolutely, but relatively.
— ὑπηρέται τοῦ λόγου] *ministri evangelii* (the doctrine κατ᾽
ἐξοχήν, comp. Acts viii. 7, xiv. 25, xvi. 6, xvii. 11). These
were the Twelve and other μαθηταί of Christ (as according to
Luke also the Seventy), who were *in the service* of the gospel
for the purpose of announcing it. Comp. iii. 7; Acts vi. 4;
Col. i. 23; Acts xxvi. 16; 1 Cor. iv. 1. Others (Erasmus,
Castalio, Beza, Grotius, Maldonatus, *al.*, including Kuinoel)
take τοῦ λόγου in the sense of the *matter* concerned, of the
contents of the history spoken of (see on Acts viii. 21); but
it would be just as inappropriate to ὑπηρέται as it would
be quite superfluous, since τοῦ λόγου must by no means be
attached to αὐτόπται also. Finally, it is a mistake to refer it
to *Christ* in accordance with John i. 1. So Origen, Athanasius, Euthymius Zigabenus, Valla, Calovius, and others,
including Stein (*Kommentar,* Halle 1830). It is only *John*
that names Christ ὁ λόγος. — Theophylact, moreover, aptly
observes: ἐκ τούτου (namely, from καθὼς παρέδοσαν ἡμῖν
κ.τ.λ.) δῆλον, ὅτι οὐκ ἦν ὁ Λουκᾶς ἀπ᾽ ἀρχῆς μαθητὴς, ἀλλ᾽
ὑστερόχρονος· ἄλλοι γὰρ ἦσαν οἱ ἀπ᾽ ἀρχῆς μαθητευθέντες . . .
οἳ καὶ παρέδοσαν αὐτῷ κ.τ.λ. By ἡμῖν the writer places himself in the *second* generation; the *first* were the immediate
disciples of Christ, οἱ ἀπ᾽ ἀρχῆς αὐτόπται καὶ ὑπηρέται. This
ὑπηρέται, however, is not chosen for the sake of placing the
Twelve on an equality with *Paul* (Acts xxvi. 16). As though
the word were so characteristic for *Paul* in particular! Comp.
John xviii. 36; 1 Cor. iv. 1.

Ver. 3. Apodosis, which did not begin already in ver. 2. —
ἔδοξε κἀμοί] in itself neither excludes nor includes inspiration. Vss. add to it: *et Spiritui sancto.* By the use of
κἀμοί Luke places himself in the same category with the
πολλοί, in so far as he, too, had not been an eye-witness; "sic
tamen ut etiamnum aliquid ad ἀσφάλειαν ac firmitudinem

Theophilo conferat," Bengel. — παρηκολουθ.] *after having from the outset followed everything with accuracy.* Παρακολ., of the *mental* tracing, *investigating,* whereby one arrives at a knowledge of the matter.   See the examples in Valckenaer, *Schol.* p. 12 ; Dissen, *ad Dem. de Cor.* p. 344 f.   Comp., moreover, Thucyd. i. 22. 2 : ὅσον δυνατὸν ἀκριβείᾳ περὶ ἑκάστου ἐπεξελθών. — πᾶσιν] namely, those πράγμασι, not *masculine* (Syr.). — ἄνωθεν] not : *radicitus,* fundamentally (Grotius), which is comprised in ἀκριβ., but : *from the first,* see on John iii. 3.   From the beginning of the history it is seen that in his investigation he started *from the birth of the Baptist,* in doing which, doubtless, he could not but still lack the authentic tradition of ver. 2.   Nevertheless the consciousness of an advantage over those πολλοί expresses itself in παρηκ. ἄνωθεν. — καθεξῆς] *in orderly sequence,* not out of the order of time, in which they occurred one after the other.[1] Only Luke has the *word* in the N. T. (viii. 1 ; Acts iii. 24, xi. 4, xviii. 23) ; it occurs also in Aelian, Plutarch, *et al.,* but the older classical writers have ἐφεξῆς. — κράτιστε Θεόφιλε] See Introd. § 3.   That in Acts i. 1 he is addressed merely ὦ Θεόφιλε, proves nothing against the titular use of κράτιστε. See on the latter, Grotius.

Ver. 4. Ἵνα ἐπιγνῷς] *ut accurate cognosceres ;* see on Matt. xi. 27 ; 1 Cor. xiii. 12. — περὶ ὧν κατηχήθης λόγων] The attraction is not, with the Vulgate and the majority of commentators, to be resolved into : τῶν λόγων, περὶ ὧν κατηχήθης, as the contents of the instruction is put with κατηχεῖσθαι in the accusative (Acts xviii. 25 ; Gal. vi. 6), and only the more remote object to which the instruction relates is expressed by περί (Acts xxi. 21, 24), but into : περὶ τῶν λόγων, οὓς κατηχήθης : that thou mightest know *in respect of the doctrines, in which thou wast instructed,* the unshaken certainty.   Comp.

---

[1] In the case of this καθεξῆς the Harmonists of course make the reservation, that it will be "conditioned at one time more by a chronological interest, at another time more by that of the subject-matter," Lichtenstein, p. 73.   Thus they keep their hand free to lay hold now of the one, now of the other, just as it is held to suit.   The assertion, often repeated, in favour of the violences of harmonizers, that in Luke the arrangement by subject-matter even predominates (Ebrard, Lichtenstein), is absolutely incompatible with that καθεξῆς.

Köstlin, p. 132, and Ewald. The λόγοι are not the πράγματα, *res* (comp. ver. 2), as is usually supposed; but it is just the specifically Christian *doctrines*, the individual parts of the λόγος, ver. 2 (τῶν λόγων τῆς πίστεως, Euthymius Zigabenus), that stand in the most essential connection with the *history* of Jesus and from it receive their ἀσφάλεια; in fact, they are in great part themselves essentially history. — κατηχήθης is to be understood of *actual instruction* (in Acts xxi. 21 also), not of hearsay, of which, moreover, the passages in Kypke are not to be explained. *Who* had instructed Theophilus— who, moreover, was assuredly already a Christian (not merely interested on behalf of Christianity, as Bleek supposes)—we know not, but certainly it was not *Luke* himself (in opposition to Theophylact). — τὴν ἀσφάλειαν] *the unchangeable certainty*, the character not to be shaken. Comp. τὴν ἀσφάλειαν εἶναι λόγου, Xen. *Mem.* iv. 6. 15. The position at the end is *emphatic*. According to Luke, therefore, by this historical work, which he purposes to write, the doctrines which Theophilus had received are to be set forth for him in *their immoveable positive truth;* according to Baur, on the other hand, the ἀσφάλεια which the writer had in view was to be this, that his entire representation of primitive Christianity sought to become conducive to the conciliatory interest (of the second century), and always kept this object in view. This is purely imported. Luke wrote from the dispassionate consciousness that Christianity, as it subsisted for him as the Pauline contents of faith, had its firm basis of truth in the evangelical history of salvation.

Ver. 5. The periodic and Greek style of the preface gives place now to the simple Hebraizing mode of presentation in the preliminary history,—a circumstance explained by the nature of its Jewish-Christian sources, which withal were not made use of without being subjected to manipulation, since Luke's peculiarities in expression pervade even this preliminary history. How far, however, the lofty, at times truly lyrical beauty and art of the descriptions are to be reckoned due to the sources themselves or to Luke as working them up, cannot be decided. — Observe, moreover, how the evangelical tradition gradually pushes back its beginnings from the emergence of the Baptist (Mark) to the γένεσις of Jesus (Matthew), and even to the conception of His forerunner (Luke). — ἐγένετο] *extitit*, emerged in history. Comp. on Mark i. 4. — ἱερεύς τις] therefore not high priest. — On the twenty-four *classes of priests* (מַחְלֹקֶת, in the LXX. ἐφημερία, also διαίρεσις, in Josephus also ἐφημερίς), which, since the time of Solomon, had the temple-service for a week in turn, see Ewald, *Alterth.* p. 315 ; Keil, *Archäol.* I. p. 188 f. — Ἀβιά] 1 Chron. xxiv. 10. From this successor of Eleazar the eighth ἐφημερία had its name. — The *chronological employment* of this notice for the ascertaining of the date of the birth of Jesus would require that the historical character of the narratives, given at ver. 5 ff., ver. 26 ff., should be taken for granted; moreover, it would be necessary withal that the year and (as every class came in its turn *twice* in the year) the approximate time of the year of the birth of Jesus should already be otherwise ascertained. Then, in the computation we should have to reckon, not, with Scaliger (*de emendat. tempor.*), forward from the re-institution of the temple-service by Judas Maccabaeus, 1 Macc. iv. 38 ff., because it is not known which class at that time began the service (see Paulus, *exeg. Handb.* I. p. 83 ; Wieseler, *chronol. Synopse*, p. 141), but, with Salomon van Til, Bengel, and Wieseler, backward from the destruction of the temple, because as to this the date (the 9 Abib) and the officiating class of priests (Jojarib) is known. Comp. also Lichtenstein, p. 76. — καὶ γυνὴ αὐτῷ] (see the critical remarks) *scil. ἦν.* — ἐκ τῶν θυγατ. Ἀαρ.] John's descent on both sides was priestly. Comp. Josephus, *Vit.* v. 1. See Wetstein. — Ἐλισάβετ] Such was also the name of Aaron's wife, Ex. vi. 23 (אֱלִישֶׁבַע, *Deus juramentum*).

Ver. 6 f. Δίκαιοι] *upright*, such as they ought to be according to God's will. — ἐνώπιον τ. Θεοῦ] a familiar Hebraism : לִפְנֵי יְהוָֹה, characterizing the ἀληθής δικαιοσύνη (Euthymius Zigabenus), which is so not perchance merely according to human judgment, but *before the eyes of God*, in God's presence, Gen. vii. 1 ; Acts viii. 21 ; Judith xiii. 20. Comp. Augustine, *ad Marcell.* ii. 13. — πορευόμενοι κ.τ.λ.] a more precise expla-

nation of the foregoing, likewise in quite a Hebraizing form
(1 Kings viii. 62, *al.*), wherein δικαίωμα is *legal ordinance*
(LXX. Deut. iv. 1, vi. 2, xxx. 16 ; Ps. cxix. 93, *al.; * see on
Rom. i. 32, v. 16), ἐντολή joined with δικ. (Gen. xxvi. 5 ;
Deut. iv. 40) is a *more special* idea. The distinction that
ἐντολή applies to the *moral*, δικαίωμα to the *ceremonial* pre-
cepts, is arbitrary (Calvin, Bengel, and others). We may add
that the popular testimony to such δικαιοσύνη does not exclude
human imperfection and sinfulness, and hence is not opposed
to the doctrine of justification. — ἄμεμπτοι] not equivalent to
ἀμέμπτως, but *proleptic:* so that they were blameless. Comp.
1 Thess. iii. 23 ; Winer, p. 549 f. [E. T. 778 f.]. — The
Attic καθότι, here as at xix. 9, Acts ii. 24, Tobit i. 12,
xiii. 4, corresponding to the argumentative καθώς : *as then,
according to the fact that,* occurs in the N. T. only in Luke. —
προβεβηκότες ἐν ταῖς ἡμ.] *of advanced age,* בָּאִים בַּיָּמִים, Gen.
xviii. 11 ; Josh. xxiii. 1 ; 1 Kings i. 1. The Greeks say
προβεβηκὼς τῇ ἡλικίᾳ, Lys. p. 169, 37, τοῖς ἔτεσιν (Machon
in *Athen.* xiii. p. 592 D), also τὴν ἡλικίαν, and the like
(Herodian, ii. 7. 7 ; comp. 2 Macc. iv. 40 ; Judith xvi. 23),
see Wetstein, and Pierson, *ad Moer.* p. 475. Observe that
κ. ἀμφ. προβ. κ.τ.λ. is no longer connected with καθότι, but
attached to οὐκ ἦν αὐτ. τέκν. by way of further preparation
for the marvel which follows.

Ver. 8 f. Ἐγένετο . . . ἔλαχε] thus without interposition of
καί. Both modes of expression, with and without καί, are
very frequent in Luke. See generally, Bornemann *in loc.* —
κατὰ τὸ ἔθος τῆς ἱερατ.] *according to the custom of the priest-
hood,* does not belong to what precedes (Luther, Kuinoel,
Bleek), to which ἔθος would be inappropriate, but to ἔλαχε
τοῦ θυμιᾶσαι ; the *usual custom,* namely, was, that the priest
of the class on service for the week, who was to have the
honourable office of burning incense, *was fixed* every day *by
lot,* just as in general the several offices were assigned by lot.
See Tr. *Tamid,* v. 2 ff. ; Wetstein, and Paulus, *exeget. Handb.;*
Lund, *Jüd. Heiligth.,* ed. Wolf, p. 804 f. *How the casting
of lots took place,* see Gloss. *Joma,* f. 22, 1, in Lightfoot,
p. 714. — The *genitive* τοῦ θυμιᾶσαι (not to be accented

θυμιᾶσαι[1]) is governed by ἔλαχε. See Matthiae, p. 800;
Ellendt, *Lex. Soph.* II. p. 2. On the *mode* of burning incense,
see Lightfoot, p. 715; Lund, *l.c.* p. 618 ff.; Leyrer in Herzog's
Encykl. XII. p. 506 ff. With this office specially divine
blessing was conceived to be associated (Deut. xxxiii. 10 f.);
and during it John Hyrcanus received a revelation, Josephus,
Antt. xiii. 10. 3. — Whether, we may ask, are we to understand here the *morning* (Grotius) or the *evening* (Kuinoel)
burning of incense? The *former*, as the casting lots has just
preceded. — εἰσελθὼν κ.τ.λ.] can neither be something that
follows after the ἔλαχε τ. θυμ. (so Luther and others, de
Wette and Bleek), nor can it belong *merely* to θυμιᾶσαι
(so Winer, p. 316 [E. T. 443], and Glöckler, following the
Vulgate), in which case the words would be quite idle. Rather
must they be, in the same relation as the following καὶ πᾶν
τὸ πλῆθος . . . ἔξω τῇ ὥρᾳ τοῦ θυμιάματος, an essential portion
of the description. It is, namely, the moment *that preceded*
the ἔλαχε τοῦ θυμιᾶσαι: the duty of burning incense fell to
him, *after he had entered into the temple of the Lord.* After
his entrance into the temple he received this charge. — εἰς τὸν
ναόν] not εἰς τὸ ἱερόν (see on Matt. iv. 5), for the altar of
incense, the θυσιαστήριον, ver. 11, stood in the *sanctuary*
(between the table of shewbread and the golden candlestick).

Ver. 10. And now, while this burning of incense (symbol
of adoration; see Bähr, *Symbol.* I. p. 463–469; Leyrer, *l.c.*
p. 510 f.) allotted to him was taking place in the sanctuary,
the entire multitude of the people (which expression does not
exactly presuppose a festival, as Chrysostom, Chemnitz, and
Calovius hold) was found (ἦν) in the forecourts, silently pray-
ing. This was implied in the arrangements for worship; see
Deyling, *Obss.* III. p. 343 f.; Leyrer, *l.c.* p. 509. — τοῦ
θυμιάματος] not: *of burning incense* (θυμίασις), but: *of incense*
(see ver. 11; Rev. v. 8, viii. 3, 4; Wisd. xviii. 21; Ecclus.
xlv. 6; 1 Macc. iv. 49; 2 Macc. ii. 5; Plat. *Pol.* ii. p. 373 A,
Legg. viii. p. 847 C; Herod. i. 198, iv. 71, viii. 99; Soph.
O. R. 4), namely, *at which this was burnt.*

Vv. 11, 12. Ὤφθη] not a *vision*, but a real *angelic appear-*

---

[1] Comp. generally, Lipsius, *Gramm. Unters.* p. 38 ff.

ance, xxii. 43. — ἐκ δεξιῶν] on the propitious side of the altar,
at which Zacharias was serving. See Schoettgen, and Wetstein,
ad Matt. xxv. 33; Valckenaer *in loc.* — ἄγγελος] *an angel.*
Who it was, see ver. 19. — φόβος ἐπέπεσεν ἐπ' αὐτ.] Comp.
Acts xix. 17 ; Ex. xv. 16 ; Judith xv. 2; *Test. XII. Patr.*
p. 592.   Among the Greeks usually found with *a dative*, as
Eur. *Andr.* 1042 : σοὶ μόνα ἐπέπεσον λῦπαι.

Vv. 13, 14. Εἰσηκούσθη κ.τ.λ.] By ἡ δέησίς σου cannot
be meant the petition *for offspring* (yet so still Olshausen, de
Wette, Bleek, Schegg, following Maldonatus and many others);
for, as according to ver. 7 it is not to be assumed at all that
the pious priest *still* continued *now* to pray for children, so
least of all can he at the burning of incense in his *official*
capacity have made such a *private* matter the subject of
his prayer ; but ἡ δέησίς σου must be referred to the prayer
just made by him at the priestly burning of incense, in
which also the whole of the people assembled without were
associated (ver. 10).   This prayer concerned the highest
solicitude of all Israel, namely, the *Messianic deliverance of the*
people (Augustine, Euthymius Zigabenus, Erasmus, Jansen,
Calovius, Ewald, and others), ἐλθέτω ἡ βασιλεία σου.   The context which follows is not opposed to this, but on the contrary
the connection is : " Has preces angelus dicit exauditas ; jam
enim prae foribus esse adventum Messiae, cujus anteambulo
destinatus sit is qui Zachariae nasciturus erat filius," Grotius.
— καλέσεις κ.τ.λ.] see on Matt. i. 21. — Ἰωάννης is the
Hebrew יְהוֹחָנָן or יֹוחָנָן (*God is gracious*, like the German
Gotthold).   The LXX. have Ἰωνά (2 Kings xxv. 23), Ἰωνάν
(Neh. vi. 18), Ἰωανάν (Neh. xii. 13 ; 2 Chron. xvii. 15,
xxiii. 1), Ἰωάνης (2 Chron. xxviii. 12). — γένεσις here is
birth (often so in the Greek writers and in the LXX.);
Xen. *Ep.* 3 : ὁδοῦ ἀνθρωπίνης ἀρχὴν μὲν γένεσιν, τέλος δὲ
θάνατον.

Ver. 15. Μέγας ἐνώπ. τ. κυρ.] A designation of a *truly*
great man; "talis enim quisque *vere* est, qualis est coram
Deo," Estius.   Comp. on ver. 6. — καὶ οἶνον κ.τ.λ.] Description of a נָזִיר, as those were called, who had for the service of
God bound themselves to abstain from wine and other intoxi-

cating drinks (Num. vi. 3), and to let the hair of their head
grow.   John was a Nazarite, not for a certain time, but for life,
like *Samson* (Judg. xiii. 5) and *Samuel* (1 Sam. i. 12).   See
in general, Ewald, *Alterth.* p. 96 ff. ; Saalschütz, *Mos. R.*
p. 361 f.; Keil, *Archäol.* I. § 67 ; Vilmar in the *Stud. u.
Krit.* 1864, p. 438 ff. — τὸ σίκερα (שֵׁכָר), which does not
occur in the Greek writers, is any exciting drink of the nature
of wine, but not made of grapes; Lev. x. 9 and frequently in
the LXX.   It was prepared from corn, fruit, dates, palms
(Pliny, *H. N.* xiv. 19), and so forth.   Eusebius, *Praep.
Evang.* vi. 10, has the genitive σίκερος. — ἔτι ἐκ κοιλίας κ.τ.λ.]
ἔτι never stands for ἤδη, but: *of the Holy Spirit* [1] *he shall be
full even from his mother's womb,* so that thus already *in* his
mother's womb (see Origen) he shall be filled with the Spirit.
A pregnant form of embracing the two points.   Comp.
Plutarch, *consol. ad Apoll.* p. 104 : ἔτι ἀπ᾽ ἀρχῆς ἠκολούθηκεν
(having therefore already followed ἐν ἀρχῇ).   Doubtless the
leaping of the child in the mother's womb, ver. 41, is conceived of as a manifestation of this being filled with the
Spirit.   Comp. Calovius and Maldonatus.

Vv. 16, 17.   Working of John as a preacher of repentance,
who as a moral reformer of the people (comp. on Matt. xvii. 11)
prepares the way for the Messianic consummation of the
theocracy. — ἐπιστρέψει] for through sin they have turned
themselves away from God. — κύριον τ. Θεὸν αὐτ.] not the
Messiah (Euthymius Zigabenus, and many of the older commentators), but *God.* — καὶ αὐτός] He will turn many to God,
and *he himself* will, etc. — προελεύσεται] not: *he will emerge
previously* (de Wette), but: *he will precede* (Xen. *Cyr.* vi. 3, 9),
go before Him (Gen. xxiii. 3, 14 ; Judith ii. 19, xv. 13). —
ἐνώπ. αὐτοῦ] can only, in accordance with the context, be
referred to *God* (ver. 16), whose preceding herald he will be.
The prophets, namely, look upon and depict the setting in of
the Messianic kingdom as the entrance of Jehovah into the
midst of His people, so that thereupon *God Himself* is *repre-*

---

[1] It is quite arbitrary in Olshausen to support the rationalistic opinion that
the expression here is to be understood not of the distinctive *Holy Spirit*, but of
the holy *power of God* in general.

sented by the Messiah; Isa. xl.; Mal. iii. 1, iv. 5 f. Comp. Tit.
ii. 13. In the person of the entering Messiah Jehovah Himself enters ; but the Messiah's own personal divine nature is
not yet expressed in this ancient-prophetic view (in opposition
to Gess, *Pers. Chr.* p. 47). Incorrect, because in opposition
to this prophetic idea, is the *immediate* reference of αὐτοῦ
to the *Messiah* (Heumann, Kuinoel, Valckenaer, Winer), as
regards which appeal is made to the emphatic use of הוּא,
αὐτός, and *ipse* (comp. the Pythagorean αὐτὸς ἔφα), whereby
a subject not named but well known to every one is designated (Winer, p. 152 [E. T. 182 f.]). — ἐν πνεύματι κ.
δυνάμ. Ἠλ.] furnished therewith. Spirit and power (power
of working) of Elias (according to Mal. iii. 23 f.) is, as a
matter of course, *God's* Spirit (comp. ver. 15) and *divine*
power, but in the peculiar character and vital expression which
were formerly apparent in the case of *Elias*, whose antitype
John is, not as a miracle-worker (John x. 41), but as preacher
of repentance and prophetic preparer of the way of the Lord.
— ἐπιστρέψαι κ.τ.λ.] according to Malachi, *l.c.: in order to
turn fathers' hearts to children;* to be taken literally of the
restoration of the *paternal love,* which in the moral degradation
of the people had in many grown cold. Comp. Ecclus.
xlviii. 10 and Fritzsche *in loc.* Kuinoel incorrectly holds
that πατέρων means the *patriarchs,* and that the meaning is
(similar to that given by Augustine, *de civit. D.* xx. 29 ;
Beza, Calovius, and others) : " *efficiet, ut posteri erga Deum
eundem habeant animum pium, quem habebant eorum majores.*"
Comp. also Hengstenberg, *Christol.* III. p. 674, and Bleek.
The absence of any article ought in itself to have warned
against this view ! — καὶ ἀπειθεῖς ἐν φρον. τ. δικ.] sc. ἐπιστρέψαι. The discourse passes over from the special relation
to the general one. ἀπειθεῖς is the opposite of τῶν δικαίων,
and therefore is not to be understood of the *children* (Olshausen),
but of the *immoral* in general, whose characteristic is *dis-
obedience,* namely towards God. — ἐν φρονήσει] connected
immediately in a pregnant way with the verb of direction,
in which the thought of the *result* was predominant. See
Kühner, II. p. 316. " Sensus eorum, qui justi sunt, in

conversione protinus induitur," Bengel. φρόνησις (see Arist.
Eth. Nic. vi. 5. 4), *practical intelligence.* Comp. on Eph. i. 8.
The *practical element* follows from ἀπειθεῖς. — ἑτοιμάσαι] *to
put in readiness,* etc. Aim of the ἐπιστρέψαι κ.τ.λ., and so
final aim of the προελεύσεται κ.τ.λ. — κυρίῳ] *for God,* as at
vv. 16, 17. — λαὸν κατεσκευασμ.] *a people adjusted, placed in
the right moral state* (for the setting up of the Messianic
kingdom), is related to ἑτοιμάσαι as its *result.* " Parandus
populus, ne Dominus populum imparatum inveniens majestate
sua obterat," Bengel.

Ver. 18. Like Abraham's question, Gen. xv. 8. — κατὰ τί]
According to what. Zacharias asks after a σημεῖον (ii. 12),
in conformity with which he should know that what had been
promised (τοῦτο)—in other words, the birth of a son, with
whom the indicated destination of Elias should associate itself
—had really occurred.

Vv. 19, 20. The angel now discloses to Zacharias *what
angel he is,* by way of justifying the announcement of penalty
which he has then to add. — Γαβριήλ] גַּבְרִיאֵל, *vir Dei,* one of
the seven angel-princes (שָׂרִים) or archangels (comp. Auberlen
in Herzog's *Encykl.* IV. p. 634[1]), who stand for service at the
throne of God (ἐνώπιον τ. Θεοῦ), as His primary servants
(ὁ παρεστηκώς, comp. thereon Rev. viii. 2, and see Valckenaer),
Dan. viii. 16, ix. 21. Comp. Fritzsche on Tob. xii. 15.
"*Nomina* angelorum ascenderunt in manum Israelis ex
Babylone," Ros Hassana, f. 56, 4; Enoch 20. See later
Jewish fictions in respect to Gabriel, set forth in Eisenmenger,
entdecktes Judenth. II. p. 363 ff., 378 ff., 390, 874. — σιω-
πῶν] It is only the subsequent κ. μὴ δυνάμ. λαλῆσαι that
defines this more precisely as *dumbness,* which, however, is not
apoplectic caused by the terror (Paulus), nor the consequence
of the agitating effect of the vision (Lange), which consequence
he himself recognised as a punishment; but it is a *miraculous*
penalty. — ἀνθ᾽ ὧν] *for the reason* (by way of retribution)
that; xix. 44; Acts xii. 23; 2 Thess. ii. 10; Hermann, *ad*

[1] Hofmann, *Schriftbew.* I. p. 343 f., makes some unimportant objections
against the accuracy of the explanation of *archangels.* See in opposition to
him, Hahn, *Theol. d. N. T.* I. p. 286.

Viger. p. 710 ; Ellendt, *Lex. Soph.* I. p. 170.   The difficulties
felt on account of the *harshness* of this measure (Paulus,
Strauss, Bruno Bauer, comp. also de Wette), with which the
impunity of others, such as Abraham and Sarah, has been
compared, are, when the matter is historically viewed, not to
be got rid of either by the assumption of a greater guilt
which the Omniscient recognised (Calvin, comp. Lange, *L. J.*
II. 1, p. 65, and even as early as Augustine), or by an
appeal to the lesser age of Zacharias (Hoffmann), and the like;
but to be referred to the counsel of God (Rom. xi. 33 f.),
whose various measures do not indeed disclose themselves to
human judgment, but at any rate admit of the reflection that,
the nearer the dawn of the *Messianic* time, the more inviol-
ably must the requirement of *faith in the promise*—and the
promise was here given through an *angel* and a *priest*—come
into prominent relief. — οἵτινες] qualitative (Kühner, II. p.
407), *ita comparati ut,* wherein is implied a reference that
justifies the penal measure. — εἰς τ. καιρὸν αὐτ.] denotes the
space of time appointed for the λόγοι, till the completion of
which it is still to hold that their fulfilment is setting in.
Comp. the classical ἐς καιρόν, εἰς χρόνον, εἰς ἑσπέραν, and the
like, Bernhardy, p. 216.   See also xiii. 9.

Ver. 21. The priests, especially the chief priests, were
accustomed, according to the Talmud, to spend only a short
time in the sanctuary; otherwise it was apprehended that they
had been slain by God, because they were unworthy or had
done something wrong.   See *Hieros. Joma,* f. 43, 2 ; *Babyl.* f.
53, 2 ; Deyling, *Obss.* III. ed. 2, p. 455 f.   Still the un-
usually long delay of Zacharias, which could not but strike
the people, is sufficient *in itself* as a reason of their wonder.
— ἐν τῷ χρονίζειν αὐτόν] not *over* (ἐπί, iv. 22, *al.*), or *on
account of* (Mark vi. 6, διά), but *on occasion of* his failure to
appear.   So also Ecclus. xi. 21 ; Isa. lxi. 6.   Rightly,
Gersdorf, Ewald, render : *when he,* etc.

Vv. 22, 23. Ἐπέγνωσαν, ὅτι ὀπτασίαν κ.τ.λ.] by the
inference *ab effectu ad causam;* and very naturally they recognise as the latter an appearance of God or an angel, since,
in fact, it was *in the sanctuary* that the dumbness had come

on, and the agitating impression might even cause death,
Judg. vi. 23, *al.* In spite of the οὐκ ἠδύνατο λαλῆσαι,
Olshausen thinks that this ἐπέγνωσαν does not refer to the
silence of Zacharias, but probably to the excitement in his
whole appearance, which Bleek also mixes up. — αὐτός, *he on
his part,* corresponding to that which *they* perceived. — ἦν
διανεύων αὐτοῖς] he was employed in making signs to them
(Ecclus. xxvii. 22 ; Lucian, *V. H.* 44), namely, that he had
seen a vision. — ὡς ἐπλήσθ. κ.τ.λ.] namely, the week in which
the class of Abia (see ver. 5) had the temple service. On the
verb, comp. ver. 57, ii. 6, 21 f.; also Gal. iv. 4; Eph. i. 10. —
εἰς τ. οἰκ. αὐτοῦ] ver. 39 f., also ver. 56 : εἰς τ. οἶκον αὐτῆς.

Ver. 24 f. Μετὰ δὲ ταύτ. τ. ἡμέρ.] in which this vision had
occurred, and he had returned at the end of the service-week
to his house. Between the return and the conception we are
not to place an indefinite interval. — περιέκρυβεν ἑαυτήν] *she
hid herself,* withdrew her own person completely (περί, see
Valckenaer) from the view of others. — μῆνας πέντε] is of
necessity to be understood of *the first,* not of *the last* five
months of pregnancy (in opposition to Heumann). See vv. 26,
36, 56, 57. — λέγουσα· ὅτι κ.τ.λ.] the *reason* which was
uttered by her for this withdrawal ; hence ὅτι is not recitative,
but to be rendered *because,* as at vii. 16 : *because thus hath the
Lord done to me in the days, in which He was careful to take
away my reproach among men.* Her reflection, therefore, was
to this effect : " seeing that her pregnancy was the work *of
God,* whose care, at the setting in of this state of hers, had
been directed towards removing from her the reproach of
unfruitfulness, she must leave to God also the announcement of her pregnancy, and not herself bring it about. God
would know how to attain His purpose of taking away her
reproach." And God knew how to attain this His purpose.
After she had kept herself concealed for five months, there
occurred in the sixth month, ver. 26 ff., the annunciation to
Mary, in which the condition of Elizabeth was disclosed to
Mary, so that she rose up (ver. 39 ff.), etc. Hence the opinions
are not in accordance with the text, which represent Elizabeth
as having kept herself concealed from *shame* at being with

child in her old age (Origen, Ambrose, Beda, Theophylact,
Euthymius Zigabenus), or in order that she might first *assure
herself* of her condition (Paulus), and might in the meantime
apply herself to devotion (Kuinoel), or to afford no handle to
curiosity (Schegg), or "quo magis appareret *postea repente*
graviditas" (Bengel), or even because it was necessary to
keep herself *quiet* during the first months of pregnancy (de
Wette). No; it was because with resignation and confidence
she awaited the emerging of the divine guidance. — αἷς]
without repetition of the preposition. See Bernhardy, p. 203 ;
Bornemann, *Schol.* p. 5 ; Kühner, *ad Xen. Mem.* ii. 1. 32. —
ἐπεῖδεν] *looked to it*, i.e. *took care for it.* So more frequently
ἐφοράω is used of the providence of the gods in the classical
writers; Herod. i. 124; Soph. *El.* 170. Comp. Acts iv. 29.
— τὸ ὄνειδός μου] Comp. Gen. xxx. 23. Unfruitfulness was
a *disgrace*, as being a token of the divine disfavour (Ps. cxiii. 9 ;
Isa. iv. 1, xliv. 3, xlvii. 9; Hos. ix. 11); the possession of many
children was an honour and blessing (Ps. cxxvii., cxxviii.).
Comp. the view of the Greeks, Herod. vi. 86 ; Müller, *Dor.* II.
p. 192. — ἐν ἀνθρώποις] belongs to ἀφελεῖν ; *among men* she
had dishonour.

Vv. 26, 27. Τῷ ἕκτῳ] see ver. 24. — Ναζαρέτ] According
to Matthew, *Bethlehem* was the dwelling-place of Joseph and
Mary. See on Matt. ii. 23, Remark, and Schleiermacher,
L. J. p. 51 ff. — ἐξ οἴκου Δαυίδ] applies not to Mary and
Joseph (Chrysostom, Theophylact, Euthymius Zigabenus, Beza,
Calovius, and others, including Wieseler in the *Stud. u. Krit.*
1845, p. 395), but merely to the latter, ii. 4, iii. 23 ff. The
descent of Mary from David cannot at all be proved in the
N. T. See on Matt. i. 17, Remark 2. Comp. on ver. 36,
ii. 4 f.

Vv. 28, 29. Εἰσελθών] namely, ὁ ἄγγελος (see the critical
remarks). Paulus erroneously puts it : " *a person who came in*
said to her." — κεχαριτωμένη] *who has met with kindness* (from
God).[1] Well remarks Bengel : "non ut mater gratiae, sed ut

---

[1] Observe the ingenious similarity of sound in the words χαῖρε κεχαριτωμένη.
Plays on words of a like kind are found among Roman Catholics with the contrasts of *ave* and *Eva*.

filia gratiae." See ver. 30; and on χαριτόω in general, see
Eph. i. 6. — On εὐλογ. σὺ ἐν γυναιξ. in the *Textus receptus*
(but see the critical remarks), see Winer, p. 220 [E. T. 308].
It would be not a *vocative*, like κεχαριτωμένη, but a *nominative*,
as the added σύ indicates : *The Lord is with thee, blessed* (κατ᾽
ἐξοχήν) *art thou among women.* — Ver. 29. The *Recepta* (but
see the critical remarks) would have to be explained : *but she,
when she looked upon him, was terrified at his saying,* so that
ἰδοῦσα only appears as an accessory element of the narrative,
not as jointly a reason of her terror (in opposition to Bornemann, de Wette, and others), which would rather be simply
ἐπὶ τῷ λόγῳ αὐτοῦ, as is shown by the text which follows
καὶ διελογίζετο κ.τ.λ. — ποταπός] *qualis, what sort of a :* a
question of wonder. Comp. on Mark xiii. 1 f. In accordance
with its *whole tenor* raising her to so high distinction the
greeting was to her enigmatical.

Ver. 31. See on Matt. i. 21.

Ver. 32 f. Μέγας] Comp. ver. 15. And *what* greatness
belonged to *this* promised One, appears from what is said in
the sequel of His future ! — υἱὸς ὑψίστου κληθήσ.] Description
of His recognition as *Messiah*, as whom the angel still more
definitely designates Him by καὶ δώσει κ.τ.λ. The name Son
of God is not explained in a metaphysical reference until
ver. 35. — τὸν θρόνον Δαυ. τοῦ πατρ. αὐτοῦ] *i.e.* the royal
throne of the Messianic kingdom, which is the antitypical
consummation of the kingdom of David (Ps. cxxxii. 11, cx.),
as regards which, however, in the sense of the angel, which
excludes the bodily paternity of Joseph, David can be meant
as ὁ πατὴρ αὐτοῦ only according to the *national theocratic*
relation of the Messiah as David's son, just as the *historical*
notion of the Messiah was once given. The mode in which
Luke (and Matthew) conceived of the Davidic descent is plain
from the genealogical table of ch. iii., according to which
the genealogy passed by way of Joseph as *foster-father.* — εἰς
τοὺς αἰῶνας] from Isa. ix. 6 ; Dan. vii. 13 f. The conception
of an *everlasting* Messianic kingdom (according to Ps. cx. 4)
is also expressed in John xii. 34 ; comp. the Rabbins 'in
Bertholdt, *Christol.* p. 156. The *"house of Jacob"* is not to

LUKE.   T

be idealized (Olshausen, Bleek, and others: of the *spiritual* Israel) ; but the conception of the kingdom in our passage is Jewish-national, which, however, does not exclude the dominion over the Gentiles according to the prophetic prediction (" quasi per accessionem," Grotius). — βασιλ. ἐπί] as xix. 14 ; Rom. v. 14.

Ver. 34 f. *How is it possible that this shall be the case ?* [1] namely, τὸ συλλαβεῖν ἐν γαστρὶ καὶ τεκεῖν υἱόν, Euthymius Zigabenus. — οὐ γινώσκω] comp. Matt. i. 18 ; Gen. xix. 8 ; Judg. xi. 39 ; Num. xxxi. 17, *since I have sexual intercourse with no man.* In this sense the pure maiden *knows* no man. As, however, she is betrothed, ver. 27, her reply shows that she has understood the promise of the angel rightly as soon to be fulfilled, and not to be referred to her impending marriage with Joseph, but as independent of the marriage that was soon to take place. The ἄνδρα οὐ γινώσκω is thus simply the confession of the *immaculate virgin conscience,* and not (a misunderstanding, which Mary's very *betrothal* ought to have precluded) *the vow of perpetual virginity* (Augustine, *de virgin.* 4, Gregory of Nyssa, Grotius, Jansen, Maldonatus, Bisping, and others), or the *resolution* to that effect (Schegg). — πνεῦμα ἅγιον] In accordance with the nature of a proper name, without the article. Moreover, see on Matt. i. 18. — ἐπελεύσεται ἐπὶ σέ] *will descend upon thee* (Acts i. 8). This, as well as ἐπισκιάσει σοι, *will overshadow thee* (Acts v. 15), is—the former without figure, the latter figuratively—a designation of the connection producing the pregnancy, which, however, is not conceived of in the form of copulation, for which the words are euphemistic expressions (Paulus, von Ammon, and older commentators), or yet under the notion of a bird which covers its eggs (Theophylact, comp. Grotius).[2] Certainly the ex-

---

[1] This question is only appropriate to the virgin heart as a question of *doubt* on the ground of conscious impossibility, and not as an actual wish to learn the *how* (τὸν τρόπον τοῦ πράγματος, Theophylact) ; comp. already Augustine : " *inquirendo* dixit, non *desperando*," whereas the meaning of the question of Zacharias, ver. 18, is the converse.

[2] Approved also by Delitzsch, *bibl. Psychol.* p. 116 f., and Bleek. But this conception is here very much out of place, and is not implied even in מְרַחֶפֶת, Gen. i. 2, which, besides, has nothing to do with the passage before us.

pressions are correlates of γινώσκω, but as regards the *effect*,
not as regards the form, since ἐπελεύσ. expresses simply the
descent of the Spirit, and ἐπισκιάσ. the *manifestation* of divine
power associated therewith in the form of a cloud (after the
manner of the Old Testament theophanies, Ex. xl. 45 ; Num.
ix. 15 ; 1 Kings viii. 10 ; comp. also Luke ix. 34). Augustine
and other Fathers have quite mistakenly laid stress in ἐπισκ.
on the notion of *coolness* (in contrast to procreation in lust) ;
comp. σκιάζειν τὸ καῦμα in Alciphr. iii. 2. — δύναμις ὑψίστου]
without the article : *power of the Highest* will overshadow thee,
will be that, which shall overshadow thee.   This will set in
in immediate consequence (καί) of the πνεῦμα ἅγιον ἐπελεύσεται ἐπὶ σέ.   Strict dogmatic expositors, such as Theophylact, Calovius, have rightly (comp. xxiv. 49) *distinguished*
between the Holy Spirit and the power of the Highest, but in
doing so have already imported more precise definitions from
the dogmatic system by explaining the power of the Highest
of the *Son of God*, who with His majesty filled the body that
had been formed by the Holy Spirit, and thus have, by a
more precise description of the formation of the body, broken
in upon the delicate veil which the mouth of the angel had
breathed over the mystery.[1] — τὸ γεννώμενον ἅγιον] *the holy
thing that is being begotten* shall (after His birth) be called Son
of God.   Most interpreters take τὸ γεννώμενον as *that which
is to be born* (comp. ver. 13), which view, moreover, has drawn
after it the old addition ἐκ σοῦ from Matt. i. 16.   But the
context which immediately precedes points only to the *begetting*
(Bengel, Bleek) ; and to this also points the *neuter*, which
applies to the embryo (comp. on Matt. i. 20, and see Fritzsche,
ad Aristoph. Thesm. 564), as well as the parallel Matt. i. 20.
The subject, we may add, is τὸ ἅγιον, not τὸ γεννώμ. (Kuinoel :

[1] Calovius : "Supervenit Spiritus non quidem σπερματικῶς sed δημιουργικῶς,
guttulas sanguineas Mariae, e quibus concipienda caro Domini, *sanctificando,
easdem foecundas reddendo, et ex iisdem corpus humanum efformando.*" Justin,
Apol. I. 33, already rightly gives the simple thought of the chaste and delicate
representation : κυοφορῆσαι παρθένον οὖσαν πεποίηκε.   Schleiermacher, *L. J.* p. 62,
erroneously affirms that the representation of Luke admits the possibility of
Jesus being thought of as conceived with the participation of Joseph.   It absolutely excludes any such notion.

" proles veneranda " = τὸ γεννώμ. τὸ ἅγιον), as also Bornemann
assumes, when he (comp. de Wette) takes ἅγιον predicatively :
" proles tua, *cum divina sit*." Not as *holy*, but as *begotten by
God's power* (διό), is the fruit of Mary called the Son of God.
Hofmann, *Schriftbew.* I. p. 117, explains : it shall be called
holy, *Son of God*, so that those two appellations are to correspond to the two members of the preceding promise. So
already Tertullian, as also Bengel and Bleek. But the asyndetic form, in which υἱὸς Θεοῦ would be subjoined, tells against
this view all the more, that we should of necessity, in direct
accordance with what precedes (καὶ δύναμις κ.τ.λ.), expect καὶ
υἱὸς Θεοῦ, especially *after* the verb, where no reader could
anticipate a second predicate without καί. Comp. Justin,
c. *Tryph.* 100 : διὸ καὶ τὸ γεννώμενον ἐξ αὐτῆς ἅγιόν ἐστιν
υἱὸς Θεοῦ.

Ver. 36 f. Confirmation of the promise by the disclosure of
Elizabeth's pregnancy, which, in fact, was also a deviation
from the order of nature (ἐν γήρει), and so far presented an
analogy, although only in an inferior sense. "En domesticum
tibi exemplum !" Grotius. After ἰδοὺ κ.τ.λ. an ἐστί was as
little needed as an εἰμί at ver. 38. — συγγενίς] The *nature* of
this relationship, which is not at variance with John i. 36,
although questioned by Schleiermacher and others, is wholly
unknown. It is, however, possible that Mary was of the
stock of *Levi* (so Faustus the Manichean in Augustine, c. *Faust.*
xxiii. 9 ; and recently, Schleiermacher, *Schr. d. Luk.* p. 26 ;
Hilgenfeld, Ewald, *Gesch. Chr.* p. 177, and others), as the
Test. XII. Patr. p. 542 makes the Messiah proceed from the
stock of Judah (Joseph) and (comp. p. 546) from the stock of
Levi.[1] — On the late form συγγενίς, see Lobeck, *ad Phryn.*
p. 451 f. ; and on the Ionic form of dative γήρει, Winer,
p. 60 [E. T. 73 f.]. — οὗτος] subject : *and this is the sixth
month.* — ὅτι οὐκ ἀδυνατ. κ.τ.λ.] Confirmation of that which

---

[1] Thus the descent from the Davidic and priestly race might have been used
for the glorification of Jesus. But from the height of the history of Jesus so
little importance was attached to things of this nature that only the *Davidic*
descent, as it was necessary in the case of the Messiah, had stress laid on it, and
the family of *Mary* was not expressly specified at all. Comp. Ewald, *Gesch.
Chr.* p. 177 f.

has just been said of Elizabeth by the omnipotence of God.
It is to be observed (1) that οὐκ ... πᾶν do not belong to one
another, but of πᾶν ῥῆμα it is said : οὐκ ἀδυνατήσει (Fritzsche,
Diss. II. *in* 2 Cor. p. 24 f.); further, (2) that the proposition
is a *general* one ; hence the *future*, which, however, is purposely chosen with a view to what was announced to Mary ;
see Dissen, *ad Dem. de Cor.* p. 369 ; (3) that there exists no
reason for abandoning the purely Greek meaning of ἀδυνατεῖν,
to be unable (Rettig in the *Stud. u. Krit.* 1838, p. 210), any
more than of ῥῆμα, *utterance* (ver. 38), especially with the
reading παρὰ τοῦ Θεοῦ (see the critical remarks). Hence
the meaning is not : " *With God nothing is impossible ;* "
but rather : *not powerless* (but of success and efficacy) *shall
any utterance on the part of God be.* So also Gen. xviii.
14. Comp. Beza : " ῥῆμα, *i.e.* quicquid Deus semel futurum
dixerit."

Ver. 38. *Behold the handmaid of the Lord !* without a
verb. Comp. ver. 36, v. 12, 18. — γένοιτο] λοιπὸν οὐ μόνον
ἐπίστευσεν, ἀλλὰ ηὔξατο γενέσθαι αὐτῇ, καθὼς ὁ ἄγγελος
εἴρηκε, Euthymius Zigabenus ; " eximio fiduciae exemplo,"
Grotius.

REMARK.—The natural explanation of the annunciation to
Mary (Paulus) is at variance with the evangelic account ;
and as the latter unfolds simply, clearly, and delicately an
external procedure, the objective is not to be rendered subjective and transferred, as a reciprocal operation of the theocratic Spirit of God and the emotional feeling of the Virgin,
by means of poetic colouring to the soul of the latter (Lange,
L. J. II. 1, p. 67). As history, believed even as it is related,
the narrative arose, and that too independently of the preliminary history of Matthew, and even incompatibly with it,[1]—in
consequence of the circumstance that the divine sonship of
Jesus was extended to His bodily origination (see on Matt.
i. 18), an idea, which gave shape to legends dissimilar in character and gaining currency in different circles. Thus, *e.g.*, it
is clear that the history, adopted at Matt. i. 19 ff., of Joseph's
perplexity and of the angelic message which came to him
does not presuppose, but excludes the annunciation to Mary ;
for that Mary after such a revelation should have made no

[1] Comp. Schleiermacher, *L. J.* p. 59 ff.

communication to Joseph, would have been not less psychologically unnatural, than it would have been a violation of the bridal relation and, indeed, of the bridal duty;[1] and to reckon on a special revelation, which without her aid would make the disclosure to her betrothed, she must have been expressly directed by the angelic announcement made to her, in order to be justified in deferring the communication of her pregnancy to her betrothed. We make this remark in opposition to the arbitrary presuppositions and shifts of Hug (*Gutacht.* I. p. 81 ff.), Krabbe, Ebrard, and others. According to the view invented by the last-named, it is assumed that Joseph had learned Mary's pregnancy, immediately after the appearance of its earliest signs, from the *pronubae* ("suspicious women"); that *immediately* there ensued the appearance of the angel to him, and *forthwith* he took her home; and that for all this a period of at most fourteen days sufficed. Mark and John have rightly excluded these miracles of the preliminary history from the cycle of the evangelical narrative, which only began with the appearance of the Baptist (Mark i. 1); as, indeed, Jesus Himself never, even in His confidential circle, refers to them, and the unbelief of His own brothers, John vii. 5, and in fact even the demeanour of Mary, Mark iii. 21 ff., is irreconcilable with them.[2] —*The angelic announcement made to Zacharias,* which likewise withdraws itself from any attempt at natural explanation (Paulus, Ammon), appears as a parallel to the annunciation to Mary, having originated and been elaborated in consequence of the latter as a link in the chain of the same cycle of legends after the analogy of Old Testament models, especially that of Abraham and his wife. As in the case of the annunciation to Mary the metaphysical divine Sonship of Jesus, so in the announcement to Zacharias the extraordinary divine destination and mission of John (John i. 6) is the real element on which the formation of legend became engrafted; but to derive the latter merely from the self-consciousness of the

---

[1] Lange, *L. J.* II. p. 83 f., rightly acknowledges this, but, following older writers, thinks that Mary made the communication to Joseph before her journey to Elizabeth, but that he nevertheless ("the first Ebionite") refused to believe her. This is not compatible with Matthew's narrative, especially i. 18. And what Lange further (p. 89) adds, that during Mary's absence a severe struggle arose in his soul, and this state of feeling became the medium of the revelation made to him, is simply *added.*

[2] Schleiermacher is right in saying, *L. J.* p. 71 : " These occurrences have been entirely without effect as regards the coming forward of Christ or the origination of faith in Him."

church (Bruno Bauer), and consequently to take away the objective foundation of the history, is at variance with the entire N. T. and with the history of the church. For the formation of the legend, moreover, the historical circumstances, that John was the son of the priest Zacharias and Elizabeth, and a son born late in life, are to be held fast as *premisses actually given by history* (in opposition to Strauss, I. p. 135), all the more that for these simple historical data their general notoriety could not but bear witness. This also in opposition to Weisse and B. Bauer, who derive these traditions from the laboratory of religious contemplation. Further, as to what specially concerns *the late birth* of John, it has its historical precedents in the history of Isaac, of Samson, and of Samuel; but the general principle deduced from such cases, " Cum alicujus uterum claudit, ad hoc facit, ut mirabilius denuo aperiat, et non libidinis esse quod nascitur, sed divini muneris cognoscatur" (*Evang. de Nativ. Mar.* 3), became the source of unhistorical inventions in the apocryphal Gospels,[1] as, in particular, the apocryphal account of the birth of Mary herself is an imitation of the history of John's birth.

Ver. 39. The angel's communication, ver. 36, occasions Mary to make a journey to Elizabeth, and that *with haste* (μετὰ σπουδῆς, comp. Mark vi. 25; Ex. xii. 11; Herod. iii. 4, iv. 5); for how much must her heart have now urged her to the interchange of the deepest feelings with the friend who, in like manner, was so highly favoured! Thus it is not merely " ne negligeret signum," etc., Grotius. From Elizabeth she receives the confirmation of that which the angel had announced to her concerning Elizabeth. But before her departure the great promise of ver. 35 is already fulfilled to herself. With extraordinary delicacy the promised conception is not related in its realization (comp., on the other hand, ver. 24), and the veil of the unparalleled marvel is not attempted to be raised; but vv. 41—44 and the whole triumph of Mary, ver. 46 ff., presuppose that she appears before Elizabeth already as the mother of the Messiah, bearing Him in her womb. She herself is only made certain of the miracle, which has already occurred in her case, by the

---

[1] See, in general, R. Hofmann, *das Leben Jesu nach d. Apokr.* 1851; also Gelpke, *Jugendgesch. des Herrn*, 1842 (who, moreover, gives the *Jewish* legends).

inspired communication which at once meets her from the mouth of her friend. Bengel is singularly arbitrary in transferring the conception, which in any case lies between vv. 38 and 39, to the moment when the child leaped in the womb of Elizabeth, which he concludes from γάρ in ver. 44. — εἰς τὴν ὀρεινήν] *into the mountain-region*—κατ᾽ ἐξοχήν, Aristot. *H. A.* v. 28; Judith i. 6, ii. 22, iv. 7, *al.*; Plin. *H. N.* v. 14. The mountainous country in the tribe of *Judah* is meant. See Robinson, *Pal.* II. p. 422 ff., III. p. 188 ff. — εἰς πόλιν Ἰούδα] *into a city of the tribe of Judah.* Luke does not give any more precise definition, and therefore it is to be assumed that he himself had no more precise knowledge. Jerusalem, the capital, is certainly not meant (in opposition to Ambrose, Beda, Camerarius); which is clear, not indeed from the want of the article (comp. ii. 4, 11; Bornemann *in loc.*), but from the unprecedented designation itself (in 2 Chron. xxv. 28 the reading is very doubtful, see the LXX.), and from the εἰς τὴν ὀρείνην [less] appropriate to Jerusalem. It *may* have been the priestly city of *Hebron*, Josh. xxi. 11 (Baronius, Beza, Grotius, Lightfoot, Wolf, Rosenmüller, and others); but that it is meant *as a matter of course* under the "city of Judah" (see Ewald, p. 182), is not to be assumed, because in that case πόλιν could not dispense with the article (to the *well-known* city of Judah). Others (Valesius, *Epp.* 669; Reland, *Pal.* p. 870; Wetstein, Paulus, Kuinoel, Crome, *Beitr.* p. 45, *et al.*; comp. also Robinson, *Pal.* III. p. 193, and Ritter, *Erdk.* XV. p. 641) have regarded *Juda* as itself the name of the city: holding that it was the priestly city יֻטָּה or יֻטָּה (Josh. xxi. 16, xv. 55; comp. Robinson, II. p. 417), so that the name is wrongly written. We should have to refer this inaccuracy to Luke himself; but the whole hypothesis is an unnecessary makeshift.

Ver. 41. Τὸν ἀσπασμ. τ. Μαρ.] *the greeting of Mary.* See vv. 40, 44. This greeting on the part of Mary (not the communication of the angelic announcement, ver. 26 ff., as Kuinoel and others import) caused *the leaping of the child* (comp. Gen. xxv. 22), and that as an exulting expression of the *joy* of the latter (ver. 44, vi. 23) at the presence of the

Messiah[1] now in the womb of His mother. Elizabeth immediately *through the Holy Spirit* recognises the cause of the
leaping. Comp. Hofmann, *Weissag. u. Erfüll.* II. p. 251 f.
Calvin, Michaelis, Paulus, Olshausen, and many others reverse
the matter, holding that the *mental agitation* of the *mother*
had operated on the child (comp. also Lange, II. 1, p. 86),
and that this circumstance had only afterwards, ver. 44,
become significant to the mother. Analogous to the conception in our passage is *Sohar Ex.* f. xxiii. 91 f., xxv. 99 :
" Omnes Israelitae ad mare rubrum plus viderunt quam
Ezechiel propheta ; imo etiam *embryones, qui in utero matris
erant, viderunt id, et Deum S. B. celebrarunt.*" A *symbolical*
significance, expressive, namely, of the thought, that at the
appearance of a higher Spirit the ideas that lie still unborn in
the womb of the spirit of the world and of the people are
quickened (Weisse), is foreign to the narrative,—a modern
abstraction.

Ver. 42 f. Ἀνεφώνησε] *She cried out* (only occurring here
in the N. T. ; comp. 1 Chron. xv. 28, xvi. 5 ; 2 Chron. v. 12 ;
Polyb. iii. 33. 4 ; frequent in Plutarch), expressing the *outburst* of the being filled by the Spirit. — ὁ καρπὸς τ. κοιλ. σου]
Designation of the *embryo*, that Mary bears in her womb. For
the expression, comp. Gen. xxx. 2 ; Lam. ii. 20. — καὶ πόθεν
κ.τ.λ.] *sc.* γέγονεν. After the first outburst now follows a
certain *reflection*, a humble pondering, from what cause (πόθεν,
comp. on Mark xii. 37) she was deemed worthy of this great
happiness : ἀναξίαν ἑαυτὴν τῆς τοιαύτης ἐπιδημίας τῆς δεσποί-
νης ὁμολογεῖ, Euthymius Zigabenus. — ἵνα κ.τ.λ.] not equivalent
to τὸ ἐλθεῖν τὴν μητ. κ.τ.λ., but *telic : that the mother of my
Lord* (the Messiah, comp. Ps. cx. 1) *should come to me*,—this is
the τοῦτο, in reference to which she asks πόθεν μοι. Comp.
on John vi. 29, xvii. 3.

Ver. 44 f. Γάρ] specifies the ground of knowledge, on which
she declares Mary as the mother of the Messiah. She had

___

[1] Older Lutherans (see Calovius) have wrongly used this passage as a proof of
the *fides infantum.* There is, in fact, here something unique in character and
miraculous. The child of Elizabeth has already in the womb the Holy Spirit,
ver. 15.

the discernment of this connection *through the Holy Spirit*, ver. 41. — ὅτι] may either be the specification of the reason attached to μακαρία (Vulgate, Luther, Erasmus, Beza, Lange, and others), or the statement of the contents to πιστεύσασα (Grotius, Bengel, Paulus, Kuinoel, Bornemann, de Wette, Ewald, Bleek, and others). The latter is the correct view, since the conception—the chief point of the λελαλημένα, which Elizabeth has in view—is no longer future, but has already taken place. Hence: *for blessed is she who has believed, that there shall be a fulfilment to all* (ver. 31 ff.), etc. As to τελείωσις, comp. Judith x. 9 ; John xix. 28.

Ver. 46 ff. An echo of the lyrical poetry of the Old Testament, especially of the song of praise of Hannah the mother of Samuel (1 Sam. ii.). This psalm-like effusion from the heart of Mary (the so-called *Magnificat*) divides itself into four strophes, namely, (1) vv. 46–48 (as far as αὐτοῦ) ; (2) ver. 48 (from ἰδού onward) as far as ver. 50 ; (3) vv. 51–53 ; and (4) vv. 54, 55. Each of these four strophes contains three verses. See Ewald, p. 181. — ἡ ψυχή μου] the mediating organ between πνεῦμα and body (Beck, *bibl. Seelenl.* p. 11 ff.; Delitzsch, *bibl. Psychol.* p. 222) which receives the impressions from without and from within, and here expresses by means of the mouth what has taken place in the πνεῦμα (hence ἠγαλλίασε in the *aorist*). The πνεῦμα is " the highest and noblest part of man, whereby he is qualified to grasp incomprehensible, invisible, eternal things ; and is, in brief, the house within which faith and God's word abide," Luther (*Ausl.* 1521). Comp. Hahn, *Theol. d. N. T.* I. p. 411 ff. That the spirit of Mary exulted full of the *Holy* Spirit, was self-evident for the evangelist after ver. 35 ; an observation, such as that of ver. 41, concerning Elizabeth : ἐπλήσθη πνεύματος ἁγ., would now have been inappropriate in reference to Mary. ἀγαλλιάω, in the *active*, is only found here and at Rev. xix. 7 (Lachmann, Tischendorf), which reason, however, does not warrant the conjecture of ἀγαλλιάσεται (Valckenaer, Bretschneider). — σωτῆρι] *benefactor.* " Is est nimirum σωτήρ, qui salutem dedit," Cicero, *Verr.* ii. 63. — ὅτι ἐπέβλεψεν ἐπὶ τ. ταπ. τ. δούλ. αὐτ.] as at 1 Sam. i. 11. Comp. Ps. xxxi. 8 ;

also Luke ix. 38. The expression of the adjectival notion by means of the substantive (comp. 2 Kings xiv. 26 ; Ps. xxiv. 18) places the quality in the foreground. See Fritzsche, *ad Rom.* I. p. 367 f. ; Bernhardy, p. 53. Mary means the lowliness of her person, in spite of which she is chosen of God to such greatness. She was in fact only an insignificant maiden from the people, an artisan's betrothed bride. — ἀπὸ τοῦ νῦν] *from henceforth;* for *now,* after Elizabeth's inspired words, no further doubt could remain to Mary respecting her condition as mother of the Messiah ; *from henceforth,* therefore, she could not but be the object of the general congratulation, whereof Elizabeth herself had just made a beginning. — πᾶσαι αἱ γενεαί] *all generations.*

Ver. 49 f. *Because the Mighty One did to me great things,* in making me the mother of the Messiah. — καὶ ἅγιον κ.τ.λ.] not for οὗ τὸ ὄν. ἅγιον (Luther, Castalio, Bengel, and many, including Kuinoel), but lyrically unperiodic : *and holy is His name!* Hence, also, a full stop is not to be placed after δυνατός (Lachmann, Tischendorf, Bleek), but only a comma. To the *might* the *holiness* attaches itself. — εἰς γενεὰς κ. γενεάς] Comp. Isa. li. 8 ; 1 Macc. ii. 61 ; *Test. XII. Patr.* p. 568 : *unto generations and generations, i.e.* ever onward from one generation to the following. The *Recepta* εἰς γενεὰς γενεῶν would mean : *to the uttermost generations;* these would be conceived of as forming a *superlative.* Analogous Greek superlative designations, especially from the dramatic writers, may be seen in Brunck, *ad Oedip. R.* 466 ; Bernhardy, p. 154. — τοῖς φοβουμ. αὐτ.] *sc.* ἐστι. It denotes the essence of theocratic piety. Comp. Ex. xx. 6 ; Ps. ciii. 7.

Ver. 51 ff. Mary now sees the Messianic catastrophe, which God will bring about by means of her son, and she announces it prophetically *as having already happened;* for she bears in fact the accomplisher of it already in her womb, and thus the work of God, which He is to execute, is before her enlightened gaze *already as good as completed ;* in *that* way she sees and describes it.—The *catastrophe itself* is the restoration of the state of things to the divine rightful order, *the overthrow of the Gentiles and the exaltation of the deeply-oppressed theocratic people* (comp. vv. 68, 71, 74); the former are set forth by the words ὑπερηφάνους, δυνάστας, πλουτοῦντας; the latter, by ταπεινούς and πεινῶντας. This intended concrete application of the general expressions is put beyond doubt by ἀντελάβετο Ἰσραὴλ κ.τ.λ., ver. 54 f. — ὑπερηφάνους] such as are *arrogant in the thoughts of their heart;* διανοίᾳ is the dative of more precise definition; and on the notion (thinking and willing as directed outwards), comp. Beck, *Seelenl.* p. 58; on καρδία as the centre of the spiritual and psychic life, Delitzsch, *bibl. Psychol.* p. 248 ff.; finally, in διεσκόρπ. the haughty are conceived of as *congregated* and keeping together; comp. Matt. xxvi. 31; Acts v. 37; Ps. lxxxix. 10. "That through Christianity the proud were humbled" (de Wette), is not the thought expressed by Mary, but a generalization of it, as is also the "confusio *diabolicae* superbiae" (Calovius and others), and the like. Comp. Ecclus. x. 14 ff. — Ver. 52. *He has cast down rulers from thrones,* does not apply to the demons and Pharisees (Theophylact), but to the Gentile holders of power. Comp. on the idea of the overthrow of thrones in the times of the Messiah, Wisd. v. 23; Enoch xxxviii. 4, and Dillmann thereon. — Ver. 53. ἀγαθῶν] not merely *means of subsistence* (Valckenaer, Bornemann, de Wette), but earthly *possessions* in general, among which the means of subsistence *are included.* Comp. xii. 18 f. De Wette, moreover, is in error in saying (comp. Olshausen) that it is *spiritual* hunger and *spiritual* satisfying that are to be thought of, and that the rich are a type of the *wise men of this world.* The whole is to be taken literally; the idealizing is not warranted according to the context. Comp. Ps. xxxiv. 11. — ἐξαπέστ. κενούς] So that they *retain* nothing of their possessions, and have *received* nothing from the Messiah. On the expression, comp. xx. 10 f.; Job xxii. 9; Judith x. 11; Hom. *Il.* ii. 298, *Od.* xiii. 214.—For descriptions of the divine inversion of relations from the classical writers, see Wetstein and Bornemann.

Ver. 54 ff. What was expressed *descriptively* in vv. 51–53, and that by means of antitheses, is now definitely and particularly condensed in ἀντελάβετο Ἰσραὴλ παιδὸς αὐτοῦ (comp. Isa. xli. 8 f.), which is the *summary* of what has been previously said. The *aorist* is to be taken quite like the previous aorists. — ἀντελάβετο] *He has interested Himself for Israel His servant* (עָבֵד). Comp. on ἀντελάβ., Acts xx. 35; Thuc. iii. 22; Diod. Sic. xi. 13. Euthymius Zigabenus explains it: ἐπεσκέψατο τὸν Ἰσραηλιτικὸν λαὸν, τὸν δοῦλον αὐτοῦ. Others, including Paulus, Glöckler, Kuinoel, take παιδός as *filii* (comp. Ex. iv. 22; Hos. xi. 1). But the *theocratic* notion of *sonship* is never expressed by παῖς (not even in Acts iii. 13). — μνησθῆναι ἐλέους] not: "*ita ut perpetuo memor sit*," etc. (Kuinoel, Bleek), but: *in order to be mindful* of mercy. We have to note the connection with the ἕως αἰῶνος emphatically put at the end. God has interested Himself for Israel, *in order to be mindful of mercy even to eternity*, in order never again to forget mercy. — καθὼς ἐλάλ. πρὸς τ. πατ. ἡμ.] not indeed a parenthesis, but an inserted clause, which makes one feel that the telic μνησθῆναι ἐλέους takes place in consequence of the divine *truthfulness*. — τῷ Ἀβραὰμ κ. τ. σπέρμ. αὐτ.] Dativus *commodi* to μνησθῆναι. Comp. Ps. xcviii. 3; Xen. *Cyr.* i. 4. 12; Bornemann, *Schol.* p. 14 f. It *might* belong to ἐλάλησε (Euthymius Zigabenus, Erasmus, Luther, Calvin, Beza, Kuinoel), since λαλεῖν may be joined as well with πρός as with a dative; but against this may be urged κ. τῷ σπέρματι αὐτοῦ, which denotes[1] the whole posterity of Abraham without limitation, and therefore cannot be included in apposition to πρὸς τοὺς πατέρας ἡμῶν. — Observe, moreover, that here (comp. ver. 72) Abraham, the progenitor of the race, is conceived of as jointly affected by and interested in the destiny of his descendants; Isa. xxix. 22 f.; Mic. vii. 20. Comp. John viii. 56; *Test. XII. Patr.* p. 587. Abraham *liveth* unto God, xx. 38. — ἔμεινε δὲ κ.τ.λ.] but not until the delivery of Elizabeth (in opposition to Calvin, Maldonatus, and others); see ver. 57.

REMARK 1. — The harmonizers, even the most recent, have adopted very different ways for the fitting of this history into the narrative of Matthew. According to Lange, *L. J.* II. 1, p. 84 ff., Mary is driven to Elizabeth by her grief at being

---

[1] In what manner it was the σπέρμα Ἀβραάμ that actually received the compassion (Rom. iv., Gal. iv.), was not here the question.

Ebionitically misjudged and discarded by Joseph; according
to Hug, *Gutacht.* I. p. 85, Ebrard, Riggenbach, and others, she
made the journey immediately after her marriage, which took
place a few days after the beginning of her pregnancy! Luke
says and knows nothing of either view.

REMARK 2.—The historical character of the Visitation of
Mary stands or falls with that of the Annunciation. But the
psychological and moral impossibility, that Mary, after the
certainty as to her condition acquired while she was with
Elizabeth, and after the theocratic inspiration with which she
declares herself blessed on account of that condition, should
not have made any communication at all to Joseph on the subject (as must nevertheless, according to Matthew, be assumed,
so that thus our narrative and that of Matt. i. 18 ff. exclude one
another); further, the utter want of any trace elsewhere of such
an intimate and confidential relation as, according to our
history, must have subsisted between the two holy families;
moreover, the design of the narrative to invest Jesus with a
singular glory, according to which even the yet unborn John
signifies his rejoicing homage before the Messiah when but
just conceived in His mother's womb; the circumstance, not to
be explained away (see the untenable suggestion of Lange, p.
92), that it is only after the leaping of the babe that Elizabeth
receives the Holy Spirit, and by means of this Spirit recognises
from that leaping the mother of the Messiah as such; the
hymnic scene annexed thereto, the *poetic* splendour and truth
of which lifts it out of the *historical* sphere, in which subsequently the house of Mary was not the abode of the faith that
is here proclaimed from the mouth of the Virgin with so lofty a
triumph (Mark iii. 31; John vii. 3),—all this is not adapted to
support or to uphold its historical character, even apart from
the fact that tradition has not even conveyed to Luke the
name of the mountain-town. The apocryphal poor and pale
copy of the Annunciation and the Visitation may be seen in
the *Protevang. Jacobi,* c. xi., xii.; according to which, moreover,
—quite differently from the course followed by the modern
Harmonists,—it is not till after the visitation, only in the sixth
month of pregnancy, when Mary is recognised as in this condition and called to account by Joseph, that she asserts her
innocence, and then the dream-revelation of the angel is imparted to Joseph (ch. xiii. f.).

Ver. 57 f. Τοῦ τεκεῖν αὐτ.] genitive governed by ὁ χρόνος:
the time, which had to elapse until her delivery. Comp. ii. 7,

22 ; Gen. xxv. 24. — ὅτι ἐμεγάλυνε κ.τ.λ.] *that He has magnified* (Matt. xxiii. 5 ; 2 Cor. x. 15 ; 1 Sam. xii. 24), namely, by this birth still bestowed, contrary to all expectation, in which they saw a proof of especially great divine compassion. The *expression* is quite as in Gen. xix. 19.— συνέχαιρον] *they rejoiced together with* her. Others, like Valckenaer (following the Vulgate): they *congratulated* her (see on Phil. ii. 17). The former is more appropriate on account of ver. 14; and comp. xv. 6, 9.

Ver. 59 f. With the circumcision was associated the *giving of the name,* Gen. xxi. 3. See Ewald, *Alterth.* p. 110. Among the Greeks and Romans it took place on the *dies lustricus.* See Dougtaeus, *Anal.* II. p. 44 f. ; Hermann, *Privatalterth.* § 32. 17.— ἦλθον] The subject is evident of itself, namely, the persons pertaining to the circumcision : " amici ad eam rem vocati," Grotius. Any Israelite might be the circumciser (in case of necessity even a woman, Ex. iv. 25). See Lund, *Heiligth.,* ed. Wolf, p. 949 ; Keil, *Archäol.* I. p. 307 f. — ἐκάλουν] They actually uttered this name (this took place immediately after the circumcision was performed ; see Lund, *l.c.,* Buxtorf, *Synagog.* 4) : but the mother (for the father was still dumb) took exception to it, ver. 60. " Vere enim incipit actus, sed ob impedimenta caret eventu," Schaefer, *ad Phoen.* 81 ; Buttmann, *neut. Gr.* p. 178 [E. T. 205]. —The naming of the child after the *father* (Tob. i. 9 ; Joseph. *Antt.* xiv. 1. 3) or after a *relative* (ver. 61 ; Lightfoot, p. 726) was very common, as it was also among the Greeks (Hermann, *l.c.* 18). On ἐπί, comp. Neh. vii. 63 ; Plut. *Demetr.* 2. The idea is : *in reference to.* — οὐχί, ἀλλὰ κληθ. Ἰωάνν.] The usual supposition (Paulus, Kuinoel, Ebrard, Bleek, following Calvin and others), that Zacharias after his return from the temple made known to Elizabeth by writing the words of the angel, ver. 13, is the more arbitrary, the less it is in keeping with the miraculous impress of the whole history. Theophylact is right in saying : ἡ δὲ Ἐλισάβετ ὡς προφῆτις ἐλάλησε περὶ τοῦ ὀνόματος; and Euthymius Zigabenus : ἐκ πνεύματος ἁγίου καὶ αὐτὴ τὸ ὄνομα τοῦ παιδὸς μεμάθηκε (comp. Origen and Ambrose), and this, indeed, at the moment

of that ἐκάλουν, ver. 59, else it would not be easy to perceive
why she should not at the very beginning have carried out
the giving of the divinely-appointed name.

Ver. 62 f. Ἐνένευον] They conveyed by signs to him the
question (τό, see Krüger, *ad Xen. Anab.* iv. 4. 17 ; Kühner,
II. p. 138), how (τί = τί ὄνομα, comp. Aesch. *Ag.* 1205) he
perchance (ἄν, see Winer, p. 275 [E. T. 386]) would wish
that the child (αὐτό, see the critical remarks) should be
named.   The *making signs* does not presuppose *deafness and
dumbness* (Chrysostom, Theophylact, Euthymius Zigabenus,
Jansen, Maldonatus, Lightfoot, Grotius, Wolf, and others,
including Ewald), against which may be urged ver. 20 ; nor
is it to be explained by the fact, that we are inclined to com-
municate by means *of signs* with dumb people as with deaf
people (Bengel, Michaelis, Paulus, Olshausen, de Wette),
which can only be arbitrarily applied to Zacharias, since he
had only been dumb for a short time and people had previously been accustomed to *speak* with him.   Probably it was
only from the wish *to spare the mother* that the decision of
the father, who had all along been listening to the discussion,
was called for not aloud, but by signs. — αἰτήσας] ὁμοίως διὰ
νεύματος, Euthymius Zigabenus. — πινακίδιον] probably a little
tablet covered with wax.   Tertullian, *de idolol.* 23 : " Zacharias
loquitur in stylo, auditur in cera." — ἔγραψε λέγων] *scripsit
haec verba.*   Comp. 2 Kings x. 6 ; 1 Macc. viii. 31, xi. 57.
A Hebraism (לֵאמֹר).   On the same usage in the Syriac, see
Gesenius in Rosenmüller's *Rep.* I. p. 135.   An example from
Josephus is found in Kypke, I. p. 211 ; Krebs, p. 98.   The
return of speech does not occur till ver. 64.   Comp. vv. 20,
13. — Ἰωάννης ἐστὶ τ. ὄν. αὐτοῦ] Shortly and categorically, in
the consciousness of what had been already divinely determined : יוחנן שמו.   " Non tam jubet, quam jussum divinum
indicat," Bengel. — ἐθαύμ.] because Zacharias agreed with
Elizabeth in a name foreign to the family.

Ver. 64. Ἀνεῴχθη . . . γλῶσσα αὐτοῦ] *a zeugma ;* in the
case of the tongue ἐλύθη may be mentally supplied ; comp.,
on the other hand, Mark vii. 35.   This recovery of speech is
to be regarded not as the effect of lively emotion (Gell. v. 9 ;

Val. Max. i. 8. 3), or of the deliverance of his soul from the reproach that had oppressed it (Lange), or of his own will (Paulus), but of *divine causation* (ver. 20).

Ver. 65 f. An historical digression, narrating the impression which these marvellous events at the circumcision produced in wider circles. — φόβος] not *amazement*, but *fear*, the first impression of the extraordinary (comp. Mark iv. 41 ; Acts ii. 43). — αὐτούς] applies to Zacharias and Elizabeth. On περιοικεῖν τινα, comp. Herod. v. 78 ; Xen. *Anab.* v. 6. 16 ; Plut. *Crass.* 34. — διελαλεῖτο] *were mutually talked of,* Polyb. i. 85. 2, ix. 32. 1. — τὰ ῥήματα ταῦτα] *these utterances,* which had occurred with such marvellous significance at the circumcision of the child from ver. 59 to ver. 64 ; ii. 19. — ἔθεντο ... ἐν τῇ καρδ. αὐτῶν] Comp. שִׂים עַל לֵב (1 Sam. xxi. 12), and the Homeric τίθημι ἐν στήθεσσι, ἐν φρεσί, and see Valckenaer *in loc.* They made those utterances the subject of their further reflection. Comp. ii. 19. — τί ἄρα] *quid igitur,* under these circumstances, according to these auspices, what *then now* will, etc. ; see Klotz, *ad Devar.* p. 176 ; Nägelsbach, *Anm. z. Ilias,* ed. 3, p. 10 f. Comp. viii. 25, xii. 42. On the *neuter* τί, which is more in keeping with the uncertainty and the emotion of the inquirers than τίς, comp. Acts xii. 18 ; Schaefer, *Melet.* p. 98 ; Bornemann, *Schol.* p. 15. — καὶ γὰρ χεὶρ κυρίου ἦν μετ᾽ αὐτοῦ] An observation of Luke, in which he would indicate that the people *rightly* asked this question, expecting something unusual of the child : *for also* (καὶ γάρ, see the critical remarks) *the hand of the Lord was with him.* The emphasis rests on χεὶρ κυρίου, which, with καί, makes known to us the mighty help of God (so χεὶρ κυρίου very frequently in the O. T. ; comp. also Hermann, *ad Vig.* p. 732) as *in keeping with* the ominous phenomena. Others, like Storr, Kuinoel, Paulus, Ewald, place these words too in the mouth of those asking the question (so also Rettig in the *Stud. u. Krit.* 1838, p. 219, who, following the *Recepta,* places a colon after καί : *and others said*). But this reflective specifying of *a reason* would have been superfluous in the mouth of those people, and little in keeping with the emotion of their question. And instead of ἦν they would have said ἐστί, in-

ferring, namely, the help of God from the events at the circumcision ; while the καί would be but tame and cumbrous.

Ver. 67. After the historical episode of ver. 65 there now follows, in reference to εὐλογῶν τ. Θεόν, ver. 64, the hymn itself (the so-called *Benedictus*) into which Zacharias broke forth, and that on the spot (Kuinoel erroneously suggests that it was only composed subsequently by Zacharias). At the same time the remark ἐπλήσθη πνεύμ. ἁγ. is repeated, and the hymn is in respect of its nature more precisely designated as *prophecy.* It is, like that of Mary, ver. 46 ff., constructed *in strophes,* containing five strophes, each of three verses. See Ewald. — προεφήτευσε] denotes not merely prediction, but the utterance of revelation generally stimulated and sustained by the Spirit, which includes in it prediction proper. See on 1 Cor. xii. 10.

Ver. 68 f. Zacharias' hymn of praise concerns the great *cause,* which his new-born son is to serve — the *Messianic deliverance* and *blessing* of the people, which he now at once looks upon *as already accomplished,* for in his new-born son there has, in fact, already appeared the preparer of the way for the Messiah (ver. 16 f.). Comp. on ver. 51. The entire hymn bears the *priestly* character, which even the apostrophe to the infant, ver. 76, does not efface. — εὐλογητὸς κ.τ.λ.] sc. εἴη. Comp. Ps. xli. 14, lxxii. 18, cvi. 48. — λύτρωσιν (comp. ii. 38) applies primarily to the Messianic deliverance under its *political aspect.* Comp. vv. 71, 51 ff. ; Plut. *Arat.* 11 : λύτρ. αἰχμαλώτων. With this, however, Zacharias knew (comp. also ver. 16 f.) that the religious and moral regeneration of the people was inseparably combined, so as to form the one Messianic work, vv. 75, 77, 79.[1] The ἐπεσκέψ. is absolute, as in Ecclus. xxxii. 17 : *he has looked to,* he has made an inspection. Comp. Acts xv. 14. — ἤγειρε] still dependent upon ὅτι. — κέρας σωτηρίας] *a horn of deliverance* (genitive of apposition), *i.e. a strong, mighty deliverance,* according to the

[1] Hofmann appropriately remarks, *Weissag. u. Erfüll.* II. p. 253 (in opposition to Olshausen), that the purity of the Messianic views of Zacharias consists in the unadulterated reproduction of *Old Testament* knowledge.

figurative use of the Hebrew קֶרֶן, 1 Sam. ii. 10 ; Ps. xviii. 3,
lxxxix. 18, cxxxii. 16 f., cxlviii. 14 ; Ecclus. xlvii. 5, 7, 11, *al.* ;
Gesenius, *Thes.* III. p. 1238 ; Grimm on 1 Macc. ii. 48.   See
Rabbinical passages in Schöttgen, *Hor.* p. 258 f.   κέρας·
ἡ ἰσχὺς παρὰ τῇ θείᾳ γραφῇ, ἐκ μεταφορᾶς τῶν ζώων τῶν
καθωπλισμένων τοῖς κέρασι καὶ τούτοις ἀμυνομένων, Suidas.
Comp. the Latin *cornua addere, cornua sumere*, and the like.
It is true that Jensius (*Ferc. lit.* p. 34), Fischer (*de vit. Lex.*
p. 214), and Paulus find the reference in the *horns of the
altar of burnt-offering* which served as an asylum (1 Kings
i. 50, ii. 28 ff.; Bähr, *Symbol.* I. p. 473 f.; Knobel on Ex.
xxvii. 2).   But apart from the inappropriate relation to the
frequent use of the O. T. figure elsewhere, how inadequate for
the due and distinct expression of the Messianic idea would be
the conception of the mere protection, which was afforded by
the laying hold of the horns of the altar ! — ἤγειρε] *excitavit*,
i.e. according to the context, *he has made to grow up* (ἐξανα-
τελῶ, Ps. cxxxii. 17). — τοῦ παιδὸς αὐτοῦ] Acts iv. 25.

Ver. 70. No parenthesis. — τῶν ἁγίων] not used substantivally (Bornemann), but see Bernhardy, p. 322 ; Krüger,
§ 50. 9. 7. — ἀπ' αἰῶνος] not *absolutely*, as though there had
been prophets even *ab orbe condito* (" imo per os Adami,"
Calovius), but *relatively ;* when the *oldest* prophets emerged
(and Moses already was such an one), was the commencement
of prophecy *since the beginning of the world.*   Comp. Gen.
vi. 4 ; Acts iii. 21 ; Longin. 34 : τοὺς ἀπ' αἰῶνος ῥήτορας.

Ver. 71 f. Σωτηρίαν] might be attached to ἐλάλησε, ver. 70
(Beza, Grotius, Ewald, and others), but it is simpler to retain
καθὼς κ.τ.λ. as a parenthetical clause, like ver. 55, so that
κέρας σωτηρ., ver. 69, is resumed by σωτηρίαν (yet only as to
the fact, without the figure) for the sake of adding the more
precise definition.   Such a resumption may occur with δέ (Rom.
iii. 22) and without it (Rom. iii. 26).   See generally, Kühner,
ad Xen. Mem. i. 1. 1.   Without δέ the expression is more
rhetorical. — The *enemies* and *haters* are the *heathen,* as in
ver. 51 ff., not the demons, sin, and the like. — ποιῆσαι]
Infinitive of the *aim,* as at ver. 54.   In this our deliverance
God designed to show mercy to (μετά, עִם, ver. 58, x. 37) our

fathers (comp. ver. 55, deeply afflicted by the decline of their people), and to remember (practically, by the fulfilment of what was therein promised) His holy covenant. Euthymius Zigabenus : διαθήκην γὰρ λέγει τὴν ἐπαγγελίαν· μνήμην δὲ αὐτῆς τὴν περάτωσιν. Vv. 73–75. Ὅρκον] neither accusative of more precise definition (Calvin, Beza, L. Bos, Rosenmüller), nor governed by μνησθῆναι (Euthymius Zigabenus, Olshausen, Bleek [1]), but climactic apposition to διαθήκης ἀγ. αὐτοῦ, in which the accusative is attracted by ὅν, Matt. xxi. 42 ; 1 Cor. x. 16 ; Buttmann, neut. Gr. p. 247 [E. T. 288]; Bornemann, Schol. p. 16 f. — πρός] denotes the swearing to. Comp. Hom. Od. xiv. 331, xix. 288. The expression with the dative is more usual. See the oath itself in Gen. xxii. 16–18. — τοῦ δοῦναι κ.τ.λ.] in order to grant to us, the purpose, on account of which God swore the oath. — ἐκ χειρὸς κ.τ.λ.] more precisely defines the previous ἀφόβως, and that as regards its objective relation. On the accusative ῥυσθέντας (not dative), see Bornemann, l.c. ; Pflugk, ad Eur. Med. 815; Krüger, Gramm. Unters. III. § 148. — Ver. 75. Religious-moral restoration of the people of God. As to the distinction between ὁσιότης and δικαιοσύνη (Plat. Prot. p. 329 C), see on Eph. iv. 24. Holiness is the divine consecration and inner truth of righteousness, so that the latter without the former would be only external or seeming; both together constitute the justitia spiritualis.

Ver. 76 f. Ἔπειτα μεταβαίνει τῇ προφητείᾳ καὶ πρὸς ἑαυτοῦ παῖδα Ἰωάννην, Euthymius Zigabenus. — καὶ σὺ δέ] but thou also (see the critical remarks). See Hartung, Partikell. I. p. 181 f. ; Ellendt, Lex Soph. I. p. 884. The καί places the παιδίον—for even of him he has only what is great to say—on a parallel with the subject, to which hitherto in his song of praise to God his prophetic glance was directed (with the Messiah), and δέ is the continuative autem. — προπορ. γὰρ πρὸ προσώπου κυρ.] as at ver. 17, hence κύριος is God.

---

[1] Μιμνήσκεσθαι is not seldom joined with an accusative by the classical writers (Hom. Il. vi. 222 ; Herod. vii. 18 ; Soph. O. R. 1057), but never in the N. T., although it is so in the LXX. and Apocrypha.

— ἑτοιμάσαι ὁδοὺς αὐτοῦ] see on Matt. iii. 3.— τοῦ δοῦναι
κ.τ.λ.] Aim of ἑτοιμάσαι κ.τ.λ., and so final aim of προπορεύσῃ
... κυρίου.— ἐν ἀφέσει ἁμαρτ. αὐτ.] In *forgiveness of their sins*,
which is to be imparted to them through the Messiah (see
ver. 78 f.) for the sake of God's mercy (which is thereby
satisfied ; διὰ σπλ. ἐλ. Θεοῦ), they are to discern deliverance ;
they are to discern that salvation comes through the
Messianic forgiveness of sins (comp. on Mark i. 4), and to
this knowledge of salvation John is to guide his people.
Accordingly, ἐν ἀφ. ἁμ. αὐτ. does not belong to σωτηρίας
alone (τῆς γινομένης ἐν τῷ ἀφεθῆναι κ.τ.λ., Euthymius
Zigabenus, Beza, Bengel, Kuinoel, Olshausen, Baumgarten-
Crusius, de Wette, Bleek, and others), but to γνῶσιν σωτηρίας
(Theophylact) = γνῶναι σωτηρίαν ἐν ἀφ. τ. ἁμ. αὐτ. So also
Luther, Ewald, and others. Calvin aptly remarks: "Prae-
cipuum evangelii caput nunc attingit Zacharias, dum *scientiam
salutis in remissione peccatorum positam esse* docet."

Ver. 78 f. *Διὰ σπλάγχνα ἐλέους κ.τ.λ.*] is not to be
separated from what precedes by punctuation, but to be
immediately connected with ἐν ἀφ. ἁμ. αὐτ. : ἐν ἀφέσει δὲ
ἁμαρτιῶν ... τῇ διδομένῃ διὰ τὴν συμπάθειαν τοῦ ἐλέους
αὐτοῦ, Euthymius Zigabenus. Comp. Theophylact. The
reference to all that is said from προπορεύσῃ onwards,
ver. 76 (Grotius, Kuinoel, de Wette, and others), is the more
arbitrary, in proportion to the natural and essential connection that subsists between the forgiveness of sins and God's
compassion. — διά] not *through,* but *for the sake of,* see on
ver. 77 ; σπλάγχνα is not merely, according to the Hebrew
רחמים (see Gesenius), but also in the Greek poetical language, the seat of the *affections,* as, for instance, of anger
(Arist. *Ran.* 1004) and of *sympathy* (Aesch. *Ch.* 407). So
here. Comp. Col. iii. 12 ; Phil. ii. 1. ἐλέους is genitivus
qualitatis, and Θεοῦ ἡμῶν depends on σπλάγχνα ἐλέους : *for
the sake of the compassionate heart of our God.* — ἐν οἷς]
instrumental : by virtue of which. — ἐπεσκέψατο ἡμᾶς ἀνατολὴ
ἐξ ὕψ.] to be taken together : *has visited us,* etc., has become
present to us with His saving help (comp. Xen. *Cyr.* v. 4. 10;
Ecclus. xlvi. 14 ; Judith viii. 33 ; Luke vii. 16). It is

appropriate to ἀνατ. ἐξ ὕψ., as the latter is *personified*. The figurative designation of the Messiah: *Dayspring from on high*, is borrowed from the rising of the *sun* (Rev. vii. 2; Matt. v. 45; Hom. *Od.* xii. 4; Herod. iv. 8), or as is more in keeping with the ἐξ ὑψίστου, from the rising of a bright-beaming *star of the night* (Num. xxiv. 17; Valck. *ad Eur. Phoen.* 506), not (in opposition to Beza, Scultetus, Lightfoot, Wetstein) from an ascending *shoot* (צֶמַח, Isa. iv. 2; Jer. xxiii. 5, xxxiii. 15; Zech. iii. 8, vi. 12), against which may be urged ἐξ ὕψ. and ἐπιφᾶναι.[1] Comp. Isa. ix. 2. — ἐπιφᾶναι] Infinitive of the aim. On the form see Lobeck, *ad Phryn.* p. 25 f. — τοῖς ἐν σκότει κ. σκ. θαν. καθημ.] *those who sit in darkness and* (climactic) *the shadow of death*—a picturesque delineation of the people totally destitute of divine truth and the true ζωή (ἡμῶν, ver. 79). — *The shadow of death* (צַלְמָוֶת) is such a shadow as surrounds *death* (personified), and they are sitting *in* this shadow, because death is ruling among them, namely, in the *spiritual* sense, the opposite of the true life whose sphere is the light of divine truth. Moreover, comp. Isa. ix. 2, and on Matt. iv. 16; on καθημ. also, Nägelsbach, *Anm. z. Ilias*, ed. 3, p. 65. — τοῦ κατευθῦναι κ.τ.λ.] The aim of ἐπιφᾶναι κ.τ.λ., and so the final aim of ἐπεσκέψατο κ.τ.λ. Comp. on τοῦ δοῦναι, ver. 77. "Continuatur translatio, nam lux *dirigit* nos," Grotius. Observe also the correlation of τοὺς πόδας with the preceding καθημένοις. — εἰς ὁδὸν εἰρήν.] *in viam ad salutem* (Messianam) *ducentem.* εἰρήνη = שָׁלוֹם, opposite of all the misery denoted by σκότος κ.τ.λ. (hence not merely *peace*). It has another sense in Rom. iii. 17. But comp. Acts xvi. 17.

Ver. 80. A summary account (comp. Judg. xiii. 24) of the further development of John. More particular accounts were perhaps altogether wanting, but were not essential to

---

[1] Bleek wishes to combine the two senses, and infers from this that the source whence Luke drew was Greek and not Hebrew, because צמח would not have admitted a reference to the rising of the sun. But the whole mixing up of two incongruous figures is excluded by ver. 79; hence the inference drawn by Bleek (see also his *Einleit.* p. 277 f.), and approved by Holtzmann, falls to the ground. The source may have been Greek; but if it was Hebrew, צמח need not have stood in it.

the matter here. — ηὔξανε] the *bodily* growing up, and, connected therewith : ἐκρατ. πνεύμ., the *mental* gaining of strength that took place εἰς τὸν ἔσω ἄνθρωπ. (Eph. iii. 16). Comp. the description of the development of Jesus, ii. 40, 52. ψυχῇ is not mentioned, for the πνεῦμα is the ἡγεμονικόν, in whose vigour and strength the ψυχή shares. Comp. Delitzsch, *Psychol.* p. 217. — ἦν ἐν τοῖς ἐρήμοις] in the well-known desert regions. It is *the desert of Judah* κατ᾽ ἐξοχήν that is meant (see on Matt. iii. 1). In that desert dwelt also the *Essenes* (Plin. *N. H.* v. 17). How far their principles and *askesis,* which at least could not have remained unknown to John, may have indirectly exercised an influence on his peculiar character, cannot be determined ; a true Essene this greatest and last phenomenon of Israelitish prophecy certainly was not ; he belonged, like some God-sent prophet higher than all partisan attitudes in the people, to the whole nation. — ἀναδείξεως αὐτοῦ πρὸς τ. ᾽Ισρ.] *His being publicly made known to Israel,* when he was announced to the Israelites as the forerunner of the Messiah. This was done on the command of God by John himself. See iii. 2–6. ἀνάδειξις is the making known (*renuntiatio*) of official nomination ; Polyb. xv. 26. 4 ; Plut. *Mar.* 8 ; see Wetstein. Comp. x. 1.

CHAPTER II.

VER. 3. *ίδίαν*] Lachm. Tisch. have *ἑαυτοῦ*, following B D L א**
Eus. An interpretation, which is further found completely in
D (*ἑαυτοῦ πατρίδα*). א* has *ἑαυτῶν*. — Ver. 5. *μεμνηστ.* See on
i. 27. — *γυναικί*] is wanting in B C* (F) D L ≅ א, min. vss.
Fathers. Deleted by Lachm., and now also again by Tisch.
An addition; *ἐμνηστευμένη* was objectionable, hence *γυναικί* was
added, and in part *ἐμνηστευμ.* was even deleted (Ver. Verc. Colb.).
There was less probability that offence might be taken after
Matt. i. 24 at *γυναικί.* Cyril of Jerusalem expresses himself too
obscurely in this respect. — Ver. 7. *τῇ φάτνῃ*] *τῇ* is wanting in
preponderating witnesses. It is deleted by Lachm. Tisch. The
article was added here and at ver. 12, in order to designate the
definite manger, *i.e.* the well-known manger of the Saviour. —
Ver. 12. *κείμενον*] B L P S ≅ א** min. Syr. utr. Vulg. codd. It.
Eus. Arnob. and Tisch. have *καὶ κείμ.*; *καί* was easily inserted to
connect the two participles. — Ver. 14. *εὐδοκία*] A B* D א, Goth.
Sax. Vulg. It., Fathers, have *εὐδοκίας.* So Lachm. and Tisch.
Recommended by Beza, Mill, Bengel, and others. There is
considerable evidence on both sides, but it preponderates in
favour of the genitive. Now, as the unfamiliar expression
ἄνθρωποι εὐδοκίας is not to be put down to the account of the
transcribers, but, on the contrary, these, not apprehending the
symmetry of the passage, had after the analogy of *δόξα* and
εἰρήνη sufficient inducement to put instead of *εὐδοκίας* the nominative likewise, *εὐδοκίας* is to be preferred. — Ver. 15. *καὶ
οἱ ἄνθρωποι*] is wanting in B L ≅ א, min. Syr. Perss. Ar. p. Copt.
Sahid. Arm. Vulg. It. Eus. Aug. Bracketed by Lachm.
Deleted by Tisch. But the homoeoteleuton (*ἄγγελοι* . . . *ἄνθρωποι*) the more easily gave occasion to the omission, as the
words are superfluous and there was no motive for their
addition. — Ver. 17. *διεγνώρισαν*] Lachm. Tisch. have *ἐγνώρισαν,*
following B D L ≅ א, min. Eus. But the syllable ΔΙ after *δέ*
was more easily passed over than added, especially as the simple
form was present in ver. 15. — Ver. 20. Instead of *ὑπέστρεψαν,*
Elz. has *ἐπέστρεψαν*; and at ver. 21, instead of *αὐτόν*: *τὸ παιδίον,*

in opposition to preponderant evidence. — Ver. 33. Ἰωσὴφ καὶ
ἡ μήτηρ αὐτοῦ] B D L ℵ, min. vss. (also Vulg.) Or. and several
Fathers have ὁ πατὴρ αὐτοῦ κ. ἡ μήτηρ. So Griesbach and Tisch.
(who after μήτηρ retains αὐτοῦ). The mention of the *father* gave
offence, and *in this place* the name might be introduced instead
of it, but not appropriately also at ver. 48. — Ver. 37. ὡς]
Lachm. and Tisch. have ἕως, in accordance with A B L ≅ ℵ*
min. Copt. Sahid. Ar. p. Vulg. codd. It. Aug. Rightly ; the
ὡς, frequently used in the case of numbers, intruded itself. —
Ver. 38. αὕτη] on preponderant evidence, and because καὶ αὕτη
presented itself mechanically from ver. 37, is to be deleted,
with Lachm. and Tisch. — ἐν Ἱερουσ.] ἐν is wanting in B ≅ Π ℵ,
min. vss. (including Vulg. ms. and codd. It.) and Fathers, and
is condemned by Griesb., deleted by Lachm. and Tisch. An
addition from misunderstanding. — Ver. 39. τὴν πόλιν αὐτῶν]
Lachm. and Tisch. have πόλιν ἑαυτῶν. In accordance with
decisive evidence ἑαυτῶν is to be adopted ; but the omission of
τήν is only attested by B D* ℵ 1. — Ver. 40. πνεύματι] has
testimonies against it of such weight, and it can so little
conceal its origin from i. 80, that with reason it is condemned
by Mill and Griesb., excluded by Lachm. and Tisch. — Ver. 42.
ἀναβάντων] Lachm. and Tisch. have ἀναβαινόντων, in accordance
with A B K L X Π ℵ, min. Vulg. codd. It. A copyist's error;
the aorist is necessary. — εἰς Ἱερος.] is wanting in B D L ℵ,
min. vss. Tisch. It betrays itself by the form Ἱεροσόλυμα as an
addition of another hand. — Ver. 43. ἔγνω Ἰωσὴφ κ. ἡ μήτηρ
αὐτοῦ] B D L ℵ, min. vss. (including Vulg. and codd. It.) Jerome
have ἔγνωσαν οἱ γονεῖς αὐτοῦ. Recommended by Griesb., adopted
by Lachm. and Tisch. Comp. also Rinck on Matt. xxiv. 36.
I regard οἱ γονεῖς αὐτοῦ as written in the margin from ver. 41.
Comp. on ver. 33. Were it original, and had Ἰωσ. κ. ἡ μήτηρ
αὐτοῦ been subsequently put for it, why should not this alteration
have been already undertaken before at ver. 41 (where only
codd. It. have : *Joseph et Maria*) ? and why should ἔγνωσαν (which
would have stood originally) not have been left ? This plural
so naturally suggested itself, even with the words of the *Recepta*,
that some witnesses for the *Recepta* (Δ, for instance) actually
read it. — Ver. 45. After εὑρόντες Elz. Scholz have αὐτόν (Lachm.
in brackets), in opposition to B C* D L ℵ, min. Arm. Aeth.
Vulg. codd. It. A current addition. — ζητοῦντες] nearly the same
witnesses have ἀναζητοῦντες. So Lachm. and Tisch. From ver. 44.

---

*The genuineness of the portion from ch. i. 5 to the end of
ch. ii.* has been *contested* by Evanson (*The Dissonance of the*

four generally received Evangelists, etc., Ipswich 1792), J. E.
Chr. Schmidt (in Henke's *Magaz.* vol. III. p. 473 ff.), Horst
(Henke's *Museum*, I. 3, p. 446 ff.), C. C. L. Schmidt (in the
Repert. f. d. Literat. d. Bibel, I. p. 58 ff.), Jones (*Sequel to
Ecclesiastical Researches*, etc., London 1803), Eichhorn, *Einl.* I.
p. 630 f. Baur reckons the section among the portions which
have been introduced into our Gospel by the agency of a
reviser (the author of the Acts of the Apostles). See his
Markusevang. p. 218 ff. But the genuineness was *defended* by
Ammon (*Nova Opusc.* p. 32 ff.), Süskind (*Symbolae*, II. p. 1 ff.),
von Schubert (*de infantiae J. Ch. historiae a Matth. et Luc.
exhibitae authentia atque indole*, Gripeswald. 1815), Reuterdahl
(*Obss. crit. in priora duo ev. Luc. capita*, Lond. 1823),
Bertholdt, Paulus, Schott, Feilmoser, Credner, Neudecker,
Kuinoel, Volkmar, Guericke, and almost all the more recent
writers. In opposition to Baur, see also Köstlin, p. 306 ff. —
The *genuineness* is rendered certain by the *external testimonies*
without exception. It is true that the section was wanting in
the Gospel of Marcion (see Tertullian, *c. Marc.* iv. 7); but
Marcion mutilated and falsified the Gospel of Luke in accordance with his dogmatic aims, and thus formed *his* Gospel,
which, according to Tertullian, Epiphanius, Origen, and others,
began : Ἐν ἔτει πεντεκαιδεκάτῳ τῆς ἡγεμονίας Τιβερίου Καίσαρος ὁ Θεὸς
κατῆλθεν εἰς Καφαρναοῦμ, πόλιν τῆς Γαλιλαίας, καὶ ἦν διδάσκων ἐν τοῖς
σάββασιν (iii. 1, iv. 31). And the *internal character* of the
section, much as it differs from the preface by its Hebraic
colouring in accordance with the sources made use of, contains
the same peculiarities of Luke as are apparent in the other
portions of the Gospel and in the Acts of the Apostles (see
Gersdorff, p. 160 ff.; Credner, I. p. 132 ff.), and betrays in the
whole peculiar character of the representation documental
sources, whose characteristic and in part highly poetic stamp
Luke with correct tact has known how to preserve in working
them up. We may add, that a reason against the genuineness
can as little be derived from Acts i. 1 as a conclusion in its
favour can be gathered from Luke i. 3. For there mention of the
Gospel is made *only as regards its main contents;* and the ἄνωθεν
at Luke i. 3 would, even if i. 5–ii. 52 were not genuine, find warrant enough in the beginning of the history from the emergence
of John and in the genealogy contained in the third chapter.

Vv. 1, 2. See especially Huschke, *üb. den z. Zeit d. Geburt
J. Chr. gehalt. Census*, Breslau 1840 (Hoeck, *Röm. Gesch.* Bd. I.
Abth. II.); Wieseler, *chronol. Synopse,* p. 73 ff. ; von Gumpach

in the *Stud. u. Krit.* 1852, p. 663 ff., where also the older literature is specified, and in his *Kritik und Antikritik*, Heidelb. 1853 ; Zumpt, *Commentatt. epigraph.* II. p. 73 ff. ; Köhler in Herzog's *Encykl.* XIII. p. 463 ff. ; Aberle in the *theol. Quartal-schr.* 1865, p. 103 ff. ; Gerlach, *d. Römischen Statthalter in Syr. u. Judäa*, 1865, p. 22 ff., 44 ff.; Strauss, *die Halben u. d. Ganzen*, 1865, p. 70 ff. ; Hilgenfeld in his *Zeitschr.* 1865, p. 408 ff.

Ver. 1. Ἐν ταῖς ἡμέραις ἐκ.] approximate specification of time in relation to the principal contents of what precedes, the birth of the Baptist. — δόγμα] *an ordinance, an edict.* Acts xvii. 7 ; Theodotion, Dan. ii. 13 ; Dem. 278. 17, 774. 19 ; Plat. *Legg.* i. p. 644 D; and the passages in Wetstein. — ἀπογράφεσθαι] *that there should be recorded,* cannot at all be meant of a mere *registration,* which Augustus had caused to be made (if also with the *design* of regulating in future a taxing of the Jews) for a statistical object, possibly with a view to the *Breviarium imperii* which he wrote with his own hand (in which " opes publicae continebantur; quantum civium sociorumque in armis ; quot classes, regna, provinciae, tributa aut vectigalia et necessitates ac largitiones," Tacitus, *Ann.* i. 11), as is held by Kuinoel, Olshausen, Ebrard, Wieseler, Ewald, and older expositors, but must, on account of ver. 2, be placed on the same footing in respect of its nature with the *census Quirinii,* and is therefore to be regarded as the direct *registration into the tax-lists,* belonging to the *census* proper (ἀποτίμησις, τίμημα) and forming its essential element, as, in fact, ἀπογράφειν, ἀπογράφεσθαι, ἀπογραφή (Acts v. 37) are the standing expressions for the *recording of estate,* whether in affairs of law-procedure (see Reiske, *Ind. Dem.* p. 63 f. ; Hermann, *Staatsalterth.* § 136. 13), or in those of taxing (Plato, *Legg.* vi. p. 754 D ; Polyb. x. 17. 10 ; and see Elsner and Wetstein). On the subject-matter itself, see Huschke, *üb. d. Census u. d. Steuerverfass. d. frühern Röm. Kaiserzeit,* Berl. 1847. — πᾶσαν τὴν οἰκουμ.] not : the whole of *Palestine* (Flacius, *Clavis;* Paulus, Hug, and others), to which the expression is never limited,[1] not even in Josephus, *Antt.*

---

[1] Justin, *c. Tr.* 78, has : ἀπογραφῆς οὔσης ἐν τῇ Ἰουδαίᾳ τότε πρώτης. But this ἐν τῇ Ἰουδ. manifestly has its reference to πρώτης. Comp. *Ap.* i. 34, p. 75 E.

viii. 13. 5, but, as the context by παρὰ Καίσαρος Αὐγούστου
imperatively requires, *the whole Roman empire* (*orbis terrarum*).
See the passages in Wetstein, and comp. Dissen, *ad Dem. de
Cor.* p. 215 ; Maetzner, *Lycurg.* p. 100. Hence the Roman
emperors were called κύριοι τῆς οἰκουμένης (Franz, *Corp.
Inscr.* III. p. 205). Luke narrates a general *census of the
empire* (Huschke) ; and even *the* limitation of the meaning
merely to a general *provincial* census (Wieseler) has no
foundation at all in the text, any more than the fanciful
suggestion of Lange (*L. J.* II. 1, p. 93), that Mary, who is
assumed as the source of information for the history of the
infancy, had, " in accordance with the policy of a lofty feminine sentiment," referred the determination of *Herod*, to under-
take a census in *Palestine*, back to the Emperor Augustus as
its originator, and that Luke, " in his kindly truth," had not
wished to alter the account, and hence had " by way of gentle
correction " inserted ver. 2.   See, in opposition to this,
Ebrard, p. 169 f.   Comp. also Auberlen, *Daniel u. d. Apok.*
p. 248 f.

Ver. 2. In a critical respect no change is to be made.
Lachmann has, indeed, struck out the article before ἀπογρ.
(in which Wieseler, and now also Tischendorf agree with
him), but the witnesses which omit it are only B D (the
latter having ἐγένετο ἀπογραφὴ πρώτη), ℵ (?) 131, Eus. ; and
how easily might ἡ, which in itself is superfluous (see Buttmann, *neut. Gr.* p. 105 [E. T. 221] ; Bremi, *ad Lys.* Exc. II.
p. 436 ff.), be merged in the last letter of αὕτη !   If ἡ is not
read, αὕτη is the subject, and ἀπογρ. πρ. is the predicate
(*this became the first* ἀπογραφή).   Beza, ed. 1, 2, 3, Pfaff,
Valckenaer have declared the entire verse to be an interpolated scholion ; but this is a violent suggestion opposed to
all the evidence.   *Conjectures* are given by Huetius : Κυϊν-
τιλίου ; Heumann : Κρονίου (= Saturnini) ; Valesius : Σατουρ-
νίνου ; Michaelis : πρώτη ἐγένετο πρὸ τῆς ἡγεμονεύοντος κ.τ.λ.,
al. ; see Bowyer, *Conject.* I. p. 117 ff. — The observation contained in ver. 2, which, moreover, is not to be put in a
parenthesis, is intended to tell the reader that this census was
the first of those held under the presidency of Quirinius, and

consequently to guard against confounding it with that
which was held about eleven years later (Acts v. 37). The
words signify : *This census was the first while Quirinius was
praeses of Syria.*[1] There was known, namely, to the reader a
second census of Quirinius (Acts, *l.c.*) ; but the one recorded
at present was the *first*, which occurred under the Syrian
presidency of this man.[2] It is true that history is at variance
with this clear meaning of the words as they stand. For at
the time of the birth of Jesus, according to the definite
testimony of Tertullian (*c. Marc.* iv. 19), *Q. Sentius Saturninus*
was governor of Syria ; *Publius Sulpicius Quirinius* did not
become so till about ten years later.[3] But this variance does
not entitle us to have recourse to explanations inconsistent
with linguistic usage or with the text. Explanations of this

[1] Not : it took place *first, when,*—came to be carried out *not earlier than* when
Quirinius, etc. Lichtenstein, p. 81 f., comes ultimately to this meaning. How
can this be expressed by πρώτη ? Instead of πρώτη Luke must have written
precisely the opposite, namely, ὕστερον, or ὕστερον δὴ ἐγίνετο κ.τ.λ. Hofmann is
similarly mistaken, *Schriftbew.* II. 1, p. 120 f.

[2] Quite definitely Justin also says, in agreement with Luke, that Christ
was born ἐπὶ Κυρηνίου (*Apol.* i. 46), and even that His birth was to be seen
ἐκ τῶν ἀπογραφῶν τῶν γενομένων ἐπὶ Κυρηνίου τοῦ ὑμετέρου ἐν Ἰουδαίᾳ πρώτου
γενομένου ἐπιτρόπου, *Apol.* i. 34 ; so that he in another erroneous manner
(see Credner, *Beitr.* I. p. 230) makes the man to be Roman procurator in *Judaea.*
This was *Coponius,* Joseph. *Bell.* ii. 8. 1.

[3] Between these two *Quintilius Varus* had been invested with this dignity,
Joseph. *Antt.* xvii. 5. 2. But the position that Quirinius had not been already
governor of Syria at an earlier date (according to Zumpt, from 4 to 1 before
Christ) must be adhered to, according to all the accounts given of him by
Josephus (especially *Antt.* xviii. 1. 1). Comp. Ewald, *Gesch. Chr.* p. 140 f.
The words ITERVM. SYRIAM. of the Tiburtine inscription are of too uncertain
interpretation, if the inscription applies to Quirinius, precisely to prove his twofold *praesidium Syriae,* since we know neither what stood after *Syriam,* etc.,
nor whether *iterum* is to be referred forward or backward. Comp. Strauss, p. 75.
What still remains of the whole damaged inscription runs thus (according
to Mommsen in Bergmann) :—

GEM. QVA. REDACTA. POT
AVGVSTI. POPVLIQVE. ROMANI. SENATV
SVPPLICATIONES. BINAS. OB. RES. PROSP
IPSI. ORNAMENTA. TRIVMPH
PRO. CONSVL. ASIAM. PROVINCIAMOP
DIVI. AVGVSTI. ITERVM. SYRIAM. ET. PH

See Bergmann, *de inscript. Latina ad P. Sulp. Quir. Cos. a 742 ut videtur
refer.* 1851.

nature, which must, nevertheless, leave untouched the incorrect statement about the taxation as an *imperial* census,
are (1) that of Herwart (*Chronol.* 241 f.), Bynaeus, Marck,
Er. Schmid, Clericus, Keuchen, Perizonius (*de Augustea orbis
terrar. descript.*, Oxon. 1638), Ussher, Petavius, Calovius,
Heumann, Storr, Süskind, and others, including Tholuck
(*Glaubwürdigk. d. evang. Gesch.* p. 184), Huschke, Wieseler,
who holds that πρώτη ἡγεμ. κ.τ.λ. means : *sooner than*
Quirinius was praeses. Comp. also Bornemann, *Schol.* p. lxvi.,
and Ewald (*Gesch. Chr.* p. 140), who compares the Sanscrit
and translates : " this taxation occurred *much earlier* (superlative) *than* when Quirinius ruled." But instead of citing
passages in which, as at John i. 15, xv. 18, πρῶτός τινος,
according to the real meaning, is *sooner than some one* (Bernhardy,
ad Dionys. Perieg. p. 770, and Eratosth. p. 122 ; Wesseling,
ad Herod. ii. 2, ix. 27 ; Schaefer, *ad Dion. Hal.* c. v. p. 228 ;
Fritzsche, *ad Rom.* II. p. 421), proofs ought to have been
adduced for such a *participial* connection as in the passage
before us ; but certainly not Jer. xxix. 2, where ἐξελθόντος κ.τ.λ.
is a genitive *absolute*, even apart from the fact that the use
of ὕστερον there cannot vouch for our πρώτη. In a similarly
erroneous manner Wieseler has adduced Soph. *Ant.* 637 f.,
701 f., 703 f. Luke would have known how to express the
meaning : *sooner than*, etc., simply, definitely, and accurately,
by πρὸ τοῦ ἡγεμονεύειν κ.τ.λ. (comp. ver. 21, xii. 15 ; Acts
xxiii. 15), or by πρίν, or πρὶν ἤ.[1]   (2) The expedient of Beza,
Casaubon (*Exercitatt. Antibaron.* p. 126 f.), Jos. Scaliger (*de
emend. temp.* 4, p. 417), Grotius, Wernsdorf (*de censu, quem
Caes. Oct. Aug. fecit*, Viteb. 1720), Deyling (*Obss.* I. ed. 3,
p. 242 f.), Nahmmacher (*de Augusto ter censum agente*, Helmst.
1758), Volborth (*de censu Quir.*, Gott. 1785), Birch (*de censu
Quir.*, Havn. 1790), Sanclemente (*de vulg. aerae Dionys. emend.*,
Rom. 1793), Ideler (*Handb. d. Chronol.* II. p. 394), Münter,
(*Stern d. Weisen*, p. 88 ff.), Neander, Hug (*Gutacht.*), and
others : that ἡγεμονεύοντ. is here to be taken in a wider
meaning, and that Quirinius had held that first ἀπογραφή in

---

[1] " Profecto mirandum est, homines eruditissimos in ejusmodi interpre-
tationum ludibria a praejudicatis opinionibus perductos labi," Valckenaer, p. 68.

Syria as *extraordinary commissioner* of the emperor, as to which
appeal is made, partly in general to the imperial favour which
Quirinius enjoyed, partly to Tac. *Ann.* iii. 48, according to
which he was nearly about that time in the East with
extraordinary commissions, partly to the analogy of the
Gallic census held by Germanicus (Tac. *Ann.* i. 31), and so
forth. This expedient would only be possible, if ἡγεμον. stood
by itself in the passage, and not τῆς Συρίας beside it. And if
ἡγεμον. were meant *proleptically*: under the *subsequent* praeses
(Lardner in Bowyer, *Conject.* I. p. 120; Münter), Luke could
hardly have proceeded more awkwardly than by thus *omitting*
the point whereon his being understood depended (it must have
been expressed in some such way as Κυρηνίου τοῦ ὕστερον
ἡγεμ. τῆς Συρίας). (3) Gerlach thinks that at the time of
Christ's birth Varus, indeed, was ἡγεμών of Syria, but Quirinius
was placed by his side as *legatus Caesaris proconsulari potestate*
for the purpose of making war upon the Homonades, and
had at that time—consequently likewise as ἡγεμών—undertaken the census, which, however, he brought to no right
conclusion, and only carried out subsequently under his second
praesidium. But granted that the Tiburtine inscription (see
upon that subject Gerlach, p. 25, 39 ff.), which Huschke
refers to *Agrippa,* Zumpt to *Saturninus,* is rightly referred,
with Sanclemente, Nipperdey, Bergmann, and Gerlach, to
Quirinius, and that a twofold legatio of the latter to Asia
took place: how could Luke with his simple and plain words
intend to designate that complicated historical relation and
leave the reader to guess it? To the latter Quirinius presented himself only as ordinary and single praeses of Syria.
Compare, moreover, what is said afterwards in opposition to
von Gumpach. (4) At variance with the text is the expedient
of Paulus, who substantially is followed by Gersdorf, Glöckler,
Krabbe, Mack (*Bericht üb.* Strauss, *krit. Bearb. d. Leb. J.*
p. 84 ff.), Hofmann, *Weissag. u. Erf.* II. p. 54, Ebrard, Lange,
L. J. II. 1, p. 94 (comp. also Tholuck, *Glaubwürdigk.* p. 184 ff.,
and Olshausen): that the word is to be accented as αὐτή
(*ipsa*): *the first recording itself took place while Quirinius,*
etc.; the issuing of the edict ensued at the time of the birth

of Jesus, but *the census itself* did not occur till under Quirinius.[1]
This is erroneous, as in fact ver. 3 relates the very *carrying
out* [2] of the ἀπογράφεσθαι, and this ver. 3 ff. must be conceived
as following immediately upon the edict. (5) Von Gumpach
lays stress on ἐγένετο,[3] whereby he regards Luke as indicating
that in ver. 1 he has spoken only of the *placing on the
register*, and would not have the same confounded with the
actual *levying of taxation*, which was *not carried into execution
until* under Quirinius. Against this it may be urged that
Luke would have known how to express the *realization*, as contrasted with *what was intended*, otherwise than by the simple
ἐγένετο, or that he would at least have placed this word, and that
with a more precise definition (ὄντως δὲ ἐγένετο, or the like), at
the head of the sentence ; as well as that he, in order to have the
ἀπογραφή recognised as something different from and later
than the mere registration, must have made use of *another*
word, and not again of ἀπογραφή so similar to the ἀπογράφεσθαι. (6) Aberle seeks by learned combination to
show that even before the death of Herod Quirinius had
actually become *praeses Syriae*, but that as *rector juventutis*
to the emperor's grandson Caius, he was still temporarily
detained in Rome by Augustus,[4] and his governorship remained

---

[1] Glöckler, Krabbe, Mack, and Tholuck, however, do not hold the accentua-
tion αὐτή as requisite, and Köhler rejects it.

[2] Ebrard, p. 177, wishes to set aside this difficulty by the explanation that
while an ἀπογράφεσθαι in the sense of a *registration* already occurred at the time
of the birth of Jesus, Luke availed himself of the double meaning of ἀπογραφή,
which also signifies the actual *census*, " *in an easy and unrestrained manner* "
to set forth how the work *begun in the registration* was *completed* in the *taxation*
of Quirinius. This is a makeshift, which imputes to Luke a very *enigmatical
and awkward* use of the word ἀπογραφή.

[3] So also does Köhler, who besides, with Hofmann and Ebrard, lays stress on
the fact that the passage runs not as ἡ πρώτη, but simply πρώτη. Luke is thus
made to say : *this taxation was completed as the first taxation*, etc.; it was,
namely, *begun* doubtless, but was soon *stopped* and was only *carried out* under
Quirinius. Comp. already Calvin and Gerlach above. Nothing of this appears
in the text, and the article with πρώτη would make no difference at all, since,
as is well known, the ordinal numbers may stand with or without an article
(Poppo, *ad Thucyd.* ii. 70. 5, iv. 90. 3, Goth.).

[4] Varus having in the meanwhile continued still to exercise the powers of
governor. As well according to Gerlach as according to Aberle, Varus is held
to have already, at the time of Christ's birth, filled the office of governor in

virtually unknown in the east and west, but is to be assigned
to the year 749. But while there is certain attestation that
he was *rector juventutis* to Caius (Tacitus, *Ann.* iii. 48), in
which post he was succeeded by Lollius (see Zumpt, p. 102),
there is no evidence at all for the assumption of a contemporary *praesidium Syriae*, which he must have held nominally
(thus somewhat like an *episcopus in partibus*). And how
should this state of things, which had remained unknown
and was only noticed by jurists and notaries for the sake of
the dating of documents, have become known to Luke in
particular, and have been left by him without any explanation,
in such a way that from his words we can only understand
the *praeses Syriae* in the primary and usual sense, according to
which the *praeses* resides in his province and administers the
same?—It is not to be inferred, moreover, from the ignorance
which Luke betrays at Acts v. 36 ff., that the addition πρώτη
proceeds not from Luke, but from an older Jewish-Christian
writer (Köstlin, p. 245); for that ignorance concerned not the
census of Quirinius, but the time of the insurrection of Theudas.
— ἡγεμον.] the general word for the post of a chief, here shown
by the context (τῆς Συρίας) to be used of the provincial chief,
praeses (proconsul). Comp. Joseph. *Antt.* xviii. 4. 2 : Συρίας
τὴν ἡγεμονίαν ἔχων. In Luke iii. 1, used of the Procurator. —
Κυρηνίου] P. *Sulpicius Quirinius* previously in the year 742
consul, *praeses* of Syria in the years 6–11 after Christ, died in
Rome in the year 21 after Christ. See Ewald, *Gesch. Chr.* p.
18 f.; Gerlach, *l.c.* His name is usually written *Quirinus;* by
others (so Wetstein, Valckenaer, Ewald, Gerlach, *al.*), *Quirinius.*
In the case of the Roman writers (especially Florus, iv. 12. 41 ;
Tacitus, *Ann.* ii. 30, iii. 22. 48) the manuscripts vary ; from
a coin and inscription, which have *Quirinus*, nothing can be
decided in view of the great doubt as to their genuineness.[1]
But it is certain that among the Greeks (Strabo, xii. 6, p. 569 ;

Syria, which, moreover, Norisius, *Cenotaph. Pis.* II. p. 82 f., and others maintained. But this is at variance with Tertullian, *l.c.*, comp. c. 7, where it can
only be regarded as a very arbitrary assumption that Saturninus is no longer
meant *as governor.*

[1] See Gerlach, p. 37, who cites another inscription, which actually reads
Quirinio, from Marini, *Act.* II. 782.

Josephus, Justin Martyr) the name is written with the termination $IO\Sigma$; and, as this manner of writing is at all events decidedly correct in our passage (C D E F, etc., including ℵ, likewise Eusebius, Chrysostom, etc.), whereas among the codices only B reads Κυρείνου (hence Lachmann reads Κυρίνου), the form *Quirinius*, which easily became confounded with the familiar Roman word Quirinus (= *Quirinalis*), is to be preferred. The confusion occurred the more easily, as *Quirinus*, Κυρῖνος (Plutarch), or Κυρίνος (Leon. phil. 1) was also a Roman name. At all events, *Luke himself* had in his mind the name *Quirinius*.

REMARK.—The statement of Luke, so far as it affirms that at the time of the birth of Christ an imperial census was taken, and that it was the first that was provincially carried out by the Syrian praeses Quirinius, is manifestly incorrect. For (1) the *praesidium* of Quirinius is placed about ten years too early; and (2) an imperial census, if such an one should have been held at all at the time of the birth of Jesus (which, however, cannot from other sources be proved, for the passages of Christian authors, Cassiodorus, *Var.* iii. 52, Suidas, *s.v.* ἀπογραφή, plainly depend on the narrative of Luke, as also does the chronologically erroneous statement of Isidor. *Orig.* v. 36. 4), cannot have affected Palestine at all,[1] since it had not yet become a Roman province, which did not happen till 759. And, indeed, the ordaining of so abnormal and disturbing a measure in reference to Palestine—a measure, which assuredly would not be carried through without tumultuary resistance—would have been so uncommonly important for Jewish history, that Josephus would certainly not have passed it over in absolute silence (*Antt.* xvii. 1. 1 does not bear on it); especially as it was not the *rex socius* himself, Herod, but the Roman governor, who was, according to Luke (in opposition to Wieseler), the authority conducting it. But (3) the holding withal of a general census of the empire under Augustus is historically altogether unvouched for; it is a matter of history (see the *Monum. Ancyran.* in Wolf, ed. Sueton. II. p. 369 ff.; comp. Sueton. *Aug.* 27) that Augustus thrice, in 726, 746, and 767, held a *census populi, i.e.* a census of the Roman citizens, but not also of the whole provinces of the empire (see, in opposition to Huschke, Wieseler, p. 84 ff.). Should we, on the

[1] See Mommsen in Bergm. p. iv. ff.

other hand, assume, with Wieseler, that the census had only the *provinces* in view and had been taken up in the different provinces in different years, and with the utmost indulgence to provincial peculiarities, — the object aimed at being the settling of an uniform system of taxation (comp. Savigny in the *Zeitschr. für geschichtl. Rechtswiss.* VI. p. 350), — the text of Luke would stand opposed to it. For, according to that text, (*a*) the *whole Roman empire is subjected to a census;* (*b*) this quite universal census is ordained *at once in the edict*, which, on Wieseler's hypothesis of the gradual and indulgent mode of its execution by the politic Augustus, would have been imprudent; and (*c*) it is represented as an *actual tax-census*, as was the well-known (according to Luke, *second*) census Quirinii, in which case the alleged indulgence is *imported*.

Nevertheless, criticism pronounces judgment on itself, when it designates the whole account as to the census as an invention of legend (Strauss; comp. Kern, *Urspr. des Evang.* p. 113 ff.; Weisse, I. p. 236), or even of Luke (B. Bauer), which is made in order to bring Mary with Joseph to Bethlehem. Comp. the frivolous opinion of Eichthal, II. p. 184 f. What a strange and disproportionate machinery for this purpose! No; *something of the nature* of a census, and that by command of the emperor, must have taken place in the Roman empire [1]—a registration, as regards which it is quite an open question whether it was taken with or without a design to the future regulation of taxation, or merely had for its aim the levying of statistics. The consolidating aims of the government of Augustus, and, in reference to Palestine, the dependence of the vassal-king Herod, take away from it all historical improbability, even apart from the analogous measure—that had already preceded it—of the survey of the whole Roman empire instituted by Augustus (Frontinus in the *Auct. rei agrar.*, ed. Goes. p. 109; Aethicus Ister, *Cosmogr.*, ed Gronov. p. 26). Further, as Quirinius was not at that time praeses, he can only have acted in this statistical measure as extraordinary commissioner, which is the less improbable, because apart from this he was then in the East by order of the emperor (see above), and because the politic Augustus very naturally as to that business put more confidence in an approved impartial commissioner than in the

[1] Possibly of the population, of the civil and military resources, of the finances, etc., as, according to Tacitus, *Ann.* i. 11, the *Breviarium totius imperii* (Sueton. *Octav.* 28, 101) of Augustus contained columns of that kind. See above on ver. 1.

reges socii themselves or in the interested proconsuls. And this action of *Quirinius* enables us to understand how tradition, in the gradual obscuring and mixing up of its recollections, should have made him *praeses Syriae* at that time, since he was so *subsequently*, and how the registration in question was made into a *census*, because *subsequently* he actually as Syrian governor [1] had charge of a census; and from this mixing up of times and matters resulted at the same time the designation of the ἀπογραφή as πρώτη, which occurred ἡγεμονεύοντος τῆς Συρίας Κυρηνίου. Thus Luke has *narrated* what actually *happened* in the *erroneous form* which it received from the tradition. But if we conceive of the ἀπογραφή as merely a *revision of the genealogical family registers* (Schleiermacher, Olshausen, ed. 1, Bleek), which probably was ordained only by the spiritual authorities, and perhaps had reference merely to the family of David, it is no longer easy to see how Luke, or the source from which he drew, could make out of it something thoroughly and specifically different. According to Schweizer in the *theol. Jahrb.* 1847, p. 1 ff., Luke has really in the passage before us, at variance with iii. 1, made Jesus be born in the year of the taxing of Quirinius, Acts v. 37, and thus long after the death of Herod, — in spite of his own distinct statement, i. 5! — The hypotheses, moreover, that Luke intended by the enrolment of Jesus (?) in the register of the Empire to point to the *universal destination* of the Redeemer (Wieseler; comp. Erasmus, Bengel, and already Theophylact and Euthymius Zigabenus), or to the *coincidence* of the birth of the Messiah and the redemption of Israel *with the political bondage of the people* (Ebrard), or to the manner in which Jesus in His mother's womb was most surprisingly dealt with *as a Roman subject* (Hofmann), are purely arbitrary creations of that subjectivity, which has the utmost delight in discovering a mystical reference behind every simple historical statement.

Ver. 3 ff. Πάντες] in the Jewish land, for which ver. 2 has prepared, and see ver. 4. Obviously only all those are meant, who did not dwell in their ἰδία πόλις; ἕκαστος is a

---

[1] Aberle, indeed, calls this in question, holding that Quirinius was at the later census merely a simple Legatus Caesaris. Although Josephus does not expressly name him ἡγεμών, he is still, in *Antt.* xviii. 1. 1, sufficiently indicated as such. Comp. Hilgenfeld, p. 413 ff. Apart from this, the expression ἡγεμονεύοντος in the passage before us is only an erroneously anticipating *reflex* of that, which *subsequently* Quirinius was *in fact*, and *notoriously*, as respects his real census attended by consequences so grave.

distributive apposition (Ameis on Homer, *Od.* x. 397). — εἰς τ. ἰδίαν πόλιν] the more precise definition is furnished by ver. 4. This statement, too, does not suit a *census* proper; for to this every one was required to subject himself at his *dwelling place,* or at *the* place where he had his *forum originis* (see Huschke, p. 116 ff.), whereas in our passage the Jewish principle of *tribe* is the basis. And if the matter were not a census, but a mere registration (see above), there was no reason for departing from the time-hallowed division of the people, or for not having the matter carried out in *Jewish form.* The actual historical state of the case shines here through the traditional dress of a census. — πόλιν Δαυ.] The city where David was born, 1 Sam. xvii. 11. — Βεθλεέμ] see on Matt. ii. 1. — ἐξ οἴκου κ. πατριᾶς Δαυ.] The tribes proceeding from the sons of Jacob were called φυλαί (מַטּוֹת); the branches proceeding from the sons of these patriarchs, πατριαί (מִשְׁפָּחוֹת); the single families of such a tribal branch, οἶκοι (בֵּית אָבוֹת). See Kypke, I. p. 213; Winer, *Realwörterb. s.v. Stämme;* Gesenius, *Thes.* I. p. 193, III. p. 1463. Joseph was thus of the family descending from David, and belonged to the same branch of the tribe to which David had belonged. A circumstantial designation of this important relationship. As to πατριά, moreover, see on Eph. iii. 15. — σὺν Μαριάμ] does not belong to ἀνέβη (Paulus, Hofmann, Ebrard), but to ἀπογράψ. beside which it stands : *in order to have himself enrolled with Mary,* etc. But that Mary had *of necessity* to share the journey with him (which was not requisite in the case of a *census,* when only the *names* of the women and children had to be *specified,* Dion. Hal. iv. 14; see Strauss, I. p. 235, and Huschke, p. 121, in opposition to Tholuck, p. 191) is the less to be supposed, as in the main the form of the execution of the ἀπογραφή was the *Jewish* one, ver. 3. Nevertheless, wives (in this case Mary as one *betrothed,* who according to Jewish law was placed on the same footing as the wife) had to be likewise *entered in the register,* which must have been a matter of Roman enactment, but for which it was not necessary that they should come personally with their husbands to the spot. We have consequently to

abide by the view that Mary undertook the journey with her
husband *voluntarily*, according to her own and Joseph's wish,
in order to remain under the protection of her betrothed (not
exactly on account of the troublous times,—an idea which
Ebrard imports). There are various arbitrary hypotheses, such
as: that she travelled with him on account of the *poll-tax*
(Huschke); that she wished still as a maiden *to represent her
father's house*, and *longed* after Bethlehem in *the theocratic
feeling of maternity* (Lange); that the command for the taxing
extended also to the *children* and contained a *definite point of
time*, just about which Mary expected her delivery (von
Gumpach). And the hypothesis that Mary was an *heiress*, who
had an estate in Bethlehem (Michaelis, Kuinoel, Olshausen;
with hesitation Bleek and Köhler), is utterly unfounded as
regards Luke in particular, since he has not the smallest
trace of any earlier connection with Bethlehem and makes
Mary in her travail not find even friendly lodging there. —
τῇ ἐμνηστ. αὐτῷ] Thus, according to Luke, she was still only
his *betrothed* (i. 27; Matt. i. 18), and the marriage was not
yet completed. At variance with Matt. i. 24. A different
form assumed by the tradition of the virgin birth. Evasive
suggestions are resorted to by Beza, Grotius, and others,
including Schegg and Bisping (that Luke expresses himself
thus, because Joseph had only *conducted* himself as one betrothed towards Mary). — οὔσῃ ἐγκύῳ] not: *because* she was
pregnant (von Gumpach), but: *who* was pregnant (Acts xxiv.
24; Rom. i. 16, and frequently). The observation forms the
transition to what follows.

REMARK.—From Mary's sharing in the journey we are not to
conclude that she likewise was of the family of David (Grotius,
Kuinoel, and others). She journeyed voluntarily with Joseph
as his future wife, and *Joseph* journeyed as a member of the
house of David. If Luke had had in his mind the thought that
Mary shared the journey as a descendant of David, he must have
written, and that at the end of ver. 5, διὰ τὸ εἶναι αὐτοὺς κ.τ.λ.
But comp. on i. 36, and on Matt. i. 17, Remark 2.

Ver. 6 f. Ἐπλήσθησαν αἱ ἡμέραι τοῦ τεκεῖν αὐτήν] comp.
i. 57. The supposition (see as early as *Protevang. Jac.* 17)

that Mary was surprised by the pains of labour *on the way*, is
set aside by the ἐν τῷ εἶναι αὐτοὺς ἐκεῖ. And probably she
had hoped to be able to finish the journey before her delivery. " Non videtur scisse, se vi prophetiae (Mic. v. 2) debere
Bethlehemi parere, sed providentia coelestis omnia gubernavit,
ut ita fieret," Bengel. — That Mary was delivered *without pain
and injury* is proved by Fathers and expositors, such as even
Maldonatus and Estius, from the fact that she herself swaddled
the child and laid it in the manger! — τὸν πρωτότοκον] See
on Matt. i. 25. The evasive suggestion resorted to, that this
word is used without reference to later born children, appears
the more groundless in view of the agreement of Matthew and
Luke. — ἐσπαργάν.] She *swaddled* him; frequently used in
Greek writers. — ἐν φάτνῃ] without the article (see the critical
remarks): she deposited him *in a manger*. Many, including
Paulus and Kuinoel, have, contrary to linguistic usage, made
of it a *stable*.[1] See, on the other hand, Gersdorf, p. 221; Bornemann, *Schol.* p. 18. — ἐν τῷ καταλύματι] *in the inn* (x. 34),
where they lodged—probably on account of the number of
strangers who were present on the same occasion. If we should
wish to understand it as : *the house of a friendly host* (for the
signification of καταλύμα is generally *a place of shelter, lodging*,
comp. xxii. 11), it would remain improbable that a *friendly
host*, even with ever so great restriction of room, should not
have made a chamber in the house available for *such* an
exigency. The text suggests nothing indicative of an inhos-
pitable treatment (Calvin).

Ver. 8 f. Ποιμένες] not οἱ ποιμένες. — ἀγραυλοῦντες] *staying
out in the open fields;* Plut. *Num.* 4; Parthen. *Erot.* xxix. 1,
and the ποιμένες ἄγραυλοι already in Homer, *Il.* xviii. 162. —

[1] That a *stable* (in opposition to Ebrard) was the place of the *birth, follows*
from ἐν φάτνῃ, διότι κ.τ.λ. It is possible that the stable was a *rock-cave*, which
an old legend (Justin. *c. Tryph.* 78 ; Orig. *c. Cels.* i. 51 ; *Protevang. Jac.* 18)
designates as the place of the birth, not without suspicion, however, by reason
of its appeal to Isa. xxxiii. 16, LXX. Moreover, that tradition transfers the
cave expressly only to the *neighbourhood* of the little town, and states withal
of Joseph : οὐκ εἶχεν ἐν τῇ κώμῃ ἐκείνῃ ποῦ καταλῦσαι, Justin, *l.c.* Over this grotto
designated by the legend Helena built the church *Mariae de praesepio.* Comp.
also Robinson, *Pal.* II. p. 284 ff. ; Ritter, *Erdk.* XVI. p. 292 ff.

φυλάσσ. φυλακάς] often conjoined also among the Greek
writers; Plat. *Phaedr.* p. 240 E; Xen. *Anab.* ii. 6. 10, and the
passages in Kypke.   Comp. שָׁמַר מִשְׁמָרוֹת, Num. i. 53, *al.*   The
plural applies to the different watch-stations. — τῆς νυκτός]
not belonging to φυλακάς, but : *by night,* definition of time
for ἀγραυλ. and φυλάσσ.—According to this statement, Jesus
cannot have been born in *December,* in the middle of the rainy
season (Robinson, *Pal.* II. p. 505 f.), as has been since the
fourth century supposed with a probable joining on of the
festival to the *Natales solis invicti* (see Gieseler, *Kirchengesch.*
I. 2, p. 287 f. ed. 4).   Just as little can He have been born on
the sixth day of January, which in the East was even earlier
fixed as the festival of the birth and baptism (still other times
fixed as the day of birth may be seen in Clement Al. *Strom.* I.
p. 339 f. Sylb.).   According to the Rabbins, the driving forth
of the flocks took place in March, the bringing in of them in
November (see Lightfoot) ; and if this is established at least
as the *usual course,* it certainly is not in favour of the hypothesis (Wieseler) that Jesus was born in *February* (750),
and necessitates precarious accessory assumptions. — ἐπέστη]
Comp. xxiv. 4; Acts xii. 7, xvii. 5.   In the classical writers
it is used also of theophanies, of appearances in dreams, and
the like, frequently since Homer (*Il.* xxiii. 106, x. 496), denoting their *sudden* emergence, which nevertheless is implied
not in the word in itself, but in the text. — δόξα κυρίου]
כְּבוֹד יְהֹוָה, radiance by which God is surrounded.   Comp. Ewald,
ad Apoc. p. 311.   *God's* glorious radiance (comp. Acts vii. 2)
had streamed down with the angel.   "In omni humiliatione
Christi per decoram quandam protestationem cautum est
gloriae ejus divinae," Bengel.

Ver. 10 ff. Παντὶ τῷ λαῷ] *to the whole* (Israelitish) people.
— ἐτέχθη ὑμῖν] *that* (that, namely) *there was born to you this
day,* etc.   The ὑμῖν, in reference to the shepherds, is *indi-
vidualizing.* — σωτήρ κ.τ.λ.] *a deliverer*—and now comes His
special more precise definition : *who is Messiah, Lord!* Χριστὸς
κύριος is not to be taken *together,* as it never occurs thus
in the N. T. — ἐν πόλ. Δαυ.] belonging to ἐτέχθη.   " Haec
periphrasis remittit pastores ad prophetiam, quae tum imple-

batur," Bengel. Mic. v. 2. — τὸ σημεῖον] the appointed sign
of recognition.[1] — βρέφος] not: *the child* (Luther), but: *a child*.
The word denotes either the still unborn child (as i. 41; Hom.
Il. xxii. 266), or, as in this case (comp. xviii. 15; Acts vii.
19 ; 1 Pet. ii. 2; also as a strong expression of the thought,
2 Tim. iii. 15) and very often in the classical writers, the new-
born child. — ἐσπαργ.] adjectival : *a swaddled child,* ver. 7.

Ver. 13 f. Πλῆθος στρ. οὐρ.] *a multitude of the heavenly
host* (צְבָא הַשָּׁמַיִם), a multitude of angels. The (satellite-) host
of the angels surrounds God's throne, 1 Kings xxii. 19;
2 Chron. xviii. 18; Ps. ciii. 21, cxlviii. 2; Matt. xxvi. 53;
Rev. xix. 14, *al.* On γίνεσθαι σύν τινι, *to be associated with
any one,* comp. Xen. *Cyr.* v. 3. 8. On στρατιά, comp. Plat.
Phaedr. p. 246 E: στρατιὰ θεῶν τε καὶ δαιμόνων. — δόξα
ἐν ὑψίστοις κ.τ.λ. According to the reading εὐδοκίας (see
the critical remarks, and Nösselt, *Exercitatt.* p. 171 ff.) :
Glory (*is,* comp. 1 Pet. iv. 11) *in the heaven to God, and on
earth salvation among men who are well-pleasing !* The angels
declare to the praise of God (ver. 13) that on account of the
birth of the Messiah God is glorified in heaven (by the angels),
and that on the earth there is now salvation among men, to
whom in and with the new-born child has been imparted
God's good pleasure.[2] They thus contemplate the Messiah's
work as having already set in with His birth, and celebrate it
in a twofold manner in reference to heaven and earth (comp.
Isa. vi. 3). Their exclamation is not a wish, as it is usually
rendered by supplying ἔστω or εἴη, but far stronger, — a
triumphant affirmation of the existing blessed state of things.
The ἐν ἀνθρώπ. εὐδοκίας (genitive of *quality,* see Winer, p. 211 f.
[E. T. 296 f.]) adds to the scene of the εἰρήνη the *subjects,*

---

[1] According to the notice σήμερον, and in view of the smallness of Bethlehem,
the sign specified by κείμενον ἐν φάτνῃ was *sufficiently certain* at once to guide
inquiry to the child in the village. Olshausen, but not the text, adds to this
the *secret impulse of the Spirit,* which led the shepherds to the right place.

[2] Olshausen (following Alberti, *Obss.*, and Tittmann, *Diss.*, Viteb. 1777) places
a stop after γῆς, so that the first clause says : "God is now praised as in heaven,
so also in the earth." This is erroneous, because, according to the order of the
words in Luke, the emphatic point would be not ἐπὶ γῆς, as in the Lord's Prayer,
but ἐν ὑψίστοις.

among whom it prevails (comp. Plat. *Symp.* p. 197 C); these,
namely, are those who believe in the Messiah, designated in
reference to God whose grace they possess, as *men who are
well-pleasing* (to Him).   Comp. *Test. XII. Patr.* p. 587 : καὶ
εὐδοκήσει κύριος ἐπὶ τοῖς ἀγαπητοῖς αὐτοῦ ἕως αἰώνων.
Observe, moreover, the correlation which exists (1) between
δόξα and εἰρήνη ; (2) between ἐν ὑψίστοις and ἐπὶ γῆς ; and
(3) between Θεῷ and ἐν ἀνθρώποις εὐδοκίας.   By ἐν ὑψίστοις
(*in regions, which are the highest of all,* xix. 38) the angels
declare what takes place in the highest heaven, whence they
have just come down.   Comp. Matt. xxi. 9 ; Wisd. ix. 17 ;
Ecclus. xliii. 9 ; Job xvi. 19 ; Heb. i. 3.— By εἰρήνη they
mean not only *peace* (usually understood of the peace of reconciliation), but the entire *salvation,* of which the new-born
child is the bearer ; comp. i. 79.—With the *Recepta* εὐδοκία,
the hymn would also consist of only *two parts,* divided by
καί,[1] which is not *for* (Bengel, Paulus, Kuinoel, and others,
comp. Theophylact), but *and.*   And the second part would
consist of two parallel clauses, of which the first lays down
the state of things in question after a purely objective manner
(ἐπὶ γῆς εἰρήνη), while the second designates it from the point
of view of God's subjectivity (ἐν ἀνθρ. εὐδοκία) : *on earth is
salvation, among men is* (God's) *good pleasure ;* ἐν ἀνθρ., namely,
would not be *in the case of* men (Matt. iii. 17 ; so usually), but
local, as previously ἐν ὑψίστ. and ἐπὶ γῆς.   Fritzsche, *ad Rom.*
II. p. 372, takes εὐδοκία as *delight ;* " in genere humano
(Messia nato) *voluptas est et laetitia.*"   But εὐδοκία nowhere
expresses this strong idea, but only the state of well-pleased
satisfaction (as Ps. cxliv. 16, LXX.), and the latter idea

[1] Nevertheless Ebrard (on Olshausen) still defends the *threefold division.*
According to him, the angels exult (1) that *in heaven* honour is given to God for
the redemption now brought about ; (2) that *upon earth* a kingdom of peace is
now founded ; (3) that *between heaven and earth* the right relation is restored,
that God's eye may again rest with good pleasure on mankind. This alleged
third clause of necessity contains somewhat of tautology ; and the text itself
by its καί and by its contrast of heaven and earth yields only *two* clauses.
Lange also, *L. J.* II. 1, p. 103, understands it in a threefold sense, but very
arbitrarily takes εὐδοκία of the divine good pleasure *manifested in a Person,*
referring to passages such as Eph. i. 5, 6.

would in this place be too weak; we could not but expect χαρὰ καὶ ἀγαλλίασις, or the like. Moreover, according to ver. 13 (αἰνούντων τ. Θεόν) it is more in harmony with the text to understand εὐδοκία on the part of God, in which case the quite usual meaning of the word (ἐπανάπαυσις τοῦ Θεοῦ, Theophylact) is retained; "quod sc. Deus gratuito suo favore homines dignatus sit" (Calvin). The opposite: Eph. ii. 3. Bornemann, Schol. p. 19 ff., considers the whole as affirmed of Christ: "Χριστὸς ὁ κύριος δόξα ἔσται ἐν ὑψίστοις ὄντι Θεῷ κ.τ.λ., h. e. Messias celebrabit in coelis Deum et in terram deducet pacem divinam, documentum (in apposition) benevolentiae divinae erga homines." But Luke himself specifies the contents as praise of God (ver. 13); and the assumption of Bornemann (after Paulus), that Luke has given only a small fragment of the hymn, is the more arbitrary, the more the few pregnant words are precisely in keeping with a heavenly song of praise.

Ver. 15 f. Καὶ οἱ ἄνθρ.] This καί is not also, but the simple and after ἐγένετο; see on v. 12. — οἱ ἄνθρωποι οἱ ποιμένες, not: the shepherd people (Grotius, Paulus, and others), against which the second article is decisive (comp. Matt. xviii. 23, xxii. 2, al.; see Bernhardy, p. 48; Kühner, II. p. 120), but a contrast to οἱ ἄγγελοι, in which case, however, we must not lay upon the expression a stress which is foreign to the connection ("totum genus humanum quodammodo repraesentantes," Bengel), but rather must adhere to the simple and artless mode of representation: after the departure of the angels the people too, the shepherds, said, etc. — διέλθωμεν] through the fields as far as to Bethlehem, Acts ix. 38, xi. 19. — δή] denotes what is definitive, without more ado. See Klotz, ad Devar. p. 395; Nägelsbach, Anm. z. Ilias, ed. 3, p. 433 f. — τὸ ῥῆμα] which has been said; ὃ ὁ κύρ. ἡμ. is an epexegesis of it. — ἀνεῦρον] they discovered (after previous search, in conformity with the direction at ver. 12). The word only occurs in the N. T. again at Acts xxi. 4, comp. 4 Macc. iii. 14; more frequently among Greek writers.

Ver. 17 f. Διεγνώρισαν] they gave exact information (διά). The word is only found besides in Schol. in Beck. Anecd.

p. 787, 15, but in the sense of accurate *distinguishing*, which
it cannot have in this place (Vulg.: *cognoverunt*); comp.
rather ἐγνώρισεν, ver. 15. At the birthplace to the parents
and others who were present they made accurate communication of the angelic utterance addressed to them, and all
who heard this communication marvelled, but Mary (ver. 19),
etc. — περὶ τῶν λαληθ.] does not belong to ἀκούσαντες
(Gersdorf), but to ἐθαύμ., with which indeed περί is very
rarely associated elsewhere; but the thought is: they fell
into amazement *in consideration of that, which*, etc. Comp. Plat.
Tim. p. 80 C: τὰ θαυμαζόμενα ἠλέκτρων περὶ τῆς ἕλξεως.

Ver. 19 f. *Δέ*] leading over to the special thing, which
Mary amidst this general amazement did — she, who, in
accordance with the revelations made to her, was more deeply
struck with the tidings of the shepherds, and saw matters in
a deeper light. She *kept* all these utterances (τὰ ῥήματα) of
the shepherds. Observe in the narrative the emphasis of
πάντα, as well as the purposely chosen adumbrative tense
συνετήρει (previously the aorist). On συντηρεῖν, *alta mente re-
positum servare*, comp. Dan. vii. 28; Ecclus. xiii. 12, xxxix. 2,
xxviii. 3. — συμβάλλουσα κ.τ.λ.] The Vulgate well renders:
conferens, inasmuch as she *put them together*, *i.e.* in silent
heart-pondering she compared and interpreted them to herself.
Comp. Plat. *Crat.* p. 348 A: συμβαλεῖν τὴν Κρατύλου μαν-
τείαν, p. 412 C; Soph. *Oed. C.* 1472; Pind. *Nem.* xi. 43;
Eur. *Or.* 1394. — ὑπέστρεψ.] to their flocks, ver. 8. — δοξά-
ζοντες καὶ αἰνοῦντες] Glorifying and giving approval. The latter
is more special than the former. — ἐπὶ πᾶσιν κ.τ.λ.] *over all
things, which they had* just *heard and seen* in Bethlehem after
such manner *as* was *spoken to them* by the angel at vv. 10–12.

REMARK.—To make of these angelic appearances a *natural*
(phosphoric) *phenomenon*, which had first been single and then
had divided itself and moved to and fro, and which the shepherds, to whom was known Mary's hope of bringing forth the
Messiah, interpreted to themselves of this birth (Paulus; comp.
Ammon, *L. J.* I. p. 203, who likewise assumes a meteor), is a
pecided and unworthy offence against the contents and purpose
of the narrative, which is to be left in its charming, thoughtful,

and lofty simplicity as the most distinguished portion of the cycle of legend, which surrounded the birth and the early life of Jesus. The truth of the history of the shepherds and the angels lies in the sphere of the idea, not in that of historical reality, although Luke narrates it as a real event. Regarded as reality, the history loses its truth, as a premiss, with which the notorious subsequent want of knowledge and *non*-recognition of Jesus as the Messiah, as well as the absolute silence of evangelic *preaching* as to this heavenly *evangelium*, do not accord as a sequel, — apart from the fact, that it is not at all consistent with Matthew's narrative of the Magi and of the slaying of the children, which is to be explained from the circumstance that *various* wreaths of legend, altogether independent one of another, wove themselves around the divine child in His lowliness.[1] The contrast of the lowliness of Jesus and of His divine glory, which pervade His entire history on earth until His exaltation (Phil. ii. 6 ff.), is the great truth, to which here, immediately upon the birth, is given the most eminent and most exhaustive expression by the living and creative poetry of faith, in which with thoughtful aptness members of the lowly and yet patriarchally consecrated class of shepherds receive the first heavenly revelation of the Gospel outside the family circle, and so the πτωχοὶ εὐαγγελίζονται (vii. 22) is already even now realized.

Ver. 21. Τοῦ περιτεμεῖν αὐτόν] The genitive, not as at ver. 22, i. 57, ii. 6, but as genitive of the *aim: in order to circumcise Him*, that He might be circumcised. Comp. Buttmann, *neut. Gr.* p. 230 [E. T. 267]. — καὶ ἐκλήθη] *was also named*, indicating the naming as *superadded* to the rite of circumcision. See Nägelsbach, *z. Ilias*, ed. 3, p. 164. And the Son of God had to become *circumcised*, as γενόμενος ἐκ γυναικός, γενόμενος ὑπὸ νόμον, Gal. iv. 4. This was the divine arrangement for His appearing as the God-man in necessary association

---

[1] In opposition to Schleiermacher, who in the case of our passage lays stress, in opposition to the mythical view, on the absence of lyrical poetry, failing to see that precisely the most exalted and purest poetry is found in the *contents* of our passage with all its simplicity of presentation ; see the appropriate remarks of Strauss, I. p. 245. Lange, *L. J.* II. p. 103, in his own manner transfers the appearances to the souls of the shepherds, which were of such elevated and supramundane mood that they could discern the joy of an angelic host ; and holds that the appearance of the angel and the glory of the Lord, ver. 9, point to a vision of the Angel of the Covenant.

with the people of God (Rom. ix. 5). There is much importation of the dogmatic element here among the older commentators.[1] — τὸ κληθὲν κ.τ.λ.] See i. 31.   Comp. Matt. i. 21,
where, however, the legend quite differently refers the giving
of the name to the angel.

Ver. 22. Women after childbirth, when the child was a
boy, were unclean for seven days, and had besides to stay at
home thirty-three days more (at the birth of a girl these
periods were doubled). Then they were bound to present in
the temple an offering of purification, namely, a lamb of a year
old as a burnt-offering, and a young pigeon or turtle-dove as
a sin-offering ; or else, if their means were too small for this,
two turtle-doves or young pigeons, the one as a burnt-offering,
the other as a sin-offering. See Lev. xii. 2 ff. ; Lund, *Jüd.
Heiligth.*, ed. Wolf, p. 751 ; Michaelis, *Mos. R.* § 192 ; Ewald,
Alterth. p. 178 f. ; Keil, *Archäol.* I. p. 296.   Accordingly
αἱ ἡμέραι τοῦ καθαρισμ. αὐτῶν : *the days, which* (*i.e.* the lapse
of them) *were appointed for their legal cleansing* (καθαρισμός,
passive, comp. ver. 14). Mary brought the offering of the
poor, ver. 24. — αὐτῶν] applies contextually (ἀνήγαγον αὐτόν)
not to the *Jews* (van Hengel, *Annot.* p. 199), but to *Mary* and
Joseph.   Comp. Euthymius Zigabenus, also Bleek.   The purification in itself indeed concerned only the mother ; but in
the case before us Joseph was, and that by means of the
presentation of the first-born son associated therewith, also
directly interested ; hence the expression *by way of synecdoche,*
which is *usually* referred to the mother *and the child* (so also
by Kuinoel, Winer, de Wette). — κατὰ τὸν νόμον M.] applies
to ἐπλήσθησαν κ.τ.λ., indicating the *legal* duration thereof. —
ἀνήγαγον, like ἀναβαίνειν of the journeying to Jerusalem. —
παραστῆσαι] All first-born sons were the property of Jehovah,
destined to the temple-service originally and before the institution of the Levites (Num. viii. 14 ff.) ; hence they had to
be *presented* in the temple to God as His special property,

_____

[1] Calovius says that Christ allowed Himself to be circumcised "tum ob
demonstrandam naturae humanae veritatem . . . tum ad *probandam e semine
Abrahae originem* . . . tum imprimis ob *meriti et redemptionis Christi certificationem.*"

but were redeemed from Him for five shekels, Ex. xiii. 2; Num. viii. 16, xviii. 15 f.; Lightfoot, p. 753; Lund, *l.c.* p. 753; Michaelis, *Mos. R.* § 227, 276; Saalschütz, *Mos. R.* p. 97.

Ver. 23. Not to be put in a parenthesis. — A very free quotation from Ex. xiii. 2. — διανοῖγον μήτραν] פֶּטֶר רֶחֶם; comp. LXX. Hardly according to the passage before us has Luke conceived, with Ambrosius and many others, that Mary brought forth *clauso utero* and only voluntarily subjected herself to this law (as Bisping still holds).

Ver. 24. Καὶ τοῦ δοῦναι] continues the narrative after the interposed sentence ver. 23: *and in order to give* an offering. —κατὰ τὸ εἰρημ. κ.τ.λ.] Lev. xii. 8. — νεοσσούς] On the later form rejected by the Atticists, νοσσούς (so Tischendorf), see Sturz, *Dial. Mac.* p. 185; Lobeck, *ad Phryn.* p. 206 f.

Ver. 25 f. Who this *Simeon* was ("primus propheta, qui diceret Christum venisse," Bengel), is utterly unknown. The supposition that he was son of Hillel, and father of Gamaliel (Michaelis, Paulus, and older commentators), who became president of the Sanhedrim in A.D. 13, does not agree with vv. 26, 29, where he appears as an *aged* man; and there is generally the less ground for entertaining it, in proportion to the frequency of the name שִׁמְעוֹן. — δίκαιος κ. εὐλαβής] Comp. Plat. *Polit.* p. 311 B: τὸ δίκαιον κ. εὐλαβές, and shortly before: ἤθη εὐλαβῆ καὶ δίκαια. The word εὐλαβής is only used in the N. T. by Luke. It denotes religious conscientiousness.[1] — παράκλησιν] The Messianic *blessing* of the nation, as its practical *consolation* after its sufferings (comp. λύτρωσιν, ver. 38), is called, according to prophetic precedent (Isa. xl. 1), in the Rabbinical literature also very often נחמה. See Vitringa, *Obs.* V. p. 83; Lightfoot and Wetstein *in loc.* The Messiah Himself: מנחם. See Schöttgen, *Hor.* II. p. 18. The same in substance is: προσδεχόμ. τὴν βασιλείαν τοῦ Θεοῦ, Mark xv. 43. — ἐπ᾿ αὐτόν] having come *upon.* — κεχρηματισμ.] a divine *responsum*, see on Matt. ii. 12. There is no hint of a *dream* (Kuinoel). — πρὶν ἤ] See on Matt. i. 18. — τὸν Χριστὸν κυρίου] comp. ix. 20: *the Messiah of God* (whom God has destined and sent as Messiah). — For

[1] Comp. Delitzsch on Heb. v. 7 f., p. 191.

the expression *to see death,* comp. Heb. xi. 5 ; John viii. 51 ;
Ps. lxxxix. 48.   On the classical use of ὁρᾶν in the sense of
experiundo cognoscere, Dorvill. *ad Char.* p. 483 ; Jacobs, *ad
Anthol.* VII. p. 108.

Ver. 27 f. *Ἐν τῷ πνεύματι*] *by virtue* of the Holy Spirit,
"instigante Spiritu," Grotius ; comp. Matt. xxii. 43. — The
expression τοὺς γονεῖς (procreators) is not appropriate to the
bodily Sonship of God, which Luke narrates, and it betrays
an original source resting on a different view.   Comp. ver. 41.
On the *form* γονεῖς, see Lobeck, *ad Phryn.* p. 69. — κατὰ τὸ
εἰθισμένον τοῦ νόμου] According to the custom prescribed by
the law. — καὶ αὐτός] *also on His part,* for the *parents* had
just carried Him in, ver. 27.   The reference to the *priest,*
" qui eum Domino sistendum amplexus erat " (Wolf ; Kuinoel
also mixes up this), is erroneous, since it is *in the bringing
in* that the child is also taken into his arms by Simeon. —
Simeon has *recognised* the *Messiah-child* immediately *through
the Spirit.*   He needed not for this " the august form of the
mother " (in opposition to Lange).

Ver. 29 ff. *Now* (after I have seen the Messiah, vv. 26, 30)
*Thou lettest Thy servant depart, O Ruler, according to Thine utter-
ance* (ver. 2), *in bliss* (so that he is happy, see on Mark v. 34) ;
now the time is come, when Thou lettest me die blessed.[1] —
ἀπολύεις] *present,* of that which is nearly an⸴ certainly impending.   There is no need to supply τοῦ ζῆν, or ἐκ τῆς γῆς, or
the like (as is usually done), as the absolute ἀπολύειν is at all
events used (comp. Soph. *Ant.* 1254 ; Gen. xv. 2 ; Num. xx. 29 ;
Tob. iii. 6), but Simeon conceives of his death figuratively as an
enfranchisement from service, as is signified by the context in
τ. δοῦλόν σου, δέσποτα.   The servant of God *dies* and is
thereby *released* from his service. — εἶδον prefixed with emphasis, in retrospective reference to ver. 26. — τὸ σωτήριόν
σου] *the deliverance bestowed by Thee,* the Messianic deliverance, which has begun with the birth of the Messiah.   Comp.
iii. 6 ; Acts xxviii. 28. — κατὰ πρόσωπον πάντ. τ. λαῶν] *in
the face of all peoples,* so that this deliverance is set forth

---

[1] Euthymius Zigabenus well remarks : μηκέτι λυπούπινον ὑπὲρ τῆς ἐλευθερίας τοῦ
Ἰσραήλ.

before all peoples, is visible and manifest to them. Comp. on κατὰ πρόσωπ., Jacobs, *ad Ach. Tat.* iii. 1, p. 612. The prophet sees the σωτήριον already in its *unfolded manifestation to all.* This is then, in ver. 32, further specially characterized as respects the two portions of the πάντων τῶν λαῶν, in which φῶς and δόξαν are appositional definitions to τὸ σωτήριόν σου : *light, which is destined to bring revelation to the heathen, and glory of Thy people Israel.* The progression of the climax lies in φῶς and δόξα. For the heathen the σωτήριον is *light,* when, namely, they come in accordance with the time-hallowed promise (Isa. ii. 2 ff., xi. 10, xliv. 5, lx. 1 ff., and many other passages), and subject themselves to the Messianic theocracy, whereby they become enlightened and sharers in the unveiling of the divine truth. For the people Israel the σωτήριον is *glory,* because in the manifestation and ministry of the Messiah the people of God attains the glory, through which it is destined to be distinguished above all peoples as the seat and possessor of salvation. Δόξαν might be included as still dependent on εἰς (Theophylact, Euthymius Zigabenus, Luther, Bleek, and others), but by taking it independently, the great destination of the σωτήριον for the people of Israel is brought into more forcible prominence. — Ver. 33. *And there was* (on the singular ἦν and the plural participles that follow, see Kühner, § 433, 1; comp. Matt. xvii. 3) *His father and His mother in amazement,* etc. In this there is no inconsistency with the earlier angelic revelations (Strauss). The thing was great enough *in itself,* and they learned it here in *another* form of revelation, the *prophetic.*

Ver. 34. Αὐτούς] the parents, ver. 33. — After he has blessed them (has in prayer promised them God's grace and salvation), he again specially addresses the *mother,* whose marvellous relation to the new-born infant he has, according to Luke, recognised ἐν πνεύματι. — κεῖται] *He is placed there,* i.e. *He has the destination,* see on Phil. i. 16. — εἰς πτῶσιν κ.τ.λ.] designates, in reference to Isa. viii. 14 (comp. Matt. xxi. 22, 44; Acts iv. 11; Rom. ix. 33; 1 Pet. ii. 6), the *moral judgment* (John iii. 19 ff.), which is to set in by means of the appearance and the ministry of the Messiah. Accord-

LUKE.   Y

ing to divine decree many must take offence at Him and *fall*
—namely, through unbelief—into obduracy and moral ruin ;
many others must *arise*, inasmuch as they raise themselves—
namely, through faith in Him—to true spiritual life. The fulfilment of both is abundantly attested in the evangelic history ;
as, for example, in the case of the Pharisees and scribes the
falling, in that of the publicans and sinners the *rising*, in that
of Paul *both ;* comp. Rom. xi. 11 ff. — καὶ εἰς σημεῖον ἀντι-
λεγόμ.] What was previously affirmed was His destination *for
others;* now follows *the special personal* experience, which is
destined for Him.   His manifestation is to be a *sign*, a marvellous token (signal) of the divine counsel, which *experiences
contradiction* from the world (see on Rom. x. 21).   The
fulfilment of this prediction attained its culmination in the
crucifixion ; hence ver. 35.   Comp. Heb. xii. 3.   But it
continues onward even to the last day, 1 Cor. xv. 25.

Ver. 35. Since the construction does not indicate that καὶ
. . . ῥομφαία is to be made a parenthesis, and since the
importance of this prophetic intimation in the address directed
to Mary is not in keeping with a mere intercalation, ὅπως κ.τ.λ.
is to be referred to καὶ . . . ῥομφαία, not to σημεῖον ἀντιλεγ.
(Kuinoel, de Wette, Ewald, and many others). — καὶ σοῦ δέ]
See on i. 76.   This καί and αὐτῆς places the anguish *of the
mother herself* on a parallel with the fate *of her Son* intimated
by σημεῖον ἀντιλεγ. ; and σοῦ δὲ αὐτῆς is a bringing of the
contrast into stronger relief than σεαυτῆς δέ.   See Schaefer, *ad
Dem. de Cor.* 319, 6. — ῥομφαίαν δὲ ὠνόμασε (not the martyr-
death of Mary, as Epiphanius and Lightfoot hold, but) τὴν
τμητικωτάτην καὶ ὀξεῖαν ὀδύνην,[1] ἥτις διῆλθε τὴν καρδίαν τῆς
θεομήτορος, ὅτε ὁ υἱὸς αὐτῆς προσηλώθη τῷ σταυρῷ, Euthymius
Zigabenus.   Similar figurative designations of pain may be
seen in Wetstein.   Bleek is mistaken in referring it to *doubts
of the Messiahship of her Son*, which for a while were to cause
division in Mary's heart.   For this thought the forcible expression would be quite out of proportion, and, moreover, unintelligible ; and the thought itself would be much too special and
subordinate, even apart from the consideration that there is no

---

[1] Comp. Hom. *Il.* xix. 125 : τὸν δ' ἄχος ὀξὺ κατὰ Φρένα τύψε βαθείαν.

direct evidence before us of *temporary* unbelief on the part
of Mary (at the most, Mark iii. 21). — ὅπως κ.τ.λ.] a divine
aim, which is to be attained by οὗτος κεῖται . . . ῥομφαία ; a
great crisis in the spiritual world is to be brought to light,
John ix. 39, iii. 19, v. 22 ; 1 Cor. i. 23 f. ; 2 Cor. ii. 15.
The conditional ἄν expresses : in order that, *when that which
is just predicted to thee sets in.* — ἐκ πολλ. καρδ.] *forth from
many hearts.* Comp. Rom. i. 17. — διαλογισμοί] not οἱ
διαλογ. ; *thoughts,* consequently what is otherwise hidden.
The revealing itself takes place through declared belief or
unbelief in Him who is put to death.

   Ver. 36 ff. Ἦν] *aderat,* as at Mark viii. 1, xv. 40 ; also 1 Cor.
xiv. 48. — After αὕτη, ver. 36, the copula ἦν is not unneces-
sarily to be supplied, in which case (so usually, as also by
Lachmann and Tischendorf) a point is placed after ver. 37 ;
but this αὕτη is the subject to which ἀνθωμολογεῖτο belongs
as verb, so that all that intervenes contains accompanying
definitions of the subject, namely thus : *This* one, *being advanced
in great age, after she had lived with a husband seven years from
her virginity, she too a widow up to eighty-four years, who
departed not from the temple, with fastings and prayers rendering
service to God night and day and having come forward at that
same hour, offered praise to the Lord,* etc.   Observe as to this—
(1) that ζήσασα . . . αὐτῆς, ver. 36, is *subordinate* to the προβεβηκ. ἐν ἡμ. πολλ. ; (2) that at ver. 37 there is to be written,
with Tischendorf and Ewald, καὶ αὐτή (not as usually, καὶ αὕτη),
so that the definition καὶ αὐτὴ χήρα . . . ἐπιστᾶσα, vv. 37, 38,
contains a further description of the woman *co-ordinated* with
the προβεβηκ. ἐν ἡμ. πολλ. ; (3) that καὶ αὐτῇ τῇ ὥρᾳ ἐπιστᾶσα (see the critical remarks) without any separation links
itself on continuously to the preceding participial definition ;
finally, (4) that καὶ αὐτή, ver. 37, *she too,* places Anna on
a parallel with Simeon ; as the latter had come forward a
pious aged man, so *she also* a pious aged woman. — προφῆτις]
Plat. *Phaedr.* p. 244 A ; Eur. *Ion.* 42, 321 ; LXX. Ex. xv. 20 ;
Isa. viii. 3, *al.*   Hebrew נְבִיאָה, an *interpretress of God,* a
woman *with the gift of apocalyptic discourse,* Rev. ii. 20 ; Acts
xxi. 9, ii. 17.   She makes use of this gift, ver. 38. — ἑπτά]

consequently a *brief* and (ἀπὸ τ. παρθεν. αὐτ.) her *only* marriage, after which she remained in widowhood, which among the ancients was accounted very honourable. See Grotius and Wetstein on 1 Tim. iii. 2, v. 9.

Ver. 37. Ἕως (see the critical remarks) ἐτ. ὀγδοήκ.: *even to eighty-four years*, she had come even to this age of life in her widowhood. Comp. Matt. xviii. 21 f. Rettig is mistaken in his judgment upon ἕως in the *Stud. u. Krit.* 1838, p. 221. Comp. Dem. 262, 5. — οὐκ ἀφίστατο κ.τ.λ.] a popular description of *unremitting* zeal (comp. Hom. *Od.* ii. 345, *Il.* xxiv. 72) in the public worship of God. Comp. xxiv. 53. — νύκτα κ. ἡμέρ.] Thus also at Acts xxvi. 7; Mark iv. 28; 1 Tim. v. 5. Elsewhere the order is inverted. Instances of both arrangements may be seen in Bornemann, *Schol.* p. 27; Lobeck, *Paralip.* p. 62 f., and from the Latin: Heindorf on *Horat. Sat.* i. 1. 77. In this place νύκτα is *prefixed* in order, as in Acts, *l.c.*, and 1 Tim. v. 5, to make the *fervency of the pious temple-service* the more prominent. The case is otherwise, where it is simply a question of definition of time, at Esth. iv. 15.

Ver. 38. Αὐτῇ τῇ ὥρᾳ] in which occurred the previously described scene with Simeon. — ἐπιστᾶσα] *having made her appearance*, namely, to speak. Comp. Aeschin. p. 65, 5; Xen. *Anab.* v. 8. 9, *Sympos.* ii. 7. The suddenness and unexpectedness in the demeanour of the aged widow is implied also here (comp. on ver. 9) in the context. On ἀνθομολογεῖσθαι (comp. LXX. Ps. lxxix. 13; 3 Macc. vi. 33), in the case of which ἀντί " referendi reprehendendique sensum habet," see Winer, *de verbor. compos. usu,* III. p. 18 ff. The *tenor* of her utterance of praise to God (τῷ κυρίῳ) is after what was related of Simeon obvious of itself, and is therefore not more precisely specified. — περὶ αὐτοῦ] ὅτι οὗτός ἐστιν ὁ λυτρωτής, Euthymius Zigabenus. *Jesus* is the subject still present, as a matter of course, in the conception of the narrator (from ver. 34 f. onwards), although not mentioned in the context (Winer, p. 132 [E. T. 180 f.]). — τοῖς προσδεχομ. λύτρωσιν] Comp. ver. 25. With the reading Ἱερουσ. *without* ἐν (see the critical remarks), *deliverance of Jerusalem* is not essentially

distinct from παράκλησις τοῦ Ἰσρ., ver. 25, comp. i. 68,
since Jerusalem is the theocratic central seat of God's people.
Comp. Isa. xl. 2. We may add, the ἐλάλει κ.τ.λ. took place on
her part likewise αὐτῇ τῇ ὥρᾳ, namely, after she had presented
her praise to God. The pious ones waiting for the Messiah are
with her in the temple, and to them all she makes communication about the child that is present. But this is not to be
conceived of as a *public utterance*, for which the limitation τοῖς
προσδεχ. would not be appropriate.

Ver. 39. Ναζαρέτ] therefore not in the first instance again
to Bethlehem. Of the Magi, of the slaughter of the children,
of the flight to Egypt, Luke has nothing. They belong to
quite another cycle of legend, which he has not followed.
Reconciliation is impossible; a preference for Luke, however,
at the expense of Matthew (Schleiermacher, Schneckenburger,
Sieffert, and others), is at least in so far well founded, as
Bethlehem was not, as Matthew reports (see on Matt. ii. 23,
Rem.), the original dwelling-place of the parents of Jesus, but
became the birth-place of the latter on occasion of the ἀπογραφή. If Bethlehem had been the original dwelling-place,
it was natural, considering the Davidico-Messianic tendency
of the legend, that no change should be made under these
circumstances. But, in opposition to the bold assumption of
the more recent exponents of the mythical theory,[1] that Jesus
was born in Nazareth, so that both the earlier residence of the
parents at Bethlehem (Matthew) and their journey thither
(Luke) are held to be the work of tradition on the basis of
Mic. v. 1 (but only Matthew bases his statement upon this
prophecy!), see on Matt. *l.c.* Even de Wette finds this probable,
especially on account of John vii. 42, comp. i. 46 ff., where
John adds no correction of the popular view. But to infer
from this that John knew nothing of the birth in Bethlehem
is unwarranted, since the tradition of Matthew and Luke,

---

[1] See also Weisse, *Evangelienfr.* p. 181 f., who holds that the reference to the
Lord's place of birth by the name of *Bethlehem* is to be understood πνευματικῶς.
Schleiermacher, *L. J.* p. 56 f., leaves the birth-place altogether doubtful; holding
that the question is wholly indifferent for our faith, which remark, however, is
inappropriate on account of the prophetic promise.

agreeing in *this* very particular, certainly suggests the pre-
sumption that the birth at Bethlehem was generally known
among the Christians and was believed, so that there was not
at all any need for a correcting remark on the part of John.

REMARK.—As the presentation of Jesus in the temple bears of
itself in its legal aspect the stamp of history, so what occurred
with Simeon and Anna cannot in its general outlines be reasonably relegated to the domain of myth (see, in opposition to Strauss
and B. Bauer, Ebrard, p. 225 ff.), although it remains doubtful
whether the prophetic glance of the seers (to whose help Paulus
comes by suggesting, in spite of the remark at ver. 33, communications on the part of Mary ; and Hofmann, p. 276, by the
hypothesis of acquaintance with the history of the birth) expressed itself so definitely as the account about Simeon purports.
The hypothesis that Luke received his information from Anna's
mouth (Schleiermacher, Neander) hangs on ver. 36 f., where
Anna is so accurately described, and consequently on so weak
a thread, that it breaks down at once when we take into account
the lesser degree of vividness and fulness of detail in the
narrative of what Anna did.

Ver. 40. Similar to i. 80, but more distinctive and more
characteristic, in keeping with the human development of the
Son of God, who was to grow up to be the organ of *truth* and
grace. Comp. ver. 52.— πληρούμ. σοφ.] the internal state of
things accompanying the ἐκραταιοῦτο ; He became a *vigorous*
child (ἐκρατ.[1]), while at the same time He became *filled,* etc.
— χάρις Θεοῦ] not to be taken of distinguished *bodily grace-
fulness* (Raphel, Wolf, Wetstein), but as : the *favour of God,*
which was *directed* upon Him. Comp. ver. 52. On ἐπ' αὐτό,
comp. Acts iv. 33.

Ver. 41 f. Τῇ ἑορτῇ] Dative of *time.* Comp. Winer, p. 195,
193 [E. T. 273, 269]. The three great festivals (Passover,
Pentecost, Tabernacles) were according to the Mosaic law to
be celebrated, although with the gradual dispersion of the
people this could not strictly be adhered to, by every male
Israelite at the national sanctuary,—an excellent means of

[1] Cyril of Alexandria says : σωματικῶς γὰρ ηὔξανε καὶ ἐκραταιοῦτο, τῶν μελῶν
συναδρυνομένων τῇ αὐξήσει. Observe that in our passage πνεύματι is not added as
at i. 80 ; the *mental* development follows in πληρ. σοφ.

maintaining and elevating the common theocratic spirit; Ex.
xxiii. 14 ff., xxxiv. 23; Deut. xvi. 16. See Ewald, *Alterth.* p.
406 ff.; Saalschütz, *M. R.* p. 421 ff. The annual *passover-
journey* was shared also by Mary, doubtless independently of
Hillel's precept to that effect (*Tanchuma*, f. 33, 4), and in virtue
of her piety (comp. 1 Sam. i. 7; *Mechilta*, f. 17, 2). As to the
Passover, see on Matt. xxvi. 2. — δώδεκα] At this age in the
case of the boy, who now was called בֶּן הַתּוֹרָה, began the
instruction in the law, the accustoming to worship, fasting,
and the like, see Lightfoot, p. 739; Wetstein.

Ver. 43 f. Τὰς ἡμέρας] the well-known seven days of festival,
Ex. xii. 15; Lev. xxiii. 6 f.; Deut. xvi. 2. — How it happened
that the parents knew nothing of the staying behind of their
son, is not expressly narrated by Luke. The charge, however,
of negligent *carelessness* (Schuderoff in the *Magaz. von Festpred.*
III. p. 63 ff., and in his *Jahrb.* X. 1, p. 7 ff.; Olshausen) is
unwarranted, as νομίσαντες δὲ αὐτὸν ἐν τῇ συνοδίᾳ εἶναι presupposes a circumstance unknown to us, which might justify
that want of knowledge. In the case of Jesus it was an irre-
sistible impulse towards the things of God, which carried Him
away to postpone His parents to the satisfaction of this instinct,
mightily stimulated as it was on this His first sojourn in Jerusalem,—a momentary premature breaking forth of that, which
was the principle decidedly expressed and followed out by Him
in manhood (Mark iii. 32 f.). — συνοδία] *company sharing the
journey.* See Kypke, I. p. 220 f. The inhabitants of one or
more places together formed a *caravan*; Strabo uses the word
also of such a company (iv. p. 204, xi. p. 528). — ἀνεζήτουν]
when they assembled together to pass the night.

Ver. 45 f. Ζητοῦντες] *present* participle: "ubi res aliqua
nondum quidem peragitur, sed tamen aut revera aut cogitatione
instituitur paraturve," Kühner, *ad Xen. Anab.* i. 3. 16. Comp.
Dissen, *ad Pind. Ol.* vii. 14, p. 81. — μεθ' ἡμέρας τρεῖς] is
reckoned, in most accordance with the text, from the point at
which the search meant by ζητ. αὐτόν began, consequently from
their return to Jerusalem, the day of this return being counted as
the first, and that of the finding as the third. Comp. the designation of the time of Christ's resurrection as "after three days."

Others explain it otherwise. "Grotius: Diem unum iter fecerant, altero remensi erant iter, tertio demum quaesitum inveniunt." So also Paulus, Bleek, and others, following Euthymius Ziga-benus. — ἐν τῷ ἱερῷ] We are to think of the *synagogue,* which "erat prope atrium in monte templi," *Gloss. Joma,* f. 68, 2 ; Lightfoot *in loc.* ; Deyling, *Obss.* III. ed. 2, p. 285 f. — καθε-ζόμενον] The Rabbinic assertion : " a diebus Mosis ad Rabban Gamalielem non didicerunt legem nisi *stantes," Megillah,* f. 21, 1 (Wagenseil, *ad Sotah,* p. 993), according to which Jesus would thus already appear as a teacher, is rightly rejected as un-founded in the N. T., by Vitringa, *Synag.* p. 167, and more recent expositors. — ἐν μέσῳ] has its reference to the *seeking* of the parents ; Jesus was not hidden, but He sat there *in the midst among the teachers.* We may conceive of Him at the feet of a teaching Rabbi, sitting in their circle (comp. on Acts xxii. 3). In this there is nothing extraordinary to be discerned,[1] since Jesus was already a *" son of the law "* (see on ver. 42). But to find here a sitting *on an equality* with the teachers [2] (Strauss, comp. de Wette) is not in accordance with the text, since the report would not otherwise have limited the action of the child to the ἀκούειν and ἐπερωτ. — ἐπερωτ. αὐτούς] The Rabbinical instruction did not consist merely in teaching and interrogating the disciples, but these latter themselves also asked questions and received answers. See Lightfoot, p. 742 ff.; Wetstein *in loc.* The questioning here is that of the pure and holy desire for knowledge, not that of a guest mingling in the conversation (in opposition to de Wette).

Ver. 47 ff. Ἐπὶ τῇ συνέσει καὶ κ.τ.λ.] *over* His understanding in general, and especially over His answers. — ἰδόντες] Joseph and Mary. They *were astonished ;* for they had not expected

[1] Lange, II. 1, p. 130, invents the idea that " the genius of the new humanity soared above the heroes of the old decorum."

[2] So also older dogmatic writers. "Ceu doctor doctorum," says Calovius, who specifies the fourfold aim : ob *gloriae templi posterioris illustrationem,* Hag. ii. 10 ; ob *adventus sui manifestationem ;* ob *sapientiae divinae demonstra-tionem ;* ob *doctorum informationem.*—Into what *apocryphal* forms the con-versation of Jesus with the doctors might be fashioned, may be seen in the *Evang. infant.* 50 ff. Even by Chemnitz He is said to have discoursed already *" de persona et officiis Messiae, de discrimine legis et evangelii,"* etc.

to find Him either *in this place,* or *so occupied.* — ἡ μήτηρ αὐτοῦ]
not merely because maternal feeling is in general more keen,
quick, and ready to show itself, nor yet because Joseph had
not been equal to this scene (Lange), but rightly in accordance
with Luke's view of the maternal relation of Mary.   Bengel:
"non loquebatur Josephus ; *major erat necessitudo matris.*" —
τί ὅτι] *wherefore ?*   See on Mark ii. 16. — ἐν τοῖς τοῦ πατρός
μου] *i.e. in the house of my Father.*   See examples of this well-
known mode of expression in Lobeck, *ad Phryn.* p. 100.   So,
following Syr. and the Fathers, most modern commentators.
Others, such as Castalio, Erasmus, Calvin, Maldonatus, Jansen,
Wolf, Loesner, Valckenaer, Rosenmüller, Bornemann, de Wette,
Ewald, *al.: in the affairs of my Father.*   This also is linguistically correct.   See 1 Tim. iv. 15 ; Bornemann, *Schol.*
p. 29 ; Bernhardy, p. 210 ; Schaefer, *Melet.* p. 31 f.   But as
Jesus in His reply refers expressly to the *search* of the parents,
which He represents as having been made *needlessly,* it is most
natural to find in this answer the designation of the *locality,*
in which they ought to have known that He was to be found,
without seeking Him in *rebus Patris.*   He might also be *elsewhere.*   To combine both modes of taking it (Olshausen, Bleek)
is *a priori* inappropriate. — δεῖ] as *Son.*   This follows from
τοῦ πατρός μου.   This breaking forth of the consciousness of
Divine Sonship [1] in the first saying which is preserved to us
from Jesus, is to be explained by the power of the impressions which He experienced on His first participation in the
holy observances of the festival and the temple.   According
to ver. 50, it must not have previously asserted itself thus
amidst the quiet course of His domestic development ("non
multum antea, nec tamen nihil, de Patre locutus erat," Bengel
on ver. 50), but now there had emerged with Him an *epoch* in
the course of development of that consciousness of Sonship,—
the first bursting open of the swelling bud.   Altogether foreign
to the ingenuous, child-like utterance, unnatural and indeli-

---

[1] At all events already in Messianic presentiment, yet not with the conception
fully unfolded, but in the dawning apprehension of the child, which could only
very gradually give place to clearness, ver. 52.

cate, is the intention *of drawing a contrast* which has been
imputed to Him : τῆς γὰρ παρθένου τὸν Ἰωσὴφ πατέρα
εἰπούσης αὐτοῦ, ἐκεῖνος φησίν· οὐκ αὐτός ἐστιν ὁ ἀληθής
μου πατήρ, ἢ γὰρ ἂν ἐν τῷ οἴκῳ αὐτοῦ ἤμην, ἀλλ᾽ ὁ Θεὸς
ἐστί μου πατήρ, καὶ διὰ τοῦτο ἐν τῷ οἴκῳ αὐτοῦ εἰμί, Theophylact. Erroneous in an opposite manner is the opinion of
Schenkel, that the boy Jesus named God His Father, "*just as
every pious Jewish child might do.*" Such a conclusion could
only be arrived at, if He had said τ. πατρὸς ἡμῶν ; but with
Jesus in the connection of His entire history τ. πατρός μου
points to a higher individual relation. And *this* too it was,
which made the answer unintelligible to the parents. What
every pious Jewish child might have answered, they would
have understood. See, besides, Keim, *geschichtl. Chr.* p. 48 f.

Ver. 50 f. If the angelic announcement, i. 26 ff., especially
vv. 32, 35, and ii. 10 ff. (comp. especially ver. 19), be historical, it is altogether incomprehensible how the words of Jesus
could be unintelligible to His parents. Evasive explanations
are given by Olshausen, and even Bleek and older expositors
(that they had simply not understood the *deeper* meaning of
the unity of the Son and the Father), Ebrard (that Mary had
no inner perception of the fact that the Father's word could
become so *absolutely exclusive* a comfort of souls, and be so even
in the boy), and others. Schleiermacher, *L. J.* p. 78, gives a
candid judgment. — ὑποτασσόμ. αὐτοῖς] That mighty exaltation of the consciousness of divine Sonship not only did not
hinder, but conditioned with moral necessity in the youthful
development of the God-man *the fulfilment of filial duty*, the
highest proof of which was subsequently given by the *Crucified
One*, John xix. 26 ff. — ἡ δὲ μήτηρ κ.τ.λ.] significant as in ver.
19 ; διατηρεῖν denotes the careful preservation. Comp. Acts
xv. 29 ; Gen. xxxvii. 11.

REMARK.—The rejection of this significant history as a myth
(Gabler in *Neuest. theol. Journ.* III. 1, 36 ff. ; Strauss, Weisse,[1]

---

[1] Weisse interprets it *allegorically:* that the youthful spirit of Christianity
withdrew itself from the care and the supervision of its parents, *i.e.* from the
restrictions of Jewish law and from the wisdom of the ancestral schools, etc.

I. p. 212 ff.), as regards which the analogies of the childhood of
Moses (Joseph. *Antt.* ii. 9. 6; Philo, *de vita Mos.* II. p. 83 f.)
and of Samuel (1 Sam. iii.; Joseph. *Antt.* v. 10. 4) have been
made use of, is the less to be acquiesced in, in proportion to
the greatness of the impression that must naturally have been
made on the Son of God, in the human development of His
consciousness of fellowship with God, at His first taking part
in the celebration of the festival in the grand sanctuary of the
nation,[1] and in proportion to the unadorned simplicity of the
narrative and its internal truth as contrasted with the fabulous
disfigurements of it in the apocryphal *Evangelium infantiae*, and
even with the previous portions of the history of Luke himself.
Comp. Schleiermacher, *L. J.* p. 80 f. The objection of an unnatural mental precocity applies an unwarranted standard in
the case of Jesus, who was κατὰ πνεῦμα God's Son.

Ver. 52. Comp. 1 Sam. ii. 26. — ἡλικίᾳ] not *age* (so Vulgate,
Luther, Erasmus, and most expositors), which would furnish
an intimation altogether superfluous, but *growth, bodily size*
(Beza, Vatablus, Grotius, Er. Schmid, Bengel, Ewald, Bleek,
and others). See on Matt. vi. 27; Luke xix. 3. Comp.
ηὔξανε καὶ ἐκραταιοῦτο, ver. 40. "Justam proceritatem nactus
est ac decoram," Bengel. Luke expresses His *mental* (σοφίᾳ)
and *bodily* (ἡλικίᾳ) development.[2] In favour of this explanation we have also the evidence of 1 Sam. *l.c.:* ἐπορεύετο
μεγαλυνόμενον, which element is here given by ἡλικίᾳ. —
χάριτι] *gracious favour*, as at ver. 40. But here, where one
twelve years old is spoken of, who now the longer He lives
comes more into intercourse with others, Luke adds καὶ ἀνθρώποις. Comp. 1 Sam. *l.c.:* וְטוֹב גַּם עִם־יְהֹוָה וְגַם עִם־אֲנָשִׁים; *Test.*
XII. Patr. p. 528. Observe, moreover, that the *advancing* in
God's gracious favour assumes the sinless perfection of Jesus
as *growing*, as in the way of *moral development*. Comp. on Mark

---

[1] Comp. Beyschlag, *Christol. d. N. T.* p. 45.

[2] In this place he prefixes σοφίᾳ, because he has just related so brilliant a
trait of the mental development of Jesus. — What shifts, moreover, have been
resorted to, especially since the time of Athanasius and Ambrose, to fence
with reservations the *progress* of Jesus in wisdom in such a way as to leave *no*
progress, but merely a successive *revealing* of His inherent wisdom, or else only
a growth in the wisdom to be attained *through human experience* (scientia
acquisita)!

x. 18.   But this does not exclude child-like innocence, and
does not include youthful moral perplexities.   Comp. Keim,
geschichtl. Chr. p. 110 ff.   It is a *normal* growth, from child-
like innocence to full holiness of the life.   Comp. also Beyschlag, *Christol. d. N. T.* p. 47 ff.

END OF VOL. I.

MORRISON AND GIBB, EDINBURGH,
PRINTERS TO HER MAJESTY'S STATIONERY OFFICE.

Just published, in demy 4to, Third Edition, price 25s.,

BIBLICO-THEOLOGICAL LEXICON OF NEW TESTAMENT GREEK.

By HERMANN CREMER, D.D.,

PROFESSOR OF THEOLOGY IN THE UNIVERSITY OF GREIFSWALD.

TRANSLATED FROM THE GERMAN OF THE SECOND EDITION

(WITH ADDITIONAL MATTER AND CORRECTIONS BY THE AUTHOR)

By WILLIAM URWICK, M.A.

'Dr. Cremer's work is highly and deservedly esteemed in Germany. It gives with care and thoroughness a complete history, as far as it goes, of each word and phrase that it deals with. . . . Dr. Cremer's explanations are most lucidly set out.'—*Guardian.*

'It is hardly possible to exaggerate the value of this work to the student of the Greek Testament. . . . The translation is accurate and idiomatic, and the additions to the later edition are considerable and important.'—*Church Bells.*

'A valuable addition to the stores of any theological library. . . . It is what it claims to be, a Lexicon, both biblical and theological, and treats not only of words, but of the doctrines inculcated by those words.'—*John Bull.*

'We very heartily commend this goodly volume to students of biblical literature.'— *Evangelical Magazine.*

'We cannot find an important word in our Greek New Testament which is not discussed with a fulness and discrimination which leaves nothing to be desired.'— *Nonconformist.*

'Cremer's Lexicon is, and is long likely to be, indispensable to students whether of theology or of the Bible, and must always bear witness to his scholarship, erudition, and diligence.'—*Expositor.*

'A work of immense erudition.'—*Freeman.*

'This noble edition in quarto of Cremer's Biblico-Theological Lexicon quite super-sedes the translation of the first edition of the work. Many of the most important articles have been re-written and re-arranged. . . . We heartily congratulate Mr. Urwick on the admirable manner in which he has executed his task, revealing on his part adequate scholarship, thorough sympathy, and a fine choice of English equivalents and definitions.'—*British Quarterly Review.*

'As an aid in our search, we warmly commend the honest and laborious New Testament Lexicon of Dr. Cremer.'—*London Quarterly Review.*

'The judiciousness and importance of Dr. Cremer's design must be obvious to all students of the New Testament; and the execution of that design, in our judgment, fully establishes and justifies the translator's encomiums.'—*Watchman.*

'A majestic volume, admirably printed and faultlessly edited, and will win gratitude as well as renown for its learned and Christian Author, and prove a precious boon to students and preachers who covet exact and exhaustive acquaintance with the literal and theological teaching of the New Testament.'—*Dickinson's Theological Quarterly.*

LANGE'S COMMENTARIES.

(Subscription price, nett), 15s. each.

THEOLOGICAL AND HOMILETICAL COMMENTARY
ON THE OLD AND NEW TESTAMENTS.

Specially designed and adapted for the use of Ministers and Students. By Prof. JOHN PETER LANGE, D.D., in connection with a number of eminent European Divines. Translated, enlarged, and revised under the general editorship of Rev. Dr. PHILIP SCHAFF, assisted by leading Divines of the various Evangelical Denominations.

OLD TESTAMENT—14 VOLUMES.

I. GENESIS. With a General Introduction to the Old Testament. By Prof. J. P. LANGE, D.D. Translated from the German, with Additions, by Prof. TAYLER LEWIS, LL.D., and A. GOSMAN, D.D.

II. EXODUS. By J. P. LANGE, D.D. LEVITICUS. By J. P. LANGE, D.D. With GENERAL INTRODUCTION by Rev. Dr. OSGOOD.

III. NUMBERS AND DEUTERONOMY. NUMBERS. By Prof. J. P. LANGE, D.D. DEUTERONOMY. By W. J. SCHROEDER.

IV. JOSHUA. By Rev. F. R. FAY. JUDGES and RUTH. By Prof. PAULUS CASSELL, D.D.

V. SAMUEL, I. and II. By Professor ERDMANN, D.D.

VI. KINGS. By KARL CHR. W. F. BAHR, D.D.

VII. CHRONICLES, I. and II. By OTTO ZÖCKLER. EZRA. By FR. W. SCHULTZ. NEHEMIAH. By Rev. HOWARD CROSBY, D.D., LL.D. ESTHER. By FR. W. SCHULTZ.

VIII. JOB. With an Introduction and Annotations by Prof. TAYLER LEWIS, LL.D. A Commentary by Dr. OTTO ZÖCKLER, together with an Introductory Essay on Hebrew Poetry by Prof. PHILIP SCHAFF, D.D.

IX. THE PSALMS. By CARL BERNHARDT MOLL, D.D. With a new Metrical Version of the Psalms, and Philological Notes, by T. J. CONANT, D.D.

X. PROVERBS. By Prof. OTTO ZÖCKLER, D.D. ECCLESIASTES. By Prof. O. ZÖCKLER, D.D. With Additions, and a new Metrical Version, by Prof. TAYLER LEWIS, D.D. THE SONG OF SOLOMON. By Prof. O. ZÖCKLER, D.D.

XI. ISAIAH. By C. W. E. NAEGELSBACH.

XII. JEREMIAH. By C. W. E. NAEGELSBACH, D.D. LAMENTATIONS. By C. W. E. NAEGELSBACH, D.D.

XIII. EZEKIEL. By F. W. SCHRÖDER, D.D. DANIEL. By Professor ZÖCKLER, D.D.

XIV. THE MINOR PROPHETS. HOSEA, JOEL, and AMOS. By OTTO SCHMOLLER, Ph.D. OBADIAH and MICAH. By Rev. PAUL KLEINERT. JONAH, NAHUM, HABAKKUK, and ZEPHANIAH. By Rev. PAUL KLEINERT. HAGGAI. By Rev. JAMES E. M'CURDY. ZECHARIAH. By T. W. CHAMBERS, D.D. MALACHI. By JOSEPH PACKARD, D.D.

THE APOCRYPHA. *(Just published.)* By E. C. BISSELL, D.D. One Volume.

NEW TESTAMENT—10 VOLUMES.

I. MATTHEW. With a General Introduction to the New Testament. By J. P. LANGE, D.D. Translated, with Additions, by PHILIP SCHAFF, D.D.

II. MARK. By J. P. LANGE, D.D. LUKE. By J. J. VAN OOSTERZEE.

III. JOHN. By J. P. LANGE D.D.

IV. ACTS. By G. V. LECHLER, D.D., and Rev. CHARLES GEROK.

V. ROMANS. By J. P. LANGE, D.D., and Rev. F. R. FAY.

VI. CORINTHIANS. By CHRISTIAN F. KLING.

VII. GALATIANS. By OTTO SCHMOLLER, Ph.D. EPHESIANS and COLOSSIANS. By KARL BRAUNE, D.D. PHILIPPIANS. By KARL BRAUNE, D.D.

VIII. THESSALONIANS. By Drs. AUBERLIN and RIGGENBACH. TIMOTHY. By J. J. VAN OOSTERZEE, D.D. TITUS. By J. J. VAN OOSTERZEE, D.D. PHILEMON. By J. J. VAN OOSTERZEE, D.D. HEBREWS. By KARL B. MOLL, D.D.

IX. JAMES. By J. P. LANGE, D.D., and J. J. VAN OOSTERZEE, D.D. PETER and JUDE. By G. F. C. FRONMÜLLER, Ph.D. JOHN. By KARL BRAUNE, D.D.

X. THE REVELATION OF JOHN. By Dr. J. P. LANGE. Together with double Alphabetical Index to all the Ten Volumes on the New Testament, by JOHN H. WOODS.

CHEAP RE-ISSUE OF
STIER'S WORDS OF THE LORD JESUS.

To meet a very general desire that this now well-known Work should be brought more within the reach of all classes, both Clergy and Laity, Messrs. CLARK are now issuing, for a limited period, the *Eight* Volumes, handsomely bound in *Four*, at the *Subscription Price* of

TWO GUINEAS

As the allowance to the Trade must necessarily be small, orders sent either direct or through Booksellers must *in every case* be accompanied with a Post Office Order for the above amount.

'The whole work is a treasury of thoughtful exposition. Its measure of practical and spiritual application, with exegetical criticism, commends it to the use of those whose duty it is to preach as well as to understand the Gospel of Christ.'—*Guardian.*

New and Cheap Edition, in Four Vols., demy 8vo, *Subscription Price* 28s.,

THE LIFE OF THE LORD JESUS CHRIST:

A Complete Critical Examination of the Origin, Contents, and Connection of the Gospels. Translated from the German of J. P. LANGE, D.D., Professor of Divinity in the University of Bonn. Edited, with additional Notes, by MARCUS DODS, D.D.

'We have arrived at a most favourable conclusion regarding the importance and ability of this work—the former depending upon the present condition of theological criticism, the latter on the wide range of the work itself; the singularly dispassionate judgment of the Author, as well as his pious, reverential, and erudite treatment of a subject inexpressibly holy. . . . We have great pleasure in recommending this work to our readers. We are convinced of its value and enormous range.'—*Irish Ecclesiastical Gazette.*

BENGEL'S GNOMON—CHEAP EDITION.

GNOMON OF THE NEW TESTAMENT.

By JOHN ALBERT BENGEL. Now first translated into English. With Original Notes, Explanatory and Illustrative. Edited by the Rev. ANDREW R. FAUSSET, M.A. The Original Translation was in Five Large Volumes, demy 8vo, averaging more than 550 pages each, and the very great demand for this Edition has induced the Publishers to issue the *Five* Volumes bound in *Three*, at the *Subscription Price* of

TWENTY-FOUR SHILLINGS.

They trust by this still further to increase its usefulness.

'It is a work which manifests the most intimate and profound knowledge of Scripture, and which, if we examine it with care, will often be found to condense more matter into a line than can be extracted from many pages of other writers.'—Archdeacon HARE.

'In respect both of its contents and its tone, Bengel's Gnomon stands alone. Even among laymen there has arisen a healthy and vigorous desire for scriptural knowledge, and Bengel has done more than any other man to aid such inquirers. There is perhaps no book every word of which has been so well weighed, or in which a single technical term contains so often far-reaching and suggestive views. . . . The theoretical and practical are as intimately connected as light and heat in the sun's ray.'—*Life of Perthes.*

In Twenty-four Handsome 8vo Volumes, Subscription Price £6, 6s. 0d.,

Ante-Nicene Christian Library.

A COLLECTION OF ALL THE WORKS OF THE FATHERS OF THE CHRISTIAN CHURCH PRIOR TO THE COUNCIL OF NICÆA.

EDITED BY THE

REV. ALEXANDER ROBERTS, D.D., AND JAMES DONALDSON, LL.D.

MESSRS. CLARK are now happy to announce the completion of this Series. It has been received with marked approval by all sections of the Christian Church in this country and in the United States, as supplying what has long been felt to be a want, and also on account of the impartiality, learning, and care with which Editors and Translators have executed a very difficult task.

The Publishers do not bind themselves to *continue* to supply the Series at the Subscription price.

The Works are arranged as follow :—

FIRST YEAR.
APOSTOLIC FATHERS, comprising Clement's Epistles to the Corinthians; Polycarp to the Ephesians; Martyrdom of Polycarp; Epistle of Barnabas; Epistles of Ignatius (longer and shorter, and also the Syriac version); Martyrdom of Ignatius; Epistle to Diognetus; Pastor of Hermas; Papias; Spurious Epistles of Ignatius. In One Volume.
JUSTIN MARTYR; ATHENAGORAS. In One Volume.
TATIAN; THEOPHILUS; THE CLEmentine Recognitions. In One Volume.
CLEMENT OF ALEXANDRIA, Volume First, comprising Exhortation to Heathen; The Instructor; and a portion of the Miscellanies.

SECOND YEAR.
HIPPOLYTUS, Volume First; Refutation of all Heresies, and Fragments from his Commentaries.
IRENÆUS, Volume First.
TERTULLIAN AGAINST MARCION.
CYPRIAN, Volume First; the Epistles, and some of the Treatises.

THIRD YEAR.
IRENÆUS (completion); HIPPOLYTUS (completion); Fragments of Third Century. In One Volume.
ORIGEN: De Principiis; Letters; and portion of Treatise against Celsus.

CLEMENT OF ALEXANDRIA, Volume Second; Completion of Miscellanies.
TERTULLIAN, Volume First; To the Martyrs; Apology; To the Nations, etc.

FOURTH YEAR.
CYPRIAN, Volume Second (completion); Novatian; Minucius Felix; Fragments.
METHODIUS; ALEXANDER OF LYcopolis; Peter of Alexandria; Anatolius; Clement on Virginity; and Fragments.
TERTULLIAN, Volume Second.
APOCRYPHAL GOSPELS, ACTS, AND Revelations; comprising all the very curious Apocryphal Writings of the first three Centuries.

FIFTH YEAR.
TERTULLIAN, Volume Third (completion).
CLEMENTINE HOMILIES; APOSTOlical Constitutions. In One Volume.
ARNOBIUS.
DIONYSIUS; GREGORY THAUMAturgus; Syrian Fragments. In One Volume.

SIXTH YEAR.
LACTANTIUS; Two Volumes.
ORIGEN, Volume Second (completion). 12s. to Non-Subscribers.
EARLY LITURGIES & REMAINING Fragments. 9s. to Non-Subscribers.

Single Years cannot be had separately, unless to complete sets; but any Volume may be had separately, price 10s. 6d.,—with the exception of ORIGEN, Vol. II., 12s.; and the EARLY LITURGIES, 9s.

Just published, in post 8vo, price 7s. 6d.,

THE PREACHERS OF SCOTLAND FROM THE SIXTH TO THE NINETEENTH CENTURY.

TWELFTH SERIES OF CUNNINGHAM LECTURES

By W. G. BLAIKIE, D.D.,

PROFESSOR OF APOLOGETICS AND PASTORAL THEOLOGY, THE NEW COLLEGE, EDINBURGH.

'Exceedingly interesting and well worth reading both for information and pleasure. . . . A better review of Scottish preaching from an evangelical standpoint could not be desired.'—*Scotsman.*

Just published, in crown 8vo, price 3s. 6d.,

SECOND EDITION, REVISED

THE THEOLOGY

AND

THEOLOGIANS OF SCOTLAND,

CHIEFLY OF THE

𝔖eventeenth and 𝔈ighteenth Centuries.

Being one of the 'Cunningham Lectures.'

By JAMES WALKER, D.D., CARNWATH.

'These pages glow with fervent and eloquent rejoinder to the cheap scorn and scurrilous satire poured out upon evangelical theology as it has been developed north of the Tweed.'—*British Quarterly Review.*

'We do not wonder that in their delivery Dr. Walker's lectures excited great interest; we should have wondered far more if they had not done so.'—Mr. SPURGEON in *Sword and Trowel.*

In Two Vols., 8vo, price 21s.,

A SYSTEM OF BIBLICAL THEOLOGY.

BY THE LATE

W. LINDSAY ALEXANDER, D.D., LL.D.,

PRINCIPAL OF THE THEOLOGICAL HALL OF THE CONGREGATIONAL CHURCHES IN SCOTLAND.

'A work like this is of priceless advantage. It is the testimony of a powerful and accomplished mind to the supreme authority of the Scriptures, a lucid and orderly exhibition of their contents, and a vindication, at once logical, scholarly, and conclusive, of their absolute sufficiency and abiding truthfulness. It is a pleasure to read lectures so vigorous and comprehensive in their grasp, so subtle in their dialect, so reverent in spirit, and so severely chaste in their style. There are scores of men who would suffer no loss if for the next couple of years they read no other book than this. To master it thoroughly would be an incalculable gain.'—*Baptist Magazine.*

'This is probably the most interesting and scholarly system of theology on the lines of orthodoxy which has seen the light.'—*Literary World.*

'This has been characterised as probably the most valuable contribution which our country has made to theology during the present century, and we do not think this an exaggerated estimate.'—*Scottish Congregationalist.*

'Oh, that Scotland and Congregationalism had many worthies like Dr. Lindsay Alexander! . . . The ripe man, full of rich experience and heavenly knowledge, will prize each leaf, and give himself a glorious drilling as he masters chapter by chapter.'—Mr. SPURGEON in *The Sword and Trowel.*

GRIMM'S LEXICON.

Just published, in demy 4to, price 36s.,

GREEK-ENGLISH LEXICON OF THE NEW TESTAMENT,

BEING

Grimm's Wilke's Clavis Novi Testamenti.

TRANSLATED, REVISED, AND ENLARGED

BY

JOSEPH HENRY THAYER, D.D.,

BUSSEY PROFESSOR OF NEW TESTAMENT CRITICISM AND INTERPRETATION IN THE
DIVINITY SCHOOL OF HARVARD UNIVERSITY.

EXTRACT FROM PREFACE.

'TOWARDS the close of the year 1862, the "Arnoldische Buchhandlung" in Leipzig published the First Part of a Greek-Latin Lexicon of the New Testament, prepared, upon the basis of the "Clavis Novi Testamenti Philologica" of C. G. Wilke (second edition, 2 vols. 1851), by Professor C. L. WILIBALD GRIMM of Jena. In his Prospectus Professor Grimm announced it as his purpose not only (in accordance with the improvements in classical lexicography embodied in the Paris edition of Stephen's Thesaurus and in the fifth edition of Passow's Dictionary edited by Rost and his coadjutors) to exhibit the historical growth of a word's significations, and accordingly in selecting his vouchers for New Testament usage to show at what time and in what class of writers a given word became current, but also duly to notice the usage of the Septuagint and of the Old Testament Apocrypha, and especially to produce a Lexicon which should correspond to the present condition of textual criticism, of exegesis, and of biblical theology. He devoted more than seven years to his task. The successive Parts of his work received, as they appeared, the outspoken commendation of scholars diverging as widely in their views as Hupfeld and Hengstenberg; and since its completion in 1868 it has been generally acknowledged to be by far the best Lexicon of the New Testament extant.'

'I regard it as a work of the greatest importance. . . . It seems to me a work showing the most patient diligence, and the most carefully arranged collection of useful and helpful references.'—THE BISHOP OF GLOUCESTER AND BRISTOL.

'The use of Professor Grimm's book for years has convinced me that it is not only unquestionably the best among existing New Testament Lexicons, but that, apart from all comparisons, it is a work of the highest intrinsic merit, and one which is admirably adapted to initiate a learner into an acquaintance with the language of the New Testament. It ought to be regarded as one of the first and most necessary requisites for the study of the New Testament, and consequently for the study of theology in general.'—Professor EMIL SCHÜRER.

'This is indeed a noble volume, and satisfies in these days of advancing scholarship a very great want. It is certainly unequalled in its lexicography, and invaluable in its literary perfectness. . . . It should, will, must make for itself a place in the library of all those students who want to be thoroughly furnished for the work of understanding, expounding, and applying the Word of God.'—*Evangelical Magazine.*

'Undoubtedly the best of its kind. Beautifully printed and well translated, with some corrections and improvements of the original, it will be prized by students of the Christian Scriptures.'—*Athenæum.*